FIFTH EDITION

CONSULTATION, COLLABORATION, AND TEAMWORK FOR STUDENTS WITH SPECIAL NEEDS

PEGGY DETTMER

Professor Emeritus, Kansas State University

LINDA P. THURSTON

Kansas State University

NORMA DYCK

Professor Emeritus, Kansas State University

Boston ▪ New York ▪ San Francisco
Mexico City ▪ Montreal ▪ Toronto ▪ London ▪ Madrid ▪ Munich ▪ Paris
Hong Kong ▪ Singapore ▪ Tokyo ▪ Cape Town ▪ Sydney

Executive Editor: *Virginia Lanigan*
Editorial Assistant: *Scott Blaszak*
Executive Marketing Manager: *Amy Cronin Jordan*
Editorial Production Service: *Chestnut Hill Enterprises, Inc.*
Manufacturing Buyer: *Linda Cox*
Cover Administrator: *Linda Knowles*
Electronic Composition: *Omegatype Typography, Inc.*

Library of Congress Cataloging-in-Publication Data

Dettmer, Peggy.
　　Consultation, collaboration, and teamwork for students with special
needs / Peggy Dettmer, Linda P. Thurston, Norma Dyck.—5th ed.
　　　　p.　cm.
　　Includes bibliographical references and indexes.
　　ISBN 0-205-43523-8
　1. Children with disabilities—Education—United States. 2. Special
education—United States. 3. Educational consultants—United States. 4.
Teaching teams—United States. I. Thurston, Linda P. II. Dyck, Norma.
III. Title.

　　LC4031.D47 2005
　　371.9'0973—dc22

　　　　　　　　　　　　　　　　　　　　　　　　　　　　2004014660

CONTENTS

PART II   PROCESSES FOR EDUCATORS WORKING TOGETHER

CHAPTER FOUR

Communication Processes for Consultation, Collaboration, and Teamwork   97

CHAPTER FIVE

**Problem-Solving Strategies for Collaborative
School Consultation**   126

CHAPTER SIX

Management and Assessment of Collaborative School Consultation   158

PART III   CONTENT OF WORKING TOGETHER FOR STUDENTS' SPECIAL NEEDS

CHAPTER SEVEN
Working Together for Students from Diverse Populations   199

CHAPTER EIGHT

Working Together for Students with Disabilities   220

CHAPTER NINE

Working Together for Students with High Ability   248

CHAPTER TWELVE

Putting It All Together with Collaborative School Consultation and Teamwork   360

PREFACE

As educators, we prepare students to become knowledgeable, caring, ethical, productive, self-fulfilled individuals in an increasingly complex, diverse, and interconnected world. When we instruct, coach, counsel with, evaluate, and mentor our children and youth, we are more aware with each teaching experience that every student is a minority of one and has special needs. Addressing these needs will require strong, secure partnerships among general and special education teachers, families, school administrators, support personnel, and the entire community.

Consultation, collaboration, and teamwork are vital elements in achieving the goals that frame our mission. These processes of collaborating and teaming may seem simplistically basic in our profession; in truth, however, they are complex and challenging. Working together can bring changes that unsettle established school patterns. Then, too, there are times when educators want and need to work alone and it makes good sense to do so. However, when collaborative school consultation and focused teamwork are applied with skill, will, and optimism, they have the potential to create positive ripple effects for all students throughout the educational system.

An explosion of information has propelled us from the last century into this one. Our students now must learn to use this information wisely and to generate new *ideas* for their future. They will need to be guided by strong ethical principles and behaviors that uphold and model those principles. They will be seeking to have a voice through self expression of their interests, talents, and abilities in various forms. Imagination and sensible risk-taking behavior can be a catalyst. Good leadership and followership skills can guide them in working together. Human relationships will be, more than ever, the most important matrix at work, in the community, and at home. It is important that students develop interrelationship skills and observe educators model those skills effectively.

This book is designed to serve as a bridge between theories of human relationships in school contexts and practices in serving special needs of students to prepare them for a solid future. It is organized into four main parts, focusing in turn on contexts, processes, content, and then a synthesis of the three. Each chapter includes ideas and activities to guide a single reader, or groups of readers, through the subtleties and intricacies of powerful interactive processes.

Part One's three chapters comprise the *Context* section. Chapter 1 introduces collaborative school consultation and describes key elements in planning, implementing, evaluating, and preparing for consultation and collaboration roles. Constructive uses of the inevitable and valuable differences among adults are discussed as they affect interactions in school environments. Chapter 2 includes a short summary of school reform and current movements for standards and accountability, along with a brief background of school consultation and collaboration, and a quick look at theoretical and research foundations. Then several collaborative school consultation structures are developed and analyzed. Chapter 3 focuses on school and home collaborations in which family members are partners with teachers, and students are active in self-direction and self-assessment of their learning.

Part Two focuses on process skills and problem-solving tools needed for effective consultation and collaboration. Chapter 4 addresses verbal and nonverbal communication, and gives techniques for dealing with resistance, anger, and conflicts among educators. Chapter 5 offers strategies for group problem solving, group consensus, and a ten-step problem-solving process for collaborative consultation that can be implemented readily by school personnel. Chapter 6 targets management of stress and time, data organization, record-keeping practices, and coordination of collaborative interactions. Techniques for evaluating consultation and collaboration outcomes are provided.

In Part Three, Chapter 7 highlights the roles of collaborative school consultation in serving culturally and linguistically diverse (CLD) students and their families. The educational needs of English language learners (ELL) are targeted, along with those of special populations such as migrant families, military families, rural and isolated communities, home-schooled students, and more. Chapter 8 stresses co-planning as the key component of successful co-teaching of students with disabilities and identifies ways of adapting and modifying instruction for them so that *no child is left behind*. Chapter 9 describes differentiation and facilitation of instruction for students who are exceptionally able and talented so that *no child is held behind* in developing capabilities and talents.

In Part Four, Chapter 10 highlights roles of school administrators, special education directors, paraeducators, and other school personnel in collaborative consultation and team participation for students with special needs. The need for professional development to prepare for collaborative school consultation is emphasized. Chapter 11 explores opportunities to serve special needs of students through interagency collaboration, support personnel, outside resources, and technology in learning environments beyond the conventional school setting. Chapter 12 promotes leadership and advocacy as integral parts of consulting, collaborating, and co-teaching. Ethics of collaborative consultation are examined, and competencies for successful consulting, collaborating, and working as team members that have been featured throughout the book are summarized. The chapter closes with emphasis on the possibilities for multiplier benefits and positive ripple effects to be gained from collaborative school consultation and teamwork, and a call for construction of a personally professional development plan for fulfilling these roles.

Each of the 12 chapters begins with a defining, three-element **Graphic**—a triangle within a circle within a square—to introduce content, process, and context themes for that chapter. **Focusing Questions** direct attention to major issues addressed in the chapter and encourage the reader to be alert for their appearance. A list of **Key Terms** is presented in alphabetical order as an advance organizer for their development in the chapter. A topical **Vignette** sets the stage for chapter themes.

Application boxes at particular places in the reading provide opportunity to ponder, practice, discuss, and apply material at that point in the chapter. The **Tips** section offers practical suggestions relevant to that chapter's content. The **Chapter Review** parallels the Focusing Questions to summarize and reflect on major chapter topics. Activities **To Do and Think About** encourage extension and application of the material. Each chapter concludes with a section, **For Further Reading,** to assist those who want to study particular topics in more depth or to explore related topics.

The past several decades have produced mountains of information, with technology as the driving force for that production. Now it is time for the *information* to spawn constructive *ideas* and for us to be guided by *ideals* founded on strong principles and solid ethics. We must *think* with the *information* that has been gathered, *teach* with the *ideas* generated, and work together as *teams* to promote our *ideals.* As educators in schools, homes, and communities, when we effectively cross the t's to think and teach as teams, and dot the i's of information, ideas, and ideals, we will be serving all learners' needs best.

ACKNOWLEDGMENTS

Previous editions of this book were dedicated to: graduate students who would be working collegially with other educators, students, and families; practicing educators who were being called on to collaborate with colleagues in new ways; educators for the future who will inherit problems not yet solved but also the progress made by their predecessors; and the multifarious agencies providing the array of services so vital to students with very special needs. It seems fitting now to dedicate this fifth edition to these children and adolescents who are educated by so many caring and dedicated people in a variety of ways.

We wish to recognize all those individuals who have contributed to the thinking and writing that molded these pages. In a collaborative process it is not easy to tell where the contribution of one appears, another interfaces, and yet another goes on from there. This demonstrates once again the complexity and the beauty of working together toward lofty aims. The shared perceptions and suggestions of students, families, teaching colleagues, reviewers, and editorial staff have been an important part of the process and the product. That is what collaborative consultation and teamwork are all about.

We extend our appreciation to the reviewers: Joy Fuqua, Fort Hays State University; Lois M. Jircitano, Western Kentucky University; and Robbie Ludy, Buena Vista University. We thank Kari Woods, Jane Jacquart, and Ann Knackendoffel for insights they contributed to the book and the instructor's guide. We also want to give special, posthumous recognition to Jane More Loeb for her pen-and-ink drawings. Jane influenced many in her lifetime with her teaching, examples, and illustrations.

Our aim for this book and its earlier editions has been to promote school consultation, collaboration, and teamwork as a means of transforming school learning environments into settings where education is special for *each* student and *all* educators are successful in their complex, demanding roles. We hope that the material presented here and in the instructor's guide will be practical and helpful to those who use it.

CHAPTER ONE

CONSULTATION, COLLABORATION, AND TEAMWORK IN SCHOOLS

Consultation ⟶ Collaboration

Teamwork

Life presents many situations for which we do not have all the information and expertise we need to meet the challenges. In today's increasingly interdependent and specialized world it is unlikely that any one person possesses enough knowledge and ability for every circumstance. So it is reasonable and prudent that we consult, collaborate, and work in teams with others to attain our goals.

Consultation services are routine in fields as varied as business, medicine, law, industry, fashion, construction, decorating, and finance. Consultants may even have their own consultants! *Collaboration* is emphasized frequently in a wide range of work settings from professions to trades to government to community affairs. *Teamwork* is regarded as an efficient, productive way of achieving goals. Put all three of these together in a school context, and educators have a powerfully interactive climate in which to address student strengths and needs.

Until recent years productive interactions by adults in school settings were more occasional and happenstance than frequent and planned. Allocation of time for interaction, practical structures for working together, preparation needed for these less familiar roles, and careful assessment of the outcomes have been the exception, not the routine. Increasing complexities of teaching and demands for school improvement and accountability underscore the need for processes and content that help us work together effectively in diverse school contexts.

We begin each of the twelve chapters with a figure that highlights that chapter's context, process, and content. For example, in Chapter 1 teamwork is the emphasis of the context square. Collaboration is the focus of the process circle. Consultation appears in the content triangle.

Focusing questions guide the reading of each chapter. Opening vignettes set the contextual stage. (See footnote accompanying the first vignette, which applies to all other vignettes as well.) Applications appearing throughout the chapters are for individual reflection and, where apropos, for group discussion. Tables and figures provide organization, visual representations, and practical checklists for implementing the material. Reviews at the chapter ends match the focusing questions to summarize the chapter's material. A section of To Do and Think About activities allows further exploration and learning by doing and sharing. The materials listed in For Further Reading guide readers to more information about that chapter's main topics.

FOCUSING QUESTIONS

1. What perspectives on consultation, collaboration, and teamwork are appropriate for the educational context?

2. What is collaborative school consultation and what is it not?

3. What are the major elements in working together as consultants, collaborators, and active participants in teaching teams?

4. What major differences among educators' styles and preferences influence interactions in the school context?

5. How do adult differences affect consultation, collaboration, and teamwork?

6. In what ways might adult differences be used constructively to better serve all students' learning needs?

KEY TERMS

autonomy	consulting teacher	professional development
client	cooperation	role clarification
collaboration	coordination	role delineation
communication	co-teaching	role parity
consultant	personality	school context
consultation	preferences	teamwork
consultee	preservice teachers	

VIGNETTE 1.A

The setting is the faculty room of a typical high school where three faculty members are sharing school news and airing their concerns.[1]

English Teacher: I'm getting another special education student next week—with severe learning disabilities this time. I guess this is more fallout from Public Law 94-142 or IDEA 1997 or inclusion, or whatever. So I'll have this student in my composition and literature classes, along with the student with behavior disorders I've been coping with all semester, and state assessments, and NCLB, and on and on.

Math Teacher: (grinning) Must be because you're doing such a great job. (serious tone) But I know what you mean. Our special ed teachers aren't taking these kids out of our classes as much as they did when I first started teaching. But that was before we'd ever heard the word *inclusion* or No Child Left Behind.

English Teacher: Well, they say a "consulting teacher" is coming to our next departmental meeting to talk about our role in helping these students with special needs. I understand we're going to be asked to collaborate—whatever that takes—along with all the other things we do, of course.

Physical Education Teacher/Coach: Hmmm, don't those two words cancel each other out? "Consult" and "collaborate," that is. I believe you English teachers call that an oxymoron. Now, I'd be inclined to *consult* a tax accountant for some expert advice, but isn't *collaboration* where everyone works together to accomplish goals? And as for *teamwork,* I can tell you what a difficult process that is when you have a group of independent thinkers and free spirits who like to do things their own way and want to be the star!

English Teacher: Frankly, I'm not interested in word games or coaching problems right now. I'm more concerned about finding out where the time is going to come from to do one more thing. And I want to know who will have the bottom-line responsibility for which students, and when, and where. And how!

Math Teacher: Right. I had some concerns about including all students in my instruction and testing. I think we need more help to pull it off, and I hope we get it.

Coach: You said it! Sounds like it will be quite a challenge for all of us.

[1]We recommend that those using this book with a group read each of the chapter vignettes aloud, with readers contributing their parts in a conversational tone and manner. In this way the situations will be more likely to seem relevant and facilitative rather than artificial and contrived.

PROFESSIONAL AUTONOMY, PROFESSIONAL COLLEGIALITY

Teaching is a multidimensional activity. This complex, demanding role has never been easy and it is becoming more challenging each year. School personnel are bombarded with more and more responsibilities, and the public is raising expectations for student achievement. Cosmetic alteration of existing programs and practices will not be enough to address the complex issues and multiple concerns.

In the past, teachers worked alone in their classrooms for the most part. They marked attendance forms, took lunch counts, and completed other daily procedures, then closed their classroom door and taught the required content to their students. They tried to handle each learning situation with minimal outside help. To ask for assistance would have been tantamount to showing insecurity or demonstrating incompetence in carrying out their duties. Hardy teachers of eight grades in one-room schoolhouses had managed without help, hadn't they?

FIGURE 1.1   "I feel so alone!"

By Jane More Loeb

Even in modern times teachers are somewhat removed from other adults and tend to function autonomously, having little rich, meaningful dialogue with professional colleagues during school. In a poll of over 1,000 teachers conducted by *Learning* magazine and reported by the Education Commission of the United States more than a decade ago, 78 percent of the respondents said that isolation from their colleagues was a major or moderate problem (Turner, 1987). Teachers may go through an entire school day without speaking to other adults in a reflective, planful way (Eisner, 1988). The absence of dialogue with peers is consistently recognized as a problem that contributes to teachers' feelings of isolation and inhibits their inclination to modify classroom practices (Johnson & Pugach, 1996). Chunking of the typical school day further insulates teachers from sources of ideas beyond their own background of experiences. This is particularly evident at the high school level where teachers might have five classes and several different preparations as they interact with more than 100 students daily (see Figure 1.1).

So even though schools are multidimensional centers of activity and could be described as very social places, the individual teacher may feel stranded on a crowded island devoid of adult interactions and professional stimulation. Nevertheless, while teachers may wish for more small-group meetings on mutual interests, and desire regular grade-level meetings, along with frequent chances to observe other teachers, and richer opportunities for inservice training, many are not prepared for engaging in collaborative efforts. Some comment candidly that they did not choose a teaching career to work all that much with adults. Others feel that teaming up with co-teachers or consulting teachers will be perceived as a sign of professional weakness or lack of confidence in their abilities. Also, too little time is available for the concentrated effort that productive interaction requires, and opportunities are rare for observing educators in other school settings to learn new ideas and revitalize enthusiasm.

When teachers do have time and opportunity to interact with colleagues, it is likely to be during professional development sessions. Unfortunately, these activities often are too highly structured and short-lived to allow meaningful interaction. Many are scheduled at the end of a hectic day, when teachers are tired, wanting to reflect a bit on their teaching day, to set the stage for the next day, and then to turn their attention toward home or community activities. Now and then teachers are visited in their classrooms by supervisors, administrators, student teachers, and sometimes parents. However, these occasions tend to create more feelings of anxiety and defensiveness than support and collegiality.

Some school systems do encourage co-teaching as a way of allowing teachers to support each other and broaden their teaching repertoires. But well-intentioned efforts to co-teach too often result in turn-teaching—"You teach this part of the lesson and then take a break or make the copies for next hour, while I handle the part coming up."

■ ■ ■ ■ ■ ▬▬

APPLICATION 1.1
COLLEGIALITY HELPS

Using Figure 1.1 to stir your thinking, recall one or more times when feelings of isolation seemed almost overwhelming, and collegial interaction would have "saved the day."

Professionals cannot be coerced into being collegial (Wildman & Niles, 1987). Teachers who are accustomed to being in charge and making virtually all the day-to-day decisions in their classrooms cannot be ordered to just go out and collaborate with each other or co-teach to any meaningful degree. Along with incentive and time, they need structure, practice, encouragement, and positive feedback about their effectiveness to perform these sophisticated, demanding functions.

DESCRIBING COLLABORATIVE SCHOOL
CONSULTATION AND CO-TEACHING

Just what *is* school consultation? Collaboration in schools? Team teaching or co-teaching? And how can these functions nurture effective partnership among teachers, families, and communities for all students, particularly for those with special learning and behavior needs?

Working definitions of *consultation, collaboration,* and *co-teaching* for school settings must be general enough to apply to a wide range of school structures and circumstances, yet flexible enough for useful adaptation to each context of local school needs. *Webster's Third New International Dictionary, unabridged* (1976), and *Webster's New Collegiate Dictionary, 8th edition* (1996), include a wealth of synonyms for these terms and many other related words such as *communication, cooperation,* and *coordination.* These words complement each other to form a conceptual foundation for consultation, collaboration, and teamwork in schools. Examples of helpfully explanatory words are:

consult: Advise, seek advice, confer, confab, huddle, parley, counsel, deliberate, consider, examine, refer to, group, communicate, review, apply for information, take counsel, discuss, seek the opinion of, talk over a situation or subject with someone.

consultation: Advisement, care, counsel, conference, or formal deliberation.

consulting: Deliberating together, asking advice or opinion of, or conferring.

consultant: One who gives professional advice or services in a field of special knowledge and training, or simply one who consults, or consults with, another.

consultee: As described in social science literature, the mediator between consultant and client (Tharp, 1975).

client: Individual, group, agency, department, community, or sometimes even a nation receiving benefits from the services of a consultant. (*Target* is occasionally used as a synonym.)

collaborate: Labor together or work jointly (especially in an intellectual endeavor); assist, associate, unite, pool.

teamwork, teaming: A number of persons associated in some joint action when they work cooperatively together. Joining forces or efforts, with each individual contributing a clearly-defined portion of the effort, but also subordinating personal prominence to the efficiency of the whole.

communication: The art of expressing ideas, the act of transmitting, giving, or exchanging information or opinions by writing, speech, or signs.

cooperation: The act of uniting, banding together, combining, concurring, agreeing, consenting, or conjoining; to work or act with others willingly and agreeably for common purpose or benefit.

coordination: Bringing elements into a common action, movement, or condition; synchronizing, attuning, adjusting, combining in harmonious relation.

co-teaching: Two or more teachers planning and implementing instruction, typically in an inclusive classroom setting.

Useful Definitions

In order to fit a variety of school contexts and student needs, the following definitions frame concepts in this book:

> **Collaborative school consultation is interaction in which school personnel and families confer, consult, and collaborate as a team to identify learning and behavioral needs, and to plan, implement, evaluate, and revise as needed the educational programs that are expected to serve those needs.**

The collaborative consultant in schools is defined here as follows:

> **A collaborative school consultant is a facilitator of effective communication, cooperation, and coordination who confers, consults, and collaborates with other school personnel, support personnel, students, and families on a team that addresses special learning and behavioral needs of students.**

All who are involved—consultant(s), consultee, and client, are collaborators working together in a combined effort to address identified needs. For example, in the vignette at the beginning of this chapter, the client is a new student who has a learning disability. The learning disabilities consultant will serve the student indirectly, for the most part, by collaborating with the classroom teacher who will be the consultee and the provider of direct services to the student. Some services might be provided by the learning disabilities consultant to the student, but for the most part the direct service is given primarily by the classroom teacher.

Consultation has become an integral part of helping professions, with each one offering a unique perspective to the process (Bramlett & Murphy, 1998). In every profession it involves sharing of expertise, and those in the consultant role do not hold claim to all the expertise. Competent consultants also listen and learn. They sometimes help consultees discover what they already know. They help others recognize their own talents and trust their own skills.

To collaborate is to labor together. Collaborators do not compromise and cooperate so much as they confer and contribute. Compromise can imply giving up some part of, or conceding, something. Cooperation might be mutually agreeable to all involved, but is not necessarily designed for mutual benefit (Welch, 1998). Collaboration, however, means adding to and making more so that all benefit.

Reports from school districts throughout the United States identify collaboration as a key variable in the successful implementation of inclusive education (Villa & Thousand, 2003, p. 22). In a study of more than 600 educators, collaboration was the only variable predicting positive attitudes toward inclusion among general and special educators (Villa, Thousand, Meyers, & Nevin, 1996).

In collaboration all are involved as active partners. The differentiated tasks can be allocated among individuals with various skills to contribute. Sometimes collaboration means recognizing differences and finding ways to accommodate those differences. The collaborative process is enriched by diversity among the collaborators—diversity of experience, perspectives, values, abilities, and interests. Individual differences of adults who consult and collaborate are rich ingredients for successful collaborations. The great need to recognize and maximize adult differences and use them constructively in group work will be addressed later in the chapter.

The concept of co-teaching as team partners in school settings is receiving increased attention among school professionals. Teamwork is working for the good of the whole— where individual preferences are subtended or set aside for the larger cause. Many heads and hearts are better than one, and the pooled experience, talent, knowledge, and ideas of a group are even better than the sum of the individual parts. Various forms for team teaching exist and and there are many different terms used to describe the process: *team teaching, co-teaching, cooperative teaching,* and *collaborative teaching* (Welch, 1998). Welch and Sheridan (1995) suggest that team-taught instruction can be microlevel staff development when each teacher models new skills for the other.

As part of a team, each co-teacher contributes a clearly defined portion of the effort that comes together to create a complete plan of action. Although some would regard consultation and collaboration as confounding terms that should not be used together, the more persuasive argument is that collaboration involves mutual problem-solving with interaction from the consultant. Idol, Paolucci-Whitcomb, and Nevin (1986) used the terms together to describe an interactive process enabling people with diverse expertise to generate creative solutions for problems in which they have mutual interest. Kampwirth (1999) asserts that both terms have evolved sufficiently so that they can indeed be used together.

How Consultation, Collaboration, and Team Teaching Differ

All three processes—consultation, collaboration, and co-teaching, as they occur in the school context, involve interaction among school personnel, families, and students working together to achieve common goals. However, subtle distinctions can be made.

In school consultation, the consultant contributes specialized expertise toward an educational problem, and the consultee delivers direct service utilizing that expertise. Consultants and consultees begin to collaborate when they assume equal ownership of the problem and solutions. Collaboration is a way of working in which power struggles *and* ineffectual politeness are perceived as detrimental to team goals. Friend and Cook (1992) distinguish between consultation and collaboration by describing collaborations as styles or approaches to interactions that occur during the consultation process. They propose that a collaborative approach can be used at some stages of consultation and not others, and with some consultees but not others. In their view collaborative consultation must be voluntary, with one professional assisting another to address a problem concerning a third party. They emphasize that successful consultants use different styles of interaction under different circumstances within different situations.

Teamwork fuels group spirit, develops process skills that help teachers interact in more productive ways, and fosters a more intellectual atmosphere (Maeroff, 1993). One of the best examples of teamwork is in a musical ensemble. Whether one is accompanying, performing with a small group, or playing with an orchestra, band, or choir, it is the united effort that creates the musical experience. Musicians of many instruments are not brought together to play the same note. Doing so would make the music only louder, not richer and more harmonious! In similar fashion, co-teachers work in concert, not usually in perfect unison, to create an effective learning experience for all students in the class. Consultation, collaboration, and co-teaching provide consultants, consultees, and teaching partners with the opportunities to engage in a "strengths" type of interaction, with each person using and building on the strengths of the others.

■ ■ ■ ■ ■ ▬▬

APPLICATION 1.2
IDENTIFYING TEACHER RESPONSIBILITIES

List all the various responsibilities you can think of that a teacher typically performs during the course of a school year. Use your recollections of student days, college coursework, student teaching, and any teaching experience that you have had. Along with instruction and curriculum preparation, include assessment, management, extracurricular, supervisory, and maintenance responsibilities. Expect to come up with 100 or more!

If you team up with other teachers in various grade levels, content areas, and specialized roles to do this activity, the combined lists could become be a colorful and impressive collage of teaching responsibilities. The process itself will be an example of teamwork, with each person adding information from his or her own perspectives and experiences. And so—collaborative consultation!

What Collaborative School Consultation *Is*

Educators—including special education teachers, classroom teachers, school administrators, related services and support personnel, as well as parents—consult, collaborate and work as team members when they take part in one or more of these:

- Discussing students' needs.
- Listening to colleagues' concerns about a teaching situation.
- Helping identify and define educational problems.
- Facilitating problem solving in the school setting.

- Promoting classroom alternatives as first interventions for students with special learning and behavior needs.
- Serving as a medium for student referrals.
- Demonstrating instructional techniques.
- Providing direct assistance to classroom teachers who have students with special learning and behavior needs.
- Leading or participating in professional development activities.
- Assisting teachers in designing and implementing behavior change programs.
- Sharing resources, materials, and ideas with colleagues.
- Participating in co-teaching or demonstration teaching.
- Engaging in assessment and evaluation activities.
- Serving on curriculum committees, textbook committees, and school advisory councils.
- Following up on educational issues and concerns with colleagues.
- Easing colleagues' loads in matters involving students' special needs.
- Networking with other professionals and outside agencies.

What Collaborative School Consultation *Is Not*

School consultation is *not* therapy, nor is it counseling for the consultee (Brown, Wyne, Blackburn, & Powell, 1979). The focus must be upon educational concerns relevant to the needs of the client, not the problems or needs of the consultee. West and Idol (1987), and Morsink, Thomas and Correa (1991) differentiate consultation from counseling by describing consultation as focused on issues, while counseling is focused on individuals. Conoley and Conoley (1982) caution that the consultant must talk about the client, not the consultee.

The consulting teacher is *not* the equivalent of a resource teacher with more free time to spend in interaction with general classroom teachers (Huefner, 1988). Furthermore, the consultant role is not always the responsibility of the educational specialist. Collaboration among professional colleagues is *not* talk or discussion for its own sake. It does not involve taking on the authority of school administrators, and it should not be a substitute for the individual teacher's accountability (Smith, 1987). It must not be supervisory or judgmental.

Importantly, collaborative school consultation must *not* be intended as a money-saving mechanism for serving included students. The movie "Educating Peter," an HBO Academy Award-winning documentary film that aired on television several years ago failed to clarify the array of related services and support personnel that were assembled to design and manage that school situation (*CEC Today,* 1993, p. 86). So the high cost and total number of personnel who contributed to Peter's successful inclusion in that general third grade classroom were not apparent to the casual viewer.

■ ■ ■ ■ ■

APPLICATION 1.3
COLLABORATING TO IDENTIFY TEACHER RESPONSIBILITIES

Using the list of teacher responsibilities you compiled in Application 1.2, sort the list under headings for tasks, such as instructional, curricular, managerial, logistical, evaluative, and supportive. Then look at which ones might take place most productively in collaborative contexts. For example, under a responsibility of ordering books and supplies classified as managerial, teams of teachers might collaborate to pool their library allocations and plan orders of materials that can be shared or used for team teaching. Asterisk (*) those with collaborative potential and add others, such as "organizing cross-grade tutors and study-buddies" or "engaging families in preparing a notebook of community resources."

ROLE RESPONSIBILITIES IN COLLABORATIVE SCHOOL CONSULTATION

When contemplating collaborative consultation roles, educators often express their concerns with these questions:

- Who *am* I in this role?
- How do I carry out responsibilities of the role?
- How will I know whether or not I am succeeding?
- How can I prepare for such a role?

First, it is necessary for central administrators and policy-makers to justify and authenticate the need for consultative and collaborative roles. Then building level administrators must stress the importance of the consulting role and ensure consultant parity among other teaching staff. A key variable in justifying and authenticating the role is allocating sufficient time and suitable places for interactions to take place.

Teachers will need encouragement to share enthusiastically with consulting teachers the responsibilities for all students. Related services personnel and support personnel will need to be integrated into a school consultation context. Families must receive information about the service roles and be assured that such type of service is appropriate for their child. Students should be an integral part of the interaction and have opportunities to be consultants and consultees as well as clients. Ultimately, communities must support the purposes and anticipate the potential benefits from consultation, collaboration, and co-teaching.

VIGNETTE 1.B

Now consider another event. This one takes place a short time after Vignette 1.A, described earlier. Three special education teachers are talking together in the school district's conference room before their special education director arrives for a planning meeting..

Learning Disabilities Teacher: I understand we're here to decide how we're going to inform staff and parents about the consultation and collaboration practices we'll be implementing soon. But I think we'd better figure out first just what it is we *will* be doing in these roles.

Behavioral Disorders Teacher: Definitely. I have a really basic question. What am I going to do the first week, even the first day, as a consulting teacher? I understand you had some training in collaboration and consulting in your former position out-of-state, but this is new to the rest of us.

Gifted Education Teacher: I agree. I've been thinking about all those personal styles, and teaching styles, and subject areas we will be dealing with. Teachers won't all like or want the same things.

Learning Disabilities Teacher: I doubt this is something we can become experts in very quickly. From what little I've had a chance to read about the term *collaborative school consultation,* the secret for success is good process skills.

Gifted Education Teacher: Yes, but at the same time we have to take into account the materials and methods that each student needs in order to learn. I'm a bit apprehensive about it all, but I'm willing to try it.

Behavioral Disorders Teacher: I guess I am, too. I've been thinking for some time now that our current methods of dealing with learning and behavior problems are not as effective and efficient as they should be. I think we must be optimistic about the possible benefits both students *and* teachers could receive from this method of helping students learn.

Interchangeable Roles and Responsibilities

Consultants become consultees when they seek expertise and information from a classroom teacher, school psychologist, administrator, parent, or resource person in the community. On some occasions a general education teacher is consultant for a special education teacher in order to contribute information about a student's problems within a classroom context not available to the special education teacher. In another instance, a parent might act as consultant for a situation in which the principal functions as consultee to help a teacher client with a classroom situation.

A student could be consultant to a teacher consultee in a situation where the family is the client because the family situation is accentuating the student's school problems. The student might contribute to problem identification and interventions, with the teacher providing direct service to parents.

The client of a consultation is typically an individual; however, clients also can be a group or team of individuals, such as a family or a within-class group of students. On occasion the client might even be an entire staff, school system, or community.

Individuals who are consultants (specialists), consultees (mediators), or clients (targets) in one consultative situation may exchange roles under different circumstances. For example, a special education teacher might be a consultant for one situation and consultee in another. The student is typically the client, or target, for the direct and indirect services of consultee and consultant, but in some cases the student could be a consultee or consultant. Consultation may be initiated by a special education teacher, school administrator, supervisor, or support service professional who has determined that a student's learning or behavior need requires attention from a collaborative team. It also might be initiated by a teacher, parent, or student acting in a consultee role. In either case, both parties—consultant and consultee—share responsibility for working out a plan to help the client (Heron & Harris, 1982.)

Although roles and responsibilities may vary among individuals from situation to situation, with appropriate role delineation a collaborative spirit can prevail. Collaboration to achieve a common goal generally produces more beneficial results than isolated efforts by an individual. The whole of the combined efforts then is greater than the sum of its parts

(Slavin, 1988). It is the basic idea that two heads are better than one, and several heads are better yet. The consultation process channels each individual's strengths and talents toward serving the client's needs. (See Figure 1.2, mixing and matching roles among the three columns to fit various school contexts.)

Initiating Collaborative School Consultation

School improvement issues, social concerns, and economic conditions may have convinced educators that consultation, collaboration, and teamwork are promising practices for helping students with special needs, but conversion of paper plans and philosophies to func-

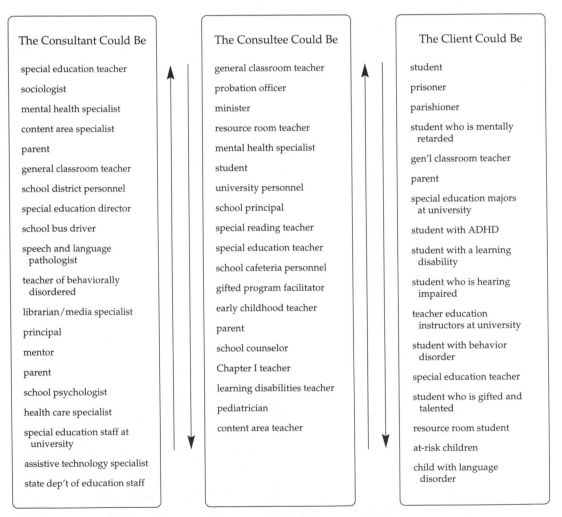

The Consultant Could Be	The Consultee Could Be	The Client Could Be
special education teacher	general classroom teacher	student
sociologist	probation officer	prisoner
mental health specialist	minister	parishioner
content area specialist	resource room teacher	student who is mentally retarded
parent	mental health specialist	gen'l classroom teacher
general classroom teacher	student	parent
school district personnel	university personnel	special education majors at university
special education director	school principal	student with ADHD
school bus driver	special reading teacher	student with a learning disability
speech and language pathologist	special education teacher	student who is hearing impaired
teacher of behaviorally disordered	school cafeteria personnel	teacher education instructors at university
librarian/media specialist	gifted program facilitator	student with behavior disorder
principal	early childhood teacher	special education teacher
mentor	parent	student who is gifted and talented
parent	school counselor	resource room student
school psychologist	Chapter I teacher	at-risk children
health care specialist	learning disabilities teacher	child with language disorder
special education staff at university	pediatrician	
assistive technology specialist	content area teacher	
state dep't of education staff		

FIGURE 1.2   Interchangeable Roles in Collaborative School Consultation

tioning systems is not simple. Questions in Vignette 1.B above that were put forth in the school district conference room raise practical concerns:

- Where do I begin as a school consultant?
- What do I do the first day on the job? The first week?
- Let me see a sample schedule for the first week. The first month, also.
- Where am I to be headed by the end of the year?

■ ■ ■ ■ ■ ▬▬▬▬▬▬▬▬▬▬▬▬▬▬▬▬▬▬▬▬▬▬▬▬▬▬▬▬

APPLICATION 1.4
CHANGING ROLES

Each one in a group of three educators receives a red or blue or yellow card. Red cards signify consultant roles, blue are consultees, and yellow are clients. Each person takes a plain card that has a designated role on it from the list in Figure 1.2. Those who are blue card consultees think of a situation, and with their assigned roles all three work out the details of who would do what when. Then the colored cards are switched. The new consultee thinks of another situation, and all three work through that one. The last switch of colored cards will be an opportunity to practice a third role. This application illustrates the interchangeability of roles for a variety of situational combinations.

Other questions and concerns that are likely to surface include:

- Will I have the opportunity to work with students at all? That is why I chose teaching as a career.
- Where's my room? Will I get office space and supplies?
- Will at least a small group of students fit into that space for some group work?
- Will I be regarded as an important part of the teaching staff?
- I think I will need special preparation for consultation, so where do I get it?
- How will I be evaluated in this role, and by whom?
- If consulting ultimately prepares consultees for direct delivery of special education services, *am I working myself out of a job?*

Those who will be engaging in consultation services primarily as consultees may be thinking:

- Will this process make me look and feel incompetent?
- How much of my ever-dwindling time with all my students be eroded by this method of service?
- When in the world will I find time and space to interact with these folks?

Participants in consultation and collaboration must be able to voice their concerns and feelings of insecurity as they sort out the dynamics of their new roles. School administrators have the responsibility of initiating open, candid expression of concerns and encouraging intensive discussion about the issues.

KEY ELEMENTS IN CONSULTING
AND COLLABORATING

Four elements of collaborative school consultation processes are pictured in the clocklike Figure 1.3:

- **Delineation** of roles
- **Framework** for structuring the roles
- **Evaluation** for assessment of outcomes
- **Preparation** for the roles

Within the four categories, twelve key areas need to be addressed. The sequence of the twelve is very important. Note the starting point in Figure 1.3. In many school contexts, educators begin "too late in the day" to implement consultation, collaboration, and teamwork. In other words, the call for commitment—shown at the "five p.m." position, is not the starting point. If an attempt is made to start there rather than with preparation in the "early morning hours of the clock," failure of school consultation will be all but assured. Educators in all educational contexts—administrators, teacher educators, teachers, and support staff—must begin very early in the process, with preparation as the first step. This preparation should take place at all levels—preservice, graduate, and inservice.

Role Delineation

The starting point for collaborative school consultation is with careful *preparation* for roles. With that point emphatically made, we will, however, discuss role delineation first in order to put the need for that preparation into perspective.

A specific school role such as counselor, general classroom teacher, specialist in learning disabilities, speech pathologist, or facilitator for the gifted program does not designate a particular consultative role. Rather, the consultation role emanates from a situational need. For example, the consultant, consultee, or client role might be assumed by a parent who provides information to the school administrator, or by a learning disabilities teacher who helps the coach assess a student athlete's learning problem, or by a mentor who provides the gifted program facilitator with material for development of a gifted student's potential.

The consultee teams up with and collaborates with the consultant to provide direct service to the client. The client role belongs to the one with the identified need or problem. The total concept reflects the contemporary approach to special services where student needs, not student labels, determine the service and delivery method, and an array of services is targeted and made available to address those needs.

Role Clarification.   The first subpart to be addressed in role delineation is clarification of the role. Until educators become comfortable with the concepts of consultation, collaboration, and educational teams, ambiguous feelings about it all may persist. Teachers and school staff sometimes are not sure why there are consulting teachers or what these people are supposed to be doing. For example, a facilitator in a consulting role for gifted programs in a large urban high school for several years kept hearing variations on the same concern—"Just how *do* you spend your day with only 30 students on your caseload? After all, they *are* fast

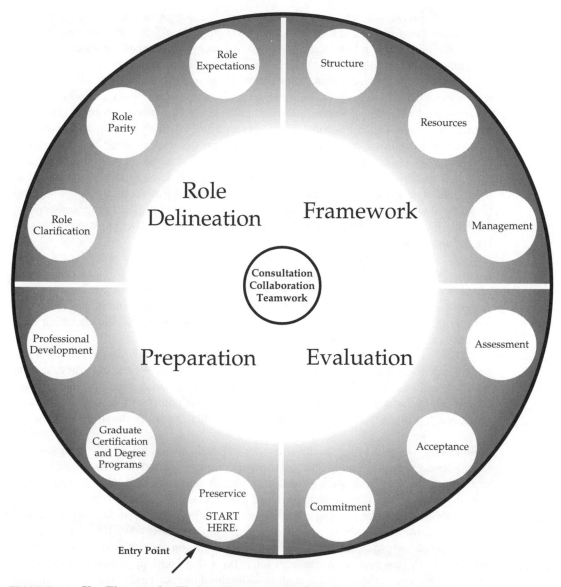

FIGURE 1.3   Key Elements for Working Together Effectively (proceeding clockwise)

learners." So the facilitator developed a job matrix to categorize the planning, implementation, and evaluation aspects and expectations of the role, and shared it with teaching colleagues and administrators (Hay, 1984).

Classroom teachers may even blame their own heavy responsibilities on the seemingly lighter caseloads of consulting teachers. One high school English teacher told a newly-appointed consulting teacher, "If you were back in your classroom teaching English instead of 'facilitating' for a few high ability students, my own student numbers wouldn't be so high." Paradoxically, consulting teachers often have excessively demanding workloads when travel time among schools, and preparing or locating special curriculum and materials, are taken into account. If their workload is too great, the effectiveness of their services will be diminished severely because little time and energy will remain for the coordination and communication activities that are integral to consultation success.

Seamless instructional plans for students' learning and behavioral needs require extensive knowledge of role responsibilities among all involved (Allington & Broikou, 1988). A classroom teacher and a reading specialist may have information to share in addressing a struggling reader's strengths and deficits, yet may know relatively little about each other's curriculum, educational priorities, or expectations for the student. They must coordinate their efforts, or those efforts may be counterproductive. In one unfortunate case, a reading specialist was instructing a fifth-grader with reading problems to slow down and read more deliberately, while the learning disabilities specialist was encouraging him to read much more rapidly and was thinking about making a referral for gifted program services. The student, a pleasant and cooperative child, was trying valiantly to please both teachers simultaneously.

Although there has been minimal study of general education teachers' roles as collaborators with special educators, some research does suggest a gap between teacher perceptions of actual and ideal performance in collaborative roles. Harris and Zetlin (1993) emphasize that collaborative consultation requires people to relinquish their traditional roles in order to share skills and to rotate their assignments in ways that expand educational experiences for both students and the adults involved.

Consultees may question a consultant's ability to address their unique classroom situation, especially if the consultant is young and inexperienced. As one classroom teacher put it when asked about involving the special education consulting teacher, "I'd never ask for *her* help. What does she know about a full classroom of students? She's never dealt with more than five or six at a time, and she never has taught in a regular classroom."

Role Parity.   Along with role ambiguity and misunderstanding, special education consulting teachers may feel an absence of role parity. They may feel as if they do not belong to any one school or faculty. They may feel minimally important to students and the educational system, or cut off and isolated from general classroom teachers because of differing responsibilities, and from special education colleagues because of distance and schedules.

Substitutes might not be provided for consulting teachers when they are absent. In fact, these teachers may be pulled out of their own roles on occasion to substitute for absent classroom teachers, or to perform other tasks that come up suddenly. Consulting teachers have been asked to guide visitors on a school tour, drive the school bus, and perform secretarial tasks. Meanwhile, classroom teachers are not going to wait with open arms for consulting personnel to come and save them. Inevitably, school bells ring, classroom doors open, and the school day commences. Life, and school, will go on every day for students and their teachers with or without support from others. All of this conveys a message of diminished parity for the consulting role and a subtle or not-so-subtle impression of non-importance.

Role confusion and inequality can cause stress and may lead to burnout eventually. Teachers who feel like "second-class" colleagues, not accepted or appreciated as a vital part of the staff, may develop defenses that erode their effectiveness. Some who travel extensively in their cars from school to school have been dubbed "windshield" personnel in some areas. These problems are accentuated by the misconception that consultants have no own-ership in student welfare and development. Ongoing recognition and reinforcement of con-sulting teacher contributions toward student success are important for credibility of the role and professional morale, and students served indirectly by the consultant tend not to be viewed as "belonging" to the consultant.

Role Expectations.   Sometimes colleagues have unreasonable expectations for the con-sultant role, anticipating instant success and miraculous student progress in a very short while. When results with students are slower than the consultees have hoped, or do not hap-pen at all, their attitudes may range from guarded skepticism to open disapproval of the con-sultation approach.

　　These educators may expect too much, or too little, from the consulting role. A school consultant cannot be a panacea for every student's difficulties. Teachers may wish to see re-sults too soon, or neglect to monitor results and then let ineffective service drag on too long. Consultees may exploit consultants by expecting them to "fix" the student, and if this does not happen, then downplay consultation as a flop. Consulting teachers may expect and want to work only with students, not adults. "I was trained to work with kids, and that's what I enjoy," confessed one consultant when assigned to an indirect service role. The team ap-proach may be awkward for an educator at first, not only for a consultant, but for the con-sultee as well. Unrealistic and unreasonable expectations must be set aside in the early planning stages of school consultation methods. Consultants should set reasonable goals for themselves and not try to do too much.

　　Sometimes the most difficult part of a support role is backing out once the consultee experiences success in meeting the client's needs (Stainback & Stainback, 1988). It is highly unlikely that effective consultation will mean elimination of the position, as some consult-ing teachers fear. The more successful that consultation services are, the more teachers and administrators are prone to value them for both their immediate contribution and their long-range positive ripple effects. As one example, students missed in initial referrals could be targeted and benefited by the interaction among classroom teachers and consulting teachers (Dyck & Dettmer, 1989).

　　The involvement of as many school personnel as possible through needs assessments, interviews, professional development, and both formal and informal communications, will minimize unwarranted expectations for consulting roles. Building successful collaborations with more receptive and cooperative colleagues at first will generate confidence in the con-sultant and respect for the approach by the reluctant and the resistant.

Framework

A framework for school consultation, collaboration, and teamwork calls for structures that provide time and facilities in which to meet, and management of the details so consultation is as convenient and nonintrusive as possible. Structure will be addressed in more detail in Chapter 2, and time and resource management in Chapter 6.

Structure.   Consultants need a structure within which to carry out their roles and respon-sibilities. It is one thing to design a hypothetical method of consultation, quite another to de-sign multiple methods for different situations, and an even greater challenge to select and put into motion the right method for each situation. This is easier if preceded by role clarification and assurance of role parity and appropriate role expectations.

The consultant will want to formulate several methods for consultation and collaboration in a variety of grade levels, subject areas, special needs categories, and school, community, and family contexts. The consultation structure should fit the context of the system. It also should provide a workable model, which will be addressed in Chapter 2. Consultants should design their own consultation method to custom-fit school needs. A poll of teachers asking how they would use a consulting teacher is a good way to begin. Studying and observing team teaching, and collaborative and consultative structures, from other school systems also is helpful.

Resources.   One of the most overwhelming and frustrating obstacles to school consultation is lack of time for consultation to occur. Scarcity of time is a major deterrent to success of the collaborative consultation process (Idol-Maestas & Ritter, 1985; Johnson, Pugach & Hammittee, 1988; McLoughlin & Kelly, 1982; Speece & Mandell, 1980). Idol (1986) recommends that resource teachers have at least one-third of their school time available for consultations. In an earlier study by Neel (1981), 48 percent of the special education teachers queried reported that they have no time scheduled for consultation and are expected to provide consultation services beyond regularly scheduled teaching hours. Most often they must use their own planning time for consultation, which is not an ideal way to instill positive attitudes toward the consultation approach.

Many special education teachers and classroom teachers have reported that their school day is simply not designed to accommodate collaboration (Idol-Maestas, 1983; Stainback & Stainback, 1988). Even if the consultant can arrange and coordinate a schedule for meeting with consultees and following up on results, it can be next-to-impossible to arrange significant blocks of consultee time for collaboration. Working out such a plan is one of the most formidable tasks facing a consultant, particularly one who also has direct teaching responsibilities at specific times.

Administrators must assume responsibility for allocating time needed by consultants and consultees to collaborate and co-teach. If they lend their authority to this endeavor, school personnel will be more willing to brainstorm ways of getting together. Schenkat (1988) points out that if working conditions in schools could be restructured to allow greater flexibility in scheduling, teachers could find the time to collaborate with colleagues. This would help build bridges between special education and general education, while expanding services to all students who have special needs.

Unfortunately, when consulting teachers first initiate consultation and collaboration, it is very likely that these activities will have to come out of their own time—before school, after school, during lunch hours, perhaps even on weekends. Even so, this *temporary* accommodation should be replaced as soon as possible with a more formal allocation of time during the school day. This is not only for their well-being, but to emphasize that consultation and collaboration are not simply add-on services to be carried out by a zealous, dedicated few.

When time *is* arranged for a consultation, facilities must be made available in which to conduct the consultation. The area should be pleasant, quiet, convenient, and relatively private for free exchange of confidences. Such a place is at a premium in a bustling school community.

Management.   There is a risk of letting fiscal issues, rather than student needs, dictate the service delivery method. The caseload issue must be addressed carefully. Assigning large caseloads to consulting teachers may save money in the short run, but could cost more eventually if student performance does not improve or if teachers burn out as a result (Huefner, 1988). Problems related to caseload are complex. For example, the average time needed to complete one Individual Education Program (IEP) has been assessed as 6.5 hours (Heron & Kimball, 1988; Price & Goodman, 1980). A consulting teacher with an overwhelming caseload of students and time-consuming responsibilities such as development of IEPs will have little or no time to consult and collaborate. Although direct service can be a strategy for easing into indirect service, the load must be manageable. If a consulting teacher's caseload is too great, direct service is inadequate, possibilities for indirect services are minimal, and the program is self-defeating.

One model, the Resource/Consulting Teacher Program (Idol-Maestas (1983), which will be discussed further in Chapter 2, incorporates 20 to 40 percent of the consulting teacher's school day into consultation-related activities. These include discussing educational problems, presenting ideas for use in regular classrooms, inservice, observation, performing curriculum-based assessment, demonstrating instructional techniques (Wiederholt, Hammill, & Brown, 1983), and coordinating the program.

A consultant must be very organized and efficient. Greenburg (1987) notes a number of studies indicating that while resource teachers may be committed to direct service as their major activity, considerable portions of their time are required for record-keeping, paperwork, and teacher consultant responsibilities (Evans, 1980; McGlothlin, 1981; Miller & Sabatino, 1978). Consulting teachers manage and monitor consultee use of materials as varied as books, tests, kits, tapes, films, and media equipment. They help teachers develop systems of observation, monitoring, and assessment, along with performing these activities themselves. Their paperwork, scheduling, and communication systems must be efficient and effective. Techniques for managing these activities will be presented in Chapter 6.

Recommended caseload numbers vary depending on school context, travel time required, grade level, exceptionalities and special needs served, and structure of the consulting method. The numbers must be kept manageable to fulfill the intent and promise of consultation and collaboration. The key lies in documenting carefully all consultation activities *and* making note also of those which should have happened but did not, due to time constraints. Consultants must negotiate with their administrators for reasonable caseload assignments and blocks of time in which to consult, collaborate, and co-teach.

Evaluation and Support

The third of four key elements in school consultation features evaluation and support. Educators will need to document the effectiveness of consultation and collaboration in order to ensure continuing support for this kind of educational service. School personnel are understandably skeptical of indirect service if it does not demonstrate its usefulness. They may be involved initially because they are told to, or because they have been talked into giving it a try, but their interest will wane if positive results are not forthcoming.

Assessment.   Assessment is vital to the success of collaborative school consultation. School personnel will be more accepting of this service delivery if its effectiveness can be demonstrated through appropriate interpretation of valid data. In keeping with the philosophy of collaboration, evaluation of the consultation should be designed cooperatively by personnel from varying roles.

Very few evaluation measures have been readily available in the published research on education-based consultation (Tindal & Taylor-Pendergast, 1989); a few of these are rating scales of judgments that represent a variety of skills and activities, and estimates of engaged time that note the activities required or demanded. Administrators, advisory council members, and policy-makers will need to study carefully the few procedures that are available for assessment, and beyond that, use their skills to design more helpful and practical assessment techniques that fit their school context and consultant role responsibilities.

Not only should processes and content be evaluated, but the context of the school setting as well. For example, a consultant may have excellent communication skills and a wealth of content with which to consult and collaborate, but if no time is provided for interaction, there will be few positive results. Consultants will want to evaluate every stage of the process to keep heading in the right direction. (Assessment will be addressed further in Chapter 6.)

Evaluation should include a variety of data-collection methods to provide the kinds of information needed by target groups. Consultation and collaboration practices must not be judged inadequate for the wrong reasons or under erroneous assumptions. If time has not been allocated for the interactions, if staff have not had preparation and encouragement, and if administrator support is lacking, those elements should be targeted for improvement before consultation service is faulted.

Acceptance.   Participation in collaborative programs must be voluntary for all involved in order for the programs to be accepted (Friend & Cook, 1990). Administrator acceptance and encouragement will help to a great extent. Broadcasting successes and promoting the benefits of consultations and collaborations that have taken place may get a collaborative consultation bandwagon rolling and the most influential of the reluctants on board. Most important, however, is involving people right from the start in needs assessments, planning efforts, evaluations, inservice presentations, and personal contacts to instill ownership and even arouse a little curiosity. Techniques and incentives for promoting acceptance of consultation, collaboration, and teamwork through professional development will be discussed in Chapter 10.

Commitment.   Consultation signals change. Collaboration requires practice. Co-teaching means sharing the ownership. These realities make involvement by school personnel more difficult, and attainment of their commitment more challenging. Consultation in the minds of many general educators remains associated with exclusive special education programs and assistance in mainstreamed classes. If teachers resent having more responsibility for special education students, they may blame school consultation and consultants for this situation. Consultees and support personnel need to develop a plan and a vision to share responsibilities for educating students who have special needs. Most of all, they need significant administrator support and encouragement for doing so. (This issue will be discussed in more depth in Chapter 10.) Those who consult must seize every opportunity to cultivate commitment by all for making it work.

Preparation

Now we return to the *initial* phase of the process. (See again Figure 1.3 on p. 15.) Preparation programs for mastering the skills of school consultation and collaboration are a necessity. Opportunities and incentives must be provided for three populations:

- Preservice students, who should prepare to be consultees and potential consultants.
- Graduate students in degree programs, who should develop skills in consulting and in preparing others to be consultants and consultees.
- Inservice teachers, who should prepare for roles as consultees and advocates for integrating consultation and collaboration into their school contexts.

Skills of the consultant and consultee are enhanced through professional development, coaching and feedback in process and content skill areas.

Preservice Preparation.   Teacher preparation programs do not often include consulting processes such as group problem solving, communication skills, and conflict resolution. Not so many years ago, studies revealed that collaborative consultation preparation for preservice teachers in college and university programs was the exception rather than the rule (Lilly & Givens-Ogle, 1981). Some progress has been made since that time, but much more is needed. Friend and Cook (1990) stress that preservice teachers need an understanding of the conditions for collaboration, and this is not typically a part of teacher education program curricula. They will need knowledge about and skills for sharing resources, sharing participation, and sharing accountability. Otherwise, they are being set up to fail, particularly in schools implementing collaborative practices.

Another much neglected area in preservice teacher preparation is family involvement. Novice teachers should have experiences in relating to families as valuable team members while they are still formulating their teaching philosophies and strategies (Kerns, 1992).

Phillips, Allred, Brulle, and Shank (1990) propose that collaboration and consultation skills can be cultivated by teacher educators at the preservice level. They recommend that teacher preparation programs provide introductory education courses in which general and special education preservice teachers participate jointly in practicum experiences that serve a diverse range of children's needs. However, this approach requires concerted effort by college and university personnel, many of whom have not prepared themselves to engage in collaboration and consultation functions, let alone to facilitate development of these behaviors in their students.

Some veteran educators may be nervous about having novice teachers address consultation practices before they have experienced real-world teaching. Nevertheless, the seeds of awareness can and should be planted early to bear fruit later in important ways. After all, for most new teachers there is not much time for experience to be acquired between that last day of their teacher education program and the first day of stepping into the classroom virtually alone as an autonomous professional with their assigned students.

Graduate Certification and Degree Programs.   If teachers are not trained in consultation, they will tend to shy away from pertinent feedback and provide only broad generalizations or retreat into paperwork associated with the role (Gersten, Darch, Davis, & George, 1991). Kauffman (1994) stresses that special education teachers who are being prepared to consult and collaborate with general educators must have special instructional and behavior management expertise or their input will have little meaning beyond that of the general educators.

The number of preparation programs for consulting teachers is increasing (Dickens & Jones, 1990; Gersten, Darch, Davis, & George, 1991; Thurston & Kimsey, 1989;), but universities have far to go to meet the needs. Some states require development of consultation skills for teacher certification. Inclusion of this training in standards for accreditation of teacher education programs would be one way to encourage more emphasis on collaborative school consultation and collaboration at the graduate and preservice levels. School administrators should recruit those who welcome the opportunity to work with adults as well as students in school settings.

Each training program will be unique; however, a basic program for collaboration should include:

- Delineating their roles
- Creating a framework that allows them to fulfill their roles
- Evaluating their effectiveness
- Helping prepare colleagues for collaborative consultation even as they expand their own proficiencies

Preparation programs must provide experiences well beyond the "mentioning" mode of training that offers only superficial exposure to a large amount of information and minimal or no practice with complex ideas and behaviors. Course syllabi should include not only the conventional learning strategies of lecture, reading, and discussion, but a strong focus on experiential content. Small-group activities, simulations and role-plays, interviewing, assessments, videotaped consultation practice, reaction and reflection papers, resource searches, and practice with the tools and strategies of technology will help educators to be more comfortable and capable in interactive school roles.

Professional Development.   Friend and Cook (1990) assert that teachers are being set up to fail when they enter the profession with content expertise and method but without skills for working effectively with colleagues. The lack of preparation for consultation is compounded by a dearth of empirical studies that might provide evidence for or against various components of consultation training. However, movements such as school restructuring and school improvement have stimulated some efforts such as those reported by Rule, Fodor-Davis, Morgan, Salzberg, and Chen (1990). In their study, Rule and colleagues identified the need for administrative support, technical assistance, and follow-up assistance, as well as the inservice training. Through inservice and other professional development activities, consultation and collaboration programs can be tailored to each school context.

INDIVIDUAL DIFFERENCES AMONG ADULTS IN SCHOOL ENVIRONMENTS

A patchwork quilt is made up of various colors, textures, sizes, and designs. If every piece were identical, the quilt would be drab and dull. Interesting, lively patchworks are those in which each piece contributes its uniqueness to the overall collage of colors and textures. Even if a few of the colors or textures clash, when assembled into an overall design the result is a vibrant, colorful structure to brighten any setting.

In much the same way schools are patchworks of attitudes, personalities, values, preferences, and interests. Each individual in the school setting is different, with every one contributing uniqueness to invigorate the whole. People may differ markedly and sometimes even take serious issue with one another, but the contributions of variety can be quite remarkable.

Educators attend to individual differences and preferences among students when planning for their learning needs, but too often overlook the beauty and value of patchwork quilt-type differences among the *adults* with whom they work. Constructive use of individual differences among school personnel is extremely important within the collaborative school environment.

It is easy in the busy and public but relatively autonomous school setting to overlook the impact that differing professional values, teaching styles, and personal interests of colleagues have on working together. Unfortunately, study of adult differences and attention to constructive use of those differences is, for the most part, neglected in teacher preparation programs. Yet the school arena sparkles with variability among individuals of all ages.

VIGNETTE 1.C

(Comments at various times of the school day in hallways and gathering areas):

"I was eager to try that teaching strategy in our school. Why don't other people on the faculty want to give it a shot? It's been working so well with the faculty across town. . . ."

"Here we go again. Another change to spin us around for our latest ride on the school improvement merry-go-round. . . ."

"Why are some people so negative toward new ideas before they even try them or give them a chance?. . . ."

"We just never see eye-to-eye on anything in our department. It's really frustrating. . . ."

"Seems like we do the same old thing, with people falling in line like sheep to stay together. Why not strike out for new ground? I say, let's take some risks and do something different for a change. . . ."

"I just can't figure out where that parent is coming from. . . ."

"*Another* meeting? They drag on and on, and we have nothing to show for all the time and effort we wasted. . . ."

"What a frantic mess that conference was! Not enough time even to figure out what the problem is, much less arrive at some sensible solutions. . . ."

"Wasn't that a great meeting? We're off to a good start. Now our next step should be. . . ."

Valuing Differences among Adults

Much of the seemingly random variation in human behavior is actually quite orderly and consistent, because it is based on the way people prefer to use their perception and judgment (Keirsey & Bates, 1978; Lawrence, 1993). If one person views the world and reacts to it in ways unlike another, it is because that person processes information differently. Different viewpoints contribute diverse insights which help broaden understanding of problems and generate promising alternatives for problem solutions.

It is easy and convenient, but myopic, to endorse only one way of doing something—one's own—while wondering why everyone else is not clever enough and agreeable enough to concur and fall into step. However, a situation perceived one way by one educator might be looked upon quite differently by another.

■ ■ ■ ■ ■ ▬▬▬▬▬▬▬▬▬▬▬

APPLICATION 1.5
PUTTING THE PIECES TOGETHER

The leader prepares several puzzles ahead of time. Pictures of adults interacting, schoolroom pictures, or pictures of children working or playing, are effective. There should be one puzzle for each 5 or 6 people and the size should be 8½ × 11 or larger. A light-colored, 1-inch "frame" around each picture should be left intact, and the rest of each picture cut into enough large pieces so every participant can have at least 2 or 3 pieces. After dividing into groups of 5 or 6 people, one person is designated responsibility for the frame. Every participant (including the frame-holder) takes several pieces of the disassembled puzzle. (The puzzle pieces should be large enough that several words can be written on them with a dark felt pen.) The group engages in discussion about their similar and different characteristics and preferences. The person with the frame writes characteristics around the frame that *everyone* in the group shares—for example, "We are all female," or "We all *don't* have a cat." Next, each person writes on each one of his or her pieces a different personal characteristic that belongs to no one else in the group—for example, "I was born in a taxicab en route to the hospital," or "Brussels sprouts is my favorite vegetable," or "I have a tattoo."

The group then assembles the puzzle, talks about it, and shares the information with all other groups. When displayed with an interaction-focused title, the assembled and glued puzzles make an effective bulletin board display or a two-sided mobile. All could be arranged into a group mobile and hung from the ceiling or doorway. (Occasionally puzzles may be handed out that are missing a piece or two. This metaphorically illustrates the "missing element" in a group that decreases their effectiveness.)

Thinking Together in Different Ways

In order to serve students best, educators do not need to think alike—they need to think *together*. The process of thinking together divergently is not an oxymoron—it can be very productive. Understanding and valuing the uniquenesses of adults in their orientations toward the world, and their styles and preferences for processing information, are key factors in the success of collegial relationships. Educators who make conscientious efforts to respect the individualism and independence of their students need to respect and protect these rights for their colleagues and the parents of their students as well.

One of the most overlooked but crucial factors in teacher preparation is the ability to relate constructively to others, including colleagues, by responding to them and their preferences and needs with emotional maturity (Jersild, 1955). Hunter (1985) urged teachers to move toward dialectical thinking. This would not mean abandoning one's own position, but building correction into one's own viewpoints by taking the opposing view momentarily. Hunter urged all to "come out of armed camps . . . where we're not collaborating, so that 'I understand why you think it's right for your students to line up while I think it's better for them to come in casually'" (Hunter, 1985, p. 3). She stressed that when educators show respect for others' points of view, they model the cooperation students need for their lives and work in the future.

Today's students will be leaders in a shrinking global community. It is vital that educators prepare them to function successfully in diverse, multicultural societies. The most effective way of doing this is to model such skills every day in the school setting with their colleagues and their students' families. Collaborative consultation and co-teaching roles are natural and appropriate vehicles for modeling constructive use of individual differences among people of all ages.

Recognizing Individual Preferences and Styles

During the 1970s, 1980s, and 1990s numerous methodologies and instruments were developed to help people understand human behavior and improve human relationships. A number of these instruments have been used in such diverse social service areas as education, counseling (for marriage and family, personal, and career needs), religion, business and industry, and others.

Assessment of individual differences can take place with one or more instruments among a wide range of existing tools and techniques, including Gregorc's instrument for profiling learning style (Gregorc & Ward, 1977), aptitude-treatment interaction theories relating individual differences to instructional method, Kolb cognitive style concepts (Kolb, 1976), the McCarthy (1990) 4MAT system, the Dunn and Dunn learning style assessment (Dunn & Dunn, 1978), and the Myers Briggs Type Indicator (Myers, 1962) to name only a few of the more prominent examples. Each of these systems has been used in a variety of contexts to increase awareness and understanding of human preferences that influence behavior. To balance the zeal of those who support each system, there are others who caution against overgeneralizing and oversimplifying complex human attributes through techniques such as self-report assessment and dichotomous interpretations—for example, concrete/abstract, morning/evening, extrovert/introvert, or impulsive/reflective comparisons. Nevertheless, Carl Jung, eminent Swiss psychologist on whose work the well-known Myers Briggs Type Indicator (MBTI) is based, professed in a convincing way that people differ in fundamental ways even though all have the same instincts driving them from within (Jung, 1923).

Personality distinguishes an individual and characterizes him or her in relationships with others. It results from inner forces acting upon and being acted upon by outer forces (Hall & Lindzey, 1978). Any one of a person's individual instincts is not more important than any one of another person's instincts. What *is* important is the person's own *preferences* for personal functioning. These individual preferences provide the "patchwork quilt" of human interaction that can be so constructive and facilitative for teamwork and group problem solving. For example, a person who looks for action and variety, shares experiences readily, prefers to work with others, and tends to get impatient with slow, tedious jobs, is indicating preferences that are quite different from one who prefers working alone, laboring long and hard on one thing, and seeking abundant quiet time for reflection. As another example, an individual who is interested in facts, works steadily and patiently, and enjoys being realistic and practical, contrasts helpfully with one who prefers to generate multiple possibilities, attends to the whole aspect of a situation, and anticipates what will be said or done.

Yet again, a person who needs logical reasons, holds firmly to convictions, and contributes intellectually while trying to be fair and impartial has different type preferences from one who relates freely to most people, likes to agree with others, and cultivates enthusiasm within the group. Finally, an individual who likes to have things decided and settled, functions purposefully, and seeks to make conditions as they "should be," does not have the same type preferences as one who has a more live-and-let-live attitude, leaving things open and flexible with attitudes of adaptability and tolerance.

Every person is equipped with a broad spectrum of attributes and could use them as needed, but typically *prefers* to focus intensively upon one or the other at a time. Murphy (1987) explains this point by using the example of color. Just as red cannot be blue, one cannot *prefer* both polarities simultaneously. One might prefer having a red car, but could live with a blue one if circumstances necessitated having it. If a person prefers to apply experiences to problems, that person cannot also prefer to apply imagination to those problems. But he or she can call forth imagination if need be, and may benefit from practicing the process of imagining or supposing in order to use that approach more productively.

Remarkably, one's less preferred functions can contribute to productivity and self-satisfaction because they provide balance and completeness. They are the well-springs of enthusiasm and energy. Being a person's most childlike and primitive functions, least-preferred functions can be quite helpful by creating a certain awkwardness and unrest that cultivates innovation. However, people do call upon their preferred functions when ease, comfort, and efficiency are most important.

Self-Study of Preferred Styles and Functions

Until individuals engage in self-study, they are prone to view others through the biased and distorted lenses of their own unrecognized needs, fears, desires, anxieties, and sometimes hostile impulses (Jersild, 1955). School consultants should reflect on their own values and preferences before attempting to work intensively with other people's preferences (Brown, Wyne, Blackburn, & Powell, 1979).

When educators do reflect, they make comments such as these:

"I have lots of skills, but I don't seem to get them put together to do what I want."

"I am fed up with these reports that have to be done on such short notice. If data are turned in hastily and carelessly, what is their value?"

"I worked really hard on that project, and then everybody else seemed to forget that the ideas were mine when it came time to give out recognition."

"Should I state my views, or wait and see what everyone else thinks and then fall in line?"

"It seems like all I do with this faculty is put out fires."

"If I didn't show up tomorrow, I'm not sure any of my colleagues would notice or care, so long as there is a substitute teacher here to corral the kids."

Self-study can be undertaken through a variety of methods and settings, including group work, role playing,reading, conferences and workshops. Personality, temperament, and learning style tools such as those named earlier in this chapter are useful when discussed in staff development sessions or department meetings with small-group activities that highlight the rich variety inherent in human nature. Of course, no single journal article, book, conference, or training package will provide sufficient material to fully understand the sophistication and complexity of individual differences.

As stated earlier, oversimplification and overgeneralization of complex constructs such as personality must be avoided. Conclusions should not become labels. Rigid interpretations must give way to open mindedness and respect. With these cautions, teachers *can* begin to deal with their colleagues more effectively and serve their students more success-fully (Dettmer, 1981). As an additional incentive, it usually is lots of fun!

It is not necessary to use a formal personality assessment to explore the constructive use of individual differences. There is value in keeping the exploratory process informal and somewhat fuzzy. The goals are to increase self-understanding in a nonthreatening manner and to broaden one's ability to respect and truly value differences in others. The Application activities in this chapter can be used as catalysts for discussing the constructive use of adult differences in school settings.

Self-study helps educators become more aware of their own attributes and weave their own best qualities into new combinations for helping students who have diverse interests and learning needs (Dettmer, 1981). Too few teacher preparation programs provide opportunities for this important self-exploration. Conoley (1987) was an early advocate in promoting aware-ness of individual differences among collaborating adults as key to the theory and practice of school consultation. Stephen Safran (1991) criticized the shortsightedness of researchers who omit factors such as personality, interpersonal affect, and "domineeringness," from their re-search designs that focus on consultation and collaboration. Joah Safran (1991) stressed the need for parity in collaborative relationships. Also, Salzberg and Morgan (1995) contend that personality variability is an important issue but the topic was noticeably absent when they re-searched teacher preparation for working with paraeducators.

In the Special Education Consulting Project directed by Dyck, Dettmer, and Thurston at Kansas State University from 1985 through 1988, on analyzing pre- and post-test data, one area of greatest gain shown by participants was "Awareness of self as a crucial variable in the consultative process." Other high rates of improvement were noted in "Ability to mon-itor and change my own behavior as needed to increase my effectiveness," and "Skill when communicating for problem solving."

CONSTRUCTIVE USE OF ADULT DIFFERENCES IN CONSULTATION AND COLLABORATION

Teachers often differ dramatically in their preferences. A collaborative school consultation might involve one teacher who pays close attention to detail, examining every test score and asking questions about particular assignments, and another who scarcely looks at the test scores, preferring instead to solicit verbal, generalized assessment of the student's capabil-ities from other professionals. A study by Lawrence and DeNovellis (1974) revealed that teachers with different preferences tend to behave differently in the classroom.

Later, Carlyn (1977) studied the relationship between personality characteristics and teaching preferences of prospective teachers. Some are more interested in administrative functions and others have a strong need for independence and creativity. Some prefer plan-ning school programs, while others enjoy working with small groups of students. Some peo-ple like action and variety more than quiet and reflection. Some like to work with others in groups, whereas others prefer to work alone or with one person. Some people get impatient with slow jobs and complicated procedures. Others can work on one thing for a long time, and they resent interruptions. Carlyn concluded in her study that teachers of different personality type preferences also preferred different kinds of teaching situations. These kinds of preferences and values help explain why some teachers will experiment with mod-ifications and materials, while others resist or just never seem to get around to doing it.

When a group of educators with different type preferences collaborate, they have the opportunity to contribute a variety of strengths within the interaction. Those who like to bring up new possibilities and suggest ingenious ways of approaching problems will bene-fit from having other people supply pertinent facts and keep track of essential details. When some are finding flaws and holding to an existing policy, others contribute by selling the idea, conciliating, and arousing enthusiasm (Myers, 1980b).

APPLICATION 1.6
SHARING A PROFESSIONAL EXPERIENCE

In a small group of 5 or 6 people, describe an experience from your teaching or schooling in which you put forth significant effort, but ended up feeling unappreciated, unreinforced, and perhaps a bit of a failure in that instance. After all in the group have shared a personal example (with each having the privilege of passing up the opportunity if they prefer not to share), discuss how members of the group felt about each other's disappointing professional experience, and demonstrate caring for their disappointment, *especially* if it was not something that would have bothered you all that much.

Opposite types may or may not attract, but they definitely need to be available in order to attain maximum team productivity. However, managing differences elegantly is a tremen-dous challenge for a consultant or consulting teacher. As stated earlier, the primary goal in consulting, collaborating, and working as a team is not to think alike, but to think *together.* Each person's individual preferences and values are important to the effectiveness of inter-action. Differences in schools and classrooms are not just disagreements between adult and child, or teacher and student, or administrator and teacher or paraeducator and consulting teacher. They reflect differing orientations to the world, individual learning styles, personal values, and individual work habits. These differences, when understood and appreciated, can be constructive for serving student needs.

USING ADULT DIFFERENCES TO FACILITATE
TEAM INTERACTION

Good teamwork calls for the recognition and use of certain valuable differences among all members of the team (Kummerow & McAllister, 1988; Myers, 1974). The most effective teams do not agree all the time, but they use individual differences constructively (Kum-merow & McAllister, 1988; Truesdell, 1983). Individuals have far more potential than they use at any one time, and the power of this potential in team settings is exponential.

Some researchers and practitioners focus on the need for collaborators to view prob-lems from mutual perspectives and shared frames of reference using a common language

(Friend & Cook, 1990; Lopez, Dalal, & Yoshida, 1993). These mind sets are without doubt important for rapport-building and initiating exploration of a problem or need. However, greatest team success will come from division of labor and efforts toward mutual respect of members' differences, from openness to the contributions of others no matter how they differ, and from facilitative communication that respects and accommodates a variety of verbal and nonverbal styles.

Needing to view matters through a shared lens, yet doing so with different eye structures, may be a conundrum but nevertheless a useful one. As Lopez et al. (1993) note, consultants and consultees must understand how divergent points of view may predispose them to see problems in conflicting ways. What needs to be said beyond that, is that the divergency is an asset in problem solving and not a liability, when utilized by skilled collaborators. Educators can learn a great deal from talking with colleagues with whom they differ both theoretically and methodologically (Gallessich, 1973). With a common vocabulary and a framework of respect for individuality, teamwork can be much more productive.

Differences When Communicating

Many communication problems among team members are due to individual differences. A statement that seems clear and reasonable to one person may sound meaningless or preposterous to another (Myers, 1974). One may want an explicit statement of the problem before considering possible solutions. Another member of the team might want at least the prospect of an interesting possibility before buckling down to facts. Yet another may demand a beginning, a logically arranged sequence of points, and an end (*especially* an end, Myers cautions). Still another will really listen only if the discussion starts with a concern for people and any direct effects of the issue on people. Myers stresses, "It is human nature not to listen attentively if one has the impression that what is being said is going to be irrelevant or unimportant" (Myers, 1974, p. 4). Communication is such a critical part of successful consultation and collaboration that it will be the focus of concern in Chapter 4.

Differences When Problem Solving

Individual differences play a significant role in the development and efficient use of problem-solving skills. Some individuals are very accurate in problem identification, and others may need very little time to come up with possible solutions. One person may focus more on the problem and the facts, while another focuses on process and the meaning behind the facts. If an individual needs to solve a problem alone, he or she must manage multiple perspectives, but problem-solving by a well-mixed team of individuals enables most perspectives to be represented efficiently. The adage "many heads are better than one" applies here. With pooled experiences, interests, and abilities, problem solving is enriched.

No specific preference is predictive of success in communication or problem solving within the group, and research shows that teams with a complete representation of types outperform virtually any single-type or similar-type team (Blaylock, 1983). The likelihood of having such team versatility is better than might be expected, for a single group composed of several individuals will contain many, if not most, preference types.

■ ■ ■ ■ ■ ▬▬

APPLICATION 1.7
USING INDIVIDUAL DIFFERENCES CONSTRUCTIVELY

Choose a favorite lesson or subject area and imagine that you and a consultee will be team-teaching this material. How would you go about this? Although it would be important to know something about your co-teacher's style and preferences, are there things you should study about *yourself* first before embarking on this collaborative endeavor? How can you share that information pleasantly and agreeably with your colleague, and then learn comparable information about that person, in order to team co-plan and co-teach more effectively?

USING ADULT DIFFERENCES TO FACILITATE EDUCATIONAL COLLABORATION

The phrase, "a little knowledge is a dangerous thing," should be heeded when addressing the issue of knowledge about individual differences. First and foremost, consultants can work from knowledge of personality assessment or learning style concepts without having the formal profiles of individuals in that group; in fact, they probably *should* do so. It is not always possible, necessary, or even desirable to ascertain people's preferences with a standardized instrument. The most important need is to develop the attitude that human differences are not behaviors acted out with intentions of irritating and alienating each other. Rather, they are systematic, orderly, consistent, often unavoidable realities of the way people prefer to use their perception and judgment. *Each set of preferences is valuable, and at times indispensable, in every field.*

Well-researched personality or temperament theory does not promulgate labeling of individuals. Learning styles theory and right-left brain function research have fallen victim on occasion to unwarranted use of labels—"He's so right-brained, that he can't . . ." and "She's a concrete sequential, so she won't. . . ." The world probably does not need any more labels for individuals, and this is particularly cogent in the field of special education.

■ ■ ■ ■ ■ ▬▬

APPLICATION 1.8
PREFERRED RECOGNITION AND REWARD

Form groups of four to six and discuss ways in which you would like to be recognized, and perhaps rewarded, reinforced, or even praised, for something you did that required effort and skill. Then talk over with the group the variations in outcomes that different individuals prefer. How might this affect a work context such as the school and the teaching profession? How could you provide reinforcement to people who have different preferences from yours?

It is inappropriate and unjust to assume too much from analysis of individual differences. No generalization should be applied to a single case, for any case could be an anomaly. As an example, Hammer (1985) stresses that a book (*Moby Dick,* for example) can be read in different ways by different people. One reader may have an eye toward the narrative as a thrilling sea adventure, while another may appreciate the symbolism of the whale. The danger is in *assuming* what pleases others and how it pleases, to the point of denying opportunities for other experiences. Teachers who assume that "her type does not like to read," may stop offering her books. If a teacher believes that a student will not enjoy a particular kind of learning experience, he may be denying the student necessary opportunities to develop (Hammer, 1985). These lessons were learned "the hard way" in uses and misuses of learning styles theory by others before us and should not have to be repeated and relearned.

All good teaching methods have value for some students at certain times and in particular places. By the same token, each method will be received differently by each student (Murphy, 1987). Valuing individual differences will require more than merely tolerating them. It means accepting the fact that people *are* different and the world is the better for the diversity (Murphy, 1987). Teacher preparation programs must be more enterprising and effective in preparing graduates to have a superlative ability for understanding individual differences among educator-colleagues as well as students. Much more research is needed on the constructive use of individual differences, especially in the area of school consultation, collaboration, and working in professional teams.

■ ■ ■ ■ ■

APPLICATION 1.9
WHAT IS YOUR PREFERENCE?

Group participants into triads or quads. Allow three minutes to discuss each of these preference sets. Ask:

Would you rather vacation in the Bahamas, or in Alaska, and why?
Would you rather work in elementary school or secondary school, and why?
Would you prefer to explore deep ocean or deep space, and why?
Would you rather win a new car or a new, installed kitchen, and why?

Then with the whole group share some interesting and unusual things you learned about each other.

TIPS FOR WORKING TOGETHER IN SCHOOLS

1. Value, *really* value, and not just give token approval or lip service to consultation and collaboration as tools for improving long-range planning and coordination among educators.
2. Do not wait to be approached for consultation, collaboration, and teamwork.
3. Try not to press for one's own solutions to school needs, educators' needs, or student needs. Strive instead for collaborative efforts to problem-solve together.

4. Refrain from assuming that colleagues are waiting around to be "saved."
5. Call on building administrators when you are in the building, leaving brief notes that you stopped by, if they are unavailable.
6. Do not share problems or concerns with classroom teachers unless they can have significant input or you have a suggestion for them that might help.
7. Carry your share of the load in contributing to work schedules, school social functions, faculty meetings, and other professional obligations and courtesies.
8. Attend extra-curricular functions of assigned schools as much as possible, and offer to help out if feasible.
9. Have lunch, workroom breaks, and informal visits with building staff often.
10. Attend monthly grade level/departmental meetings to interact with colleagues and to learn of their needs and concerns.
11. Ask for help when you are facing a problem, because it has a humanizing, rapport-building effect.
12. Visit every teacher in the building regularly.
13. Leave the door open, both figuratively and literally, for future partnerships and collaborations.
14. Don't be seen or perceived in your area(s) as doing little or nothing.
15. Know when to stay in the consultation, and recognize situations in which it is time to wrap it up.
16. "Dress for success" in each setting, matching your level of dress with the context in order to establish parity.
17. Listen to the other person's point of view. Seek to understand the person's ideas and meaning.
18. Encourage each member of a collaborative group to share knowledge and perceptions about an issue, in order to establish a solid framework in which to discuss the issue.
19. Take the time to assess preferences of consultees before deciding upon a consultation method.
20. Encourage input from as many sources as possible when deliberating upon a difficult problem, in order to take advantage of many styles, preferences, and cultural perspectives.
21. Appreciate perceptions and preferences different from one's own by engaging in a dialectical conversation. Do not feel that it is necessary to change your position, or to convert the other person to your position.
22. When students with special needs are included in general education classrooms, share with receiving teachers any helpful information about the students' learning styles and preferences. But take care not to stereotype students or alter teacher expectations inappropriately.
23. Everyone is not an expert at everything. Find ways to acknowledge and use suggestions from others.
24. Respect the rights of others to hold different beliefs. While one may not agree with others, one must assume they are acting in ways they believe appropriate.
25. Really care about other persons' feelings and ideas, and show it through actions.
26. Be available—and available—and available.

CHAPTER REVIEW

1. Consultation, collaboration, and co-teaching involve sharing expertise and concerns, laboring together, and planning and working together as a team to identify students' special needs and implement programs that facilitate learning and achievement.

2. Collaborative consultation in school contexts can be described as interaction in which school personnel and parents confer and collaborate as a team within the school context to identify learning and behavioral needs, and to plan, implement, and evaluate educational programs for serving those needs. The school consultant is a facilitator of effective communication, cooperation, and coordination who confers and collaborates with other school personnel and parents in a team effort to serve the special learning and behavioral needs of students.

3. Key elements in school consultation and collaboration are role delineation, a framework for these activities, evaluation and support of the efforts, and preparation for consultation and collaboration. A consultant, consultee (or mediator), and client (or target) in one school-related situation may function in any of the other capacities under different circumstances. Several questions reflect the immediate concerns of consultants and consulting teachers: What do I do? How do I begin? What is my schedule for a week? How will I know I am succeeding? How can I prepare for this kind of role?

4. Most educators are attuned to the need for responding to individual differences of their students; however, little attention has been given to individual differences among school personnel and ways in which those differences affect the school context and professional interactions.

5. Adult differences affect professional interactions in communicating, identifying problems, generating solutions to problems, and evaluating performance.

6. Problems caused by disharmony between opposite types can be lessened when the basis of the disagreement is understood. Adult differences can be used to advantage in teamwork and problem solving. When all preferences are available through contribution of varying preferences among team members, all facets of a problem can be studied and a wide range of options generated.

TO DO AND THINK ABOUT

1. Using material in this chapter, a dictionary, interviews, recollections from teaching experiences, discussion with colleagues or classmates, and any other pertinent references, formulate a description and philosophy about collaborative school consultation which reflects your viewpoint at this time.

2. Interview three school professionals (elementary, middle school, and high school levels if possible) and two parents to find out their views of collaborative school consultation and teamwork among school educators. You can approach this in one of two ways—by giving interviewees definitions if they ask "What do you mean?" Or you can encourage them to share their own perceptions of the terms to define them in their own way. Compare the interview results, and make inferences. Note any indication of willingness to collaborate or glimmer of budding interest in consultation, and determine how these positive signs might be followed up productively.

3. Make strips of the three parts of Figure 1.2 on cardboard, and insert the three cut strips into slits in a cardboard frame, creating a three-part sliding scale for a mix-and-match of roles to facilitate discussion.

4. Discuss ways provocative issues related to individual preferences and styles might be explored without endangering professional collegiality and school spirit.

5. Visit with colleagues or classmates about ope-nended topics such as:
   - What do I think is good and what is not good about being a teacher?
   - What changes do I hope will take place in education in the next ten years, and how will I need to change if they do happen?
   - What are my best attributes as a teacher?

- What teaching strengths do I value in others?
- (If group members know each other well enough)—What teaching strengths within this group do I value most?

6. What questions or concerns about collaborative consultation are uppermost in your mind now?

FOR FURTHER READING

Brown, D., Pryzwansky, W. B., & Schulte, A. C. (1991). *Psychological consultation: Introduction to theory and practice.* Needham Heights, MA: Allyn & Bacon. Chapters 6 and 7, on roles of consultants and consultees.

Conoley, J. C., & Conoley, C. W. (1982). *School consultation: A guide to practice and training.* New York: Pergamon Press. One of the earlier books on school consultation, with helpful forms to accompany basic information.

Hay, C. (1984). One more time: What do I do all day? *Gifted Child Quarterly, 28*(1), 17–20. A secondary level gifted program facilitator's response to colleagues.

Henning-Stout, M. (1994). Consultation and connected knowing: What we know is determined by the questions we ask. *Journal of Educational and Psychological Consultation, 5,*(1), 5–21.

Hoy, W. K. (1990). Organizational climate and culture: A conceptual analysis of the school work place. *Journal of Educational and Psychological Consultation, 1*(2), 149–168.

Jersild, A. T. (1955). *When teachers face themselves.* New York: Teachers College Press, Columbia University.

Jung, C. G. (1923). *Psychological types.* New York: Harcourt Brace.

Keirsey, D., & Bates, M. (1978). *Please understand me,* (2nd ed.) Del Mar: CA: Prometheus Nemesis.

Kummerow, J. M., & McAllister, L. W. (1988). Team-building with the Myers-Briggs Type Indicator: Case studies. *Journal of Psychological Type, 15,* 26–32.

Lawrence, G. (1993). *People types and tiger stripes: A practical guide to learning styles,* (3rd ed.). Gainesville, FL: Center for Applications of Psychological Type, Inc.

Morsink, C. V., Thomas, C. C., & Correa, V. I. (1991). *Interactive teaming: Consultation and collaboration in special programs.* New York: Macmillan. Chapter 4 on understanding roles and perspectives of team members.

Myers, I. B. (1980). *Gifts differing.* Palo Alto, CA: Consulting Psychologists Press.

Thomas, C. C., Correa, V. I., & Morsink, C. V. (2001). *Interactive teaming: Enhancing programs for students with special needs* (3rd ed.). Upper Saddle River, NJ: Prentice Hall. Unit I on context and foundations for interactive teaming.

Yocum, D. J., & Cossairt, A. (1996). Consultation courses offered in special education teacher training programs: A national survey. *Journal of Educational and Psychological Consultation, 7*(3), 251–258.

■ ■ ■ ■ ■

CHAPTER TWO

FOUNDATIONS AND FRAMEWORKS FOR COLLABORATIVE SCHOOL CONSULTATION

Structures ←—→ ▲ ←—→ Interrelationships

↑
Learning Environments

Consultation, collaboration, and teamwork probably began around cave fires ages ago. As people learned about the ideas of others in the group and expressed their own opinions, they honed skills of communication and collaboration. As they planned hunting and food-gathering forays, and then began to plant and harvest, they developed strategies for teamwork. They most likely assessed their processes and outcomes to achieve greater success the next time.

Collaborative work groups have sustained and improved the quality of life from early ages to modern times with ever-escalating significance and consequence. Interpersonal skills now are becoming more and more essential for our survival and progress in an increasingly complex, interconnected world. All members of every society must interact effectively and work together cooperatively if the world is to flourish. Educators who are successful in using these sophisticated skills will model for young people the processes they need to survive and prosper in the world they will inherit.

The opening graphic for this chapter again accentuates the three organizational features of the book. The content (triangle) for Chapter 2 features structures (triangle) in the context (square) of learning environments, and interrelationship processes (circle).

FOCUSING QUESTIONS

1. How do educational reform and school improvement issues signal the need for collaborative school consultation?
2. What is the concept of the inclusionary school?
3. What is the significance of No Child Left Behind (NCLB) for collaborative school consultation?

4. Are there theoretical and research bases for collaborative school consultation and what is its history?

5. What structural elements are key components in developing collaborative consultation methods to fit school contexts for serving student needs?

6. What models of consultation, collaboration, and teamwork have evolved in education?

7. How might educators tailor existing models and other structural elements into useful school consultation methods for their school contexts?

KEY TERMS

American with Disabilities Act (ADA)
approach
collaborative school consultation
IDEA (Public Law 101-476)
IDEA 1997
inclusion/full inclusion
intersubjectivity
least restrictive environment (LRE)

mainstreaming
method
mode
model
No Child Left Behind (NCLB)
perspective
prototype
Public Law 94-142
regular education initiative (REI)

Resource/Consulting Teacher Program model (R/CT)
School Consultation Committee model
Stephens/systems model
system
triadic model
Vermont Consulting Teacher Program model

VIGNETTE 2A

The setting is a school administration office where the superintendent, the principal, and the special education director are having an early-morning conference.

Special Education Director: I've assigned five people on our special education staff to begin serving as consulting teachers in the schools we targeted at our last meeting.

Principal: I understand the high school is to be one of those schools. I'm all for trying a new approach, but at this point I'm not sure my staff understands how this method of service is going to affect them.

Superintendent: Are you saying we need to spend a little more time at the drawing board and get the kinks out of our plan before tossing it out to the teachers?

Principal: Yes, and I think the parents also will want to know what will be happening.

Special Education Director: I've been compiling a file of theoretical background, research studies, program descriptions, even some cartoons and witty sayings, that focus on consultation and collaboration approaches. Let me get copies of the most promising material to you and the principals of the other targeted schools. Perhaps we should plan in-service sessions for teachers and awareness sessions for parents before we proceed.

Superintendent: That sounds good. Draft an outline and we'll discuss it at next week's meeting. I'll get the word out to the other principals to be here.

SCHOOL IMPROVEMENT ISSUES

During the 1970s, 1980s, and 1990s educators witnessed an explosion of reports, proposals, and legislative mandates calling for educational reform. During the 1970s the issues focused on accountability, lengthening of school days and years, and increased investments of time, money, and effort in education. Demands for cost containment and growing concerns over labeling of students fueled interest in a merger of general education and special education. The primary impetus for the merger was the mainstreaming movement with the concept of least restrictive environment (LRE) catalyzed by passage of Public Law 94-142 (that is, put forth by the 94th Congress as their 142nd piece of legislation). After that legislation was passed, educators could no longer arbitrarily place individuals with disabilities in a special school or self-contained classroom. A continuum of service options was to be available and the type of service or placement was to be as close to the normal environment as possible, with general education teachers responsible for the success of those students. In order to meet this new responsibility, teachers were to receive help from special education personnel.

During the second wave of reform in the 1980s the individual school became the unit of decision making. This promoted the development of collegial, participatory environments among students and staff, with particular emphasis on personalizing school environments and designing curriculum for deeper understanding (Michaels, 1988). One component of this second wave was school restructuring. Many states initiated some form of school restructuring; however, few schools truly were restructured. Where restructuring efforts occurred, they tended to be idiosyncratic in that they were carried out by a small group of teachers, creating only marginal changes (Timar, 1989).

A position paper issued by Will (1986), former director of the U.S. Office of Special Education and Rehabilitative Services, stated that too many children were being inappropriately identified and placed in learning disabilities programs. In that paper Will called for *collaboration* between special education personnel and general education personnel in providing services within the general classroom. Thus the Regular Education Initiative (REI), referred to by some educators as the General Education Initiative (GEI), precipitated major changes in the way education is delivered. All students, with the exception of those with severe disabilities, were from that time to be served primarily in a regular education setting. The rationale for the REI was that:

- The changes would serve many students not currently eligible for special education services.
- The stigma of placement in special education programs separate from age peers would be eliminated.
- Early intervention and prevention would be provided before more serious learning deficiencies occur.
- Cooperative school-parent relationships would be enhanced (Will, 1986).

In 1986 P.L. 94-142 was amended by P.L. 99-457, which mandated free appropriate education for preschool children from ages 3–5 with disabilities. An Individualized Family Service Plan (IFSP) was required for each child served, thus extending the concept of the IEP to provide support for child *and* family (Smith, 1998).

In 1990, early in the third wave of reform, Public Law 94-142 was amended by passage of Public Law 101-476, the Individuals with Disabilities Education Act (IDEA). That legislation's primary elements were:

- All references to handicapped children were changed to children with disabilities.
- New categories of autism and traumatic brain injury (TBI) were added, to be served with increased collaboration among all special education teachers, classroom teachers, and related services personnel.
- More emphasis was placed on requirements to provide transition services for students 16 years of age and older.

Two distinct groups emerged to advocate for REI—the high incidence group speaking for learning disabilities, behavioral disorders, and mild/moderate mental retardation, and the low-incidence group speaking for students with severe intellectual disabilities. A few in the latter group even spoke out for the elimination of special education altogether (Fuchs and Fuchs, 1994). Both groups shared three goals:

- To merge special and general education into one inclusive system
- To increase dramatically the number of children with disabilities in mainstream classrooms
- To strengthen the academic achievement of students with mild and moderate disabilities, as well as that of underachievers without disabilities.

To achieve these goals, total restructuring of schools would be needed. "Increasingly, special education reform is symbolized by the term 'inclusive schools'" (Fuchs & Fuchs, 1994, p. 299).

The *America 2000* report presented in 1991 by President George H. W. Bush and Secretary of Education Lamar Alexander, and the 1994 federal school reform package known as *Goals 2000* signed into law by President Clinton, identified goals to be met in the nation's schools by the year 2000. The latter report stipulated that home and school partnerships are essential for student success. After these reports were publicized, public pressure to improve schools escalated. Also in 1990 the Americans with Disabilities Act (ADA) was passed, prohibiting discrimination against persons of all ages with disabilities in transportation, public access, local government, and telecommunications. It required schools to make all reasonable accommodations for accessibility of students with disabilities and extended provisions concerning fairness in employment to employers who do not receive federal funds (Smith, 1998).

In 1997, after much study and discussion nationwide, reauthorization and amendments of IDEA, or P.L. 105-17, was approved by Congress and signed into law by President Clinton. This legislation, known as IDEA 1997, contained:

- Provisions for improved parent/professional partnerships
- Requirement for states to provide mediation for parents and schools in resolving differences
- Required training by states for paraeducator training to prepare for their roles
- Required participation by general education teachers on IEP teams when students are or will be placed in a general education classroom

- Increased cost-sharing among agencies with reduced financial burdens for special education locally
- Accountability of education for students with disabilities by way of participation in state and district-wide assessment programs
- Assurance that children with disabilities will not be deprived of educational services as result of dangerous behavior, while enabling educators to more easily remove them from current educational placement if needed
- Strengthened disclosure requirements, with families having greater access to their children's records, and more information available in the IEPs
- Revamping of ways in which school districts receive federal funding, with elimination of the child count formula, and gradual reliance on census data with more accountability for poverty

In general the special education community was pleased with components of IDEA 1997. A few concerns remained, not the least of which was the *increase,* not a much hoped-for decrease, in the paperwork that so erodes the time and morale of special educators.

Inclusionary Schools

The concept of inclusion which has swept the nation in recent years did not suddenly emerge out of a vacuum. It emanated from the long line of special education movements briefly described above, that have grown out of concern for more appropriate education for all students. Inclusive schools *include* students with special needs in the total school experience, rather than "exclude" them by placing them in special schools or classrooms. The movement toward inclusion in the 1990s was built on this early foundation. In full inclusion, support services come to the student in the general education setting. In partial inclusion students may be served in another instructional setting when appropriate for their individual needs, but receive most of their instruction in the general education setting.

From its quiet beginning, the inclusionary movement snowballed into a popular position in which special education and regular education would merge into the unified school system envisioned in earlier decades as the remedy for separate, stigmatizing, and very expensive special education. Proponents of an inclusionary school system make the case that *all* students are unique individuals with special needs requiring differentiated individual attention; therefore, practices used effectively for exceptional students should be considered for use with all students (McLeskey, Henry, & Hodges, 1998; Stainback & Stainback, 1984).

Essential Elements for Success of Inclusion.   The term "inclusion" has been erroneously viewed by many professionals as a synonym for the least restrictive environment (LRE) as mandated by federal legislation. However, legislation does not define inclusion or a unified educational system, just as it did not include the term mainstreaming. Instead, inclusion is one of several alternatives within a continuum. Formal definitions that do exist differ based on the interest group fostering the definition.

Mainstreaming placed students with disabilities in general education settings only when they could meet traditional academic expectations with minor adaptations (Beakley, 1997); however, inclusive schools integrate students with special needs into their home schools with grade peers whether or not they can meet traditional standards. Special services are brought to the students instead of having students removed, or "pulled out," to go to the special services (Waldron & McLeskey, 1998). "No students, including those with disabilities, are relegated to the fringes of the school by placement in segregated wings, trailers, or special classes (Stainback & Stainback, 1998, p. 34).

To further describe the concept of inclusion, selected definitions from the literature appear below:

- Inclusion: The commitment to educate each child to the maximum extent appropriate in the school and classroom he or she would otherwise attend (Rogers, 1993). The current focus for inclusion is on location of instruction and grouping of students. It is arbitrary across states and across districts within a state, and ideally it involves a regular teacher and a special education teacher co-teaching in one classroom (Beakley, 1997).
- Full (or Total) Inclusion: The belief that instructional practices and technological supports are presently available to accommodate all students in the schools and classrooms they would otherwise attend if not disabled (Rogers, 1993).
- Inclusive Schools: Schools where all members accept their fair share of responsibility for all children, including those with disabilities. Aids and resources are utilized where needed regardless of official classifications of disability (Fuchs & Fuchs, 1994).

Characteristics of Inclusive Schools.   The National Center on Educational Restructuring and Inclusion (NCERI) conducted a study in 1994 to determine the status of the inclusion movement. Although most students with disabilities continued to be educated in separate settings, inclusion programs were being implemented in many states across the country. NCERI researchers determined that the following six factors are necessary for inclusion to succeed (Lipsky, 1994):

- Visionary Leadership. School leaders must have a positive view about the value of education for students with disabilities, and an optimistic view of teachers who can change and schools that can accommodate the needs of students with special needs. An overriding attitude that all children can benefit from inclusion is important.
- Collaboration. Successful inclusion presumes that "no one teacher can or ought to be expected to have all the expertise required to meet the educational needs of all students in the classroom" (Lipsky, 1994, p. 5). The processes of consultation, collaboration, and co-teaching are recognized as essential for effective inclusion programs.
- Refocused Use of Assessment. Inclusive schools tend to use more authentic assessment measures with a focus on monitoring student progress.
- Supports for Staff and Students. Two essential support factors reported in the study are systematic staff development, and flexible planning time for special education personnel and general educators to meet and work together. Families are involved in the planning processes. Other useful supports include assignment of school aides, curriculum adaptation, therapy services integrated into the regular school program, peer supports, computer technology, and other assistive devices.
- Funding. Funding formulas in many states need to be changed in order for inclusion to be implemented successfully.
- Effective Parental Involvement. Inclusive programs place emphasis on substantive parent involvement through family support services and the development of educational programs that engage parents as co-learners with their children.

The survey also highlighted classroom practices of co-planning and co-teaching. These will be discussed more fully in Chapter 8.

Effective Inclusionary Schools.   Inclusive schools emphasize learning for all students, with teachers and staff working together to support a learning climate in which all students can succeed. An important criterion for judging the success of inclusion is that the students with disabilities make at least as much progress in the inclusionary setting as they would in an exclusionary setting. Making comparable progress would ensure the placement in the least restrictive environment (Waldron & McLeskey, 1998). Salend and Duhaney (1999) found that students without disabilities did not evidence interference in their academic performance, and had several social benefits for them. Hobbs and Westling (1998) also cite studies which found that children with disabilities fare better in academic skills than students in special classes, and inclusion does not have a detrimental effect on students without disabilities. They purport that the success of inclusion depends on effective collaboration among professionals, and to this end they recommend use of a collaborative problem-solving model.

All educators share responsibility for student achievement and behavior. There must be total commitment from principal to school custodian (Federico, Herrold, & Venn, 1999). Teachers refer to "our kids," rather than "your kids" and "my kids." Paraeducators provide continuity and support for students, teachers, and families. They participate actively on the team and help with planning and delivery of appropriate services.

Every inclusive school looks different, but is characterized by a sense of community, high standards, collaboration and cooperation, changing roles and an array of services, partnership with families, flexible learning environments, strategies based on research, new forms of accountability, and continuing professional development (Federico, Herold, & Venn, 1999; Working Forum on Inclusive Schools, 1994). In a qualitative study of inclusive elementary school programs, Wood (1998) found that in the initial stages of inclusion teachers maintained discrete role boundaries through an informal but clear division of labor. However, as the school year progressed, role perceptions became less rigid as the teaming became more cooperative.

Concerns About Inclusion.   In spite of considerable research that indicates positive results, inclusion has not been perceived positively by all educators. Critics point to situations where teachers receive little to no assistance and sometimes are not even informed about the nature of their students' disabilities. Some contend that special education teachers have difficulties managing educational programs of their students when they are dispersed among several classrooms.

In some schools several children with severe disabilities are assigned to the same classroom. This does not represent a typical classroom situation because perhaps only one child in 100 will have severe disabilities. This situation can create an extremely frustrating environment for the classroom teacher (Rogers, 1993).

VanTassel-Baska (1998) notes that studies in gifted and talented education within inclusionary settings are limited, but those that exist reveal some troubling trends. Research shows that students with high ability and remarkable talents too often do not receive instruction that is appropriately intensive enough for their needs in the inclusionary classroom. This concept will be addressed in detail in Chapter 9.

Problems develop in inclusionary settings when children with disabilities are "dumped wholesale" into classrooms, with budget cuts and no planning and collaboration. Special educators lament loss of control over the learning environment and fear loss of specialized services for students with disabilities (Salend & Duhaney, 1999). In addition, a backlash is surfacing among some parents of nondisabled who feel their children's education is being compromised.

All in all, teachers' responses to inclusion programs are complex, are shaped by multiple variables, and change over time (Salend & Duhaney, 1999). So while cautious educators may applaud the intent of inclusion and the gains from inclusionary settings for all students, teachers, and families, they will not want to regard inclusion as a panacea. Narrow definitions, myopic practices, and most of all, failure to prepare school personnel in collaborative and co-teaching strategies will short-circuit well-meaning intentions for those with special needs.

No Child Left Behind

The No Child Left Behind Act passed by the U.S. legislature in 2001, and signed by President George W. Bush on January 8, 2002, mandates requirements and adds specificity to the 1965 Elementary and Secondary Education Act noted earlier in the chapter. The goals of this legislation are as lofty, and in all probability as undoable, as President Clinton's Goals 2000, mandating, among other things, that "All Children Will Enter School Ready to Learn."

The 35th annual Phi Delta Kappa/Gallup Poll of the public's attitudes toward the public schools indicates that only 24 percent of respondents said they know a great deal or a fair amount about NCLB and 76 percent said they know very little or nothing at all about it (Rose & Gallup, 2003). In spite of this lack of knowledge, NCLB has unleashed a flurry of gear-ups for testing, test preparation, high-profile reports of schools making or failing to make adequate progress, and calls for more accountability from the schools to succeed or let students be schooled elsewhere.

Metaphors, mostly denigrating, have been put before the public to accentuate flaws in the thinking behind this Act. To mention only one, NCLB has been dubbed a "Trojan horse" (Bracey, 2002 Rose, 2003) that comes bearing promises but carries hidden problems. Elmore (2003), who has labeled NCLB as the single largest nationalization of education policy in the history of the United States, points out the Act's overinvestment in testing and underinvestment in capacity-building among teachers and schools to provide high-quality instruction to students. He also notes ungrounded theories of improvement, weak knowledge about how to mend failing schools, poor incentives for quality and performance, and policymaking by remote control.

Lewis (2002) reminds educators of students with special needs of what they already know, which is: no new set of laws and mandates can ensure that children served by IDEA will not be left behind. Smith (2003) adds to this prompt the reality that the range of human variation will doom NCLB to fail, compounded by that other reality of the 9/91 factor: between birth and 19th birthday, children spend only 9 percent of their time in school and 91 percent elsewhere. Requiring schools to make up for all differences in children's nature and the conditions of their nurture is, as Smith puts it, absurd.

The NCLB Act contains several more subtle topics beyond the most publicized issues of adequate yearly progress (AYP), high-stakes testing in reading and math only (with science to be added in 2006), inclusion of children with disabilities in all testing, and school improvement requirements. It sets up the public for a plethora of bad reports about schools. It demands that teachers will be judged competent by acquisition of a teaching certificate, and it mandates school reform without the wherewithal to make significant changes.

Collaborative consultants must be vigilant in monitoring effects of NCLB and assertive in demanding that the right things are carried out for the right purposes. Teacher certification programs must include preparation for the collaborative and team roles so important for inclusionary settings. School administrators must make community members and family members integral parts of school improvement efforts. School psychologists and counselors must provide their expertise and reasoned judgment to assessment issues and interpretations. In all these areas and more, educators must work diligently to ensure that NCLB will hold promise, not punishment, for caring educators and their students.

A BRIEF HISTORY OF SCHOOL CONSULTATION

Having noted the strong emphasis on the need for collaborative school consultation brought out in educational reform and the school improvement movements, it is appropriate to examine its history briefly. The advent of special education may date back to the mid-nineteenth century, when state after state (Rhode Island in 1840, then Massachusetts in 1852, followed in time by the others) passed compulsory school attendance laws mandating formal education for every school-age child regardless of disability, giftedness, or other special need. Now the school doors open each morning, bells ring, students congregate, and classes begin. Students in these classes have many special learning and behavior needs. Up to one-third of all school-age children can be described as experiencing difficulty in school by reason of special needs. If the significant learning needs of gifted students are included, this figure increases substantially.

These realities, along with various social issues of the times, have spurred interest in school consultation, collaboration, and teamwork. The result has been an escalating number of conferences, publications, research studies, pilot programs, federal and state grants, training projects, as well as development of several teacher preparation programs, for understanding and applying consultation and collaboration practices in schools.

Collaborative School Consultation before 1970

School consultation probably originated in mental health and management fields (Reynolds & Birch, 1988). Caplan (1970) had developed consultation programs to train staff members for working with troubled adolescents in Israel at the close of World War II. Building upon Caplan's work, mental health services escalated and moved into school settings, where consultation services of school psychologists produced promising results. The role of consultation in school psychology was broadened to encourage collaborative relationships (Gallessich, 1974; Pryzwansky,1974). Such relationships were nurtured to help teachers, administrators, and parents deal with future problems as well as immediate concerns.

The first direct explication of a consulting teacher service delivery model for students with mild disabilities was by McKenzie, Egner, Knight, Perelman, Schneider, and Garvin in 1970. This group described a program for preparation of consulting teachers at the University of Vermont and a plan for implementing a consulting teacher model in the state (Lilly & Givens-Ogle, 1981).

By the mid-1960s the term *school consultation* was listed in *Psychological Abstracts* (Friend, 1988). School counselors began to promote the concept of proactive service, so that by the early 1970s consultation was being recommended as an integral part of contemporary counseling service. This interest in collaborative relationships on the part of counselors and psychologists reflected a desire to influence individuals, groups, and systems that most profoundly affect students (Brown, Wyne, Blackburn, & Powell, 1979). Examples of consulting in the areas of speech and language therapy, and in hearing-impaired and visually-impaired programs, date from the late 1950s. Emphasis on teacher consultation for learning disabled and behavior-disordered students surfaces in the literature as early as the mid-1960s. At that time consultants for the most part were not special educators, but clinical psychologists and psychiatric social workers.

In 1965, passage of the Elementary and Secondary Education Act (ESEA) authorized funding and made specific provisions for students with disabilities (Talley & Schrag, 1999). Reauthorizations in 1988 and 1994 mandated parent involvement and coordination in programs such as Head Start, encouraging school and community-linked services through the Community Schools Partnership Act. Consultation and collaboration became essential factors in coordinating the array of services provided for students with special needs. (Coordination efforts will be discussed further in Chapter 11.)

The behavioral movement, which was gaining momentum in the late 1960s and early 1970s, fueled interest in alternative models for intervention and the efficient use of time and other resources. This interest sparked development of a text by Tharp and Wetzel (1969) in which they presented a triadic consultation model using behavioral principles in school settings. This triadic model is the basic pattern upon which many subsequent models and methods for consultation were constructed.

By 1970 the special education literature contained references to a method of training consulting teachers to serve students in special education at the elementary level (McKenzie, Egner, Knight, Schneider, Perelman, & Garvin, 1970). The Vermont Consulting Teacher Model, using a consulting teacher to serve students with mental handicaps, was put into place in 1970 (Haight, 1984).

Collaborative School Consultation from 1970 to 1999

As noted earlier, the decade of the 1970s was a very busy time in the field of special education. Intensive special education advocacy, federal policymaking for exceptional students, and technological advancements affected special education practices for handicapped students (Nazzaro, 1977). The Education for All Handicapped Children's Act (EHA) was passed in 1975 and signed by President Gerald Ford, reauthorized in 1990 as the Individuals with Disabilities Education Act (IDEA), and amended as IDEA 1997. These legislative actions contained national guidelines on service delivery of education for students with disabilities (Talley & Schrag, 1999). One of the many guidelines was prescription of multidisciplinary and multidimensional services to be coordinated for maximizing student learning and development.

By the mid-1970s consultation was regarded as a significant factor in serving students with special needs. Special education became a major catalyst for promoting consultation and collaboration in schools (Friend, 1988).

By the mid-1980s consultation had become one of the most significant educational trends for serving students with special needs. To analyze the trend, a questionnaire was sent by West and Brown (1987) to directors of special education in the fifty states. Thirty-five state directors responded. Twenty-six of the respondents stated that service delivery models in their states include consultation as an expected role of the special educator. The 26 states reported a total of ten different professional titles for consultation as a job responsibility of special educators. About three-fourths of the respondents acknowledged the need for service delivery models that include consultation. However, only seven stated that specific requirements for competency in consultation were included in their policies.

As interest in school consultation escalated in the 1980s, the National Task Force on Collaborative School Consultation, sponsored by the Teacher Education Division of the Council for Exceptional Children, sent a publication to state departments of education with recommendations for teacher consultation services in a special education services continuum (Heron & Kimball, 1988). Guidelines were presented for: Development of consultative assistance options; definition of a consulting teacher role with pupil-teacher ratio recommended; and requirements for preservice, inservice, and certification preparation programs. The report included a list of education professionals skilled in school consultation and a list of publications featuring school consultation.

By 1990 a new journal focusing on school consultation, *Journal of Educational and Psychological Consultation,* appeared in the literature. A pre-convention workshop sponsored by the Teacher Education Division (TED) of the Council for Exceptional Children (CEC) on school consultation and collaboration programs and practices was a featured event at the 1990 annual CEC conference in Toronto.

Early leaders in school consultation reconceptualized models to fit more appropriately with inclusionary schools and expanded roles of school personnel. Caplan's mental health consultation model evolved into mental health collaboration as a better choice of practice for school-based professionals (Caplan, Caplan, & Erchul, 1995). Bergan (1995) similarly described an evolution of the school psychologist's behavioral consultation focus on assessment, labeling, and placement activities to an expanded role of consultative and collaborative problem solving for students' needs. The framework for behavioral consultation was reconceptualized to become a case-centered, problem-solving approach that could be teacher-based, parent-based, or conjoint-based (parent-teacher) consultation in which the consultee's involvement is critical to the success of positive client outcomes (Kratochwill & Pittman, 2002).

In the field of education for gifted students, discussion of consultation practices has been minimal, although it promises to be one of the most viable fields for extensive use of collaborative consultation. Dettmer (1989), Dettmer and Lane (1989), and Idol-Maestas and Celentano (1986) have stressed the need for collaborative consultation practices to assist with learning needs of gifted and talented students. Dyck and Dettmer (1989) suggest methods for facilitating learning programs of twice exceptional, gifted learning-disabled students within a consulting teacher plan.

Collaborative School Consultation After 2000

The general public in the new millennium is becoming more and more aware that teaching is not just a responsibility of professional educators within the school's walls. Community members and resource personnel beyond school walls are needed as collaborators and team members to help in planning and directing rich, authentic learning experiences for students.

Also gaining prominence is an awareness of the need for collaboration among general and special education teachers that gives students opportunities for learning and practicing skills related to the standards set forth by governing bodies. Teaming across classrooms is being utilized by many dedicated teachers as an approach that can bring students closer to achieving those standards (Kluth & Straut, 2001).

The early decades of this millennium will be a critical period for professional educators in learning to work together and to *enjoy* doing it. It will be very important for them to model such behaviors for their students, who will be expected to work collaboratively as adults in their careers and community roles. Family involvement, with strong partnerships between home and school educators, is an essential part of helping students become strong, ethical leaders for the future.

THEORETICAL AND RESEARCH BASES OF COLLABORATIVE SCHOOL CONSULTATION

Is school consultation theory-based as a practice or an atheoretical practice related to a problem-solving knowledge base? Differing points of view exist.

West and Idol (1987) propose that school consultation is theory-based if identified across more than one literature source focusing upon the relationship between consultant and consultee. On the other hand, if identified by problem-solving methods, then it is knowledge-based in the area of problem-solving.

West and Idol identify ten prominent models of consultation, of which six are founded on clearly distinguishable theory or theories: mental health, behavioral, process, advocacy, and two types of organizational consultation. They designate a seventh as a collaborative consultation model having the essential elements for building theory because it features a set of generic principles for building collaborative relationships between consultants and consultees.

Is there a research base for collaborative school consultation? During the 1980s when interest in collaboration and consultation was escalating, many analyses and discussions of school consultation took place. Heron and Kimball (1988) have identified an emerging research base that includes:

- Theory and models (West & Idol, 1987);
- Methodology (Gresham & Kendell, 1987);
- Training and practice (Friend, 1984; Idol & West, 1987);
- Professional preferences for consultation service (Babcock & Pryzwansky, 1983; Medway & Forman, 1980);
- Guidelines (Salend & Salend, 1984);
- Competencies for consultations (West & Cannon, 1988).

Gresham and Kendell (1987) summarize most consultation research as descriptive, which is useful for identifying key variables in consultation processes and outcomes, but not for determining interactions between variables or directions of influence upon the outcomes of consultation. They stress that consultation research must assess the integrity of consultation plans, since many plans are not being implemented by consultees as designed (Witt & Elliott, 1985). Fuchs, Fuchs, Dulan, Roberts, and Fernstrom (1992) share views stated by Pryzwansky (1986) that many studies on consultation are poorly conceptualized and executed. Conducting the research well requires careful planning, attention to detail, interpersonal skills, flexibility, positive relationships with school personnel, and research skills (Fuchs et al., 1992).

West and Idol (1987) point out that efforts to conduct research in the complex, multi-dimensional field of school consultation are impeded by lack of psychometrically reliable and valid instrumentation and controls.

Without question there should be more research to ascertain effects of collaborative consultation and to understand more about the variables related to those effects. Methodological weaknesses to be overcome in pertinent research are omission of control or comparison groups, use of inappropriate control or comparison groups, use of only one consultant, use of only one dependent measure (Bramlett & Murphy, 1998; Medway, 1982), lack of objective data, absence of follow-up data, little information about consultants' training and experience, and possible experimenter bias (Fuchs, et al., 1992; Pryzwansky, 1986).

Gresham and Kendell (1987) found little empirical evidence to show that what people are calling consultation actually *is* consultation. They urged researchers to define the research variables more explicitly, control them more carefully, and measure them more accurately. Witt (1990) contended that research on collaboration is a dead end unless it can be shown that collaboration is related to important student outcomes.

According to findings of Slesser, Fine, and Tracy (1990), much of the research on school consultation heretofore has examined behaviors specific to particular models. They propose that further research is needed to examine specific behaviors and attitudes of more successful consultants compared with those less successful, because it is likely that many school consultants initiate their own integration of different models. Indeed, that customization will be a recommendation given in this book.

One promising area of exploration is the topic of intersubjectivity. Since the 1980s and the rediscovery and analysis of Lev Vygotsky's work, this aspect of social learning has captured the attention of educational psychologists. The intersubjective attitude is one of negotiation and joint construction of meaning, based on a commitment to build shared meaning by finding common ground and exchanging interpretations (Woolfolk, 2001). Colleagues with an intersubjective attitude assert their own positions while respecting those of others and working together to co-construct useful perspectives. Recall the discussion of adult differences and variety of styles in teamwork presented in Chapter 1.

STRUCTURAL ELEMENTS OF COLLABORATIVE SCHOOL CONSULTATION

Overlapping philosophies of consultation have evolved out of a blending of consultation knowledge and practices from several fields. This overlap creates a tangle of philosophy and terminology which could be problematic for educators endeavoring to develop viable school consultation structure. So it is helpful to sort out the myriad consultation terms, theories, research findings, and practices, and recast them into useful structures.

When addressing issues, it is tempting for educators to slip into "educationese", (convoluted and redundant phrases), "jargon," (in-house expressions that approximate educational slang), and "alphabet soup" (acronyms that appear to lay people to be a form of code). But if collaborative school consultation is to be accepted by teachers and school administrators, it must be presented in bold, clear language. This requires careful attention to semantics, or the study of meaning and ways meaning is structured in language.

Collaborative consultation is a blend of six elements—system, perspective, approach, prototype, mode,and model, which will synthesize into a method with goodness of fit for the particular educational situation. (See Figure 2.1.) These six elements are framed as:

- *System*—entity of many parts serving common purpose
- *Perspective*—a particular viewpoint
- *Approach*—preliminary step toward a purpose
- *Prototype*—pattern
- *Mode*—form or manner of doing
- *Model*—an example

Characteristics of the six elements can be illustrated by words and pictures to fit any local context.

For brevity and clarity the six elements are designated by the upper-case form of their first letter—for example, System is marked with *S*. (When two elements begin with identical letters, some other prominent letter in the word is used.) Thus the six categories are designated as *S* (system), *P* (perspective), *A* (approach), *R* (prototype), *E* (mode), and *M* (model).

Systems

The word *system* (S) denotes a complex unity composed of many diverse parts for a common purpose. The most natural system within which to conduct school consultation and collaboration is, obviously, the school. However, educators are involved not only in the academic or cognitive aspect of student development, but also in physical, emotional, so-

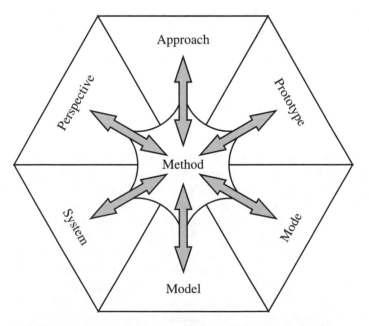

FIGURE 2.1   Structure for Collaborative School Consultation

cial, and life-orientation aspects. Educators include not only teachers, but parents, related services and support personnel, other caregivers, and the community in general.

Systems (S) in which educators function to serve special needs of students include: home and family, community, medical and dental professions, mental health, social work, counseling, extracurricular, and advocacy and support groups. Other systems with which consultants and collaborators might be involved from time to time in addressing very specialized needs are therapy, industry, technology, mass communications, cultural enrichment, and special interest areas such as talent development.

Perspectives

A *perspective,* (P), is an aspect or object of thought from a particular viewpoint. Consultation perspectives that have evolved in education and related fields include: Purchase; doctor-patient; and process. In some sources these categories are referred to as approaches, and in others they appear as models. Here, however, we differentiate them as perspectives.

A *purchase* perspective is one in which the consumer shops for a needed or wanted item. The consumer, in this case the consultee, "shops for" services that will help that consultee serve the client's need. For example, the teacher of a developmentally delayed student might ask personnel at the instructional media center for a list of low-vocabulary, high-interest reading material with which to help the student have immediate success in reading. The purchase perspective makes several assumptions (Neel, 1981); (1) That the consultee describes the need precisely; (2) the consultant is in the right "store" to get something for that need; (3) the consultant has enough "inventory" (strategies and resources) to fill the request, and (4) the consultee can assume the costs of time, energy, or modification of classroom procedures.

As a consumer the consultee is free to accept or reject the strategy or resource, using it enthusiastically, putting off trying it, or ignoring it as a "bad buy." Even if the strategy is effective for that case, the consultee may need to go again to the consultant for similar needs of other clients. Many things have to go right in order for this perspective to work, so the consultee must think through the consequences of the purchase technique (Schein, 1969). Little change can be expected in consultee skill as a result of such consumer-type interaction. Thus the overall costs are high and the benefits are limited to specific situations.

The *doctor-patient* perspective casts the consultant in the role of diagnostician and prescriptor. The consultee knows there is a problem, but is not in a position to correct it. Consultees are responsible for revealing helpful information to the consultant. Again, this perspective makes several assumptions: (1) The consultee describes the problem to the consultant accurately and completely; (2) The consultant can explain the diagnosis clearly and convince the consultee of its worth; (3) the diagnosis is not premature; and (4) the prescribed remedy is not *iatrogenic* (a term from the medical profession that describes professionals' actions which turn out to be more debilitating than the illness they were designed to treat). An iatrogenic effect from educational services would create more problems for student, educators, or school context than the initial condition did. For example, an iatrogenic effect created by having consulting teachers take gifted students from their general classrooms to attend gifted program activities could be resentment and antagonism felt toward them by their peers and perhaps even by their classroom teachers.

A classroom teacher might use a doctor-patient perspective by calling on a special education teacher and describing the student's learning or behavior problem. The consultant's role would be to observe, review existing data, perhaps talk to other specialists, and make diagnostic and prescriptive decisions. As in the medical field, there is generally little follow-up activity on the consultant's part with the doctor-patient perspective, and the consultee does not always follow through with conscientious attention to the consultant's recommendations.

In a *process* perspective, the consultant helps the client perceive, understand, and act upon the problem (Neel, 1981; Schein, 1969). Consultative service does not replace the consultee's direct service to the client. In contrast to the purchase and doctor-patient perspectives, the consultant neither diagnoses nor prescribes a solution. As Neel puts it, the consultee becomes the consultant's client for that particular problem.

Schein (1978) sorts process consultation into two types—a catalyst type in which the consultant does not know a solution but is skilled toward helping the consultee figure out one, and the facilitator type where the consultant contributes ideas toward the solution. In both catalyst and facilitator types of process consultation the consultant helps the consultee clarify the problem and develop solutions. Skills and resources used to solve the immediate problem may be used later for other problems. Assumptions are: (1) The consultee can diagnose the problem; (2) The consultant is able to develop a helping relationship; (3) The consultant can provide new and challenging alternatives for the consultee (who is the consultant's immediate client) to consider; and (4) Decision-making about the alternatives will remain the responsibility and privilege of the consultee. In the process perspective for consultation, the consultee who needs help with a student or school situation collaborates with a consultant to identify the problem, and explore possible alternatives. They work as a team to develop a plan of action. The consultee then implements the plan.

All three of these perspectives—purchase, doctor-patient, and process—have strengths; therefore, each is likely to be employed at one time or another in schools (Vasa, 1982). One factor influencing the adoption of a particular perspective is the nature of the problem (West, 1985). For example, in a non-crisis situation the consultee may value the collaborative approach. However, all three have limitations as well. In crisis situations the consultee may need a quick solution, even if temporary, for the problem. In such cases the purchase or doctor-patient perspectives would be preferred. Situations that immediately affect the physical and psychological well-being of students and school personnel require immediate attention and cannot wait for process consultation. However, when process consultation is employed regularly, many of the skills and resources that are developed for solving a particular problem can be used again and again in situations involving similar problems. This makes process consultation both time-efficient and cost-effective for schools.

Approaches

An *approach* (A) is primarily a *formal* or an *informal* step toward a purpose. Formal consultations occur in preplanned meetings such as staffings, conferences for developing Individual Education Plans (IEPs), arranged interactions between school personnel, and organized staff development activities. They also include scheduled conferences with parents, related services personnel, and community resource personnel.

In contrast, informal consultations often occur "on the run." These interactions have been called "vertical consultations" because people tend to engage in them while standing on playgrounds, in parking lots, at ball games, even in grocery stores. They are dubbed "one-legged consultations" when they occur in hallways with a leg propped against the wall (Hall & Hord, 1987; McDonald, 1989). Conversations also take place frequently in the teacher workroom. This aspect will be addressed more fully in Chapter 12 as a type of informal staff development. It is very important to designate informal interactions as consultations because they *do* require expenditures of time and energy on the part of both consultant(s) and consultee(s). Highlighting them as consultations helps establish the concept of school consultation and enhance efforts toward constructing a suitable framework for the practices of consultation and collaboration. Informal consultations should be encouraged because they can initiate more planful, productive consultation and collaboration. Sometimes they become catalysts for meaningful inservice and staff development activities. In other cases they may initiate team effort that would have been overlooked or neglected in the daily hustle and bustle of school life.

Prototypes

A *prototype* (R) is a pattern. Consulting prototypes include mental health consultation, behavioral consultation, advocacy consultation, and process consultation.

The *mental health* prototype has a long history (Conoley & Conoley, 1988). The concept originated in the 1960s with the work of psychiatrist Gerald Caplan. Caplan conceived of consultation as a relationship between two professional people in which responsibility for the client rests on the consultee (Hansen, Himes, & Meier, 1990). Caplan (1970) proposed that consultee difficulties in dealing with a client's problems usually are cased by any one, or all, of four interfering themes:

- Lack of knowledge about the problem and its conditions
- Lack of skill to address the problem in appropriate ways
- Lack of self-confidence in dealing with the problem
- Lack of professional objectivity in approaching the problem

The consultant not only helps resolve the problem at hand, but enhances the consultee's ability to handle similar situations in the future. Caplan's most important intervention goal is to enhance the consultee's professional objectivity so that the consultee does not identify subjectively with the client, or try to fit the client into a category and assume an inevitable outcome (Conoley & Conoley, 1982). When the mental health prototype is used for consultation, consultee change may very well precede client change. Therefore, assessment of success should focus on consultee attitudes and behaviors more than on client changes (Conoley & Conoley, 1988). School-based mental health consultation is characterized by consultant attention to teacher feelings and the meaning the teacher attaches to the student's behavior (Slesser, Fine, & Tracy, 1990).

The *behavioral consultation* prototype is also intended to improve the performance of both consultee and client. Behavioral consultation is characterized by clear, explicit problem-solving procedures (Slesser, Fine, & Tracy, 1990). It is based on social learning theory, so skills and knowledge contribute more to consultee success than unconscious themes such as objectivity or self-confidence (Bergan, 1977). Behavioral consultation probably is more familiar to educators and thus is more easily introduced into the school context than is a mental health consultation prototype. The consultant is required to define the problem, isolate environmental variables that support that problem, and plan interventions to reduce the problem. Bergan (1995) recounts the evolution of a problem-solving model that he based on the theoretical approach of behavioral theory founded in an empirical research tradition. His four-stage model of a consultative problem-solving process was grounded on successful identification of the problem as the first stage. Problem analysis, implementation, and evaluation followed this stage.

Conoley and Conoley (1988) regard behavioral consultation as the easiest prototype to evaluate, since problem delineation and specific goal-setting occur within the process. Evaluation results can be used to modify plans, and to promote consultation services among other potential consultees. Cipani (1985) notes that behavioral consultation can fail to bring results when it focuses on problematic social behavior, such as aggression or being off-task, when that behavior really emanates from poor or inadequate academic skills.

Organizational consultation features individuals together in small-group formation and small, incremental steps over long periods of time to implement programs and solve problems. The more who are involved, the greater the probability of implementing planned changes (Truesdell and Lopez, 1995).

In *advocacy consultation* the client is the community, not the established organization (Gallessich, 1974), with the consultant serving the "client" directly as trainer and catalyst, and indirectly as advocate (Raymond, McIntosh, and Moore, 1986). This concept is considered by some to be quite political, with one group trying to overcome another for a greater share of the finite resources. Advocacy consultants stress that power, influence, and politics are the motivating influences behind human behavior (Conoley & Conoley, 1982). They need specific consulting skills for organizing people and publicizing events to serve special needs appropriately, which can include seeking due process for clients.

The *human relations* prototype, like the advocacy prototype is an organizational type of consultation. It is based on how influences of the work environment have impact on personal growth, and is designed to increase organizational productivity and morale (Gallessich, 1982).

Process consultation is sometimes included as a sixth prototype, along with mental health, behavioral, organizational, advocacy, and human relations consultation. But in this book it was included above as a perspective, and therefore will not be treated as a prototype.

Modes

A *mode* (E) is a particular form or manner of doing something. Modes for school consultation can be regarded as direct consultation for the delivery of service to clients, or indirect consultation for delivery of service to clients through consultees.

In a *direct* mode the consultant works directly with a special-needs student. For example, a learning disabilities consulting teacher or a speech pathologist specialist might use a technique with the student, while a parent or classroom teacher consultee observes and assists with the technique. Direct service to students usually is carried out for students subsequent to a referral (Bergan, 1977). The consultant may conduct observations and discuss the learning or behavioral need directly with the student (Bergan, 1977; Heron & Harris, 1987). The consultant becomes an advocate and the student has an opportunity to participate in decisions made pertinent to that need. Another example of direct service is teaching coping skills to students for their use at home or at school (Graubard, Rosenberg, & Miller, 1971; Heron & Harris, 1987).

The *indirect* service delivery mode calls for "back-stage" involvement among consultants and consultees to serve client needs. The consultant and consultee interact and problem-solve together. In doing so the consultant provides direct service to the consultee, who then provides related direct service to the client. School consultation typically is regarded as indirect service to students through direct work with their teachers or parents (Lilly & Givens-Ogle, 1981); however, variants of service delivery are possible in particular circumstances.

It is in this arena that some of the most significant changes have occurred since the enactment of Public Law 94-142, and, more recently, the inclusionary movement.

Models

Models (M) are patterns, examples for imitation, representations in miniature, descriptions, analogies, or displays. A model is not the real thing, but an approximation of it. It functions as an example through which to study, replicate, approximate, or manipulate intricate things. Models are useful for examining things or ideas when they are too big to construct (such as a model of the solar system) or too small to copy (a DNA molecule). They help explain and illustrate things that cannot be replicated because they are too costly (a supersonic jet plane), too complex (the United Nations system), or too time-intensive (travel to another galaxy). Such qualities make the model a useful structure on which to pattern the complex human processes of school consultation and collaborative teamwork.

Some of the more well-known models adopted or modified for school consultation over the past 25 years are:

- Triadic model
- Stephens/systems model
- Vermont Consulting Teacher Program model
- School Consultation Committee model
- Resource/Consulting Teacher Program model
- Collaborative consultation model

The *triadic model,* developed by Tharp and Wetzel (1969), and Tharp (1975) is the classic consultation model from which many school consultation models have evolved. It includes three roles—consultant, consultee (or mediator), and client (or target). In this most basic of the existing consultation models, services are not offered directly, but through an intermediary (Tharp, 1975). The service flows from the consultant to the target through the mediator. The consultant role is typically, although not always, performed by an educational specialist such as a learning disabilities teacher or a school psychologist. The consultee is typically, but not always, the classroom teacher. The client or target is usually the student with the learning or behavioral need. An educational need may be a disability or a talent requiring special services in order for the student to approach his or her learning potential. The triadic model requires both consultant and consultee to take ownership of the problem and share accountability for the success or failure of the program that is developed (Idol, Paolucci-Whitcomb, & Nevin, 1995). See Figure 2.2.

When studying the triadic model, or any other consultation model, it is important to recall the discussion in Chapter 1 about school consultation roles. Roles are interchangeable among individuals, depending upon the school context and the educational need. For example, on occasion, a learning disabilities consulting teacher might be a consultee who seeks information and expertise from a general classroom teacher consultant. At another time a student might be the consultant for a resource room teacher as consultee, and parents as the clients, or targets for intervention that is intended to help their child. Tharp gives the following example:

> Ms. Jones the second-grade teacher may serve as mediator between Brown, the psychologist, and John, the problem child. At the same time, she may be the target of her principal's training program and the consultant to her aide-mediator in the service of Susie's reading problem.

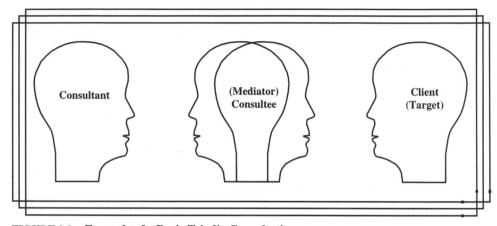

FIGURE 2.2 Example of a Basic Triadic Consultation

The triadic model, then, describes relative position in the chain of social influence (Tharp, 1975, p. 128).

Tharp identifies several advantages of the triadic model (Tharp, 1975), including the clarity it provides in delineating social roles and responsibilities, and the availability of evaluation data from two sources—mediator behavior and target behavior. However, it may not be the most effective model for every school context and each content area with the process skills and resources that are available. Advantages and disadvantages of using a triadic model of school consultation are included in Application 2.1, p. 60.

The *Stephens/systems model* constructed by Stephens (1977) is an extension of his directive teaching approach (Heron & Harris, 1982). It includes five phases:

- Assessment, observation, data collection
- Specification of objectives, problem-identification
- Planning, finding ways of resolving the problem
- Implementation of the plan, measurement of progress
- Evaluation, data analysis.

Baseline data are collected on target behaviors. Then interventions are planned, and additional data are collected in order to compare intervention effects. If the plan of treatment is not effective, further assessment

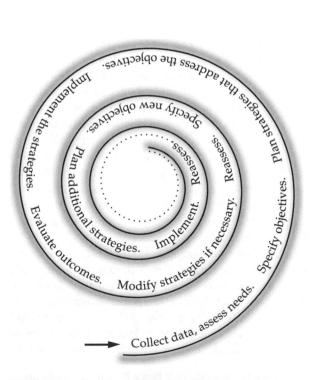

FIGURE 2.3 Interpretation of the Stephens/systems model

is conducted (Figure 2.3). The consultant helps the consultee devise criterion-referenced assessments or coding devices (Heron & Harris, 1987). This helps consultees become an integral part of the program and acquire skills to use after the consultant leaves. If interventions for one behavior or learning need are effective, then other target behaviors can be selected for modification, beginning with the first step in the model. Other advantages of using the systems model, as well as possible concerns to be considered, are included in Application 2.1, page 61.

The *resource/consulting teacher program model* (R/CT) was implemented at the University of Illinois and replicated in both rural and large urban areas (Idol, Paolucci-Whitcomb, & Nevin, 1986). It is based on the triadic model, with numerous opportunities for interaction among teachers, students, and parents. The resource/consulting teacher offers direct service to students through tutorials or small-group instruction and indirect service to students through consultation with classroom teachers for a portion of the school day. Students who are not staffed into special education programs can be served along with exceptional students mainstreamed into general classrooms. Parents are sometimes included in the consultation. (Figure 2.4.)

In the R/CT model, emphasis is placed on training students in the curricula used within each mainstreamed student's general classroom (Idol-Maestas, 1983). Close cooperation and collaboration between the R/CT and the classroom teacher are required so that teacher expectations and reinforcement are the same for both resource room and regular class setting

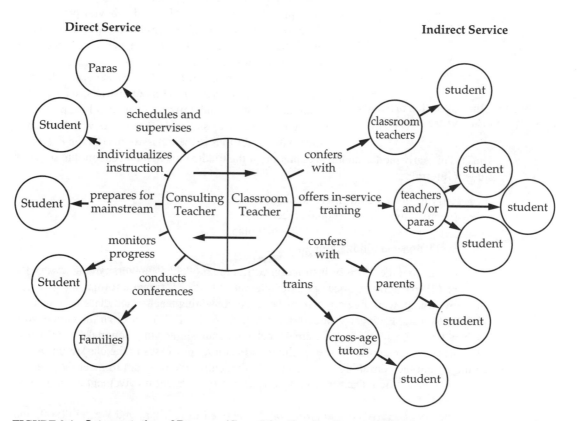

FIGURE 2.4   Interpretation of Resource/Consulting Teacher Program Model

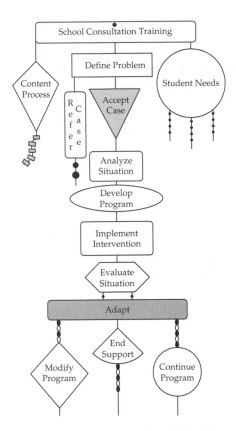

FIGURE 2.5   Interpretation of School Consultation Committee Interaction

(Idol-Maestas, 1981). Advantages and disadvantages of the R/CT model are included in Application 2.1, page 61.

The *School Consultation Committee model* (McGlothlin, 1981) provides an alternative approach for school consultation in the form of a School Consultation Committee model. The committee typically includes a special education teacher, a primary classroom teacher, an upper-grade classroom teacher, the building principal, and persons involved in ancillary and consultant roles. After a one-day training session conducted by an outside consultant, the committee meets as frequently as needed in order to screen referrals, assess problems and develop plans, and evaluate the results of those plans. The consultant remains available to help the committee as needed (McGlothlin, 1981). See Figure 2.5.

The School Consultation Committee is a familiar approach for school personnel who have had experience on preassessment, student improvement, or prereferral teams. It is a meeting of the minds, where responsibilities are shared in a group effort to produce desired outcomes. Such an approach addresses learning and behavior problems in the general classroom before considering special education eligibility. Advantages and disadvantages of this model are given in Application 2.1, page 62.

The *Vermont Consulting Teacher Program Model* is a collaborative effort of local school districts, state department of education, and university personnel for providing consultative services statewide to teachers who have children with disabilities in their classrooms (Heron & Harris, 1987). This early model, another adaptation of the triadic model, includes four phases after student referral:

- Entry level data-collection and diagnosis
- Specification of instructional objectives
- Development and implementation of a plan
- Evaluation and follow-through

There are three forms of instruction within the model: (1) university coursework for teachers, (2) specialized workshops as an alternative to the coursework format, and (3) consultation through working partnerships between consulting teacher and classroom teacher (Knight, Meyers, Paolucci-Whitcomb, Hasazi, & Nevin, 1981). Through the coursework teachers learn principles of measurement, behavior analysis, and instructional design. These principles then are applied to the teaching and learning processes in the classroom. A key feature is that the consulting teacher must individualize the program to meet the specific needs of the classroom teacher (Heron & Harris, 1987). Parent involvement is an integral component of the model.

The *collaborative consultation model* is derived from Tharp and Wetzel (1969) and Tharp (1975) and includes three components—(C)consultant, M(mediator), and (T)target

(Idol, Paolucci-Whitcomb, & Nevin, 1995). It conceptualizes the consultant and consultee as equal partners with diverse expertise—identifying problems, planning intervention strategies, and implementing recommendations with mutual responsibility (Idol, Paolucci-Whitcomb, & Nevin, 1986; Raymond, McIntosh, & Moore, 1986). The communication is not hierarchical or one-way. Rather, there is a sense of parity that blends the skills and knowledge of both consultant and consultee, with disagreements viewed as opportunities for constructive extraction of the most useful information (Idol, Paolucci-Whitcomb, & Nevin, 1995). In addition, there is the expectation that both consultant and consultee will work directly with the student. In research to investigate teacher responses to consultative services, Schulte, Osborne, and Kauffman (1993) found that teachers indicate collaborative consultation services are viewed as an acceptable alternative to resource rooms by most, and a quite desirable alternative by some. However, scheduling and teacher time can impose limits on success.

Pryzwansky (1974) suggested the basic structure of the collaborative approach by emphasizing the need for mutual consent on the part of both consultant and consultee, mutual commitment to the objectives, and shared responsibility for implementation and evaluation of the plan. The consultant, mediator, and target have reciprocally reinforcing effects on one another, which encourages more collaborative consultation at a later date (Idol-Maestas, 1983). Each collaborator, as part of the team, contributes a clearly defined portion of the effort so that all comes together to create a complete plan or solution.

Collaborative consultation can be blended with other approaches for particular contexts. One teacher in a small school with as many as six different lesson preparations who is coaching a different sport each season finds a combination of the collaborative and triadic models very time efficient. It can be conducted informally, utilizes both consultant and consultee knowledge efficiently, and has the aspect of confidentiality that is so important in a small, rural school (Figures 2.6 and 2.7).

Idol, Nevin, and Paolucci-Whitcomb (1995) describe several features that demonstrate the effectiveness of collaborative consultation:

- Learners with special needs can be served better when teachers generate and merge strategies and ideas through collaboration.
- Educators can acquire the skills to collaborate effectively.

Consultant   Consultant   Consultee   Consultee   Client

FIGURE 2.6   Interpretation of Triadic School Consultation

FIGURE 2.7   Interpretation of Collaborative School Consultation Based on a Triadic Model

- Collaborative solutions are more successful than those developed individually.
- Positive changes occur in school systems in the form of more team teaching, enhanced skills and attitudes of collaborators, and improvements of learning and social skills among learners with special needs. (See Application 2.1, page 62 for more aspects concerning this model.)

Variations of collaborative consultation include, but are not limited to, the following:

1. The Adaptive Learning Environments Model (ALEM). This is one of the earliest of the more recent variations. The goal of ALEM is to eliminate the need for pull-out programs by providing classroom alternatives that address learning needs of all students. Extensive collaboration among parents, teachers, administrators and other professionals is critical for the success of ALEM.

2. Class-Within-A-Class (CWC). This is an innovative delivery model that strives to reduce dependence on pull-out programs by serving learning disabled students full-time in general classes. Special education teachers go into the classrooms during instruction to collaborate and consult with the teacher and provide additional support to students with learning disabilities in the class.

3. Success-for-All (SFA). It is a comprehensive program aimed at preschool and primary levels. Its main purpose is to prevent failure by assuring reading success during the early school years. Individual tutoring, cross-age grouping, and extensive collaboration are important features of this program.

4. Mainstream Training Project (MTP). This uses inservice training for preparing classroom teachers at the secondary level to serve students who have learning difficulties. When classroom teachers have been trained in using effective teaching methods for students with learning and behavior problems, special education consultants work closely with them to monitor student progress and assist in implementation of newly-learned teaching techniques.

5. Schoolwide Enrichment Model (SEM). It is designed to provide more challenging learning experiences for gifted and talented students in the regular classroom. Classroom teachers are supported by consultation services from facilitators for gifted programs. Teachers and facilitators collaborate in providing gifted and talented students with curriculum options and alternatives such as flexible pacing, enrichment, personalized instruction, and challenging group experiences.

6. Resource Consultation Model. The concept was developed originally by Curtis, Curtis, and Graden (1988) and adapted for education of gifted students. With this model consultation becomes a problem-solving process shared by all school personnel in which the primary goal is to use limited and expensive resources more effectively and efficiently to better serve students (Kirschenbaum, Armstrong, & Landrum, 1999). In this model, consultation can occur at one of three levels—collaboration on a less formal and less structured basis; assistance from gifted education personnel (which turns out to be used 85 percent of the time); or team intervention if several school personnel will be affected, such as on a matter involving acceleration.

7. *Instructional consultation* is a merger of collaborative consultation processes and instructional psychology knowledge (Rosenfield, 1995): When instruction is diagnosed, and any instructional components detrimental to the learner are identified and corrected, the learner will improve. Assumptions about learning difficulties must be reexamined and trust must be established between teacher and school psychologist. Implementation of interventions takes place in the classroom, as intervention and assessment are more closely woven together.

8. In the *Special Education Consultant Teacher* model (Goldberg, 1995), linking relationships are established among the consulting teacher, other professionals, parents, and teachers. These linking relationships allow for delivery of direct and indirect services, with the consulting teacher affecting a spectrum of educational services. Certain conditions must be in place within the system if the model is to be effective, including mutual expertise, access to collaborative interactions, fluency with a shared professional vocabulary, time control, and administrator support.

DEVELOPMENT AND APPLICATION OF STRUCTURES FOR COLLABORATIVE SCHOOL CONSULTATION

Any plan for collaborative school consultation should take into account the school's needs by including facets from all the components that have been introduced:

S. System (school systems, other social systems)

P. Perspective (purchase, doctor-patient, process)

A. Approach (formal, informal)

R. pRototype (mental health, behavioral, advocacy, human relations)

E. modE (direct, indirect)

M. Model (triadic, Stephens/systems, Resource/Consulting Teacher Program, School Consultation Committee, Vermont Consulting Teacher Program, collaborative consultation and variant models).

The most relevant factors of these six key components can be synthesized into an appropriate method for serving special needs of the client as they occur. Once again, refer to Figure 2.1. Note that the Method area in the middle draws from each of the six descriptive elements to synthesize components into a viable method for formulating collaborative consultations.

Educators will recognize the need for having all six elements—systems, perspectives, approaches, prototypes, modes, and models—understood and available for potential combination into appropriate methods for serving special needs of students within every school context. *Locally-developed methods* for addressing *special learning needs* are the most effective practices that educators can employ.

■ ■ ■ ■ ■ ▬▬

APPLICATION 2.1
BUILDING STRUCTURES FOR COLLABORATIVE CONSULTATION

A helpful activity for thinking about complex functions is the thought problem. Thought problems, as practiced by eminent scientists such as Einstein, take place in the mind, not in the laboratory or classroom. The idea is to manipulate variables and concepts mentally, "seeing" them from all angles and deferring judgment until all conceivable avenues have been explored. A thought problem is an opportunity to reflect upon something intently before presenting it for discussion and critique by others. Much of the time this type of activity precedes engagement in complex processes such as collaborative consultation.

The following activity is a thought problem with several parts, one for each of the models described earlier. This exercise encourages you to be *very* "Einsteinian" as you reflect on school consultation, and manipulate and embellish your images of the models.

First, study again the brief descriptions of the models. Then select one from the following and arrange its components mentally to create a graphic way of illustrating a consultation method that could be useful in your school context. Einstein used trains, clocks, kites, rushing streams, even swirling tea leaves to ponder interesting phenomena and conceptualize his ideas. You may find it helpful to use computer graphics, illustrations, building blocks, toy people, or other special effects as you manipulate the elements of your ideas. Here are examples for starters:

TRIADIC TYPES OF MODELS

1. How might you show the interactions intended for the triadic model? One enterprising consultant drew a bow, with arrow poised for flight toward a target. The bow represents the consultant, the arrow is consultee, and the bull's-eye is the problem or need. Another created a restaurant scene, with the consultant as behind-the-scenes cook, the consultee as the cook-and-server, and the client as the diner. A third person devised the graphic in Figure 2.2. How would *you* visualize an interactive graphic for a triadic type of consultation or one of the variations on the triadic model? Note the following:

Advantages	**Possible Concerns**
A way to get started with consultee	Little/no carry-over to other situations
Quick and direct	and problems
Informal and simple, keeps problems	Needed again for same or similar
in perspective	situations
Objectivity on the part of the consultant	Only one other point of view expressed

Advantages	Possible Concerns
Student anonymity if needed	Expert consultation skills needed
Appropriate in crisis situations	by consultant
Time-efficient	May not have necessary data available
May be all that is needed	Little or no follow-up
Can lead to more intensive	Tendency to blame lack of progress
consultation/collaboration	on consultant

STEPHENS/SYSTEMS TYPES OF MODELS

2. For the Stephens/systems model, one illustrator organized the steps into a spiral model beginning with assessment of needs and concluding with reevaluation. Another viewed the model as a baseball field, with pitcher's mound as where the action (assessment) begins, then the batter's box, first, second, third bases, and home plate serving as the model's steps. Another developed the steps into a BINGO! on the Bingo card. (See Figure 2.3.)

Advantages	Possible Concerns
Each step in concrete terms	Extensive paperwork
Follows familiar IEP development system	Assumes spirit of cooperation exists
Collaborative	Time-consuming
Changes easily made	Might become process-for-process sake
Formative and developmental	May seem "much ado about little"
Strong record-keeping	Assumes training in data-keeping
Avoids the "expert" role	and observation
Has an evaluation component	Multiple steps overwhelming
Much accountability	to busy teachers
Provides whole picture of need, plan,	Delayed results
and results	

RESOURCE/CONSULTING TEACHING
TYPES OF MODELS

3. Now try depicting the process of interaction provided by the Resource/Consulting Teacher Program. (See Figure 2.4.)

Advantages	Possible Concerns
Provides direct and indirect service	Energy-draining
Parent involvement	Time often not available
"In-House" approach to problems	Scheduling difficult
Opportunity for student involvement	High caseloads for consulting teacher
Compatible with non-categorical/	Indirect service not weighted as heavily
interrelated methods	as direct
Ownership by many roles	Training needed in effective interaction
in problem-solving	Delayed, or no, reinforcement
More closely approximates	for consultant
classroom setting	Administrator support and cooperation
Spreads the responsibility around	essential
Opportunity to belong as a	
teacher/consultant	
Opportunity for regular contact between	
consultant/consultee	

SCHOOL CONSULTATION COMMITTEE TYPES OF MODELS

4. You might want to develop a more linear design for the School Consultation Committee model. One possibility is a mobile design (see Figure 2.5), and another could be a computer-type flow chart tailored to illustrate local school procedures.

Advantages	**Possible Concerns**
Administrator involved	Only one day of training for special
Multiple sources of input	assignment
Skill gains from other teachers	Time-consuming
Familiar to those using preassessment/	Possible resentment toward specialized
building team	expertise
Time provided for professional interaction	Potential for too much power from some
Many points of view	committee members
Good for major problem-solving	Solution might be postponed
Focuses on situations of the school context	Confidentiality harder to ensure
Involves a number of general	Indirect, not direct service to student
education staff	Could diffuse responsibility so no one
Can minimize problems before they get	feels responsible
too serious	

COLLABORATIVE TYPES OF MODELS

5. Note the development of the triadic school consultation model (see Figure 2.6) into a collaborative consultation model (see Figure 2.7). How might that look to you in your educational context?

Advantages	**Possible Concerns**
Fits current reform movements	Little or no training in collaboration
Professional growth for all through	Lack of time to interact
shared expertise	Working with adults not preference
Many ideas generated	of some educators
Maximizes opportunity for constructive	Requires solid administrator support
use of individual differences	Takes time to see results
among adults	
Allows administrator to assume	
facilitative role	
Parent satisfaction	

■ ■ ■ ■ ■ ▬▬▬▬▬

APPLICATION 2.2
FORMULATING AN OUTLINE FOR A MODEL

After creating your own graphics in Application 2.1, explain their main parts in words. Then reread the advantages and concerns section for your model that accompanied the illustration of it in this book, testing your graphics to see if they maximize important benefits and minimize potential shortcomings of each.

■ ■ ■ ■ ■

APPLICATION 2.3

SELECTING AN APPROPRIATE MODEL FOR SPECIFIC SITUATIONS

Nine practice situations for school consultation, collaboration, and/or teamwork are presented below. There are no right or wrong methods for addressing the needs presented by these situations. But each should be addressed by targeting several issues:

1. Is this a situation in which consultation and collaboration will be beneficial for the client? (If the answer is yes, proceed to next points.)
2. Who best fits the consultant, consultee, and client roles in each?
3. How might interaction among the roles be structured? What should happen first? Who will do what? When would the interaction most likely conclude? (Do not dwell on the specific consultation process at this time. That is addressed in Chapter 5.)
4. Determine the structural elements that will be included in the method you develop for addressing each of the situations:
   4.1 In what contextual *system* (school, home, medical, etc.) will the consultation be conducted?
   4.2 Will the most helpful *perspective* be a purchase, a doctor-patient, or a process relationship?
   4.3 Should the *approach* be formal or informal?
   4.4 Is the most descriptive *prototype* the mental health, behavioral, process, advocacy, or human relations pattern?
   4.5 Will the consultation be provided in a direct or an indirect service delivery *mode?*
   4.6 Which *model* seems to serve the need and fit with the other five consultation components best?
5. What may be major obstacles in carrying out collaborative school consultation and teamwork? Major benefits? Remember that positive ripple effects may occur that contribute significantly to instances beyond this situation.

POINTS TO CONSIDER WHEN ADDRESSING THE SITUATIONS

A. One person may decide that the best way to address the need is with the *triadic* model and a *purchase* perspective, using *indirect* service from the consultant to the client, in an *informal, mental health* prototype of interaction within the *school system.*
B. Another person may address a client's need appropriately by choosing the *School Consultation Committee* model similar to preassessment teams or school building teams, with a *process* perspective, in a *formal* and *direct* way, using the *behavioral* prototype in the *school system.*
C. Yet another individual or group may approach a particular problem through a *collaborative consultation* model, with a *process* perspective, using *direct* service to the client from both consultant and consultee, in a *formal* way that approximates an *advocacy* prototype, in a system of a *community work setting.*
D. To carry out the Application 2.3 task, recall that the methods of consultation should include facets of each of the six structural elements that will best meet the student's special needs.

SITUATIONS FOR THE APPLICATION ACTIVITY

1. Clarisse is a new 10-year old student placed in the TMR program. The teacher quickly learned that she prefers to observe rather than participate, and will not join in group activities. In her previous school, according to parents, she had been allowed to lie on the floor most of the

day so she would not have tantrums over participation. Her new teacher and para want Clarisse to demonstrate her capabilities, but do not want her to get off to a bad start in the new school and do not want parents to feel negative toward the new teachers. The teacher knows this is a crucial time for Clarisse and wonders what to do.

2. The speech pathologist has been asked by the gifted program facilitator to consult with her regarding a highly gifted child who has minor speech problems, but is being pressured by parents and kindergarten teacher to "stop the baby talk." The child is becoming very nervous and at times withdraws from conversation and play. How can the speech pathologist structure consultation and collaboration?

3. A school psychologist is conferring with a teacher about a high school student she has just evaluated. The student is often a behavior problem, and the psychologist is discussing methods for setting up behavior limits with appropriate contingencies and rewards. The teacher makes numerous references to the principal as a person who likes teachers to be self-sufficient and not "make waves." How should the school psychologist handle this?

4. A fifth-grade student with learning disabilities (LD) is not having success in social studies. The student has a serious reading problem, but is a good listener and stays on task. The LD resource teacher suspects that the classroom teacher is not willing to modify materials and expectations for the child. The teacher has not discussed this situation with the LD teacher, but the student has. Parent-teacher conferences are next week. What should happen here, and who will make it happen?

5. Parents of a student with learning disabilities have asked the special education consulting teacher to approach the student's classroom teacher about what they think is excessive and difficult homework. The parents say it is disrupting their home life and frustrating the student. How can this situation be addressed?

6. A high school learning disabilities consultant is visiting with a principal at the principal's request. The principal expresses concern about the quality of teaching of two faculty members and asks the consultant to observe them and then provide feedback. How should the consultant handle this situation?

7. A local pediatrician contacts the director of special education and asks her to meet with local doctors to discuss characteristics and needs of children with disabilities. How should this opportunity be structured for maximum benefit to all?

8. Schoolwide achievement tests will be administered soon. Under IDEA regulations, special education students are to be included in these assessments or documentation must be made as to reasons for excluding them. The consulting teacher is conferring with the classroom teacher of several mainstreamed students with learning disabilities about their readiness for these tests. The demands of NCLB loom in the minds of both teachers.

9. An energetic new teacher is full of ideas, which often are initiated with little planning or step-by-step instruction for students. She allows the students to be self-directed and to move from one activity to another as their interests direct them. A slow-learning student is floundering in this unstructured setting. The special education director has been alerted to the situation by the school principal, who had been approached by the student's mother with her concerns. There is no other classroom at the student's grade level in this school to which the student might be transferred, and now that several weeks of school have gone by, it probably is too late to consider such a step. What might be done?

TIPS FOR STRUCTURING COLLABORATIVE
SCHOOL CONSULTATION

1. Be knowledgeable about the history and outcomes of school improvement and reform movements.
2. Keep up to date on educational issues and concerns.
3. Be aware of education legislation and litigation.
4. Be on the alert for new methods or revisions of existing methods through which consultation and collaboration can occur in your school context.
5. Create specific ways that teachers can get your help.
6. Read current research on school consultation and collaboration, and highlight references to these processes in other professional material you read.
7. Visit programs where models different from those in your school(s) are being used.
8. Find sessions at professional conferences that feature different models and methods, and attend them to broaden your knowledge about educational systems.

CHAPTER REVIEW

1. School reform movements which highlight the need for consultation and collaboration include the regular education initiative, school improvement movements, inclusion, restructuring and reform efforts.

2. Many professional educators and parents have contended that students with disabilities should not be excluded from their neighborhood school programs and student peer groups. This movement, called inclusion, is another effort to define and operationalize the concept of least restrictive environment. It is tied to broader school reform movements that have evolved over the last three decades.

3. The No Child Left Behind legislation passed in 2001 stipulates that schools will demonstrate adequate yearly progress by its students. The public is unsure about the meaning and purpose of this legislation, while special education teachers are wary of its impact on students with special needs.

4. School consultation evolved from practices in the mental health and medical services fields. The earliest uses of school consultation were in areas of speech and language therapy, and services for visually-impaired and hearing-impaired students. Differing points of view are held about the existence of a theoretical base of school consultation. Some researchers consider school consultation theory-based if the relationship between consultant and consultee can be identified across more than one literature source. Research in school consultation and collaboration has been conducted to assess situational variables, outcome variables, and organizational change. There is a need for more reliable and valid instrumentation, more specific definition of variables, and more careful control of variables during the research.

5. Structural elements to develop effective methods of school consultation can be categorized as: Systems (institutions and contexts); Perspectives (purchase, doctor-patient, problem-solving); Approaches (formal, informal); Prototypes (mental health, behavioral, advocacy, human relations); Modes (direct, indirect); and Models (see 6 below).

6. Several collaborative consultation models are: Triadic model, Stephens/systems model, Resource/Consulting Teacher program model, School Consultation Committee model, Vermont Consulting Teacher program model, and the collaborative consultation model. Variants of the collaboration consultation model include the Adaptive Learning Environments Model (ALEM), Class-Within-A-Class (CWC), Success-For-All (SFA), Mainstream Training Project (MTP), Schoolwide Enrichment Model (SEM), and Resource Consultation Model.

7. Educators should introduce into their school context a structure combining consultation, collaboration, and co-teaching that is tailored in a fashion using the system, perspective, approach, prototype, mode, and model that suit the specific setting.

TO DO AND THINK ABOUT

1. Using material in this chapter and Chapter 1, a dictionary, interviews, recollections from teaching experiences, discussion with colleagues or classmates, and any other pertinent references, formulate a description and philosophy about collaborative school consultation which builds upon the one you developed in Chapter 1 and which reflects your viewpoint at this time.

2. Pinpoint several changes that have occurred in special education during the past twenty years, and suggest implications for school consultation methods.

3. Locate articles focusing on consultation, collaboration and teamwork, summarize the highlights, and prepare a "fact sheet" or information bulletin for other school staff, including administrators.

4. Have the complete articles from which you shared information in number 3 available for any who might ask to read the entire work.

5. Brainstorm with a group to list current issues and major problems in education. After generating as many ideas as possible, mark those that seem most amenable to solutions afforded by consultation, collaboration, and teamwork. You might want to asterisk those that in the past have "belonged" to special education, and discuss what part general education plays in dealing with those issues now.

6. Visit schools where consultation and collaboration play an integral role in serving students' special needs. Using the information related to Figure 2.1, analyze the consultation systems, perspectives, approaches, prototypes, modes, and models that seem to be in use in those schools. Then summarize the results into brief, innovative descriptions of the methods that seem to have evolved from the synthesis of these components.

FOR FURTHER READING

Bassett, D. S., Jackson, L., Ferrell, K. A., Luckner, J., Hagerty, P. J., Bunsen, T. D., & MacIsaac, D. (1996). Multiple perspectives on inclusive education: Reflections of a university faculty. *Teacher Education and Special Education, 19*(4), 355–386.

Brown, D., Pryzwansky, W. B., & Schulte, A. C. (1991). *Psychological consultation: Introduction to theory and practice.* Needham Heights, MS: Allyn & Bacon. Chapters 1, 2, and 3 in particular.

Conoley, J. C., & Conoley, C. W. (1982). *School consultation: A guide to practice and training.* New York: Pergamon Press, Inc.

Educational leadership. (December 1994/January 1995), *52*(4). Topical issue on the inclusive school.

Erchul, W. P., & Martens, B. K. (1997). *School consultation: Conceptual and empirical bases of practice.* New York: Plenum.

Fuchs, D., Fuchs, L. S., Dulan, J., Roberts, H., & Fernston, P. (1992). Where is the research on consultation effectiveness? *Journal of Educational and Psychological Consultation; 3*(2), 151–174.

Journal of Educational and Psychological Consultation. All issues. and in particular Volume 1, Number 4, 1990, and Volume 3, Number 2, 1993.

Morsink, C. V., Thomas, C. C., & Correa, V. I. (1991). *Interactive teaming: Consultation and collaboration in special programs.* New York: Merrill. Chapter 2 in particular.

Scruggs, T. E., & Mastropieri, M. A. (1996). Teacher perceptions of mainstreaming/inclusion, 1958–1995: A research synthesis. *Exceptional Children, 63*(1), 59–74.

Smith, J. D. (1998). The history of special education: Essays honoring the bicentennial of the work of Jean Itard. *Remedial and Special Education, 19*(4), entire issue.

Stanovich, P. J. (1999). Conversations about inclusion. *Teaching Exceptional Children, 31*(6), 54–58.

CHAPTER THREE

WORKING TOGETHER WITH FAMILIES AND STUDENTS

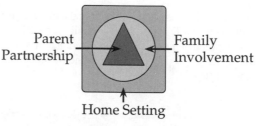

Education must be a shared responsibility. Education of the whole child requires solid, well-functioning partnerships among school, community, and family.

Family members are a child's first and most influential teachers. Educators need to understand family involvement as a way to enhance their work and improve student learning (Lueder, 1998). Too often the conventional pattern of relationships between schools and parents is limited to the role of parents as donors or classroom volunteers. This pattern must be transformed by recognizing families and communities as equal partners in preparing students for adult life. This perception is the key to family-centered practices that strengthen and promote competence in students, families, and communities.

It is now time to cultivate home–school collaborations that will allow both school educators and home educators to fulfill their commitments to develop each child's potential. Home–school partnerships provide students the best opportunity for overcoming risks and disabilities, and to achieve their full potential in a complex, challenging world.

In this chapter, parent partnerships are the content focus (triangle in the opening graphic). We will explore processes (circle) of family involvement with schools as they emanate from the home setting context (square).

FOCUSING QUESTIONS

1. What legislation has mandated parent involvement and supported family empowerment in schools?

2. How does involvement by families in home–school partnerships benefit students, their families, teachers, their schools, and communities?

3. In what ways has family involvement matured into family partnership and collaboration?

4. What are barriers to home–school collaborative partnerships?

5. How can educators examine their values and attitudes toward families in order to build collaborative relationships?

6. What do teachers need to know to be better prepared to work with families of culturally and linguistically diverse students?

7. How can school personnel initiate and individualize partnerships with families?

8. How should students with special needs be involved in planning for their own learning?

KEY TERMS

cultural and linguistic
   diversity (CLD)
cultural competence
efficacy
empowerment

equal partnerships model
family-focused
   collaboration
home–school collaboration

Individual Family Service
   Plan (IFSP)
parent involvement
parent partnerships

VIGNETTE 3

The setting is a junior high school. The learning disabilities teacher has just arrived at the building, hoping to make some contacts with classroom teachers before classes begin, when the principal walks out of her office briskly, with a harried look.

Principal: Oh, I'm glad you're here. I believe Barry is part of your caseload this year, right? His mother is in my office. She's crying, and says that everybody's picking on her son.

LD Consultant: What happened?

Principal: He got into an argument with his English teacher yesterday, and she sent him to me. After he cooled down and we had a talk, it was time for classes to change, so I sent him on to his next class. But he skipped out. The secretary called and left word with the baby-sitter to inform the mother about his absence. He must have really unloaded on her, because she's here, quite upset, and saying that the teachers do not care about her son and his problems. Could you join us for a talk?

LD Consultant: Okay, sure. (Enters the principal's office and greets Barry's mother.)

Mother: I am just about at my wits' end. It's not been a good week at home but we've made an effort to keep track of Barry's work. Now this problem with his English teacher has him refusing to come to school. Sometimes I feel that we're at cross purposes—us at home and you at school.

LD Consultant: We certainly don't want this to happen. I'd like to hear more about your concerns, and the problems Barry and his teachers are having. Is this a good time, or can we arrange for one that is more convenient for you?

Mother: The sooner, the better. I don't want Barry missing school, but with the attitude he has right now, it wouldn't do him any good to be here.

LD Consultant: Let's discuss some strategies we can work on. We are all concerned about Barry, and we need for him to know that.

MANDATES FOR FAMILY INVOLVEMENT

School partners need to be aware of several legislated mandates intended to assure and strengthen educational partnerships between home and school. The Education for All Handicapped Children Act of 1975 (P.L. 94-142) prescribes several rights for families of children with disabilities. Succeeding amendments have extended those rights and responsibilities.

Legislation mandating family involvement is part of EACHA, the Handicapped Children's Protection Act, Early Intervention for Infants and Toddlers (Part H of P.L. 99-457), and the Individuals with Disabilities Education Act (IDEA, P.L. 101-476). Passage of P.L. 94-142 in 1975 guarantees families the right to due process, prior notice and consent, access to records, and participation in decision making. To these basic rights the 1986 Handicapped Children's Protection Act adds collection of attorney's fees for parents who prevail in due process hearings or court suits. The Early Intervention Amendment was part of the reauthorized and amended P.L. 94-142. Passed in 1986, it provides important provisions for children from birth through five years and their families. Part H addresses infants and toddlers with disabilities or who are at-risk for developmental delays. Procedural safeguards for families were continued and participation in the Individualized Family Service Plan (IFSP) was added.

The IFSP is developed by a multidisciplinary team with family members as active participants. Part B, Section 691, mandates service to all children with disabilities from ages three to five, and permits noncategorical services. Children may be served according to the needs of their families, allowing a wide range of services including parent training. This amendment fosters collaboration based on family-focused methods. The legislation speaks of families in a broad sense, not just a mother–father pair as the family unit. Families' choices are considered in all decisions.

The 1990 amendments under P.L. 101-476 increased participation by children and adults with disabilities and their families. An example is the formation of community transition councils with active participation of parents in the groups. Subsequent court decisions and statutory amendments have clarified and strengthened parental rights (Martin, 1991). The spirit of the law is met when educators develop positive, collaborative relationships with families.

The Individuals with Disabilities Education Act (IDEA) Amendments of 1997 were signed into law in June of 1997 after two years of analysis, hearings, and discussion. This reauthorization of IDEA, as Public Law 105-17, brought many changes to P.L. 94-142. Parent participation in eligibility and placement decisions, and mediation as a means of resolving parent–school controversies are two critically important areas of change. P.L. 105-17 strengthens the involvement of parents in all decision making involving their children (National Information Center for Children and Youth with Disabilities, 1997). This legislation added to the impetus of Goals 2000: Educate America Act featuring parent involvement and participation in promoting the social, emotional, and academic growth of children as one of its eight goals. More recently, the No Child Left Behind (NCLB) legislation sets forth several goals for schools, including closing achievement gaps between privileged and disadvantaged students, improving teacher preparation, instituting accountability systems for schools, teachers, and students, and setting academic standards with required testing to determine student progress (Hanna & Dettmer, 2004).

EDUCATIONAL RATIONALE
FOR FAMILY INVOLVEMENT

A student's school, family, and community provide overlapping spheres of influence on behavior, development, and achievement. The collaborative team should include all three spheres, with the student at the center.

Strong home–school relationships support student development and learning (Epstein, 1995; Hansen, Himes, & Meyer, 1990; Reynolds & Birch, 1988). Extensive research about the effects of family involvement demonstrates that parent involvement enhances students' chances for success in school and significantly improves their achievement. Students improve in terms of both academic behavior and social behavior, with higher attendance rates and lower suspension rates. They have higher test scores, more positive attitudes toward school, and higher completion rates for homework (Christenson & Cleary, 1990).

Children are not the only beneficiaries of family involvement. Family members benefit from improved feelings of self-worth and self-satisfaction, and increased incentive to enhance the educational environment of the home (Murphy, 1981). They have the opportunity to learn skills that help with their child's needs, such as behavior management techniques and communication strategies. As parents work with teachers, they have opportunity to provide input about their children's interests and needs and to express their own wisdom. Teachers learn more about their students' backgrounds. They receive support from family members who are valuable sources of information about their children's interests and needs and can provide encouragement to their children as they study and learn.

School systems benefit from home–school collaboration through improved attitudes toward schools and advocacy for school programs. A positive home–school relationship helps others in the schools and the community. Family involvement increases positive communication among all who are involved on the education team. It augments opportunity for school program success (Shea & Bauer, 1985), and enhances school and community accountability for serving special needs (Turnbull, Turnbull, & Wheat, 1982). These points all provide strong evidence that "reaching the family is as important as reaching the child" (Rich, 1987a, p. 64).

Family Empowerment

Special education laws and changes in laws do require significantly new and different ways of working with families. Empowerment is the goal (Royster & McLaughlin, 1996; Turnbull & Turnbull, 1997). Staples suggests this definition of empowerment: "An ongoing capacity of individuals and groups to act on their own behalf to achieve a greater measure of control over their lives and destinies" (Staples, 1990, p. 30). In their research with families of children in early intervention services, Thompson, Lobb, Elling, Herman, Jurkiewicz, and Hulleza (1997) looked at "pathways to family empowerment":

- Family-level empowerment, in management of day-to-day situations;
- Service-level empowerment, in families working with the systems of professionals and agencies; and
- Community/political level empowerment, in parent advocacy for improved services to all children with special needs (pp. 99–113).

To maximize all levels of empowerment of families with children with special needs, educators will want to hold timely meetings with appropriate interagency attendance, help families identify and build their social support systems, and provide models and mentors for parents to learn and adopt skills in each of the three levels.

MOVING FROM PARENT INVOLVEMENT TO PARTNERSHIPS WITH FAMILIES

Educational consultants and their colleagues must be aware of the realities facing today's families. Challenges in working with families today are very different from those faced a decade or two ago. Significant changes have taken place in society, along with new educational legislation and new demands for accountability for student outcomes. Poverty levels, births to unwed adolescent parents, and the numbers of nonbiological parents as primary caretakers (foster care, grandmothers, extended family, adoptive parents, and so on) have increased. In addition, there are increasing numbers of cultural minority families. Families can include single parents, parents with disabilities, gay and lesbian parents, families in poverty, and blended and extended families.

Many families are overwhelmed by family crises and normal life events; many face multiple and prolonged stressors such as long work hours, illness and disability, and multiple responsibilities. Many are discouraged and burned out. Multiple cultures and languages, differences in perceptions of the role and value of education, multiple stressors, and economic and educational barriers will make family collaboration a challenge for many consultants and many families. Educational legislation and social reality call for recognition of all types of families in school–home collaboration to achieve positive educational outcomes for children. This inclusiveness gives educators the opportunity and flexibility to work collaboratively with persons who may be helpful and supportive of the child's success in school.

Broadened Conceptualization of Family

Changing times and changing families require new ideas, new languages, and new models. The first step in these changes is to think in terms of *family* rather than parent. Many children do not live with both parents, or with either biological parent. Part H and Section of 619 of IDEA refer to *families* rather than parents. A broad, inclusive definition of family should be used by consultants who are collaborating with adults responsible for the development and well-being of children with special needs.

This new, inclusive definition of the family was suggested to the Office of Special Education and Rehabilitation Services (OSERS) by the Second Family Leadership Conference:

> A family is a group of people who are important to each other and offer each other love and support, especially in times of crisis. In order to be sensitive to the wide range of life styles, living arrangements, and cultural variations that exist today, family . . . can no longer be limited to just parent/child relationships. Family involvement . . . must reach out to include mothers, fathers, grandparents, sisters, brothers, neighbors, and other persons who have important roles in the lives of people with disabilities (Family and Integration Resources, 1991, page 37).

Educational legislation and social reality call for recognition of all types of families in school–home collaboration for positive educational outcomes for children. This inclusiveness gives educators the opportunity and flexibility to work collaboratively with persons who may be helpful and supportive of the child's success in school. The critical issue for student learning is not any existing or perceived difference between home and school, but the successful relationship between them. Home and student must not be separated from school and teacher (Christenson & Cleary, 1990).

Beyond Involvement to Collaboration

It is possible for families to be involved in the school life of their children without being collaborative. Although the two terms—*collaboration* and *involvement*—have been used interchangeably in the literature, collaboration goes beyond involvement. Educators too often regard involvement as giving parents information, conducting parenting classes, and developing advocacy committees. However, this kind of involvement does not assure that family needs and interests are being heard and understood. It does not signify that educators are setting program goals based on family members' concerns and input. It might involve parents in a narrow sense, but not in *working together* to form a home–school partnership.

It is important to distinguish between parent involvement and family collaboration in this way:

- Parent involvement is parent participation in activities that are part of their children's education, for example, conferences, meetings, newsletters, tutoring, and volunteer services.
- Family collaboration is the development and maintenance of positive, respectful, egalitarian relationships between home and school. It includes mutual problem solving and shared decision making.

Values Inherent in Home–School Collaboration

Collaboration with families adds a dimension to home–school relationships. Not only should family members be involved with schools, educators must be involved with families. Metaphorically speaking, a one-way street becomes a two-way boulevard to provide an easier road to "Success City" for students. Family-focused home–school collaboration is based on these principles:

- Families are a constant in children's lives and must be equal partners in all decisions affecting their educational programs.
- Family involvement includes a wide range of family structures.
- Diversity and individual differences among people are to be valued and respected.
- All families have strengths and coping skills that can be identified and enhanced.
- Families are sources of wisdom and knowledge about their children.

Effective family-centered help-giving is comprised of elements of relationship and of participation (Dunst, 2000). Central to family-centeredness is the respect for family concerns and priorities, issues of family competence and assets, and utilization of family and community resources and supports.

Hammond (1999) lists these characteristics of family-centered programs: Flexible programming; individualizing services for families; communication; developing and maintaining relationships; building family–staff collaboration; and respecting the family's expertise and strengths. This is a tall order for educational consultants, but new, empowering relationships and better outcomes for students depend on this shared sense of respect and care.

BARRIERS TO COLLABORATION WITH FAMILIES

Changing families make traditional methods of recruiting parent participation somewhat problematic. Barriers can include teacher factors, lack of organizational cultural competence, and family historical, attitudinal, or perceptual factors. Issues of work, transportation, and child care influence family participation. School systems and educators also create barriers when they relegate parents to a passive role in their child(ren)'s education.

Demographic data show that in recent years there has been a big drop in the proportion of people who have children in schools. National forums such as the Public Agenda reports reveal that educators are out of touch with typical views of parents and the public, which does not mean that any group is right or wrong, just that they are disturbingly far apart (Brandt, 1998). School consultants who recognize potential barriers to home–school collaboration will be better prepared to use successful and appropriate strategies to bridge the gap between home and school.

Virtually all families care about their children and want them to succeed, so they are eager to obtain better information from schools. In that same vein, just about all teachers and administrators would like to involve families (Epstein, 1995). However, Phelps (1999) contends that many teachers are apprehensive about working with families, and this negatively shapes their attitudes. A study by Bennett, DeLuca, and Bruns (1997) did report positive teacher attitudes toward parent involvement, with young teachers in the sample more positive than experienced teachers.

In reviewing research about parent involvement, Bennett, DeLuca, and Bruns (1997) conclude that, although family involvement is endorsed by educational professional organizations and is considered best practice, it is more theory than actual practice. Epstein (1995) calls this the "rhetoric rut." Why is home–school involvement more an ideal than a reality? Barriers to effective collaboration can be programmatic, school and consultant related, or family related. Finders and Lewis (1994) suggest that family involvement practices too often use a deficit approach model, that is, programs are based on the assumption that educators are the experts and family involvement is for the purpose of remediation. Bennett, Deluca, and Bruns (1997) stress the need for parents to be included as respected and equal members of the team, and they stress that improved communication with families can have positive effects on the inclusion experience. Administrators must use creative scheduling to allow time for this communication, and teachers need to access the resources that will make inclusion and collaboration work. All too often a general school climate of mistrusting parents can inhibit collaborative efforts. The school context is a powerful determinant of home–school interactions and partnerships (Phelps, 1999). Administrators should encourage teachers to initiate contact with families by providing resources and safe environments for partnership activities. Healing relationships with parents and neighborhoods seem directly related to the ability of teachers and school administrators to reflect on their own practices and move toward a family empowerment model (St. John, Griffith, & Allen-Hayes, 1997).

Culturally and Linguistically Diverse Families

Active parent and community involvement in educational programs for culturally and linguistically diverse (CLD) students is essential, yet the growing differences between cultural and linguistic backgrounds of school personnel and their students makes home–school collaboration a challenge. Persistent portrayal of CLD families as deficient in knowledge, skills, and abilities necessary to ready children for school is a huge barrier to active parent participation. Misconceptions about parental concern for their children's schooling are all too prevalent among school personnel (deValenzuela, Torres, & Chavez, 1998).

Another barrier to parent involvement is basing programs on middle-class values, expectations, and behaviors to the exclusion of minority families, their languages, and their cultures. Consultants must understand that there are differing views between home and school regarding parents' appropriate roles in the education of their children.

August and Hakuta (1997) describe patterns of parental involvement (parent behaviors that support education) of Puerto Rican families, Chinese American families, and Mexican American families. Studies reveal that parent behaviors fostering child learning may not be visible to school personnel.

Consultants need to help school personnel accommodate differences in families— families of children with disabilities, poverty-level families, CLD families—and consider that they are not homogeneous groups. Educators need to respond in individually relevant ways rather than to make assumptions about families based on language, ethnicity, and background.

Thurston and Navarrete (2003) surveyed 263 mothers on welfare to learn about their parent involvement practices. Only 22 percent of these mothers had completed high school, and a majority of those having children with disabilities had received special services themselves as students. Despite this, 70 percent reported good relationships with the teachers of their children, and there was no significant difference between mothers of children having disabilities and those of children having no disabilities. The group was nearly unanimous in expressed interest for getting involved in their children's schooling. Fewer than 3 percent were uninterested. The researchers suggest that educators focus on the strengths families bring to home–school partnerships and serve in a strong advocacy role for families in poverty.

Fox, Vaughn, Wyatte, and Dunlap (2002) remind educators that parents are involved with their children's education twenty-four hours a day, seven days a week. These researchers interviewed twenty culturally diverse family members about the impact of children with problem behaviors on families. They found three issues that educators should keep in mind when collaborating with parents:

- Family members had difficulty coming to terms with their child's disability;
- Having support of a genuinely caring person is very important;
- Problem behavior has a pervasive impact on all aspects of family functions.

This pervasive impact was investigated by Park, Turnbull, and Turnbull (2002), who analyzed the literature to discover the impact of poverty on quality of life among families of children with disabilities. They found five domains of impact: health, productivity, physical environment, emotional well-being, and family interactions. They suggest that educators act as advocates for poverty-level families of children with disabilities. Educators need to learn more about full-service models and collaborate actively with related service providers and community networks. If they become knowledgeable about services and advocate for broader services and access, collaborative efforts with parents will be more successful, to the benefit of students, families, and school personnel.

Classrooms today have increasing numbers of students from culturally and linguistically diverse backgrounds. Education consultants must remember that disability is a culturally and socially constructed phenomenon. Each culture and society defines the parameters of what is considered normal, with some cultures having a broader or different definition of disability than that accepted in American schools (Linan-Thompson & Jean, 1997). This may be one reason minority parents tend to be less involved and less informed about their child's school life than mainstream parents. It is important to learn from family members how their beliefs and practices will affect programs for children with special needs. Educational consultants who work with families must be aware of the family's perceptions of disability. Linan-Thompson & Jean (1997) suggest taking time to learn about family perceptions of special needs, carefully and thoroughly explaining the whole special education process, using informal assessments in addition to formal assessment tools (which helps explain the disability in other than formal terms), and discovering and using parents' preferred forms of communication (written, informal meetings, video- or audiotapes).

Traditional approaches to reaching out to families are not always appropriate for families from cultural and noncultural minority groups. Research reveals cultural differences in the utilization of services and the stated needs of families having children with disabilities or other risk factors (Arcia, Keyes, Gallagher, & Herrick, 1992; Sontag & Schacht, 1994). Educators must develop cultural competence (Anderson & Goldberg, 1991; Cross, 1996; Lynch & Hanson, 1992; Mason, 1994). Cultural competence means accepting, honoring, and respecting cultural diversity and differences. Then individualization of educational programs for students can be done in a manner that respects the family's culture. Cross (1996) suggests that professionals learn about cultures they serve by observing healthy and strong members of the different groups. Other recommendations include spending time with people of that culture, identifying a cultural guide, reading the literature (professional as well as fiction) by and for persons of the culture, attending cultural events, and asking questions in sensitive ways.

Bruns and Fowler (1999) recommend that educators give special recognition to cultural preferences in transition planning. Traditional parental roles of teacher, information source, decision maker, and advocate for transition planning may not be appropriate for or sensitive to all families. They suggest transforming these roles to guide, information specialist, decision maker, and ally. They also recommend inviting extended family members, friends, and community members to take part in education-related decisions as a way to meet diverse beliefs, values, and traditions of cultural groups. As educators develop cross-cultural competencies and increasingly collaborate with families culturally or linguistically different from themselves, they should remember that one approach does not fit all ranges of diversity (Parette & Petch-Hogan, 2000).

Lynch and Hansen (1992), Huff and Telesford (1994), and Cross (1988) suggest that school personnel use these strategies when collaborating with families from diverse cultural groups:

1. Acknowledge cultural differences and become aware of how they affect parent–teacher interactions.

2. Examine one's own personal culture, such as how one defines family, desirable life goals, and behavior problems.

3. Recognize the dynamics of group interactions such as etiquette and patterns of communication.

4. Explore the significance of the child's behavior in relation to his or her culture.

5. Adjust collaboration to legitimize and include culturally specific activities.

6. Learn about the families. Where are they from and when did they arrive? What cultural beliefs and practices surround child rearing, health and healing, and disability and causation?

7. Recognize that some families may be surprised by the extent of home–school collaboration expected in the United States.

8. Learn and use words and forms of greetings in the families' languages.

9. Work with cultural mediators or guides (relative, church member, neighbor, or older sibling) from the families' cultures to learn more about the culture and facilitate communication between school and home.

10. Ask for help in structuring the child's school program to match home life, such as learning key words and phrases used at home.

Well-publicized policies at the district level encouraging home–school collaboration are vital in providing opportunities for minority family members to become full partners with teachers, but effective structures and strategies often do not exist (Chavkin, 1989; Lynch & Stein, 1987). Lightfoot (1981) suggests that traditional methods of parent involvement such as PTA meetings, open house, or newsletters permit little or no true collaboration, constructing instead a "territory" of education that many parents are hesitant to invade. Concern, awareness, and commitment on the part of individuals in the educational system are beginning steps in challenging the limitations that inhibit collaboration between teachers and families who have language, cultural, or other basic differences.

Historical, Attitudinal, and Perceptual Factors in Partnerships

The success of family collaboration activities is based on partnerships developed and maintained by using the relationship and communication skills to be described in Chapter 4. However, other barriers overshadow the need for effective communication. They surface as formidable challenges to educators even before lines of communication with parents are established. Such barriers can be classified as perceptual, attitudinal, or historical. Examples are time limitations, anticipation of negative or punishing interactions, denial of problems, blaming, or a personal sense of failure in parenting and teaching (Swap, 1987).

Parents of children with learning and behavior problems can be effective change agents for their children; therefore, the question is not whether to involve them, but how to do it (Shea & Bauer, 1985). Although family members may want very much to play a key role in encouraging their children to succeed in school, they may be inhibited by their own attitudes or circumstances. Many parents, while very concerned about their child's education, are fearful and suspicious of schools, teachers, and education in general (Hansen, Heimes, & Meier (1990). They may fear or mistrust school personnel because of their own negative experiences as students. Or they may have experienced a history of unpleasant experiences with other professionals, so that current school personnel fall heir to that history.

Parents of children with special needs face many economic and personal hardships. Work schedules and health concerns prevent some parents from participating in school activities (Leitch & Tangri, 1988). Low-income families may have difficulty with transportation and child care, making it hard to attend meetings or volunteer in school, even when they would like to do so (Thurston & Navarette, 1996).

The single parent, already burdened with great responsibilities, is particularly stressed in parenting a child with special needs. The role can be overwhelming at times. When working with the single parent, school personnel will need to tailor their requests for conferences and home interventions, and to provide additional emotional support when needed (Conoley, 1989).

Many types of disability are very expensive for families, and the impact on the family budget created by the special needs of a child may produce new and formidable hardships. Sometimes families arrive at a point where they feel their other children are being neglected by all the attention to the special needs child. This adds to their frustration and stress. In addition, children with special needs and their families are vulnerable to stereotypes of society about physical, learning, or behavioral disabilities. They feel the impact of their family's dependence on others for services (Schulz, 1987). The ways in which families cope with the frustrations and stress influence their interaction with school personnel. Providing support networks can help them cope with the situation (Morsink, Thomas, & Correa, 1991).

Family members may avoid school interactions because they fear being blamed as the cause of their children's problems. Sometimes teachers do blame parents for exacerbating learning and behavior problems: "I can't do anything here at school because it gets undone when they go home!" But blaming does not facilitate development of mutually supportive relationships. Family members are very sensitive to blaming words and attitudes by school personnel. A teacher, who is also part of a therapeutic foster family, reported that he felt "blame and shame" after a school conference regarding the child with emotional and behavior problems who had been his foster child for two months.

Judging attitudes, stereotypes, false expectations, and basic differences in values also act as barriers and diminish the collaborative efforts among teachers and families. It is difficult to feel comfortable with people who have very different attitudes and values. Families and teachers should make every effort not to reproach each other, but work together as partners on the child's team. Educators, including teachers and parents, must abandon any posture of blaming or criticism, and move on to collaboration and problem solving. It is important to remember that it does not matter where a "fault" lies. What matters is who steps up to address the problem.

Collaboration requires respect, trust, and cooperation. However, as noted in Chapter 1, with respect to individual differences, and, as will be addressed in Chapter 4, regarding rapport-building, collaboration need not require total agreement. Educators cope with value differences in positive ways when they:

1. Remember that a teacher's place is on the parent's side as a team member working for a common goal, the child's success.

2. Become aware of their own feelings of defensiveness. Taking a deep breath and putting the feelings aside will help to continue building positive relationships. If that is not possible, they should postpone interactions until the defensiveness can be handled.

3. Remember that the focus must be on the needs and interests of families and their children, not on their values. It is important to attack the problem, not the person.

4. Accept people as they are and stop wishing they were different. This applies to parents as well as to their children.

5. Remember that most families are doing the best they can. Parents do not wake up in the morning and decide, "I think today I will be a poor parent."

6. Respect families' rights to their values and opinions. Different values do not mean better or poorer values. It is not possible to argue family members out of their values, and teachers do not have the right to do so.

7. Demonstrate the qualities of open-mindedness and flexibility.

8. Remember that parents develop a deeper commitment to schools when they are included in a way meaningful to them (St. John, et al., 1997).

BRIDGE BUILDING FOR SUCCESSFUL HOME–SCHOOL COLLABORATION

Friendly, positive relationships and honest, respectful communication can help bridge the barriers that might exist in home–school collaboration. The goal of collaboration is to promote the education and development of children by strengthening and supporting families. Keeping this in mind, consultants will remember that collaboration is not the goal but the means to the end. Strategies that have proven to be sturdy bridges to circumvent barriers are: Focusing on family strengths; using appropriate communication skills; and promoting positive roles for family members.

Focusing on Family Strengths

The traditional emphasis of education in past years has been a pathology- or deficit-based model. The philosophy of family-focused services and collaboration emphasizes the empowerment approach rather than focusing on what is going wrong. Instead of focusing on the child's or family's problem, collaborators focus on family members and the strength acquired through their experiences. This encourages the developmental progress of the child as well as healthy reactions to problems and crises and competent life management (Waters & Lawrence, 1993).

Using Appropriate Communication Skills

Bridges to circumvent language and communication barriers are difficult to construct. Chapter 4 describes communication skills that are important in building and maintaining collaborative relationships with adults in the lives of students with special needs. Consultants will want to use rapport-building skills to build trust and confidence in the collaborative relationship, and to recognize and reduce their own language and communication barriers. Those who communicate with family members should use these guidelines:

- Be aware of voice tone and body language.
- Be honest and specific.
- Give one's point of view as information, not the absolute truth.
- Be direct about what is wanted and expected.
- Do not monopolize the conversation.
- Listen at least as much as talk.
- Do not assume one's message is clear.
- Stay away from educational or psychological jargon.
- Attack the problem, not the person.
- Focus on positive or informational aspects of the problem.
- Have five positive contacts for every negative one.
- Always be honest; do not soft-pedal reality.

Providing Social Support

Families rely on informal and formal social support networks for information and guidance they need to carry out responsibilities for child rearing, children's learning, and child development. Schools can provide a rich array of child, parent, and family support in the form of information and environmental experiences to strengthen family and child competence and influence student outcomes. Parenting supports include information and advice that can strengthen existing parenting knowledge and skills and facilitate acquisition of new competencies (Dunst, 2000).

For families of children with disabilities, supports are a crucial aspect of family-focused collaboration. Workshops, newsletters, informational meetings, provision of emotional support, and multigenerational gatherings are examples of formal supports needed by families. Schools are instrumental also in promoting informal support systems for families. According to extensive research by Dunst (2000) and his colleagues, informal support demonstrates a stronger relationship to many child, parent, and family outcomes than does formal support. Thus, consultants should encourage activities that help families develop informal support networks such as parent-to-parent groups and informal multiple-family gatherings.

Promoting Positive Roles for Family Members

Family members play a range of roles from purveyor of knowledge about the child to advocates for political action. No matter what role is taken by individual family members, educational consultants should remember that families are:

- Partners in setting goals and finding solutions;
- The best advocates and case managers for the child with special needs;
- Individuals with initiative, strengths, and important experiences; and
- The best information resource about the child, the family, and their culture.

Within any role along the wide continuum of family members, the consultant must respect and support the courage and commitment of family members to struggle with the challenges of daily living faced by all families. Recognizing, supporting, and reinforcing interventions on behalf of the child with special needs will promote an increased sense of competency and help create a safe, nurturing environment for children, while maintaining the unique cultural and ethnic characteristics of their family unit (Berg, 1994; Waters & Lawrence, 1993).

Supporting and reinforcing families in their chosen roles is not always easy. Members in multiproblem families often are viewed as having defective or faulty notions of parenting, no problem-solving skills, and an array of psychopathology (Berg, 1994). Even for families having different values and expectations, and risk factors such as poverty or drug/alcohol involvement, Waters and Lawrence (1993) recommend that professionals focus on strengths. Figure 3.1 lists other suggestions for developing bridges to overcome potential or real barriers in collaboration.

Family Partners in IEP and IFSP Planning

The Individual Education Plan (IEP), Individual Family Service Plan (IFSP), or Individual Transition Planning (ITP) conference can be a productive time or a frustrating experience. Parents may be emotional about their child's problems, and teachers apprehensive about meeting with the parents (Reynolds & Birch, 1988). A number of researchers have found that too little parent involvement in team decision making, particularly relating to IEP, IFSP, and ITP development, is a major problem in special education programs (Boone, 1989; Pfeiffer, 1980).

School consultants will improve school–home collaboration in these areas if they provide family members with information and preparation for the meeting. Consultants can communicate with family members by phone, letter, or informal interview to inform them about names and roles of staff members who will attend, the typical procedure for meetings, ways they can prepare for the meeting, contributions they will be encouraged to make, and ways in which follow-up to the meeting will be provided.

FIGURE 3.1   Suggestions for Building Bridges to Successful Home–School Collaboration

- Keep in mind that the family usually has concerns and issues that have nothing to do with you personally and that you may not know about.
- Be sensitive to the language levels, vocabularies, and background of the family and adjust your language, but be yourself.
- Get enough information, but not more than you need. You don't want to appear "nosy."
- Focus discussions on factors you can control.
- Find out what has been tried before.
- Listen so that you are completely clear about the family's concerns.
- Honor confidentiality.
- Remain open to new approaches and suggestions. Each family is different.
- Set concrete, measurable goals. Communication is clearer and measures of success are built in and promote collaboration.
- Wait until the family asks for help or until a good relationship is established before making suggestions.
- Help families solve their own problems and allow them to become, or develop the skills to become, their child's own case manager.

(Adapted from PEATC, 1991b)

Turnbull and Turnbull (1997, p. 233) list eight components that an IFSP/IEP conference should include:

- Preparing in advance
- Connecting and getting started
- Sharing visions and great expectations
- Reviewing formal evaluation and current levels of performance
- Sharing resources, priorities, and concerns
- Developing goals and objectives (or outcomes)
- Specifying placement and related services
- Summarizing and concluding

Figure 3.6 (Dettmer, 1994), presented on page 91, outlines specific ways parents can be involved in IEP, ITP, or IFSP development and implementation before, during, and after the IEP conference. These lists could be printed in the school handbook and shared again with participating families before conferences.

Osborne and deOnis (1997) suggest five actions for schools to take to involve families in the education of students:

- Actively welcome families in overt ways, such as posting friendly signs.
- Invite and support a range of involvement activities.
- Break down existing barriers, such as negative school recollections.
- Educate parents and the community about school policies and procedures.
- Keep parents informed with all the communication formats available.

When parents and teachers work together as equals, they have more opportunities to express their own knowledge and can come to respect each others' wisdom. Siblings need information about disabilities, opportunities to talk about their feelings, time to hear about the experiences of other siblings of children with disabilities, people with whom to share their feelings of pride and joy, and ways to plan for the future (Cramer, et al., 1997).

Kay and Fitzgerald (1997) suggest that parents and teachers collaborate on action research to systematically explore a problem or issue. They believe this partnership helps parents and teachers learn more about the others' perspectives and can lead to alliances that result in making improvements in programs and schools. Project DESTINY in Vermont used monthly parent support groups, enhancing teachers' attitudes and skills at working cooperatively with parents, and involving parents in weekly planning meetings at school to empower parents of students with emotional and behavioral disabilities (Cheney, Manning, & Upham, 1997). Timberland Elementary School in Fairfax County, Virginia, used multilingual parent liaisons to build a bridge between the school and neighboring families in need (Halford, 1996). The parent liaison begins with home visits with the goal of helping families address their problems and foster an environment that is supportive of their children's learning. The Best Practice Project in Chicago (Daniels, 1996) generated genuine teacher–parent partnerships that supported learning for children and leadership development for parents and teachers. Whether collaborative efforts are ongoing communication or complex family involvement programs, underlying all types of involvement are the efforts of trusting and respecting educators.

DEVELOPING HOME–SCHOOL PARTNERSHIPS

There is great variation in individual practices for home–school collaboration. Effective collaboration efforts depend on attitudes of teachers, their beliefs about the family role and the efficacy of family involvement, and their comfort level and communication skills. Educators may believe in family partnerships, but they may not know how to involve family members in a systematic and egalitarian manner.

Family involvement is usually conceptualized from family member perspectives (Wanat, 1997). In her study with 57 parents, Wanat found that parents did not distinguish between involvement at school and at home and they had specific ideas about what constituted meaningful involvement. One parent in her study summarized legitimate parent involvement as "everything you do with the child because education involves a lot more than just sitting at school." It would be well for education consultants to remember this statement when they work collaboratively with parents.

Citing the growing body of empirical and theoretical literature on the importance of school and family relationships, Conoley (1989) notes that educators wanting to collaborate with families must determine whether the family has an intact decision-making system. If it does not, a successful outcome is doubtful. Single-parent families place stress on the decision-making system, and for collaborative efforts to produce results, the interactions must fit the single parent's time and energy level. Also, families stressed by poverty or substance abuse will be less available to consult and collaborate with school personnel.

The crucial issues in successful learning are not between home *or* school, and parent *or* teacher, but the relationship between each pair of variables (Seeley, 1985). When school personnel collaborate with family members, they nurture and maintain partnerships that facilitate shared efforts to promote student achievement. The more that family members become partners with teachers and related services personnel, the smoother and more consistent the delivery of instruction to the student can be (Reynolds & Birch, 1988). As families and teachers plan together and implement plans of action, they find that working as a team is more effective than working alone (Shea & Bauer, 1985). Each can be more assured that the other is doing the best for the child (Stewart, 1978).

■ ■ ■ ■ ■ ▬▬▬▬▬▬▬▬▬▬▬▬▬▬▬▬▬▬▬▬▬▬▬▬▬▬▬

APPLICATION 3.1
READING CENTER FOR FAMILIES

Visit a school library, or revisit your own school library, and find a corner that could be outfitted as "Parent/Family Reading Center." (Try to find a quiet, pleasant place but not *too* out-of-the-way.) Display an attractive painting, a plant, perhaps a snapshot display of recent school events, along with a small table, comfortable chairs, and, of course, books and periodicals. These should be focused on interests and needs of families, parents, day-care providers, grandparents, and home–school projects. Promote the center at parent–teacher meetings and parent conferences. Perhaps meet with a group of parents there on a nonconfidential matter (planning the yearly social event, initiating a coupon drive for playground equipment, and so forth). Work into the plan the school personnel who would be responsible for upkeep, checkout and returns, and materials acquisition. Some of this might even be accomplished by students.

Five Steps for Collaborating with Families

Five basic steps will assist school personnel in developing successful home–school partnerships:

Step 1: Examining one's own values
Step 2: Building collaborative relationships
Step 3: Initiating home–school interactions
Step 4: Individualizing for parents
Step 5: Evaluating home–school collaboration

Step 1: Examining One's Own Values

Value systems are individualistic and complex. They are the result of nature and the impact of experiences on nature. People need to apply information and logic to situations that present values different from their own. Kroth (1985) provides an example. He notes that a significant amount of research indicates a positive effect on children's academic and social growth when teachers use a daily or weekly report card system to communicate with parents or guardians. This information provides logical support for interaction among teachers and family members on a regular, planned basis.

School personnel must guard against setting up a climate of unequal relationships. It is vital to recognize that parents are the experts when it comes to knowing about their children, no matter how many tests educators have administered to students, or how many hours they have observed them in the classroom. If professional educators are perceived as *the* experts, and the *only* experts, false expectations may create unrealistic pressure on them. Some family members find it difficult to relate to experts. So a beautiful "boulevard of progress" becomes a one-way street of judging, advising, and sending solutions.

The first step in collaborating with families is to examine one's own values. Figure 3.2 is a checklist for examining one's values and attitudes toward parents and other family members.

Communicating messages of equality, flexibility, and a sharing attitude will facilitate effective home–school collaboration. The message that should be given to parents of students with special needs is, "I know a lot about this, and *you* know a lot about that. Let's put our information and ideas together to help the child."

The checklist in Figure 3.3 serves as a brief self-assessment to test the congruency of attitudes and perceptions with the two-way family collaboration discussed earlier. Inventorying and adjusting one's own attitudes and perceptions about families are the hardest parts of consulting with them. Attitudes and perceptions about families and their roles in partnerships greatly influence implementation of the consulting process.

School personnel also must keep in mind that family members are not a homogeneous group; therefore, experiences with one family member cannot be generalized to all other parents and families. There is evidence that mothers and fathers react differently to their exceptional children (Levy-Shiff, 1986). Furthermore, parental stress seems to be related to the child's developmental age and parental coping strengths (Wikler, Wasow, & Hatfield, 1981).

Step 2: Building Collaborative Relationships

The second step in collaborating with families is building collaborative relationships. As will be emphasized in Chapter 4, basic communication and rapport-building skills are essential

FIGURE 3.2   Examining Own Values

Instructions: Rate belief or comfort level, from 1 (very comfortable or very strong) to 5 (very uncomfortable or not strong at all).

How comfortable do you feel with each?

5 parents or others who are overly protective
4 teachers who think they are never wrong
3 families who send their children to school without breakfast
2 teachers who get emotional at conferences
1 teachers who do not want mainstreamed students
1 open discussions at family meetings
2 parents who have lost control of their children
1 volunteers in the classroom
5 conflict
3 being invited to students' homes
3 using grades as a behavior management tool
3 family members who call every day
4 teachers who do not follow through
1 students attending conferences
1 principals attending conferences
1 parents who do not allow their children to be tested
1 different racial or ethnic groups
1 family members who do not speak English
3 others who think special needs children should be kept in self-contained classrooms
5 teachers who think modifying curriculum materials or tests is watering down the lessons
4 family members who drink excessively or use drugs
1 administrators who do not know your name
5 criticism

How strongly do you believe the following?

1 Family members should be able to call you at home.
1 Newsletters are an important communication tool.
1 Family members should volunteer in the classroom.
3 General classroom teachers can teach students with special needs.
1 All children can learn.
1 Family members should come to conferences.
4 Resistance is normal and to be expected in educational settings.
5 Children in divorced families have special problems.
3 Family resistance is often justified.
3 Teacher resistance is often justified.
3 Family influence is more important than school influence.
1 Medical treatment should never be withheld from children.
5 Children with severe disabilities are part of a supreme being's plan.
5 Sometimes consultants should just tell others the best thing to do.
1 Consultants are advocates for children.
1 Teachers should modify their classrooms for children with special needs.
5 It is a teacher's fault when children fail.
5 Consultants are experts in educating special needs children.
5 Some people do not want children with special needs to succeed.

Do you think all teachers, administrators, counselors, psychologists, parents, grandparents, social workers, and students would have responded as you did? What happens when members of the same educator team have different views?

FIGURE 3.3   Self-Assessment of Attitudes and Perceptions Concerning Families and Family Collaboration

Rate yourself on the following, from 1 being "very little" to 5 being "always."

1. I understand the importance of parent involvement.   1 2 3 4 (5)
2. I recognize the concerns parents may have about working with me.   1 2 3 (4) 5
3. I recognize that parents of students with special needs may have   1 2 3 4 (5)
   emotional and social needs I may not understand.
4. I recognize and respect the expertise of families.   1 2 3 4 (5)
5. I feel comfortable working with families whose values and attitudes   1 2 3 4 (5)
   differ from mine.
6. I am persistent and patient as I develop relationships with families. 1 2 3 4 (5)
7. I am comfortable with my skills for communicating with families.   1 2 3 4 (5)
8. I am realistic about the barriers for me in working with families.   1 2 3 4 (5)
9. I find it difficult to understand why some families have the attitudes 1 (2) 3 4 5
   they have.
10. I recognize that some family members will have problems interact-   1 2 3 4 (5)
    ing with me because of their experience with other teachers.

for establishing healthy, successful relationships with family members. To briefly preview, these are the most important skills for educators in interacting with families:

- responsive listening
- assertive responding
- mutual problem solving

Prudent teachers avoid words and phrases that may give undesirable impressions of the children or the special needs with which they are concerned (Shea & Bauer, 1985). They listen for the messages given by parents and respond to their verbal and nonverbal cues.

In communicating with families, school personnel must avoid jargon that can be misunderstood or misinterpreted. Parents often feel alienated by professional educators and one common cause is words (*program, site*) and acronyms (IFSP, ITBS,) that pepper the conversation without explanation of their meaning (Soodak & Erwin, 1995). Some professional educators seem unable, or unwilling, to use jargon-free language when they communicate with lay people (Schuck, 1979). Choices of words can ease, or inhibit, communication with parents, and professional educators must respect language variations created by differences in culture, education, occupation, age, and place of origin (Morsink, Thomas, & Correa, 1991).

Teachers and administrators often find that one of the most important, but difficult, aspects of developing relationships with parents is listening to them. The challenge lies in listening to parents' messages even though they might disagree strongly with family members, and their attitudes and values might differ significantly from those of the families. Although the quality of the interaction should be a primary focus in parent relationships, the numbers and variety of initiated communications are important as well. Hughes and Ruhl (1987) found that most teachers averaged fewer than five parent contacts per week, but 27 percent averaged from 11–20 parent contacts per week. Phone calls, introductory and welcoming

FIGURE 3.4   Ascertaining Family Interests

Families! We want to learn more about you so that we can work together helping your child learn. Please take a few minutes to respond to these questions so your voice can be heard. It will help the Home–School Advisory Team develop programs for families, teachers, and children.

Check those items you are most interested in.

____ 1. Family resource libraries or information centers
____ 2. Helping my child learn
____ 3. Support programs for my child's siblings
____ 4. Talking with my child about sex
____ 5. Helping with language and social skills
____ 6. Mental health services
____ 7. Talking with another parent about common problems
____ 8. Respite care or babysitters
____ 9. My role as a parent
____ 10. Classes about managing behavior problems
____ 11. Making my child happy
____ 12. Managing my time and resources
____ 13. Making toys and educational materials
____ 14. Reducing time spent watching television
____ 15. What happens when my child grows up
____ 16. Recreation and camps for my child
____ 17. State-wide meetings for families
____ 18. Vocational opportunities for my child
____ 19. Talking to my child's teacher
____ 20. Talking with other families
____ 21. Learning about child development
____ 22. Things families can do to support teachers
____ 23. Home activities that support school learning
____ 24. Information about the school and my child's classes
____ 25. Helping my child become more independent
____ 26. Others?

_____

_____

_____

Thanks for your help!

Name of family member responding to this form:

_____

Child's name: _____

letters, newsletters, parent-to-parent calendars, and note pads with identifying logos all have been used effectively by educators to initiate partnerships. Each note, phone call, conversation, or conference, whether taking place in a formal setting or on the spur of the moment at the grocery store, should reflect the willingness and commitment of school personnel to work with parents as they face immense responsibilities in providing for the special needs of their child.

An effective partner–educator provides support and reinforcement for family members in their family roles. In addition to listening to family members and recognizing their expertise, it is crucial to support parents by giving them positive feedback about their efforts toward the child's education. Many parents spend more time with their children who have disabilities than with those who do not (Cantwell, Baker, & Rutter, 1979). Families often get very little reinforcement for parenting, particularly for the extra efforts they may expend in caring for children with special needs. They should be encouraged and commended for providing three types of parental engagement at home that are consistently associated with student performance at school:

- organizing and monitoring the student's time;
- helping with homework; and
- discussing school matters with their child (Finn, 1998).

Too many families hear very few positive comments about their children. They may feel guilty or confused because of their children's problems. Examples of support and reinforcement that teachers use include thank-you notes for helping with field trips, VIP (Very Important Parent) buttons given to classroom volunteers, supporting phone calls when homework has been turned in, and happygrams when a class project is completed. It is important for teachers to arrange and encourage more regular, informal contacts with parents. Family members often report being put off by the formality inherent in some scheduled conferences, particularly when they are limited to ten minutes, as they often are, with another child's family waiting just outside (Lindle, 1989).

Ask parents for preferred modes of communication. Phone calls are appropriate for positive reports, but should not be used to discuss weighty concerns. Notes sent home can promote consistency in expectations and help teachers and family members develop a common language (Bos, Nahmias, & Urban, 1999). Some consultants have found e-mail and school Web site access an effective way to communicate with families. However, many families do not have access to this technology.

One innovative program is the Trans*Parent* Model (Bauch, 1989) in which teachers use a computer-based system called Compu-Call that stores messages in a computer. It directs the autodialer to place calls either to all families or to specific groups. The purpose of these calls can be to describe learning activities, explain homework assignments, or suggest ways that families can support the child's home study. Parents call any time from anywhere and get the information they need. The system helps families help their children who are having problems or on extended absence from school keep up with the schoolwork.

Family members often become frustrated when they do not understand the subjects their children are attempting to master. A program of Family Math encourages parents and children to work together as a team in evening sessions involving a "hands-on" approach to learning math concepts and logical thinking (Lueder, 1989). Family literacy programs that are established in some communities enable parents to help children with their schoolwork

(Nuckolls, 1991). Some schools have set up an evening computer literacy program in which families can learn together and reinforce each other as they gain skills in educational technology. Parents are not the only ones who put energy and time into such programs. The programs require a level of school personnel involvement that challenges the staff, but the positive ripple effect of having family members play more active roles in their child's education makes the effort worthwhile.

Step 3: Initiating Home–School Interactions

Parents want their children to be successful in school. Even parents who are considered "hard to reach," such as nontraditional, low-income, and low-status families, usually want to be more involved (Davies, 1988). Most, however, wait to be invited before becoming involved as a partner in their child's education. Unfortunately, many have to wait for years before someone opens the door and provides them the *opportunity* to become a team member with others who care about the educational and social successes of their children. Parent satisfaction with their involvement is directly related to perceived opportunities for involvement (Salisbury & Evans, 1988). They are more motivated to carry on when they are aware that the results of their time and energy are helping their child learn. School personnel who are in a position to observe these results can provide the kind of reinforcement that parents need so much.

When parents are welcome in schools and classrooms, and their child's work and experiences are meaningful to them, parents often experience new aspirations for themselves and for their children (St. John, et al., 1997).

Step 4: Individualizing for Families

Special education professionals are trained to be competent at individualizing educational programs for students' needs. Nevertheless, they may assume that all parents have the same strengths and needs, thereby overlooking the need to individualize parent-involvement programs (Schultz, 1987). By using the assessments discussed earlier, and taking care to avoid stereotypes and judgments, they will be more successful in involving parents as partners in their child's learning program.

Christensen and Cleary (1990) confirm that successful home–school consultation includes mutual problem identification, mutual monitoring of effects of involvement, and active sharing of relevant information. Successful work with parents calls for establishing respectful and trusting relationships, as well as responding to the needs of all partners. The degree to which parents are placed in an egalitarian role, with a sense of choice, empowerment, and ownership in the education process, is a crucial variable in successful collaboration (Cochran, 1987; Peterson & Cooper, 1989).

Step 5: Evaluating Home–School Collaboration

Evaluation of efforts to provide opportunities for collaboration in schools can indicate whether or not families' needs are being met and their strengths are being utilized. Evaluation also shows whether needs and strengths of educational personnel are being met. Assessment tools used after a workshop, conference, or at the conclusion of the school year allow school personnel to ask parents, "How did we do in facilitating your learning of the new information or accessing the new services?" Some teachers use a quick questionnaire, to be completed anonymously, to see if the activity or program fulfilled the goals of the home–school collaboration. If data show that the activity gave families the information they needed, provided them with the resources they wanted, and offered them the opportunities they requested, educators know whether or not to continue with the program or modify it.

Educators also should evaluate their own involvement with families. This means assessing the use of family strengths and skills to facilitate educational programs with children who have special needs. Did teachers get the information they needed from families? How many volunteer hours did parents contribute? What were the results of home tutoring on the achievement of the resource room students? What changes in family attitudes about the school district were measured? Chapter 6 contains information about procedures for evaluating collaboration efforts. Note again that the purpose of family collaboration is to utilize the unique and vital partnership on behalf of their children.

■ ■ ■ ■ ■ ▬▬▬▬▬▬▬▬▬▬▬▬▬▬▬▬▬▬▬▬▬▬▬▬▬▬▬▬▬▬▬▬▬▬▬▬

APPLICATION 3.2

Meet in groups of four or five teachers. Discuss the situation below and then make a list of things you would *not* want to have happen during the ensuing conference:

The parent of a fifth-grade girl is having difficulty with her schoolwork, especially math and spelling. The parent has tried hard to help, but both parent and child become frustrated when working on the homework. The parent feels she needs more attention at school to relieve the pressure of learning the material at home. The parent has requested a conference.

Next, regroup as parents. Make another list of what you as *parents* do not want to happen during parent conferences.

Then, compile both lists into overall "Do and Don't" help sheets. Perhaps they might be embellished with illustrations.

Find practical uses for these help sheets.

Equal Partnership Model

Teachers use interviews, checklists, and more complex assessment instruments to solicit information about parent needs. Parents have much to communicate to school personnel about their children, the child's needs within the family, and the "curriculum of the home" (Bevevino, 1988, p. 15). This can include parent–child conversation topics, how leisure reading is encouraged, deferral of immediate gratifications, long-term goals, how homework is assisted and assessed, what TV is watched and how it is monitored, how affection and interests in the child's accomplishments are demonstrated. Bevevino stresses that this curriculum, just like the one in school, varies in amount and quality, with both home and school curricula functioning as important multipliers of the other's effects.

If school personnel plan workshops, classes, and materials that are not based on family interests and needs, a message is communicated that educators know more about their needs than they do; then the family involvement is not a true partnership. An example of a needs and interests assessment is included in Figure 3.5.

The equal partnership model stresses the importance of providing opportunities for family members to use their strengths, commitment, and skills to contribute as full partners to the education of their children. This relationship is not based on a deficit model of blame and inequality. Families appreciate having their special efforts recognized, just as teachers do. Multiyear research by St. John and colleagues (1997) showed mixed results when parents were not treated as full partners in the education of their children.

Tools for assessing parent strengths are similar to those for assessing needs. Interviews and checklists are useful in determining what types of contributions families can bring

FIGURE 3.5   Family Member Participation Checklist

Families! We need your help. Many of you have asked how you can help provide a high-quality educational program for your children. You have many talents, interests, and skills you can contribute to help children learn better and enjoy school more. Please let us know what you are interested in doing.

_____ 1. I would like to volunteer in school.
_____ 2. I would like to help with special events or projects.
_____ 3. I have a hobby or talent I could share with the class.
_____ 4. I would be glad to talk about travel or jobs, or interesting experiences that I have had.
_____ 5. I could teach the class how to _____.
_____ 6. I could help with bulletin boards and art projects.
_____ 7. I could read to children.
_____ 8. I would like to help my child at home.
_____ 9. I would like to tutor a child.
_____ 10. I would like to work on a buddy or parent-to-parent system with other parents whose children have problems.
_____ 11. I would like to teach a workshop.
_____ 12. I can do typing, word-processing, phoning, making materials, or preparing resources at home.
_____ 13. I would like to assist with student clubs.
_____ 14. I would like to help organize a parent group.
_____ 15. I want to help organize and plan parent partnership programs.
_____ 16. I would like to help with these kinds of activities:

At school _____

At home _____

In the community _____

Your comments, concerns, and questions are welcome. THANKS!

Name: _____

Child's Name: _____

How to Reach You: _____

to the partnership. These assets can be conceptualized along four levels of involvement (Kroth, 1985), from strengths which all family members have, to skills that only a few family members are willing and able to contribute. For example, all parents have information about their children that schools need. At more intensive levels of collaboration, some family members are willing and able to tutor their children at home, come to meetings, help make bulletin boards, and volunteer to help at school. At the highest level of collaboration, only a few parents can be expected to lobby for special education, serve on advisory boards, or conduct parent-to-parent programs. A number of parent advocates of children with learning and behavior disorders have made impressive gains in recent decades toward state and national focus on the rights of children with special needs. They have formed organizations, identified needs, encouraged legislation, spoken for improved facilities, and supported each other through crises. In many instances they have involved pediatricians, community agency leaders, and businesses in special projects for children with special needs.

By considering family member strengths as well as needs and interests, educators will be focusing on the collaborative nature of parent involvement. An example of an interest assessment form is provided in Figure 3.4 on page 86. As stated earlier, involvement is not synonymous with collaboration. Developing a workshop on discipline or a volunteer program without assessing strengths, needs, and goals demonstrates a failure to respect the partnership between school and home. True partnership features mutual collaboration and respect for the expertise of all parties.

FIGURE 3.6   Checklist for Families in Developing IEPs

Throughout the year:
> Read about educational issues and concerns.
> Learn about the structure of the local school system.
> Observe your child, noting work habits, play patterns, and social interactions.
> Record information regarding special interests, talents, and accomplishments, as well as areas of concern.

Before the conference:
> Visit the child's school.
> Discuss school life with the child.
> Talk with other families who have participated in conferences to find out what goes on during the conference.
> Write down questions and points you would like to address.
> Review notes from any previous conferences with school staff.
> Prepare a summary file of information, observations, and products that would further explain the child's needs.
> Arrange to take along any other persons that you feel would be helpful in planning the child's educational program.

During the conference:
> Be an active participant.
> Ask questions about anything that is unclear.
> Insist that educational jargon and "alphabet soup" acronyms be avoided.
> Contribute information, ideas, and recommendations.
> Let the school personnel know about the positive things school has provided.
> Ask for a copy of the IEP if it is not offered.
> Ask to have a follow-up contact time to compare notes about progress.

After the conference:
> Discuss the conference proceedings with the child.
> Continue to monitor the child's progress and follow up as agreed on.
> Reinforce school staff for positive effects of the planned program.
> Keep adding to the notebook of information.
> Be active in efforts to improve schools.
> Say supportive things about the schools whenever possible.

STUDENT PARTICIPATION IN CONFERENCES

The student has the greatest investment and most important involvement in deciding on and constructing an individual education plan for learning. Indeed, it is counterproductive to formulate goals and objectives without involving the student in the conference as a member of the planning team.

Shea and Bauer (1985) stress several benefits from having students participate in conferences for their individualized programs:

- Awareness that parents and teachers are interested in them and working cooperatively;
- Information from teachers and family members about their progress;
- Feeling of involvement in the efforts toward personal achievement;
- A task-oriented view of improving their performance.

Shea and Bauer recommend discussing advantages of the student's participation with family members and encouraging their support. If there are strenuous parental objections, the issue should be explored for reasons and possible impact on the student's success in school.

Turnbull and Turnbull (1997) offer a four-step I-PLAN to enhance student participation. The steps in the plan for which the students are trained are:

- *Inventory* to show perceived strengths, areas of improvement needed, and goals and choices for learning. This information is provided in an inventory sheet that the student takes to the conference.
- *Provide Your Inventory* Information includes learning how and when to provide the information during the conference.
- *Listen and Respond* includes development of effective listening and responding skills.
- *Name Your Goals* has the student name the goals agreed on before the conference ends.

Parent partnerships can be particularly difficult to cultivate at the secondary level. Much of the reluctance stems from attitudes of teen-age students who would just "die" of humiliation if their parents were seen at school. Other teens might counter a teacher's efforts to have family members involved with "Go ahead, but they won't care/come/participate," "They have to work," "They don't care," and so on. Parents pick up on these attitudes and acquiesce to them, and teachers are hard-pressed to find the time for changing these attitudes (McGrew-Zoubi, 1998).

In some middle-school settings, where traditional parent–teacher interactions and conferences have been perceived as more problematic than problem solving, an innovative student-centered model for conferencing has been developed and tried. In this model, a structure is developed, students are helped to prepare for their own conferences, this new format is communicated to parents and colleagues, and procedural operations are developed (Countryman & Schroeder, 1996). In the planning, development, and evaluation phases of this new approach, teachers found that students should have more participation in developing conference scripts, they needed a log to help them organize their products, and they must not overlook including such classes as art, family and consumer science, and modern languages or those subjects would not get discussed. One additional finding was students' expressed need to see how teachers evaluated them before it was revealed at the conference.

Hanna and Dettmer (2004) provide a ten-step plan for getting students ready to guide their parent–student–teacher conference. Student and teacher should discuss these steps and prepare for them, even rehearse them, in advance of the scheduled conference.

1. Determine the purpose(s) of the conference.

2. Formulate goals for the conference and prepare the invitation to family members. In the invitation, family members should be clued as to what to expect and ways to contribute.
3. Develop an agenda and determine location, seating plan, introductions format, and possible opening and closing remarks.
4. Select samples of work and pertinent information that focus on accomplishments, interests, and any major concerns. Consider responses in anticipation of questions or concerns that parents might bring up.
5. Rehearse a simulated conference.
6. At conference time, explore ideas for further learning and achievement.
7. Set reasonable goals.
8. Adhere to the time schedule, summarize, and close on a positive note.
9. Determine follow-up and follow-through procedures for attaining the planned goals.
10. Evaluate the event with rubrics designed specifically for the purpose.

A student-guided conference must not be hurried. A thirty-minute segment of time might be reasonable. Busy teachers, particularly those at the secondary level with dozens of students, will need strong administrator support and innovative scheduling ideas to make student-guided conferences effective. But for a courageous, energetic, and innovative school staff, student-guided parent conferences can promote meaningful ownership by students in their own learning. Students and other participants also can benefit from an assessment of the conference outcomes by using rubrics designed for the purpose (see Hanna & Dettmer, 2004) that has parallel forms for teacher/convenor and parent/family member. This triangulation of data adds richness and depth to the evaluation process concerning the conference experience.

MAINTAINING HOME–SCHOOL COLLABORATION AND PARTNERSHIPS

Home–school collaboration is mandated; it is challenging; it is rewarding. Students, schools, and families are strengthened with appropriate outreach efforts and partnership activities when they are based on the values and practices of the family-focused approach.

Family-centered interventions, support, and advocacy are suggested by several researchers who have looked at diverse families and students with disabilities. One recommended model is the family empowerment model in which schools recognize that the family is the child's first teacher, that learning is a life-long endeavor, and that all families want the best for their children and can have a positive, significant impact on their children's education.

In proposing guidelines for educator collaboration, Melaville and Blank (1991) have several useful suggestions for successful home–school collaboration:

- Involve all key players.
- Choose a realistic plan or strategy.
- Establish a shared vision.
- Agree to disagree on some issues and processes.
- Make promises you can keep.
- Keep your "eyes on the prize."
- Build ownership for all individuals and units.
- Avoid technical difficulties (language problems, getting hung up on paperwork or details).
- Share the success.

FIGURE 3.7 **"Keep parents informed"**

By Jane More Loeb

Educators have two choices in collaborating with families: to see school as a battleground with an emphasis on conflict between families and school personnel, or to see school as a "homeland" environment that invites power sharing and mutual respect, and with collaboration on activities that foster student learning and development (Epstein, 1995).

TIPS FOR HOME AND SCHOOL COLLABORATION

1. Establish rapport with families early in the year. Call right away, before problems develop, so that the first family contact is a positive one.
2. Invite families in to talk about their traditions, experiences, hobbies, or occupations.
3. Send home "up slips," putting them in a different format from the "down slips" that families sometimes receive, and have conferences with families because the student is performing *well* in the classroom.
4. When sharing information with families, "sandwich" any necessary comments about problems or deficits between two very positive ones.
5. During interaction with families, notice how your actions are received, and adapt to that.
6. When interacting with families, never assume anything.
7. When several staff members will be meeting with family members, make sure each one's role and purpose for being included in the meeting will be understood by the parents.
8. Introduce families to all support personnel working with the child.
9. Build interpersonal "bank accounts" with frequent deposits of good will to families. The "interest earned" will be better outcomes for students.
10. Send out monthly newsletters describing the kinds of things the class is doing, and school news or events coming up. Attach articles families would be interested in. Have a "Family Corner" occasionally, for which families provide comments or ideas.
11. Encourage volunteering in the classroom to read stories, help with art lessons, listen to book reports, or give a lesson on an area of expertise such as a job or hobby.
12. Invite families to help students find resource materials and reference books on research topics in the library.
13. Send follow-up notes after meetings. Put out a pamphlet about home–school collaboration in IEP planning conferences.
14. Provide classroom teachers with handouts that can be useful during conferences.
15. Have a Home Book notebook of pictures, activities, and stories about class that students take turns sharing at home.

16. Put a Family Board at the entrance of the building for posting ideas of interest to families, examples of class activities, and pictures.
17. Involve parents and siblings, babysitters, and grandparents to all class parties.
18. Write the right notes. Say thanks, confirm plans, ask for opinions, praise work, give good news, give advance notice of special events and classroom needs (see Figure 3.7).
19. Have families from other countries or culture groups talk to students about their customs and culture.
20. Ask families what their family goals are, and respond with how those goals are being met by the classroom curriculum.

CHAPTER REVIEW

1. The variable with the most significant effect on children's development is family involvement in the child's learning. Educational professionals are integral parts of children's lives, but families are the link of continuity for most of them. Parents and other family members and caregivers are the decision makers for their children, whose futures are largely dependent on the continued ability of their parents to advocate for them. Numerous mandates and passages of legislation have recognized this relationship and provided for involvement by families in the educational programs of students who have special learning and behavioral needs. Educators must be partners with families of students with special needs. This is a demanding and challenging responsibility; however, educators are committed to such a partnership because it fulfills a legal right of families.

2. Research confirms the benefits of the partnership for children, families, and schools. Involvements mean teacher involvement as well as family involvement. This becomes collaboration and mutually respectful, committed teamwork. The No Child Left Behind legislation, with its goals of closing achievement gaps for students who are disadvantaged and closely monitored accountability systems, will be closely watched by involved parents in the years to come.

3. Educational consultants have begun to focus successfully on family strengths by broadening the concept of parent involvement to parent partnership, by using appropriate communication skills, and by promoting positive roles for family members. These enhanced perceptions recognize family needs and promote family competence.

4. Educators and families encounter numerous barriers to home–school collaboration, including underutilization of services, lack of organizational cultural competency, and differing attitudes, history, values, culture, and language. Examining their own culture and values as potential barriers to understanding will enable them to address the diversity they experience during collaboration.

5. Educators must clarify their own values in order to respect the values of others. Checklists, structured value-clarification activities, or thoughtful consideration help educators identify their specific values about education, school, and home–school collaboration.

6. Using rapport-building skills and communication skills such as responsive listening, assertive responding, inclusive conferencing techniques, and mutual problem solving will convey respect for family members and willingness to collaborate with them. Patience and quiet, calm persistence are needed.

7. Educators should provide a variety of opportunities for families to become involved with the school. These opportunities should be based on family strengths, expertise, and needs. Family strengths represent contributions that they can make to the partnership. The needs of parents are those interests and needs they have concerning their families.

8. Home–school collaboration is not complete without including students as partners in their learning programs. They can be involved in setting their own learning goals, assessing their progress, and guiding their student conferences for family members.

TO DO AND THINK ABOUT

1. Brainstorm to identify family characteristics that would be encouraging to a consultant or teacher who has students with learning or behavior disorders. Then develop plans for interaction and involvement with families that would cultivate those characteristics.

2. Identify problems inherent in the three interactions below. Then suggest what could and should have been said differently by the teacher in scene A, by the parent in scene B, and by the consultant in scene C.

Scene A.

Parent: What's this about suspending my child from your class for three days? I thought you people were supposed to be teaching kids instead of letting them sit and waste time in the principal's office.

Teacher: You're being unreasonable. You don't understand our rules and neither does your child. Your child needs to learn some manners and plain, old-fashioned respect!

Scene B.

Teacher: I'm calling to tell you that your son caused a disturbance again in my class. I would like you to meet with me and his counselor.

Parent: He's always been an active kid. Can't you people learn to handle active, curious children without always dragging us parents into it?

Scene C.

Parent: How can I get Bobby to settle down and do his homework without a battle every night? It's driving us crazy.

Consultant: I'm glad you're concerned, but I think he will be okay if you just keep on him. Don't worry, he's a bright kid and he'll snap out of this phase soon. Just be glad your other three aren't dreamers like he is.

3. Plan a booklet that could be used by consultants to improve home–school communication and collaboration. Report on what will be included, how it can be used, and how it will be helpful.

FOR FURTHER READING

Berg, I. K. (1994). *Family-based services: A solution-focused approach.* New York: W. W. Norton.

Berger, E. H. (2000). *Parents as partners in education: Families and schools working together.* Upper Saddle River, NJ: Prentice-Hall.

Educational Leadership, 55(8). Topical issue, Engaging Parents and the Community in Schools, May 1998.

Elkind, D. (1994). *Ties that stress: The new family imbalance.* Cambridge: Harvard University Press.

Fine, M. (1990). Facilitating home–school relationships: A family-oriented approach to collaborative consultation. *Journal of Educational and Psychological Consultation, 1*(2), 169–187.

Gorman, J. C., & Balter, L. (1997). Culturally sensitive parent education: A critical review of quantitative research. *Review of Educational Research, 67*(3), 339–369.

Gruskin, S., Silverman, K., & Bright, V. (1997). *Including your child.* Washington, D.C.: Office of Educational Research and Improvement, U.S. Department of Education.

Harry, B., Kalyanpur, M., & Day, M. (1999). *Building cultural reciprocity with families: Case studies in special education.* Baltimore, MD: Brookes.

Hildebrand, V., Phenice, L. A., Gray, M. M., & Hines, R. P. (2000). *Knowing and serving diverse families.* Upper Saddle River, NJ: Merrill.

Ingoldsby, B. B., & Smith, S. (1995). *Families in multicultural perspective.* New York: Guilford.

Lueder, D. C. (1998). *Creating partnerships with parents: An educators' guide.* Lancaster, PA: Technomic.

Martin, R. (1991). *Extraordinary children—ordinary lives.* Champaign, IL: Research Press.

Sue, C. W., and Sue, D. (1990). *Counseling the culturally different: Theory and practice* (2nd ed.). New York: Wiley.

Turnbull, A. P., & Turnbull, H. R. (1998). *Families, professionals, and exceptionality* (3rd ed.). Upper Saddle River, NJ: Merrill/Prentice-Hall.

Wolf, J. S., & Stephens, T. M. (1989). *Parent/teacher conferences: Finding common ground. Educational Leadership, 47*(2), 28–31.

CHAPTER FOUR

COMMUNICATION PROCESSES FOR CONSULTATION, COLLABORATION, AND TEAMWORK

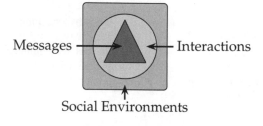

Communication is one of the greatest achievements of humankind. A vital component of human relationships in general, it is also the foundation of cooperation and collaboration among educators. Communication is not over when one delivers a message. Communication involves talking, listening, managing interpersonal conflict, and addressing concerns together. Components of successful communication are understanding, trust, autonomy, and flexibility. Effective communicators withhold judgment and minimize efforts to control the path of communication.

While problems and conflicts are unavoidable elements of life, good communication skills facilitate problem-solving and resolution of conflicts. Ineffective communication creates a void that breeds misunderstanding and distrust. Elements of trust, commitment, and effective interaction are critical for conflict-free relationships. Effective communication becomes a foundation for cooperation and collaboration among school personnel, parents, students, and others involved in education.

The graphics for this chapter's topic of communication feature *messages* as content (triangle), and *interactions* as processes (circle). *Social environments* are the context (square).

FOCUSING QUESTIONS

1. What is a primary reason people fail in collaborative efforts?
2. What are key components of the communication process?
3. How does one establish rapport in order to facilitate effective communication?
4. What are major verbal and nonverbal skills for communicating effectively?
5. What are the primary roadblocks to communication?
6. How can a school consultant be appropriately assertive and cope with resistance when the need arises?
7. What are effective methods of dealing with resistance, negativity, and anger?
8. What techniques and skills are useful for conflict management?

KEY TERMS

anger
assertiveness
body language
communication
conflict management

empathy, empathic
negativity
nonverbal communication
paraphrasing
rapport

resistance
Responsive Listening
   Checklist
roadblocks to communication
verbal communication

VIGNETTE 4

The setting is the hallway of a junior high school in midafternoon, where the general math instructor, a first-year teacher, is venting to a colleague.

Math Teacher: What a day! On top of the fire drill this morning and those forms that we got in our boxes to be filled out by Friday, I had a disastrous encounter with a parent.

Colleague: Oh, one of those, huh?

Math Teacher: Jay's mother walked into my room right before fourth-hour, and accused me of not doing my job. It was awful!

Colleague: (frowns, shakes head)

Math Teacher: Thank goodness there weren't any kids around. But the music teacher was there telling me about next week's program. This parent really let me have it. I was stunned, not only by the accusation, but by the way she delivered it. My whole body went on "red alert." My heart was pounding, and that chili dog I had for lunch got caught in my digestive system. Then my palms got sweaty. I could hardly squeak out a sound because my mouth was so dry. I wanted to yell back at her, but I couldn't!

Colleague: Probably just as well. Quick emotional reactions don't seem to work very well in those situations. I found out the hard way that it doesn't help to respond at all during that first barrage of words. Sounds like you did the right thing.

> **Math Teacher:**   Well, it really was hard. So you've had things like this happen to you?
>
> **Colleague:**   Um-humm. I see we don't have time for me to tell you about it, because here come our troops for their next hour of knowledge. But I can tell you all about it later if you want. Come to my room after school and we'll compare notes—maybe even plan some strategies for the future just in case. And, by the way, welcome to the club!

COMMUNICATION FOR EFFECTIVE SCHOOL RELATIONSHIPS

People typically communicate in one form or another for about 70 percent of their waking moments. They spend about 10 percent of that time writing, 20 to 40 percent speaking, and 45 to 65 percent listening (Bolton, 1986). Unfortunately, lack of effective communication skills is a major reason for work-related failure.

Teachers manage many kinds of relationships in their work with children with special needs. Some relationships grow throughout the year or over several years, others are established and stable, while still others are new, tentative, and tenuous. No matter what the type of relationship, and no matter whether it is with families, colleagues, paraeducators, or other human service providers, communication is the key to successful relationships.

A supportive, communicative relationship among special education teachers, general classroom teachers, and parents is critical to the success of mainstreamed children with special learning needs. Trends in education emphasize the necessity for greatly strengthened communication among all who are involved with the student's educational program. Special educators who are to serve as consultants and team members for helping students with special needs succeed, must model and promote exemplary communication and interaction skills.

Consulting is not a one-person exercise. A consultant will pay a high price for a "Rambo" style of interaction ("My idea can beat up your idea," or "I'm right and that's just the way it is"). Communication that minimizes conflict and enables teachers to maintain self-esteem may be the most important and most "delicate" process in consulting (Gersten et al., 1991.) Unfortunately, development of communication skills is not typically included in the formal preparation of educators. Because the development and use of "people skills" is the most difficult aspect of collaboration for many educators, more and more educators are stressing the need for specific training in consulting and communication skills to serve special needs students.

Challenges of Communication

Communication requires three elements:

- A message;
- A sender of the message, and
- A receiver of the message.

Semantics play a fundamental role in both sending and receiving messages. A person who says, "Oh, it's no big deal—just an issue of semantics" is missing a major point. The semantics frequently *are* the issue and should never be taken for granted. The vital role of semantics in consultation, collaboration, and teamwork was introduced in Chapter 2 and will be important in this chapter, with its focus on communication skills.

Body language also plays a key role in communication. Studies of kinesics, or communication through body language, show that the impact of a message is about 7 percent verbal, 38 percent vocal, and 55 percent facial. The eyebrows are particularly meaningful in conveying messages.

Placing, or removing, a chair barrier would be another aspect of communication. We communicate nonverbally much of the time and in many more ways than we tend to realize. Nonverbal modes of communication include use of space, movements, posture, eye contact, attendance to time, positions of feet and legs when sitting, use of furniture, facial expressions, gestures, mannerisms, volume of voice, rate of voice, and level of energy (Gazda, Asbury, Balzer, Childers, Phelps, & Walters, 1999).

In order to communicate effectively, the message sender must convey the purpose of the message in a facilitative style with clarity to the receiver. As the noted theologian John Powell put it, "I can't tell you what you *said,* but only what I *heard.*" Miscommunication breeds misunderstanding. A gap in meaning between what the message sender gives and what the message receiver gets can be described as distortion at best, or as communication trash in extreme cases. A person may send the message, "You look nice today," and have it understood by the receiver as, "Gee, then I usually don't look very good." A classroom teacher wanting to reinforce efforts of the learning disabilities teacher might say "Gerry seems to get much better grades on tests in the resource room," but the resource teacher may hear, "You're helping too much and Gerry can't cope outside your protection." (See Figure 4.1, which graphically illustrates a potential range of distorted communication.)

Vague semantics, distorted messages, and psychological filters disrupt the message as it passes (or doesn't pass) between the sender and the receiver. Examples of filters are differing values, ambiguous language, stereotypes and assumptions, levels of self-esteem, and personal experiences. Static from preconceived ideas works constantly to prevent people from hearing what others are saying and provide only what people want to hear (Buscaglia, 1986). This can be demonstrated with the well-known game of "Gossip." Players stand in a long line or a circle, while one of them silently reads or quietly receives a message. Then that person whispers the message to the next one, and that message continues to be delivered to each one in turn. After passing through the filters of many people and stated aloud by the very last one, the message in most cases

FIGURE 4.1 Miscommunication

By Jane More Loeb

is drastically different from the original message. The game results are usually humorous. Real-life results are not always so funny.

■ ■ ■ ■ ■ ▬▬▬▬▬▬▬▬▬▬▬▬▬▬▬▬▬▬▬▬▬▬▬▬▬▬▬▬▬▬▬▬▬▬▬▬▬

APPLICATION 4.1
SENDING, RECEIVING, AND SHARING MESSAGES

In groups of three, with one person designated as Interviewer, another as Interviewee, and the third one Responder, conduct three-minute interviews to learn more about each other. After each interview change roles, so that each has a turn to serve in all three capacities. Each Responder may make brief notes to use during a one-minute Share Time to introduce his or her Interviewee to the whole group. Use questions of this nature, or others given by the convener: What are your special talents? Apprehensions? Pet peeves? Successes you have had? Long-range goals? Things you want to learn more about?

Ethnic and Gender Differences in Communication

Language is the window through which the reality of others' experiences is revealed. Gender and ethnicity are other factors that may cloud that window and lead to systematic misjudgments in interpreting communication. Misunderstanding may not be due simply to miscommunication. Other factors such as the sex or cultural background of the sender or the receiver may be responsible. Examples of gender differences in conversational style affecting both sender and receiver of the message are discussed by sociolinguist Deborah Tannen (1994; 1991). Her research describes differences in communication styles between females (both girls and women) and males (both boys and men):

- Amount of time listening versus talking
- Interrupting
- Physical alignment during conversation
- Use of indirectness and silence
- Topical cohesion

For example, men's and boys' conversations tend to be diffuse, while those of women and girls are more tightly focused with minimal topics. Educational consultants should be aware that such types of communication style differences may lead them to be misunderstood or cause them to misunderstand their consultees.

The caveat for gender also applies to cross-cultural interactions. Most consultants are aware that different languages or different dialects may have different words for the same object. Some languages have no direct translations for terms we use in education and so must be translated indirectly.

Conversational style is a major component of ethnicity (Tannen, 1994). Different cultures use silence, interruption, proximity, eye contact, facial expression, and intonation to communicate ideas and feelings that consultants may not perceive. For example, in the Midwest it may be considered rude to interrupt; however, overlap or simultaneous group talk is the norm in some ethnic cultures or regional areas of the United States. The Athabaskans in

Alaska value silence highly and devalue what they perceive as excessive talk (Scollon, 1985). Unwary educational consultants in such cases could lose much esteem for engaging in consultations in the same manner as they might do elsewhere. As discussed specifically in Chapter 3 and elsewhere throughout the book, consultants will continue to be challenged by the cultural diversity of collaborators. Increasing diversity among colleagues, families, and communities requires that educational consultants recognize and continuously consider the impact of culture on communication in their work.

SKILLS FOR COMMUNICATING

In order to be effective communicators, senders and receivers of messages need skills that include rapport-building, responsive listening, assertiveness, tools for dealing with resistance, and conflict-management techniques. With well-developed communication skills, consultants and consultees will be able to engage more effectively in collaborative problem-solving.

Five major sets of skills are integral to successful communication:

- Rapport-building skills
- Responsive listening
- Assertion skills
- Conflict management skills
- Collaborative problem-solving skills

Rapport-building is the first step in establishing a collaborative relationship. Responsive listening skills enable a person to understand what another is saying and to convey that the problems and feelings have been understood. When listening methods are used appropriately by a consultant, the consultee plays an active role in problem solving without becoming dependent on the consultant.

Assertion skills include verbal and nonverbal behaviors that enable collaborators to maintain respect, satisfy their professional needs, and defend their rights without dominating, manipulating, or controlling others. Conflict management skills help individuals deal with the emotional turbulence that typically accompanies conflict. Conflict management skills also have a multiplier effect of fostering closer relationships when a conflict is resolved. Collaborative problem-solving skills help resolve the conflicting needs so that all parties are satisfied. Problems then "stay solved," and relationships are developed and preserved. Problem solving is discussed in Chapter 5.

Rapport-Building to Enhance Communication

Collaboration with other professionals that is in the best interest of students with special needs often means simply sitting down and making some joint decisions. At other times, however, it must be preceded by considerable rapport building. Successful consultation necessitates good rapport between the participants in the consulting relationship. Johnson and Johnson (1987) contend that it is more difficult to reject ideas offered by persons who are liked and respected than by those who are disliked. It is important to keep in mind that both the consultant and the consultee should provide ideas toward solving the problem. Respect must be a two-way condition for generating and accepting ideas. Rapport building is vital for building an appropriate consultation climate.

When we take time to build positive relationships with others that are based on mutual respect and trust, others are more likely to:

- Want to work with us
- Care about our reactions to them
- Try to meet our expectations
- Accept our feedback and coaching
- Imitate our behavior

We are more likely to:

- Listen to and try to understand their unique situations
- Accept them as they are and not judge them for what they are not
- Respond appropriately to their concerns and criticisms
- Advocate for, and support and encourage them in their efforts on behalf of, students with special needs

What behaviors are central to the process of building a trusting, supportive relationship? When asked this question, many teachers mention trust, respect, feeling that it is okay not to have all the answers, feeling free to ask questions, and feeling all right about disagreeing with the other person. People want to feel that the other person is *really* listening. Trust is developed when one addresses the concerns of others and looks for opportunities to demonstrate responsiveness to others' needs.

Respecting differences in others is an important aspect of building and maintaining rapport. Although teachers and other school personnel are generally adept at recognizing and respecting individual differences in children, they may find this more difficult to accomplish with adults. Accepting differences in adults may be particularly difficult when the adults have different values, skills, and attitudes. Effective consultants accept people as they really are rather than wishing they were different. Rapport building is not such a formidable process when the consultant respects individual differences and expects others either to have this respect or to develop it (Margolis & McGettigan, 1988).

Responsive Listening Skills

Plutarch said, "Know how to listen and you will profit even from those who talk badly." Shakespeare referred to the "disease" of *not* listening. Listening is the foundation of communication. A person listens to establish rapport with another person. People listen when others are upset or angry, or when they do not know what to say or fear speaking out will result in trouble. People listen so others will listen to them. Listening is a process of perpetual motion that focuses on the other person as speaker and responds to that other person's ideas, rather than concentrating on one's own thoughts and feelings. Thus, effective listening is *responsive listening* because it is responding, both verbally and nonverbally, to the words and actions of the speaker.

Listening responsively and empathically is associated with the development of trust and understanding (Margolis & Brannigan, 1986; Nichols & Stevens, 1957) and with effective consulting practices (Gutkin & Curtis, 1982). It improves relationships, promotes exploration of prospective solutions (Egan, 1982), minimizes resistance (Murphy, 1987), and fosters collaboration (Idol-Maestas, Lloyd, & Lilly, 1981). Although most people are convinced of the importance of listening in building collegial relationships and preventing and solving problems, few are as adept at this skill they would like or need to be. There are several reasons for this. First, most people have not been taught to listen effectively. They have been taught to talk—especially if they are teachers, administrators, or psychologists. Educators are good at talking and regard it as an essential part of their roles. But effective talkers must be careful not to let the lines of communication get tangled up in a tendency to talk too much or too often.

Listening helps keep the "locus of responsibility" with the one who owns the problem (Gordon, 1977). Therefore, if one's role as a consultant is to promote problem-solving without fostering dependence on the part of the consultee, listening will keep the focus of the problem-solving where it belongs. Listening is important in showing empathy and acceptance, two vital ingredients in a relationship that fosters growth and psychological health (Gordon, 1977).

Responsive, effective listening enables one to gather information essential to one's role in the education of children with special needs. It helps others feel better, often by reducing tension and anxiety, increasing feelings of personal well-being, and encouraging greater hope and optimism. This kind of listening encourages others to express themselves freely and fully. It enhances one's value to others, and often contributes significantly to positive change in others' self-understanding and problem-solving abilities.

Listening can prevent or minimize misunderstandings that occur in schools when educational roles are overloaded with responsibilities. It is very difficult for one person to understand the variety and complexity of another's problems. The receiver of a communication cannot know the sender's experiences or the nuances of the message. Listening helps one person "experience" the other's attitudes, background, and problems.

Listening is difficult also because it is hard to keep an open mind about the speaker. People may be hesitant to listen because they think listening implies agreeing. Openness certainly is important in effective communication. However, listening is much more than just hearing. Consultants must demonstrate tolerance toward differences and appreciation of richly diverse ideas and values while they are engaged in consulting relationships. A consultant's own values about child rearing, education, or the treatment of children with special needs become personal filters that make it difficult to really listen to those whose values are very different. For example, it may be hard to listen to a consultee parent who thinks it is appropriate for a very gifted daughter to drop out of school at the age of sixteen to help on the family farm because "She'll be getting married before too long and farm work will prepare her to be a wife better than schoolwork ever can." It takes discipline to listen to comments such as this when your mind is reacting negatively and wants to put together some very pointed arguments. A good rule of thumb to remember in such cases is that "when we add our two cents' worth in the middle of listening, that's just about what the communication is worth!" (Murphy, 1987).

Listening is very hard work. If the listener is tired or anxious or bursting with excitement and energy, it is particularly hard to listen carefully. Feelings of the listener also act as filters to impede listening. Other roadblocks to responsive listening are making assumptions about the message (mind-reading), thinking about our own response (rehearsing), and reacting defensively.

Improving listening skills can help establish collaborative relationships with colleagues, even those with whom it is a challenge to communicate. When consultants and consultees improve their listening skills, they have a head start on solving problems, side-stepping resistance, and preventing conflicts.

There are three major components of responsive listening:

- Nonverbal listening (discerning others' needs and observing their nonverbal gestures)
- Encouraging the sending of messages (encouraging others to express themselves fully)
- Showing understanding of the message (reviewing what they conveyed), or paraphrasing

Nonverbal Communication

The successful collaborative consultant models facilitative nonverbal communication, or body language, during interactions and attends carefully to the body language of others. Nonverbal communication can be organized into six categories: eye contact; gestures; paralanguage (volume, rate, pitch, and pronunciation of the verbal communication); posture; overall facial expression; and, a new category added to the traditional five already named, clothing and setting for the interaction (White, 2000).

Eyes and the brows above them are expressive instruments for conveying thoughts as well as feelings. Gestures send signals, and facial expressions disclose thoughts and feelings. When gestures and facial expressions do not match verbal content, mixed signals result. For example, teachers send mixed signals when they smile as they outline class rules and procedures, but display stern faces when introducing a learning activity. A consulting teacher might err similarly when interacting with parents or co-teachers. Voice tone, pitch, volume, and speed can affect the receiver of a message in positive or negative ways.

Slouching posture or turning away will imply lack of interest or rejection. Clothing worn by educators should be comfortable, of course, but also should be chosen to suit the environment. In Chapter 1 the importance of paying attention to one's physical appearance was noted. The consulting teacher, told by her colleagues at one school that she "dressed to supervise, not to work," learned to "dress down" for that setting, with sneakers and no jewelry. For her afternoon schedule in a school with a more dressy style, she changed to heeled shoes, a blazer, and a scarf or necklace. Not expecting to notice much difference, she was amazed to find more acceptance with her role at both schools.

Nonverbal Listening Skills.   Responsive listeners use appropriate body language to send out the message that they are listening effectively. Some body language cues reflect ethnic background (Schein, 1969). Nonverbal listening behavior of a good listener is described by Tony Hillerman in his 1990 best-seller *Coyote Waits:* "Jacobs was silent for awhile, thinking about it, her face full of sympathy. She was a talented listener. When you talked to this woman, she attended. She had all her antennae out. The world was shut out. Nothing mattered but the words she was hearing" (Hillerman, 1990, pp. 148–149).

Nonverbal listening may be less than effective for those people who do several things at once, such as watch a television show and write a letter, or talk to a colleague and grade papers, or prepare supper while listening to a child's synopsis of the day. This is because nonverbal components of listening should demonstrate to the speaker that the receiver is respecting the speaker enough to concentrate on the message and is following the speaker's thoughts to find the *real* message. Careful listening conveys attitudes of flexibility, empathy, and caring, even if the speaker is using words and expressions that cloud the message. A person who is attentive leans forward slightly, engages in a comfortable level of eye contact, nods, and gives low-key responses such as "oh," and "uh-huh," and "umm-humm." The responsive listener's facial expression matches the message. If that message is serious, the expression reflects seriousness. If the message is delivered with a smile, the listener shows empathy by smiling.

The hardest part of nonverbal listening is keeping it nonverbal. It helps the listener to think about a tennis game and remember that during the listening part of the "game," the ball is in the speaker's court. The speaker has the privilege of saying anything, no matter how silly or irrelevant. The listener just keeps sending the ball back by nodding, or saying "I see" or other basically nonverbal behaviors, until he or she "hears" the sender's message. This entails using nonverbal behaviors and "listening" to the nonverbal as well as the verbal message of the sender. The listener recognizes and minimizes personal filters, perceives and interprets the filters of the sender, and encourages continued communication until able to understand the message from the sender's perspective. Responsive listeners avoid anticipating what the speaker will say and *never* complete a speaker's sentence.

After listeners have listened until they really hear the message, understand the speaker's position, and recognize the feelings behind the message, it is their turn to speak. But they must be judicious about what they do say. Several well-known, humorous "recipes" apply to this need.

- Recipe for speaking—stand up, speak up, then shut up.
- Recipe for giving a good speech—add shortening.
- It takes six letters of the alphabet to spell the word *listen*. Rearrange the letters to spell another word that is a necessary part of responsive listening.[1]
- In the middle of listening, the *t* doesn't make a sound.

Verbal Listening Skills.   Although the first rule of the good listener is to keep one's mouth shut, there are several types of verbal responses that show that the listener is following the thoughts and feelings expressed by the speaker. Verbal responses are added to nonverbal listening responses to communicate that the listener understands what the other is saying from that speaker's specific point of view. Specific verbal aspects of listening also keep the speaker talking. There are several reasons for this that are specific to the consulting process:

- The consultant will be less inclined to assume ownership of the problem.
- Speakers will clarify their own thoughts as they keep talking.
- More information will become available to help understand the speaker's point of view.
- Speakers begin to solve their own problems as they talk them through.
- The consultant continues to refine responsive listening skills.

Three verbal listening skills that promote talking by the speaker are inviting, encouraging, and questioning cautiously. Inviting means providing an opportunity for others to talk, by signaling to them that you are interested in listening if they are interested in speak-

[1]Did you get *silent*?

ing. Examples are "You seem to have something on your mind," or "I'd like to hear about your problem," or "What's going on for you now?"

Verbal responses of encouragement are added to nodding and mirroring of facial responses. "I see," "Uh-hum," and "Oh" are examples of verbal behaviors that encourage continued talking. These listener responses suggest: "Continue. I understand. I'm listening." (Gordon, 1977)

Cautious questioning is the final mechanism for promoting continued talking. Most educators are competent questioners, so the caution here is to use minimal questioning. During the listening part of communication, the message is controlled by the speaker. It is always the speaker's serve. Intensive and frequent questioning gives control of the communication to the listener. This is antithetical to the consulting process, which should be about collaboration rather than power and control. Questions should be used to clarify what the speaker has said, so the message can be understood by the listener—for example "Is this what you mean?" or "Please explain what you mean by 'attitude problem.'"

Paraphrasing Skill.   Responsive listening means demonstrating that the listener understands the essence of the message. After listening by using nonverbal and minimal verbal responses, a consultant who is really listening probably will begin to understand the message of the speaker. To show that the message was heard, or to assess whether or not what was "heard" was the same message the sender intended and was not altered by distortion, the listener should paraphrase the message. This requires the listener to think carefully about the message and reflect it back to the speaker without changing the content or intent of the message.

There is no simple formula for reflecting or paraphrasing, but two good strategies are to be as accurate as possible and as brief as possible. A paraphrase may begin in one of several ways: "It sounds as if . . ." or "Is what you mean . . . ?" or "So, it seems to me you want (think) (feel) . . ." or "Let me see if I understand. You're saying . . ." Paraphrasing allows listeners to check their understanding of the message. It is easy to mishear or misinterpret the message, especially if the words are ambiguous. Correct interpretation of the message will result in a nod from the speaker, who may feel that at last someone has really listened. Or the speaker may correct the message by saying, "No, that's not what I meant. It's this way . . ." The listener may paraphrase the content of the message. For example, "It seems to me that you're saying . . ." would reflect the content of the message back to the speaker. "You appear to be very frustrated about . . ." reflects the emotional part of the message. It is important to use the speaker's words as much as possible in the paraphrase words and to remain concise in responses. By paraphrasing appropriately, a listener demonstrates comprehension of the message or receipt of new information. This aspect of hearing and listening is essential in communication, and in assertion, problem-solving, and conflict management as well.

Just by recognizing a consultee's anger, or sadness, or frustration, a consultant can begin to build a trusting relationship with a consultee. The listener doesn't necessarily have to agree with the content or emotion that is heard. It may appear absurd or illogical. Nevertheless, the consultant's responsibility is not to change another's momentary tendency; rather, it is to develop a supportive working relationship via effective communication, paving the way to successful cooperation and problem-solving while avoiding conflict and resistance.

Parents often comment that they have approached a teacher with a problem, realizing they didn't want a specific answer, but just a kindly ear—a sounding board, or a friendly shoulder. Responsive listening is important in establishing collaborative relationships and maintaining them. It is also a necessary precursor to problem-solving in which both parties strive to listen and get a mutual understanding of the problem before it is addressed.

So when is responsive listening to be used? The answer is—*all* the time. Use it when establishing a relationship, when starting to problem-solve, when emotions are high, when the conversation doesn't seem to be getting anywhere, and when the speaker seems confused, uncertain, or doesn't know what else to do.

This complex process may not be necessary if two people have already developed a good working relationship and only a word or two is needed for mutual understanding. It also may not be appropriate if one of the two is not willing to talk. Sometimes "communication postponement" is best when you are too tired or too emotionally upset to be a responsive listener. When a consultant cannot listen because of any of these reasons, it is not wise to pretend to be listening, while actually thinking about something else or nothing at all. Instead, a reluctant listener should explain that he or she does not have the energy to talk about the problem now, but wishes to at a later time, for example: "I need a chance to think about this. May I talk to you later?" or "Look, I'm too upset to work on this very productively right now. Let's talk about it first thing tomorrow." Figure 4.2 summarizes responsive listening skills that help avoid blocked communication.

FIGURE 4.2   Responsive Listening Checklist

	Yes	No
A. *Appropriate Nonverbals*		
1. Good eye contact	_____	_____
2. Facial expression mirrored	_____	_____
3. Body orientation toward other person	_____	_____
B. *Appropriate Verbals*		
1. Door openers	_____	_____
2. Good level of encouraging phrases	_____	_____
3. Cautious questions	_____	_____
C. *Appropriate Responding Behaviors*		
1. Reflected content (paraphrasing)	_____	_____
2. Reflected feelings	_____	_____
3. Brief clarifying questions	_____	_____
4. Summarizations	_____	_____
D. *Avoidance of Roadblocks*		
1. No advice-giving	_____	_____
2. No inappropriate questions	_____	_____
3. Minimal volunteered solutions	_____	_____
4. No judging	_____	_____

(Thurston, 1989)

Roadblocks to Communication

Roadblocks (Gordon, 1977) are red flags to interaction, halting the development of effective collaborative relationships. They may be verbal behaviors or nonverbal behaviors that send out messages such as, "I'm not listening," or "It doesn't matter what you think," or "Your ideas and feelings are silly and unimportant." Roadblocks discourage the speaker and erode feelings of being able to handle problems, complete tasks, or live up to standards (Gordon, 1977).

Responsible school consultants most assuredly do not intend to send blocking messages. But by being busy, not concentrating, using poor listening skills, or allowing themselves to be directed by filters such as emotions and judgment, well-meaning consultants inadvertently send blocking messages.

Nonverbal Roadblocks.   Nonverbal roadblocks include facing away when the speaker talks, displaying inappropriate facial expressions such as smiling when the sender is saying something serious, distracting with body movements such as repetitively tapping a pencil, and grading papers or writing reports while "listening." Interrupting a speaker to attend to something or someone else—the phone, a sound outside the window, or a knock at the door—also halts communication and contributes in a subtle way toward undermining the spirit of collaboration.

Verbal Roadblocks.   Gordon (1977) lists twelve verbal barriers to communication. These have been called the "Dirty Dozen," and they can be grouped into three types of verbal roadblocks that prevent meaningful interaction (Bolton, 1986):

- Judging
- Sending solutions
- Avoiding others' concerns

The first category, judging, includes criticizing, name-calling, and diagnosing or analyzing why a person is behaving a particular way. False or nonspecific praise, and evaluative words or phrases, send a message of judgment toward the speaker. "You're not thinking clearly," "You'll do a wonderful job of using curriculum-based assessment!" and "You don't really believe that—you're just tired today," are examples of judging. (Notice that each of these statements begins with the word "you.") Avoiding judgment about parents or others helps teachers avoid deficit-based thinking, which hurts everyone it touches (Lovett, 1996). Nonjudgmental communication conveys fairness and equity, which is a vital component of a collaborative relationship.

Educators are particularly adept with the next category of verbal roadblocks—sending solutions. These include directing or ordering, warning, moralizing or preaching, advising, and using logical arguments or lecturing. A few of these can become a careless consultant's entire verbal repertoire. "Not knowing the question," Bolton (1986, p. 37) says, "it was easy for him to give the answer." "Stop complaining," and "Don't talk like that," and "If you don't send Jim to the resource room on time . . ." are examples of directing or warning. Moralizing sends a message of "I'm a better educator than you are." Such communication usually starts with "You should . . ." or "You ought to. . . .". When consultees have problems, the last thing they need is to be told what they *should* do. Using "shoulds" makes a consultant sound rigid and pedantic. Avoid giving the impression that you are more concerned with rules or shoulds than with the relationship with the consultee.

Avoiding others' concerns is a third category of verbal roadblocks. This category implies "no big deal" to the message receiver. Avoidance messages include reassuring or sympathizing, such as "You'll feel better tomorrow" or "Everyone goes through this stage," or interrogating to get more than necessary information, thereby delaying problem solving. Other avoidance messages include intensive questioning in the manner of the Grand Inquisition, and humoring or distracting, "Let's get off this and talk about something else." Avoiding the concerns others express sends the message that their concerns are not important.

Advising, lecturing, and logical argument are all too often part of the educator's tools of the trade. Teachers tend to use roadblock types of communication techniques frequently with students. The habits they develop cause them to overlook the reality that use of such tactics with adults can drive a wedge into an already precarious relationship. Consultants must avoid tactics such as assuming the posture of the "sage-on-the-stage," imparting wisdom in the manner of a learned professor to undergraduate students, lecturing, moralizing, and advising. Unfortunately, these methods imply superiority, which is detrimental to the collaborative process.

Other powerful roadblocks to communication are: too much sending, not enough receiving; excessive kindness (Fisher, 1993); reluctance to express negative information (Rinke, 1997); and inadequate feedback, that is, the sender is not told whether the message is received, acknowledged, or understood (Fisher, 1993). When consultants use roadblocks, they are making themselves, their feelings, and their opinions the focus of the interaction, rather than allowing the focus to be the issues, concerns, or problems of the consultee. When they set up roadblocks, listeners do not listen responsively or encourage others to communicate clearly, openly, and effectively. Because it is so easy to inadvertently use a communication block through speaking, it is wise to remember the adage, "We are blessed with two ears and one mouth, a constant reminder that we should listen twice as much as we talk." Indeed, the more one talks, the more likely a person is to make errors, and the less opportunity that person will have to learn something.

Terms and Labels as Roadblocks.   Inappropriate use of terms and labels can erect roadblocks to communication. Educators should adhere to the following points when speaking or writing about people with disabilities ("Guidelines for Reporting," 1996):

1. Do not focus on the disability, but instead on issues affecting quality of life for the individual, such as housing, affordable health care, and employment opportunity.
2. Do not portray successful people with disabilities as superhuman, for all persons with disabilities cannot achieve this level of success.
3. Do not use generic labels such as "the retarded" or "the deaf," but say "people with mental retardation" or "people who are deaf."
4. Emphasize abilities and not limitations, such as "uses a wheelchair," rather than "wheelchair-bound."
5. Terms such as *physically challenged* are considered condescending, and saying "victim of" is regarded as sensationalizing.
6. Do not imply disease by saying "patient" or "case" when discussing disabilities resulting from prior disease.

7. Show people with disabilities as active participants in society.
8. Use accurate terms—for example, *cleft lip* and not *hare lip, a person with cerebral palsy* and not *spastic* (because the muscles are spastic, not the people), *a person with epilepsy* and not *an epileptic,* a *stroke survivor* and not a *stroke victim.*
9. Refrain from stigmatizing terms such as *retardate, deviant, handicapped, crippled, victimized by,* or *afflicted with.*

Acceptable, contemporary terminology facilitates active listening and improves verbal communication.

Assertiveness

By the time the consultant has listened effectively and the collaborative relationship has been developed or enhanced, many consultants are more than ready to start talking. Once the sender's message is understood and emotional levels are reduced, it is the listener's turn to be the sender. Now the consultant gets to talk. However, it is not always easy to communicate one's thoughts, feelings, and opinions without infringing on the rights, feelings, or opinions of others. This is the time for assertiveness.

Being assertive involves achieving your goals without damaging the relationship or another's self-esteem (Katz & Lawyer, 1983). The basic aspects of assertive communication (Sundel & Sundel, 1980; Alberti & Emmons, 1974; Thurston, 1987) are:

Use an "I" message instead of a "you" message.
Say "and" instead of "but."
State the behavior objectively.
Name your own feelings.
Say what you want to happen.
Express concern for others.
Use assertive body language.

Open and honest consultants say what they want to happen and what their feelings are. That does not mean they always get what they want. Saying what you want and how you feel will clarify the picture and assure that the other(s) won't have to guess what you want or think. Even if others disagree with the ideas and opinions, they can never disagree with the feelings and wishes. Those are very personal and are expressed in a personal manner by starting the interaction with "I," rather than presenting feelings and opinions as truth or expert answer.

In stating an idea or position assertively, consultants should describe the problem in terms of its impact on the consultant, rather than in terms of what was done or said by the other person. "I feel let down" works better than "You broke your part of the agreement." If a consultant makes a "you" statement about the consultee which the consultee thinks is wrong, the consultant will only get an angry reaction and the consultant's concerns will be ignored.

Concern for Others during the Interaction.   Expressing concern for others can take many forms. This skill demonstrates that although people have thoughts and feelings which differ from those of others, they can still respect the feelings and ideas of others. "I realize it is a tremendous challenge to manage thirty-five children in the same classroom." This statement shows the consultant understands the management problems of the teacher. As the consultant goes on to state preferences in working with the teacher, the teacher is more likely to listen and work cooperatively. The consultee will see that the consultant is aware of the problems that must be dealt with daily. "It seems to me that . . ." and "I understand . . ." and "I realize . . ." and "It looks like . . ." are phrases consultants can use to express concern for the other person in the collaborative relationship. If the consultant cannot complete these sentences with the appropriate information, the next step is to go back to the listening part of the communication.

How to Be Concerned and Assertive.   Assertive people own their personal feelings and opinions. Being aware of this helps them state their wants and feelings. "You" sentences sound accusing, even when that is not intended, which can lead to defensiveness in others. For example, saying to a parent, "You should provide a place and quiet time for Hannah to do her homework," is more accusatory than saying, "I am frustrated when Hannah isn't getting her homework done, and I would like to work with you to think of some ways to help her get it done." Using "and" rather than "but" is very important in expressing thoughts without diminishing a relationship. This is a particularly difficult assertion skill. To the listener the word "but" erases the preceding phrase and prevents the intended message from coming through.

It is important to state behavior specifically. By describing behavior objectively, a consultant or consultee sounds less judgmental. It is easy to let blaming and judgmental words creep into language. Without meaning to, the speaker throws up a barrier that blocks the communication and the relationship.

■ ■ ■ ■ ■ ▬▬▬▬▬▬▬▬▬▬▬▬▬▬▬▬▬▬▬▬▬▬▬▬▬▬▬▬▬▬▬▬▬▬▬▬▬▬

APPLICATION 4.2
COMMUNICATING POSITIVELY

Compare the first statement with the second one:

1. "I would like to have a schedule of rehearsals for the holiday pageant. It is frustrating when I drive out to work with Maxine and Juanita and they are practicing for the musical and can't come to the resource room."
2. "When you don't let me know ahead of time that the girls won't be allowed to come and work with me, I have to waste my time driving and can't get anything accomplished."

In reflecting on these statements, which one is less judgmental and accusatory? Can these two contrasting statements create differing listener attitudes toward the speakers? For many listeners the judgmental words and phrases in the second sentence ("you don't let me know," "won't be allowed," "waste my time") sound blaming. They introduce a whole array of red flags.

Assertive communication includes demonstrating supportive body language. A firm voice, straight posture, eye contact, and body orientation toward the receiver of the message will have a desirable effect. Assertive body language affirms that the sender owns his or her own feelings and opinions but also respects the other person's feelings and opinions. This a difficult balance to achieve. Body language and verbal language must match or the messages will be confusing. Skills for being assertive are listed in Figure 4.3.

What we say and how we say it have a tremendous impact on the reactions and acceptance of others. When consultants and consultees communicate in ways that accurately reflect their feelings, focus on objective descriptions of behavior and situations, and think in a concrete manner about what they want to happen, assertive communication will build strong, respectful relationships. Assertive communication is the basis for solving problems and resolving conflicts.

The Art of Apologizing.   Sometimes, despite good communication skills and careful relationship-building and problem-solving, consultants make errors and mistakes. Good consultants never blame someone else for communication breakdowns; they accept responsibility for their own communication. This is demonstrated when a consultant says "Let me explain in a different way" instead of "Can't you understand?" Good consultants also use the art of apologizing.

One of the biggest misconceptions in the area of consultation and collaboration is that apologizing puts consultants and teachers at a disadvantage when working with colleagues and parents. It is simply not true that strong, knowledgeable people never say they're sorry. In fact, apologizing is a powerful strategy because it demonstrates honesty and confidence. Apologizing offers a chance to mend fences in professional relationships. Some suggestions from psychologist Barry Lubetkin (1996) about how to apologize include allowing the person you've wronged to vent her or his feelings first, apologize as soon as possible, don't say "I'm sorry, but . . . ," and say it once and let that be enough. Most importantly, apologies are empty if you keep repeating the behavior or the mistake.

FIGURE 4.3   Assertiveness Checklist

	Usually	Sometimes	Never
1. Conveys "I" instead of "you" message			
2. Says "and" rather than "but"			
3. States behavior objectively			
4. Says what he/she wants to have happen			
5. States feelings			
6. Expresses concern			
7. Speaks firmly, clearly			
8. Has assertive posture			
9. Avoids aggressive language			

MANAGING RESISTANCE, NEGATIVITY, ANGER, AND CONFLICT

Communication is the key to collaboration and problem-solving. Without back-and-forth discussions, there can be no agreement. Problem-solving often breaks down because communications break down first, people are not paying attention, or they misunderstand the other side, or emotions were not dealt with as a separate and primary issue.

In problem solving it is critical to separate the person from the problem. Collaborative consultants will find themselves often needing to deal with emotions, as well as any errors in perceptions or communication, as separate issues which must be resolved on their own. Emotions may take the form of resistance, anger, negativity, or outright conflict. If emotions are not recognized and dealt with skillfully, they may become barriers to effective communication when they are experienced by the consultant or consultee. Sometimes, regardless of how diplomatic people are in dealing with the emotions of others, they run into barriers of resistance in their attempts to communicate.

It is estimated that as much as 80 percent of problem-solving with others is getting through the resistance. Resistance is a trait of human nature that surfaces when people are asked to change. Researchers have found that people resist change for a number of reasons. They may:

- Have a vested interest in the status quo
- Have low tolerance for change
- Feel strongly that the change would be undesirable
- Be unclear about what the change would entail or bring about
- Fear the unknown

A wise person once suggested, "How can we ask others to change when it is so hard to change ourselves?" Resistance often has nothing to do with an individual personally or even with a new idea. The resistance is simply a reaction to change of any kind. Change implies imperfection in the way things are being done, and this makes people defensive. However, it is good to remember the adage from some wise person, "Change is the only thing that is permanent."

Why Educators Resist

It is human nature to be uncomfortable when another person disagrees. It is also human nature to get upset when someone resists efforts to make changes, implement plans, or modify systems to be more responsive to children with special needs. The need for change can generate powerful emotions. Most people are uncomfortable when experiencing the strong emotions of others. When someone yells or argues, the first impulse is to become defensive, argue the other point of view, and defend your own ideas. Although a school consultant may intend to remain cool, calm, and collected in the interactions that involve exceptional children, occasionally another individual says something that pushes a "hot button" and the consultant becomes upset, angry, or defensive.

Special education consulting teachers who have been asked to describe examples of resistance they have experienced toward their roles provide these examples:

Consultees (classroom teachers) won't share how they feel.

They act excited about an idea, but never get around to doing it.

They won't discuss it with you, but they do so liberally with others behind your back.

They may try, but give up too soon.

They take out their frustrations on the students.

They are too quick to say that a strategy won't work in their situation.

They dredge up a past example where something similar didn't work.

They keep asking for more and more details or information before trying an idea.

They change the subject, or suddenly have to be somewhere else.

They state that there is not enough time to implement the strategy.

They intellectualize with a myriad of reasons it won't work.

They are simply silent.

They just prefer the status quo.

When resistance spawns counter-resistance and anger, an upward spiral of emotion is created that can make consulting unpleasant and painful. Bolton (1986) describes resistance as a push, push-back phenomenon. When a person meets resistance with more resistance, defensiveness, logical argument, or any other potential roadblock, resistance increases and dialogue can develop into open warfare. Then the dialogue may become personal or hurtful. Nobody listens at that point, and a potentially healthy relationship is damaged and very difficult to salvage.

How to Deal with Resistance and Negativity

An important strategy for dealing with resistance and defensiveness is to handle one's own defensiveness, stop pushing so that the other person will not be able to push back, delay reactions, keep quiet, and *listen.* This takes practice, patience, tolerance, and commitment. It is important to deal with emotions such as resistance, defensiveness, or anger before proceeding to problem-solving. People are not inclined to listen until they have been listened to. They will not be convinced of another's sincerity and openness, or be capable of thinking logically, when the filter of emotions is clouding their thinking.

Negative people and negative emotions sap the energy of educational consultants. Reactions to negativity, to conflict, and to resistance can block communication and ruin potentially productive relationships. It is important to remember that negative people are not going to change. The person who has to change is the consultant.

The first point is to refrain from taking negativity personally. Such individuals just may be having a bad time at that point in their lives. A positive approach would be to deal with negativity as a challenge from which much can learned about working with people. When there is a breakthrough in the communication and problem solving, such folks can become one's staunchest ally and supporter.

Accommodating negative or resistant school colleagues or family members of students at their best times and on their turf can be a first step toward this alliance. Communicating in writing is a good way to diffuse emotional reactions and convey the message one wishes to send. Following up later and remaining patient will model a spirit of acceptance spiced with invincibility yet grounded in purpose.

For application of practical techniques, William Ury, of the Program on Negotiation at Harvard Law School, stresses that one of the keys to working with difficult people is controlling one's own behavior (Ury, 1991). The natural reaction to resistance, challenges, and negativity is to strike back, give in, or break off the communication. A negative reaction to resistance leads to a vicious cycle of action and reaction and leads to communication and relationship breakdowns. Instead of reacting, seek to regain a mental balance and stay focused. His suggestion is, don't react.

Ury (1991) provides two strategies for curbing one's own natural reactions to resistance and negativity. The first is to "go to the balcony." This means distancing oneself from the action-reaction cycle. Step back and take a deep breath and try to see the situation objectively. Imagine yourself climbing to the balcony overlooking the stage where the action-reaction drama has been taking place. Here, you can calmly look at the situation, with a detached or third-party perspective. Going to the balcony means removing yourself from your natural impulses and emotions. Remember, when your "hot buttons" get pushed or when you find yourself getting emotional and reacting, instead of acting, go to the balcony!

Another strategy Ury (1991) suggests is to keep your eyes on the prize. Dealing with emotional and difficult situations in collaborative efforts usually diverts us from our goals and causes distress, so always keep your mind on the larger picture. In the collaborative consultant's case, the prize is optimal developmental and educational outcomes for students with special needs. If we remember that the communication process is crucial to the relationships among the stakeholders in a student's education, we will remember that diversions are worth dealing with and the eventual outcome is well worth the process.

Consultants must "hear their way to success" in managing resistance. This may take five minutes, or months of careful relationship building. Colleagues cannot always avoid disagreements that are serious enough to create anger and resistance. A comment or question delivered in the wrong manner at the wrong time may be the "hot button" that triggers the antagonism. Consider remarks such as these:

"If you want students to use good note-taking skills, shouldn't you teach them how to take notes?"

"Not allowing learning disabled students to use calculators is cruel."

"Why don't you teach in a way that accommodates different learning styles?"

"You penalize gifted students when you keep the class in lockstep with basal readers."

Such remarks can make harried, overworked classroom teachers defensive and resentful. If an occasion arises in which a teacher or parent becomes angry or resistant, responding in the right way will prevent major breakdowns in the communication that is needed.

Why People Get Angry

Anger is felt when a situation is perceived as unfair or threatening and the person angered feels helpless to rectify that situation (Margolis, 1986). Differences of opinions, values, and behaviors exacerbate these feelings. Coyle (2000) explains anger as a secondary feeling that follows frustration, unmet expectations, loss of self-respect, or fear. The anger is accompanied by anxiety and powerlessness, changing into feelings or actions of power and fight. And sometimes "people vent their anger at those giving them the most help because they feel comfortable directing it there. In most instances, angered people feel unjustly victimized and blame others for their pain and anguish" (Coyle, 2000, p. 43).

How to Deal with the Anger.   Unresolved conflict leads to anger, which undermines morale and thwarts productivity. It is important for the collaborative consultant to respond appropriately to angry people. A first rule is to address the problem rather than the person, then seek to find a shared goal with the angry person. Defer judgment and together explore options. When an angry person is loud and belligerent, speak more softly and calmly. Listen intently with responsiveness, not reaction.

Margolis (1986) recommends that educators learn about those who are angry and get to know them as people, not problems. When they meet with the angry person, they should succinctly state a general and slightly ambiguous purpose for the meeting and ask if that purpose is satisfactory. The tone must be empathic, with careful phrasing of questions and brief summaries at key points during the problem-solving phase. The final summary with agreements and commitments should be written down to provide a record for later referral if necessary. Margolis reminds educators to congratulate all for what they have accomplished during the interaction.

■ ■ ■ ■ ■ ▬▬▬▬▬▬▬▬▬▬▬▬▬▬▬▬▬▬▬▬▬▬▬▬▬▬▬▬▬▬▬▬▬▬▬▬

APPLICATION 4.3
MANAGING RESISTANCE

Construct a problem situation involving another person that could happen, or *has* happened, in your school context and interact with a colleague to try these communication techniques:

Dismiss the negativity with "You may be right," and keep moving forward. Be assertive, i.e., "I am bothered by discussing the negative side of things." Ask for complaints in writing (because some people don't realize how negative they sound). Ask for clarification, also, by suggesting that the person describe the problem and clarify the desired outcome. This leads people to thinking about positive actions. Don't defend attacks, and invite criticism and advice instead. Ask what's wrong. Look for interests behind resistance, negativity, and anger by asking questions. Tentatively agree by saying "that's one opinion."

Switch roles and try another episode. Then have a debriefing session to critique the interactions.

Why Conflict Occurs in School Contexts

Conflict is an inevitable part of life. It occurs when there are unreconciled differences among people in terms of needs, values, goals, and personalities. If conflicting parties cannot give and take by integrating their views and utilizing their differences constructively, interpersonal conflicts will escalate. School consultants and collaborators are not exempt from the dysfunction that often accompanies conflict. So it is important for them to develop tools for transforming vague and ambiguous sources of conflict into identified problems that can be solved collaboratively. Lippitt (1983) suggests that conflict, as a predictable social phenomenon, should not be repressed, because there are many positive aspects to be valued. Conflict can help clarify issues, increase involvement, and promote growth, as well as strengthen relationships and organizational systems when the issues are resolved. Gordon (1977) contends it is undesirable to avoid conflict when there is genuine disagreement, because resentments build up, feelings get displaced, and unpleasantries such as backbiting, gossiping, and general discontent may result.

Reasons for Conflict among Educators.   Teachers, administrators, and parents face many possible occasions for conflict when they are involved with educating children who have special needs. Some conflicts occur because there is too little information or because misunderstandings have been created from incorrect information. These instances are not difficult to resolve because they require only the communication of facts. Other areas of conflict arise from disagreement over teaching methods, assessment methods, goals, and values. Parent goals and teacher goals for the exceptional student may differ significantly, and support personnel may add even more dimensions to the conflict. For example, if a child is instructed by the reading specialist to read more slowly, urged by the learning disabilities teacher to read more rapidly, required by the classroom teacher to read a greater amount of material, and ordered by the parent to get better grades or *else,* effective communication is tenuous or nonexistent, and conflict is inevitable. Some conflict can even be beneficial if it clears the air of lingering disagreement and doubt so that conflicting parties can move ahead. But if differences cannot be resolved through formal or informal conflict-resolution processes, then relationships will surely disintegrate.

Perhaps the most difficult area of conflict relates to values. When people have differing values about children, education, or educator roles within the learning context, effective communication is a challenging goal. As discussed earlier in this chapter, rapport building, listening, and paraphrasing are significant in building relationships among those whose values conflict. The most important step is to listen courteously until a clear message about the value comes through, demonstrating respect for the value even if it conflicts with yours. Then it is time to assert your own values and, along with the other person, try to reach a common goal or seek a practical issue on which to begin problem-solving.

How to Resolve School-Related Conflicts

Some conflicts, particularly those involving values, are difficult to prevent and may seem at the time to be unresolvable. However, if all can agree to common goals or common ground for discussion, conflicts can be resolved.

When emotions or conflict inhibit the communication process, first listen responsively and acknowledge what is being said. The other side appreciates the sense of being heard and understood, and the consultant will gain a vivid picture of their interests and concerns. A useful strategy is to focus on interests rather than positions as a way to circumvent potential conflicts during the communication process.

Gordon (1977) and many others suggest that conflict resolution can follow one of three paths:

- I win, you lose.
- You win, I lose.
- I win, you win.

The first two paths are frequently taken because people fear conflict and wish to avoid it. The third path, with the win/win outcome, is hard because those involved must confront

their emotions and the emotions of others, and work diligently to turn conflict into cooperation. This method focuses on needs rather than solutions. It is based on two-way communication with lots of listening. During conflict situations, the immediate purpose of interaction
is improving communication, not changing points of view.

"Always think win/win" is one of Stephen Covey's (1989) seven habits of highly effective people and is a crucial element of effective relationships and problem-solving in educational and community settings. If you can't come to a true win/win agreement, Covey
suggests, it is better to go for no deal at all. This allows you to preserve the relationship and
the possibility for a win/win pact in the future. Win/win agreements flow from solid relationships, and taking time to develop a strong level of trust is essential for mutual collaboration. We must resist the urge to succeed at the expense of the other person. This forms a
relationship that is open to success on both sides in the future.

Covey (1989) suggests a four-step process for the win/win approach:

1. Try to see the situation from the other person's perspective.
2. Identify the key issues and concerns involved.
3. Make a list of the results that you would consider a fully acceptable solution.
4. Look for new options to get those results.

Resolving conflicts within an "everybody wins" philosophy requires listening skills
described earlier in the chapter to find common ground. In dealing with emotions of the
speaker, the listener must concentrate with an open mind and attend to the speaker's feelings as well as the facts or ideas that are part of the message. The listener must strive to hear
the whole story without interrupting, even if there are strong feelings of disagreement. Conflict usually means that intense emotions are involved. Only by concentrating on the message with an open mind can all parties begin to deal with the conflict. Emotional filters often
function as blinders. If the emotions cannot be overcome, the best tactic is to postpone the
communication, using assertive responses to do so.

Listening establishes a common intent and develops a starting attitude. Listening to
one who is upset helps that person focus on a problem rather than an emotion. Listening lets
people cool down. Bolton (1986) calls this the spiral of resistance, suggesting that if one listens with empathy and does not interrupt, the speaker's anger or high emotion will dissipate.
Without saying a word, the listener makes the speaker feel accepted and respected.

It is hard to argue with someone who does not argue back. It is hard to stay mad or
upset with someone who seems to understand and empathize. Each time a person listens, a
small victory for the advancement of human dignity has been achieved (Schindler & Lapid,
1989). Only after emotions are brought into the open and recognized can all parties involved
move on to seek a common goal.

Barriers to communication among educators and families may sometimes be specific
conditions such as learning disabilities of adults involved. When education consultants work
with parents, paraeducators, or other adults who may have a learning disability themselves,
some suggestions for improving communication are:

- Break large tasks or bodies of information into smaller ones.
- Give information in a very structured manner.
- Offer "organizational tools" such as notes, colored files or flyers for color coding,
  paper for taking notes or printed notes.

- Be very careful about being critical.
- Offer plenty of positive feedback, when warranted.
- Encourage them to tape meetings or instructions.
- Communicate frequently and offer information in smaller segments.
- Frequently test the accuracy of communication by asking them to repeat or rephrase what was said.

The initial intent for resolving a conflict should be to learn. This enables all factions to increase mutual understanding and think creatively together. Most people could agree to such a start because it does not address goals or values. It does not even require agreement that a problem exists. It simply establishes the intent to learn by working together. Establishing intent for dialogue should follow the reduction of emotional responses. Of course, as discussed earlier, it is important to avoid roadblocks at all stages of the process.

Consultants and consulting teachers must put aside preconceived notions about their own expertise and learn from those who often know the student best—parents and classroom teachers. Such consultees respond positively to open-ended questions that let them know they are respected and needed. When consultants open their own minds, they unlock the potential of others.

■ ■ ■ ■ ■

APPLICATION 4.4
PRACTICE MAKES PERFECT, OR EASIER, AT LEAST!

With a partner, practice the following uncomfortable or embarrassing situations. Use the Figures in this chapter as checklists to monitor verbal and nonverbal communication, for both sending and receiving.

1. Ask a person who drops by to come back later.
2. Say "no" to someone who is urging you to help with a project.
3. Answer the phone when you have about three things going on (voice tone and rate being particularly pertinent here).
4. Receive a compliment graciously.
5. Deliver a compliment so that it is not a distorted message.
6. Ask a colleague to please (for once!) be on time.
7. Enter a roomful of people who are probably unknown to you.
8. Respond when someone has interrupted you.
9. Break into the conversation when someone has monopolized the discussion to everyone's frustration.
10. Apologize for an oversight or ill-chosen remark you made.

Now, as you feel more confident in these real-life "peak" and "pit" situations, practice using them until they become second nature.

After listening constructively, consultants need to help establish ground rules for resolving the conflict. The ground rules should express support, mutual respect, and a commitment to the process. Again, this requires talking and listening, dialoguing, and keeping an open mind. It is important not to dominate the dialogue at this time and, by the same token, not to let the other person dominate the conversation. This part of the communication might be called "agreeing to disagree," with the intent of "agreeing to find a point of agreement." It is important to share the allotted interaction time equitably and in a way that facilitates understanding. Consultants must use precise language without exaggerating points, or, as discussed earlier, flaunting "educationese" or taking inappropriate shortcuts with jargon and "alphabet soup" acronyms.

Dealing with conflict productively also requires asserting one's ideas, feelings, or opinions. While listening enables the consultant to understand the speaker's perspectives, wants, and goals, assertion skills allow consultants to present their perspective. This often follows a pattern of listen—assert—listen—assert—listen, and so on, until both parties have spoken and have been heard.

Although there may be resistance after each assertion, it will gradually dissipate so that *real* communication and collaboration can begin to take place. Only after this process has happened can collaborative goal setting and problem-solving occur. Figure 4.4 summarizes useful steps for managing resistance and conflict.

FIGURE 4.4   Checklist for Managing Resistance and Conflict

A. *Responsive Listening*

   1. Had assertive posture   _____

   2. Used appropriate nonverbal listening   _____

   3. Did not become defensive   _____

   4. Used minimal verbals in listening   _____

   5. Reflected content   _____

   6. Reflected feelings   _____

   7. Let others do most of the talking   _____

   8. Used only brief, clarifying questions   _____

B. *Assertiveness*

   9. Did not use roadblocks such as giving advice _____

  10. Used "I" messages   _____

  11. Stated wants and feelings   _____

C. *Recycled the interaction*

  12. Used positive postponement   _____

  13. Did not problem-solve before emotions were controlled _____

  14. Summarized   _____

  15. Set time to meet again, if applicable   _____

Welch (2001) outlines the O.F.T.E.N. strategy, a variation of the useful Awareness Wheel approach (Miller, Miller, Nunnally, & Wackman, 1991), employed extensively in counseling situations. The first step in the O.F.T.E.N. technique is describing one's observation of a problematic situation. Next comes articulation of how one feels about the situation by using "I messages." Then thinking is shared by participants to reveal their observations and feeling. Expectations for the situation are articulated by all, with consensus and understanding of the expectations. To complete the process, participants brainstorm ways to meet the expectations, compromising when necessary, to develop a plan of who does what, when, and where. This final phase includes a contingency plan in case the actions are not carried out. The O.F.T.E.N. strategy is easy to remember and convenient to use when a formal procedure for conflict resolution is required.

There is a well-known story of a man who had three sons. He stipulated in his will that the oldest son should inherit half his camels, the middle son should get one-third of the camels, and the youngest should be the new owner of one-ninth of his camels. When the old man died, he owned seventeen camels. But the sons could not agree on how to divide the camels in accordance with their father's will. Months and months of bitter conflict went by. Finally the three young men sought the advice of a wise woman in the village. She heard their complaints and observed their bitterness and felt sorry that brothers were fighting and putting the family into turmoil. So she gave the brothers one of her camels. The estate then was divided easily according to the father's wishes. The eldest took home nine camels, the second put six camels beside his tent, and the youngest took home two camels. The men were happy, the father's last wishes were honored, and the wise woman took her own camel back and led it home.

Conflict management is the process of becoming aware of a conflict, diagnosing its nature, and employing an appropriate problem-solving method in such a way that it simultaneously achieves the goals of all involved and enhances relationships among them. If the consulting relationship is treated as a collaborative one in which each person's needs are met (the win/win model), then feelings of self-confidence, competence, self-worth, and power increase, enhancing the overall capacity of the system for responding to conflict in the future. The win/win relationship is based on honesty, trust, and mutual respect—qualities stressed earlier as vital to a successful consulting relationship. Win/win allows all involved parties to experience positive outcomes. The model works best when all parties use effective communication skills (Fisher & Ury, 1991).

The opposite of successful conflict management is avoiding conflict, ignoring feelings, and bypassing the goals of others. The relationship becomes adversarial, if it is not already so, because for someone to win, another must lose. When conflicts are approached with responsive listening and dealt with honestly and openly, the underlying problem or need can be resolved.

When engineers stress collaboration, they often use the bumblebee analogy. According to the laws of aerodynamics, bumblebees cannot fly. But as everyone knows, they do. By the same token, some might say that groups cannot function productively because of the conflicts, personal agenda, and individual preferences that exist among the members. But they do. Groups of people play symphonies, set up businesses, write laws, and develop IEPs for student needs. An understanding of adult individual differences, styles, and preferences, as discussed in Chapter 1, will encourage participants in consultation and collaboration to listen more respectfully and value differences among colleagues. This knowledge, when combined with responsive listening, avoidance of roadblocks, and assertiveness, will enable consultants to deal with resistance and conflict productively. Conflict management puts these skills to practical use in educational settings of school and home.

Educational consultants maximize their effect on the lives and education of children with special needs by using good communication skills. They should always keep in mind the ancient rule we instill in children for crossing the street: "Stop, Look, and Listen." For the collaborative school consultant it means:

- Stop talking, judging, and giving advice.
- Look at the long-term outcome of good communication (keep eyes on the prize).
- Listen to parents, colleagues, and others who work in collaboration for children with special needs.

The stop, look, and listen rule sets up consultants for success—in establishing collaborative relationships, in developing rapport, in dealing with conflict and emotions, and in solving problems.

TIPS FOR COMMUNICATING EFFECTIVELY

1. Avoid communication roadblocks. Research shows that positively worded statements are one-third easier to understand than negative ones (Rinke, 1997).
2. Listen. This helps dissipate negative emotional responses and often helps the other person articulate the problem, perhaps finding a solution then and there.
3. Use assertion. Say what you feel and what your goals are.
4. Be aware of your "hot buttons." Knowing your own responses to certain "trigger" behaviors and words will help you control natural tendencies to argue, get defensive, or simply turn red and sputter.
5. Attend to nonverbal language (kinesics, or body language) as well as to verbal language when communicating.
6. Don't "dump your bucket" of frustrations onto the other person. Jog, shout, practice karate, but avoid pouring out anger and frustration on others. Instead, fill the buckets of others with "warm fuzzies" of empathy and caring.
7. Develop a protocol within the school context for dealing with difficult issues and for settling grievances.
8. Deal with the present. Keep to the issue of the current problem rather than past problems, failures, or personality conflicts.
9. Use understanding of individual differences among adults to bridge communication gaps and manage conflicts in educational settings.
10. Advocate for training that focuses on communication, problem solving, and conflict management.

CHAPTER REVIEW

1. The primary reason people fail in collaborative efforts is because of communication problems. It is too often assumed that communication skill develops with no special attention to the complexities of social interaction.

2. The sender, the message, and the receiver are three key components of the communication process. Each component is vital. When a message is missent or misheard, many distortions occur which prevent open, honest communication. This

happens because of differences in values, language, attitudes, perceptions, gender, ethnicity, and history of sender and receiver.

3. Rapport-building requires respect for differences in others, trust, feeling all right about not having all the answers, and being comfortable even when there is disagreement.

4. Major skills in effective communication are responsive listening, asserting, managing conflict, and collaborative problem-solving. Both verbal and nonverbal components are included in these skills. The skills form the basis of a respectful, egalitarian relationship and a successful team on behalf of the student with special needs. They pave the way to effective problem-solving and mutual collaboration.

5. Communication can be hampered by verbal roadblocks and nonverbal roadblocks. Verbal roadblocks include responses which are judging, responses that send solutions, and responses that avoid the concerns of others. Nonverbal roadblocks include body language that conveys lack of empathy and concern.

6. Assertive communication allows speakers to state their own views, feelings, and opinions without impeding the ongoing consulting process. Assertiveness means stating one's wants or feelings by starting sentences with "I," using "and" rather than "but," and showing concern for the other person. Resistance sometimes occurs when a speaker is assertive. This resistance is a natural reaction to the request for change. It can be managed by using a combination of assertiveness and responsive listening.

7. Conflict arises when members of educational teams have different feelings, values, needs, and goals. Conflict resolution should follow a win/win model if collaborative efforts are to be maintained. Listening instead of arguing, establishing ground rules, and seeking a common goal will help bring teams to the problem-solving stage without any "losers."

8. Resistance, anger, and negativity are residuals of disagreements and unwanted change. Consultants will want to remain calm and listen, using strategies such as "going to the balcony" and "hearing their way to success."

TO DO AND THINK ABOUT

1. Discuss the following:

   What type of roadblock does each of these comments set up?

   > What you need is more activity. Why don't you develop a hobby?

   > You are such a good friend. I can count on you.

   > Let's talk about something more positive.

   > I know just how you feel.

   > Why did you let her talk to you that way?

   Which of these lines create resistance and defensiveness?

   > What you should do is . . .

   > Do you want to comment on this?

   > Everyone has problems like that.

   > That's a good thought.

   > You mean you'd actually do that?

   > Let's change the subject.

   > What should I do?

   What assertive statements could be made for each situation?

   > A colleague talks to you about his personal problems and you can't get your work done.

   > The paraeducator comes in late frequently.

   > During a committee meeting one member keeps changing the subject and getting the group off task.

   > A colleague wants to borrow some material but has failed to return things in the past.

   > During a phone conversation with a wordy parent, you need to get some information quickly and hang up soon.

   > The class next door is so rowdy that your class can't work.

2. Discuss these basic assumptions about communication for consultation and add more to the list.

   The reactions of others depend on your actions, word choices, body language, and listening skills.

   People generally want to do a good job.

   People have a powerful need to "save face."

   No one can force another person to change.

   Learning to communicate, be assertive, and facilitate conflict resolution is awkward at first.

3. During initial attempts at paraphrasing, the process often feels and sounds awkward and phony. What might be done about that?

4. Practice the following situations:

   expressing anger in constructive ways;

   getting the interaction back on task;

   stating a contrasting view to a supervisor-type;

   recommending a better way of doing something;

   asking again, and again, for materials you loaned some time ago that you need now.

5. Restate the following message so the language is assertive but nonthreatening to the receiver.

   "You penalize gifted students when you keep the class lockstepped in the basal texts and the workbooks."

   "If you want students to use good note-taking skills, you should teach them how to take notes."

   "Not allowing students to use calculators is terribly outmoded."

   "It is not fair to insist that learning disabled students take tests they cannot read."

FOR FURTHER READING

Bolton, R. (1986). *People skills: How to assert yourself, listen to others, and resolve conflicts.* New York: Simon and Schuster.

Fisher, R., & Ury, W. (1991). *Getting to yes: Negotiating agreement without giving in.* New York: Penguin.

Gazda, G. M., Asbury, F. R., Balzer, F. J., Childers, W. C., Phelps, R. E., & Walters, R. P. (1999). *Human relations development: A manual for educators* (6th ed.). Boston: Allyn & Bacon.

Johnson, D. W., & Johnson, F. P. (2000). *Joining together: Group theory and group skills* (7th ed.). Boston: Allyn & Bacon.

Rinke, W. J. (1997). *Winning management: 6 fail-safe strategies for building high-performance organizations.* Clarksville, MD: Achievement Publishers.

Smith, D. K. (1996). *Taking charge of change: 10 principles for managing people and performance.* Reading, MA: Addison-Wesley Publishing Co.

Stone, D., Patton, B., & Heen, S. (1999). *Difficult conversations: How to discuss what matters most.* New York: Random House.

CHAPTER FIVE

PROBLEM-SOLVING STRATEGIES FOR COLLABORATIVE SCHOOL CONSULTATION

Educational Needs → ▲ ← Problem-Solving Strategies

↑ Educational Settings

Using a structured process for collaborative school consultation is like preparing food according to a recipe. After the fundamentals of cooking have been mastered, one can adapt those procedures to just about any setting, preference, or creative impulse. In similar fashion, a basic "recipe" for consultation and collaboration can be adapted to any school context, grade level, content areas, or special learning need. Just as a recipe should be adaptable for individual preferences, so should collaborative consultation structure be flexible and adaptable to fit the needs of individual students in their school contexts.

When educators exercise ingenuity in constructing teaching and learning strategies, schools are better contexts in which all can perform at their best. Collaborative school consultation is an ideal scenario for incorporating problem-solving techniques which cultivate flexible, divergent thinking.

This chapter's content (triangle) targets the educational needs of students. Processes (circle) to be explored are problem-solving strategies, some tried-and-true, and others rather new. Contexts are educational settings where learning is to take place.

FOCUSING QUESTIONS

1. What are fundamental components in a problem-solving process?
2. Why is problem identification so important in collaborative consultation?
3. What basic steps should be included in the collaborative school consultation process?
4. What kinds of things should consultants and consultees say and do during their professional interactions?

5. What problem-solving techniques are particularly helpful for collaborative consultation and teamwork?

6. What interfering themes and hurdles can hinder problem-solving?

KEY TERMS

brainstorming	interfering themes	problem identification
concept mapping	lateral thinking	problem-solving process
follow-through	metaphorical thinking	Six Thinking Hats thinking
follow-up	POCS (problem, option,	
idea checklist	consequence, solution)	

THE PROBLEM-SOLVING PROCESS

Educators must exercise perception and judgment in order to ascertain student needs, set reasonable goals, and select the most efficient means of addressing those needs and goals (Lanier, 1982). This will require development and ongoing improvement of problem-solving skills. Problem-solving ability comes more naturally and easily to some than to others. There is not any one specific formula or "recipe." Furthermore, problem-solving skills, particularly as used by groups, can be improved with training and practice.

Pugach and Johnson (1995) suggest two general categories for problem solving in the context of teacher collaboration: (1) schoolwide problems and (2) specific student problems. Full inclusion is an example of schoolwide problem solving undertaken in a collaborative way by all school staff. Specific student needs are the more common type of issue that teachers deal with in a problem-solving mode. However, both categories of problems provide an opportunity to broaden the educational options for students with special needs.

Pugach and Johnson (1995) suggest also that another important outcome of collaborative problem solving on a systemwide basis is development of a support structure for teachers to improve classroom instruction. For this kind of professional development it is helpful to begin with a study of a fundamental problem-solving process. Gordon (1977) outlines several general components that are important for solving problems effectively:

- Identification and definition of the problem
- Generation of alternative solutions
- Evaluation of alternative solutions
- Decision-making
- Implementing the decisions
- Following up to evaluate the solution

These components include the basic elements of the problem-solving processes most frequently employed in a wide variety of business and professional areas.

VIGNETTE 5

The setting is the office area of an elementary school, where a special education staff member has just checked into the building and meets a fourth-grade teacher.

Classroom Teacher: I understand you're going to be a consulting teacher in our building to work with learning and behavior disorders.

Consulting Teacher: That's right. I hope to meet with all of the staff very soon to find out your needs and how we can work together to address those needs.

Classroom Teacher: Well I, for one, am glad you're here. I have a student who is driving me and my other twenty-four students up the wall.

Consulting Teacher: How so?

Classroom Teacher: Well, since she moved here a few weeks ago she's really upset the classroom system that I've used for years, and used quite successfully, I might add.

Consulting Teacher: Is she having trouble with the material you teach?

Classroom Teacher: No, she's a bright child who finishes everything in good time, and usually does it correctly. But she's extremely active, almost frenetic as she busy-bodies around the room.

Consulting Teacher: What specific behaviors concern you?

Classroom Teacher: Well, for one thing she tries to help everyone else when they should be doing their own work. I've worked a lot on developing independent learning skills in my students, and they've made good progress. They don't need to have her tell them what to do.

Consulting Teacher: So her behavior keeps her classmates from being the self-directed learners that they can be?

Classroom Teacher: Right. I have to monitor her activities constantly, which means diverting my attention from all the other students. She bosses her classmates in the learning centers and even on the playground. At this rate she will soon be having serious difficulties with peer relationships.

Consulting Teacher: Which of those behaviors would you like to see changed first?

Classroom Teacher: Well, I need to get her settled into some activities by herself rather than bothering other students.

Consulting Teacher: What have you tried until now to keep her involved with her own work?

Classroom Teacher: I explain to her what I expect and then try to reinforce appropriate behavior with things she likes to do.

Consulting Teacher: We could make a list of specific changes in behavior you'd like to see, and work out a program to accomplish them. In fact, the technique of webbing might help us explore the possibilities. How about doing one together on this chart paper? Then we will have a record of our ideas. (Consultant and teacher work together to make the web and begin a plan.) . . . There's the bell. Want to meet tomorrow to add any second thoughts to our chart and finalize this plan?

Classroom Teacher: Sounds good. I'd like to get her on track so the class is more settled. Then other children will like her better and she'll be able to learn other things, too. We could meet right here tomorrow, if that's O.K. with you. It helps a lot to have someone to talk with about this and work out a plan.

A problem-solving process that reflects high levels of communication, cooperation, and coordination will allow educators to share their expertise related to the problem. Learning and behavior problems are not always outcomes of student disabilities. Many students are simply "curriculum-disabled" (Conoley, 1985), requiring a modified or expanded approach to existing curriculum in order to function successfully in school (Pugach & Johnson, 1990). To modify the settings for learning and make accommodations in the educational environment, educators must identify those aspects of students' educational curriculum that are interfering with their development.

The POCS Concept for Problem Solving

The concept of collaborative problem solving that draws upon effective communication, cooperation, and coordination is demonstrated succinctly by the POCS (*Problem, Options, Consequences, Solution*) problem-solving method (Thurston, 1987):

- *Problem* Identification (P)
- Generating *Options* (O)
- Determining the *Consequences* (C)
- Planning the *Solution* (S)

A POCS worksheet for taking notes on generated ideas can help consultants when used as a problem-solving guide (See Figure 5.1).

FIGURE 5.1   The POCS Method of Problem Solving

Problem: _____

Expected Outcome: _____

Options	*Consequences*
1. _____	_____
2. _____	_____
3. _____	_____
4. _____	_____
5. _____	_____
6. _____	_____

Chosen Solution: _____

Responsibilities and Commitments: _____

Follow-up Date and Time: _____

(by Linda P. Thurston)

The Problem.   The first and most critical step in the POCS method of problem solving is to identify the problem (Bolton, 1986; Schein, 1969). The most sophisticated teaching methods and the most expensive instructional materials are worthless if the student needs are misidentified or overlooked. It can even be argued that an inaccurate definition of the problem situation has potential for iatrogenic effects. These effects hurt more than help, just as identifying an illness incorrectly can result in inappropriate treatment and can delay or deny use of a better treatment.

Problem identification requires special emphasis if the consultation process is to produce results. Bergan (1995) stresses that when problem identification is successful, the consultation is much more likely to come to a successful conclusion.

In earlier research Bergan and Tombari (1976) determined that for problem identification, consultation variables such as interview skills, flexibility, and efficient work modes have greatest impact on problem solving. They concluded that consultants who are skilled in problem analysis are the most able to identify appropriate target behaviors and develop workable interventions. Information on a student's behaviors, discrepancies between current and desired performance, and baseline data are needed to determine the level of potential target behaviors (Polsgrove & McNeil, 1989).

Multisourced information about student needs provides a more accurate perspective on learning and behavior problems, along with information about the settings in which they are demonstrated, the severity and frequency of the problems, and the persons who are most affected by those behaviors (Polsgrove & McNeil, 1989). Obtaining information from multiple sources requires effective communication skills by all who can contribute information. Communication is such an important aspect of successful school consultation that it was addressed separately in Chapter 4. Expressing thoughts and feelings with clarity and accuracy entails effective listening and appropriate assertiveness. The problem will never be solved if all parties think they are working on different issues. Problems are like artichokes—they come in layers. Only after the outside layers are stripped away can problem-solvers get to the heart of the matter. Good listening facilitates movement to the heart of the problem.

Options.   Problem solving also involves generating options to solve the problem. Divergent thinking is important in order not to get stuck in routines and answers. Some consultants find it helpful to encourage the person who "owns" the problem to make the most suggestions. For example, if the problem is making a decision about post-secondary education for a student with learning disabilities, the student and the parents should be encouraged to generate the most options. This is important for several reasons. When people participate in decision-making, they feel more ownership toward the results than when the decision is forced on them. Also, as explained by Johnson and Johnson (1987), people are more apt to support decisions they helped create than those imposed on them, regardless of the merit of the idea.

An important second reason for prompting the owner of the problem to give initial suggestions is that consultants should avoid giving advice and being presented or perceived as the expert. Several researchers have shown that a nonexpert approach to educational consulting is especially effective in special education (Idol-Maestes, Lloyd, & Lilly, 1981; Margolis & McGettigan, 1988). The suggestions and opinions of others need to be listened to with respect and fully understood before additional suggestions are offered.

Finally, teachers and others are more likely to be resistant if the problem-solving process is perceived as advice-giving by the consultant. Problems that come up in school consultation often reveal the need for changed classroom practices. (Recall that resistance was discussed in Chapter 4.) Advice-giving and hierarchical structure may be unintentionally communicated if consultants promote the options generated as their ideas. If a consultant is regarded as *the* expert, there is pressure on that consultant and false expectations are created. It is hard to win in this kind of situation. The best practice for the consultant is to communicate equality, flexibility, and a sharing attitude. Three questions assess the equality that is or is not present in a professional consulting relationship:

- Does the consultant recognize the consultee's expertise and opinion?
- Does the consultant encourage the consultee to generate ideas and make decisions?
- Do consultees feel free to *not* do as the consultant might recommend?

Eager, competent consultants who are ready to solve problems and produce quick results, instant cures, and dramatic increases, too often jump in and try to solve problems alone. Consultees may react with resistance or negativism, or perhaps even hostility, by hiding their feelings and withdrawing, blaming others if things do not work out.

It is difficult for consultants to avoid the "quick fix." But a quick fix is inappropriate (DeBoer, 1986). It is demeaning to the one who has been struggling with the problem. Others need to feel that the consultant fully understands their unique situation and the source of their frustrations before they are ready to participate in problem solving and listen to the suggestions of colleagues. Consultants must listen before they can expect to be listened to and treated with parity or approached voluntarily by consultees.

All learning situations and all students are unique. In response to a question about classroom management, a wise high school teacher replied, "I don't know all the answers, because I haven't seen all the kids." While students and situations may appear similar in some ways, the combinations of student, teacher, parents, and school and home contexts are unique for each problem. Furthermore, in many cases, people with problems already have their answers. They just need help to clarify issues or an empathic ear to face the emotional aspects of the concern. If people keep talking, they often can solve their own problems. Joint problem-identification and idea-generating assures that professional relationships are preserved. Then professional communication is enhanced and professionals maintain a greater feeling of control and self-esteem.

Good consultants do not "solve" problems—they see that problems get solved. So they facilitate problem solving and "nix the quick fix." As Gordon (1977) asks, whose problem is it? Who *really* owns the problem? Busy consultants do not need to take on the problems of others, and such action would inhibit consultees from learning and practicing problem-solving skills. Everyone who owns a part of the problem should participate in solving it. That may involve collaboration among several people—teachers, administrators, vocational counselors, students, parents, and others. Consultants and consultees should focus on the problem rather than on establishing ownership for the problem. All individuals will need to attend carefully to minimizing roadblocks and maximizing assertion and listening skills, as was discussed in Chapter 4.

Consequences.   Effective consultants facilitate problem solving in such a way that all members of the group feel their needs are being satisfied, and an "equitable" social and professional relationship is being maintained (Gordon, 1977). Members of the problem-solving team work together to evaluate all the suggestions made, with each presenting disadvantages and merits of the suggestion from their own perspectives. Agreement is not necessary at this point, because the barriers and merits important to each person are taken into account. Honest and open communication, using good listening skills and an appropriate level of assertiveness, are vital at this step.

Solution.   The problem-solving group selects a workable solution all are willing to adopt, at least on a trial or experimental basis. The consultant promotes mutual participation in the decision. Group members more readily accept new ideas and new work methods when they are given opportunity to participate in decision-making (Gordon, 1977). Many times a complex problem can be solved as each person in the group discovers what the others really want or, perhaps, fear. Then solutions can be formulated to meet the goals and protect the concerns of all involved.

Better decisions are made with a cool head and a warm heart (Johnson, 1992). Johnson suggests asking oneself if the decision helps meet the *real* need. Real needs are based on reality, not illusion or wishful thinking, and on personal and professional goals. Next, one should ask, What information do I need? Do I have enough information to create options I may not have realized before this? Have I thought of the consequences of each option? Have I *really* thought through the options?" Taking time to ask all the necessary questions is a key to Johnson's (1992) decision-making process. Asking many questions helps make options and choices obvious.

Problem-Solving Roles

In collaborative problem solving, whether using the POCS method or another effective method, the role of the consultant is to facilitate interaction and teamwork. This necessitates skills of good listening, assertive responses, and successful resolution of conflicts, as discussed in Chapter 4. Collaborative school consultation encourages collective thinking for creative and imaginative alternatives and allows all involved to have their feelings and ideas heard and their goals met. The ultimate goal for effective problem solving is to provide the best education possible for students with special needs. At this point it may be helpful to review the descriptions of consultation, collaboration, and teamwork presented in Chapter 1, and consider several examples that differentiate the three interactive processes.

Problem Solving with Consultation.   A preschool teacher is concerned about a child in the group who is not fluent in speech, so the teacher asks the speech pathologist to help determine what to do about it. The speech pathologist consults with the teacher, getting more information about the observed behavior, and makes additional observations. The consultant then uses her expertise in speech pathology to address the teacher's questions.

In another instance, a speech pathologist provides individual therapy for a preschool child who has articulation errors or fluency disorders. The speech pathologist wants to know how these speech patterns are affecting the child's social development as well as performance in pre academic skills such as letter naming and sound discrimination. The speech pathologist asks the teacher to serve as a consultant regarding this issue, and the preschool teacher provides the information requested.

Problem Solving with Collaboration.   The preschool teacher and the speech pathologist are both concerned about a child's generalization of speech skills learned in speech therapy sessions. The two teachers meet to discuss their mutual concern. Both parties discuss their observations and engage in problem-solving activities to identify the problem clearly and select possible solutions. Both parties agree to make some changes in their respective settings to solve the problem. If the solutions do not work, they are committed to try other possibilities.

In another situation, a teacher of students with behavioral disorders, along with the school counselor, three classroom teachers, and a student's parents, meet to discuss the behavior of that student. The individuals involved in the meeting engage in problem solving to formulate a plan for addressing the problem. Each individual has a role to play in implementing the plan.

Problem Solving with Teamwork.   A special education teacher and a general classroom teacher engage in co-teaching, a form of teamwork unique to classroom settings. The teachers meet weekly to engage in co-planning. During the co-planning they decide when, where, and how to share responsibilities for meeting the instructional needs of all students in the classroom during a specified class period each day. Each teacher uses his or her areas of expertise and strength whenever feasible. The co-teachers come to consensus on evaluation systems and assign grades for all students by mutual agreement. They no longer speak of "my students" or "your students" and instead they speak of, plan for, and teach "our students."

In another situation, a team of professionals provides services for severely and profoundly disabled infants and toddlers. Each professional has an area of expertise and responsibility. The social worker has the leadership role because she is responsible for most family contacts and often goes into homes to provide additional assistance for families. The nurse takes responsibility for monitoring the physical well-being of each child and keeps in close contact with other medical personnel and families. The speech pathologist works with the children to develop speech and language skills. The occupational therapist is responsible for teaching the children self-help skills. The physical therapist follows through with the medical doctor's prescribed physical therapy. Special education teachers provide language stimulation and modeling, coordinate schedules, and facilitate communication among the team, which meets twice weekly to discuss individual cases.

THE TEN-STEP PROCESS FOR COLLABORATIVE SCHOOL CONSULTATION

Now that the fundamentals of problem identification, options, consequences, and solution finding have been discussed, and distinctions among problem solving with (1) a major focus on consultation, (2) problem solving that emphasizes collaboration, and (3) problem solving with a team have been described, the ten-step process for collaborative school consultation will be introduced. This process, outlined in Figure 5.2, can help consultants and consultees communicate effectively and coordinate their efforts efficiently so that they can successfully identify educational problems and design programs for students' needs.

Step 1: Preparing for the Consultation

As consultants plan and prepare for consultation and collaboration, they focus on the major areas of concern. They prepare helpful materials and organize them in order to use collaborative time efficiently. It is useful to distribute information beforehand so that valuable interaction time is not consumed reading new material. But they must take care to present that

FIGURE 5.2   The Ten-Step Process for Collaborative School Consultation

1. Prepare for the consultation.
   1.1 Focus upon major topic or area of concern.
   1.2 Prepare and organize materials.
   1.3 Prepare several possible actions or strategies.
   1.4 Arrange for a comfortable, convenient meeting place.

2. Initiate the consultation.
   2.1 Establish rapport.
   2.2 Identify the agenda.
   2.3 Focus on the tentatively defined concern.
   2.4 Express interest in the needs of all.

3. Collect and organize relevant information.
   3.1 Make notes of data, soliciting from all.
   3.2 Combine and summarize the data.
   3.3 Assess data to focus on areas needing more information.
   3.4 Summarize the information.

4. Isolate the problem.
   4.1 Focus on need.
   4.2 State what the problem is.
   4.3 State what it is not.
   4.4 Propose desirable circumstances.

5. Identify concerns and realities about the problem.
   5.1 Encourage all to listen to each concern.
   5.2 Identify issues, avoiding jargon.
   5.3 Encourage ventilation of frustrations and concerns.
   5.4 Keep focusing on the pertinent issues and needs.
   5.5 Check for agreement.

6. Generate solutions.
   6.1 Engage in collaborative problem-solving.
   6.2 Generate several possible options and alternatives.
   6.3 Suggest examples of appropriate classroom modifications.
   6.4 Review options, discussing consequences of each.
   6.5 Select the most reasonable alternatives.

7. Formulate a plan.
   7.1 Designate those who will be involved, and how.
   7.2 Set goals.
   7.3 Establish responsibilities.
   7.4 Generate evaluation criteria and methods.
   7.5 Agree on a date for reviewing progress.
   7.6 Follow through on all commitments.

8. Evaluate progress and process.
   8.1 Conduct a review session at a specified time.
   8.2 Review data and analyze the results.
   8.3 Keep products as evidence of progress.
   8.4 Make positive, supportive comments.
   8.5 Assess contribution of the collaboration.

9. Follow through and follow up on the consultation about the situation.
   9.1 Reassess periodically to assure maintenance.
   9.2 Provide positive reinforcement.
   9.3 Plan further action or continue the plan.
   9.4 Adjust the plan if there are problems.
   9.5 Initiate further consultation if needed.
   9.6 Bring closure if goals have been met.
   9.7 Support effort and reinforce results.
   9.8 Share information where it is wanted.
   9.9 Enjoy the communication.

10. Repeat or continue consultation as appropriate.

(Peggy Dettmer, Norma Dyck, & Kari Woods)

material as tentative and still open to discussion. It is not always expedient to plan in great detail prior to consultations. Sometimes consultations happen informally and without notice—between classes, during lunch periods, or on playgrounds. While educators usually will want to accommodate colleagues on these occasions, they also need to look beyond them for opportunities to engage in more in-depth sessions.

Consultants need to give each collaborator enough advance notice and time to prepare. They will want to provide convenient and comfortable settings for the interaction, arranging seating so there is a collegial atmosphere with no phone or drop-by interruptions. Serving coffee and tea can help set congenial, collegial climates for meetings.

Step 2: Initiating the Consultation

Consultants need to exert much effort in this phase. When resistance to consulting is high, or the teaching staff has been particularly reluctant to collaborate, it is difficult to establish first contacts. This is the time to begin with the most receptive staff members in order to build in success for the consulting program. Rapport is established by addressing every consultee as special and expressing interest in what each one is doing and feeling. Teachers should be encouraged to talk about their successes. The consultant needs to display sensitivity to teachers' needs and make each one feel important. The key is to *listen.*

The consultant will want to identify the agenda and keep focusing on the concern. It is helpful to have participants write down their concerns before the meeting and bring them along. Then the consultant can check quickly for congruence and major disagreements.

Step 3: Collecting and Organizing Information

The data should be relevant to the issue of focus. However, data which might seem irrelevant to one person may be the very information needed to identify the real problem. So the consultant must be astute in selecting appropriate data that include many possibilities but do not waste time or resources. This becomes easier with experience, but for new consultants, having too much information is probably better than having too little.

Since problem identification seems to be the most significant factor in planning for special needs, it is wise to gather sufficient data from multiple sources. A case study method of determining data sources and soliciting information is particularly effective in planning for students who have special learning and behavior needs. See Figure 5.3 for a case-study format that recognizes up to 16 data sources of information for problem-solving to address a student's needs. The more of the 16 that are tapped, the more easily and clearly the need is identified.

Step 4: Isolating the Problem

As discussed earlier, the most critical aspect of problem solving is identifying and defining the problem at hand. Bolton (1986) emphasizes that consultants and consultees must define the problem by focusing on the need, not the handy solution. Without problem identification, problem-solving cannot occur (Bergan, 1995; Bergan & Tombari, 1976). The most common problem-solving error is to short circuit the problem definition step and hasten to traditional solutions rather than developing individually tailored solutions (Conoley, 1989, p. 248). Henning-Stout (1994) notes that less experienced consultants in particular tend to spend insufficient time with the consultee on the nature of the problem and proceed too quickly to developing "the plan."

Step 5. Identifying Concerns and Stating Realities Relevant to the Problem

All concerns and viewpoints related to the problem should be aired and shared by each participant. A different viewpoint is not better or worse, just different. An effective consultant keeps participants focusing on the student need by listening and encouraging everyone to respond. However, a certain amount of venting and frustration is to be expected and accepted. Teachers and parents will demonstrate less resistance when they know they are free to express their feelings without retaliation or judgment. Consultants should remain nonjudgmental and assure confidentiality, always talking and listening in consultees' language.

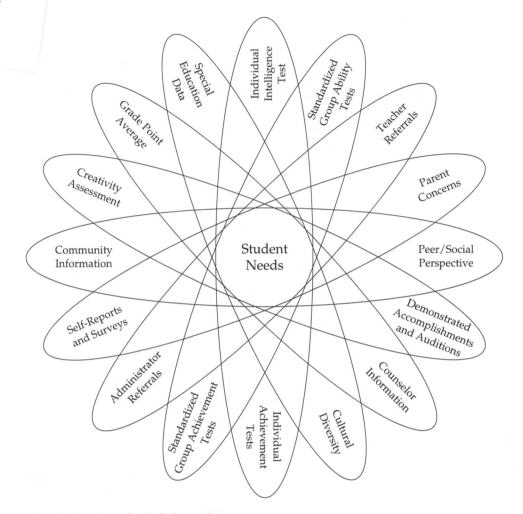

FIGURE 5.3   Case Study Information

As information is shared, the consultant will want to make notes. It is good to have everyone look over the recorded information from time to time during the consultation as a demonstration of trust and equality, as well as a check on accuracy. (A log format for recording information and documenting the consultation will be provided in Chapter 6.)

Step 6: Generating Solutions

Now is the time for creative problem solving. If ideas do not come freely, or if participants are blocking productive thinking, the consultant might lead the group in trying one or more of the techniques described later in the chapter. A problem-solving technique not only unleashes ideas, it sends a message about the kind of behavior that is needed to solve the problem. "Straw votes" can be taken periodically if that helps the group keep moving toward solutions. "Thinking outside the box" and combining ideas are desirable processes at this stage. Two productive activities are to have brief discussions focusing on benefits and on concerns. These two sharing periods should be initiated with the word stems "I like. . . ." (where the benefits are shared), and "I wish . . ." or "How to . . . ?" (where the concerns are shared). At this stage the group should modify, dismiss, or problem solve for each concern.

Step 7: Formulating the Plan

After solutions have been generated, wishes and concerns aired, and modifications made, the revised solution is ready to be formulated into a plan. Participants must remain on task. They need to be reinforced positively for their contributions. Consultants will want to be ready to make suggestions, but they should defer presenting them so long as others are suggesting and volunteering. They must avoid offering solutions prematurely or addressing too many issues at one time. Other unhelpful behaviors are assuming the supervisor/expert role, introducing one's own biases, and making suggestions that conflict with existing values in the school context.

As the plan develops, the consultant must make clear just who will do what, and when, and where. Evaluation criteria and methods that are congruent with the goals and plan should be developed at this time, and arrangements made for assessment and collection of data on student progress. A vital element to success in collaborative problem-solving will be the commitment by *all* participants to follow through with the plan, which will appear as Step 9.

Step 8: Evaluating Progress and Process

This step and the final two steps frequently are overlooked. Consultation and collaboration experiences should be followed by assessment of student progress resulting from the collaborative plan, and also by evaluation of the collaborative consultation process itself. Several figures in Chapter 6 are useful for this purpose.

The consultant will want to make positive, supportive comments while drawing closure to the interaction, and at that time can informally evaluate the consultation with consultee help, or formally evaluate by asking for brief written responses. This is a good time also to plan for future collaboration.

Step 9: Following Through and Following Up the Consultation

Of all ten steps, this may be the most neglected. Ineffective consultation often results from lack of follow-up service (Neel, 1981). It is in the best interest of the client, consultee, consultant, and future opportunities for consultation to reassess the situation periodically. Participants will want to adjust the student's program if necessary, and initiate further consultation if the situation seems to require it. Informal conversations with consultees at this point are very reinforcing. During the follow up, consultants have opportunities to make consultees feel good about themselves. They can make a point of noting improved student behaviors and performance, as well as positive effects that result from the collaboration. Also, they may volunteer to help if things are not going as smoothly as anticipated, or if consultees have further needs. The sweetest words a consultee can hear are, "What can I do to help you?" However, this question *must* be framed in the spirit of: "What can I do to help you *that you do not have the time and resources to do?*" and NOT as, "What can I do for you that you do not have the skill and expertise to accomplish?" Consultants should follow through immediately on all promises of materials, information, action, or further consultation, and take special steps to reinforce things that are going well. Figure 5.4 is an example of a form that could be used.

Step 10: Repeating the Consultation If Needed

Further consultation and collaboration may be needed if the plan is not working, or if one or more parties believes the problem was not identified appropriately. On the other hand, consultation also may be repeated and extended when things are going well. The obvious rationale here is that if one interaction helped, more will help further. This is very reinforcing for processes of consultation, collaboration, and teamwork. It encourages others to participate in the consultation and collaboration activity.

FIGURE 5.4   Memo to Follow Through on Collaborative Consultation/Teamwork

From: _____ to _____
                    (consultant)   (consultee/s)

Date: _____ Re: _____

I am eager to follow through on the plan which we developed on the date above, and also to assist in other ways that may have occurred to you since then.

How do you feel things have progressed since that time? Please be forthright.

_____

_____

What else may I do to help?

_____

_____

                                        (List here any times, descriptions, etc., that would
                                        help me respond specifically to your needs.)

_____   Information   _____

_____   Resources   _____

_____   Meet again   _____

_____   Classroom visit   _____

_____   Conference with: _____

Thank you so much! I enjoy working with you to serve our students and schools.

What to Say during the Consultation

The ten-step consultation procedure, committed to memory or stapled into one's plan book, is a good organizational tool and a reassuring resource for the consultant, particularly for those engaging in their first consultations. Of course, the consultant does not want to parrot points from an outline as though reading from a manual for programming a videocassette machine! But by practicing verbal responses that are helpful at each step, it will become more natural and automatic to use facilitative phrases when the need arises. Each number for the phrase sets below corresponds to a numbered step of the ten-step consultation process outlined above.

1. *When planning the consultation.* (Comments in this step are made to oneself.)

   (What styles of communication and interaction can I expect with these consultees?)

   (Have I had previous consultations with them and if so, how did these go?)

   (Do I have any perceptions at this point about client needs? If so, can I keep them under wraps while soliciting responses from others?)

   (What kinds of information might help with this situation?)

2. *When initiating the consultation.* (In this step and the rest of the steps, say to the consultee—)

   You're saying that. . . .

   The need seems to be. . . .

   May we work together along these lines . . . ?

   So the situation is. . . .

   I am aware that . . .

   What can we do in regard to your request/situation. . . .?

3. *When collecting information*

   Tell me about that. . . .

   Uh-huh. . . .

   What do you see as the effects of . . . ?

   Let's see now, your views/perceptions about this are. . . .

   Tell me more about the background of. . . .

   Sounds tough. . . .

   To summarize our basic information then,. . . .

4. *When isolating the problem*

   The major factors we have brought out seem to be. . . .

   Are we asking the right questions?

   What do you perceive is the greatest need for . . . ?

   What circumstances have you noted that may apply . . . ?

   Are there other parts to the need that we have not considered?

   So to summarize our perceptions at this point. . . .

   Are we in agreement that the major part of this issue is. . . .?

5. *When identifying the concerns and stating the realities*

   You say the major concern is. . . .

   How do you feel about this?

   But I also hear your concern about. . . .

   You'd like this situation changed so that. . . .

   How does this affect your day/load/responsibility. . . .?

   You are concerned about other students in your room. . . .

   What are some ways to get at . . . ?

   You're feeling . . . because of. . . .

   This problem seems formidable. Perhaps we can isolate part of it. . . .

   Would you say that . . . ?

   Perhaps we can't be sure about that. . . .

   The major factors we have brought out seem to be. . . .

   If you could change one thing, what would you change first?

6. *When generating possibilities*

   How does this affect the students/schedule/parents?

   Do we have a good handle on the nature of this situation?

   We need to define what we want to happen. . . .

   How would you like things to be?

   What has been tried so far?

   What happened then?

   Is this the best way to get it done? The only way?

   How could we do this more easily?

   Could we try something new such as . . . ?

   Could you add to what has been said?

   What limitations fall upon things we might suggest?

   Let's try to develop some ideas to meet the need. . . .

   Your idea of . . . also makes me think of. . . .

7. *When formulating a plan*

   Let's list the goals and ideas we have come up with.

   So, in trying . . . you'll be changing your approach of. . . .

   To implement these ideas, we would have to. . . .

   We have considered every possibility brought forth, so which shall it be?

   The actions in this situation would be different, because. . . .

   We've discussed both alternatives carefully and now it's time to choose.

   We need to break down the plan into steps. What should come first? Next?

   When is the best time to start with the first step?

8. *When evaluating progress*

   Have we got a solid plan?

   One way to measure progress toward the goals would be. . . .

   Some positive things have been happening. . . .

   How can we build upon these gains?

   Now we can decide where to go from here. . . .

   In what ways did our getting together help?

   I can see [the student] progress every day.

   You're accomplishing so much with. . . .

   How could I serve you and your students better?

9. *When following up and interacting with colleagues*

   How do you feel about the way things are going?

   We had set a time to get back together. Is that time still O.K., or should we make it sooner?

   I'm interested in the progress you have observed.

   I'm following up on that material/action I promised.

   I just stopped by. . . .

   Since we bumped into each other. . . .

   I wondered how things have been going for you.

   How are things in your corner of the world these days?

   I'm glad you've hung in there with this problem.

   You've accomplished a lot, which can be overlooked when you're with it every day.

   You know, progress like this makes teachers look very good!

10. *If repeating the consultation*

    Should we have another go at discussing . . . ?

    Perhaps we overlooked some information that would help. . . .

    We got so much accomplished last time. How about getting together again to . . . ?

    That's a fine progress report. Would another plan session produce even more fantastic results?

■ ■ ■ ■ ■

APPLICATION 5.1
USING THE TEN-STEP CONSULTING PROCESS

1. Select one or more of the following situations and simulate a school consultation experience, using the ten-step process and any of the application phrases that seem appropriate:

   Situation A: A ninth-grade student is considered lazy by former teachers, has failed several courses, and cannot grasp math concepts. He has difficulty locating information but can read and understand most material at his grade level. He is never prepared for class, seldom has pencil and paper, and loses his assignments. Yet he is pleasant, seemingly eager to please, and will try things in a one-to-one situation. His classroom teachers say he will not pass, and you have all decided to meet about this. How will you, the learning disabilities consulting teacher, address the situation?

Situation B: You are attending an IEP meeting on behalf of a third-grade student who is emotionally disturbed and classified as having borderline mental retardation. You believe she should be placed in a general classroom with supportive counseling service and re-evaluated in a year. The other staff participants feel she should have been in special education placement with mainstreaming into music, art, and physical education. The mother is confused about the lack of agreement among school personnel. How will you address the concerns of all in this situation, particularly the mother?

Situation C: A sixth-grade student's mother is known as a perfectionist. Her son, who has been identified for the gifted program, did not receive all A's on the last report card, and she has requested a conference with you as the classroom teacher, the principal, and the school psychologist. How will you address this situation?

Situation D: A first-year kindergarten teacher has learned that one of her students will be a child with cerebral palsy. Although the child's history to date has included continuous evaluation, home teaching, group socialization experiences, special examinations, and therapy sessions as well as family counseling for three years, the teacher is nervous about her responsibilities with this child. As the speech pathologist, how will you build her confidence in caring for the kindergartner's language needs, and her skill in helping the child to develop her potential?

Situation E: The special education director and middle-school building administrator have been asked by a group of general education teachers and special education teachers to meet with them. The director and the principal sense that this group has been chosen informally by the entire teaching staff to be their spokespersons. They know that these teachers and their colleagues are caring and conscientious educators. The representative group wants to discuss the grave concerns they have about including all students with special needs in the high-stakes standardized tests to be given in a few weeks. As they voice the concerns, ask how best to prepare the students for these tests, and question what is to be done with the results of the tests, how might the special education director and building administrator react and respond?

What to Consider if Group Problem Solving Is Not Successful

There is no universal agreement on what makes consultation effective, and little empirical support exists to guide consultants as to what should be said and done in consultation (Gresham & Kendell, 1987; Heron & Kimball, 1988), However, the ten steps outlined above have worked well for many consultants and consulting teachers. If this method of ten steps does not work, consultants should ask several questions.

- Were feelings addressed?
- Was the problem defined accurately?
- Did all parties practice good listening skills?
- Were the nitty-gritty details worked out?
- Were any hidden agendas brought to light and handled?
- Were all participants appropriately assertive?
- Was the consultation process evaluated?

- Could any other problem-solving tools facilitate the process?
- Was there follow-up to the consultation?
- Should we convene in groups to practice problem-solving techniques?

■ ■ ■ ■ ■

APPLICATION 5.2
FOR A FURTHER CHALLENGE

As a team effort with several colleagues who share your grade level and subject area, construct a scenario to demonstrate the ten-step collaborative school consultation process at your teaching level and in your content area(s). Role-play it for others, stopping at key points—for example, after problem identification, and again after formulation of the plan, to ask the observing group what they might do at that point. If several promising alternatives are suggested, try each one and follow it to its conclusion, in the manner of the choose-an-adventure books that children like to read.

What techniques worked best? How did individual differences influence the consultation? Were these individual differences used constructively, and if not, what could have been done instead?

TOOLS FOR GROUP PROBLEM-SOLVING

In support of collaborative consultation in schools, Nevin, Thousand, Paolucci-Whitcomb, and Villa (1990) describe it as a process whereby teams with diverse expertise generate creative solutions to mutually defined problems. The collaborative format of working together and drawing upon collective expertise to solve problems is widely practiced in the business and professional world. In their efforts to use the best ideas of bright, innovative minds, astute leaders employ a number of group problem-solving techniques. These techniques allow individuals to extend their own productive thinking powers and enhance those of their colleagues by participating in structured group problem solving activities. However, such techniques are yet to be relied on to much extent in educational settings, where autonomy and self-sufficiency have traditionally been more convenient than collaboration and teamwork.

One innovative proposal for developing collaboration skills is one of the most frequently used problem solving activities in the public school—the IEP process. The shared thinking in which the interactive IEP team engages is a collaborative method of solving problems (Clark, 2000).

Simulated IEP conferences might be used as staff development tools for enhancing consultation and collaboration as members of the IEP team. The team could be assigned to develop an Individual Educational Plan for an imaginary colleague wanting to do an advanced, independent study on the subject of autism and then share the information with others in the district. They would collaborate in assigned roles—family member, facilitator of the study, and special subject (autism in this case) instructor. As they prepared the statement of level of performance (capability and motivation toward completing the program while working full-time), justification for placement (ability and need to do an independent study), "annual goals," measurable objectives, due dates with persons responsible for support, and evaluation methods, they would be collaborating as a caring team of home and school members.

Another way to incorporate IEPs into problem solving, with great promise for benefiting overworked teachers, is to identify and implement ways that electronic technology can expedite efficient IEP development, revisions, and storage. The use of technology-based IEPs and the impact of student-led IEPs were featured as preconvention workshops at the Council for Exceptional Children annual conference in April, 2001.

A great number of easy-to-use problem-solving techniques suitable for group participation are available. These include, but certainly are not limited to: brainstorming, lateral thinking, Six-Thinking Hat Thinking, concept mapping, idea checklists, and metaphorical thinking. Others include: jigsaw, reciprocal teaching, compare and contrast, SCAMPER, Plus-Minus-Interesting, role play, TalkWalk, and more. Many teachers have incorporated these kinds of group problem solving activity into their curriculum planning for students often, but have overlooked the potential that the techniques have for collaborating with adults more effectively and pleasurably. We will present a few brief descriptions and application activities here.

Brainstorming

Brainstorming is a mainstay of creative problem-solving methodology. It facilitates generating many unique ideas. When a group is brainstorming, participants should be relaxed and having fun. There are no right or wrong responses during the process, because problems seldom have only one right approach. No one may critique an idea during the brainstorming process. All ideas are accepted as plausible and regarded as potentially valuable. Each idea is shared and recorded. In large group sessions, it is most efficient to have a leader for managing the oral responses, and a recorder for getting them down on a board or chart visible to all.

The well-known rules developed by Osborn (1963) for brainstorming are:

1. Do not criticize any ideas at this time.
2. The more wild and zany the ideas, the better.
3. Think up as many ideas as possible.
4. Try to combine two or more ideas into new ones.
5. Hitchhike (piggyback) on another's idea. A person with a hitchhike idea should be called on before those who have unrelated ideas.

Note that when coaching others (children in particular) in brainstorming techniques, it is good to introduce them to the "humanitarian principle" before the very first session. This means that no idea will be accepted if it is obviously harmful to others. So, a response to "What are new ways to use old bricks?" that came out as "To drown kittens," (typically followed by a pause for chuckles or shocked expressions from peers along with quick glances to observe teacher reaction), would be answered by a brief but firm "Sorry, we abide by the humanitarian principle here." Then the teacher could move quickly on without accepting that idea, and yet would remain true to rules 1 and 2 of a brainstorm activity.

Brainstorming is useful when the group wishes to explore as many alternatives as possible and defer evaluation of the ideas until the options have been exhausted. People who can not resist the urge to critique ideas during brainstorming must be reminded that evaluation comes later. Leaders should call on volunteers quickly.

When the flow of ideas slows, it is good to persevere a while longer. Often the second wave of thoughts will contain the most innovative suggestions. Each participant should be encouraged to contribute.

■ ■ ■ ■ ■

APPLICATION 5.3
USING THE BRAINSTORM TECHNIQUE

A brainstorming session would be appropriate for this situation: A first-grade student has read just about every book in the small, rural school. The first-grade teacher and gifted program facilitator brainstorm possibilities for enhancing this student's reading options and augmenting the school's resources as well.

Lateral Thinking

The conventional method of thinking is vertical thinking, in which one moves forward mentally by sequential and justifiable steps. Vertical thinking is logical and single-purposed, digging down more deeply into the same mental hole. Lateral thinking, on the other hand, digs a "thinking hole" in a different place. It moves out at an angle, so to speak, from vertical thinking to change direction, attitude, or approach so that the problem can be examined in a different way (deBono, 1986).

Lateral thinking should not replace vertical thinking, but complement it. While many educators emphasize vertical thinking at the expense of more divergent production, both are necessary to arrive at creative solutions for complex problems. The ability to use a lateral thinking mode by suspending judgments and generating alternatives should be cultivated by school personnel.

■ ■ ■ ■ ■

APPLICATION 5.4
USING THE LATERAL THINKING TECHNIQUE

Lateral thinking could be useful in this situation:

> A high school student with learning disabilities has a serious reading problem, but teachers in several classes are not willing to make adjustments. The teachers have not discussed any problems with you, the resource teacher, recently but the student has. How might you as consultant, and student as consultee, think of ways to approach the situation and modify classroom practices to help this student succeed? To think laterally, the consultant might regard the teachers as clients, and consult with the student about ways of reinforcing teachers when they *do* make things easier. The student would be modifying the behavior of teachers, in contrast to a vertical thinking tactic of asking teachers to modify student behavior.

Six Thinking Hat Thinking

This thinking tool also was developed by deBono as a nonargumentative and creative way to think through issues (deBono, 1985). Six colored hats—white, yellow, black, red, green, and blue—are "put on" as a way to encourage helpful kinds of thinking about a problem from many different angles. With the white hat on, participants gather information. The yellow hat is for looking at positives, values, and benefits. The red hat allows sharing of emotions and feelings about the issue. With the green hat, one can think "outside the box" for new possibilities. The blue hat is a management and procedures reminder. Finally, the black hat provides a devil's advocate perspective.

■ ■ ■ ■ ■ ▬▬▬▬▬▬▬▬▬▬▬▬▬▬▬▬▬▬▬▬▬▬▬▬▬▬▬▬▬▬▬▬▬▬▬

APPLICATION 5.5
THINKING WITH SIX HATS

Have fun in a group exploring all sides of a problem, for example, the pros and cons of the NCLB legislation, or the use of a particular technology with students who have disabilities, using Six Hat Thinking. Make paper hats to wear or hold up when one wishes to make a point, or when the leader calls for a particular hat-color perspective.

The hats also can be assembled into a bulletin board collage for display as a reminder to maximize different styles of thinking and responding to issues. This would be another practical example of the constructive use of adults' individual differences.

Concept Mapping

Concept mapping (referred to by some as mind-mapping, semantic mapping, webbing, or trees of knowledge or information) is a tool for identifying concepts, showing relationships among them, and reflecting upon the degree of generality and inclusiveness that envelopes them (Wesley & Wesley, 1990). The technique allows users to display ideas, link them together, elaborate upon them, add new information as it surfaces, and review the formulation of the ideas. The process begins with one word, or issue, written on paper or the chalkboard and enclosed in a circle. Then other circles of subtopics, ideas, words, and concepts are added to that central theme by lines or spokes that connect and interconnect where the concepts relate and interrelate. More and more possibilities and new areas open up as the webbing grows. Relationships and interrelationships that can help verbalize problems and interventions are recorded for all participants to see. If the concept map is left on display, the process can go on and on as more ideas are generated and added.

Concept mapping is taught to students for reading comprehension at all grade levels. Buzan (1983) offers strategies for mind mapping in which learning techniques such as note-taking can be structured to show interrelationships easily. Many students in gifted programs have been introduced to the concept of webbing to focus on a problem of interest and plan an independent study. Sometimes college students are encouraged to try mind-mapping by combining lecture notes and text reading to study for exams. Concept-mapping is a powerful tool. Not only is it useful for enhancing individual learning, but for leading to more meaningful and productive staff development (Bocchino, 1991). Figure 2.4 in Chapter 2 could be considered the initial stage of a concept map as it graphically portrays rudiments of a Resource/Consulting Teacher model. The figure could be developed further by extending the webbing with schedules, roles, resources, and interconnections.

■ ■ ■ ■ ■ ▬▬▬▬▬▬▬▬▬▬▬▬▬▬▬▬▬▬▬▬▬▬▬▬▬▬▬

APPLICATION 5.6
USING THE CONCEPT MAPPING TECHNIQUE

A classroom teacher has agreed to work with a student new to the district and identified as behavior-disordered. The student has acceptable social skills in some instances and is friendly and cooperative. But he also requires individual instruction, is working about two years below grade level, and makes remarks impulsively to other students, which give teachers cause for concern. During previous visits with the teacher, she indicated that things were going well. Now, in the middle of November, she asks to see you, as consultant for behavioral disorders, immediately. She is upset, saying things such as "It just isn't working," and "I've tried so hard," but she has not described the problem. How might concept-mapping or webbing help in this situation?

Idea Checklist

Checklists that suggest solutions for problems can be created from sources such as college texts, teaching manuals, and instructional media manuals. More unusual checklists include referral agency listings, gift catalog descriptions, instructional resource center guides, and even Yellow Pages sections of various directories. By asking a question, such as "How can we help Shawn improve in math proficiency?" and scanning a Yellow Pages section or an off-level teaching manual, new ideas may emerge. Several chapters of this book contain checklists for a variety of educational purposes.

■ ■ ■ ■ ■ ▬▬▬▬▬▬▬▬▬▬▬▬▬▬▬▬▬▬▬▬▬▬▬▬▬▬▬

APPLICATION 5.7
USING THE IDEA CHECKLIST

A high school sophomore, 17 years old and in the educable mental retardation program, is ready for a vocational training program. As EMR resource teacher, you believe the Vocational Rehabilitation Unit's four-month job training program would be the most appropriate program for the student. However, the parents feel very protective of their son and are concerned that the environment will be noncaring. They resist suggestions that he leave their home. How might an idea-checklist process help during this consultation?

Metaphorical Thinking

Metaphors are mental maps that permit the connection of different meanings through some shared similarity. They appear often in spoken and written communication. For example, the sentences "Life is a loom," "The fog swallowed the ship," and "Last June my flower garden was a paintbox of colors" are metaphorical. They connect unlike things in order to explain. People use metaphors to sort out their perceptions, evaluate, express feelings, and reflect on the purpose of things in order to make better sense of their world (Deshler, 1985).

The metaphor uses one subject to strengthen and deepen the understanding of another. As staff development tools, metaphors can guide groups in change processes. They are useful to generate new ideas, and teach new concepts (Garmston, 1994). Pollio (1987) suggests that some of the most important scientific, philosophical, and technical insights were conceived from an imaginative image. One of his examples is Einstein seeing himself as a passenger on a light ray and holding a mirror in front of him, an image that helped him form the theory of relativity.

In similar, albeit less dramatic fashion, educators can use metaphors to connect two different viewpoints so one idea can be understood by means of the other. Metaphorical thinking, and the process of developing positive metaphors for education, can stimulate creative problem solving by school personnel.

■ ■ ■ ■ ■

APPLICATION 5.8
EXPLORING THE POWER OF METAPHORICAL THINKING

With a group of your colleagues generate free-association responses to open-ended phrases such as, "Life is a _____." (e.g., Zoo. Journey. Pressure cooker. Bank. Car lot. Battle. Party.) "School is a _____." (e.g, Prison. Twelve-act play. Family. Game.) A second part of the activity is to continue on from that image, e.g., "If life is a *zoo,* then teachers are _____, and students are _____." "If school is a twelve-act play, students are _____, teachers are _____, principals are _____." Open-ended phrases then could move to topics such as "Team teaching is like _____, and teachers are the _____." "Inservice days are a _____ (battery charge?) and teachers are the (dead batteries now all charged up?)." (Metaphors can be served as tart lessons sweetened with humor and a twist of wry!)

Other Collaborative Activities

A number of collaborative activities for children's learning are just as promising for facilitating interchange, reciprocity, and a community of learning among adults (Brown, 1994).

Jigsaw.   Participants in this learning method developed by Aronson (1978) undertake independent, collaborative research on a topic of mutual interest. The technique can be used by a school faculty, a school district staff, or other group of teachers and area specialists to find background material and possible alternatives for solutions to academic and behavioral problems. The group decides on the central theme(s) of the issue and several subtopics. Then the large group divides into smaller groups. Each small group conducts research on one subtopic and shares that knowledge by teaching it to others. In this way all have a part in the problem solving. Time and energy of busy professionals are used to maximum benefit. Redundancy of effort is minimized. Most importantly, a collaborative synergy develops that improves their ability to problem-solve in other situations.

Reciprocal Teaching.   In reciprocal teaching, six or so participants form a group and each member takes a turn leading a discussion about an article, video, position paper, staff development presentation, or other material they have read and want to understand more fully. The leader begins with a question and summarizes the discussion at the end. Clarification for understanding and predictions about future content can be requested by the leader when appropriate (Brown, 1994). With this technique, group cooperation helps ensure understanding by all members, with the less well-informed learning from those who are more knowledgeable.

One example of using reciprocal teaching could be to have a team of teachers read relevant material and then explore possibilities for adapting classroom settings to accommodate students with attention deficit and hyperactivity disorder. The synergistic discussion may open new avenues for addressing this complex concern.

Compare and Contrast.   Each small group identifies terms and phrases that define differing perspectives of an issue—for example, reading methods, math methods, tracking or mainstreaming, inclusion or pull-out programs, graded or ungraded systems. One compare-and-contrast session might draw out aspects of the two-part item, "what general classroom teachers don't know about special ed curriculum, and what special ed teachers don't know about general curriculum." An organization of the results completes the exchange, with all participants leaving the session more informed and reflective about the issues. A technique such as brainstorming or POCS could be employed during a later staff development event to make use of compare-and-contrast findings.

SCAMPER.   The SCAMPER technique was developed by Eberle (1984) as a built-in mnemonic device to brainstorm in practical situations. For example, using SCAMPER to preplan a transition program for a teen with mental retardation from school into a work area could create a number of possibilities: S, what can be substituted?; C what can be combined?; A, what adaptations?; M, how modified, magnified, multiplied, or minified?; P, how put to other uses or purposes?; E, what could be eliminated?; and R, how could things be rearranged or interchanged?

Plus-Minus-Interesting.   This simple process can be completed in a half-hour or so, often stimulating rearrangement of perspectives and sometimes recasting values placed on those perspectives. As an example, in a school considering the use of active senior citizens as reading aides, the collaborative team would generate a three-part list of the pluses, the minuses, and things which are interesting and which the team would like to investigate further before making a decision. It is not necessary that the pluses exceed the minuses, and sometimes the interesting feature may ultimately be determined as the most promising. The discussion which PMI instigates can assist problem solving (deBono, 1973).

Role-Play.   A fundamental purpose of role-playing as a problem solving practice is to produce new perspectives. For example, in a teacher-parent conflict, the teacher would take the role of the parent, and the parent that of the teacher. Participants have specific parts to play. At a critical part in the interaction the leader stops the players and has the whole group explore options that would be possible from that point. Then new solutions may emerge (Torrance & Safter, 1999). In role-playing the convener must be skilled and facilitative, so that the players participate intently without self-consciousness.

Concentric Circle or Fishbowl.   A small circle of participants discusses an issue while a larger circle on the outside of that one listens and then discusses. This technique encourages participation by members usually reticent to respond, and stimulates lively discussion. Issues must be well-chosen and articulated clearly to the group.

In-basket Techniques. These are simulations of situations that may come to the consulting teacher's mailbox or message board. The basket contains requests or questions that need action. Since there are typically no right or wrong answers, the technique is good for engaging in a multiperspective discussion during which the teacher describes the situation and invites input. General issues that do not require confidentiality would be most suitable for this approach.

Case Studies. Problems gleaned from professional literature or composed by participants are given to the group. Members react to the question "What seems to be going on here?" and then prepare individual plans or one group plan for next steps. One member coordinates discussion of the various plans to enhance the group's flexibility in problem solving.

Role Rotation. Here the participants have the opportunity to consider the issue in question from a completely different perspective. For example, a classroom teacher might participate as an administrator. A learning disabilities consultant could take the role of a parent. Application 1.1 in Chapter 1 is an exercise that lends itself to role rotation.

TalkWalk. In this unique form of small-group interaction the participants engage in collegial dialogue focused on instructional and curricular issues while they walk together in an open environment (Caro & Robbins, 1991). The fresh air, physical and mental exercise, and exploration of ideas leads to free thinking and expression. This technique can be used as part of a workshop or simply as an informal arrangement among colleagues.

Caro and Robbins suggest that groups of two or three work best. TalkWalk provides educators with 4 Es for problem solving: *Expertise* from collective experience; *Enrichment* to improve sense of self-worth and problem-solving capacity; *Expediency* to obtain rapid solutions through assistance; *Exercise* to bring a fresh attitude and perspective to the problem. One walk, for example, might focus on the group's vision for students who are in transition from school to work and independent living. An outcome of the talk could be a plan that will help make the vision become real.

Finding Solutions to Problems Using Multiple Intelligences

One unique way to generate many perspectives and, perhaps, arrive at some clever solutions for problems is to frame the questions in terms of Gardner's (1993) well-known multiple intelligence categories. For example, to build interest, rapport, and skills for team-teaching among staff with no experience doing it, these questions could help with planning efforts:

Linguistic: How can we use words and stories to describe team-teaching?

Logical–mathematical: How might we measure the benefits and drawbacks of a team-teaching approach in our school?

Musical: Should we create a team song or cheer?

Spatial: Should we make a physical map of where everything will be and what more, or less, we should include in the spaces we will share?

Interpersonal: What kinds of differences in interests, preferences, values, and personal habits would be important to discuss before embarking on a team-teaching mission?

Intrapersonal: How would I describe my feelings about giving up some of my professional autonomy and sharing many of my ideas and techniques?

Bodily–kinesthetic: How can we move throughout the room, arrange materials, and get students' attention when we are teaching together in the same spaces?

Naturalistic: Will our school environment accommodate team-teaching so that students are comfortable, parents are satisfied, and teachers are positive about the experience?

Interaction Formats

Collaborating consultants will want to know how to set up a variety of group formats for stimulating interaction among professionals. (See Figure 5.5) Some of the most useful ones are as follows.

Buzz groups.   Buzz groups work well in a group of 50 or fewer. This format ensures total participation and is easy to set up. The leader presents a topic or problem, provides minimal directions for subgrouping by twos or threes, and invites everyone to consider all aspects of the problem in the time allowed. The main disadvantage is a high noise level if the physical space is small.

Huddles.   Huddles work best with groups of five or six discussants. The leader arranges the groups, defines the topic, announces the time limit (six minutes works well), and gives

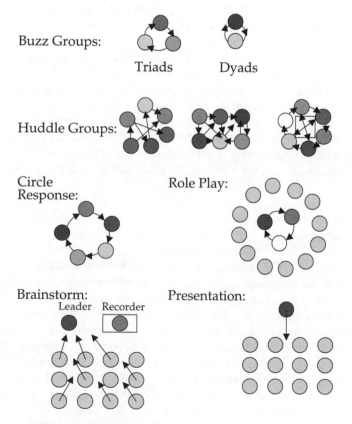

FIGURE 5.5   Interaction Structures

a two-minute warning that time is expiring. Each group designates its own reporter. The leader usually passes from group to group facilitating and encouraging if needed. In this structure the participants tend to build on colleagues' contributions. The reporting process can vary, from a simple "most important points" to ranking of major points, to a written summary that is collected by the leader.

Circle Response.   Small groups of collaborators sit in a circle. The designated leader begins by stating or reiterating the topic. The response pattern moves to the left, with each taking a turn or saying "I pass." At the end of a stipulated time, the leader summarizes the ideas and integrated thinking of the group.

Others.   An enterprising consultant also could consider structured role play, a structured or unstructured interview forum, reader's theater, research-and-report, and a film talk-back session as ways of encouraging interaction and information exchange among educators.

THEMES THAT CAN INTERFERE

Caplan (1970) proposed that consultants' difficulties in dealing with clients' problems usually are caused by any one, or all, of four interfering themes. These themes are conflicts related to life experiences which can interfere with problem solving and are difficult to address because of their negative effects (Caplan & Caplan,1993). They are:

- Lack of knowledge about the problem and its conditions: The educator may not have the knowledge needed to address student needs and related factors.
- Lack of skill to approach the problem in appropriate ways: A teacher may not have the skills or resources needed to deal with student problems.
- Lack of self-confidence in dealing with the problem: Due to inexperience, self-doubt, or even fatigue or illness, the teacher may lack confidence and self-esteem.
- Lack of professional objectivity in approaching the problem: This may cause problems for an educator in assessing and handling the teaching or learning situation (Sandoval, 1996).

Collaborative school consultation is a viable arena in which to address these four themes that threaten to interfere with the educator's ability to serve student needs. For example, some teachers might show lack of knowledge by over- or under-identifying students for special education because of stereotypical thinking. Others show lack of skill by failing to modify curriculum for those with disabilities, or by inappropriately using a strategy such as cooperative learning. Lack of confidence can generate resistance to new plans and inflexibility toward new ideas. Lack of objectivity is demonstrated when educators equate student situations to another situation in their own lives or to former students and their situations.

When collaborating, consultants should use every opportunity to reinforce the efforts and successes of classroom teachers and also to convey a desire to learn from them and their experiences. Too often classroom teachers, the ones occupying the lowest position in an hierarchy of specialists (Pugach, 1988), and parents, who can be somewhat removed from the school setting, are overlooked when possibilities for solutions to learning and behavior problems are explored.

When communicating and cooperating with consultees to identify the learning or behavior need, it is important that consultants avoid sending messages intimating that classroom teachers and parents are deficient in skills that only special education teachers can provide (Friend & Cook, 1990; Huefner, 1988; Idol, Paolucci-Whitcomb, & Nevin, 1986). Nurturance of communication skills and cooperative attitudes will encourage feelings of parity and voluntariness among all school personnel and parents during the problem-solving process. Students assigned to resource settings in other schools for part of the week or school day may have teachers there who never communicate about them and their work. This is a serious drawback to some cluster group arrangements where students travel from one school to another with no planned interaction among school personnel taking place.

Coordination of collaborative effort is vital. Special education teachers who cannot identify basal reading curriculum used in various levels, and classroom teachers who cannot identify the nature of instruction taking place in the resource room, make problem identification more difficult (Idol, West, & Lloyd, 1988). Their lack of shared knowledge may even intensify the problem. All parties must think about their own roles in the problem situation, and endeavor to learn from each other by interacting, deferring judgment, and coordinating their services.

A team approach is a productive way to assess the context, conditions, interfering themes, and circumstances surrounding the student's needs and the school programs designed to meet those needs. It has been noted that astronomers from all parts of the world collaborate often because there is no one place from which every part of their "work area," the sky, can be observed. This analogy applies to educators and parents as they address each child's total needs in the cognitive, affective, physical, and social domains to develop learning and behavior goals.

Those goals become building blocks for decision making. Without goals, decision making is like a hammer without nails. Educators have long-range and short-term goals. Students have Individual Education Plans (IEPs) with yearly goals and short-term goals. Schools have mission statements and educational aims. Both school aims and student goals should be used for making decisions in educational environments. A goal motivates action and provides direction for that action. Reviewing goals helps educators stay focused and sort out the things that are important from those that are not.

Hurdles to Overcome

Educators with experience as consultants describe several problems that can interfere with the success of consultation, collaboration, or teamwork among educators. By recognizing them as possibilities but not necessarily expecting them to occur, consulting teachers can be ready to sidestep or step over potential hurdles such as:

- Loss of touch with the students when not in direct service with them
- Uncertainty about what and how to communicate with those who resist or resent collaboration
- Being regarded as a teacher's aide, "go-fer," or quick-fix expert
- Having consultation regarded as a tutorial for students
- Territoriality of school personnel
- Rigid curriculum and assessment procedures
- Unrealistic expectations (either too high or too low) toward the role

- Not having enough information or appropriate materials to share
- Being perceived as a show-off, or a bossy expert, or an interloper
- Running into veils of professional politeness that shield consultees from genuine commitment
- Difficulty managing time and resources, which often happens
- Lack of training for the role
- An excessive caseload that short-circuits effectiveness
- Too many "hats" to wear in the role
- Most of all, resistance of colleagues toward change of any kind

Knowing the potential hurdles can help educators keep them from becoming insurmountable barriers by ensuring that there are role delineation, a consultation framework, adequate evaluation of the process, and careful preparation to develop the necessary skills. Some of the mystique surrounding special education and support services is reduced when classroom teachers become familiar with the techniques and are led to appreciate and understand special education roles.

■ ■ ■ ■ ■

APPLICATION 5.9
POSITIVE AND NOT-SO-POSITIVE CONSULTATIONS

Assess which of the following consultation contacts were positive and which were not so positive. Why were the positive consultations successful? Why were some of them less successful than the consultant and consultee wished? What might have been done to improve the outcome? What still might be done?

1. Primary level teachers and I sat down and discussed what materials they thought would be good to order and place in the resource room, for their use as well as mine. Everyone had a chance to share needs, express opinions, and make recommendations.
2. An undergraduate asked me about my student teaching and substituting days. She was feeling very down and unsure of her teaching abilities. I reassured her by telling of some things that had happened to me (and why). I encouraged her to find a dependable support system, and gave her some ideas and things to think about.
3. A kindergarten child was staffed into my program, but the teacher wouldn't let me take her out of "her" class time. So I arranged to keep the child after school. The first night I was late coming to fetch the child, and the teacher blew up about it.
4. The music teacher asks students who cannot read to stand up in class and read, and then pokes fun at them. I approached the teacher about the situation, but the teacher wanted nothing to do with me, and after that made things worse for the students.
5. One of the teachers I have spent several weeks with stopped me in the hall yesterday to ask for an idea to use in her class that next hour. Before she finished putting her question into words, she thought of an idea herself, and she still thanked me!
6. In visiting with the principal about alternatives in altering classroom assignments, it ended with his screaming at me for finding fault with his staff, which I had not done.

7. I give a sticker every day to a student with learning disabilities if he attends and does his work in the resource room. His classroom teacher complained to the principal because "other students work hard and don't get stickers."

8. I participated in a parent conference in which the parent wanted to kick the daughter out of the house and into a boarding school. It ended with the daughter agreeing to do more work at home, and the mother agreeing to spend one special hour a week just with her daughter.

TIPS FOR PROBLEM SOLVING THROUGH COLLABORATIVE CONSULTATION

1. Have materials and thoughts organized before consultations and develop a list of questions that will help ferret out the real problem.

2. Be prepared for the meeting with a checklist of information typically needed. Do not be reluctant to say that you do not have *the* answer. If it is something you should know, find out when you can and get back to the person who asked.

3. Have strategies and materials in mind that may be helpful to the situation, but do not try to have all the answers. This discourages involvement by others.

4. Do not offer solutions too readily, and try not to address too much or too many topics at once.

5. Avoid jargon, and shun suggestions that conflict with policies or favored teacher practices.

6. Make it a habit to look for something positive about the teacher, the class, and the student, and comment on those things. Use feedback as a vehicle that can provide *positive* information, not just negative comments.

7. Don't try to "fix it" if it is not "broken."

8. Don't wait for the consultee to make the first move. But do not expect that teachers will be enthused or flattered to have questions asked about their classrooms and teaching methods.

9. When a teacher asks for advice about a student, first ask what the teacher has already observed. This gets the teacher involved in the problem and encourages ownership in serving the student's special need. Whenever possible, use the terms *we* and *us,* not *I* and *you.*

10. Know how to interpret test results and how to discuss those results with educators, parents, and students.

11. When possible, provide parents with samples of the child's schoolwork to discuss during the conference. Refrain from talking while they peruse the materials. Have a list of resources ready to share with parents for help with homework, reinforcements, and study tips. When providing materials, explain or demonstrate their use, and then keep in touch so that no problems develop.

12. Maintain contact with teachers during the year. You may find that the teacher has detected an improvement that is directly related to your work, and this reinforcement will be valuable for you and your own morale.

13. Remember that minds, like parachutes, work best when they are open.

CHAPTER REVIEW

1. While many variants of a problem solving process exist, basic steps are similar for all. They include identifying the problem(s), generating options, analyzing consequences, and developing plans for solutions. When these steps have been taken, implementation of the plan and follow-up activity can occur.

2. Problem identification is the most critical phase of problem solving. Information from multiple sources, and collaborative input by a team of educators will help identify the real problem and facilitate its solution.

3. Ten important steps in a problem solving consultation are: planning; initiating the consultation; collecting information; identifying the problem; generating options and alternatives; formulating a plan; evaluating progress and process; following through and following up; interacting informally; and repeating if necessary.

4. Consultants will benefit from practicing key phrases to use during each phase of the consultation.

5. Divergent production of ideas during problem solving can be enhanced by the use of techniques and tools such as brainstorming, idea checklists, lateral thinking, Six Thinking Hat thinking, concept-mapping, idea checklists, and metaphorical thinking. Other tools for interaction include jigsaw, reciprocal teaching, compare-and-contrast, role-play, TalkWalk, and more. Teachers often use these techniques with students, but may overlook the possibilities they present for professional activity. Collegiality and collaboration are enhanced by the use of a variety of interaction formats such as buzz groups, huddle groups, circle responses, role-plays, panels, and interviews.

6. Themes identified by Caplan (1970) that can interfere with productive problem solving are lack of knowledge, lack of skill, lack of self-confidence, and lack of professional objectivity.

TO DO AND THINK ABOUT

1. When consultants introduce themselves to consultees, what are four or five things they can mention about themselves in order to develop rapport?

2. Discuss at least five things a consultant does *not* want to happen while consulting and collaborating, along with the conditions that might cause these unwanted events, and how the conditions might be avoided or overcome. Who has the most control over whether these unwanted events will or will not happen?

3. For a challenging assignment, select a school issue or student problem and create a method for engaging in consultation by designating a system, perspective, approach, prototype, mode, and model, as discussed in Chapter 2. Carry out the consultation as a role-play or simulation, using the ten steps and verbal responses provided in this chapter. In a "debriefing" session with your colleagues, discuss which parts of the consultation process were most difficult, some possible reasons, and what could be done to make the consultation successful.

4. Develop a file of humor and satire about consultation that would be helpful in developing rapport with colleagues or in getting a potentially difficult meeting off to a friendly start. For example, consider these, some of which are new and others that have been around for awhile.

   "The consultant is one who drives over from the central office and borrows your watch to tell you what time it is." Or, "The consulting type pulls up to a place, pops off, and pulls away." Or, in a pictorial spoof using the triadic model satirically, show a consultee leaning his arm over a high cliff in an attempt to save a client who is dangling precariously from a small tree limb. The consultee jerks his head toward the professional mountain-climber consultant just behind him and shouts down to the unfortunate client, "The expert here recommends that you not let go of my hand!" Then make a strong point that this is the way collaborative school consultation is *not* to happen!

Think of ways humor and satire can be used to the consulting teacher's advantage for initiating interaction and developing rapport with consultees, particularly those who are a bit skeptical about the value of collaborative consultation. If you have a humorous bent or the creative urge, make up a joke, cartoon, or comic strip about consulting or collaboration that could be used to defuse resistance and build rapport among consultation group members.

FOR FURTHER READING

Beebe, S. A., & Masterson, J. T. (1994). *Communicating in small groups: Principles and practices* (4th ed.). New York: Harper Collins.

Clark, S. G. (2000). The IEP process as a tool for collaboration. *Teaching Exceptional Children, 33*(2), 56–66.

Corey, M. S., & Corey, G. (1992). *Groups: Process and practice* (4th ed.). Pacific Grove, CA: Brooks Cole.

Davis, G. A., & Rimm, S. B. (1998). *Education of the gifted and talented.* Englewood Cliffs, NJ: Prentice Hall. Chapters on creativity and thinking skills.

DeBoer, A. (1997). *Working together: The art of consulting and communicating.* Longmont, CO: Sopris West.

DeBoer, A., & Fister, S. (1998). *Working together: Tools for collaborative teaching.* Longmont, CO: Sopris West

deBono, E. (1973). *Lateral thinking: Creativity step by step.* New York: Harper & Row.

deBono, E. (1985). *Six thinking hats.* Boston: Little, Brown.

Giangreco, M. F. (1993). Using creative problem-solving methods to include students with severe disabilities in general classroom activities. *Journal of Educational and Psychological Consultation, 4*(2), 113–135. Provides specific examples of using the Osborn-Parnes Creative Problem-Solving process for instructional inclusion relevant to students with intensive educational needs.

Haynes, M. E. (1988). *Effective meeting skills: A practical guide to more productive meetings.* Los Altos, CA: Crisp.

Hobbs, T., & Westling, D. L. (1998). Promoting successful inclusion through collaborative problem solving. *TEACHING Exceptional Children,* Sept/Oct, 1998, Presents five key components of a structured problem-solving process and a number of professional practices to maximize success of the process.

Jayanthi, M., & Friend, M. (1992). Interpersonal problem solving: A selective literature review to guide practice. *Journal of Educational and Psychological Consultation, 3*(1), 39–53. A review of literature on variables that could facilitate or constrain interpersonal problem-solving processes.

Mills, G. E., & Duff-Mallams, K. (2000). Special education mediation: A formula for success. *Teaching Exceptional Children, 32*(4), 72–78.

Morris, A. (1999). Teamwork. New York: Lothrop, Lee, & Shepard. A delightful children's book describing teamwork as a group from any culture or walk of life that works together and plays together. Photos from fifteen different countries and activities as diverse as college students laying sandbags to contain a river in the United States, to whitewashing a temple roof in Thailand. The book could be used as a prelude to a group problem-solving meeting, or with students to explain the concept of team-teaching when it is introduced into their classroom.

Osborn, A. F. (1963). *Applied imagination: Principles and procedures of creative problem-solving.* New York: Charles Scribner.

Starko, A. (2001). *Creativity in the classroom: Schools of curious delight* (2nd ed.). Mahwah, NJ: Lawrence Erlbaum.

CHAPTER SIX

MANAGEMENT AND ASSESSMENT OF COLLABORATIVE SCHOOL CONSULTATION

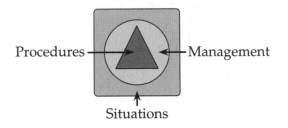

Schools are bustling arenas of activities that often seem to have little to do with books and studies. Not only do school personnel teach students in academic settings, they also feed them, transport them, keep records, counsel and advise, dispense materials and resources, address social and health problems, and much, much more. If the services of various school-related roles such as librarian, speech pathologist, school psychologist, social worker, nurse, were included, the list of responsibilities would be even more daunting.

In this complex hubbub the demands on educators can be overwhelming. Stress and fatigue take a toll, with burnout and attrition from the teaching profession an all too frequent result. The challenge of accountability is a heavy burden. High-stakes testing takes its toll on teachers as well as on students. But role-related stress can be minimized and heavy responsibilities controlled by managing time and resources wisely and by assessing outcomes of services provided.

In this chapter the content (triangle) focus is on procedures that make collaborative school consultation more efficient and enjoyable. Management processes (circle) are the key, used in the situations context (square).

FOCUSING QUESTIONS

1. What aspects of their roles cause school personnel to be vulnerable to stress and burnout?
2. What management and organizational techniques can help consultants and collaborators perform their roles effectively?
3. What procedures for conducting meetings, interviews, and observations contribute to consultation and collaboration success?

4. How can collaborating school consultants manage records and resources efficiently?

5. How are evaluation data helpful in developing and improving collaborative consultation, and who will want to use the data for accountability and decision making?

6. When should evaluation plans for collaborative school consultation be developed and implemented?

7. What are the important contexts, processes, and content area elements to be evaluated in collaborative school consultation? Are there parallels to the way teachers gather data about students' skills?

KEY TERMS

attrition	formative assessment	single agenda meetings
behavior observations	interview	(SAM)
burnout	observation	stress management
caseload	portfolio assessment	summative assessment
consultation log or journal	self-assessment	time management

STRESS AND BURNOUT AMONG EDUCATORS

Rising costs, public criticism, low morale, and an avalanche of regulations and paperwork create pressures on educators that erode their ability to prepare students for a successful future. Some remain in the profession and juggle their daily routines within a burgeoning agenda of reform and mandates. Others burn out and leave the profession. Still others simply "fizzle out," "rust out," or "coast out." The latter go through the motions of their profession in lackluster fashion, just getting by until retirement age arrives or opportunity for a better situation comes along. These educators create situations that are particularly penalizing for students who have special needs and are the most vulnerable to effects of uninspired teaching.

One of the most difficult aspects of the No Child Left Behind Act is its requirement that schools staff all classrooms with highly qualified teachers, even as it is becoming harder and harder to keep teachers who are prepared. Steep attrition in the first few years of teaching is a well-recognized situation, with about a third of new teachers leaving the profession within five years (Darling-Hammond, 2003). Sadly, teacher turnover is 50 percent higher in high-poverty schools than in low-poverty schools (Ingersoll, 2001).

As advocates for children with special learning and behavior needs, special education teachers may set unreasonably high expectations for themselves and others. Lack of role clarity, and discrepancy between their own role perceptions and the expectations of others, contribute to this syndrome (Bensky, Shaw, Gouse, Bates, Dixon, & Beane, 1980). Dettmer (1982) identifies lack of recognition and reinforcement for their work, along with heavy responsibilities without much decision-making authority, as additional stressors for special education personnel.

There may be a cyclical or reciprocal relationship between teacher stress and student behavior (Shaw, Bensky, & Dixon, 1981). For example, short term results of teacher stress such as irritability, inability to concentrate, disorganization, and poor management of work flow can affect the behavior and performance of students. The overwhelming responsibilities and pressures of working with special needs students make teachers particularly vulnerable to stress and burnout, and the severity varies by service-delivery model.

Minimizing Stress of Professional Responsibilities

Burnout can come about from physical and emotional exhaustion. Prolonged stress or the buildup of stressors causes fatigue and frustration. Up to 50 percent of educators have indicated they may leave the profession because of burnout (Raschke, Dedrick, & DeVries, 1988), and burnout disproportionately affects special education teachers and others in helping professions (Maslach, 1982; Pines & Aronson, 1988). There are three basic components of burnout:

1. Emotional exhaustion ("I'm tired and irritated all the time. I am impatient with my students and colleagues.")
2. Depersonalization ("I am becoming emotionally hardened; I start to blame the students or their families for all the problems.")
3. Reduced accomplishment ("I feel like I'm not making a difference for my students.")

The result can be attrition, alienation, cynicism, and physical problems such as heart disease, hypertension, ulcers, headaches, and psychosomatic illnesses.

Stressors that cause stress reactions are many and varied. For the consultant, stressors could be a new special education regulation, a change in job description, an angry parent, or a student who is behaving in a violent manner. Most educators do have a vast repertoire of coping skills, and we all know that stress in general is a normal life event. Eustress (Schultz, 1980) is a proactive, positive response to a stimulus, such as that experienced by artists, entertainers, athletes, speakers, and yes, teachers, before going "on stage," that helps us perform at our best. It can even help us learn and grow. People who have experienced some stress probably are more likely to have good coping skills and to be understanding of others under stress than people who have not.

On the other hand, distress (anxiety, sorrow, pain, trouble) wears us down physically and emotionally. People become less capable of recognizing and responding to the needs of others in supportive ways when they are distressed. Busy, committed educators will never be able to reduce or eliminate all the stressors in their lives, but they can develop some specific coping strategies so that a balance between stress and coping can be achieved and burnout can be avoided.

Developing positive adaptive strategies is crucial to maintaining emotional and physical health. The techniques individuals use depend on their preferences, lifestyle, and skills. Consultants and consultees must learn to "work smarter, not harder" to accomplish goals for students who are at risk of failure in school. Consultants also must take care of themselves so they do not lose their commitment and enthusiasm, and students with special needs do not lose their good, caring teachers. Recall the words of the flight attendant who instructs, "First put on *your* oxygen mask and *then* put on the baby's mask." We cannot take care of others if we are in no shape to help.

Building mutually supportive networks will minimize, if not eliminate, feelings of isolation and helplessness in the demanding role of school consultant. It helps to talk things out with others and get a new perspective when tackling complex responsibilities inherent in meeting special needs. A support system is an effective outlet for frustration and provides a backup in times of crisis. One group of special education staff makes a commitment to meet each Friday at a centralized place for lunch and lively conversation. Ground rules stipulate there will be no talking about students, schools, or staff in that public place. The camaraderie and conviviality of the weekly event, looked on favorably by district administrators, provide an effective support system for teachers whose roles invite stress.

■ ■ ■ ■ ■ ▬▬▬▬▬▬▬▬▬▬▬▬▬▬▬▬▬▬▬▬▬▬▬▬▬▬▬▬▬▬▬▬▬▬▬▬

APPLICATION 6.1
STRATEGIES FOR REDUCING STRESS

What if burnout has happened or is at least in the glowing embers stage? What if you feel low self-esteem, and emotional and physical exhaustion now? These strategies may help.

1. Talk to someone, give a positive comment, share ideas.
2. *Pretend* you are O.K. Remember that problems in life are inevitable, demonstrating that we are alive and still functioning. Smile. Stand up straight and walk with a bouncy step. Wear bright, happy clothes—a funny tie, or long, dangling earrings shaped like dinosaurs or pea pods or clowns.
3. Sit in the warm, fresh air. Natural light helps the body function better.
4. Laugh out loud. Each person should have his or her "laugh ration" every day for mental and physical health. Listen to a comedy tape. Read a joke book. Watch children play.
5. Move, stretch, walk, jog. Mild exercise gets the blood flowing and transports more oxygen throughout the body, helping you feel alert and alive.
6. Play energetic, happy music. Classical music is best. Listening to sixty-cycle music such as that by Bach, Handel, and Mozart has been shown to increase alpha brain wave, the relaxation wave length (Douglass & Douglass, 1993). On the other hand, rock music is tiring and tends to drain energy away.
7. Break the routine. Take a different route when driving to work. Let others' cars cut in front of your car and feel smug about it. Rearrange your schedule or your furniture. Take a vacation if you can and when you do, leave worries and cares behind. Give yourself over to relaxation and rejuvenation.
8. Schedule appointments with yourself. Keep a jar of little treats in a handy place, such as encouraging statements, chocolates, or envelopes with a $5 bill inside, to be good to yourself every now and then.
9. Use reminders to help remember these and other prevention and intervention strategies. They could be colored ribbons, stick-on happy faces, ads from magazines, letters to yourself. Put the reminders on your tote bag or briefcase, on your watch, calendar, or rear view mirror.
10. Remind yourself often that prevention and remediation of stress and burnout are the concern of the individual, not family or friends or colleagues. Each must become aware of the factors and variables in his or her own personal formula of strategies for keeping the flame of motivation alive.

MANAGEMENT OF TIME

When school consultants are asked about the biggest obstacle to their role, the majority respond, "Time!" A study released by the Council for Exceptional Children in October, 2000 (*CEC Today,* 2000) reported that current special education teaching conditions have pushed the field into crisis. Time required to complete overwhelming paperwork, high caseloads, lack of administrator support, and lack of qualified special education teachers are targeted as major issues. Teachers stress that they need more time for collaborative planning, and 15 percent of the respondents reported that they have *no* time for individualized instruction. Only 26 percent have more than three hours for individualized instruction. When administrators are not familiar with special education, the unfortunate result can be failure to allow time for planning and collaborating, vital components of instructional accommodations and modifications.

Time is indeed a critical factor in the plans and purposes of educators, particularly for school consultants and consultees in their complex roles. Studies have shown that school consultants have considerable time pressures from attending meetings, preparing and planning, administering tests, communicating, observing, evaluating, and problem solving (Nelson & Stevens, 1981; Tindal & Taylor-Pendergast, 1989). Time is a precious, nonrenewable commodity, with many school consultants prone to "timelock" in which claims on time have grown so demanding that it seems impossible to wring one more second out of the crowded calendar (Keys, 1991).

Caseload is a key factor in managing time and arranging schedules. One consultant devoted 76.8 hours over 13 weeks to just one case. The experience of Idol (1988) and others suggests that special education consultants should serve a maximum of 35 students. Those having both direct and indirect service roles should have their ratios classified for each category, and students receiving consultation services as well as direct services should be counted twice. The solution, if there is one, lies in how we choose to use the time available to us.

Time is not adaptable, but people are. An ancient Chinese proverb says, "You cannot change the wind, but you can adjust the sail." Time-management skills can be learned and improved. Because time management is primarily about choices, it is very personal, and the best management plan for one may not be the best for another. A basic five-step plan is useful for practicing time management:

1. Analyze one's current use of time.
2. Establish goals and priorities.
3. Plan time and work.
4. Use positive time-management techniques.
5. Review results and reinforce successes.

Most consultants, when asked specifically how they use their time, rely on memory or perceptions. However, to make significant improvements in time management, busy consultants must accurately observe *and record* their use of time. Time logs are a valuable way to observe personal use of time. Consultants may choose to use a diary time log, recording everything they do, when they do it, and how long it takes. Another option is to record time in 15-minute segments, or use a matrix which lists times of the day in segments and lists elements of the consulting role. The matrix can be used to check off quickly those responsibilities that were being done in each segment, and time spent on each activity can be totaled at the end of the day. When recording use of time, remember to begin early in the day, not waiting until the end of the day to try to remember it all.

It is helpful to review long-term goals daily. They should be posted on the desk, the wall, or in a planner. This simple activity, according to Douglass and Douglass (1993), helps one stay focused. Long-term goals should be subdivided into short-term goals, weekly goals, and daily goals. To minimize the gap between long-term and short-term goals, Douglass and Douglass (1993) suggest:

1. Keep a master "to do" list with priority codes that match the items to your goals.
2. Assign a due date to each project. Due dates keep tasks from being put off and foster a sense of completion when accomplished.
3. Estimate time required to complete the task or the project.

Putnam (1993) offers a number of practical tips for making every minute count, including:

- Think of oneself as a time manager.
- Establish goals, stay focused, and make long-range plans.
- Take time to make time, so that there are fewer time-management issues later on.
- Delegate routine tasks to students, aides, or parent volunteers when possible.
- Minimize procrastination.
- Learn to say "no." *Practice* saying "no" until it feels firm and sincere.

Time-management practices encourage efficient use of abilities and strengths. The purpose of time management is not to get *everything* done, but to accomplish professional and personal goals (Maher, 1985). Being busy is not the same as being productive. Time management is a skill that can be learned and improved. (See Figure 6.1 for one consulting teacher's Weekly Organizer form.)

Finding Time for Collaboration and Teaming

Managing time and schedules in order to conduct consultation and collaborate effectively is one of the biggest challenges for school consultants. In Cawelti (1997) teachers report their instruction improves when they work in teams. But they need to have the time available in order to do that. Many educators believe outcomes-based education and performance-based assessment are promising innovations for schools, but acknowledge that each requires additional teacher plan time. How to accomplish that is as yet unresolved. Three examples from comments by teachers as reported by Voltz, Elliott, Jr., and Cobb (1994) are less than optimistic:

> Our schedules are so tight, there is no time during the regular school day for planning together or discussion.
>
> Timing is the greatest problem. There is just no time for classroom teachers and resource teachers to communicate. . . .
>
> . . . when the resource teacher and I needed to confer and we had to do it on our own time . . . we had an essential conference with the resource teacher in the lavatory and me on the floor outside the door, talking through the door . . . (p. 534).

WEEKLY ORGANIZER

Dates: _____ to _____

Week at a Glance				
Monday /	Tuesday /	Wednesday /	Thursday /	Friday /

To Do (Priority)	To See	
	Person/Place	Time

To Do (Eventually)	To Phone/E-mail	
	Person	Phone number/E-mail address

☺ Notes & Reminders ☺

--Reproduced with permission by author   ©Jane Jacquart 2003

FIGURE 6.1   Weekly Organizer Form

These comments are consistent with a number of other studies investigating barriers to consultation, collaboration, and teaming (Davis, 1983a; Fullan & Miles, 1992; Idol-Maestas & Ritter, 1985). Time emerges as the key issue inherent in every school-change analysis for the past decade (Raywid, 1993), with successful schools differing from unsuccessful ones in the frequency and extent to which teachers interact and collaborate about materials and instruction. Raywid (1993) found that approaches to finding time included freeing up existing time, restructuring or rescheduling time, using existing time better, or buying time. Examples from her research include:

- Teachers sharing the same lunch period with their plan period after lunch, which results in 90 minutes of shared time per day.
- Teachers interacting while students leave the building a few hours weekly to perform community service.

- Substitutes hired with money saved by increasing class sizes by one or two students.
- Day-long staff development for 3 to 5 days per year in some districts.
- Compensatory time for teachers participating in 2- to 3-day planning sessions during breaks between terms.
- Staff-development days, from as many as 5 or more instructional days waived by state legislatures.
- Lengthened instructional days.
- Special talents and skills programs provided by specialists, or hobby days for students while teachers meet to collaborate and plan.
- University personnel working in partnership to provide activities that free up teachers to interact.

Raywid stresses that teachers cannot be expected to give up time for working together when they are exhausted at the end of the school day, or when they have their own personal activities, or when they are uncomfortable about the way their class might be handled in their absence.

Other educational leaders offer additional strategies for creating time to collaborate. These include working with the Parent-Teacher Organization to implement volunteer substitute-teacher programs that free up teachers, revising school schedules to provide shared planning time, releasing teachers who collaborate from other school duties such as lunch and bus supervision, providing other supervisors for times such as assemblies and student activities, and implementing peer-tutoring programs across classes. Many innovative ideas are available for carving out time to collaborate and team; however, the ideas themselves require significant amounts of time to plan, implement, and coordinate effectively.

West (1990) offers a number of strategies for increasing collaboration time that have been used successfully at elementary, middle, and junior and senior high levels, including:

- Bringing large groups of students together for speakers, films, or plays;
- Using volunteers such as grandparents, parents, community leaders, and retired teachers;
- Hiring a permanent "floating substitute";
- Having the principal set aside one day per grading period as "collaboration day," with no other activities on this day;
- Having the principal or another staff supervisor teach a period a day regularly;
- Having students working on independent or study activities while clustered in large groups under supervision;
- Having faculty vote to extend the instructional day twenty minutes for two days a week in a collaboration period.

In an education update from the Association for Supervision and Curriculum Development (ASCD, 2000), finding time for collaborating is described as "not a question of know-how, but of want-to." One thing teachers do want is for collaborative time to be part of the school day, not after school or on Saturdays. The sharing of materials and ideas, asking big questions, doing joint planning, and making presentations to one another is good staff development activity. When teachers focus on producing rubrics, creating strategies for improvement, and analyzing assessment data, they refrain from using their collaborative planning time for routine activities such as grading papers.

■ ■ ■ ■ ■ ▬▬▬▬▬▬▬▬▬▬▬▬▬▬▬▬▬▬▬▬▬▬▬▬▬▬▬▬▬▬▬▬▬▬▬▬

APPLICATION 6.2
USING TIME WISELY

Physicists define time as nature's way to keep everything from happening at once! By planning time and managing time-wasters, educators can be more productive and less stressed. These strategies can be helpful:

1. Make a "To Do" list—monthly, weekly, and/or daily lists. Make each list at the same time of day on the same kind of paper. Write down all that needs to be done and plan all activities, even those such as talking with friends or playing with the family. Then prioritize the list. Lakein (1973) suggests "ABC-ing" the list, with A as top priority. for only those which *must* be done. Designate B priorities as "nice if done," and C jobs as "maybe later." You might even end up with a D or "So What?" list.

2. Say "no" when you need to. Avoid saying "Well . . . ," or "I'll think about it." Certainly avoid, "I will if you can't find anyone else," because they won't. Responding with "This is so important that it needs more attention than I can give it now," is often very effective.

3. Rearrange personal schedules. Do the most difficult tasks at your peak efficiency time.

4. Plan for bits of time. Keep "can do" lists for periods of 5 minutes, 15 minutes, and 30 minutes. When waiting for a meeting to start, or classes to begin, do something on your list. This is a good chance to get some C or short B priority things done. And, it is reasonable at times to sit and think, read a mystery, or listen to music. Time spent relaxing is not wasted time.

5. Delegate. This is the perfect solution for C priorities, if a helper is available. Teachers are habituated into functioning autonomously, but others may be just waiting for a chance to contribute and develop their own skills.

6. Break mountains of work into molehills. Do a task analysis or break down the job into smaller steps that you can complete with satisfaction.

7. Set deadlines and time limits. Plan a treat for accomplishing a task by deadline. Time limits help get things done efficiently and prevent simple tasks from becoming major projects. It prevents letting the intentions to clean out one drawer become major cleaning of the whole desk, file cabinet, and book shelves.

8. Organize desk and office area. MacKenzie (1975) describes the "stacked desk syndrome," in which the desk is so cluttered with things-not-to-forget that one cannot find things, concentrate, or work efficiently.

9. Handle the C tasks sensibly. If they can't be delegated or ignored, try putting them on the extra-minutes list. If that is not an option, consider bartering, pooling resources, and consolidating activities.

10. Overcome procrastination. Entire books have been written about this phenomenon, but most of us put off reading them! The hardest part is simply getting started on the task.

11. Take less time to do routine things. For example, make a list of tasks that require attention once a month, twice a month, weekly, and daily. Look at the list. What would happen if the daily list became a weekly list, the weekly list moved to semi-monthly, and the twice-monthly to once a month? Probably nothing drastic. It may not be necessary to vacuum weekly, or wash twice a week, or grade every worksheet, or communicate with parents weekly. If so, fine, but if not, do it less often and use that time to work on A activities or special activities for students and colleagues.

12. Get a "Do Not Disturb" sign, and use it without guilt. Some teachers have had great success making and using work-status cubes for their desk *and* even encouraging their stu-

dents to do the same. Faces on one's cube can convey messages such as "Please Do Not Disturb Right Now," "I need help," "This is not a good day for me, so be patient, please," or "May I help someone?"

13. Plan time for yourself. Busy educators often devote much time and energy to taking care of others at the expense of neglecting themselves. Take time to relax, visit with others in the building, talk to a child, read a book, go for a walk, sketch a picture.

14. Plan rewards to reinforce one's own efficiency and any measurable progress toward goals. Many teachers are quite goal-directed but fail to build self-rewards into their *own* self-management (Davis, 1983b).

Techniques for Meetings, Interviews, and Observations

Who has not winced at the thought of yet another meeting? Meetings, interviews, and classroom observations take precious time as well as physical and mental energy. Tremendous amounts of collective time and energy are wasted when people are trapped in unproductive meetings. Educators who want to work smarter, not harder, should set goals for conducting group interactions that are efficient and productive for all.

Conducting Efficient Meetings.   Consulting educators are busy, but classroom teachers may be the most overextended of all. Many classroom teachers find that the total time for having all their students together for a class period is appallingly short. Consultation and collaboration will be accepted more readily when consultees know that consultants respect their time and their students' time. So a meeting should be planned only if it promises to contribute significantly in serving client needs.

The first rule in planning an efficient meeting is to ask, "Do we really need to have this meeting?" If the answer is *not* a resounding "Yes," then the business probably can be handled a more efficient way, perhaps by memo, phone, e-mail, or brief face-to-face conversations with individuals. Good reasons for having a meeting are:

- Meeting legal obligations (such as an IEP conference).
- Problem-solving with several people representing a variety of roles.
- Brainstorming so that many ideas are put forth.
- Reconciling conflicting views.
- Providing a forum for all to be heard.
- Building a team to implement educational decisions.

Unnecessary meetings waste school time. They also erode participants' confidence in the value of future meetings that may be called. Sigband (1987) recommends that meetings be held only when there is verifiable need, basing each meeting on an overall purpose and series of objectives. Only people who can make a definite contribution need to be there. An agenda should be prepared, and the meeting room and any needed equipment should be ready. Most important, the meeting must begin on time and end on time, or early if possible.

Preparing for the Meeting.   Leaders or chairs of meetings will be more prepared and organized if they follow a planning checklist. (See Figure 6.2 for an example.) The planning

FIGURE 6.2   Checklist to Prepare for Meetings

Date: _____   Place: _____

Time: _____   Topic: _____

Participants: _____

Goals for Meeting: _____

_____

_____

Preparation of Room: Preparation for Participants:

_____   Overhead projector   _____   Nametags

_____   Screen, bulbs, cord   _____   Pads and pens

_____   Chalkboard, chalk   _____   Handouts

_____   Charts, pens, tape   _____   Agenda

_____   Tape recorder, tapes   _____   Ice-breaker activity

_____   Podium, lectern   _____   Map of location

_____   Tables, chairs   _____   Refreshments

_____   Breakout arrangements   _____   Follow-up activity

_____   Other?   _____   Other?

Room Arrangement: _____

_____

_____   (Sketch of Room)

_____

_____

sheet should include general planning points such as date, time, participants, and goals. Checklists designed to stipulate preparations for the room and to note participant needs also will be useful.

Participants.   After determining a need for a meeting, leaders and chairs will want to request attendance from only those who can contribute. They should keep the group as small as possible, adhering to the rule of thumb that the more people involved, the shorter the meeting should be. Experts on group interaction recommend that the maximum for problem-solving is five, for problem identification about ten, for hearing a review or presentation as many as thirty, and for motivation and inspiration as many as possible. If a group includes more than six people, it is likely that not everyone will have an opportunity to speak.

Agenda.   Chairpersons for meetings should develop an agenda that reflects the needs of all participants. Sometimes e-mail can be used to solicit agenda items from those who will participate. It is often helpful to send out an agenda in advance. The agenda items could be given in question format as a variation now and then. For example, rather than "Scheduling for the Resource Room," the issue might be "How can we craft a fair, workable schedule for use of the resource room on M-W-F?"

With an agenda distributed beforehand, participants will be more productive and less apprehensive. Sometimes leaders of large-group meetings draw upon a teaching technique of placing a short, high-interest activity, relating to the topic but needing little explanation, on the chalkboard or overhead screen. Participants focus on the task as they arrive, thereby becoming centered on the meeting topic as they do so. Meetings are more effective when participants can anticipate the task. (See Figure 6.3 for an example of a pre-meeting communication to prepare participants.)

It is important to allocate time for each item on the agenda. Estimating the time needed for each item will allow the chair to monitor progress during the meeting. It is counterproductive to focus too long on early items and fail to get to the last ones. If more important items are placed far down the agenda and time becomes short, it might even appear that they have been put there by the convener to avoid action or decision-making. Consultants seeking to build collaborative interactions among their colleagues will not want that to happen.

FIGURE 6.3   Checklist to Prepare Participants

Date: _____   Place: _____

Time Start: _____   Time End: _____   Topic: _____

Roles: Facilitator: _____

Recorder: _____

Timekeeper: _____

Other Participants: _____

Agenda for Meeting: _____

_____

_____

_____

_____   Minutes of Prior Meeting Attached _____

_____   Advance Preparation Needed_____

_____   Next Planned Meeting _____

At the Meeting

Action	Person(s) Responsible	Target Date	Done

Seating Arrangements.   Comfortable chairs and seating arrangements that facilitate inter-action are important factors in the success of a meeting. Full-size chairs (not kindergarten furniture) with a little padding, but not too much, should be provided. For best interaction, there should be an arrangement where all can face each other. A circle for six to ten people, a U-shape with peripheral seating if there is to be a visual presentation, and a semi-circle of one or more rows for large groups work well (Lawren, 1989).

Participant Responsibilities.   Along with the responsibility of each participant to interact and help problem-solve, brainstorm, or decide, three other responsibilities are important—chair, recorder, and timekeeper. In many cases the consultant will take care of all three roles, partic-ularly if the meeting includes only two or three people. However, if the meeting is long, or the issues are complex and there is much discussion and brainstorming, it is efficient for the chair to ask another participant to record the plans and decisions. One potentially useful strategy for getting the most out of a meeting is to take notes, whether or not they are required. This fo-cuses attention and keeps the writer active yet still. Even adults sometimes find it hard to sit still and listen when there are so many other things vying for one's energy and attention.

During the Meeting.   Whether the meeting involves two or twenty persons, all participants should be made to feel that they have important contributions to make. All should listen at-tentively to each other, think creatively and flexibly, and avoid disruptive communication such as jokes, puns, sarcasm, or side comments (Gordon, 1974). Talking and whispering in subgroups can be particularly distracting. Ironically, some teachers who will not tolerate such behavior by their students in the classroom are the biggest offenders. Astute group lead-ers have various ways of handling this disagreeable occurrence. They might go over to the offenders and stand alongside or between them, direct questions to them, or request a re-sponse from them. Each participant in a meeting should be thinking at all times, "What will help move us ahead and solve the problem," and "What does the group need and how can I help?" (Gordon, 1974).

Compromise for consensus is not always the best solution. It may reflect a weak de-cision, a watered-down plan, or failure by some participants to express their concerns as firmly as they should. During the meeting leaders should encourage opposing views so that they do not surface later when the matter has been closed. If any participant wishes to dis-sent, the time to do so is in the meeting, not in hallways after the matter has been decided. Of course, many consultations and collaborations involve only two individuals—consultant and consultee. But procedures recommended for groups of several or more are often perti-nent to interactions between only two individuals as well.

Winding Up the Meeting.   The timekeeper should be consulted frequently but quietly, so the meeting can end on time. When time is up, the leader should review any key decisions and, if needed, set the time and place for the next meeting, perhaps with a preliminary overview of that agenda. If a meeting's agenda and progress become sidetracked, leaders should redirect the group's attention by making a point to refocus the discussion (Raschke, Dedrick, & DeVries, 1988).

Minutes of the Meeting.   Sometimes committees are chided for keeping minutes to waste hours! Minutes should reflect the group's decisions about what is to be done, by whom, and by what date, but need not include each point of the discussion. Minutes are a record for naming those who will have a responsibility, for describing plans and decisions, and for listing projected dates for completion of tasks. This is an important aspect of the consultation which must not be slighted.

Assessment of the Meeting.   Some time should be reserved at the end of the meeting to discuss progress made and to evaluate the effectiveness of the meeting. Participants should be thanked for coming and for their active participation. Finally, there should be follow-up on any actions assigned.

Single Agenda Meetings (SAM).   When educators have a single topic that can be handled in a quick meeting before or after school, they can structure the meeting with a single agenda meeting (SAM) process. After becoming familiar with this process, team members will be able to have short SAM meetings without much ado. However, they should not try to squeeze a large agenda or issue into the SAM format. (See Figure 6.4.)

Conducting Effective Interviews.   School consultants often need to interview school personnel, community resources, and family members to plan programs for helping students with special needs. Interviewees can provide information for case studies and formulation of learning goals. They help generate options and alternatives for special needs, and provide data for program evaluation.

Successful interviews require effective communication skills (see Chapter 4), and postures of onedownsmanship, parity, and cooperativeness. Queries such as "Tell me more," and "Could you expand on that?" and "Let me see if I understand what you are saying" are examples of the responsive listening and paraphrasing that help to elicit the most useful information.

FIGURE 6.4   Single Agenda Meetings (SAM)

Date and Time

Problem Statement: _____

_____

_____

_____

1. Background information	5 minutes
2. Possible solutions (each individually writes ideas)	5 minutes
3. Share and select solution	12 minutes
4. Assign action items and schedule next meeting	5 minutes

(1995, Curriculum Solutions, Inc., adapted by permission)

The interviewer should take notes, allowing interviewees to look them over at the conclusion of the interview. If a tape-recording is desired, the interviewer must ask permission beforehand to make one. Some feel it is best to avoid taping, because respondents are often less candid if their comments are being recorded.

Interviews must be conducted ethically, collegially, and for a purpose not attainable by less intrusive, time-consuming methods. Keys to a successful interview by the school consultant are asking the right questions and valuing the expertise of the interviewee. A follow-up interaction soon after the interview session is affirming and reassuring, thus facilitating further collaboration.

Making Prudent Observations.   Consultants often need to observe a student, groups of students, or an entire program in operation. This is not an easy professional task. Consultants who go into classrooms to observe can expect some discomfort and anxiety on the teacher's part. There may be latent resentment because the consultant is free to visit other classrooms, something many teachers would like but are rarely given the opportunity to do.

Consultants can facilitate the process of observation and ease the minds of those being observed in several ways. First, they should provide a positive comment upon entering the room, and then sit unobtrusively where the teacher has designated. They should avoid getting involved in classroom activities or helping students. Effective observers can blend into the classroom setting so they are hardly noticed. Regular visits minimize the likelihood of having students know who is being observed and for what reason. It is a sad thing to hear a student say, "Oh, here's that learning disabilities teacher to check up on Jimmy again." Records of behaviors must be done in code so that the physical aspects of writing, watching, and body language of the consultant do not reveal the intent of the observation. Each consultant should develop a personal coding system for recording information. Sometimes observers watch the targeted student for one minute, and then divert their attention to another student for one minute, continuing the process with other peers. In this way the student's behavior can be compared with that of classmates. The consultant may teach a lesson and have the classroom teacher observe. This can be helpful for both consultant and consultee.

An observer should exit the room with a smile and a supporting glance at the teacher. Then very soon after the observation, the observer will want to get back to the classroom teacher with positive, specific comments about the classroom, feedback on the observation, and suggestions for entering into problem solving. Although consultants do not observe in classrooms for the purpose of assessing teacher behaviors and teaching styles, it would be myopic to assume that they do not notice teaching practices which inhibit student success in that classroom. When the practices seem to be interfering with student achievement, the consultant might ask the consultee in a non-threatening, onedownsmanship way whether the student achieved the goals of the lesson. If not, is there something the teacher would like to change so this could occur? Then what might the consultant do to help?

To avoid gathering inaccurate information, consultants will want to make repeated observations. In doing so they can use the opportunity to obtain additional information on antecedents to the problem (Cipani, 1985).

Achieving rapport with a consultee, while targeting a teaching strategy for possible modification, requires utmost finesse by consultants. The observer should make an appointment as soon as possible for providing feedback and continuation of the problem solving.

MANAGEMENT OF CONSULTATION RECORDS AND RESOURCES

A prominent space scientist commented that physicists can lick anything, even gravity, but the paperwork is overwhelming. Special education teachers can relate to that. They cite excessive paperwork and record-keeping, along with insufficient time in which to do it, as major causes of stress and burnout. Writing and monitoring IEPs, individual pupil record-keeping, and completion of records and forms rank high as major usurpers of their personal and professional time (Davis, 1983a). Components of the IDEA reauthorization will require even more.

When asked to estimate the amount of time they spend performing their responsibilities, resource teachers often overestimate the time spent on direct pupil instruction and staffings and underestimate their preparation for instruction and clerical duties such as record-keeping. If teaching is to be an important service profession, careful record-keeping is essential. Record-keeping must be written into the consultant's role description as an important responsibility, with time allowed for its accurate completion. Who would want to be treated by a doctor who did not write down vital information after each visit, or served by a lawyer who failed to record and file important documents? The key for educators is to manage their paperwork so that it does not manage them. Developing efficient systems and standardized forms for record-keeping will help educators, and consultants in particular, work smarter and not harder.

Using a Consultation Journal or Log

One of the most important formats for consultants to develop is a consultation log or journal. Consultants can record the date, participants, and topic of each consultation on separate pages, along with a brief account of the interaction and the results agreed on. Space should be provided for follow-up reports and assessment of the consultation. (See Figure 6.5 for a sample format.) Records should be kept for the time spent in consultation and any positive results accomplished, if consultation is to gain credibility as an essential educational activity. Although consultants cannot control the type of records required, they can exercise a good bit of control over processes and procedures for collecting and using information (Davis, 1983a).

One caution is due in regard to consultation logs. Important points of the discussion about student needs and progress might be entered in the log. However, no diagnostic classification or plan that necessitates parent permission should be recorded (Conoley & Conoley, 1982). Confidentiality of the information must be preserved. Consultants will want to develop procedures for coding that will ensure confidentiality, yet identify pertinent information efficiently.

Memos and Professional Cards

A consultation memo is a communication tool and also a record of that communication. It should be as brief as possible and very clear, or it will confound rather than convey the message (Cleveland, 1981). Receivers will pay more attention to a memo that synthesizes the information and expresses it in simple terms. Jargon, acronyms, excess verbiage, and cryptic sentences are to be avoided. Contrary to some practice, memos should be drafted and then rewritten in best form, rather than dashed off hastily and flung into a mailbox. This is

FIGURE 6.5   Consultation Journal Format

Client (coded): _____ Consultee (initials): _____

Initiator of Consultation: _____

General Topic of Concern: _____

_____

Purpose of Consultation: _____

_____

_____

Brief Summary of Consultation: _____

_____

_____

_____

Steps Agreed On—By Whom, by When: _____

_____

_____

_____

Follow-up: _____

_____

Most Successful Parts of Consultation: _____

_____

Consultation Areas Needing Improvement: _____

_____

Satisfaction with consultation process (1 = least, 5 = most)

1. Communication between consultant and consultee   _____

2. Use of collaborative problem solving   _____

3. Consultee responsiveness to consultation   _____

4. Effectiveness of consultation for problem   _____

5. Impact of consultation on client   _____

6. Positive ripple effects for system   _____

particularly relevant to electronic memos, which will be discussed in a later chapter. The writer should put the message simply, telling just enough and no more, have facts (times, dates, meeting rooms, descriptions, names) accurate, stick to the point and make the memo as grammatically correct and aesthetically pleasing as possible without spending hours at the task.

Consultants will find it helpful to include a personalized logo on the memo forms they use to communicate with consultees. This logo identifies the consultant at a glance. A busy recipient immediately recognizes its source and can make a quick decision about the need to respond now or at a later time. It personalizes professional interaction by providing a bit of information about the consultant, a humorous touch, or the creative element that educators enjoy and appreciate. A carefully designed logo can promote consultation, collaboration, and team effort in a positive light.

Another item that improves consultant efficiency is the professional card. Business cards have been a mainstay for communicating basic information in many professions and can be useful in education as well. Administrators can increase the visibility of their staff and enhance staff morale by providing them with attractive, well-designed professional cards. Educators find these cards helpful when they interact with colleagues at other sites, or when they attend conferences and conventions. The cards are convenient for quickly jotting down requests for information. They help build communication networks among colleagues with similar interests, and even promote one's own school district.

Organizing a Consultation Notebook

Consultants often use a looseleaf notebook divided into sections with index tabs. The sections can be categorized by buildings served, students served, or teachers served. One very organized consulting teacher had a section of "Best Times to Meet with Teachers," listing days and times available for every teacher with whom she collaborated. Each consultant will want to develop the style that works best in his or her school context and role. Figure 6.6 is a list of suggestions for a special education consultant's notebook sections. Figure 6.7 shows a different format used by a consulting teacher for learning and behavioral disabilities. Consultants may not want or need all of these sections, and may come up with others of their own they would like to include. Personalization for the role and school context again determines its usefulness.

A primary responsibility of the consultant is to ensure confidentiality of information for both student and staff. This can be accomplished in at least two ways—coding the names with numbers or symbols while keeping the code list in a separate place, and marking person-specific files as confidential. A "Confidential" rubber stamp prepared for this purpose can be used to alert readers that the information is not for public viewing. These practices, along with the usual protection of information and data, and the practice of seeing that the recorded information is as positive and verifiable as possible, are common-sense rules that should be sufficient for handling all but the most unusual cases.

An itinerant consulting teacher who serves several schools may want to prepare a simple form stating the date, teacher's name and child's code, along with the topic to be considered, for each school. The list can be scanned before entering the building, so that no time is lost in providing the consultative or teaching service. Some consulting teachers block off

FIGURE 6.6   Consultation Notebook Format

Appointments:	One for week, one for year.
"To-do" lists:	By day, week, month, or year as fits needs. List commitments.
Lesson plans:	If delivering direct service, outline of activities for week.
Consultation logs:	Chart to record consultation input and outcomes (Figure 6.5)
Phone call log:	Consultation time by phone.
Observation sheets:	Coded for confidentiality.
Contact list:	Phone numbers, school address, times available.
Faculty notes:	Interests, social and family events and dates, teaching preferences of staff.
Schedules:	For faculty, paras, support staff, regular school events.
Student list:	Coded for confidentiality, birth dates, IEP dates, other helpful data.
Student information:	Anecdotal records, sample products, events, awards, interests, birthdays, talents.
Medication records:	If part of responsibilities.
Materials available:	Title, brief description with grade levels, location.
Services available:	School and community services for resources.
State policies:	Guidelines, procedures, names and phone numbers of agencies/ personnel.
School policies:	Brief description of school policies regulations, handbook.
Procedural materials:	Forms, procedures, for standard activities.
Evaluation data:	Space and forms to record data for formative and summative evaluation (discussed later in this chapter) and coded if confidential.
Idea file:	To note ideas for self and for sharing with staff and parents.
Joke and humor file:	To perk up the day, and for sharing with others.
Three-year calendar:	For continuity in preparing, checking, and updating IEPs.
Pockets:	For carrying personalized memos, letterhead, stamps, hall passes, paper, professional cards.

and color-code regular meeting times and teacher responsibilities. This practice permits a clearer picture of available consultation times. Another helpful strategy is development of a comprehensive manual that includes standard procedures and forms used in the school district and required by the state.

Consultation Schedules.   The consultant schedule is a vital tool. It not only allows the consultant to organize time productively, but demonstrates to administrators and other school personnel that the school consultant is goal-directed, productive, and facilitative. Schedules should be left with secretaries of all buildings assigned to the consultant, and posted in teacher workrooms so that colleagues have easy access to the information.

FIGURE 6.7   Consulting Teacher's Notebook

Table of Contents

1. Student Information
   1.1 Personal Information
   1.2 Student Profiles
   1.3 A Quick Look at IEPs
   1.4 Student Schedules
   1.5 Medication Records

2. School Information
   2.1 Faculty-Staff Roster(s)/Faculty Notes
   2.2 Master Schedule(s)
   2.3 School Calendar(s)
   2.4 School Policies/School Handbook(s)

3. Calendars
   3.1 Daily To-Do Lists
   3.2 Personal Calendars (Weekly, Yearly)
   3.3 IEP Review Dates
   3.4 Three-Year Evaluation Dates

4. Forms
   4.1 Personal Motif Memos
   4.2 Consultation/Collaboration Request

   4.3 Observation Sheets
   4.4 Weekly Teacher Progress Report
   4.5 Consultation Logs

5. Lesson Plans
   5.1 Weekly Lesson Plans
   5.2 Student Matrix Worksheet
   5.3 Class Co-planning Sheet
   5.4 Unit Co-planning Sheet
   5.5 Co-teaching Planning Sheet
   5.6 Para schedule and responsibilities

6. Consultation/Collaboration
   6.1 Advantages of Consultation/
       Collaboration
   6.2 Tips for Consultation/Collaboration
   6.3 Completed Consultation Logs
   6.4 Consultation Evaluation Forms
   6.5 Personal Journal

7. Resource Listing

Consultations and collaborative experiences can be keyed on the consultant's schedule with code letters for efficiency. One consulting teacher uses this code in her notebook:

- ID   informal discussion, spontaneous meeting
- PM   planned, formal meeting
- PC   phone conversation
- MM   major meeting of more than two people
- FT   follow-through activity
- SO   scheduled observation

Standardized forms are helpful for collecting and using basic information. The forms that produce multiple copies may be more expensive in the short run, but can save valuable time and energy in the long run. The time spent on developing systems and standardizing conventional forms will be well-spent. It frees up more time and energy for individualizing and personalizing the instruction for special needs of the students.

Commercial resources are available which provide sample letters and forms adaptable to a variety of educational purposes, from writing a letter of congratulations to answering concerns and criticisms (Tomlinson, 1984). Although educators will not want to use these patterns verbatim, they can get a "jump start" in preparing some of the more difficult communications.

Coordination and organization of student files, consultation logs, school procedures, and schedules will necessitate more time for paperwork at the outset, but once the procedures are set up, they will be time-efficient and cost-effective in the long run.

Organizing and Distributing Materials

Many school districts now have extensive instructional resource centers where school personnel can check out a variety of material for classroom use. Even with the busiest resource center in full operation, consultants usually have their own field-related materials and information about special areas that teachers want and need. With little or no clerical help, and often little storage space available beyond the seats, floor, and trunk of their own vehicles, traveling school consultants need to develop a simple, orderly check-out system for loaned materials, or soon the consultant will have little left to use and share.

Materials belonging to the schools should be marked with a school stamp, and personal materials should be labeled with a personal label. Library pockets and check-out cards facilitate check-out and return. The consultant should keep an up-to-date inventory of available materials within both personal and school libraries that are loanable and specific to student needs. Before traveling to a school, the consultant can scan the check-out file for due dates, and stop by classrooms or put memos into message boxes asking for their return. Efficient consultants leave request cards so school staff can let them know of their needs. They also periodically assess the usefulness of their materials by querying teachers and students who used them. These kinds of interactions build positive attitudes toward collaboration and teamwork, promote the effectiveness of school consultation, and extend the ripple effect of special services.

ASSESSMENT AND EVALUATION OF COLLABORATIVE SCHOOL CONSULTATION

A collaborative school consultation program requires evaluation just as any other educational program does. Indeed, evaluation is particularly important in programs in which there is a strong focus on abstract skills and outcomes. Consultants cannot know if the consultation activities are effective unless they conduct some type of evaluation. Administrators and policymakers cannot support their programs unless meaningful data are available.

Conoley and Conoley (1982) articulate the critical importance of evaluation to consultants with the following statement:

> It will make little difference to a consultee organization if the consultant does everything with textbook perfection. The decision-makers are interested in positive outcomes in terms of cost, increased services, or staff feedback. Consultants must be prepared not only to provide assistance to others who are planning, implementing, and evaluating programs (i.e., program consultation) but must also *give priority* [emphasis added] to such activities in their own service delivery systems (p. 82).

Engaging in an on-going systematic assessment process is the best way to make sure appropriate decisions are made.

VIGNETTE 6

The setting is the conference room of a special education program office where the principal, the director of special education, the special education consulting teacher, and a parent are seated.

Principal: Mrs. James, I have asked Mrs. Garcia, our director of special education, and Mr. Penner, our special education consulting teacher, to meet with us today to help address your questions. I've explained to them that you're concerned about the new program for your daughter. As I understand your concerns, you feel she is not learning as much as she did last year when she went to the resource room for special help. Is there anything you would like to add?

Parent: Well, I don't like to complain, but I just don't understand this new way of doing things for her. I was glad when she qualified for special education, because I thought she would finally get some help. Now she isn't getting it any more. Besides that, I wonder how this consulting program affects the other children. As you know, I am president of the local Parent Teachers Association, and questions about the special education program have come up at several of our meetings. I told parents I would try to get more information from you.

Consulting Teacher: I've been working closely with your daughter's classroom teacher this year, and we've worked out some special learning activities in the classroom such as cooperative learning. She loves that, and when she needs a little extra help we've arranged for a sixth-grade girl to tutor her. Besides that, she goes to the resource room for math.

Special Education Director: I understand the placement team agreed to all these special experiences at the IEP meeting last spring.

Parent: Yes, I know we agreed to try them, but I don't think they are working. I'd like more evidence that this is the right way to educate children who have learning problems.

Principal: Mr. Penner, do you have data that we can show Mrs. James?

Consulting Teacher: Well, I could get some test scores from teachers, I guess.

Special Education Director: Our consultation program is rather new. I believe it is already producing some positive outcomes, but it's evident that we must provide more documentation of the results. We'll need a more structured evaluation plan to get the appropriate data for assessing our results.

Principal: I agree. Thank you for being involved with your daughter's program, Mrs. James, and thanks for helping us think through what we need to do. After we do some further work on this topic, may we call on you to collaborate with us on developing a more specific plan?

Components of an Evaluation Plan

A model of consultation evaluation is shown in Figure 6.8. The model features the accumulation of information for two primary purposes—formative evaluation and summative evaluation. Formative evaluation is used when making decisions to modify, change, or refine a program during its implementation. Summative evaluation documents the attainment of program goals and is used most often by administrators in determining whether or not programs should be started, dropped, maintained, or chosen from among several alternatives (Popham,

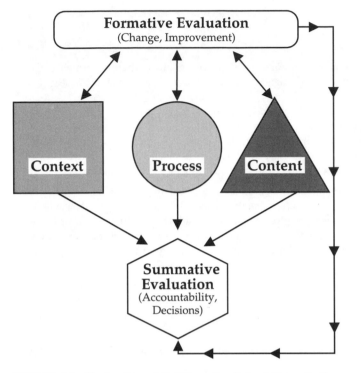

FIGURE 6.8   Evaluation of Collaborative School Consultation

1988; Posavac & Carey, 1989; Scriven, 1967). Data gathered during formative evaluations are often included as part of summative evaluation data.

The key in selecting evaluation procedures is to consider the purposes of assessment—the questions that need to be answered. Formative assessments provide information for making changes and improvements. The focus is upon individual concerns and the local school context. Summative evaluations are used to make decisions about program goals; therefore, they require collection of data from larger groups. Formative and summative evaluations also differ in the audiences to whom the results will be targeted and the way in which those results will be communicated (Popham, 1988). We propose that a good consultation evaluation will include context, processes, and content of consultation. These three elements are used for both formative and summative purposes. Examples of questions that might be addressed in each situation are presented in Figure 6.9.

FIGURE 6.9   Purposes of Assessment and Evaluation

	Focus on:	**FORMATIVE** **Change/improvement**	**SUMMATIVE** **Accountability**
Context	*Program success*	*Development/change* What program aspects should be changed to fit this school and community?	*Status decisions* Should the consulting program continue next year?
Process	*Consultation skills*	*Growth/development* What interpersonal management skills need to be changed?	*Self-analysis* Do I have the skills to be an effective consultant?
Content	*Student/client progress*	*Growth/progress* Are achievement and behavior improving?	*Placement decisions* Does the student need more or less restrictive service?

Developing an Evaluation Plan

Consultants should identify data-collection methods clearly in the initial stages of program development and at the beginning of each school year thereafter. A consultant who does not decide how to evaluate the program until the end of the school year will be working harder, not smarter. Summative evaluation procedures should be extensive enough to document achievement of each annual goal. This language probably sounds familiar, for that is exactly what is required when an IEP is developed. The similarity is not coincidental. Principles guiding IEP development must guide all good program development.

Once goals are determined, consultants can begin to list the types of data needed and determine ways of obtaining the data. Much of the data will exist within classrooms, in student files, or in school computer data banks. The challenge is to know what is needed and plan a strategy for collecting and summarizing the data in a meaningful, time-efficient way.

> Anita, a certified learning disabilities teacher, was excited about the prospects for the coming school year. Her school had set goals to address the educational needs of students at risk and to decrease the number of students labeled as disabled. Since many of these formerly labeled students were placed in LD programs, she volunteered to change her program delivery model to consultation and collaboration, with only limited resource room services. It was a challenge for which she hardly knew where to begin.
>
> Anita had studied literature on consultation and collaboration and she knew that the first step was to think through the program goals. She also knew it would be important to gather appropriate data so she and her administrators could decide whether or not their goals were met by this program change. She carefully considered the types of data that she would gather throughout the school year in order to make a good decision about the effectiveness of the program. As she thought about her evaluation plan, she also wanted to make sure she continued to improve her consultation skills during the year. So she included several goals that addressed that need.

Her plan is shown in Figure 6.10.

Sources of Information

The evaluation plan should contain at least one measure to document achievement of each program goal and a projected time line for gathering the information. Many different sources of information should be used, including but not limited to:

- Direct observations of behavior
- Portfolios of student work
- Long-term projects
- Parent input
- Related services personnel reports
- Student self-assessment records
- Logs and journals of consultation activities
- Progress charts
- Interviews
- Videotaped conferences
- Anecdotal records
- Student grades
- Counselor input

FIGURE 6.10 **Consultation Evaluation Plan**

Program Goals	Evaluation Procedures	Dates
Student progress in general classroom, with grades no less than D.	Curriculum-Based Measurement Grade reports Student portfolios	Daily 9-wks Ongoing
Increase in skills of teachers for teaching special needs students.	In-service evaluation	Each session
Student use of study skills classroom.	Classroom observation Teacher reports	9-wks 9-wks
Positive interaction with peers and teachers in classroom settings.	Classroom observation Behavior rating scale	Ongoing 9-wks
Parent satisfaction with child's school experiences.	Questionnaire	Dec.–May
Teacher satisfaction with consultation services.	Self-assessment checklists and rating forms	9-wks
Teacher use of suggested materials and methods in teaching.	Classroom environment checklist	Sep., Jan., May
Consultant use of effective communication and problem-solving.	Videotapes, behavior rating form, consultation verbal analysis system	9-wks
More student service with less labeling.	Consultation activity report Consultation log	Daily By need

Assessment methods and procedures should be as objective and unbiased as possible. Sometimes unbiased opinions and objectivity are not easily attained. For example, a consultant might ask consultees to complete checklists such as the ones presented in this chapter, but respondents may not be willing or able to offer objective opinions. As noted earlier, lack of objectivity can be an interfering theme in working with the special needs of students. Consultees sometimes give high ratings indiscriminately. This failure to discriminate may be due to fear of the consequences of being truthful (such as losing a colleague's friendship) or not knowing enough about the questioned behavior to offer a constructive opinion. High ratings are of little benefit for evaluation, and if inaccurate, they may be another example of an iatrogenic effect, compounding problems rather than creating solutions. For these reasons, consultants need information from multiple sources, in different circumstances within the context, and at varying times throughout the school year.

The following points list key elements in developing an effective evaluation plan:

1. It should be an ongoing process.
2. Multiple sources of information should be used.
3. Valid and reliable methods of gathering information should be used.

4. It should be limited to gathering data that will answer pertinent questions and document attainment of consultation goals.
5. It should be realistic, diplomatic, and sensitive to diversity issues.
6. Legal and ethical procedures, including protection of rights of privacy, must be followed.
7. Anonymity of respondents should be maintained whenever possible.
8. It needs to be cost-effective in time and money. For example, whenever possible, existing data should be used.

Evaluating the Contexts of Collaborative School Consultation

Contextual evaluation is based on the premise that educational events occur in a context and the elements of the context play important parts in determining whether or not educational processes result in the desired outcomes (Field & Hill, 1988). It acknowledges the interdependence of all aspects of the school experience, including teachers, parents, students, administrators, classroom environment, school facilities, policies, procedures, and legal requirements.

Contextual evaluation should consider the impact of students on teachers as well as the impact of teachers on students. It must assess the effect of teachers on consultants as well as the effect of consultants on teachers. It also should provide information on the professional interactions among individuals involved within the consultation environment(s).

Contextual evaluation is discussed here as it might be applied by individual consultants or collaborators. Administrators interested in a more extensive discussion of contextual appraisal for special education evaluation will find the work of Field and Hill (1988) a helpful reference.

Evaluators will want to give careful attention to environmental factors that are related to student outcomes (Ysseldyke & Christenson, 1987). These factors include:

- *School district conditions* such as teacher-pupil ratio, extent of emphasis on basic skills, amount of homework, emphasis on test taking, grading policies;
- *Within-school conditions* such as class size, school ambience, leadership from the principal, cooperative environment, collaborative staff relations, degree of structure, classroom rules and procedures; and
- *General family characteristics* such as socio-economic status, educational level, use of out-of-school time, and peer groups outside the school.

Assessment of student characteristics and general classroom conditions is needed in order for a consultant to determine whether or not any mismatch between student characteristics and classroom situation is a factor in the problem. If the classroom environment is a problem, analysis of the information can be used to formulate appropriate solutions. Information about student progress will be discussed later under content of consultation, because student academic and behavior change is the most valid measure of the effectiveness of content.

The major contextual element to be assessed is the classroom learning environment in which the student is expected to function. Bender (1988) suggests that educational placement teams conduct extensive evaluations of every classroom in the building at least every five years, keeping the information available for the use of preassessment team members, consultants, and other school staff. He articulates the importance of this type of assessment information for consultants:

> . . . some of the most useful services presently performed by special education consultants depend on knowledge about the standard functioning of general classrooms. When a consultant visits a class to observe the student and to consult, prior knowledge of what general types of strategies are commonly used in that class is likely to greatly enhance the consultant's ability to make meaningful strategy suggestions. (Bender, 1988, p. 19)

Other reasons for including this type of assessment in the evaluation plan are: (1) it is recognized that planning for instruction based on student learning styles and characteristics alone has been unsuccessful (Bender, 1988; Bursuck & Lessen, 1987; Ysseldyke & Christenson, 1987); (2) research on effective instruction now provides useful information for determining which elements of the classroom environment should be evaluated (Bursuck & Lessen, 1987; Ysseldyke & Christenson, 1987); and (3) the assessment has the potential to help classroom teachers better understand their own needs in facilitating learning for students with special needs (Bender, 1988).

Evaluating the Processes of Collaborative School Consultation

One of the most important reasons for conducting process evaluation is to glean information for professional development. According to some authorities, self-assessment and self-direction are preferred methods of professional development for teachers (Bailey, 1981). The rationale for self-assessment applies even more to school consultants than to teachers, because in most school contexts there will be few, if any, opportunities for consultants to receive any assistance from administrators or supervisors. Without some type of self-assessment, a consultant may perpetuate ineffective processes and the quality of the consultation may decline over time. The value of engaging in self-assessment of one's consultation is illustrated by this journal entry of a graduate student in consultation:

> Before involvement in the consulting project at this university, I had never seriously examined my communication skills. The videotaping has been the hardest for me; however, I have come to realize the importance of it and I have gained a better insight into areas that can be improved.
>
> The first videotape recording was a real eye-opener, revealing lack of skill in handling resistance. The second recording surprised the consultee, as she realized that during the consultation she had thought of a solution to the problem for herself. The third videotape revealed more areas in need of work: Conflict resolution, assertiveness, and controlling facial responses. I feel I did a good job of using the problem-solving technique, and the best part was to hear two consultees say they were going to use it themselves in problem situations. They feel it helped them focus on the problem and think of real solutions. It gave them a base from which to work.
>
> Setting time limitations is something I'm not comfortable doing. I would rather allow the consultee enough time to work through feelings and identify the issues. However, looking back over my consultation log, I see that six of the consultations took more than 45 minutes and might well have concluded earlier if I had set time limits.
>
> Now that I have identified this baseline of strengths and weaknesses, I have set the following goals to achieve by the end of the school year:

1. Reduce resistance from consultees to no more than one time in twenty.
2. Resolve conflicts at least 80% of the time.
3. Use assertive behavior during consultation 100% of the time.
4. Eliminate inappropriate facial responses.
5. I will videotape consultation episodes every nine weeks and tabulate the target behaviors to see if I am making progress in reaching my goals.
6. I will use a simplified version of the Consultant Behaviors Checklist to get feedback from my consultees every nine weeks.
7. I will periodically interview consultees after consultation episodes to gather more immediate feedback about the target behaviors I am trying to improve.

Self-Assessment Procedures

While many individuals engage in some self-appraisal or mental reflection, few do so systematically. Thus, the assessment or appraisal might not lead to meaningful improvement. Effective self-assessment should consist of a systematic, comprehensive program in which the consultant can gain information that leads to improvement or to a change of behavior.

The following suggestions for developing a self-assessment program are adapted from the work of Bailey (1981).

1. *Gain a philosophical overview of self-assessment.* Understand that self-assessment is not synonymous with the accountability required by administrators. Its purpose is personal change and improvement, and you should not share the results with supervisors unless you want to. The activities may not be easy to do, and some are rather time-consuming. They require selection of objective methods to gather data, in order to be most effective. Data should be collected in several consulting sessions with different types of consultees and various problem situations.

2. *Use media for self-assessment.* An objective way of gaining feedback about your behavior is to monitor it through use of audio- or videotaped material. Students in consulting preparation programs often are reluctant initially to use this type of feedback, but most are grateful later for its helpfulness. These tips for preparing and analyzing videotapes are helpful:

2.1 Set the consultee at ease by explaining the purpose of the videotape recording.

2.2 Do a few "trial runs" before involving a consultee, in order to become comfortable with the video camera and accustomed to seeing yourself on tape.

2.3 Don't focus on traits that have nothing to do with the quality of consultation. Taping distorts one's voice and visual image, so don't worry about them.

2.4 Observe or listen to the tape several times, each time focusing observations on just one or two behaviors.

2.5 Tabulate behavior using a systematic observation method so the information can be interpreted meaningfully and progress followed objectively.

2.6 Be sensitive to the rights of privacy of the consultee. Arrange the seating during a videotape-recording session so that you face the camera and the consultee's back is to the camera.

2.7 Do not show the tape to an audience without receiving signed permission from the consultee.

3. *Identify the important consultation skills to be observed.* Merely watching and listening to oneself with the help of media will not provide enough information to guide personal development. Specific skills must be designated for recording the observation. Checklists and rating forms such as the Consultant Behaviors Checklist (see Figure 6.11) can be used to identify behaviors to observe while viewing or listening to the taped consulting sessions. These checklists were developed from lists of important consulting behaviors described by researchers in the field.

4. *View or listen to taped consulting sessions and tabulate observation data.* Systematic behavioral observation techniques discussed later in this chapter are useful for observing

FIGURE 6.11 Collaborative Consultant Behaviors Checklist

Consultant _____ Observer _____ Date _____

	yes	needs work	does not apply
1. *Welcome*			
Sets comfortable climate	____	____	____
Uses commonly understood terms	____	____	____
Is nonjudgmental	____	____	____
Provides brief informal talk	____	____	____
Is pleasant	____	____	____
2. *Communication Exchange*			
Shares information	____	____	____
Is accepting	____	____	____
Is empathic	____	____	____
Identifies major issues	____	____	____
Keeps on task	____	____	____
Is perceptive, providing insight	____	____	____
Avoids jargon	____	____	____
Is encouraging	____	____	____
Gives positive reinforcement	____	____	____
Sets goals as agreed	____	____	____
Develops working strategy	____	____	____
Develops plan to implement strategy	____	____	____
Is friendly	____	____	____
3. *Interpretation of Communication*			
Seeks feedback	____	____	____
Demonstrates flexibility	____	____	____
Helps define problem	____	____	____
Helps consultee assume responsibility for plans	____	____	____
4. *Summarizing*			
Is concise	____	____	____
Is positive	____	____	____
Is clear	____	____	____
Sets another meeting if needed	____	____	____
Is affirming	____	____	____

consultant behavior, just as they are useful in observing student behavior in the classroom. Tabulate only one or two behaviors in each viewing, perhaps starting with a verbal behavior such as the number of times you said "O.K." or a nonverbal behavior such as looking away from the consultee. After tabulating the target behaviors, summarize strengths and behaviors that should be improved.

5. *Write down goals and objectives.* Prioritize the behaviors needing change and write behavioral objectives for them. Remember to state some type of criterion such as saying "O.K." no more than two times in a 20-minute consultation session. Include dates for achievement of each objective.

6. *Select strategies to help make the needed changes.* Formulate the strategies from material presented in other chapters of this text.

7. *Gather feedback and chart progress in achieving goals.* Periodic checks to determine whether or not you are making progress in the self-selected area for change are essential. It is very easy to believe erroneously that the change has taken place if this step is bypassed. If goals focus on verbal skills, audio tapes probably will be sufficient for follow-up data, but if they include nonverbal skills, use of videotapes should continue. Perhaps it would be most efficient to reevaluate consultation skills at every marking period for students. The advantage of using consultee feedback is that consultee information can be contrasted with the consultant's own information. If there is much discrepancy between the two sets of information, causes of the discrepancy need to be determined.

8. *When a criterion is met, a self-reward is due for a job well done!* The objective data can be shared with a supervisor. The consultant may wish to chart consultation growth just as student progress growth is documented. Charts tell the story much more quickly than a list of numbers or a narrative description. Self-assessment should be an on-going process propelled by realistic expectations.

Records of Collaborative Consultation Activities

Administrators are interested in more than how effectively consultants communicate or engage in problem-solving. They want to know about practical issues such as how the consultant uses time, how many consultees have been helped, the types of problems addressed, and whether or not the consultation services were helpful to the consultees.

Consultants should keep records of consultation activities in order to answer these types of questions. The consulting log in this chapter is a useful form for documenting these data. Those who want to develop their own forms would find the work of Tindal and Taylor-Pendergast (1989) a helpful reference. It may be productive also to check with one's administrator to find out what specific information would be most desired. Busy consultants should not spend time collecting information that is not wanted or needed.

> One special education consultant in an inclusive school avoided the confusion that resulted from many people going in and out of each classroom every day by devising a system to record these activities. In each classroom she placed record forms that were completed by each person who went into the classroom to consult or provide special services to a student with disabilities. These individuals were asked to "log in" by entering the date, time, name,

and a brief comment regarding the student(s) with disabilities during the time in the classroom. Later, the data were sorted in various ways for final reports.

Evaluating the Content of Collaborative School Consultation

The content of consultation consists of the problem solutions, instructional techniques, or behavioral interventions selected through the consultation process. The content can be judged effective if the goals of the consultation are achieved. In school consultation the goals usually address improved achievement or behavior.

School consultants need training in the traditional approach of examining students through use of formal and informal testing procedures to identify their special learning needs. Skill in observing classroom performance, as differentiated from performance in a testing situation, is also necessary.

Curriculum-Based Assessment (CBA).   The most functional approach to making these observations is Curriculum-Based Assessment (CBA). It is important to identify accurately the student's current level of performance in the classroom and monitor progress in a systematic, on-going manner. Standardized tests are not designed for this type of monitoring. Curriculum-Based Assessment is the most appropriate approach for the purpose (Bender, 1988; Bursuck & Lessen, 1987; Deno, 1987; Wang, 1987).

"There is nothing new about curriculum-based assessment. In many respects it is like coming home to traditional classroom instruction" (Tucker, 1985, p. 199). What *is* new are more precise and practical ways of examining student progress in the classroom curriculum. The basic concept of CBA is use of the actual curriculum materials, or the course of study adopted by a school system, in making the assessment (Tucker, 1985). CBA differs from traditional testing, which uses material representing a composite of items taken from many different curricula. While standardized tests tell us how students perform in relation to a large reference group, CBA tells us how students perform in the classrooms where they are expected to function. Since most school consultants will be addressing problems that occur in general classrooms, they will need this type of information to formulate good solutions to problems and to document effectiveness of their efforts.

Consultants can choose among several ways to conduct CBA. Although teacher-made tests and criterion-referenced tests provide information about content mastery, portfolios and Curriculum-Based Measurement provide information to monitor progress in larger domains over time. All the procedures have valid uses. The method chosen will depend on the circumstances within the school and should be the most valid, reliable, and efficient method for a given purpose. Although Curriculum-Based Measurement meets these criteria, it is limited to measurement of basic skills and cannot be used to monitor many other valuable educational goals. Caution should be taken in adopting commercially prepared CBA measures because they probably will not be accurate measures of the curriculum in a particular school. Criterion-referenced tests that accompany the textbooks adopted by school personnel would be appropriate CBA measures for a consultant to use.

Some school districts and states require a type of CBA for all students. A term commonly used for this practice is *outcomes-based education* (OBE). OBE requires schools to state the outcomes they expect from their efforts. These outcomes are often stated as processes as well as products. Although school districts might state very broad outcomes, such as "all students will be good communicators in a complex world," the outcomes become more narrow as they are stated at the building and classroom levels. For special educators, the IEP is an outcomes-based document for a single individual. For a school that utilizes the principles of outcomes-based education, the information generated for that program might be sufficient for evaluation needs. The consultant would need only to gain access to the information as it applies to the program being evaluated.

Other CBA measures are informal reading inventories (assuming the reading materials are taken from school texts), and mastery tests in content subject matter. Many special educators are familiar with approaches to evaluation of student learning such as Precision Teaching (Lindsley, 1964) and Data-Based Instruction (Mercer & Mercer, 1993). These approaches require specification of observable and measurable objectives which can be recorded as the number of correct and incorrect movements or responses per minute. One-minute probes are given daily and the scores are plotted on charts. The charts are analyzed frequently to observe trends indicating whether instructional program changes are needed. A variation of this approach was developed and refined at the University of Minnesota (Deno, 1987). This CBA system is called Curriculum-Based *Measurement* (CBM), emphasis added to differentiate it from other forms of CBA.

Portfolio Assessment.   Other types of student performance, including sample worksheets, copies of projects, extra-credit reports, and samples of artwork, can be collected into portfolios to help document the content of consultation. Evaluation of such products is an alternative that has much potential for assessing a wide range of student abilities and needs.

Portfolio assessment focuses on both process and the product of learning. It is authentic in purpose and task, multidimensional, and contributes to an ongoing learning process. The material can be continuously evaluated, streamlined, and sent with the student from grade level to grade level as visible evidence of growth and improvement. It provides an effective vehicle for partnership in learning between teacher and student and contributes valuable support material for staffings and parent conferences.

Problems to be overcome in using this alternative form of assessment center around the additional work, storage space, patience, and time for teacher interaction with each student. A school consultant can ease the load of a teacher who wishes to use portfolio assessment by working as a team member to consult with students as they reflect on their work, and by collaborating with the teacher to develop ways of organizing and using the procedure.

Portfolios must provide some measure of objectivity to be reliable indicators of growth or progress toward goals in a working portfolio. Teachers need to organize a systematic process of securing samples to put into the portfolio. For example, writing samples might be gathered once each month, dated, and placed in chronological order in the portfolio. Then the samples can be easily viewed to show progress toward the goal. Additional objectivity and evaluation are provided with use of a rubric. Rubrics are lists for standards or outcomes that guide the evaluation process. They are often in the form of rating scales. Figure 6.12 provides an example of a rubric for the product, process, and content of writing. Ideally, the rubric is completed and discussed in a conference between the student and teacher at regular intervals during the school term. The completed rubrics are kept in the portfolio for future reference and modified as growth takes place (Swicegood, 1994).

FIGURE 6.12   Example of Rubric for Portfolio Assessment

WRITTEN EXPRESSION RUBRIC				
	EMERGING	**GROWING**	**MASTERED**	**EXPANDED**
WRITING PRODUCT				
Handwriting				
Grammar				
Spelling				
Capitalization				
Paraphrasing				
WRITING PROCESS				
Idea generation				
Brainstorming				
Organization of ideas				
Editing skills				
Error correction				
Final draft				
WRITING CONTENT				
Sentence development				
Paragraph organization				
Paragraph development				
Overall length of writing				
Use of words				
Fluency of writing				
Variety of purposes				

COMMENTS:

Implementation of a portfolio assessment system in collaboration with students and colleagues includes the following steps:

1. Collaborate with students by giving them a voice in planning, organizing, and assessing the portfolio collection.
2. Determine types of contents to be included (with flexibility for adding new types that may be determined later).
3. Prepare formats to organize portfolio contents, such as a table of contents or a summary sheet.
4. Determine criteria for evaluating the contents.
5. Determine the final destination of the portfolio and its contents.
6. Arrange for a safe, secure storage space.
7. Rehearse discussion and critique of the portfolio before conference.

Maintaining Student Academic Records.   If consultants have been using curriculum-based assessment and systematic behavioral observation procedures, a summary of the information can provide a summative record of consultation content. This information can report the number of goals met or not met, student grades or test scores, and interviews with teachers and parents.

A disadvantage of using records such as portfolios for assessment is the immense volume of material generated for consultants who monitor the progress of a caseload of thirty or more students. One solution to this dilemma is to require students to keep their own portfolios of their work (Wolf, 1989). This strategy seems especially valuable for use by consultants for gifted and talented students in content areas of art, music, design, written expression, computer programming, and other subjects which do not lend themselves easily to conventional forms of assessment.

Another method involves collaboration among classroom teacher, special education consultant, *and student* to develop criteria for assessing portfolio products, selecting the best or most representative ones, and removing others. Thus the portfolio volume is reduced while the student is gaining valuable self-assessment skills. Students skilled in using computers can store their products in a computer file.

Recording Behavior Observations.   Finding solutions to classroom behavior problems constitutes one of the major content areas of consultation. Consultants will need to gather objective information to document behavior changes. Systematic behavior observations, as well as subjective measures such as rating scales and checklists, should be used for this purpose. Rating scales or checklists can be developed for the context, or commercially prepared instruments can be used after careful selection to fit context needs.

Several individuals, such as classroom teachers, parents, teacher aides, or peer tutors, can be asked to complete the rating scales. There are two advantages in asking the classroom teacher. First, the behaviors to observe can be more closely targeted. Second, teachers can be encouraged to focus attention on behaviors not previously considered. Bursuck and Lessen (1987) emphasize that a combination of behavioral observation by a consultant and completion of a behavior checklist by the teacher will be preferable to either one alone.

For example, it is not sufficient to observe that the student does not pay attention or is noisy. The educator needs to know precisely the rate and frequency of the behaviors and under what conditions the student displays the behaviors. Systematic, direct observation of the student in the environments in which the problems occur is the best assessment procedure for gathering the information.

■ ■ ■ ■ ■ ■

APPLICATION 6.3
DEVELOPING A TEACHER PORTFOLIO

Educators can benefit from building their own professional portfolios. In doing do they demonstrate to students the value and importance of portfolios. The portfolio can be presented as an example of productivity when they are evaluated by a supervisor or an administrator. Last, but not to be overlooked—they can be fun to build!

Possibilities for portfolio products abound. A few are lesson plans that worked well; videotapes of classroom activity highlights; sample tests; effective worksheets or packets; an original teaching or grading technique; sketch of an unusual bulletin board so it won't be forgotten; list of professional books read; any articles published in newsletters, newspapers, or other professional outlets; documentation of consultation episodes (coded for confidentiality); descriptions of team teaching activities; photos of special class sessions; original computer software that worked well; a highly effective management technique; notes from parents or students that were reinforcing; goals for the semester or school year; special achievements by students. The list could go on and on.

Develop a plan for your teacher portfolio. Include a table of contents and perhaps rubrics for showing growth and progress toward professional goals. Do not overlook collaborative experiences in your collection. Decorate the folio in your personal style!

Data collected on specific behaviors can help collaborators set goals, plan programs, and evaluate interventions. In preassessment and problem-solving it is much easier to deal with "is at least 15 minutes tardy 85% of the time," or "screams and kicks heels on the floor an average of 6 times per day," or "writes 90% of the 4s, 5s, and 7s backward," or "regularly completes math assignment accurately in less than half the time allocated," than it is to work collaboratively on problems described as "irresponsible," "aggressive," "has problems writing numbers," and "fast worker."

Several methods of behavior measurement are useful for consultants:

- frequency recording,
- interval recording,
- time sampling,
- duration.

Each method begins with identifying and defining a specific, concrete behavior or a set of behaviors to be observed.

Behavior should be defined so precisely that when measured by two different people, the numbers will be virtually the same, assuring reliability of the measurement. Two people measuring "aggression" or "irresponsibility" or "speedy work" would not be likely to have very high interrater reliability of the measurement! Sometimes it will take several visits to the classroom, or a visit to the classroom by several different consultants, to develop an observable and measurable definition of the behavior.

Audio- or Videotape Records.   Another possibility for accumulating records of student behavior, particularly social behavior in the classroom, is the use of audio- or videotaped sessions (Minner, Minner, & Lepich, 1990), which can be part of a student's portfolio. "Teachers have told us that tapes are especially useful when showing parents how their son or daughter has progressed" (p. 33). This approach to data collection, while very effective, is often difficult to arrange. The suggestions discussed for using videotapes in self-assessment are applicable for this situation. Consultants should be very cautious about protecting the confidentiality of the observed student as well as other students in the classroom.

BENEFITS FROM EVALUATION OF COLLABORATIVE SCHOOL CONSULTATION

Teacher involvement in consultation and collaboration must not be perceived as a sign of weakness or inadequacy. Instead, consultees should be commended for taking advantage of services provided to help both educators and students succeed. Involvement in consultation and collaboration must be rated as a strength on the performance evaluations of school personnel by administrators and supervisors. School personnel should be involved in developing and implementing consultation practices and assessing their outcomes, and should conduct self-assessment of their consultation and collaboration. Self assessment is sometimes a painful but always a necessary practice for the consultant. The Consultation Log earlier in this chapter includes a brief self-assessment.

Videotaping, having a colleague observe and report, and often just reflecting upon one's habits are all potentially helpful ways of growing professionally. Reflection leads to insights about oneself, prompting changes in self-concept, changes in perception of an event or person, or plans for changing some behavior (Canning, 1991). One speech/language pathologist analyzed her emerging consultation skills this way:

> In my early perception of consulting I viewed myself as the expert. Experience has taught me I am not. Expert language usually is understood by very few. Knowing how to frame good questions is an invaluable tool. I used to think I knew what was best for the child. Experience again has shown me this is not so—we must all get our respective "what's bests" on the table and mediate. I felt that I needed to have all the workable solutions to the problem at hand, but this was assuming too much. I thought everyone likes and respects the "expert" and wants his or her help. I now perceive my task as one of earning the right to become part of the planning for any child. This means I must be as knowledgeable as possible, not only in my own field, but about the total environment (physical and mental) of each child. I am still learning that effective intervention takes time and careful planning.

Figures 6.13 and 6.14 provide tools for assessing the collaborative consultations. Other self-assessment questions the consultant can ask include:

- What solutions have I offered for discussion?
- What documentation have I gathered to support my opinions?
- Can I list the questions I want to ask the consultee?
- Can I listen and work cooperatively on the problem?
- Can I be honest about my feelings toward the student, the problem, and the personnel involved?

FIGURE 6.13   Consultee Assessment of Consultation and Collaboration

Please evaluate your use of the consulting teacher service provided in the _____
program by providing the following information. Respond with:

1 = Not at all	2 = A little	3 = Somewhat	4 = Considerably	5 = Much

1. The consulting teacher provides useful information. _____

2. The consulting teacher understands my school environment and teaching situation. _____

3. The consulting teacher listens to my ideas. _____

4. The consulting teacher helps me identify useful resources that help my students' special needs. _____

5. The consulting teacher explains ideas clearly. _____

6. The consulting teacher fits easily into the school setting. _____

7. The consulting teacher increases my confidence in the special programs. _____

8. I value consulting and collaborating with the consulting teacher. _____

9. I have requested collaboration time with the consulting teacher. _____

10. I plan to continue seeking opportunities to consult and collaborate with the consulting teacher. _____

Other comments: _____

_____

FIGURE 6.14   Checklist for Evaluating Collaborative Consultation

Dear _____,

Please take a few minutes to help me improve my consulting skills by completing this checklist.

Any additional comments you wish to make will be greatly appreciated. Thank you!

_____(name)_____

	A Strength	O.K.	Needs Improving
1. Helped me to be comfortable collaborating.	____	____	____
2. Communicated clearly.	____	____	____
3. Used our time productively.	____	____	____
4. Listened well.	____	____	____
5. Asked facilitating questions.	____	____	____
6. Showed understanding of my role.	____	____	____
7. Demonstrated flexibility.	____	____	____
8. Presence/time not disruptive.	____	____	____
9. I want to work together again.	____	____	____
10. Other comments:			

- Will I follow through on the plan?
- Will I document the efficacy of the plan?
- Will I try new methods and strategies?
- Will I persist in the plan?
- Will I give feedback to the consultee about the situation?
- Am I willing to ask for help or advice?

TIPS FOR MANAGING AND EVALUATING COLLABORATIVE SCHOOL CONSULTATION

1. At the end of the year, write thank-you notes to school personnel you have worked with, including principals, secretaries, and custodians. When writing notes to colleagues, sign your name in a distinctive color on pads of an individualized design. Send a note on a "reminder" memo, and staple a bag of nuts, or a Valentine cookie, or a doughnut, to it. Remember those who collaborate with you in special ways by delivering a treat to their room along with a brief note of appreciation.

2. Color-code folders for schools if you serve several. Use a file box with a card for each day to list reminders, and a schedule book. Keep an idea file of filler activities.

3. Use tubs for storage of materials. Plan ahead and put materials in the tub for one week, one month, a season, or a thematic unit.

4. Have a retrieval box in a certain place for receiving borrowed items that are returned. Keep a check-out catalog so you will know where your materials are. When materials are due, remove due-cards for the buildings where you will be that week and collect the materials while there.

5. Listen to conversations in the workroom, lunchroom, and faculty meetings. When a topic surfaces for which you have materials, offer to share. Prepare a list of instructional material that is for loaning and distribute it. Make sure grade level and sample objectives of the material are given.

6. Don't schedule yourself so tightly that you have no time for informal interactions and impromptu consultation. These can open the door for more intensive and productive collaboration. Also, be even more protective of colleagues' time than you are of your own, and make good use of it.

7. Furnish treats often. (For very nutrition-conscious schools, make the treats vegetables or fruit.)

8. Make concise checklists for procedural activities, such as general items to tell parents at conferences, or items to tell new students and their parents.

9. If doing a demonstration lesson, give the classroom teacher a paper stating the activity name, type of activity it is, and learning objectives. State your name at the bottom and specify that it comes from "Consultant ___'s Lesson Plan," thereby establishing your identity.

10. Go to classroom teachers and ask *them* for help in their area of expertise. Ask for a copy of something you have seen that would be a good addition for your file, but be sure they mean for you to use it or share it before you do so.

11. Generate alternatives to having more and more meetings, try them out, and get input from colleagues on their value. When a meeting *is* needed, and it promises to be a

difficult one, on the night before the meeting try visualizing a successful one in which everything goes very well.

12. Visit other schools and take notes on organizational systems and management techniques that could be incorporated into your system. Then prepare a summary sheet for colleagues on your return.

13. Find time to collaborate by exploring innovative ways of "making" more time and using it wisely. Schedule common lunch or preparation periods; in large districts increase class size by just one and use surplus funds to hire substitutes; have teachers match a period of early dismissal time with their contribution of equal time; have students involved in community service one afternoon a week while teachers meet.

14. Develop ways of working smarter, not harder, such as having information-exchange pools with other teachers, sharing learning centers and packets with colleagues in other attendance centers, and gathering free resources from commercial business and industry.

15. Promote instances of high-quality consultation and collaboration, not just the frequency and time spent in the activities.

16. As a consultant, portray oneself as assistant to the teacher.

17. Become more visible, visiting each classroom and making positive comments about what is going on there.

18. Always have an ear open to opportunities to help out, and spin off helping situations to become more established as a consulting teacher.

19. Be realistic and understanding about the demands that are placed upon classroom teachers, administrators, and parents in fulfilling *their* roles.

20. Be realistic about what consultants can do, and celebrate even small successes.

21. Keep school personnel wanting more consultation services, making them so valuable that if they were taken away from the schools, the role and its services would be missed.

22. Keep providing benefits for them. Again, "What can I do for you and your students that you do not have time or resources to do?" is the operative question.

23. Identify successful, exemplary consultation and collaboration practices, *especially* when they occur in your school district!

24. Work with a group of collaborating colleagues to write a guide on the use of consultation and collaboration. Present it to new faculty members, and periodically conduct refresher sessions for all professional development activities.

25. Send notes of appreciation to consultees regularly.

26. Do not expect a uniformly high level of acceptance and involvement from all, but keep aiming for it.

CHAPTER REVIEW

1. Stress that is encountered in many human service roles can lead to burnout and subsequent attrition from the field. Positive attitudes, health maintenance, supportive networks, realistic goals, relaxation, environmental changes, and taking control of one's life will minimize stress and help prevent burnout, fizzle out, rust out, and coast out among consultants and teachers.

2. Careful management of time and energy decreases stress and increases productivity for those in consultative roles. School personnel will want to establish goals to manage their resources, identify and remediate time-wasters, use positive time-management strategies, and take good care of themselves.

3. Meetings, interviews, and observations must be kept as efficient and positive as possible. With careful planning each of these activities can be more productive for consultants and collaborators. It is important to provide a comfortable meeting environment, prepare an agenda, keep minutes of decisions and plans, and assess the success of the meeting. When consultants observe in classrooms, they should demonstrate caring attitudes and provide positive support for those being observed.

4. Record-keeping systems and resource-management systems are necessary for busy consultants who serve many schools. Consultants must keep records and materials in order, maintain confidentiality, and be on the lookout for helpful material with which to consult and collaborate. Consulting journals and notebooks are tools that facilitate management of complex responsibilities. Personalized touches for memos and messages help develop rapport with consultees.

5. An evaluation program is essential for documenting the effectiveness of any educational program, making improvements, and defending the quality of the program to administrators and other decision makers.

6. During the initial stages of program development, consultants should create a plan for ongoing evaluation. Formative and summative information of the context, processes, and content of consultation must be gathered throughout the program and the school year in the most efficient manner possible. Methods of gathering data should come from multiple sources and should be as objective and unbiased as possible.

7. Formative and summative evaluation should include evaluation of consultation processes. Consultants need to engage in systematic self-assessment, in order to gain information for improving their consultation skills, because it is not likely most will have the administrator feedback and monitoring needed for professional growth in this area. They should also keep careful records of their activities, to justify the program to decision makers.

TO DO AND THINK ABOUT

1. Discuss some record-keeping and managerial tasks that most people really do not like to do, such as preparing income tax returns, and consider ways the activities could be made less unpleasant and more manageable. Then consider how these techniques could be used creatively by school consultants.

2. Describe The Perfect Meeting. What would need to be done in order for this meeting to transpire?

3. Design a weekly and daily planning sheet that has space for stating goals, listing activities in categories, prioritizing the list, and estimating times for accomplishing the activities. Try your planning sheets, and share them with others if you found them helpful.

4. Conduct a time analysis to diagnose time-management problems you may have. Use one of the methods described in this chapter or develop your own.

5. Create ideas for the following management tools, and if your present situation warrants, construct them and try them out:

   - A logo for personalized note pads or memo sheets that will identify you and feature school consultation in a positive, collaborative spirit
   - An observation checklist that would work in your school situation
   - A consultation log or journal format to record the consultation and follow through, as well as a brief assessment of the consultation
   - A table of contents for a notebook in which to organize information, data, and material needed to carry out the school consultation role
   - A system for cataloging materials to be shared with consultees, and for checking the material in and out

6. Name several consumer and decision-making target groups within a school district who are likely to ask for data to support a consultation program. What would be the most effective formats for presenting the data to each target group for its purposes?

7. Develop an evaluation plan for consultation service during the coming school year in your school setting.

8. Conduct a self-assessment of one's own consultation skills. Give careful attention to each step of the process. Make an effort to videotape the consultation in a real or simulated experience periodically. Chart behavioral data to demonstrate progress on at least two specific objectives.

9. Use the Consultation Log for at least six weeks. Meet with other consultants to modify the forms as needed, and then use the revised forms for the remainder of the school term.

10. Once a week, make it a point to take ten or fifteen minutes at the end of the day to reflect on all the important things that happened in the classroom that day. Notice how observant one becomes after engaging in this practice for a while.

FOR FURTHER READING

Bender, W. N. (1988). The other side of placement decisions: Assessment of the mainstream learning environment. *Remedial and Special Education, 9*(5), 28–33.

Collins, C. (1987). *Time management for teachers: Practical techniques and skills that give you more time to teach.* West Nyack, NY: Parker.

Conoley, J. C., & Conoley, C. W. (1982). *School consultation: A guide to practice and training.* New York: Pergamon Press. Contains more than a half-dozen forms to be used or adapted for gathering consultee feedback about the effectiveness of the consultation process.

Davis, W. E. (1983). *The special educator: Strategies for succeeding in today's schools.* Austin, TX: PRO-ED. Chapter 2 on burnout, chapter 5 on meetings, chapter 6 on paperwork, record-keeping, and time management, and chapter 8 on ethical, legal, and professional dilemmas.

Fuchs, L. S., Fuchs, D., & Hamlett, C. L. (1990). Curriculum-Based Measurement: A Standardized, long-term goal approach to monitoring student progress. *Academic Therapy, 25*(5), 615–632. Provides a reasonably detailed description of how CBM can be used to help teachers formulate effective instructional programs using the charted data to make relevant decisions.

Haynes, M. E. (1998). *Effective meeting skills: A practical guide for more productive meetings.* Los Altos, CA: Crisp.

Jusjka, J. (1991). Observations. *Phi Delta Kappan, 72*(6), 468–470.

Keyes, R. (1991). *Timelock: How life got so hectic and what you can do about it.* New York: Harper Collins.

Kozoll, C. E. (1982). *Time management for educators,* Fastback #175. Bloomington, IN: Phi Delta Kappa Educational Foundation.

MacKenzie, A., & Waldo, K. C. (1981). *About time: A woman's guide to time management.* New York: McGraw-Hill.

Maher, C. A. (1982). Time management training for providers of special services. *Exceptional Children, 48,* 523–528.

Newman, J. E. (1992). *How to stay cool, calm and collected when the pressure's on: A stress control plan for business people.* New York: American Management Association.

Sapolsky, R. (1994). *Why zebras don't get ulcers: A guide to stress, stress-related diseases, and coping.* New York: W. H. Freeman.

Sugai, G. (1986). Recording classroom events: Maintaining a critical incidents log. *Teaching Exceptional Children* (1986, Winter), 98–102.

Swicegood, P. (1994). Portfolio-based assessment practices. *Intervention in School and Clinic, 30*(1), 6–15. Provides an overview of portfolio assessment practices and their application for students with disabilities.

CHAPTER SEVEN

WORKING TOGETHER FOR STUDENTS FROM DIVERSE POPULATIONS

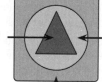

Diversity ⟶ ⟵ Awareness and Appreciation

Educational Environments

For many years, the United States was regarded as a melting pot of many races, ethnicities, religions, and cultures. Then it became stylish to refer to it as a "salad bowl." With the salad metaphor each of the many diverse populations could be perceived as contributing unique characteristics to the flavor and piquancy of the whole. But now the melting pot and salad bowl comparisons fall short of describing the ever-expanding richness of perspectives, attributes, talents, skills, and styles that epitomize this country in the twenty-first century.

The imagery of a mosaic is more illustrative of our broad spectrum of cultures. Each socioeconomic, racial, ethnic, religious, age, gender, and ability group offers unique pieces to the picture, with shared values and institutions of the whole providing the frame and the adhesive. Or we could construct a tapestry in which threads of many textures, hues, and sizes would be woven into a colorful, interesting picture. Of course there would be occasional knots, ravelings, and frays, but every thread would be valuable in providing purpose and significance to the whole design. Mosaic and tapestry metaphors for multiculturalism reflect philosophies, if not always practices just yet, that can enhance the multicultural sensitivities of every individual and catalyze a growing respect for all others.

In this chapter the primary content area (triangle) is diversity. Processes (in the circle) are awareness and appreciation, with the context (square) representing the educational environments.

FOCUSING QUESTIONS

1. How does the changing demography of contemporary classrooms relate to school consultation and collaboration?

2. What is meant by *cultural diversity,* and what terms are used for various school programs that serve culturally diverse learners?

3. What is the collaborative consultant's role for working with diverse populations and how can supportive attitudes, sensitivities, and skills for the role be developed and assessed?

4. Why should consulting teachers strive to first know their own culture before they set out to consult, collaborate, and work on educational teams in multicultural settings?

5. What are some differences in culturally diverse communication styles and belief systems that teachers may find among their students and their colleagues in education?

6. What educational practices might a consultant find helpful when working with culturally and linguistically diverse students who have special needs?

7. How can collaborative consultants promote awareness and appreciation of cultural and linguistic diversity in school settings?

8. What are special needs of students in rural and isolated areas, in areas with high rates of mobility, in military dependent contexts, and in settings where they are home-schooled?

KEY TERMS

cultural and linguistic
   diversity (CLD)

cultural and linguistic diversity
   with exceptionality(ies)
   (CLDE)

culture

English for speakers of other
   languages (ESOL)

English-language learners
   (ELL)

home schooling

macroculture

microculture

military dependent students

mobile students

multiculturalism

rural students

VIGNETTE 7.1

The instructor of a course that includes awareness and appreciation of cultural diversity distributes an activity to class members, and says, "Please move about the room to obtain a different autograph on each blank line of your paper. You may use your own name once if you qualify for that item. When your autograph form is complete, or the signal is given to stop, please sit down and interact with others near you by telling some things about your own cultural background, sharing memorable multicultural experiences you have had, and discussing places and peoples you would like to know more about.

AUTOGRAPH FORM
Obtain autographs from:

1. Someone who speaks Spanish.   _____
2. Someone who has been in more countries than you have.   _____

3. A person who owns a world atlas. _____
4. Someone who has eaten blubber (or sushi, grasshoppers, or some
    other local delicacy of a culture not your own). _____
5. A person who has driven on roads (legally) left of center. _____
6. A person who has seen a movie in a foreign language. _____
7. Someone who knows the time in Sweden right now. _____
8. A person who has studied the French or German language. _____
9. One who has or did have an international pen pal. _____
10. Someone with a friend or a relative from another culture. _____

As participants collect the autographs, and especially as they begin discussing their own experiences with other cultures and languages, the instructor is aware of the wide range of multicultural experiences within the group. Sharing these backgrounds and learning more about their experiences will be helpful in expanding multicultural understanding.

CULTURAL AND LINGUISTIC DIVERSITY (CLD)

Demographers project that by the year 2056, more than 50 percent of the U.S. population will be persons with different cultural and linguistic backgrounds from the current norm. The number of students from diverse cultures is expected to grow to 24 million, or 37 percent, of the school-age population by the year 2010. Such diversity reflects the multicultural tapestry of our population with its many colors, ideas, backgrounds, languages, lifestyles, and beliefs.

Citizens of our nation and personnel in our school systems are learning to recognize and appreciate the richness that diversity brings to the texture of community life. As Hallahan and Kauffman propose (1991):

- Cultural diversity is to be valued just as varied sizes, colors, and textures contribute to the whole.
- Common cultural values hold our society together as the framework synergizes pieces into a connected, meaningful whole.

What is culture? According to Webster's dictionaries (1976; 1996), culture is the sum total of customary beliefs, social forms, and ways of living built up by a group of human beings and transmitted from one generation to another. It is useful to think of culture as made up of six major elements (Banks, 1988; Hallahan & Kauffman, 1991):

1. Values and behavioral styles
2. Languages and dialects
3. Nonverbal communication
4. Awareness of one's cultural distinctiveness
5. Frames of reference, or normative worldviews and perspectives
6. Identification with, or feeling part of, the cultural group

These six elements coalesce into a nation's culture (the macroculture), with smaller cultures (the microcultures) providing unique variations within it (Banks & Banks, 1989; Hallahan &

Kauffman, 1991). It is appropriate to define *culture* broadly, because many demographic variables (age, gender, residence), status variables (social, educational, economic), and affiliations (formal, informal) contribute. Current uses of the word *culture* in education settings have come to relate to ethnicity, language, religion, sexual preference, economic level, demographic indicators such as ruralness, age, gender, and many other indicators of group uniqueness.

Education demographer Hodgkinson notes that the United States has more diversity in the country by race, ethnicity, income, parents' education, and other factors than it has had for many years. Different regions of the country are becoming more unlike in very important ways and a policy or practice that benefits one region may be questionable, objectionable, or unworkable in another. For example, frequently mobile students require school contexts that are not homogenized but tailored to student needs (Hodgkinson, 2000). Educational systems will be called on more and more during the next several decades to serve new pluralities with sensitivity and understanding of multicultural issues.

Cultural Diversity in the Teacher Population

The teaching force does not reflect cultural diversity and it never has. Profiles of prospective teachers continue to be primarily white females from small towns or suburban communities who attended colleges or universities not far from home and plan to return to places similar to home for their teaching career. These teachers reflect middle-class backgrounds and values and have limited experience with diverse cultures. Eighty percent of teachers surveyed by Futrell, Gomez, and Bedden (2003) felt unprepared to teach a diverse student population. Fewer than 3 percent can teach in a language other than English (Holloway, 2003).

It is essential for educators to become familiar with the cultures of the students and families with whom they work and to have preparation in interpersonal communication and problem solving with culturally diverse populations. Deans and department chairs of teacher education programs are well aware that a critical element in gaining national accreditation for their programs is demonstration of diversity in student enrollment, instructional faculty, and sites for student teaching and field experiences. Once preservice teachers are placed in schools for that first year of teaching, experienced consulting teachers have an important role in mentoring and coaching them to work effectively with culturally and linguistically diverse students. (The mentor teacher is discussed in Chapter 12.)

Terminology for Multicultural Awareness and Understanding

Changes in the language used in various professional circles to describe programs, students, and instructional strategies related to diversity may be confusing to consultants and consultees. Definitional uncertainties will need to be tolerated by consultants, who may need to ask questions or research the meaning of terms used in various local school programs related to diversity. Terms include *English-language learners* (ELL), *English-language development* (ELD), *multicultural education, English for speakers of other languages* (ESOL), *cultural and linguistic diversity* (CLD), and *culturally and linguistically diverse students with exceptionalities* (CLDE).

The term *English-language learners* (ELL) refers to students who are less than proficient in English. *English-language development* (ELD) refers to all types of instruction that promote the development of either oral or written English-language skills and abilities. This term replaces terms such as *English as a second language* (ESL) or *English for speakers of other languages* (ESOL) (Gersten & Baker, 2000). The merger of ELD with academic content instruction is often called "sheltered content instruction" (Echevarria & Graves, 1998).

Tobias (1993) suggests that one term that creates misunderstanding and can cause differential treatment of others is the phrase *minority group,* so this term is used less frequently than those just mentioned. One reason for this is the historical problem in education of mistaking ethnicity for exceptionality (Hallahan & Kauffman, (1991). For example, the word *disadvantaged* should not be coupled with the word *cultural* because a person is not disadvantaged by having an affiliation with any culture. The appropriate term for conveying meaning is *cultural diversity.* Neither should ethnic standards for one group be used as standards of another group. An ethnic group is described by Banks (1988) as one that shares a common ancestry, culture, history, tradition, and sense of peoplehood in becoming a political and economic interest group. Multicultural awareness means that people can disagree without the need to regard one side as right and the other as wrong. Tyler (1979) stresses that "right ways" of conducting particular social activities within various ethnic groups can be diametrically opposed.

MULTICULTURAL COMPETENCIES FOR COLLABORATIVE CONSULTANTS

Efforts to become more inclusive in education include increasing knowledge about cultural diversity, fostering positive attitudes toward cultural pluralism, and cultivating skills in arranging multiple learning environments that will enable individuals from every culture to realize their potential. Cultural awareness is not always a part of an educator's strengths. As an example of just one teacher's experience, Dorris (1979) describes an elementary school student of American Indian heritage who brought a printed program home from school with an illustration of the "The Pilgrims' First Thanksgiving." This child's father noted the caption under the illustration informing readers that "the Pilgrims had served pumpkin, turkey, corn, and squash to the Indians, a feast *the likes of which the Indians had never seen before.*"

Glasgow and Hicks (2003) offer suggestions for recognizing and celebrating diversity in the classroom. They provide several research-based points that consultants should remember in their work with CLD children and families and other school personnel on the education team. Selected examples include:

1. Think beyond content. English-language learners come with a variety of challenges and needs, as well as strengths.

2. Develop a critical understanding of the social-cultural context of interactions and instruction in your setting and allow this understanding to guide your work.

3. Reflect on and promote a positive ethnic identity, because all cultures add value to schools and to society.

4. Develop multicultural connections in your discipline and your community.

5. Confront your own ethnic and cultural stereotypes.

6. Become culturally literate to the highest degree possible when working in schools, communities, and school districts with significantly diverse populations.

7. Prepare for a cultural and linguistic mismatch between you and your students.

Language used within a culture is a major transmitter of the culture because it affects how people think about things (Westby & Ford, 1993). Organizations, including schools, have their own language, which becomes the medium through which perspectives, values, and beliefs are defined.

Self-Assessment of Cultural Awareness and Sensitivity

Only after we have assessed our own attitudes and values toward cultural and linguistic diversity will we be able to develop and strengthen our skills for working with diverse populations. When we hone our cross-cultural competencies, we are better consultants for consultees from diverse backgrounds. In addition, we are better equipped to promote understanding and appreciation of diverse cultural groups in the school setting. Therefore, we must examine our attitudes about cultures different from our own, taking care to ferret out any narrowness of thinking.

Sample items for assessing one's multicultural awareness are provided in Figure 7.1. The items can be used for personal reflection and self-study. Discussion and expansion of the list can provide a powerful staff-development experience. The list also could be administered as part of a study module for a teacher preparation course on consultation and collaboration, or a professional development in-service activity. Other items might be added to the checklist as a result of powerful discussions about multiculturalism and cultural diversity in schools and communities.

■ ■ ■ ■ ■ ▬▬▬▬▬▬▬▬▬▬▬▬▬▬▬▬▬▬▬▬▬▬

APPLICATION 7.1
SETTING PERSONAL OBJECTIVES FOR APPRECIATION OF DIVERSITY

After completing the checklist in Figure 7.1, select two or three of the items that you would like to incorporate into a personal plan for the school year. Set target dates and on those dates evaluate the outcomes. Treat yourself to something special for making significant progress!

Being Aware of One's Own Cultural Background

It can be argued that every consultative activity involves human diversity; therefore, a consultant's individual understanding of what diversity means will affect the collaboration and consultation processes (Clare, 2002). Clare further suggests that persons' worldviews and perspectives of diversity vary and change as a result of multicultural experiences and proximity to other groups. These experiences provide avenues for personal reflection and they shift the way consulting teachers frame collaborative efforts and educational practices.

Culturally responsive consultants are essential to the immediate and long-term success of the consultation (Ramirez, Lepage, Kratochwill, & Duffy, 1998). The first step in cultural awareness is understanding one's own culture, beliefs, and values. Educators must become comfortable with their own microcultural identification (Hallahan & Kauffman, 1991). Recogniz-

FIGURE 7.1   Examples of Multicultural Assessment Items

A = Always; U = Usually; S = Sometimes; R = Rarely; N = Never

Personal Sensitivity

_____   1. I realize that any individual in a group may not have the same values as others in the group.

_____   2. I avoid words, statements, expressions, and actions that members of other culture groups could find offensive.

_____   3. I read books and articles to increase my understanding and sensitivity about the hopes, strengths, and concerns of people from other cultures.

_____   4. I counteract prejudicial, stereotypical thinking and talking whenever and wherever I can.

School Context Efforts

_____   5. I include contributions of people of color as an integral part of the school curriculum.

_____   6. I strive to nurture skills and develop values in students and colleagues that will help members of minority groups thrive in the dominant culture.

_____   7. I know where to obtain bias-free, multicultural materials for use in my school.

_____   8. I have evaluated the school resource materials to determine whether or not they contain fair and appropriate presentation of people of color.

Parent/Community Relations

_____   9. I invite parents and community members from various cultural backgrounds to be classroom resources, speakers, visiting experts, or assistants.

_____   10. I value having a school staff composed of people from different cultural backgrounds.

_____   11. I exhibit displays showing culturally diverse people working and socializing together.

_____   12. I advocate for schools in which all classes, including special education classes, reflect and respect diversity.

ing characteristics of one's own cultural beliefs is especially important for European Americans because of their tendency to view culture through an ethnocentric lens, often believing, somewhat naively, that theirs is the primary or prevailing culture (Lynch & Hansen, 1992).

■ ■ ■ ■ ■ ▬▬▬▬▬▬▬▬▬▬▬▬▬▬▬▬▬▬▬▬▬▬▬▬▬▬

APPLICATION 7.2

REFLECTING ON ONE'S OWN CULTURAL ORIENTATION

Think about your own cultural background. What language did your great-grandparents, or more distant ancestors, speak? When did they come to this country? Why did they come? What family customs, such as holidays and food, reflect the culture of your ancestors?

Then practice effective communication skills by listening to descriptions from others about their cultural heritage. Share your cultural background information with others so that they can practice their communication skills and get to know *you* better.

After consultants develop an understanding of their own culture, values, and beliefs, they should work to enhance their abilities for acknowledging cultural differences in communication and relationships. To do this, cross-cultural communication skills are important competencies for consultants. "It may be that diversity in interpretation (different ways of knowing) is . . . a particular strength of human perception and cognition. Diversity is essential to viability in other domains—for example, human genetics—and may also be a strength in the cognitive domain" (Conoley, 1994, p. 47).

COLLABORATIVE CONSULTATION PROCESSES IN DIVERSE CULTURAL SETTINGS

Consultants have an instrumental role in bringing together diverse groups of educators, including teachers, administrators, related services personnel, families, and community members. Consultants use communication and collaboration skills to help the educational team address and resolve problems and to work for creative solutions.

Collaborative consultation and a true collaborative environment, rather than an expert model of consultation, comprise the current preferred mode of education for CLDE students (Baca & Cervantes, 1998). In this approach the expertise of one partner in the team working, for example, with CLDE students, is not valued over that of another; all are recognized as vital to the collaborative process and the education of students. One of the greatest challenges for consultants in diverse settings is understanding the consultee's frame of reference, or "entering the consultee's world" and viewing things as the consultee sees them (Soo-Hoo, 1998). Home communication patterns for students or consultees may be quite different from those they hear and see in school. Expectations between family members and teachers may be at variance. One must acquire a deep understanding of the consultee's or the client's frame of reference through ethnic study and cross-cultural materials.

Bodgan and Biklen (1998) propose that being able-bodied and working with individuals having disabilities can create tension and misunderstanding. They are careful to point out that differences do not always impinge on the staff member's effectiveness, but need to be taken into account and planned for so that potential difficulties can be avoided. Cultures throughout the world have different perceptions of disability. In some cultures, those with "disabilities" are accepted as having a place in the community with no stigma or problem but rather a talent and uniqueness to contribute. This is a challenging paradox for educators who feel strongly about providing different services for students with special needs.

Cross-cultural variations have important effects on collaborative problem solving. In their recommendations for doing fieldwork in another culture, Bogdan and Biklen (1998) provide insight that is helpful for collaborative school consultants as well. They caution that not all cultures share middle-class American definitions of terms. Carrying this concept further, in different cultures there are different rules about human communications and relationships. One such instance is that it is not acceptable in some cultures to share beliefs and opinions with people outside the group. Another is the proclivity for being quiet in the presence of authority figures. This can be disconcerting to school personnel who are trying to solicit active parent input during conferences and staffings.

Examples of ethnic-based values and behaviors that can affect group interaction are preferences regarding (Adler, 1993; Sue & Sue, 1990):

- Personal space, such as physical distance between communicants and arrangement of furniture for seating
- Body movement, including body orientation, gestures, facial expressions
- Time orientation
- Eye movement and position
- Touch
- Nonverbal vocal cues such as loudness, hesitations, inflections, and speed

The field of sociolinguistics focuses on the relationship between verbal and nonverbal communication. Areas of linguistics, anthropology, and sociology are joined to analyze the sociology of language. Interactions of language structures and social structures are examined to learn how language transmission influences attitudes and opinion (Adler, 1993).

In some cultures the way to respond to a question with finesse is to skirt the subject and arrive at it indirectly, while in a different culture being direct and forthright is admirable. As another example, in certain cultures public congratulation is offensive because group accomplishment is valued more than individual achievement, while in other cultures public congratulation would be an incentive to continue excelling. Variations of actions involving handshakes, head nods, eyebrow raising, and finger-pointing will have widely different meanings in different cultural settings.

Sue and Sue (1990) provide helpful tables of generic cultural characteristics for counseling the majority culture of the United States, and Asian, African American, Hispanic, and Native American cultures. For example, some individuals in an Asian culture may expect one-way communication from the authority figure to another person. Silence signifies respect and there are well-defined, concrete patterns of interaction. Members of a Hispanic culture may provide a different time perspective, a strong emphasis on the extended family, and typically a bilingual background. Many members of the African American culture are action oriented with a sense of peoplehood and importance placed on nonverbal behavior. Values within the Native American culture tend to stress cooperation over competitive individualism, to work toward immediate, short-range goals, and to respect creative and intuitive approaches.

Members of Hispanic, Asian, and Native American cultures promote respect for elders and authority figures, and the expectation of not speaking until spoken to. Therefore, a consulting teacher hoping to engage the family in collaborative problem solving may be met with silence or short phrases as a sign of respect, and may erroneously interpret this response as being negative or disengaged. However, as a cautionary note, generic cultural characteristics are not the be-all and end-all of cultural diversity. Any person or family may differ markedly from such generalities. Thus, any suggested description of characteristics will provide only broad brush strokes with which to begin working to achieve successful relationships as collaborators and consultants.

Labeling issues may become more pronounced during multicultural collaboration. This can be caused by real or perceived feelings of superiority, prejudice, stereotyping, and unreasonable expectations (Adler, 1993). For example, statistics documenting overrepresentation of children of color in programs for those with mental retardation and their underrepresentation in gifted and talented programs are well known by special education personnel. A more subtle but debilitating concern, however, is the lowered expectation level that educators too often have for students in minority cultures due to such data.

The socioeconomic variable that includes class, status, position, and prestige has many ramifications for teaching and learning, and may be even more obvious during collaborative endeavors. Gender and age also affect interactions, particularly when they intersect with characteristics of some culture groups. Collaborators must monitor their own behavior for use of fair and balanced gender-specific languages. For example:

- Use *persons* or *women and men,* not *men* or *mankind.*
- Use the term *homemaker,* not *housewife.*
- Avoid saying *female* doctor, *male* nurse, saying simply *doctor* or *nurse.*
- Instead of saying "He adds the balances," say "The accountant adds the balances."
- Do not avoid recognizing same-sex partnerships. Same-sex partners are usually called "partner," rather than "significant other."
- Avoid *man and wife,* replacing it with *the couple* or *husband and wife.*
- Refrain from terms like *the fair sex, woman's work, man-sized job.*
- Say "Susan is a successful executive," not "Susan is a successful lady."
- Identify someone as a *supervisor* rather than a *foreman.*
- Say "Students" or "Class," instead of "Boys and Girls."

Consultants will want to avoid negative words, using language instead that indicates a desire to help students expand their abilities, not to help them "get better." Caution must be exercised in discussing poor work, bad behavior, or poor attitudes. What is perceived as mild criticism or simply suggestion in one culture may bring about severe punishment to the child or disillusionment about the student's ability from a family of another culture. Idioms should not be used that might be misunderstood in another language, for example, "He will work his way out of this," or "Let's put this on the back burner for now, "or "We need to get her to up to speed in that," or "Students need to toe the line in her classroom," or "That's a Catch-22." Consultants should listen carefully to family members to learn more about the student and capitalize on his or her strengths, which is good strategy for any situation involving any student, for that matter.

Awareness of differences and respect for different customs within diverse cultures can become major factors in interaction within school settings and collaborative efforts by school personnel. Consulting teachers and collaborators must model respect for diversity and assist other school personnel in cultivating ethnic identities of students through classroom activities that range from more traditional through contemporary styles. This will reduce stereotyping and accommodate diversity, to the advantage of multicultural students with special needs (Heron & Harris, 1987). One powerful and constructive way educators can model respect is to convey intentions of learning *from* another culture, and not just learning *about* it.

A Chinese student studying special education in the United States was enrolled in a university course to study principles and methods of school consultation and collaboration. This student wrote:

> Since I came to the United States, I have been involved in a totally different circumstance I have never confronted before. . . . I really observe and analyze a life with different implications and features. I was puzzled at the scene in which American students rushed in and out of the classroom each day, while in China we may have more leisure time chatting or discussing among students. Classmates in China usually stand for {sic} close friends, who take years to study, work, play, and live together. Here in America, only a few faces are familiar

to me as one semester passed. . . . I sometimes feel myself retiring, quietly friendly, sensitive, modest about my abilities. This in fact reflects some aspect of culture in our society. I was nurtured to become a "good boy"—courteous and modest. Thus, I, like many other Chinese students, shun disagreements, do not force my opinions or values on other.

In considering methods for improving cross-cultural awareness and sensitivity, the best way for consultants to learn about other cultures is by learning from the people themselves, rather than *about* them as a member of a cultural group. Thus, the communication and interpersonal skills discussed in Chapter 4 are important for collaboration with partners in the education of CLDE students.

■ ■ ■ ■ ■

APPLICATION 7.3
ROLE-PLAYING TO BUILD MULTICULTURAL AWARENESS

Picture yourself living in another country with a very different culture and language from that where you currently live. For example, what if you and your family as you are now were living in a rural village in Argentina, in a fishing area in Malaysia, or in a city dwelling in Hong Kong? What would you want your new neighbors to know about you and your cultural background? What are some of your habits, beliefs, and attitudes you think might stand out and make you seem very different? Imagine that you are the parent of a child with a disability living in this place. What would you want the teacher(s) to know about your beliefs about educating children with disabilities? What would you do if the school had very different beliefs and programs? How would you want teachers to work with you on behalf of your child?

Working in Teams for Culturally and Linguistically Diverse (CLD) Students

Those who work together for CLD students should remember that students in the throes of acculturation may find the learning environment in public schools stressful and confusing (Baca & Cervantes, 1998). There may be instances when the cultural difference itself, or the disability, is not the foremost problem. It is necessary to consider the interaction of culture and language within the acculturation context and the possible effects of a disability on this interaction (Baca & Cervantes. 1998).

Success for culturally and linguistically diverse students with exceptionality(ies) (CLDE) students can be maximized by attending to promising practices that have proven effective. For example, Baca and Cervantes (1998) name four crucial elements in developing educational programs for culturally and linguistically diverse students:

- Content
- Instructional strategies
- Instructional setting
- Student behavior

These are considerations to be discussed in a consultant role with other educators who are working with CLDE students.

Teacher assistance teams are a common strategy for serving exceptional CLD students. This team should include individuals with expertise in appropriate assessment and instructional options related to the cultural and linguistic background of the students as well as the exceptionality.

Bahamonde and Friend (1999) suggest that co-teaching is a promising alternative to current practices of bilingual education. By applying best practices and knowledge from special education to bilingual education, improvements can be documented in student–student, student–teacher, and teacher–teacher relationships. Collaborative consultation is a key feature of co-teaching and more about this subject is found in Chapter 8.

Strategies for Success with CLDE Students

Howard's (2001) research found that students' perceptions and interpretations of their teachers' instruction revealed important insights into the dynamics of young African American learners. Howard suggests three specific strategies or areas that consultants could facilitate in their work with teachers of CLDE students. These areas and teacher behavior representing each area are listed below:

1. *Caring.* Demonstrate sincere concern for students. Use positive reinforcement. Express high expectations. Take time to find out about students' lives outside the classroom. Demonstrate commitment to both the academic and social development of students.

2. *Establishing community.* Encourage kindred relationships in the academic setting. Eliminate homogeneous ability groupings (both formal and informal). Establish appropriate democratic principles and promote interdependence.

3. *Creating classroom environments.* Create exciting and stimulating classroom environments. Connect course content to the students' lives. Modify style of discourse in ways that are more interactive, engaging, and entertaining for students.

Baca and de Valenzuela (1998) provide several suggestions for teachers who work with CLDE students. Their ideas hold special merit for consultants who work with a variety of students and a diverse population of professionals. Not only should consultants work to adopt their suggestions, they are in an excellent position as educational team leaders to help other professionals as well as entire school systems make changes in order to work with all students appropriately and effectively. Baca and de Valenzuela (1998) recommend:

- Integrating the nature of schooling with a holistic, interconnected program rather than compartmentalized and disjointed special programs for CLDE students
- Adopting instructional strategies known to be effective with CLD students
- Integrating assessment and instruction
- Challenging one's own unwarranted assumptions and those of the school about CLDE students and their families

Modifying Materials and Instruction for CLDE Students.   Modification of materials and instruction requires educators and all members of teams serving the CLDE student to be sensitive to the learning, language, and cultural characteristics of the student. Harris

(1998) recommends that when modifying materials four criteria should be used to determine their appropriateness:

1. Does the material reinforce learning?
2. Is the material logically sequenced?
3. Is the material comprehensible? (Does the language level of the material match the language proficiency of the student?)
4. Is the material culturally sensitive?

These are important questions for consultants to consider as they work with special and general educators and others in planning for CLDE students.

Instructional Practices for English Language Learner (ELL) Students

Effective instruction for English-language learners is more than just "good teaching." An extensive literature search and qualitative multivariate analysis by Gersten and Baker (2000) support the use of some specific techniques:

- Preteaching critical vocabulary prior to student reading
- Providing explicit instruction and guided practice in math problem solving
- Using classwide peer tutoring and other strategies that provide frequent opportunities to use oral language in the classroom
- Providing frequent, clear feedback to students
- Using approaches that structure time so students are actively engaged in academic work

Extensive analysis by Gersten and Baker (2000) indicates that instructional practices for English-language learners invariably assume students can learn English while learning academic content. A major problem with this sheltered content instruction is that time for language learning is often truncated or omitted altogether. Consultants should be aware that inadequate time for English-language development, which Gersten and Baker found to be a major problem in current practice, may be a much greater problem with ELL students who have special needs. For ensuring appropriate English-language development, the researchers recommend:

- Considering language learning and content-area learning as distinct educational goals;
- Providing time each day for English-language learners to work on all aspects of ELL; and
- Blending oral language engagement and cognitive engagement in all instruction.

Instructional variables that represent principles of best practice from the Gersten and Baker (2000) study are:

1. Building and using vocabulary as a curricular anchor
2. Using visuals to reinforce concepts and vocabulary
3. Implementing cooperative learning and peer-tutoring strategies
4. Using native language strategically
5. Modulating cognitive and language demands

See the section For Further Reading at the end of this chapter for a source that provides a fuller discussion of this topic.

Special Needs of Students in Rural and Isolated School Settings

Rural schools in remote areas are characterized by geographic isolation, cultural isolation, too few students for some kinds of grouping, too few staff members covering too many curricular and special program areas, resistance of students toward being singled out, limited resources, and, most of all, distance that necessitates great amounts of personnel time spent in travel. Some special education resource personnel spend up to half of their work day on the road (Meyen & Skrtic, 1988). The consulting teacher has become a mainstay of school districts in which miles and more miles separate students who have special learning and behavior needs.

In rural areas communication is more likely to be person-to-person rather than written or phoned as in urban settings. In rural setting teachers tend to be highly visible, therefore more vulnerable to community pressure and criticism. Rural educators are left much to themselves to solve problems and acquire skills for their roles (Thurston & Kimsey, 1989). These qualities of rural school life create advantages for consulting teacher approaches, yet there are certain disadvantages inherent in indirect service delivery. Few rural schools are fully prepared and able to meet the needs of special needs students without consultation and other indirect services. Therefore, it is necessary for consulting teachers to become intensively involved in providing learning options and alternatives for students. Consulting teachers can coordinate collaborative effort among teachers, administrators, parents, and other community members so that few resources seem like more.

In a comparative study of consultant roles and responsibilities in rural and urban areas, Thurston and Kimsey (1989) found that rural and urban teachers conduct similar consulting activities, but rural teachers have less formal recognition of their consulting roles. They seem less confident in their consulting skills than their urban counterparts. Major obstacles include:

- Too many other responsibilities
- Not enough time
- Lack of administrative support
- Too much paperwork
- Minimal professional interaction due to sparse population (although electronic communication has become increasingly helpful with this aspect)
- Long distances to travel and often poor roads and weather conditions for driving
- More lesson preparations and extracurricular duties
- The reality that differentness is more noticeable among smaller populations.

Contrasting obstacles reported by urban area consulting teachers include too many other responsibilities, too much paperwork, and disinterested parents.

Rural area students tend to be resourceful, open to a wide range of experiences, somewhat independent, and capable of self-direction. These pluses can be used to advantage by consultants in designing collaborative arrangements for special needs. Because students in rural areas often dislike being singled out, it is important to involve them in planning learning programs in which they are comfortable and interested.

Rural teachers do have advantages in carrying out their consulting roles. They often function as influential change agents. They tend to be creative and innovative problem solvers (perhaps paralleling the farmer/rancher who can fix almost anything with improvisation and what is on hand). In no other setting is the multiplier effect more useful than in rural areas having limited access and resources. These multiplier benefits (which will be discussed further in Chapter 12) can be maximized by playing on the strengths of the rural community, including smaller class sizes, more frequent interaction between students and staff, greater involvement of parents in the school and its activities, and students who participate in most phases of school life.

Special Needs of Students Who Move Frequently

With up to 20 percent of the population in the United States on the move each year, many school-age children's educational programs are disrupted. Moving and the events leading up to and following it can be traumatic for anyone; for the student with disabilities they may be particularly troublesome. Records must be forwarded, new teachers and texts and classmates assimilated, and adjustments made to home conditions of sleep, meals, and schedules while the child is getting settled in.

Wallings (1990) describes several characteristics and some major effects on families who move frequently. Such families tend to be younger with young, school-age children, and they are more apt to rent than own a home. The older the student, the more difficult a move seems to be, because adolescents are quite peer-oriented. Boys in particular are often less adept than girls at making new friends, and may be teased, bullied, or rejected. Children may feel they cannot measure up to expectations in the new school. One whose disability was accepted by peers in the former school has to begin all over again to win friends and influence adults.

Single-parent families have a particularly difficult time because there is no other adult with whom to share responsibilities and repercussions of the move. The school-age individual may be put into the position of that other needed adult without having the coping skills and maturity to manage the stress. Belonging to a minority group (for example, a black student in a white majority classroom, or a white student in a primarily black classroom) is another factor in feeling welcome and being accepted. Limited ability with English will add yet another dimension to acclimation and academic success. (Refer again to the CLD and ELL sections of this chapter.)

Neighborhood ties are disrupted by moves, and parents are adjusting to new jobs in many cases. Families who are forced to move due to eviction, ethnic or racial tension, or economic deprivation will be particularly stressed. Children and teens of agricultural workers whose work takes them to different areas with regular frequency (and many of whom participate in that work themselves) may arrive late after school has begun. They often must catch up in academic areas due to constant moves, necessitating that they forego enrolling in classes such as art, drama, and debate. Those with disabilities and other special needs beyond these apparent ones are in particular need of consultation and collaboration by those who can provide the array of services they require. Mobility is a fact of modern life and it affects not only the students and families who move, but the institutions they use (Keller & Decoteau, 2000).

Newly arriving students with special needs should be assisted by the collaborative team in handling any stress and disorientation as soon as they arrive at the new school. Special services personnel in the new school can help ease their transition. Some plans that have proven successful are (Wallings, 1990):

- Peer support groups, particularly helpful when there is seasonal influx such as migrant worker employment;
- Class emphasis on teamwork and cooperation, which will help the new students and all others in the process;
- A buddy system, which could involve matching the student with an older, confident and popular student;
- Inclusion of a variety of learning styles and methods;
- Mentors (best if adult) to serve as the new student's advocate and confidant;
- Parent support groups;
- Periodic orientation programs at various times of the year;
- In-service programs for school personnel to focus on the needs of transient students, particularly those with disabilities, in their adjustment to the new school and neighborhood.

Students with special needs due to advanced abilities also can be affected by family moves. This area has not seen much research activity; however, one study revealed that gifted students were much more concerned about making new friendships and adjusting to their new school climate than they were about their academic success (Plucker & Yecke, 1999). There seemed to be little difficulty in sustaining their academic performance, but organizational difficulties such as different qualifications for programs and reluctance of school officials to accept test scores were barriers to smooth transitions. The researchers noted that, in order to overcome these kinds of administrative hurdles, parents frequently relied on assertiveness in their interactions with school personnel.

Special Needs of Military Dependent Students

Military dependent children and youth, a group whose families often move frequently, and live with considerable stress and anxiety, are too often overlooked as a population having special needs who can benefit significantly from consultation services. When families move from site to site, they frequently become frustrated with the tangled web of records (or *no* records until they do arrive), referrals, screenings, and conferences. When school records and student information are slow to catch up with the student or are misplaced, then the *students* are at risk of being misplaced in the school programs! Parents need quick forwarding of accurate, clear student records to ease their child's transition from school to school. Coordinators for the Army's Exceptional Family Member Program in Hawaii advise parents of exceptional children to deliver copies of program records personally, especially those related to their child's IEP (Keller & Decoteau, 2000). They also recommend that parents get a personal letter from former teachers explaining to the new teachers how they worked with that child. Consultants can become a lifeline for students and their families by assisting busy classroom teachers with organization of student records and coordination of orientation activities and conferences. Consultants also can facilitate integration of students into activities with their new peers.

Much can be done in the way of making military dependent and transitory students feel welcome in new environments. They can be assigned to buddies who help with orientation to the school and integration into peer groups. Selected classmates might interview the "new kid on the block," focusing on things their new peers like to do. Teachers can plan activities in which all students participate in making a class album or collage mural, highlighting unique qualities of everyone in the class. Ethnicity is addressed by reminding students that everyone has a cultural heritage (German, Finnish, Korean, Samoan, Irish, Nigerian, and so on). Each could research his or her own heritage, and a variety of project extensions are possible.

Curricular units and learning centers that highlight a student's travels and former experiences will be instructive for other students even as they make the military family's child feel more welcome. New students' strengths can be drawn on to help remediate gaps that may have resulted from dissimilar educational programs and frequent adjustments to new situations. In addition, students who have traveled widely can be valuable resources for their classmates and teachers and they should be encouraged to do so.

As more families are separated by the deployment of fathers, or mothers, or sometimes *both* parents to trouble spots around the world, consulting teachers can become sources of assurance for anxious families who have students with special needs. These caring professionals can provide continuity in learning programs and support for the social and emotional needs of students who may feel afraid, lonely, and confused. Working in a team with families, school administrators, teachers, social service personnel, and military staff will help ensure a stable learning environment for military dependent students.

Special Needs of Students Schooled at Home

Home schooling has increased steadily throughout the past two decades. The number of home-schooled students has been estimated as 1.5 million students (*CEC Today,* 2000). More recently, other reports suggest that as many as two million students are home-schooled and tens of millions of families are becoming more and more interested in it for their children.

Parents' reasons for home schooling have been cited as academic, value-driven, or religious, aiming for flexibility, wanting to keep their student's problems such as suspension or pregnancy at home, or the desire to serve special needs such as disabilities or giftedness more intensively than programs in public schools typically do. It is believed that approximately 10 percent of home-schooled students have disabilities.

As home schooling is becoming more accepted and prevalent, educators are seeing the need to develop collaborative partnerships with families who home-school. Some parents request the use of school services, including speech therapy, foreign language classes, extracurricular activities including sports, enrichment programs, and the use of libraries and other materials. As taxpayers they are entitled to these resources and by law they are entitled to special education services for their exceptional students.

Evidence that home schooling is successful for most of the students has been documented through such means as success rates in university classes and scores on standardized tests. However, there are few safety nets for the students if home-schooling does not work. Good home-schooling experiences are built on tremendous commitments of time, effort, and often a lost second-income source by families, particularly when there are disabilities that require special attention.

The home-schooling process has benefited greatly from distance-learning curricula and from resources available on the Internet. Many home-schooling families also take advantage of nearby community colleges and universities. Some parents do not want to commit to home-schooling as a full-time activity, preferring instead to send their children to school and supplement their education with downloaded curricula or community-based experiences to give them additional opportunities for learning.

Many home-schooling families want to remain a part of the public school community, and many educators adhere to the policy that all private and home-schooling students are eligible to receive services (*CEC Today,* 2000). A growing trend is one in which personnel from public schools and homes work together to educate the child. By collaborating with school personnel for a child's special needs, families can be assured that they have provided everything the home and the school have to offer in order to give their child the greatest opportunity to succeed. Collaborative partnerships will allow both home and school educators to provide the most benefits available for students in whom they have a common interest.

Educators with Disabilities

One diverse group that seldom is discussed in educational literature is educators who have disabilities. The teaching ranks undoubtedly include individuals with disabilities—physical, learning, perhaps behavioral, but this is not a widely investigated or talked-about topic.

Adults with physical disabilities such as missing limbs, hearing or visual impairment, disfigurement, or impaired mobility do occasionally prepare for and enter the teaching profession. Young children, and sometimes socially awkward adolescents, can be quite blunt (as when a group of seventh graders queried a former war veteran, now a teacher, who has a prosthesis for the right arm, by asking "Where'd you get that thing?"); at the same time they can be remarkably accepting as they get their papers handed back to them with the prosthesis, or shake "hands" with their teacher in greeting.

Teachers who have learning problems with memory, spelling, or comprehension have opportunities to model tenacity toward achievement and to share learning strategies that have helped them succeed. They can inspire children with anecdotes about how hard it was for them to progress in college, but that by having solid goals and good habits to nudge them forward, they achieved their aim of earning a degree and obtaining teacher licensure. Adults who have overcome anxiety disorders, eating disorders, obsessive-compulsive disorders, or drug and alcohol dependency also have much to offer children and youth by modeling attitudes of coping, resilience, a regimen of good habits, and a conquering spirit.

Media cite data sources estimating that six to nine million adults have ADHD, or attention deficit with hyperactivity disorder (Adults and Attention Deficit Disorder, *New York Times,* 1997, September), and some of these millions surely are in the education profession. Meanwhile, teachers despair over helping their own students with ADHD to succeed in school. However, many adults with ADHD tend to excel in crises and have learned adaptive strategies for dealing with paperwork and details. One former salesman said he could not keep an accurate count of his merchandise, so he left that job and found fulfillment working in a restaurant and teaching reading to those with disabilities.

The incidence of disability among school personnel, the objective analyses of their abilities to handle the conditions, and discussions of the impact this has on schools and students are topics for which much more information is needed. School collaboration is an arena in which these topics can be discussed openly rather than left to linger below the surface and adversely affect communication and problem solving. Interference with problem solving by one's own problems would be an example of lack of objectivity, one of the four interfering themes (Caplan, 1970) referred to as impediments to effective teaching.

COLLABORATIVE CONSULTATION FOR SUCCESSFUL AND ETHICAL PROMOTION OF CULTURAL DIVERSITY

Educators will want to design activities that not only reduce stereotyping and prevent prejudice, but also promote contributions from culturally diverse groups. Multicultural education is *not* an activity for the last thirty minutes of school on Friday; awareness and acceptance of cultural and linguistic diversity must be infused throughout the entire school program. Consultants can be particularly facilitative and supportive in this endeavor as they assist in assessing the instructional environment and designing effective instruction for culturally diverse groups.

The hidden curriculum is a key area for developing awareness and acceptance of diversity. Informal discussions, bulletin board displays, selections read to the class, speakers brought into the classroom, all are helpful if planned carefully. Selected teaching activities can promote acceptance of and even a fascination for differences, as well as allow for different opinions and points of view and increase understanding of how people can be limited by their cultural assumptions. Consulting and collaborating teachers can designate a permanent bulletin board for multicultural news and displays. They might work with the library or media center to provide and publicize special displays and materials. Feature stories in the school newspaper and parent newsletters, along with radio spots and inserts into the daily announcements at school, can highlight diversity and multicultural events. In and of itself, the school curriculum is an ideal vehicle for developing multicultural awareness and nurturing cultural sensitivity. Consultants must work to ensure that curriculum builds and does not destroy positive attitudes and understanding.

Collaborative consultants also are in a position to encourage fuller use of diversity-focused resources within the entire community. They might bring in successful citizens representing culturally diverse groups to tell about their heritage, interests, and roles in society. They might pair these resource people with students having special needs, particularly if they have the same cultural background as the student.

Awareness, appreciation, and sensitivity toward individual differences and cultural diversity are vital attributes for consultants as they work with a wide range of resource and support personnel, teachers, parents, and the students themselves. Goals for multiculturalism are fundamental goals for ethical education programs that benefit all children. Such principles are exemplified in the City of New York's Board of Education staff-development program, and grounded in recent research on processes of teaching and learning for students with disabilities and special needs, which includes (Tobias, 1993):

- Holding high expectations for all students and believing all can learn
- Encouraging open, free sharing of beliefs, ideas, information, and feelings
- Helping students treat each other as equals without regard to cultural factors such as race, religion, ethnicity, gender, sexual orientation, or disability
- Helping students take active roles in improving their lives and the lives of those around them
- Perceiving themselves as professionals working to help children learn and develop

TIPS FOR WORKING WITH DIVERSE POPULATIONS IN SCHOOL SETTINGS

1. Learn about the values, beliefs, and traditions of other cultures in your school by attending community activities sponsored by those cultural groups.
2. Read fiction and nonfiction about people, families, and communities that are very different from your own.
3. Get to know the families of culturally and linguistically diverse students by making special efforts to reach out to them. Let them know you want to learn more about them because you care about their children.
4. Sit in on classes in bilingual education programs.
5. Develop collaborative relationships with teachers of English-language learners or culturally and linguistically diverse students with exceptionalities, even if you are not working with any of the students in their classes at the present time.
6. Make the most of opportunities to travel to new places, interact with people from other cultures, and acquire at least a rudimentary knowledge of a new language.

CHAPTER REVIEW

1. Cultural and linguistic diversity is increasing dramatically in public schools. Demographic trends are presenting major new challenges for school personnel. This will require that consultants work closely with families, community members, and professionals of diverse cultural and linguistic backgrounds.

2. Cultural diversity is reflected in the variety of customary beliefs, social forms, and ways of living built up by groups of people and transmitted from one generation to the other. Culture must be defined broadly because many demographic variables contribute to this construct.

3. Collaborative school consultants have key roles in bringing together diverse groups of educators from schools, families, and communities. Self-assessment, preceded by examination of one's own cultural affiliations, can be a basis for ongoing professional and personal development concerning diversity and self-awareness issues. In addition, assessments or checklists can be used for staff development and individual consultation work.

4. Consultants need to develop cross-cultural competencies for collaboration with adults from diverse backgrounds. These competencies must include reflection on their own cultural background and sensitivities.

5. Teachers may observe patterns of diverse communication styles and value systems among culturally diverse populations. However, they should not generalize by forming stereotypical generalizations about other culture groups.

6. Consultants should learn as much as possible about best practices for CLD, CLDE, and ELL students and combine these with best practices from special education. This will be most likely to produce the best outcomes for the student, and such commitment demonstrates true collaboration between professionals from various fields of expertise.

7. School consultants and consulting teachers are in ideal positions to infuse appreciation and recognition of diversity into the school context. They can facilitate greater parent involvement, coordinate instruction with ELL and bilingual education teachers, and collaborate in systems changes that help schools meet the needs of CLDE students.

8. Coordination of services and collaboration among school personnel and support personnel are particularly beneficial for students in rural, isolated areas, for students who are military dependents, and for those in families that move often. In the past several years, the increase in

home-schooling and parental interest in supplementing their home-schooling with public school resources has opened the door for substantive collaboration between school educators and home educators in home–school partnerships.

TO DO AND THINK ABOUT

1. Visit a family that has a different cultural or linguistic background from your own. Ask questions that will help you develop an understanding of their values, beliefs, and customs.

2. Design a bulletin board that celebrates cultural and linguistic differences in children, families, and neighborhoods. Where might you display it?

3. Interview teachers from schools with significant multicultural populations, asking them to suggest ways in which consultation and collaboration might help meet students' special needs. What steps should be taken to carry out these ideas?

4. Visit with colleagues or classmates about open-ended topics such as:
   - What do I think I would do if I were in a school where I was the only teacher whose native language was English?
   - What are my best attributes as a teacher of children with cultural and linguistic differences?
   - What cross-cultural strengths do I have? What could I improve?

FOR FURTHER READING

Association for Supervision and Curriculum Development. (1999). Partners in education: How schools and homeschoolers work together. *Education Updaqte, 41*(4), 1, 4–5.

Baca, L. M., & Cervantes, H. T. (1998). *The bilingual special education interface* (3rd ed.). Upper Saddle River, NJ: Merrill.

Gersten, R., & Baker, S. (2000). What we know about effective instructional practices for English-language learners. *Exceptional Children, 66*(4), 454–470.

Glasgow, N. A., & Hicks, C. D. (2003). *What SUCCESSFUL teachers do: 91 research-based classroom strategies for new and veteran teachers.* Thousand Oaks, CA: Corwin.

Keller, M. M., & Decoteau, G. T. (2000). *The military child: Mobility and education.* Fastback #463. Bloomington, IN: Phi Delta Kappa Educational Foundation. This little fastback provides helpful suggestions and lists other resources for attending to the needs of military children in public schools.

Soo-Hoo, T. (1998). Applying frame of reference and reframing techniques to improve school consultation in multicultural settings. *Journal of Educational and Psychological Consultation, 9*(4), 325–345. Soo-Hoo contends that literature on multicultural issues in school consultation is very limited. Culture shapes and determines behavior, influencing not only what one thinks but how how one thinks. Understanding frames of reference and reframing are important techniques for consulting in multicultural settings.

Westby, C. E., & Ford, V. (1993). The role of team culture in assessment and intervention. *Journal of Educational and Psychological Consultation, 4*(4), 319–341. Authors propose that results of educational assessment are as much or more dependent on culture of the evaluation team and their communicative interaction patterns as they are on the culture, strengths, and needs of students evaluated and their families. Available on-line at: www.crosscultured.com.

CHAPTER EIGHT

WORKING TOGETHER FOR STUDENTS WITH DISABILITIES

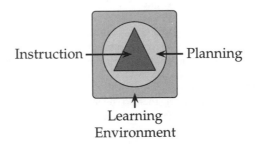

Over the years, as special educators and general educators have worked together to meet the needs of students with disabilities, it has become apparent that these students fall along a continuum of learner differences rather than constituting a separate category; teacher adjustments for learner differences can and should occur for all students, not just those with disabilities. From these realizations a new paradigm for teaching, learning, assessment, and curriculum development has emerged, called *Universal Design for Learning* (UDL). Rather than remediating students so that they can learn from a set curriculum, the UDL curriculum is made flexible to accommodate learner differences (Center for Applied Special Technology, www.cast.org, 2004).

The UDL curriculum recognizes that there is not one optimal solution for everyone; it includes alternatives to make it accessible and appropriate for individuals with different backgrounds, learning styles, abilities, and disabilities in widely varied learning contexts (Center for Applied Special Technology, www.cast.org). With such a curriculum, special educators and general educators must work together to ensure that appropriate alternatives are selected to address unique needs of students with disabilities. When curriculum alternatives are insufficient for individual students, or when a non-UDL curriculum is used, the special educator has an additional challenge of finding or creating accommodations, and in some cases modifying the learning goals for students with disabilities in accordance with their Individual Educational Plans (IEP).

Whether the classroom educator is using a UDL curriculum or not, co-planning and co-teaching remain important roles for consultants. In this chapter we will explore five aspects of working together for students with disabilities:

- Planning and delivering differentiated instruction
- Planning individualized alternatives for certain students
- Planning and making adaptations

- Planning remedial instruction
- Planning other instructional supports

In this chapter instruction is the content (triangle) feature, with processes (circle) the planning that will be needed. They take place within the learning environments (square) of the classroom setting.

FOCUSING QUESTIONS

1. What effect can Universal Design for Learning (UDL) have on teachers working together for students with disabilities?
2. How does planning for co-teaching differ from typical teacher lesson planning?
3. What are some common approaches to co-teaching?
4. How do cooperative learning techniques help students improve academic achievement and social relationships?
5. Why is it important to inform all persons involved in a student's instruction about the goals and objectives on his or her IEP?
6. Who can qualify for curriculum adaptations and what are options to consider?
7. What kinds of accommodations are appropriate to provide?
8. What are appropriate curriculum modifications for students with disabilities?
9. How can teachers use text in digital format to meet individual student needs?
10. How can remedial instruction be provided by individuals other than special educators?
11. What other instructional supports will benefit students with disabilities placed in general classrooms?
12. Why is it essential for special education teachers to monitor student classroom performance frequently in inclusive schools?

KEY TERMS

adapted outcomes	differentiated instruction	scaffolding
adapting tests	digital text	self-advocacy
adapting text materials	enhanced outcomes	Station Teaching
cooperative learning	functional outcomes	study strategies
co-planning	Interactive Lesson Planning	Teach and Monitor
co-teaching	Model	team-teaching
curriculum accommodations	Parallel Teaching	Universal Design for
curriculum adaptations	peer tutors	Learning (UDL)
curriculum modifications	remedial instruction	

VIGNETTE 8

The setting is the LD teacher's office (once the resource room where LD students came for special instruction in the former "pull-out" program). The principal arrives first, followed by a behavioral disorders (BD) teacher, two learning disabilities (LD) teachers, a speech pathologist, and a counselor. Teacher A assumes the facilitator role, teacher B functions in the recorder role, and the speech pathologist has the timekeeper role (with these roles being rotated in subsequent meetings).

Teacher "A" (facilitator):   "Who has agenda items today?"

Principal: "I want to discuss CBM and a discipline policy procedure."

Teacher "A" (facilitator):   "How much time do you need for your agenda item?"

Teacher "A" (facilitator):   (Writes the agenda item and time needed—anywhere from one to ten minutes—on a form.)

Teacher "C":   "I need ideas for working with Jason."

Teacher "A" (facilitator):   (Continues to write agenda items and time needed as each person states them . . .).

Teacher "A" (facilitator):   "All right, let's start with item 3, Jason.

Teacher "C":   "I'm concerned about Jason because he can't read the fourth-grade materials. He has a wonderful background in science and social studies. I really think his problem is that he can't read and write the material used in the classroom.

Teacher "B" (recorder):   (Writes the main points of the discussion, pertinent decisions, and future agenda items related to the issue.)

Speech Pathologist (timekeeper):   (Starts stopwatch at beginning of each item discussion and notifies the facilitator when the allotted time has been used.)

Teacher "A" (facilitator):   (After most of the items have been discussed, the time allotted for the meeting has almost expired.) "I will put the last two items on the agenda for next week. Are there other items for that meeting?"

PLANNING AND DELIVERING
DIFFERENTIATED INSTRUCTION

Co-teaching (two or more teachers planning and delivering instruction) by special educators and general educators creates new challenges for planning lessons in general classrooms. Without co-planning, co-teaching often becomes a special educator helping the classroom teacher, or "turn-taking" at best. This arrangement brings little satisfaction to either teacher and is not likely to result in the high-quality student outcomes that educators and parents desire. Reinhiller (1996) proposes that co-teaching is both art and talent, voluntary in nature, and has become widely accepted as an appropriate model for collaboration.

Typical Lesson Planning

Special educators and general educators in traditional roles plan lessons differently from one another. General classroom teachers usually plan for groups of students while special education teachers typically plan for individuals. Research conducted by a Joint Committee on Teacher Planning for Students with Disabilities (1995) indicated that general education teachers do not individualize instruction although they might differentiate by planning for *all, most,* and *a few* students. They do not typically engage in a linear planning process going from objectives to activities followed by evaluation methods, even though they usually know how to use that type of planning. They usually start planning lessons by selecting a theme or topic then planning content and activities to use with the entire class or large group. Those plans may be followed by consideration of the objectives or specific outcomes for the group and ways to evaluate them.

Special educators, on the other hand, are trained, even required by federal law, to base lesson plans on individualized learner goals. Federal laws for individuals with disabilities require multidisciplinary teams to develop plans for individuals (IEPs). The planning steps are based on traditional, linear lesson planning models—goals, objectives, activities, and evaluation. This linear process may not be the best way for co-teachers to plan lessons, nor does it reflect the way teachers typically plan lessons (Joint Committee on Teacher Planning for Students with Disabilities, 1995). General classroom teachers obviously are concerned about student learning, but they must keep their groups of students engaged in activities throughout the school day for the sake of classroom order. The challenge for co-teachers is to reconcile the individualized and group planning processes for the benefit of all students.

Co-Planning Lessons

An interactive model for planning differentiated instruction that reflects the realities of current classroom contexts and students with special needs included in the classroom is shown in Figure 8.1. The model (Dyck, Pemberton, Woods, & Sundbye, 1996) does not follow the linear approach found in many planning models. The interactive model allows teachers to plan activities, objectives, and assessments concurrently or to plan them in varying orders depending on the situation. Co-teachers can begin planning at any point in the model or they can choose to use only parts of it. It does not require that each objective be tied to a separate activity, as is usually the case in a linear planning mode. An activity can address several objectives and assessments. Likewise, one objective can be addressed by several activities and assessments. In all instances, the lesson theme, topic, or goal, often determined by the textbook, is the common element in the plan.

The Interactive Lesson Planning Model presented in Figure 8.1 addresses *nearly all* students, *most* students, and *some* individual students. As a result, the model can be successful when co-teachers plan (Dyck, Pemberton, Woods & Sundbye, 1996).

Co-teachers using the model answer the following questions when planning a lesson:

- What is the theme, topic, or goal of the lesson?
- What content is in the textbook and/or printed curriculum guide that addresses this theme, topic or goal?
- What of that content is useful to and can be learned by *all* or *nearly all* students in the class?
- What of that content is useful to and can be learned by *most* students in the class?
- What of that content is useful to and can be learned by only *some* individual students in the class?
- Which students cannot benefit from any of that content?
- How will the activities take place—whole group, small groups, individual, etc.?
- Who will be in each group or activity?

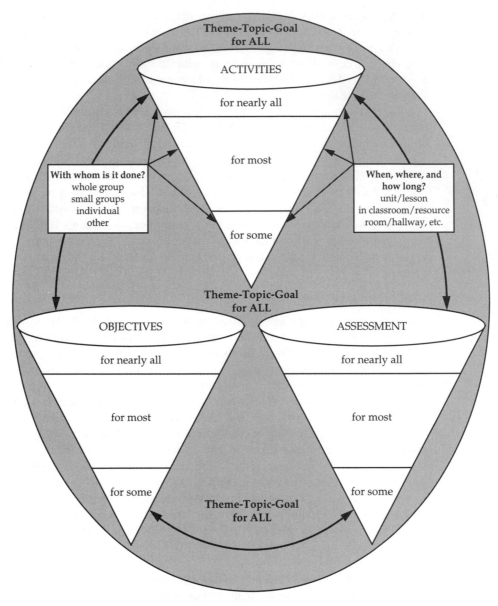

FIGURE 8.1   Interactive Lesson Planning Model

- What activities will keep *each* student motivated and busy?
- When, where, and for how long will this lesson plan be taught?
- Who is primarily responsible for each of the activities and assessments?

The answers to these questions form a basis for differentiating activities, objectives and assessments.

An example of a lesson plan using this process is shown in Figure 8.2. A narrative of the planning meeting follows. References to correlates in the Interactive Lesson Planning Model are noted in brackets. Another example using an elementary classroom is presented in *Teaching Exceptional Children* (Dyck, Sundbye & Pemberton, 1997).

Narrative for the Co-planning.   Lori and Mark decided to co-teach an American History lesson about the Battle at Gettysburg during the Civil War. [*What is the theme, topic, or goal of the lesson?*]

1. Mark provided his lecture materials from past lessons. They reviewed the lecture outlines, textbook materials and assignments. [*What content is in the textbook and/or printed curriculum guide that addresses this theme, topic or goal?*]
2. They discussed what could be eliminated or added to the original lecture and textbook material. Everyone could benefit from the lecture, even Randy who had mental retardation. Most students could read the textbook assignment, pages 254–263 except Colin who needed it read aloud and Randy who couldn't read it at all. [*What of that content is useful to and can be learned by all or nearly all students in the class?*]
3. They decided most students, with the exception of Randy, would benefit from the assignments 1 and 3 on pages 263 of the textbook. [*What of that content is useful to and can be learned by most students in the class?*]
4. Mark was concerned about the ability of some students with learning difficulties to benefit from some of the content. Lori wondered whether students with high ability would be challenged. They decided to use cooperative learning methods to deal with some of those concerns. Lori would prepare "challenge tasks" which would be required for the students with high ability although anyone could try to do them. Mark had group study worksheets they could use, but Lori recommended several changes. Mark thought of some other items that could be eliminated or added to help the students in the class who had learning difficulties.
5. Mark then volunteered to make the revisions since he had the original study worksheets on his computer. [*What of that content is useful to and can be learned by most students in the class? What of that content is useful to and can be learned or needs to be learned by only some individual students in the class?*]
6. Although Lori was assigned to be the teacher for the course, they decided Mark should present the lecture since he had done it many times previously. However, Lori would be in the class and would feel free to add information whenever it seemed appropriate to help clarify a point. [*How will the activities take place—whole group, small groups, individual, etc.?*]
7. Lori would direct the cooperative learning activities. She had already established teams in the class and this content would fit in nicely. Mark said he would have his para come into the classroom during that time. It would free him up to consult with another teacher. [*Who will be in each group or activity? What activities will we use to keep EACH student motivated and busy?*]
8. Lori felt the students needed a summative experience that would require them to demonstrate individual accountability. Mark and Lori discussed what the activity would be and Lori agreed to prepare it (a test). They would divide the tests, each grading half. When the tests were graded, Lori would record the scores in her grade book and Mark would

FIGURE 8.2   Interactive Lesson Planning Form

Theme, Topic, or Goal: *Battle at Gettysburg*   Date(s): *4/5 – 4/10*

ACTIVITIES

WHEN	WHAT	FOR NEARLY ALL	FOR MOST	FOR SOME	WITH WHOM
Mon. & Tues.	*Lecture Read pages 254–263*	*all for lecture*	*Reading all but Randy*	*Read aloud to Colin*	*Mark.*
Tues. & Wed.	*Assignments 1 and 3 on pages 263 of the textbook*		*all but Randy*		*Lori & para*
Tues. & Wed.	*Draw picture showing important people in the battle*			*Randy*	*Mark*
Thurs.	*Cooperative Learning – revised study guides.*	*all*		*challenge tasks for high achiever*	*Lori & Mark*
Fri.	*Independent Test*		*all but Randy*	*read to 3 LD*	*Lori*
Fri.	*Test in resource room*			*Randy*	*para.*

OBJECTIVES

WHEN	WHAT	FOR NEARLY ALL	FOR MOST	FOR SOME	WITH WHOM
by 4/10	*State the primary events leading up to the Battle at Gettysburg*		*all but Randy*		
by 4/10	*State primary people and events during the battle*		*all but Randy*		
by 4/10	*Answer questions about the important outcomes of the Battle*			*orally for LD and Randy*	
by 4/10	*Identify pictures of key persons and events in the Battle at Gettysburg*			*Randy*	
by 4/10	*Create a product showing the important outcomes of the Battle at Gettysburg*			*high achieving students*	

ASSESSMENT

WHEN	WHAT	FOR NEARLY ALL	FOR MOST	FOR SOME	WITH WHOM
Fri.	*Independently take written test*		*all but 3 LD & Randy*		*Lori.*
Fri.	*Take oral test*			*3 LD*	*Mark.*
Fri.	*Draw picture of key people and events*			*Randy*	*para.*

give team rewards. Mark would give the test orally to the students with learning disabilities and prepare a modified test for the para to give to Randy in the resource room. [*Who is primarily responsible for each of the activities and assessments?*]

Delivering Differentiated Instruction

Co-teaching (sometimes referred to as collaborative teaching or cooperative teaching) involves two or more teachers (usually a general education teacher and a special education teacher) who plan and deliver instruction as equals within one educational setting to one group of students. A key element of co-teaching is the shared responsibility of the teachers in both planning and delivering instruction. Co-teaching usually occurs for a set period of time such as one class period each day, certain days of the week or, as illustrated in the case above, one lesson topic. Some teachers have been misled to believe co-teaching is necessary for every inclusion situation and students should never be taken out of the general classroom for special help. However, co-teaching should only be used when it is the *best* option for meeting the needs of a significant number of students. Friend and Bursuck, (1996, p. 86–87) note: "It is relatively expensive (that is, the cost of two teachers with one group of students) and should be reserved for situations in which the number of students with disabilities in a class justifies the presence of two teachers, or the class is one in which all students with disabilities enroll (for example, in high school, it may be U.S. history)."

Co-teachers must use effective teaching practices well documented by research (ERIC, 1987a; 1987b; Bickel & Bickel, 1986, Morsink, Soar, Soar, & Thomas, 1986) which include:

1. Gain the learner's attention. Use verbal prompts such as "look here" and listen." Maintain 90 percent task engagement during teacher-directed activities.
2. Review relevant past learning. Teacher review, with correcting of homework, is recommended.
3. Communicate the goal of the lesson. Tell what is being learned and why it is important. Keep the goal statement brief.
4. Model the skill to be learned. Proceed in small steps that are not too difficult and give explicit verbal directions. Exaggerate steps as needed to call attention to the critical features.
5. Prompt for correct response. Let students practice with many correct responses. Continue until very high levels of proficiency are demonstrated. The teacher should do each step as the students are doing them, providing modeling and verbal prompts.
6. Check for skill mastery. Students perform the behavior under teacher supervision without prompting. The teacher provides feedback after every trial and watches for many successful repetitions.
7. Close the lesson. Review the skill, discuss what will be in the next lesson, or introduce independent work.

THE PLAN IN ACTION:
No matter how well the teachers plan, some co-teaching actions must be spontaneous. This reality became obvious as Lori and Mark put their plan into action. Mark presented the lecture while Lori monitored as planned. Lori spontaneously "jumped in" from time to time to clarify information. At one point she went to the chalkboard and drew a diagram to more clearly illustrate a point that seemed confusing to students. The next day, as planned, Lori took

over when the class began team study in the cooperative learning format. She instructed students to get into their teams, gave instructions for team activities and told how they could earn bonus points. Now the para was monitoring and noticed Randy needed more explanation so he wrote out the steps for Randy. Once students were engaged in teamwork, Lori and the para "cruised" the classroom, stopping to help individuals or teams as needed and providing positive reinforcement for team effort. Friday, both teachers were present while students took individual tests. The para took Randy to the resource room to help him take his special test while Mark read the test to the students with learning disabilities. He read questions orally for them when needed. He noticed two students having difficulty writing their answers and pulled them aside one-by-one to let them dictate answers to him. Then he asked them to do an additional task while the rest of the class finished their tests. Lori involved the students with high ability in other activities in the center of the classroom when they finished their tests while Mark continued to monitor the test-takers. Lori and Mark divided the tests to grade as planned.

Preparation for Co-teaching.   Teachers need to prepare the classroom before implementing co-teaching. They need to discuss their views on teaching and learning and resolve any differences. If these differences cannot be resolved, for example, direct instruction versus constructivist learning, it would be best to forego co-teaching. However, the teachers would still need to engage in regular co-planning. They need to also agree on classroom rules and routines during co-teaching. In addition, they should agree on how grades will be assigned to students Other matters to discuss are the role of paras and substitute teachers during co-teaching, how to inform parents of the new approach, and most important, scheduled planning time at least once per week.

Selecting the Best Approach.   Co-teachers can use one of several approaches to present their lessons. Some examples are Teach and Monitor, Parallel Teaching, Station Teaching, and Team Teaching. Vaughn, Schumm and Arguelles (1997) and Bauwens and Hourcade (1997) provide descriptions of other co-teaching arrangements.

Teach and Monitor.   One of the most common approaches is for both teachers to be in the classroom during instruction, but one of them takes primary responsibility for lecturing or presenting the lesson. The other teacher helps monitor performance of students and provides additional assistance to the students who need it. This approach does not require as much advanced planning as other approaches and is simple to implement. However, the teacher who circulates around the room can easily begin to feel like a" teacher's aide." One parent recently reported a situation where her child came home from school saying they had a new "student teacher" in her room. In reality, the "student teacher" was the special education teacher who was co-teaching in the classroom. This remark is not provided to minimize the role of "student teachers" but to illustrate the point that both teachers might not be recognized as co-equals by the students and as such may not be equally effective in providing instruction. In order to minimize potential limitations of the Teach and Monitor approach to co-teaching, the teachers should alternate roles regularly.

Variations of this approach are Speak and Chart or Speak and Add. With Speak and Chart one teacher lectures while the other writes the outline or notes on the chalkboard. With Speak and Add one teacher lectures while the other jumps in to add or clarify points from time to time. Duet is a planned variation of Speak and Add where each teacher takes turns presenting portions of the material in a coordinated fashion. These co-teaching structures often become blended as the prior example of Lori and Mark illustrates.

Parallel Teaching. A second form of co-teaching that is commonly practiced is parallel teaching. While both teachers plan a lesson, they split the class and each delivers the lesson to a smaller group at the same time. Parallel teaching might also require parallel curriculum, that is, both teachers teach a similar topic but one teacher teaches it at a more advanced level than the other. For example, after having read a story to the entire class, one teacher takes the highest achievers and works on a dramatization of the story while the other teacher works with the other students on vocabulary meaning and retelling the story sequence.

Station Teaching. A third method of co-teaching is Station Teaching. This approach occurs when teachers co-plan instructional activities that are presented in "stations" or learning centers. While the teachers are stationed at some of the centers, others require independent work or involvement of peer teachers or paras. Each station presents a different aspect of the lesson and allows teachers to work with small groups of students. This way each teacher works with all students in the class as they rotate through the stations.

Team Teaching. This approach is sometimes used as a synonym for co-teaching. However, it can be a model where the special education teacher joins with one or more special education teachers to form a team. This team is responsible for all of the children in the classroom or at a particular level. A variation of team teaching was observed in one school that involved ignoring the categorical labels for service of students. Instead, all students identified for special education services were assigned to special educators according to their age or grade level placement. The special educators, regardless of categorical specialization, were assigned to grade-level teams and assumed primary responsibility for all students with special needs at the assigned grade level. The special educators met weekly to discuss matters of concern. In addition, each special educator was a member of a grade level team and met regularly to discuss common issues with those team members. The special educators moved in and out of the classrooms at that grade level to co-teach as needed, to adapt materials, or sometimes to present a special lesson. The teaming processes to manage such a system are extensive. According to the teachers involved in the approach, it will not work unless there is *trust* among all the teachers and efficient *teaming* practices. The scenario at the beginning of this chapter provides an example of the system used for team meetings at this school.

A high school math teacher described a pre-algebra class that she and the teacher for learning disabilities co-teach. They have a shared planning time every other day because the school uses block scheduling. Within that time they can usually set out a general plan for the week and then attend to specific problems or coordinate activities as needed. They share actual teaching responsibility more than they use a teach-and-monitor approach. This is purposeful, so students will perceive them *both* as math teachers, and not one as math teacher with the other as special education teacher only for certain students. What this co-teacher likes best about the approach is the camaraderie she shares with another adult. It lessens her feelings of isolation. However, she is quick to point out that co-teaching in situations where partners do not share a similar philosophy of classroom management, or do not appreciate and value temperament differences, will be challenging.

Planning Cooperative Learning Lessons

Mark and Lori, in the narrative for co-planning, used cooperative learning as part of their teaching method. Cooperative learning methods have gained widespread attention for use in many classrooms and, if carefully planned, may not require the presence of the special educator in the classroom every day as illustrated in an earlier scenario. When used appropriately, the methods result in improved student achievement and improved social relationships at the same time (Johnson & Johnson, 1987; Lloyd, Crowley, Kohler, & Strain, 1988; Madden & Slavin, 1983).

The term *cooperative learning* has become associated with a variety of structured approaches that arrange classrooms so students study in heterogeneous groups to meet academic goals (Johnson & Johnson, 1987; Slavin, 1986). In most of the models, all students in the classroom are assigned to heterogeneous groups and, under the guidance of the teacher, help one another master content previously presented by the teacher. Students are held individually accountable for the content, with individual performance scores pooled to determine group rewards. Thus, all students are rewarded for helping, sharing, and working together.

Common problems and possible solutions are listed in Figure 8.3. Co-teachers may need to modify cooperative learning activities for students with learning and behavior problems in the classroom. If a modification is made, co-teachers should make sure that these two elements are present (Slavin, 1990):

1. *Group goals or positive interdependence.* The members within a group must work together in order to earn recognition, grades, rewards, and other indicators of group success.
2. *Individual accountability.* All individuals within the group must demonstrate their learning in order for the group to experience success. This accountability could involve individual test scores that are averaged for group recognition or a report in which each person contributes a specific portion. It should not be a single product without differentiated tasks, for that would be disastrous for students with severe disabilities included in the class.

When students with behavior problems are included in the classroom, special educators will need to closely monitor the experiences. It is possible the classroom teacher will need assistance to teach social skills needed for successful cooperation. Dishon and O'Leary (1989; 1990) provide useful suggestions for efficient teaching of social skills for cooperative learning. Developing and posting class rules for cooperative learning such as those shown in Figure 8.4 will be helpful to all students.

Resistance to the Concept of Co-Teaching

Consultees may resist the idea of co-teaching in overt ways or more covertly. Recall the discussion about resistance in Chapter 4. Extensions of the resistance to innovations mentioned there can surface on the topic of co-teaching as:

- We're not ready for that here. Maybe in a few years.
- I heard that was a disaster in Schmoo City.
- Wherever would we find the time to pull that off successfully?
- The kids will be totally confused.
- Isn't that wasteful, having two teachers in one room at the same time? What will the school board say about that?
- If it's such a good educational idea, why hasn't it been done before? . . . Oh, the notion of team teaching came about in the 1960s. Then why aren't we still doing it?
- Whose "neck will be on the block" if our kids' test scores are a disaster?

FIGURE 8.3   Common Problems and Possible Solutions during Cooperative Learning

LEARNING PROBLEMS

Student cannot read and/or write the material.
Have a teammate read material to the student.
Have teammates read material aloud "round robin."
Highlight main ideas and important information.

Student is hearing impaired.
Have team work in area of room with most sound control.
Seat student where lips of team members can be seen.
Provide extra teacher prompting during team study.

Student is visually impaired.
Provide more time to complete assignment.
Seat student where team discussion can be heard easily.
Reinforce efforts of team to explain information.

Student has difficulty making oral presentations.
Have student write and a team member read the report.
Allow student to pre-plan comments by assigning issue.
Have student work closely with another to offer ideas.

Student cannot do any of the group work.
Give different material to study and different quiz.
Form teams by achievement levels (is hard to manage).
Give direct teacher instruction to provide head start.

BEHAVIOR PROBLEMS

Student cannot get along with other team members.
Give team bonus points based on team cooperativeness.
Move from team to team, reinforcing right behavior.
Ignore the behavior (as team sometimes handles it well).

Student is ostracized by team members.
Use improvement points to provide equal opportunity.
Select the team for that student with care.
Place a sympathetic person on that student's team.

Student refuses to become involved in team study.
Use bonus points often to reinforce involvement.
Make every effort to involve student in the group.
Allow student to work alone, but keep door open.

Student is frequently absent or tardy.
Upon return, have student complete assignment or quiz.
Use late score for individual grade, but not team score.
Give creativity bonus if team copes well with absence.

Parents of high ability students disapprove of the strategy.
Meet with parents to explain cooperative learning.
Stress universal need to learn cooperative strategies.
Promote the concept of developing leadership skills.
Group with mental peers for some work on occasion.

FIGURE 8.4   Class Rules for Cooperative Learning

Speak to Each Other
1. Speak softly.
2. Take turns talking.
3. Limit talking to the subject of study.
4. Look at the person speaking—be a good listener.
5. Ask teammates for help before asking the teacher.
6. Disagree agreeably.

Help Each Other
7. Tell your teammates how to find answers when they need help, instead of telling answers.
8. Encourage everyone on the team to do his or her best work.
9. Make sure everyone on your team knows the material before you stop working together.
10. Don't get yourself or another person off task—pay attention to the assigned work.

- Let's shelve it for this year and come back to it later.
- I know! Let's turn the topic over to a study committee.

These kinds of resistance, voiced or displayed with descriptive body language, are called "wet-blanket" by some, and described by others as "how to chloroform innovations and promising ideas."

■ ■ ■ ■ ■ ▬▬

APPLICATION 8.1
EXPOSING KILLER PHRASES

After reading the "wet-blanket" phrases above, brainstorm independently or with a group to think of more comments that shut down creative thinking and enthusiastic participation for new ways of educating students. Focus in particular on ones that are wet-blankets on the wisps of new ideas sparked by school improvement issues.

Have a round-robin reading, with a bit of drama added, to expose these phrases by hearing them at their worst.

PLANNING FOR INDIVIDUAL STUDENTS

Special educators need a method of communicating information recorded on the IEP (Individualized Education Program) to classroom teachers, paraeducators, and other persons involved in a student's instruction. These individuals can only assume the student should meet the same goals and objectives as most students in the classroom without IEP information to guide them. It is helpful to all persons involved to have each student's IEP goals and objectives on a one-page form. Other information on the IEP should be available to teachers on request. IEP documents must be kept confidential as required by law. Other documents summarizing student goals and objectives may not be subject to the same legal limits, but the intent of confidentiality should not be violated.

Helping Teachers Use IEP Information

Consultants should devise a way to provide IEP highlights to teachers and paras without violating student's rights. One possibility is to put the information in a "locked" computer file. Only individuals who know the identification code can have access to the information. Another possibility is to put paper copies in a locked file cabinet in the classroom. The limitation of putting information in locked files is that it can be easily forgotten—*out of sight, out of mind.* Perhaps a periodic E-mail message with the relevant information and a personal note about the student's progress or lack of it would be a way to keep everyone informed about progress toward meeting IEP goals and objectives.

PLANNING AND MAKING ADAPTATIONS

Federal law requires accommodations for individuals who qualify for certain types of carefully defined disabilities. Section 504 of the Rehabilitation Act of 1973 requires public agencies to provide reasonable accommodations for individuals with disabilities, even those who do not qualify for IDEA, such as students with attention deficit disorders or other health impairments. The intent of both laws is to provide access to participation in school programs. Although the "504" and IEP plans may specify accommodations needed by individual students, consultants should help all parties involved in teaching these students in planning and preparing the accommodations.

Many authors use the terms *adaptations, accommodations,* or *modifications* interchangeably. For our purposes, curriculum adaptations involve both accommodations and modifications. Curriculum accommodations are assistive aids and supports that help the student achieve the same outcomes as most other students in the class. Examples of accommodations include reading a test to the student, writing answers dictated by the student, putting text into Braille, or providing sound amplification. Curriculum modifications involve changing the goals, activities or outcomes for students—for example, reducing the number of spelling words for a student to master.

Consultants in elementary schools should consider using the term "scaffolding" rather than accommodations. Scaffolding, as used by general educators, assumes that the external supports to enable a student to benefit from classroom learning are temporary and will be faded once the individual no longer needs them. While that is the goal of general educators and is reasonable for some students with disabilities, many individuals with disabilities will need scaffolding or accommodations for a lifetime. Consider the special needs of students who are deaf or hard of hearing.

■ ■ ■ ■ ■ ▬▬▬

APPLICATION 8.2
OBTAINING RESOURCES FOR ADAPTATIONS

Write sources listed in this book and obtained from colleagues to get more information about the strategies discussed in the chapter. Work with teachers to determine which of these strategies or skills are most needed by students in your school. Develop a comprehensive plan for including them in a systematic way, and include plans for obtaining training in their use.

Ten general areas most amenable to curriculum accommodation and modification (Munson, 1987) are:

- Instructional level
- Curricular content
- Instructional materials
- Format of directions and assignments
- Instructional strategies
- Teacher input mode
- Student response mode
- Individual instruction
- Test administration
- Grading policies

While curriculum adaptations may seem to be the most logical way of addressing special learning needs, the consultant should be aware that classroom teachers may resist suggestions for changing their lesson plans. Teachers seem to be most receptive to adapting the format of directions and assignments and making test modifications (Munson, 1986–87.) Although they view instructional adaptation as desirable, most feel they are not able to do it (Ysseldyke, Thurlow, Wotruba & Nania, 1990).

Classroom teachers might believe they do not know how to adapt instruction but the most plausible explanation is that they do not have time to do it. Consultants and collaborators must consider whether or not their suggestions for classroom modifications are reasonable and feasible for the situation. (See Chapter 4 for information about dealing with consultee resistance.)

Many of the resources available for helping teachers make classroom modifications represent the views of special educators rather than the collaborative views of classroom teachers and special education teachers. However, Figure 8.5 contains a list of modifications taken from materials prepared collaboratively by elementary classroom teachers and special education teachers. The list is a helpful resource for sharing with classroom teachers during consultations.

Digital Resources to Assist in Adaptations

When text is available in digital format, teachers can use it in a variety of ways to meet individual student needs. Digital formats are used in computers so the teacher can adapt the text for the class in a variety of ways. The print can be enlarged and printed out for students with low vision. It can be read aloud by the computer if it has the appropriate software. Teachers can request that publishers provide digital (CD-ROM) versions of materials for specific learners. Although publishers are not required by law to provide such versions, many do so as a courtesy to schools. Digital versions of text can also be found online. One of the best sources is the eText Spider at the CAST Web site (www.cast.org). The site provides tools to search selected on-line sources in order to find electronic text in the public domain that can be adapted without fear of copyright infringement. For example, we entered "Mark Twain" and received a list of about thirty publications written by him. We then selected one title at a site that would allow us to down-load the entire text free of charge.

Making Modifications

Students whose cognitive disabilities prevent them from benefiting from the general classroom curriculum, even with accommodations, need curriculum modifications. Students with mild or moderate cognitive disabilities may need adapted outcomes while students with severe cognitive disabilities will need different goals or outcomes. Whenever possible, a theme or topic being studied by the rest of the students in the classroom should also be studied by these students.

Adapted Outcomes. Students with moderate learning and behavior problems can succeed very well in most classrooms but may need modified outcomes such as reduced number of practice problems or highlighted text. Other examples: in math, the student works on the same concept but the number of required practice problems may be reduced; in social studies the teacher might mark certain parts of the text material that must be read and the remainder skimmed; in science the teacher might limit the number of concepts within a domain to be mastered. In short, these students are expected to master most but not all of the content. Most of the items listed in figure 8.5 are adapted outcomes.

Functional Outcomes. For students with severe cognitive challenges, the curriculum goals may focus on areas such as social/behavioral development, language development,

FIGURE 8.5   Suggestions for Adaptations

Instructional Level
Let student work at success rate level of about 80%.
Break task down into sequential steps.
Sequence the work with easiest problems first.
Base instruction on cognitive need (concrete, abstract).

Curricular Content
Select content that addresses student's interest.
Adapt content to student's future goals (job, college…).

Instructional Materials
Fold or line paper to help student with spatial problem.
Use graph paper or lined paper turned vertically.
Draw arrows on text or worksheet to show related ideas.
Highlight or color-code on worksheets, texts, tests.
Mark the material that must be mastered.
Reduce the amount of material on a page.
Use a word processor for writing and editing.
Provide a calculator or computer to check work.
Tape reference materials to student's work area.
Have student follow text as listening to taped version.

Format of Directions and Assignments
Make instructions as brief as possible.
Introduce multiple long-term assignments in small steps.
Read written directions or assignments aloud.
Leave directions on chalkboard during study time.
Write cues at top of work page (for example, noun = …).
Ask student to restate/paraphrase directions.
Have student complete first example with teacher prompt.
Provide folders for unfinished work and finished work.

Instructional Strategies
Use concrete objects to demonstrate concepts
Provide outlines, semantic organizers, or webbings.
Use voice changes to stress points.
Point out relationships between ideas or concepts.
Repeat important information often.
Use color-coded strips for key parts.

Teacher Input Mode
Use multi-sensory approach for presenting materials.
Provide a written copy of material on chalkboard.
Demonstrate skills before student does seat work.

Student Response Mode
Accept alternate forms of information-sharing.
Allow taped or written report instead of oral.
Allow students to dictate information to another.
Allow oral report instead of written report.
Have student practice speaking to small group first.

Test Administration
Allow students to have sample tests to practice.
Teach test-taking skills.
Test orally.
Supply recognition items and not just total recall.
Allow take-home test.
Ask questions requiring short answers.

Grading Policies
Grade on pass/fail basis.
Grade on individual progress or effort.
Change the percentage required to pass.
Do not penalize for handwriting or spelling on tests.
Use scoring templates and rubrics.

Modifications of Classroom Environment
Seat students according to attention or sensory need.
Remove student from distractions.
Keep extra supplies on hand.

(adapted from development by Munson, Riegel)

concept development, basic skills, or self-help skills. For example, if the class is studying plants, but the goals for a particular student have to do with counting and language development, he or she may count, sort, and talk about seeds. These students may also need accommodations to help them attain their goals. The primary reason for their inclusion in the class is to participate in the social context and culture of the group.

Enhanced Outcomes.   Students with high ability in classrooms also need modified curriculum.Several strategies presented in this chapter as effective practices for students with learning and behavior disorders in inclusive classrooms are identified as less appropriate for gifted students (Schatz, 1990; Robinson, 1990). For example, cooperative learning is an effective instructional strategy for a variety of reasons. However, it should not be justified for gifted students through inference that they require remediation in social skills. Nor should it be used to make gifted students available as handy tutors (Robinson, 1990). While occasional peer tutoring can be challenging and rewarding for the gifted student, it should not be used to set very able students up as surrogate teachers for other students.

When gifted students are included in general classrooms, as the majority are for most of their school day, their learning needs also must be considered. Providing appropriate learning environments for them necessitates intensive collaboration and consultation among gifted program facilitators, classroom teachers, and resource personnel so that classroom modifications and resource adaptations help gifted students develop their learning potential (see Chapter 9).

PLANNING REMEDIAL INSTRUCTION

Many special education programs have put all their resources into co-teaching, accommodations and modifications while overlooking the special needs of students with significant basic skill disabilities in need of remedial instruction. We have observed far too many parents turning to private remedial services, home schooling or employing private tutors to help their children who are not getting remediation in the schools. Special educators in public schools must provide this type of instruction for students who need it.

According to a study by Zigmond (1997), half of the students with learning disabilities in inclusive elementary schools made no progress in reading during the school year. Traditional resource rooms are not meeting these needs of students either. One-fourth of the students in pull-out programs did not make progress in reading during the school year. Neither situation is acceptable. Special education programs must provide intensive remedial instruction in basic skills for some students.

Guidelines for Remedial Instruction

Collaborating teachers must develop remedial plans indicating what skills to remediate, teaching techniques to use, who will provide the instruction, when and where it will be provided. Harris and Sipay (1990) give the following guidelines for planning remedial instruction:

- Tutoring from one to three children at a time produces best results.
- Some students must be given one-to-one tutoring to make any progress.
- A minimum of about 50 instructional hours is necessary for significant improvement.
- Three times a week will produce results, but every day is even better.
- Remedial periods should usually last from 30 to 45 minutes.

Resources for Remedial Lessons

Most special educators will not have time to provide extensive remedial instruction given all their other responsibilities. Most will need to plan the remediation and direct a paraeducator, peer tutor, or volunteer to provide the instruction. Special educators need to acquire a library of resources that provide explicit guidelines for tutors to follow. An excellent resource for this task is *Helping the Struggling Reader: What to Teach and How to Teach it* (Sundbye & McCoy, 1997). This resource provides thirty-nine teaching plans that address varying student needs from learning about sounds and letters, to using print and meaning together, to comprehension. The teaching plans are designed for one-on-one, intensive teaching, but can be adapted for use with small groups as well. An easy-to-use grid helps the teacher match types of reading difficulties with the teaching plans that are most likely to be helpful. Tutors can easily follow the teaching plans selected. The performance records for each teaching plan will help the consultant monitor student progress and make adjustments when needed.

Another resource that goes beyond reading is *Tactics for Teaching* (Lovitt, 1995). One hundred five tactics are categorized into six sections: reading, writing, spelling, mathematics, classroom management, and self-management. Each tactic provides a brief rationale for the tactic, describes the type of student with whom it would be most appropriate, an outline of procedures for implementing the technique, procedures for monitoring its use, and ways the tactic can be modified in special situations.

PLANNING OTHER INSTRUCTIONAL SUPPORTS

Consultants and collaborating teachers cannot be present in every inclusive classroom for all instruction that takes place but they can support classroom teachers in many other ways. Consultants can provide invaluable support for classroom teachers by: planning for tutors and other instructional assistants assigned to the classroom; teaching students study strategies, classroom survival skills, and self-advocacy behaviors; adapting tests and other text material; and monitoring student progress.

Planning for Peer Tutors and Other Instructional Assistants

Classroom teachers occasionally are reluctant to implement peer tutoring programs despite obvious benefits, because they must spend time and effort in gaining successful results. Since time, energy, and resources for establishing effective peer tutoring programs are considerable, consulting teachers can collaborate with teachers to develop the programs. Peer tutoring programs can be building-wide or limited to one or a few classrooms.

Jenkins and Jenkins (1986) identified the following critical components of a successful peer tutoring program:

1. Provide highly structured lesson formats for tutors to use during the tutoring session, such as packaged programs with teacher instruction.
2. When possible, use content that correlates with the classroom content. Do not expect the tutor to teach material that has not already been presented by the teacher.
3. A mastery model of instruction is preferred because it provides satisfaction to tutor and tutee.
4. Schedule tutoring sessions frequently for moderate lengths of time (about one-half hour every day at the elementary level and daily one-hour sessions at the secondary level).
5. Provide tutor training and supervision, including feedback and reinforcement to tutors and classroom teachers.

6. Keep daily performance data on instructional objectives. Other types of information can include daily assignment record, monthly calendar, diary, or log book.
7. Carefully select and pair tutors with learners. The most important selection criteria are individual characteristics such as dependability, responsibility and sensitivity.

Consideration should be given to personalities and compatibility of the tutor and tutee, congruence of schedules, gender differences (not a critical issue, but perhaps pertinent at the secondary level), tutor knowledge of content to be tutored, interests, and eagerness to participate. More highly skilled tutors are often placed with more difficult-to-teach students (Jenkins & Jenkins, 1986).

One of the most important elements of a good peer tutoring program is tutor training. The amount and type of training will vary depending on the ages and abilities of the tutors and learners. Training usually addresses topics such as information about the program, tutor responsibilities, measurement procedures, lesson structure, teaching procedures, and personal behavior. The training should include personal relationship skills such as responsive listening, conversing, and praising good effort as described in Chapter 4. It is important that the tutors be instructed in specific procedures which have been experimentally validated to assure maximum learning and minimum frustration.

An example of peer tutoring at the high school level is the H.E.L.P. room in a Midwestern high school. The program (Here to Encourage the Learning Process) was developed for students who had difficulties keeping up in general education classrooms, but who did not qualify for special education programs. Although a teacher and a para staffed the program, peer tutoring was the principal methodology. Tutors were trained over a period of several weeks in communication skills, study skills, observation skills, writing of behavioral objectives, and tutoring skills. Evaluations of the H.E.L.P. program showed positive results. Parents reported that their children were more interested in school, and teachers welcomed the assistance. Students said they were less frustrated and more successful in the classroom (Thurston & Dover, 1990).

Teaching Study Strategies

Students with learning difficulties often show marked improvement in general education classrooms after they have been taught strategies for using information presented in the classroom. Many learning strategies resemble processes more commonly recognized as study skills.

Strategies Intervention Model.   Special educators in high schools can support classroom teachers by teaching all students to use The Strategies Intervention Model (Deshler & Schumaker, 1986). The strategies are techniques, principles, or rules that enable students to learn, solve problems, and complete tasks independently. Deshler and Schumaker (1986) stress the importance of deliberately teaching for generalization across settings. If the special education teacher is collaborating with the classroom teacher, this generalization process will be much more effective than other delivery options. Perhaps the special education teacher will teach the strategies in the resource room, but the regular classroom teacher will want to take over monitoring the generalization. The classroom teacher provides explicit cues that will help the student know when to use a particular strategy and gives periodic probes to determine whether or not the student continues to use the strategy.

Central to the entire generalization process just described are regular cooperative planning efforts between the resource and regular classroom teacher. Regular communication is essential to determine the degree to which the newly-acquired learning strategies are being used in the regular classroom. In addition, in such meetings classroom teachers can be encouraged to cue students to use the strategy at the appropriate time (Deshler & Schumaker, 1986, p. 586.).

Teaching Self-Advocacy

Students with special needs should be taught how to communicate their special needs to teachers, employers and others. The self-advocacy form in Figure 8.6 was prepared by Dyck (1997) to use with secondary-level students in general classrooms. Under ideal circumstances, the special education teacher would prompt the student to take responsibility to give the form to each of her teachers and pick it up once the teacher has filled in the right hand column. This responsibility is especially important for students with learning and behavior problems. A good variation is for the classroom teacher to hand out the form the first day of class and ask every student to complete the left-hand column and return it. The teacher then looks over each form, writes responses in the right hand column and returns them to the students shortly thereafter. (It is a good idea for the teacher to photocopy the completed forms before returning them to the students.) This process provides an efficient and confidential way for teachers and students to communicate regarding special needs and preferences.

Adapting Tests

Many students with learning and behavior problems have difficulty taking tests over subject matter they have learned. As a student progresses to higher grade levels, the ability to demonstrate knowledge through tests becomes more and more important. Many consultants at upper grade levels will need to give careful attention to the test-taking skills of students with learning and behavior difficulties.

When students have difficulty taking teacher-made tests in content subjects, consultants should give attention to a number of elements about the nature of the tests and ways to either help students take the tests as written, or collaborate with the teacher to make test adaptations. Lieberman (1984) suggests the first week of each school year, beginning at about the seventh-grade level, should be devoted to teaching study skills and test-taking strategies.

Other suggestions to consider when consulting with classroom teachers about alternative test construction and administration are:

- Give frequent, timed mini-tests.
- Give practice tests.
- Have students test one another and discuss answers.
- Use alternative response forms (multiple choice, short-answer, essay).
- Back up the written tests with taped tests.
- Provide extra spacing between discussion or short-answer items.
- Underline key words in test directions as well as test items.
- Provide test-study guides featuring a variety of answer formats.
- Provide additional time for students who write slowly.
- Administer tests orally (Mercer & Mercer, 1993).

FIGURE 8.6 Self-Advocacy Form

Name _____   Course _____

What Works for Me:	What Teacher Accepts:

Class Presentations
- Allow me to tape record lectures.
- Hand out lecture outlines or objectives in advance.
- Give me copies of overheads.
- Let me sit where I can see and hear the presenter.
- _____

Tests
- Give me oral tests.
- Record test on tape.
- Allow someone to read test to me.
- Allow extra time for me to take tests or shorten the test.
- Put plenty of space for me to write on tests.
- Provide short answer and multiple choice questions.
- _____

Study Methods
- Allow more time for reading or shorten assignments.
- Let me read an easier book (_____ level).
- Provide explanations for acceptable homework form (typed, etc.).
- Check to make sure I understand directions.
- I need frequent breaks.
- I need a quiet area for study.
- Explicitly instruct me to write down my homework assignment in my notebook.
- Type handwritten teacher materials.
- Use written backup for oral directions.
- Allow me to use a calculator.
- Allow me to use a word processor with spell check.
- Break down long assignments into smaller sections for me to complete.
- I learn well in small groups.
- I don't learn well in small groups.
- I learn well in whole-class presentations.
- I need to learn with a "study buddy".
- _____

Teachers are likely to be more resistant to test adaptations than to adaptations of classroom materials. Likewise, even when they believe it is a good thing to do they are not very likely to make the adaptations themselves. Consultants can assist classroom teachers in:

- Adapting their tests by adjusting the content to be directly related to the objectives of the class.
- Changing the format so the items are easy to read, more space is allowed for discussion, or the order of items is rearranged to make them more predictable.
- Rewriting directions or providing cues such as highlighting, underlining, and enlarging.
- Providing prompts such as "Start here." or "Look at the sign on this row."
- Adjusting the readability level of the questions.
- Providing outlines or advance organizers.
- Providing spelling of difficult words.
- Allowing students to use outlines, webs, or other visual organizers (Salend, 1994).

As teachers become proficient in using more authentic assessment procedures the need for test modification will lessen. Even then, some type of accommodation is likely to be needed for some students with disabilities.

Adapting Text Materials

Many of the guidelines for adapting tests apply when adapting other text material such as textbooks, study guides, or activity sheets. Before getting started with textbook adaptations the consultant and collaborating teacher should answer the following questions:

- What are the outcomes or objectives?
- What chapters will be covered and in what order?
- When will the chapters be covered, and in what depth?
- In what setting will the text be used?
- How will the objectives be assessed?
- What is the student's reading problem—decoding, comprehension?
- What are the student's interests, strengths, and prior experiences?

Adapting text can be the most powerful accommodation teachers make but it is also the most difficult and time-consuming. "Text adaptations are not for the faint-hearted. They tend to require more time and effort on the part of the teacher than other instructional adaptations, and consequently, are less likely to be done by general classroom teachers" (Dyck, 1999, p. 3).

Characteristics of students who are most likely to benefit from adapted text fall into five broad categories. These are students who cannot:

- see print,
- read many words in the text,
- understand content in the text material,
- attend to long texts, and/or
- write print.

Once the type of adaptation needed has been determined, specific selection can be based on the student's abilities, the lesson goals, and available resources. Figure 8.7 shows a decision tree for selecting the type of text adaptation most likely to help an individual student. In general, the simplest adaptation requiring the least resources such as time and money that will help the student meet curriculum goals should be selected.

Bypass Reading.   Perhaps the most common way to adapt a text is to change the modality of text input, usually reading it aloud in person or on audiotape. Many teachers ask students to take turns reading text material aloud in a "round-robin" manner. We do not advocate this form of adaptation on a regular basis, but recognize that teachers use it because it is an easy way to bypass reading for certain students. Although relatively easy to accomplish, reading text aloud is not without problems. Tape-recorded text material, peer tutoring, and computer adaptations are often better ways to bypass reading.

Decrease Reading.   Students who can decode text, but at a very slow rate, or who have difficulty with the vocabulary meaning or concepts presented in a text need the amount or density of content decreased. Such adaptations include selecting another text with similar content but using easier vocabulary, highlighting key concepts, omitting unnecessary or distracting parts of text, or writing abridged versions of text.

Support Reading.   Sometimes students need more information than is provided in the text to help them understand it. Examples include adding definitions of key terms, adding interest to important content, and adding cues, signals, and questions that will help the student focus on the most relevant information.

Organize Reading.   Many students who are not thought of as "struggling readers," as well as those who are, will benefit from the use of graphic organizers. Much has been written about teaching students to create graphic organizers, but struggling readers may benefit most when the teacher provides such organizers before making the reading assignment.

Guide Reading.   Teachers often use study guides to help students focus on and review important content in reading assignments. They can use previews and summaries, fill-in graphic organizers, framed outlines, and structured notes as alternatives to traditional study guide formats.

Keep in mind, if a decision is made that a text needs to be adapted, student work products and tests should be similarly adapted. For example, if a student needs the amount of reading decreased by eliminating portions of the text, the student also will need decreased written product assignments. In some cases the student's Individual Education Plan (IEP) goals will also need to be revised to reflect the use of adapted text. An elaborated discussion of these concepts is available in *How to Adapt Text for Struggling Readers* (Dyck, 1999).

Monitoring Student Progress

Frequent monitoring is essential in situations where the special education teacher is not providing all of the direct instruction to students with special needs. In fact, it might be the most

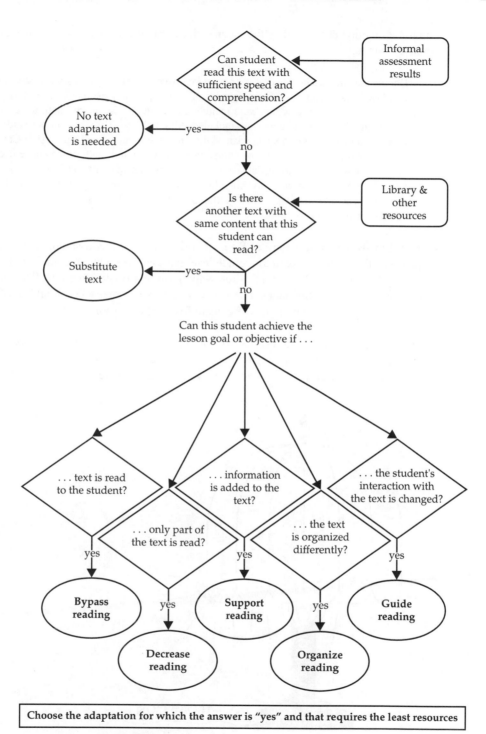

FIGURE 8.7   The Decision Tree for Adaptations

Adapted from: Dyck, N. (1999). © 1999 permission granted by Curriculum Solutions, Inc.

important function performed by the special educator in inclusive schools. Consider the example of Debbie:

> Debbie was now in her second year at an inclusive school. She had sixteen students in her caseload—mostly fourth and fifth graders. Debbie spent at least one hour each day in each classroom where her students were included. In addition, she taught math to several small groups in which her students were included. Although she felt confident her students were making satisfactory progress in basic skills, she wasn't sure. She began using Curriculum-Based Measurement (CBM) procedures, taking reading and math probes once each week. After a few weeks of charting data she realized four of her students were not making progress in reading. She had not been working directly with these students in reading and did not realize the problems they were having. She immediately took steps to make changes in those students' reading instruction.

Curriculum-Based Assessment (CBA).   Curriculum-based assessment (CBA) is an appropriate testing tool for use at any grade level but may be most beneficial in elementary schools. It has the most direct application in monitoring growth in basic skill areas such as reading, writing, and mathematics. The consultant or classroom teacher should take frequent measures using the actual materials or content from the classroom.

Monitoring Classroom Grades.   Secondary level teachers can monitor student progress by number of completed assignments and grades in general classroom courses. This information must be interpreted cautiously however, because teachers' grading standards vary

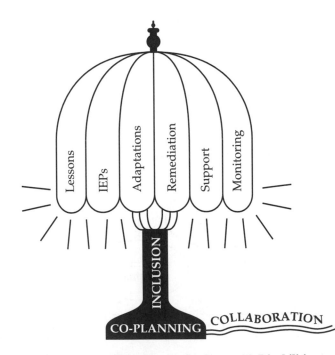

FIGURE 8.8   Co-Planning for Students with Disabilities

greatly. Special educators in inclusive schools should discuss with each teacher their grading philosophies and plan a system for grading students with adapted curriculum.

TIPS FOR COLLABORATIVE PLANNING AND TEACHING

1. Co-teaching *requires* careful planning. Planning time must be built into the restructured school day. (See Figure 8.8.)
2. Co-teachers will want to discuss their philosophies about teaching.
3. When co-teaching, clarify classroom rules and procedures such as routines for leaving the room, discipline matters, division of chores such as grading or making bulletin boards.
4. Devise a way to keep track of individuals who are providing services for students so that monitoring does not become a problem.
5. Rather than just telling classroom teachers about materials modification, *show* them. Give examples or do one for them.
6. Request demonstration lessons from classroom teachers featuring *their* most outstanding teaching techniques.
7. Offer to retype a test for a teacher (to double space, type in large print, or organize it differently) for use with a student who has a learning problem.
8. Before ordering computer software, have students try it out first. This gives them an opportunity to be consultants for teachers, and cultivates student ownership in educational planning and evaluation.
9. When preparing and distributing materials for classroom use, don't just drop them off and run. Help the teacher or student get started, and stay awhile to see how it goes.
10. Keep a supply of materials to send to classrooms for students who need reinforcement, even those with whom you don't work who could use the practice.
11. Have a favorite dozen of successful strategies available for demonstration teaching or sharing.
12. Be understanding of classroom teachers' daily trials with some mainstreamed students. Celebrate with classroom teachers even the smallest student progress.

CHAPTER REVIEW

1. Until the ideals of UDL (Universal Design for Learning) become a reality in all classrooms, special educators need to assist classroom teachers in planning, adapting, and delivering lessons.

2. Co-teaching (two or more teachers planning and delivering instruction) by special educators and general educators requires co-planning which differs from group planning models used by general educators and the linear, individual planning models of special educators.

3. The Interactive Planning Model addresses nearly all students, or most students, or some individual students, as needs dictate. As a result, the model can be successful when co-teachers plan and co-teach lessons using one or a combination of various approaches for presentation of lessons.

4. Because students work together in achieving meaningful objectives during cooperative learning activities, their achievement and social relationships can be improved at the same time.

5. Without information about a student's IEP goals and objectives, classroom teachers, paraeducators and other persons involved in a student's instruction can only assume the student should meet the same goals and objectives as most students in the inclusive classroom.

6. Federal laws specify who should be eligible for reasonable accommodations in schools.

7. Curriculum adaptations include accommodations (assistive aids and supports) and modifications (changed activities, goals, or outcomes).

8. Students whose cognitive disabilities prevent them from benefiting from the general classroom curriculum, even with accommodations, need curriculum modifications. Students with mild or moderate cognitive disabilities may need adapted outcomes while students with severe cognitive disabilities will need different goals or outcomes. Whenever possible, a theme or topic being studied by the rest of the students in the classroom should also be studied by these students.

9. Digital text can provide a variety of options for serving special needs. Some of these are available on-line.

10. Most special educators will not have time to provide extensive remedial instruction given all their other responsibilities. Most will need to plan the remediation and direct a peer tutor or volunteer to provide the instruction. Special educators need to acquire a library of resources that provide explicit guidelines for tutors to follow.

11. Consultants and collaborating teachers cannot be present in every general classroom for all instruction that takes place but they can support classroom teachers in many other ways such as: planning for tutors and other instructional assistants assigned to the classroom; teaching students study strategies, classroom survival skills, and self-advocacy behaviors; adapting tests and other text material; and monitoring student progress.

12. Frequent monitoring is essential in situations where the special education teacher is not providing all of the direct instruction to students with special needs. In fact, it might be the most important function performed by the special educators because they have no other valid way to make curriculum changes if needed. Curriculum-Based Assessment is a helpful tool in elementary schools. Teacher grades can be useful in secondary schools.

TO DO AND THINK ABOUT

1. Plan a lesson with another teacher. Then co-teach the lesson. After teaching, evaluate the processes and think about what you need to do to improve.

2. Interview teachers who co-teach to find out how they make it work. If possible, visit in their classrooms.

3. Identify a real or hypothetical student with disabilities and provide accommodations for the student during a lesson in the general classroom when you are not present.

4. Develop a plan for implementing a peer tutoring program that could be used in your school.

5. Select a real or hypothetical situation in which you would be consulting about a student with severe learning disabilities. Draft ideas that might come up for discussion regarding testing and grading. The ideas should be consistent with school policy, and facilitative, fair, and honest for the student.

FOR FURTHER READING

Center for Applied Technology (CAST). (2004). *Resources to help implement UDL and make curriculum adaptations.* Available on-line: www.cast.org.

Fennick, E. (2001). Coteaching: An inclusive curriculum for transition. *TEACHING Exceptional Children, 33*(6), 60–66. Describes how co-teaching in high school life skills classes can provide instruction for transition, job skills, and daily living skills in inclusive environments.

Friend, M., & Bursuck, W. D. (1996). *Including students with special needs: A practical guide for classroom teachers.* Boston: Allyn and Bacon.

Morocco, C. C., & Aguilar, C. M. (2002). Coteaching for content understanding: A schoolwide model. *Journal for Educational and Psychological Consultation, 13*(4), 315–347. A model for co-teaching involving collaboration between a content-area teacher and a special education teacher. Success is dependent on collaborative school structures, equal status rules for teachers, commitment to all students' learning, and strong content knowledge.

Reinhiller, N. (1996). Coteaching: New variations on a not-so-new practice. *Teacher Education and Special Education, 19*(1), 34–48. Co-teaching approaches as a collaborative model, a special education instructional strategy, and an activity are discussed. Challenges, barriers, and benefits of these innovations are delineated.

Tomlinson, C. A. (1999). *The differentiated classroom: Responding to the needs of all learners.* Alexandria, VA: Association for Supervision and Curriculum Development.

Tomlinson, C. A. (2000). *ERIC Digest on differentiation of instruction for elementary grades.* Available on-line: http://ericeece.org/pubs/digests/2000/tomlin00.html.

Vaughn, S., Schumm, J. S., & Arguelles, M. E. (1997). The ABCDEs of co-teaching. *Teaching Exceptional Children, 30*(2), 42–45.

CHAPTER NINE

WORKING TOGETHER FOR STUDENTS WITH HIGH ABILITY

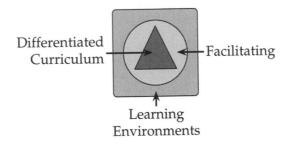

Too many educational policymakers, school administrators, and, yes, teachers, believe that students with high ability for learning do not have special educational needs; *they can get it on their own* and most of them will do just fine. Those having such views point out that many other students have immediate, major problems to be addressed by overworked teachers in busy, crowded, underfunded schools. They believe that students who can*not* "make it" without intensive special services must be served first and foremost.

However, if educators carefully think through their belief that very able students can get it on their own, they see that there is a problem with the word *it*. When that seemingly insignificant little pronoun *it* is taken to mean the basic curriculum for typical grade-level scope and sequence, then yes, most very capable students probably can, and in many cases already did, "get it" on their own. Indeed, many "got it" well before it was formally introduced in school. Or, they had quickly "gotten it" in a fraction of the time the instructor had allocated for learning it. We would conclude then that elementary and early secondary students, bound by compulsory education laws to be in school, gained little if anything while "marking time in place." For the students this is frustrating. For the world at large, it is a tremendous waste.

Educators face the challenge issued by legislated mandate to have No Child Left Behind (NCLB): Schools must show adequate yearly progress (AYP) by students or be tagged as "needs improvement," with the imminent ramifications of that label. However, there is no counterbalancing mandate that calls for having *No Child **Held** Behind* (NCHB). School boards and administrators will be pressed to focus their attention and resources on NCLB to assure adequate yearly progress in the standard curriculum by the majority of students. Students of most concern due to their special needs will be in subgroups of those with disabilities, English-language learners, and children of families who are poor (Christie, 2004). Schools striving for excellence and already ranking high in math and reading scores will feel victimized by NCLB's high-stakes testing for accountability purposes that forces teaching-to-the-test at the expense of more creative kinds of learning (Allen, 2004). All in all few concerns and resources are likely to be directed toward *developing exceptional potential* (DEP) in order that no child is *held* behind.

FOCUSING QUESTIONS

1. Why are special education programs necessary for exceptional students, whom many believe are able to "get it on their own"?

2. What student characteristics and learning needs have curriculum implications for the instruction of highly capable students?

3. In what ways can collaborative school consultation facilitate development of potential in exceptionally capable students?

4. What teaching techniques, curriculum options, and learning alternatives can schools provide for very capable and talented learners?

5. What resources beyond the school setting can be accessed to enrich and accelerate school programs?

6. How might general education teachers and special education teachers collaborate to maximize the potential of extremely able, high-achieving children and youth?

7. In what ways can families of very able students and school personnel develop partnerships for facilitating the development of student potential?

8. What ripple effects can school personnel and families expect from well-designed educational programs for students of high ability and remarkable talents?

KEY TERMS

curriculum compacting

development of exceptional
   potential (DEP)

differentiated curriculum

facilitator

flexible pacing

interest inventory

mentorship

No Child *Held* Behind
   (NC*H*B)

onedownsmanship

portfolios

preassessment

self-assessment

self-directed learning

taxonomy for a sensorimotor
   domain

taxonomy for a social domain

taxonomy of the affective
   domain

taxonomy of the cognitive
   domain

VIGNETTE 9.A

Vinny is frustrated. He loves to high-jump and he shows great promise in this activity as well as other related track-and-field events. But his elementary physical education teacher says that the high-jump bar can be set no higher than what is a comfort level for most of the class. "Why not?"

asks Vinny. "Well, I guess there are lots of reasons," the teacher responds. "The other kids can't go as high as you, and they need to work where they can be successful. So we all need to stay at that height for the limited time we have to practice. We do have only so much time to spend on the high jump. And, you know, it might discourage them to see you do lots better than they can. Then, too, think about this. They might not even like you as much if you 'show them up.' So we need for you to just go along with everyone else, and we'll wait till you get older to set the bar higher."

Ironically, this vignette probably would not happen. It involves sports, and typical schools long ago abandoned the practice of requiring very promising athletes to "mark time" until their age and grade level dictated advancement. Many factors drove this change of policy, for example, community and family pressures to compete with other schools and families, public adulation for the exceptional athlete, age–peer admiration for sports ability, and even educators' recognition of competitive sports skills as a relatively grade-irrelevant instructional area. However, parallel reasons for allowing advancement in academics to be paced by ability, not age or grade, are seldom offered.

THE REALITY OF INDIVIDUAL DIFFERENCES

Students differ, and the magnitude of these differences can be great. Some educators ignore this reality and strive to treat all students alike. They take very seriously the concept of equality and fail to consider that "there is nothing so unequal as equal treatment of unequals." Eisner (2003) questions the widely accepted assumption that the aim of schooling is to get all students to the same place at about the same time. His critical analogy of schools as railroads delivering students for expected arrival at a common destination by the time they are eighteen is sharply descriptive. Eisner asserts that the *good* school:

> does not expect all students to arrive at the same destination at the same time. Indeed, it provides conditions in which variability among students can be increased. What we ought to be doing in schools is increasing the variance in student performance while escalating the mean. In an ideal approach to curriculum and instruction—an approach in which every aspect of teaching is ideally suited to each student, and each aspect of curriculum is appropriate for the abilities students possess—variability among students will increase, not decrease (Eisner, 2003/2004, p. 650).

Students differ; therefore their learning needs differ, sometimes dramatically so. A lock-step curriculum does not provide the wide range of educational strategies and resources necessary for these differing needs. The differences cannot be eliminated; indeed, effective teaching tends to increase individual differences among students. But when instruction is effective, *all* students learn. Those who have difficulty in learning *do* achieve, and those who learn easily achieve *more* (Hanna & Dettmer, 2004). Many people do not want to be reminded of what they probably already know—that effective instruction increases the variation among students. To them it seems unfair that the "rich" tend to get "richer," while the "poor" tend to get relatively "poorer." Nevertheless, teachers are faced daily with undeniable differences in student achievement and ability to achieve, and *these differences will tend to increase with each year of schooling and good teaching* (Hanna & Dettmer, 2004). This in no way insinuates that teachers should let low achievers stay at low levels. Ethical practice requires us to maximize the achievement of all students; in other words, we should strive to have No Child Left Behind, but we must also make *every* possible effort to have *No Child Held Behind.*

Because of individual differences, students in inclusive classrooms just do not develop neatly and tidily at the same pace and at the same time. The conventional solution has been to sort and place them in classroom groups by age and grade level. But in most of these age-/ grade-level groups, we can find rather predictable percentages of students who are functioning, or capable of functioning, at two, four, six, sometimes eight grade-levels above expected achievement levels.[1] If this were a sports-focused matter, accommodations typically would be made. A precocious Vinny would not have the high-jump bar (note the adjective *high*) frozen at a designated low level until everyone else grows into his skill; he would be given time, equipment, space, instruction, and encouragement to develop his special talents. A tall, precocious freshman basketball player would not be relegated to the bench for the next one or two years if she could contribute to school victory and pride now. It is unfortunate when schools and the public forego age-/grade-level constraints for performance areas that don't really matter all that much in the overall aims of education (skills needed primarily for competitive sports events, not fitness skills needed for quality of life), but then "throttle down" bright minds that could contribute so much to quality of life for all.

CHARACTERISTICS OF LEARNERS WITH HIGH ABILITY AND TALENTS

Many educators feel strongly that too much time and other finite resources are consumed deciding *who* will be served in special programs for students with high ability, with not enough spent on *what* can be done to develop student potential. Neihart, Reis, Robinson, and Moon (2002) point to the ongoing lack of consensus about who should be designated highly able and who should not. They state that definitions among schools vary greatly and are often more attuned to the programs a school has decided to offer than to a particular definition of giftedness or talent. So, then, how do school personnel decide which students have needs that should be served with special programming or curriculum? The simplest methods seem to turn out to be the best.

Parents know their child or adolescent best, so they should participate in the determination. But this is a complex undertaking and probably not the most efficient place to start. To be more practical, consider that classroom teachers see students in a variety of "kid roles," from schoolwork to social interactions to emotional encounters to physical performances. Elementary teachers even have opportunities to observe student work in a variety of content areas. However, there *is* a major problem. Observations and evaluations of student potential, if they are to be of value, must be predicated on a condition that many schools fail to provide, making available the means by which students can *reveal* their potential. Clark (2002) aptly describes this as creating responsive, nurturant school environments so that children's abilities will "bubble up." It does not take too much imagination to recognize that such environments for learning also would give educators a head start on the infusion of differentiated curricula!

---

[1] Some would call such a group overachievers. That is a misnomer because one cannot achieve more than one does; the "overachiever" is being mislabeled as such by people who are *underexpecters.*

Identifying Exceptional Abilities and Talents

One of the attributes of programs where planners do not perseverate on identification issues is a philosophy of serving a flexible number of students if, when, and how the students need such curriculum differentiation. In such programs school personnel are called on to provide data about students' academic achievement and also to contribute information emanating from the "hidden curriculum," or that part of school life that includes participation in extracurricular activities, behaviors in settings such as hallways and lunchrooms, leadership and followership, demonstrations of innovative and creative abilities, enthusiasm for learning evidenced by attendance and completed assignments, and more. They also have input from families and students *if they seek it out.* This can be a start toward a more formal assessment of parent and student preferences.

Checklists. Ascertaining classroom teachers' perceptions of student ability is a readily available place to begin. An example of a teacher checklist for considering high performance potential is provided in Figure 9.1. The form can be used as is or, better yet, modified to fit the school setting. It also can be a tool for framing and presenting a staff development activity on characteristics and needs of high ability learners. It may be duplicated and completed for only one or a few targeted students or, even better, for the entire classroom. Items 1 through 7 reflect the types of characteristics targeted in more formal measures of aptitude. Items 8 through 12 target learning styles and items 13 through 19 performance styles. Items 20 through 25 predict creative thinking and doing. Items 26 through 30 indicate social preferences that relate to learning. The seven lettered items at the end of the numbered list supply even more evidence of exceptional ability if the student does well in spite of them.

Figure 9.2 provides an alternate checklist for building administrators. They know all students but perhaps not as many facets of student performance as do classroom teachers. They see the bigger picture and sometimes have interesting interactions with families regarding student capabilities and school programs. Administrators tend to prefer brief, succinct fact sheets, information bulletins, and, in this case, short checklists. A written formal note of explanation and request should accompany distribution of the form to them.

Teacher forms and administrator forms should include space for making additional comments. Confidentiality of the information during both distribution and collection processes must be assured.

Secondary teachers often respond well to checklists that are in question format and describe specific (and sometimes annoying) behaviors, such as:

Do you have a student (or more than one) who:

✓ Finishes what should have been a twenty-minute assignment in five minutes?
✓ Volunteers off-the-wall comments or suggestions during discussions?
✓ Is highly intolerant of stupidity, especially when perceived in an authority figure?
✓ Is impatient with sloppy or disorganized thinking to the point of rudeness?
✓ Recognizes sophisticated punch lines and gets more out of humor?
✓ Plans activities efficiently but can procrastinate to the point of desperation?
✓ Would rather argue than eat?
✓ Has probably read every book available on subjects of personal interest?

FIGURE 9.1   Teacher Referral Checklist

The following criteria are useful in assessing high potential of students. Please use one form per student to assign a value of *3* (to a considerable degree), *2* (to some degree), or *1* (to little if any degree) for each characteristic.

1. Learns rapidly and easily
2. Uses much common sense and practical knowledge
3. Retains easily what has been presented
4. Knows about many things of which other students are unaware
5. Uses a large number of words easily and accurately and appreciates word power
6. Recognizes relationships, comprehends meanings, and seems to "get more out of things"
7. Is alert with keen powers of observation and responds quickly
8. Likes difficult subjects and challenging tasks for the fun of learning
9. Asks penetrating questions and seeks out causes and reasons
10. Is a good guesser with an intuitive sense
11. Reads voraciously well beyond age level, and sets aside time for reading
12. Questions the accepted ways of doing things
13. Prefers to work independently with minimal direction
14. Has a longer attention span than age peers
15. Has little patience for routine drill and practice
16. Tends to be critical of self and others, with high standards and seeking perfection
17. Seldom needs more than one demonstration or instruction in order to carry out an activity
18. Perseveres on projects and ideas
19. Is withdrawn yet very capable when pressed
20. Demonstrates remarkable talent in one or more areas
21. Uses materials in innovative and unusual ways
22. Creates unusual stories, pictures, examples, models, or products
23. Has many interests and follows them with zeal
24. Makes extensive collections, with sustained focus
25. Invents contrivances, gadgets, and new ways of doing things
26. Prefers to be around older students or adults, communicating effectively with them
27. Has an advanced sense of humor and "gets it" when others may not
28. Influences other students to do things
29. Is serious-minded and intolerant of prolonged foolishness
30. Shows much sensitivity toward people, social issues, and right and wrong

Please check any of the following factors which apply. If present along with a number of the attributes above, they may provide additional validation of high ability.

A. A disability that affects learning and/or behavior
B. Living in a home where English is the second (or third) language
C. Transience (three or more moves) during the elementary school years
D. Social or educational isolation from resources and stimulation
E. Home responsibilities or employment that interferes with school
F. Irregular school attendance
G. Little or no interaction between school personnel and family

Additional comments:

FIGURE 9.2   Building Administrator Referral Checklist

The following criteria are useful in assessing high potential of students. Please use one form per student to assign a value of *3* (to a considerable degree), *2* (to some degree), or *1* (to little if any degree) for each characteristic.

1. Is quite advanced in academic areas   _____
2. Shows superior leadership qualities   _____
3. Demonstrates a high degree of critical thinking and prefers intellectual challenge   _____
4. Is motivated by curiosity and seems to be self directed   _____
5. Has many interests and is involved in many activities and projects   _____
6. Is full of ideas and demonstrates flexibility, originality, and resourcefulness   _____
7. Is keenly observant and questioning   _____
8. Is usually serious minded and intolerant of foolishness   _____
9. Has a high energy level with unusual perseverance   _____
10. Has family members who are intensely concerned with enrichment and acceleration in the curriculum and with the learning environment of the school   _____

Please check any of the following factors which apply. If present along with a number of the attributes above, they may provide additional validation of high ability.

A. Irregular school attendance   _____
B. Limited contact between school personnel and family   _____

Additional Comments:

Educators who work with preschool children and kindergartners relate to lists that contain characteristics such as these:

✓ Asks many questions, often on topics typically interesting to older children
✓ Demonstrates early use of a large vocabulary and multiple meanings of words
✓ Understands abstract concepts such as time, coins, larger numbers, calendars
✓ Relates experiences with great detail and makes up vivid, dramatic stories
✓ Has a long attention span and deep concentration level for such an early age
✓ Learned to read at a very young age with little or no formal teaching
✓ Expressed self in complete sentences at an early age
✓ Shows precocious interest in values, purposes, and right-and-wrong issues

Room and reminders must be left in busy classroom teachers' think time for noting characteristics of dual-or-more exceptionalities. Students with high potential may also be chronic underachievers. They may have physical disabilities or behavior disorders. Attention deficit with hyperactivity disorder (ADHD) is not uncommon among the high ability population. Cultural differences such as deference to authority or reluctance to compete against friends can force talents underground. Conditions of illness may prevent students from demonstrating their capabilities. Students causing most concern among school personnel in regard to their progress will be those in subgroups such as students with disabilities, English-language learners, and children of families who are poor (Christie, 2004).

Identification of potential among such populations of special need can be masked by problems which do not allow their abilities to "bubble up." Conversely, their abilities to compensate may mask problem areas so that those do not become apparent. The student loses both ways: Ability is not served and disability is not remediated. Collaborative consulting teachers, special education personnel, school counselors, and school psychologists must be vigilant in watching for these circumstances.

The checklist system itself imposes some limitations on validity of the information gathered. These limitations include:

- the halo effect, where generously favorable attitudes cause spuriously high ratings
- logical error, in which two characteristics—for example, high achievement and high ability, or giftedness and poor social skills—are rated similarly because of rater beliefs
- generosity error, when respondents wish for every subject to be highly rated
- severity error, when respondents think *no* one is particularly exceptional in ability
- central tendency (a rarer occurrence), in which respondents rate everyone average and avoid both ends of the extremes

The consulting teacher may find evidence of one or more of these limitations, and may have difficulty getting a decent return of the forms from distracted teachers and principals. But the efforts are rewarded even if a classroom teacher returns a form with a comment like this, "I'm not going to refer Jackie for the enrichment/acceleration program at this time. But after completing a checklist for her, I am thinking differently about her [abilities] now." Something differentiated is bound to happen for the student from that time on!

Interest Inventories.   As a part of the identification process, or after selections have been made for service in special programs and curriculum is being designed, rich data can be obtained from individual interviews in which the interviewer/consultant uses an inventory format to gather information about student interests and goals. Sometimes the interest inventory is supplemented with a learning styles inventory to determine likes and dislikes in regard to structures for the learning process. See Figure 9.3 for an informal instrument that includes both interests and learning styles to obtain rudimentary information about a student's learning wants and needs. Interviewers must bear in mind, however, that the best interest survey for any school's personnel is one that has been designed by the user(s) to fit that school setting.

Much more information will be obtained from a personal interview in which the consulting teacher serves as recording secretary or at least shares the writing responsibility, than one in which a form is just given out for the student to fill out then or later. Sometimes, to save time, an interviewing teacher may solicit the information from a group of students. One drawback to this approach, however, is that students, particularly younger ones, may mimic others' preferences rather than concentrate on making their own wishes known.

■ ■ ■ ■ ■ ▬▬

APPLICATION 9.1
WANTED: WORK

The consulting teacher for the district's gifted program headed toward the school office to announce her arrival in the building. The program was new and she had not yet assembled the identified students into a group or even met with them individually. A polite tap on her shoulder caused her to turn. A seventh-grade student whom she did not know at the time as one of the

FIGURE 9.3   Interest Inventory Format

INTEREST INVENTORY

1. Name _____ Age _____ Grade _____

2. Gender _____ Brothers/Sisters _____

3. Community type (rural, urban, small town) _____

4. School(s) attended _____

5. My favorite subject(s) in school _____

6. What I like to read about _____

7. What I like to access on the Internet _____

8. My hobbies and collections _____

9. Lessons I take _____

10. What I like to watch on TV _____

11. My favorite recreation/sport _____

12. Where I have been on trips _____

13. Where in the world I would go if I could _____

14. What I would do in the world if I could _____

15. What I like best about school _____

16. When I have free time at school I like to _____

17. What I would like to learn more about _____

18. What careers I find most interesting _____

19. What I want to think about doing as a career _____

20. What I wish _____

Rate the next set of activities by putting:
1 = "Like very much", 2 = "It's OK," 3 = "Just so-so", or 4 = "Don't like."

_____   Doing things with a group

_____   Doing things on my own

_____   Reading assignments

_____   Writing reports

_____   Doing experiments

_____   Constructing things

_____   Drawing pictures

_____   Acting out things I'm learning

_____   Listening to teachers and speakers

_____   Watching films or television

_____   Working quickly in order to get done

_____   Working at a leisurely pace

_____   Being a leader most of the time

_____   Being a follower most of the time

_____   Planning my own learning activities

_____   Evaluating my own progress and development

identified group, but who obviously recognized *her,* thrust some spiral-notebook paper into her hand and, without a word, strode on down the hall. She stepped aside to read the paper, which turned out to be two sheets stapled together, and found these words:

> **WANTED: WORK**
>
> I, as a concerned, bored student, am protesting against underestimating our abilities. I'm sorry to say that I'm writing this in math class. But what we do in here is really not worth working on. Review, review, that's all we do. This class is no challenge. If I've learned anything in this class, it is boredom. I want work. *We* want work. I have no intention of doing anything in this class except twiddle my thumbs. I've found no enjoyment in sitting here listening to the teacher repeat things I learned in 5th grade. I'm sure others feel the way I do. Please, we want a challenge.
>
> Sincerely, Ray

She turned to the second sheet and found a list of twenty-two signatures from other students, only twelve of whom were on her list for placement in the gifted program.

Analyze this situation from several perspectives—the consulting teacher's, the building administrator's, the math department teachers' in this large middle school, the petitioning student's, and those of the interesting collection of twenty-two names. What to do? Generate several options this teacher might consider, and create scenarios of most likely outcomes for each option.

Case Study Information.   The case-study format displayed in Chapter 5's Figure 5.3 shows sixteen data sources for gathering information about student interests and needs. The figure can be visualized as a "daisy" of opportunities to know students better. If each explored "petal" source is shaded with a graphite pencil or covered with a tissue paper overlay, an increasingly dark center indicates a growing assurance that student characteristics and needs will require differentiated curriculum. The daisy tool is instructive for staff development and useful in planning sessions that include school psychologists, school counselors, family members, and most importantly, the student.

NEEDS OF LEARNERS WITH HIGH ABILITY AND TALENTS FOR SCHOOL-BASED LEARNING

A simple equation can guide educators in providing special services for students:

Characteristics + Needs = Curriculum Implications.

Tomlinson's (1999) curricular prompt that "one size cannot fit all" emphasizes the need for differentiated curriculum tailored for the individual. Tailored curriculum includes these conditions:

1. Release from repetition of material already learned
2. Removal of ceilings on prescribed curriculum
3. Flexible pacing for progress through the curriculum that allows time and space for accelerative, enriching learning experiences, and provides time for learning activities with mental peers
4. Engagement in self-directed learning and self-assessment processes.

These conditions can be met through general strategies that include:

1. Release from repetition by curriculum compacting
2. Removal of ceilings by setting appropriate open-ended goals and objectives
3. Flexible pacing through the use of alternative instructional strategies, learning options, and planned learning experiences with mental peers
4. Student engagement in the learning through participation in goal-setting and planning conferences, design and production of portfolios, and student-guided assessment processes.

Wide ranges of educational experiences must be available that target general instructional objectives while appealing to a variety of student interests, talents, and goals. All students in school have the right to a challenging school-based curriculum that allows them to learn, and educators and policymakers have the unequivocal responsibility to provide it. Collaborative consultation and working in teams are key processes in making it happen.

Differentiating the School-Based Curriculum

Differentiated, challenging curriculum is the business of schools that attend to individual differences and aim for development of student potential to the fullest degree possible. Tomlinson frames and activates that business with a clear mission statement:

> What we call *differentiation* is not a recipe for teaching. It is not an instructional strategy. It is not what a teacher does when he or she has time. It is a way of thinking about teaching and learning. It is a philosophy. As such, it is based on a set of beliefs (2000, p. 6).

Educational policymakers and practitioners must make important administrative and curricular decisions for their schools and students. Will student differences in ability to learn curricular material be exhibited in kind and amount of achievement sought, or in time allocated to reach designated achievement levels (Hanna & Dettmer, 2004)? Some content (for example, reciting the alphabet or adjusting a microscope correctly) is best suited to allocating enough time for nearly all students to attain mastery. Other content can never be mastered because it is broad and open-ended (for example, analyzing rhythm and blues music or predicting the migratory patterns and feeding habits of blue whales). For the latter type of content, consulting teachers can be of particular assistance in preparation and implementation.

As teachers struggle with management and coordination issues, students often languish waiting for something interesting and challenging to happen. Some "sleep through" their classroom situations only to "wake up" later and find that they have missed important elements needed for understanding key concepts. Other students "tune out" and create their own personal diversions during the school day, sometimes by "acting out." But most simply bide the time by reading, daydreaming, playing little games such as writing class notes backward or with the other hand, analyzing and charting their teachers' idiosyncrasies, or surreptitiously interacting with friends.

Acceleration or Enrichment?

There is no need to debate the choice of accelerated curriculum over enriched curriculum, or vice versa. Curricular content that accelerates student learning *is enriching,* and curriculum that enriches *will, by definition, accelerate.*

Enriching, accelerating instructional strategies call for careful organization and coordination among general education teachers, special education personnel, resource personnel, school administrators, and families, with intensive student collaboration in their own learning programs. Classroom teachers are responsible for delivering content in differentiated, alternative, accelerated, enriched forms. They should introduce fundamentals at the levels and paces (note the plurals) that can be accomplished by each student. No one should have to repeat, repeat, and repeat again content that has already been learned. The key is *flexible pacing,* with movement through the curriculum at speeds, breadths, and depths that stimulate and challenge exceptionally able minds.

Flexible pacing of the curriculum puts a tremendous burden on classroom teachers for serving highly able students along with their responsibilities for teaching, reteaching, and providing correctives for students who have not yet achieved adequate yearly progress on district- and state-stipulated goals. Therefore, they must have assistance from special education facilitators who can seek out learning options and alternatives, coordinate them, gather resources for the learning, and design challenging curriculum. These consulting teachers for special services facilitate by collaborating with:

- teachers in the classroom to develop learning options and alternatives, and organize the individual or small group plans;
- resource personnel outside the school environment to engage them in extension of learning opportunities for students;
- school administrators to sanction and activate the extended learning programs;
- families and students to utilize the differentiated curriculum options and alternatives.

Pursuit of such lofty educational aims for the brightest and most talented students cannot be assumed by only classroom teachers or only special services facilitators. It will require "the whole village."

CONSULTATION, COLLABORATION, AND TEAMWORK ROLES WITH STUDENTS OF HIGH ABILITY

In the twenty-first century, with its wealth of information and explosion of ideas for the taking and using, and with worldwide problems threatening the welfare of all, educators must work in many different ways to prepare students for their future. Workers in business, health care, industry, agriculture, technology, sales, human services, and other career areas are collaborating and working in teams. Educators, too, must consult and collaborate, not only to do their very important work effectively, but to model these behaviors for students who will be called on to demonstrate them in their own future work.

A task force commissioned by the National Association for Gifted Children[2] (NAGC) to investigate linkage of general education and gifted education (more appropriately described as education of the gifted, but colloquially referred to as "gifted education") presented

---

[2]Note the infrequent appearance of the term *gifted* in this chapter. This values-laced term could have been avoided altogether but for necessary credits and references to the term in often-quoted educational literature and widely disseminated teaching resources.

three rationales that signal the need for school collaboration (Tomlinson, Coleman, Allan, Udall, & Landrum, 1996):

A. Collaboration between general and gifted education would facilitate balancing equity and excellence, to the benefit of all students.

B. Collaboration between the two fields would reinforce the reality of shared goals, namely, better schools, richer curriculum content, and robust learning experiences for all students. (It is important to remember that very able students spend most of their school time in general classrooms.)

C. Collaboration between the two fields would maximize strengths of both generalists and specialists to the benefit of the total school community. (Both have important roles; they are not the same roles and they ought not to be.)

As stressed earlier in the book, the "my kids/your kids" and "us/them" attitudes undermine collaborative efforts and working as teams. The NAGC task force recommended thinking of collaborative consultation metaphorically: as an orchestra with full expression of the music possible only when all parts do their best to blend and harmonize.

General Classroom Teachers.   Classroom teachers are responsible for delivering curriculum content in basic, differentiated, compacted, accelerated, and enriched forms. But they should have assistance from special services personnel such as gifted program facilitators, who may co-teach, provide resources, coordinate out-of-school learning experiences, direct mentorships, and so forth. Teachers need to understand and appreciate the characteristics, needs, and curricular implications of those with high learning ability, provide a learning environment in the classroom that nurtures high ability, draw on the assistance of special services personnel, and *release students from assignments for which they have demonstrated competence.* (See Figure 9.4). This requires that they use curriculum compacting to remove unnecessary repetition and to "buy time" for more challenging assignments. (Curriculum compacting is discussed later in the chapter.)

Special Education Facilitators.   Specialists in the education of highly capable students have responsibility for coordinating alternate learning activities, freeing up options, gathering resources, and designing responsive learning programs to challenge students appropriately. They must familiarize themselves with classroom content of all grade levels they serve, a daunting assignment but important for building rapport with classroom teachers and being most effective in collaborative conferences. They function as team members in classrooms, as consultants out of the classrooms, as communicators with administrators, and as partners in learning with students and their families. They keep records on student needs and accomplishments, and are in close contact with school counselors and school psychologists. Sometimes they provide professional development experiences for school personnel or awareness sessions for families, school boards, or community groups. On occasion it is good for them to exchange roles, as discussed in Chapter 1, by working with a classroom teacher's students while that teacher guides a small group in a complex learning activity in or out of the classroom. This lets the special education facilitator observe other students for exceptional ability and allows the class-

FIGURE 9.4   To Make Up, or Not to Make Up, Missed Work: Talking it Over

room teacher to have time away from the classroom to direct accelerative, enriching activities with a single student or a small group of students.

Building Administrators and Special Education Directors.   They are in some ways the most critical factor in the success of differentiated learning programs for students with exceptional ability. If principals do not support tailored curriculum and encourage accelerated, enriching instruction, little is likely to happen that benefits students *or* their teachers. Administrators must provide the support and safety that exceptional students need to use extended resources productively. They should commend teachers for making efforts to collaborate with colleagues and for designing differentiated curriculum strategies and materials.

Building principals must charge school psychologists and counselors to help identify special learning needs and provide assistance with curricular, social, and affective implications of those needs. They also have the responsibility to ensure that the school setting is free of disturbing violence, distracting disobedience, coercive group conformity, and numbing disdain of many students (and, woefully, some teachers) for intellectualism, "differentness," or remarkable academic performance.

Families of Very Able Students.   Legislators and policymakers have delivered the message that children and youth must enter school ready and willing to learn. This is a gargantuan order not yet filled, but family partnerships with schools can help students become ready and motivated for learning.

Parents of students who are very capable expect teachers to demonstrate expertise in meeting their child(ren)'s advanced needs. They worry about peer relationships and social acceptance, and about pressures on the child to succeed always at high levels and please everyone. They often are weary from their child's high energy levels and concerned about the future with educational choices and financial decisions to be made. Perhaps most of all they want to have their child's talents and needs recognized and addressed for as much of the school day as possible with excellent instruction that activates meaningful learning. Their collaboration as partners on planning teams is vital to curriculum planning for their child(ren) and can contribute significantly to excellence of instruction for all students.

School Counselors and School Psychologists. These roles are integral in identifying student capabilities and any problems from failure of schools to meet those needs. They provide preassessment, assessment, and postassessment information to teachers and parents. In IEP conferences they often fill the required administrator role when the principal cannot attend. They *can* be helpful with practical suggestions for resources to optimize learning if encouraged to do so, and may help conduct staff-development activities for understanding needs of very able and talented students. Secondary level counselors can be so much more to highly able students than "card shufflers" for scheduling drop/adds by overseeing their cognitive, emotional, and social needs in what are often explosive peer environments for them.

A major area of team contribution by school psychologists is in the individual education planning conference or any similar goal-setting conference for a student. Individualized education plan (IEP) goals should be open-ended, aimed at complex learning and the high-road transfer of learning that calls for application to new areas. Objectives should be developed with input by the student, and not remedial in tone but directed toward those strengths for which the IEP is warranted.

Assessment of progress on goals and objectives can be problematic for a number of reasons and school psychologists should help resolve these problems, which include:

- Difficulty in assessing high-order outcomes that cannot be measured as easily, precisely, or efficiently as basic skills and mastery outcomes;
- Challenges of choosing standardized measures for goals and objectives that are highly individualized;
- Assessing progress in situations where statistical problems, such as measuring high-order processes and a gain at upper extremes of tests normed on general populations, can occur;
- Low ceilings on many measures of achievement;
- Regression effects that can cause high scorers to obtain more typical scores on subsequent testing (which can be very hard for parents and teachers to understand and accept);
- Lack of norms for high ability populations on some tests, which reduces their reliability;
- Need for long-range goals to be pursued for many years before significant outcomes can be anticipated.

Media Specialists and Librarians. These educators are the backbone of differentiated curriculum inside the school environment. They are often the best resource for locating materials to lift students beyond mundane basal texts or help them to delve into an independent study or research project. They know where things are! And as adults they have the clout to help young students access them. By surveying teachers they can learn what kinds of materials teachers need for personalizing instruction. Librarians might challenge students to read something from every classification area of books in the library. They can help teachers build core skills practice into rich literature selections rather than rely on workbooks of mundane basals. Student presentations can be enhanced by media staff coaching. Library and media personnel should be part of any team targeting curriculum modification, independent study, research projects, individual study for testing out of courses, and other individual education plans.

Mentors and Resource Personnel.   A mentor has opportunity for such profound influence on others that the relationship must not be left to chance. Mentorships give students opportunity to apply and extend their learning beyond the available school curriculum. Mentors become role models for skills, leadership, and the zeal for continued learning. They establish advisory relationships with students even as they stimulate intellectual and practical skills development. The consulting teacher will want to take care in initiating and monitoring this very special kind of relationship. Several steps are pertinent for setting up and facilitating a mentorship (Dettmer, 1980):

1. Designate student(s) who will participate in mentorships.
2. Ascertain student interests and learning styles.
3. Locate mentors who may be matches for those interests and styles.
4. Discuss mentorship with the potential mentors to ascertain their feelings about it.
5. Temporarily make mentor/mentee matches, and initiate casual interaction between them.
6. When a match is established, involve parents and develop a very general study plan, including a plan for eventual termination of the mentorship so that neither party is offended or let down.
7. Continue to monitor progress, from a distance if possible, handling any problems immediately.
8. Evaluate the experience, with input from the student, mentor, parents, and facilitator, and bring closure as previously planned in step 6.

Other suggestions for seeking out and developing community resources for differentiated instruction are provided in Chapter 11.

Professional Development Leaders.   As noted in Chapter 1, professional development of preservice, in-service, and graduate levels is a key element for classroom teachers in the context of collaborative school consultation. First-year teachers as well as veteran teachers must be ready, willing, and able to teach high ability students who spend most of their school time in regular classrooms. Attention to special needs can have many positive spillover effects. Many teachers say their preparation for such students made them better teachers for *all* of their students.

Reis and Westberg (1994) found that Guskey's staff-development philosophy (to be discussed in Chapter 10) is significant in creating a positive response from teachers toward eliminating content (curriculum compacting) and replacing it with modified activities and content for very capable students. Guskey stresses that teacher willingness to continue changes in instructional practices is contingent on real results demonstrated by the learning success of students. In other words, activities that are successful will be repeated by the teacher, and those that are not noticeably successful will not be continued.

Other Influential Role Groups.   Policymakers, including legislators, school boards, and accrediting agencies, design laws and regulations and allocate resources for schools.

Advocates include parent groups, lobbyists for funding and lawmaking, business supporters, and other community factions interested in excellent education and the benefits good schools can provide for communities, not the least of which is real estate values! Researchers contribute new insights into learning and teaching, and in working together within the sociocultural environments of schools.

University instructors of content-area classes and teacher preparation programs prepare students to know and teach content and should include understanding of learning principals and motivation theory *as they relate to the very capable student.* Curriculum developers and textbook authors have the means of including enriching, challenging content in basal materials if they can overcome pressures from interest groups whose agenda does not include focusing space and attention on "those who can get it on their own."

Pediatricians are an overlooked group who often see children and adolescents first for conditions resulting from stress, depression, anorexia, perfectionism, and other socioemotional factors that hinder school success. Some do ask to be part of educational teams so they can learn more about the total spectrum of children's needs, and their input is a powerful resource in studying that spectrum of needs.

Media roles typically deal with good news about student achievements. Media slants on high performance can sway public opinions about needs of schools and the students who attend them, so those in such roles should be given information that enables them to perform their role ethically and supportively.

WORKING IN TEAMS TO SERVE VERY ABLE STUDENTS' NEEDS

VIGNETTE 9.B

A team meeting scheduled for September 8th is about to begin. Assembled are Maria, Andy, Kari, and Keysha. The setting is a quiet, pleasant room where preserving confidentiality will not be a problem and the meeting will not be disturbed.

Maria: Hi, everybody. I'm facilitator today, remember? Here are your blank agenda forms.[3] Let's get started. Recall the ground rules: We form the agenda by each of us stating topics we want to discuss and amount of time we think we'll need. We have a total of thirty minutes today. Kari is timekeeper and notifies us when the allotted time for each item is up. You'll have opportunity to request more time if you need it. I'll prioritize the agenda items, and be responsible for seeing that we get to all of them. This may mean denying requests for additional time or deferring a lengthy item to another time. Let's stay on topic untill we agree to take action or carry an item over to the next meeting. Andy is recorder today. He'll fill out the final group form with actions and comments recorded during the meeting, and make copies for everyone by Monday morning. Okay, what are your new agenda items for today? Andy?

Andy: I'd like to discuss moving Josh and Roberta to a different math group. Ten minutes will be enough.

[3](See Figure 9.5 for the form as it was used in another meeting.)

FIGURE 9.5   Team Meeting Agenda

Date ___9/5/00___   Time ___2:30 p.m.___

Members Present	Roles
Andy	Recorder
Lucy	_____
Sydney	Facilitator
Kari	Time-Keeper

1. Announcements, ground rules, assignment of roles and goals

2. Items for Discussion

	Estimated Time
Carry-over item: space for Lucy's group	5 minutes
Change group for Billy, Wanda & Sam	10 minutes

3. Action Plan

Action	Responsible Person	Due Date
Set up corner in music room	Lucy/Marcia	9/10/00
Math tutoring for Billy & Wanda	Andy/Kari	9/8/00
Move Sam up to reading group 5	Sydney	9/8/00

4. Future Agenda Items

Assigning reading and math grades

5. Next Meeting:

	Date	Time	Place
	10/3/00	2:30 p.m.	Media Center

Maria: Good. Kari?

Kari: I don't have anything.

Maria: Okay Keysha?

Keysha: Nothing new, but I need five minutes for the carryover item, which concerns deciding on a location for my Great Books reading group to meet.

Maria: Fine. I have a new item. I'd like to discuss moving DeShawn to a new reading group. It should only take two minutes. Now, let's begin with the carryover item from our last meeting. Keysha, where are we on that?

Keysha: About a location for my reading group to meet: It's pretty clear that our current space on the stage in the gym is not going to work. We just can't hear each other read passages and discuss them. I've done some checking with others, and I've come up with two options. I could set up an area in a corner of the music room. Louella is willing and she doesn't have any students during my reading period. I don't know where I'd store materials, though. Another option is to empty the storage room behind the stage and set up in there. Then I wouldn't have to disturb Louella. But I'd need to find more tables and chairs.

Andy: Don't worry about Louella. She's working with me and my group during that period. She did say she'd share, right?

Keysha: Yes, and I guess maybe I'm the reluctant one. You know how I like to display student work all around. Hard to do when you're borrowing someone's space.

Kari: If you use the storage room, where will all the P.E. stuff and play props go?

Keysha: That's a problem I haven't solved. Also, where to get tables and chairs.

Kari: (silently signals Maria that time is up for this item)

Maria: Time's up for this item. Do you want more?

Keysha: Yes, just one more minute.

Maria: Sure.

(The team works out a storage room alternative, including communication to be made with the custodian. Andy writes down the action item on the form.)

Maria: Good work on Keysha's concern. Now, our next item is to consider whether Josh and Roberta need to be moved to a more advanced math group. Andy, what is your concern?

Andy: Both seem to be frustrated with having to do individual drill and practice on some of the concepts I think they'll need in order to work at the next level. But they show considerable understanding of math's more complex aspects. I guess it's the proverbial rock and hard place.

Maria: I think maybe I know what's going on. Those two were student council representatives from their homerooms last year, weren't they? Remember that special civics project the reps worked on? They missed some math lessons because of that.

Andy: Okay. What if we provide some tutoring on the concepts? They should pick it up quickly and be ready to move into the advanced group before long.

Maria: Who would do that and when?

Andy: Keysha, could you spare Kari for a couple of weeks to help me catch them up? I can tell her what to do and she could work with them during class, or monitor class while I tutor.

Keysha: Yes, a couple of weeks is okay. But I really need her back by October when we start a new unit.

Kari: I'll be glad to help out.

Maria: So Kari will shift to Andy's math group for two weeks. Andy will pull together the lessons and provide instructions for Kari. Starting Monday?

Andy: Fine. Monday the 13th. (He writes down the action item on the form.)

Maria: Next up is DeShawn's reading placement. It's apparent to me we have him grouped wrong for reading. I'm not sure why. He is a super reader. It became evident in his classroom work, so I administered an informal reading inventory. He's at the seventh-grade instructional level.

Andy: Whoa! How did we miss that during grouping?

Keysha: DeShawn moved to this district just a few weeks ago. In the commotion at the start-up of the year, I think we just didn't get the initial assessment right.

Maria: What now? Should he move to group 5 on Monday?

All: Yes!

Maria: I'm his homeroom teacher. I'll make sure he makes the switch. Is there anything content-wise he needs to know before the move?

Andy: No. We're starting the illustrated classic, *20,000 Leagues Under the Sea* on Monday. It's a good time to move him. (writes down the action on the form)

Kari: (quietly signals Maria time is up)

Maria: That's all our time for today. Looks like we have everything on the agenda covered, too. Nothing to carry over. Good job, everybody! We'll meet again October 6th, same time, same place. Kari, you're scheduled to be facilitator, Andy is timekeeper, and Keysha will be recorder.

Andy: I'll have the notes for today's meeting in your boxes by Monday morning.

Maria: Have a good weekend, all!

APPLICATION 9.B

In Vignette 9.b what roles (not for the meeting, but in the larger scheme of things) do you identify among the team? What were some good features of the collaborative meeting? How was teamwork demonstrated? Do you see any areas in which improvement to the process could be made? Have you been a part of such team sessions and, if so, what would you add to an analysis of this process?

CURRICULAR IMPLICATIONS OF HIGH-ABILITY CHARACTERISTICS AND NEEDS

Recall that "Characteristics plus needs equals curricular implications." In a study of the impact of gifted programs on gifted students (Hertzog, 2003), students said their teachers engaged them in high-level thinking and created better classroom atmospheres than in general classrooms, resulting in more positive relationships between students and teachers. Less time was spent on discipline and they developed a strong work ethic while participating in the programs. They did voice some concerns about segregation from other students and labeling issues, but felt they had been provided an education enriched by challenges and mental stimulation.

In the study Hertzog quotes Mary Frasier's comment at the 2000 American Education Research Association convention that the goal of gifted education is not to give students a "better" education but to give them a more *appropriate* one. Attaining this goal is hard work, but collaborative consultation and working with colleagues in teams can help. Many minds, models, and methods will ease the work load and make it more enjoyable while carrying it.

Taxonomy of the Cognitive Domain

One structure that can be used in a variety of ways to differentiate curriculum for special needs is the well-known set of taxonomies for the cognitive and affective domains. The *Taxonomy of Educational Objectives, Handbook I: Cognitive Domain* (Bloom, Engelhart, Furst, Hill, & Krathwohl, 1956) is one of the most frequently cited publications in educational literature. It was developed as a way of classifying goals of an educational system and helping educators test achievement of the goals. Many educators are concerned that a large proportion of tests *and* teaching practices greatly overemphasize two categories—memory work and translation of material (familiar to teachers as the knowledge and comprehension levels of the cognitive taxonomy)—while largely neglecting to nurture application of knowledge and understanding to new situations (termed *high-road transfer* by educational psychologists). Intellectual assignments and activities with rich potential for transfer of learning—application, analysis, synthesis, and evaluation—are too often neglected in favor of simpler and tidier instruction, drill, practice, regurgitation, and mastery learning approaches. The latter are not the kinds of learning opportunities exceptionally able students need most to practice.

A graphic that is familiar to educators shows the taxonomy of the cognitive domain as a pyramid sliced horizontally for dividing categories of thinking by complexity. Wide slabs at the base depicting knowledge and comprehension too often usurp 80 to 90 percent of learning time and resources. But students who learn rapidly and easily should have an inverted pyramid of emphasis with the wide slabs at the top, not because they don't need knowledge and understanding, but because for the most part they have already acquired it or can do so very rapidly. Having less concentration on basic elements would free up the bulk of their learning time to be directed toward the higher orders of thinking that use known and comprehended material but go much farther with it.

Briefly described, the six categories of the very familiar taxonomy of the cognitive domain are:

■ **Knowledge:** Recalling or recognizing facts, principles, methods, and the like. Little is demanded beyond remembering material as it was presented, and many believe that this category is greatly overdone in teaching and testing.

■ **Comprehension:** Understanding meaning, as shown by paraphrasing or explaining but stopping short of deep understanding. Authors of the cognitive taxonomy averred that most school-based teaching and learning was concentrated in development of knowledge bases and comprehension. They encouraged educators to build on these learning categories by stretching the curriculum goals to aspire to higher orders of thinking.

- **Application:** Using ideas, rules, or principles in new situations, which are for the most part intended for use in real life.

- **Analysis:** Taking apart the components of a concept and showing relationships among the parts. For example, children develop this kind of thinking when they study, sort, classify, label, and organize their valued collections.

- **Synthesis:** Putting elements together in ways not demonstrated by that individual before. However, it is not truly free creative expression, because it typically occurs within limits set by the problem, materials, or structure.

- **Evaluation:** Assessing the value of goals, ideas, methods, products, materials, and such, and making purposeful judgments about them.

Taxonomy of the Affective Domain

In 1964 Krathwohl, Bloom, and Masia directed the development of the *Taxonomy of Educational Objectives, Handbook II: Affective Domain.* The original committee had recognized the need for addressing affective functions, but had been discouraged by the difficulty of designing ways of measuring them.

It is inevitable that both cognitive and affective components are involved in learning and doing.Educators want pupils to *like* to eat healthfully as well as to be able to do so, to *respect* rules of good citizenship as well as to know them, and to *value* as well as to understand management of resources. A brief description of the classification scheme for the affective domain shows the five categories, again ordered from simplest to most complex (Krathwohl, Bloom, & Masia, 1964):

- **Receiving:** Being aware of something or someone in the environment and attending at least passively to it (attending to the science teacher's lecture, the phys ed teacher's rules for safety and hygiene, a piano piece played during a recital).

- **Responding:** Reacting to the environment and responding to elements in it (noting the candidates who filed for an upcoming presidential election, seeing if the microscope is in position for slide viewing, looking at the arrangement of books on the library shelf).

- **Valuing:** Actively seeking out ways to respond (implementing the teacher's structure for a cooperative learning group and applying the rules for the activity, voluntarily following recommended steps in a physical development program).

- **Organization:** Integrating knowledge and applying information to something considered important (using text, lecture, class discussion, and media information about food safety to explain the significance for a country's economy and world trade activity).

- **Characterization by a Value or Value Complex:** Organizing values into a whole, and acting in accordance with newly acquired values or beliefs (e.g., voluntarily practicing coaches' instructions for safety and sportsmanship, and following those rules when not knowingly being observed or graded).

Taxonomy of the Psychomotor Domain

The **psychomotor domain** concerns muscular or motor skills, manipulation of materials and objects, and acts requiring coordination. Examples are ball throwing, watercolor brush strokes, sanding a birdhouse, keyboarding, and driving a car. Of course, cognitive and affective components accompany psychomotor activity. One must "know" the numerals from 1 to 100 in order to perform the motor task of saying them, and copying them neatly is often as much a function of feeling toward the task as of motor skill. Hitting a hockey puck clearly involves not only psychomotor skills in executing the techniques while skating, but knowledge of game rules and ice-relevant physics, along with interest in and commitment to the game.

It is ironic that little attention was directed by developers of the cognitive and affective taxonomies toward physical development of students, when so much emphasis in recent years has been put on motor skills needed for athletics, art, industry, and technology. But since then several psychomotor taxonomies have been developed. The Simpson (1972) taxonomic structure is appropriate for motor skills in a wide range of areas. It includes seven categories, as ordered from simplest to most complex:

- Perception: Using senses to get cues that guide motor movement.
- Set: Being set mentally, emotionally, and physically to perform a particular action.
- Guided Response: Imitating and engaging in trial and error.
- Mechanism: Performing movements with confidence and skill.
- Complex Overt Response: Performing complex movements effectively.
- Adaptation: Modifying movements to fit special situations.
- Origination: Creating new movements for appropriate situations.

Rethinking the Taxonomies for Creative, Sensorimotor, and Social Needs

Developers of the cognitive domain taxonomy did not promote their work as the be-all and end-all for processes of thinking and doing. They disdained fragmentation of educational purposes and wished to set the taxonomy at a level of generality that allowed for flexibility and growth. They hoped not to abort teachers' thinking and development of curriculum, and they surely did not wish for the taxonomies to be used as recipes, which, alas, some teachers have been prone to do. They thought of the taxonomies as fluid and unfinished, and encouraged more thought and development of the concepts.

The process of rereading these *original* works and pondering the significance of their profoundly important ideas can be a rewarding exercise for educators and often leads to new ideas about teaching and learning. For example, since the original cognitive and affective domains were conceptualized, interest in creativity has expanded, generating increased research on creative thinking and development of original products as an important part of school curriculum. Therefore, it follows that the cognitive taxonomy can be expanded appropriately to include categories for imagination and creativity while retaining the category of synthesis. And because cognitive activities of imagination and creativity are accompanied by affective components, the categories of *wonder* (in using one's imagination), and *risk-taking* (in creating a new entity) fit well into the affective domain.

Furthermore, a psychomotor taxonomy need not be limited to motor activity. In the school curriculum a physical perspective should include sensory input, with attention to sight, sound, touch, taste, and smell, and perhaps others yet to be identified, such as balance, in the school curriculum. Many teachers, particularly at the primary levels, do this already because they realize the importance of sensory input for learning.

Finally, it is well past time for including in the school curriculum an overlooked but extremely important aspect of learning and doing—the social domain. Secondary level instructors most of all can draw on social aspects of learning to enrich school learning.

Taxonomy for a Social Domain

The **social domain** pertains to sociocultural settings in and around schools, where students interact in large groups and small clusters within classrooms, on playgrounds, and in gymnasiums, labs, shops, lunchrooms, hallways, restrooms, theater stages, conference rooms, offices, and transportation vehicles. Students and teachers cultivate relationships and develop networks of relationships in this richly interactive, cooperative, and collaborative environment (Hanna & Dettmer, 2004).

A taxonomic structure for describing social behavior can be organized into eight categories:

■ **Relating:** Students relate to others by acknowledging their presence, making eye contact, attending to their words or actions, and showing that they want to be with them.

■ **Communicating:** Communicators send or receive messages from others when they speak, gesture, call, sing, signal, listen. The most overlooked aspect of the communication process, as discussed in Chapter 4, is *listening*. Messages are sent verbally and nonverbally, with body language often being the more powerful of these two types.

■ **Participating:** Joining in, volunteering for, going along with, or actively and willingly taking part in group activities, which indicates that one is ready to participate in socially constructed settings. Much of school life and later life consists of belonging to and taking part in groups.

■ **Negotiating:** Negotiation often takes place informally in play groups when children choose teams, explore give-and-take options, and take turns. Later they bargain, barter, compromise, renegotiate, all the while building skills for relating to others in positive ways. Mediation and arbitration are extensions of negotiation and precursors to setting aside personal preferences to accommodate and assimilate those of others.

■ **Collaborating:** Working together for success of the group or the project. Well-developed collaborative teamwork is a necessary skill of family, career, and community life in the twenty-first century.

■ **Adjudicating:** Conciliating and settling differences among others. Conciliation is an outcome of effective negotiation and mediation efforts. Those who communicate and negotiate effectively in social settings are more able to mediate differences for the benefit of all.

■ **Initiating:** Creating opportunities and processes for interactions, even when social risks are involved, in order to activate social action and change.

■ **Converting:** Constructing social transitions and convincing others to join in for social aims that can benefit all (Dettmer, 1997).

Taxonomic Contributions to Curriculum Differentiation

The taxonomies are powerful tools for focusing on levels of instruction that enable students to learn in increasingly complex, challenging ways.

A. When teaching at the basic (knowledge and comprehension) levels (for example, the times tables) and expecting students to attend to the lesson (receive and respond), instructors will allow sufficient time for learning the material at a stipulated competency level. Reteaching and correctives often are required. When so, *extending activities must be made available* for those who do not need to relearn or to correct.

B. When lesson objectives are aimed at higher-order thinking, instructors designate the level of achievement that is reasonable for open-ended, never-ending learning (for example, learning about and evaluating benefits of various electrical power sources for an energy-hungry nation) and determine the point at which the class must move on, thereby accepting the reality of varying levels of achievement among the group. Curriculum plans incorporate strategies such as questioning and responding cues depicted in Figures 9.6 and 9.7. Expanded versions of these starter lists can be taped into instructors' plan books and used to enhance learning episodes such as class discussion and writing assignments. During their team planning, collaborating teachers might discuss student growth in complex thinking skills and tolerance for differing opinions and values.

C. When the objectives for learning focus on creativity and innovation with wonder and risk-taking as affective complements, teachers, mentors, and content-area specialists provide

FIGURE 9.6   Good Thinking!

Who has some ideas about this?

Why do you think that occurred?

What may happen next?

If you could, what would you change about . . . ?

Who has some ideas about this?

It was good what you said. Now let's think about it this way . . .

We can't seem to solve this. How else could we approach it?

Is there anything important we left out?

Will you give an example, please?

Yes, that is a reasonable answer. Where do we go from here?

I see that you have an idea/answer. How did you arrive at it?

Could you say that another way?

What would be an exciting or innovative way to do that?

What caused . . . to . . . the way it did?

Do you agree with _____'s suggestion?

(etc.)

FIGURE 9.7   Thinking Higher, Wider, and Deeper

If you could interview a famous person, who would it be?

If you could have picked an important event in history to have attended, which would it have been, and why?

If you could have two notable persons meet for a discussion, whom would you choose, and what would you have the topic(s) be?

If you were to redo something you have written, drawn, composed, invented, how would you change it?

How would you put your feelings about something you like very much into a work of art or science?

How could you combine poetry, music, video, art, to convey what life is like or was like in a particular time and place of interest to you?

What writer, artist, or scientist would you select as a very influential person, and why?

Of things you have written, composed, drawn, performed, invented, or discovered, which did you like best and why?

What might creative expression be like in other civilizations—past, present, future?

(etc.)

flexible time limits and suspend expectations for achievement. If they feel inadequate to critique the work and provide constructive feedback, they call in experts for that aspect of the learning. Students are major participants in planning the curriculum and assessing their performance at this level, with collaborative team effort among all.

STUDENT COLLABORATION IN DIFFERENTIATED LEARNING ACTIVITIES

If educators want students to think and perform at more complex and individually expressive levels than recall, recitation, explanation, and translation, they must convey that intent to students. Very able students will accept readily the challenge to analyze, synthesize, and evaluate. With encouragement they can become partners in curriculum development rather than passive recipients. Figure 9.8 can be introduced to students as early as the primary grades. It is a tool for explaining high-order thinking and doing that builds on the knowing and understanding categories. Growth in higher-order processes as depicted on the taxonomic "plant" illustration is the right and responsibility of every learner, no matter at what ability level. Such nurturance will enable all learners to "bloom" into the most knowledgeable and productive persons they can be.

Student Portfolios

Portfolios are useful tools for increasing student collaboration in learning and assessment. The student can select categories of content to include and keep the portfolio current by choosing which materials to add and which to remove. Included content will provide sup-

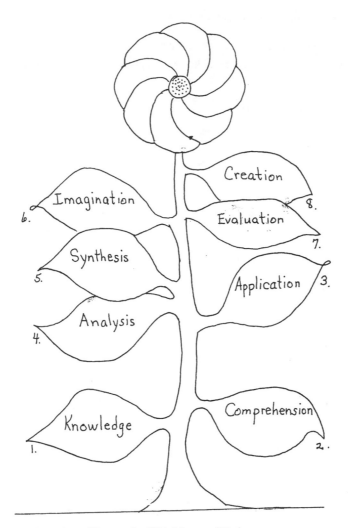

FIGURE 9.8   Blooms for Thinking and Doing

© Peggy Dettmer, 1997

portive material for differentiated curriculum opportunities and serve as a springboard for interaction during student-guided conferences with teacher and parents. Two important aspects of student portfolio development are organization through preparation of a table of contents, and development of assessment rubrics by which the contents are evaluated. A few simple steps help to start off a portfolio system smoothly:

   Step 1: Discuss the concept of portfolios with the class or group taking part and get students involved.

   Step 2: Collaborate with other teachers and with students to develop criteria for selecting portfolio contents.

Step 3: Develop a format for the table of contents and coach students on how to prepare their own so it reflects their individual interests and performances.

Step 4: Again collaborate with colleagues and students to develop criteria for evaluating the portfolio products and to involve students in designing rubrics and other assessment tools.

Step 5: Decide together the final destination of portfolio contents.

For critique of their products, students may include assessments they have requested from outside experts, favorite former teachers, or the principal. An example of a form is provided in Figure 9.9.

FIGURE 9.9   Request for Assessment

I, _____ , would like for you, _____ , to critique my _____
     (student name)   (evaluator's name)   (type of work)

It is included with this form. I have proofread, edited, revised, and improved it, and I now present it for critique and feedback from the evaluator I have chosen—You!

I am asking that you:

_____ provide comments on merits and strengths of this work.

_____ suggest any additions, deletions, revisions that could improve the work.

_____ comment on weaknesses, inaccuracies, errors, or misjudgments in the work.

_____ suggest resources I missed that would have added value to work.

_____ offer any ideas that come to mind for an extension of this work.

I will use your critique and feedback to:

_____ redo this work for the purpose of _____

_____ work more effectively on my next project which is _____

Thank you very much for your assistance! My teacher(s) and I value your help very much.

_____   _____

(student signature)   (facilitating teacher signature)

_____   _____

(date of request)   (date of returned assessment)

SELECTED INSTRUCTIONAL MODELS FOR DIFFERENTIATING INSTRUCTION

Many teaching models and instructional approaches are well-suited to curriculum differentiation for students' special learning needs, including the multiple talents models, the autonomous learner model, the multiple intelligences approach, and others. Three that include significant emphasis on collaboration among general education, special needs education, and resource personnel will be described briefly here. Others can be found among the numerous sources of materials for education of gifted students.

The Enrichment Triad

The Enrichment Triad Model (Renzulli, 1977) is one of the most widely used, longstanding models for serving very capable and talented students in inclusive schools. All students in the general classroom participate in Type 1 exploratory activities on topics of interest through learning centers, field trips, resource speakers, learning packets, and more. All students in the classroom also participate in Type 2 process-building activities to develop skills in problem solving, creative thinking, inquiry, and more.

Students who are of above average ability, motivated to learn and do, and show signs of creativity are invited to participate in Type 3 enrichment activities such as independent studies, research, and project development as would be done by professionals. Interest inventories and learning styles surveys guide construction of these intense activities. The Type 3 experiences may take place in the classroom, in a resource room with other students identified for the talent pool, or beyond the classroom with mentors and content experts. The Enrichment Triad Model is built on a solid foundation of intensive staff development and collaboration among classroom teachers and special education personnel.

Resource Consultation Model

In many schools there is little collaboration between general classroom teachers and gifted education teachers, with classroom teachers making few efforts to modify their curriculum for their most able students (Kirschenbaum, Armstrong, & Landrum, 1999). The resource consultation model calls for teachers of gifted students to work in ways that may be different from ways they have worked in the past (Ward & Landrum (1994).

The consultation occurs at different levels. In level one, teachers collaborate on an unstructured, informal basis for serving student needs. At level two they seek assistance from specialized personnel for the education of gifted students. Level three provides team intervention with several staff members involved in the decision making. Aims of the model are to enhance student academic performance for highly able learners *and* their age peers, to improve teacher competencies in providing differentiated instruction, to demonstrate effectiveness of the consultation approach, and to redefine the role of the gifted education specialist. Research studies (Landrum, 2001) show that positive spillover effects of the resource consultation model produce diverse and more frequent services to gifted students, and make the specialized services available to other students in the general classroom. Enhanced staff development results in gifted education teachers learning more about the general education program, and classroom teachers and other specialists becoming more familiar with the gifted education program.

TREAT Program Model

The TREAT Program (Treat & Dyck, 1997), is a successful model any elementary classroom teacher might use to address special needs of students with high ability in the classroom. The TREAT Program includes steps outlined in Figure 9.10. The test out option is available for

FIGURE 9.10   The TREAT Model

Testout: Any student in the class is given an opportunity to test out of a study unit.

Revise: The successful student receives a grade of "A" for the unit. The student participates in choosing what to do next and completes a contracted activity as described in steps E, A and T below.

   Enrich: The student may select from enrichment options offered by the teacher.

   Accelerate: The student may be given the option of accelerating the pace of learning subject matter material through advance placement or curriculum compacting or telescoping.

   Think-and-Do: The student, with teacher guidance, constructs an independent study in a personally meaningful content area.

any student who wants to try. The result is that some students are pleasantly surprised to discover they can successfully test out and receive the same positive benefits as the students identified as gifted. Students with less ability benefit because the teacher can provide instruction aimed at their needs without being concerned about overlooking the needs of students with high ability.

Classroom teachers can implement the TREAT Program alone, but if a special services facilitator is available the TREAT Program will be much more effective. Facilitators typically have had extensive training in understanding students with high ability and can provide special materials and guides along with knowledge about other resources available in the school and community. The facilitator and the classroom teacher generally meet regularly (preferably every week) to plan.

TAILORING THE CURRICULUM FOR HIGHLY ABLE STUDENTS

A key part of tailoring curriculum and integrating learning alternatives to fit very capable students' learning programs is to find out what they already know. It is also helpful to know the student's prior experiences with material to ascertain if the demonstrated skills have been learned rapidly and easily, or if they reflect a less complex level of much practice in recalling and rephrasing. For these purposes teachers should test their achievement levels with out-of-level (power) tests, observe and interview the student, and evaluate with as much other multisourced evidence as possible.

Preassessment and Pretesting

Pretesting can identify those who are able to move faster through content or skip it entirely (Systma, 2001). This justifies and facilitates integration of curriculum compacting as a teaching strategy for highly capable students. It also provides students with previews of upcoming units and stimulates their thinking by requiring them to draw on prior knowledge.

Some state regulations stipulate that before students can be identified formally as exceptional and receive services of special education personnel, they must have curriculum modifications in the classroom. This raises philosophical and practical issues of a chicken-first or egg-first nature. Simply put, to determine whether the classroom is appropriate for gifted students, teachers must provide differentiation that requires minimal modification, is easy to implement, and can be measured with existing evaluation tools. But if these efforts are only minimal, short-term, and made by teachers who do not have time, preparation, and resources for working with such students, they are not likely to reveal much about student capability for performing at more complex or accelerated levels. Conversely, if preassessment interventions do result in significant progress, that is even stronger evidence that the student needs differentiated learning programs a general classroom may not readily be able to provide!

The right approach in selection of preassessment strategies is necessary for determining which students need what kinds of differentiation and at what levels they will be most challenged. A few of the many examples of preassessment strategies that could be used are:

1. Pretest, and if material is known, advance to the next unit or chapter. Use the pretest grade to compare with the advanced unit grade for assessing achievement.

2. Use supplementary materials as suggested in basal textbooks for high achievers. Do this for six to nine weeks and assess growth in that area.

3. Replace assigned seatwork or homework with opportunities for more in-depth study of that subject through the use of library, Internet, or people resources. Measure the completed work after four to six weeks.

4. Allow the student to use alternate test forms such as essays, make-up-an-exam options, in-depth reaction papers, or compare-contrast papers. Use for one to three weeks and measure the product(s).

5. Allow the student to "stop off" during a particular unit of special interest and do more in-depth study, catching up with the class later through compacted curriculum and test-out opportunity. Use for one to three weeks and measure the product by teacher evaluation and, perhaps, peer evaluation.

6. Allow coursework to be undertaken in two subjects simultaneously, attending each class half-time and completing half of the assignments as determined by pretest and curriculum compacting. Measure by grading the work after using for nine to eighteen weeks.

At the end of the suggested duration times, the preassessment team should reconvene to discuss student progress. If the student is showing progress at the more rapid pace or flexible learning process, and is responding positively to the differentiation, then *more* options and alternatives can be made available. Content-area teachers, school counselors, facilitators for differentiated programs, family members, and the student should collaborate in making these decisions.

Textbook Analysis

Love of reading, interest in science, and the intrigue of mathematics have been dulled in many bright students by mundane, simplistic grade-school textbooks. Basal readers, in particular, with their readability formulas and syllable schemes have "dumbed down" stories so that children sometimes cannot even follow the meager plots and mundane story lines. Studies made in the 1990s revealed that textbooks dropped two grade levels in difficulty and 79 to 88 percent of fifth- and sixth-grade average readers could pass pretests on reading comprehension before the material was covered in the basal reader (Renzulli & Reis, 1991). Better readers were performing at 93 percent on comprehension skills pretests. A few years before that a nonprofit educational consumer agency determined that 60 percent of fifth graders in some districts could achieve a score of 80 percent or higher on a test of math content *before they opened their texts* in September. Similar findings were reported with fifth- and tenth-grade science texts and tenth-grade social studies texts.

One way to judge the suitability of basal materials for very capable students is to do a textbook analysis. Consulting teachers and classroom teachers working in teams can examine grade-level texts for enrichment material and may find they can devise instructional strategies even better for their purposes than those in the basal series.

VIGNETTE 9.C

Two groups of teachers have taken it on themselves to critique content-area textbooks as a prelude to serving on curriculum committees for selecting new textbooks. Here is an abbreviated version of their several-page reports:

Group One: We evaluated the XXX social studies text at the fifth-grade level. It is superb, having been critiqued by several consultants, university instructors, and fifth-grade teachers as well as teachers from other grade levels. Bloom's *Taxonomy* is used as a format for unit questions, with categories that include Focus, Critical Thinking, Connect, and Activity. Factual information is presented in different ways, with occasional side notes relating the historical topic to the present time. Special pages appear every so often for a unit to continue the lesson with exploration ideas or activities. One section on Making Decisions poses a problem from the past and asks "What Would You Do?" In the back is a small encyclopedia called Minipedia. Also there are an Atlas and a Time and Space Databank, which are wonderful reference tools for students and teachers. With this textbook, the teacher has an opportunity to enrich and accelerate social studies content for students.

Group Two: Our group critiqued a math text at the kindergarten level. It contains a lot of material on copying abstract symbols, on counting in isolated situations, and on analyzing pictures of objects. But kids need to work with things and learn about numbers in real-life situations. Use of concrete materials was not emphasized here. The enrichment masters seem to be for assigning more of the same when students finish their workbook pages too early, and the answers are to be written rather than circled. (To take up more time?) They represent no more cognitive effort than the regular lesson. One "gifted student" activity is provided for each unit that does offer some possibilities, but these are obscurely placed and total only nine in all. We feel that if teachers construct their lessons around material provided by this rather typical text, it's no wonder so many students get turned off by math!

Curriculum Compacting

Curriculum compacting (Renzulli & Reis, 1985) is a *must* part of differentiated curriculum. It is a strategy that consulting teachers and classroom teachers can plan and implement productively for very able students. Just as teachers condense daily lessons and assignments for children returning to school after an illness, they can compact curriculum for students who learn more quickly and easily than the majority of students. This "buys time" for students to pursue individual interests and independent study in more challenging areas of regular or accelerated curriculum.

Reis, Burns, and Renzulli (1992) provide several recommendations based on their findings from teachers who have implemented curriculum compacting:

1. Start the compacting process by targeting a small group of students for which it seems especially appropriate.
2. Select one content area where the student(s) seem most successful and in which the most resources are available.
3. Try different methods of preassessment, being flexible in experimenting with different systems and soliciting assistance from other faculty or paraeducators.
4. Compact by unit, chapter, or topic rather than by time period.
5. Decide how to document the compacted material and how to define proficiency based on staff consensus and district policy.
6. Request help from available resources in order to create a wide range of opportunities and alternatives for replacing the eliminated content.

Very able students need not always accelerate at a fast pace through the curriculum. On occasion they may welcome the opportunity to slow down and study a subject in depth and detail, catching up with the class later by completing regular assignments on a compacted basis.

Differentiated Learning Options in Inclusive Schools

An inclusive school increases responsibilities of classroom teachers to provide for learning needs of highly able students. VanTassel-Baska (1989) notes several mistaken beliefs that need to be altered regarding differentiation for highly able students. First, consultants and consultees should not assume that curriculum must *always* be different from what all learners have. Nor do all learning experiences need to be product-oriented. Then, too, one curriculum package or a single learning strategy will *not* provide all that is needed.

It cannot be denied that many teachers feel negatively toward acceleration, telescoping, or compacting of content for very capable students. Some of their concerns must be heeded, such as the possibility that vital content and needed practice will be skipped; however, most concerns are not justified. The research is clear that acceleration is *not* harmful as a general rule to the academic, emotional, or social well-being of students who already may be tuned out, bored, or discouraged. Far worse to languish for years "wanting work" as depicted in Application 9.1.

Differentiation that can be provided within schools through collaborative efforts and teaming up of consultants, teachers, parents, and resource personnel includes:

- Flexible pacing (appropriate acceleration in content and process) through curriculum compacting, telescoped units, or testing out with replacement content;
- Enriched and extended, relevant curriculum (*not* busywork or enrichment irrelevant to their strong abilities and interests);

- Group activities (seminars, special classes) that can include a significant number of interested, focused students who would enjoy a challenge, too;
- Individual arrangements for enhancement (independent study, assistance in acquiring skills needed to pursue major interests and talents, extended lab, practice, and library time).

Tomlinson (1996) recommends a curriculum model for addressing academic diversity and talent that uses a sliding scale of differentiation and adaptation much like the adjustment bar on an electronic sound machine. Asserting that no one size of hat, shoe, or curriculum fits all students, she adapts curriculum to needs of the very able by designing curriculum flexibility to include sliding levels of abstract representations, leaps of insight, open approaches, independence in planning, and a quicker pace of study. (See For Further Reading to locate a description of this approach.)

VIGNETTE 9.D

Oliver, high school senior and aspiring playwright, had never participated in a gifted program. He did not care to be tested with the district's standardized measure of aptitude and, as for the program, he commented to the facilitator, "Activities like riding in a bus 100 miles to tour the Boeing aircraft plant are not what I need." But when his drama teacher suggested that perhaps gifted program enrollment could "credential" him for having major accommodations made to his senior year curriculum, he agreed to the testing. He tested very well, and sure enough, after 11 years of "revving his motor with his brakes on" in many of his classes, he was given relatively free license to write the senior class play, to cast, stage, and direct it, conduct rehearsals, and even instruct the art department in the type of publicity material he wanted. Some teachers expressed doubts about the curricular intensity of this individual education plan, but the principal endorsed the idea with only two stipulations: the consulting facilitator could edit any objectionable parts of the script and there must be teacher supervision at rehearsals. The play, though not well attended by the students or the community, was interesting and innovative, and Oliver graduated deeming his senior year a personal success.

Classroom Enrichment Activities.   As noted earlier, most very able children spend more time with their classroom teachers than they do with specially trained resource teachers. Therefore, the general classroom curriculum is the most potentially productive place to begin planning accelerated content and enriched experiences for special learning needs.

VIGNETTE 9.E

ANNA'S ASSIGNMENT
Anna, a second-grade student reading at the sixth-grade level and just home from school in early September, laid a second-grade basal reader on the kitchen table. She announced to her mother that the class's homework assignment was to read aloud to parents the word list in the back of the book, practicing any words they did not know. Anna's mother sighed inwardly and strengthened

her resolve to request a parent conference next week to talk about the snail's pace in reading, rather than postpone her concerns until the first scheduled parent conferences in October. For now, to Anna she said, "Just put the book in your backpack and return it to school tomorrow. For your homework this evening, let's get your new dictionary and read as many pages in it as that word list takes up in the reader. We can see how many new, interesting words we find on those pages, and we will practice any that you don't know. OK?"

Classroom teachers are responsible for instructing a wide range of students and often do not have the time, resources, and facilities to recognize exceptional capabilities in a class of twenty-five or thirty students and challenge them appropriately. They want bright students to master basic skills without developing learning gaps that might impede their progress later. Teachers feel the brunt of parent pressures to provide advanced opportunities, and some become defensive when their most able students complain that lessons and materials are "boring."[4] Some do not feel prepared to teach children who may be as knowledgeable or more so in subjects than they. These situations call for a meeting of the minds among all parties for a collaborative resolution of curricular issues that could impede student progress and dampen their enthusiasm for learning.

A study by Purcell and Leppien (1998) highlights two facets of the collaborative process that can tap into its power for providing challenging instruction:

- Expectations for student learning must be discussed and made congruent.
- Interactions among school personnel must facilitate differentiated curriculum.

The researchers point out that classroom teachers need enrichment specialists to recognize their goals, understand their content areas, and demonstrate resourcefulness and communicate effectively. Enrichment specialists need classroom teachers to be flexible, willing to try new ideas, collaborative in adapting the curriculum, and participatory in monitoring performance by appropriate assessment of learning outcomes. (See Figure 9.11.)

Research by Gerber and Popp (2000) indicates that collaborative programs should be explained thoroughly to those affected by them prior to their initiation of the programs. Students in particular need carefully presented, clear explanations about the purposes and potential benefits of consultation, collaboration, and co-teaching. For example, Reinhiller (1996) cautions that students may have initial difficulty accepting two adults with equal status. Also, scheduling concerns may cause anxiety among staff and students and even spill over to family members if transportation issues and family schedules are involved. It is very important that successes of collaborative programs are disseminated to faculty, families of students, school administrators, and policymakers such as school boards and legislators. (See Figure 9.11.)

Beyond School Environments

Some arrangements that would benefit very capable students the most are accessible only outside the school setting. When students leave their school campus for enrichment, accelerated

---

[4]The "b word" as delivered by impatient students (and sometimes parents) tends to be overworked. It is likely that everyone benefits at one time or another from feeling bored, for it causes us to fall back on our own resources and develop them. But atrophy (of mind and ability) is another thing altogether. Atrophy affects one's capability and productivity for the present and future.

FIGURE 9.11   Learning Opportunities in the School Setting

- Differentiated curriculum in the classroom
- Curriculum compacting
- Use of books from the library as basal readers for both comprehension and skill building
- Telescoped curriculum where a course of study is collapsed into a shorter time frame
- Continuous progress courses, moving ahead as content and skills are acquired
- Grade skipping
- Early entrance to school (however, not permitted in some states)
- Test out
- Cross-age tutoring, with very able students teaching younger students of high ability
- Programmed instruction packages for rapid progress in areas of keen interest
- Seminars within schools or in collaboration with other schools or universities
- Advanced placement
- Mini-replications of existing research studies
- Conversations with/observations of book authors, artists-in-residence, scientists, etc.
- Enrichment activity calendars for classroom teachers with a daily enriching activity
- Resource room time for independent study, research, or project development
- Honors classes
- Dual enrollment
- Discussion groups for moral dilemmas, great books, or current issues
- Special units of study that have a concentrated international perspective
- Biographies and autobiographies, to study great leaders of past and present
- Collection and analysis of the world's wisdom (proverbs, fables, maxims, credos, etc.)
- Summer school enrichment courses
- International Baccalaureate program
- Extra classes for extra credit
- Cluster grouping to work with mental peers on advanced topics
- Extended library, lab, practice, or computer time, or more time to work on projects
- Small-group discussions and investigations with mental peers

(and more)

course work, group learning experiences, or individual arrangements, special educators and classroom teachers must assume responsibility for collaborating and communicating often to ensure that the students accomplish school district and state requirements, and continue to be involved in the life of the school. They also must deal with student supervision and liability issues. Figure 9.12 lists some of the more commonly used off-campus learning opportunities.

■ ■ ■ ■ ■

APPLICATION 9.3
SCAVENGER HUNT

Get several educator colleagues involved in a hunt to find interesting, unusual, promising resources for enriching and accelerating student learning. Allow the group a certain length of time to search in instructional media centers, libraries, museums, historical societies, university campuses, neighborhoods, or towns and bring back innovative ideas for teaching and learning. Share and discuss these potential resources among the group and try some of them with students, if possible.

FIGURE 9.12   Learning Opportunities Beyond the School Setting

- Early graduation from high school
- Early entrance to the university, with or without a high school diploma
- Career shadowing
- Academic competitions—regional, state, national, international
- Community service (sometimes for high school credit)
- Student exchange programs—urban to rural, west to east, U.S. to other countries, etc.
- Mentorships
- Tutorials with experts in a field of keen interest or exceptional talent
- Travel study programs
- Concurrent enrollment in high school courses and college courses
- Part time enrollment in vocational-technical schools to learn a trade
- University credit by examination
- College correspondence courses
- Field trips
- College level independent studies
- Internships and apprenticeships
- Periodic contributions of writing and reporting for newspaper and media
- Presentations and performances of advanced work, to audiences outside the school

(and more . . .)

BENEFITS AND BARRIERS IN COLLABORATIVE CONSULTATION FOR STUDENTS WITH HIGH ABILITY AND TALENT

Many positive benefits result from consulting and collaborating to tailor school curricula for very able learners. Teachers get to know students' interests, not just their weak areas, and begin to focus more on their strengths, not their shortcomings. As they work together to design personalized programs and free up time for learning alternatives, they provide seamless attention to special needs. Schools become more lively places for learning, staff members more enthusiastic, and families more supportive. Students are delighted to have a "voice" in their learning. Teachers find outlets for expression of their best and most creative ideas, which may be why they chose education as a career in the first place!

Potential barriers do exist, but some attention to them early on can be a means of removing them. One such barrier is that some educators may perceive a request for assistance from a facilitator of exceptionally able students as a sign of professional weakness. Here the school administrators can help by promoting use of the services as a very definite sign of teacher *strength.* Consulting teachers would do well to demonstrate respect in their interactions with classroom teachers: "What can I do for you and your students that you don't have *time and resources* to do now?" *not* ". . . that you don't have the knowledge or skills to do." Teachers may feel patronized by comments from special needs facilitators. Here is where the communicative art of onedownsmanship, or deemphasizing one's knowledge and skills during interactions, in the interest of maintaining a relationship (Caplan, 1970), can be especially useful.

Time, that irreplaceable commodity, is in short supply—another barrier. Techniques such as described in the Vignette 9.b team meeting and at other places throughout the book can help busy educators find ways of conserving time for collaborative consultation.

Educating exceptionally capable students to the fullest of their abilities is a lofty aim for schools and for the public that funds those schools. It requires solid commitment and dedication to meeting all students' special needs, provision of curriculum content that is differentiated for special needs and abilities, careful organization and management of tailored learning programs, and a supportive learning environment staffed with personnel who can ably coordinate it all. Collaborative school consultation and working as teams can create such a learning environment.

TIPS FOR WORKING TOGETHER FOR STUDENTS OF HIGH ABILITY

1. Talk with very able students to learn what has worked for them and what has not been helpful.
2. Provide teachers and administrators as much feedback as possible about good things they have done for the needs of highly capable students.
3. Seek out sources for requesting grant money to fund enrichment projects in the school. Even small amounts can be very energizing to staff and students.
4. Go to conferences for inspiration and information. For a particularly collaborative and productive experience, take along a general classroom teacher and a school administrator, school board member, or parent(s) of a student.
5. Observe other facilitators and collaborative consultants in schools that have outstanding programs for highly able students. If visiting several, select ones that use different approaches to broaden your perspective.
6. Talk with school and public librarians. Ask them to order specific books and periodicals about the needs of high-potential students that would interest parents and community members.
7. As an extension of #6, take samples of pertinent periodicals to receptionists at doctors' and dentists' offices and suggest that such publications would be popular waiting room reading material.
8. Leave characteristics/needs information sheets about exceptionally able children and youth in the staff workroom, along with a basket of treats to enjoy as teachers read.

CHAPTER REVIEW

1. Individual differences are present in every classroom. Students who by law must attend school should have instruction while they are there that enables them to learn and do new things.

2. Students who learn rapidly and easily with minimum drill and practice, and who perform at advanced levels, will require accelerated and enriched curriculum to optimize their potential. Some students are twice-or-more exceptional, having a disability or cultural or health factor that must be included in their individual education plan as additional special need(s).

3. Collaboration between general education teachers and special education facilitators should enable students to study and learn at an appropriate pace and level for much of the school day because they spend much of that day in regular classrooms. Collaboration involving school administrators will help ensure that agreed-on possibilities become realities. Collaborative partnerships with parents provide an all-important bridge of support between home and school.

4. Flexible pacing is a must for highly capable students. They should move through the curriculum

at a pace that allows them to learn new material and does not require them to review and regurgitate prior learning. Occasionally they might stop off to study a subject in more depth and catch up later with their class. In-school and out-of-school alternatives and options are as many and as diverse as the problem-solving imaginations of team members can generate. Differentiation models, such as the Enrichment Triad Model, the resource consultation model, and the TREAT Model, provide structure and coordination of special learning programs. Staff development is an integral part of these models' success.

5. Providing for differentiated curriculum to serve highly able students involves many individuals. There must be contact with a variety of people groups, from teachers to librarians to textbook authors to community-based mentors and more. This takes excellent communication skills, much organization, and considerable coordination.

6. Classroom teachers and special education teachers may want to co-teach a lesson or, perhaps, even a unit. They might exchange roles for a time, to gain new perspectives on students and the material. They can work together with the student as a partnership of three or more to plan, implement, and evaluate differentiated learning experiences.

7. Families are integral members of a special education team. Parent conferences, IEP conferences, interviews to determine family preferences, and family participation in specially scheduled events and assignments are part of family roles in education of the very able learner.

8. Well-developed programs of personalized instruction and differentiated curriculum cause many positive ripple effects. Enthusiasm for teaching may be renewed, parent support more visible, and instruction of all students enhanced.

TO DO AND THINK ABOUT

1. In collaboration with another teacher, co-plan a lesson that addresses curricular needs of highly capable students in a typical classroom. Describe extending resources that will be needed and who will obtain them. Determine how you will assess the learning (entire class and smaller group) and how you will evaluate the success of the co-teaching process.

2. Develop a hypothetical situation at the secondary level in which you consult about a student with high ability and/or talents. Draft ideas that might come up for discussion regarding planning, resource gathering, coordinating, and assessment. The ideas should be consistent with school policy, acceptable to the student's family, and, above all, appealing to the student.

3. Role-play being an enrichment program facilitator at the elementary level along with several colleagues acting as classroom teachers to prepare a collaborative plan for one week (or one month, if that is more appropriate) that provides differen-

tiated curriculum to one or more grade levels within a large elementary school. Determine how you and your colleagues will move on from articulation of the inevitable differences to a compatible and cohesive plan. Decide and practice how you could explain the plan to students and their family members.

4. Select a textbook for a grade level and curricular area that interests you. Analyze it and its instructor's manual for qualities that would make it suitable for use with students of high ability.

5. As an extension of #4, have a colleague select a contrasting text. Then each of you should describe the material's merits or deficits as if one of you were a member of a curriculum selection committee and the other were a marketing representative for the text's publisher. Suggestion: This is more enjoyable if the text has desirable qualities, so be choosy and look until you find one that does!

FOR FURTHER READING

Dettmer, P. (1991). Gifted program advocacy: Overhauling bandwagons to build support. *Gifted Child Quarterly, 35*(4), 165–171. Suggests ways in which twenty role groups can support differentiated learning programs for students with high ability and offers a fifteen-point plan of advocacy.

Hertzog, N. B. (2003). Impact of gifted programs from the students' perspectives. *Gifted Child Quarterly, 47*(2), 131–143.

Howley, A., Howley, C. B., & Pendarvis, E. D. (1986). *Teaching gifted children: Principles and strategies.* Boston: Little, Brown. This book, while not new, presents ideas that are still fresh, practical, and sometimes contrast with popular views on education of exceptionally able students, which can be enlightening. The last chapter, "Equal Opportunity: Mediocrity or Excellence?," will be particularly interesting to many readers.

Hughes, C. E., & Murawski, W. A. (2001). Lessons from another field: Applying coteaching strategies to gifted education. *Gifted Child Quarterly, 45*(3), 195–204. Offers a new definition of collaboration within the context of gifted education and explains co-teaching as a collaborative strategy. Descriptions and examples of adaptations of five models for co-teaching originally developed for students with disabilities are provided.

Kirschenbaum, R. J., Armstrong, D. C., & Landrum, M. S. (1999). Resource consultation model in gifted education to support talent development in today's inclusive schools. *Gifted Child Quarterly, 43*(1), 39–47.

Landrum, M. S. (2001). An evaluation of the Catalyst program: Consultation and collaboration in gifted education. *Gifted Child Quarterly, 45*(2), 139–151.

Neihart, M., Reis, S. M., Robinson, N. M., & Moon, S. M. (2002). *The social and emotional development of gifted children: What do we know?* Waco, TX: Prufrock.

Tomlinson, C. A. (1995). Deciding to differentiate instruction in middle school: One school's journey. *Gifted Child Quarterly, 39*(2), 77–87.

Tomlinson, C. A. (1996). Good teaching for one and all: Does gifted education have an instructional identity? *Journal for the Education of the Gifted, 20*(2), 155–174.

Treffinger, D. J. (1982). Gifted students, regular classrooms: Sixty ingredients for a better blend. *Elementary School Journal, 82*(3), 267–273. This article offers a wealth of ideas (sixty in all) for the elementary classroom teacher who wishes to enrich and accelerate content. The article suggests materials that can be found in content-related and general school publications to assist teachers with curriculum planning.

VanTassel-Baska, J. (1991). Gifted education in the balance: Building relationships with general education. *Gifted Child Quarterly, 35*(1), 20–25. This article focuses on the relationships among gifted education, special education, and general education and discusses the importance of establishing links with general education and educational reform movements.

VanTassel-Baska, J. (1998). *Excellence in educating gifted and talented learners* (3rd ed.). Denver, CO: Love. Chapter 14 provides a succinct discussion of key issues and problems in secondary programming for students of high ability. Collaborative relationships with other agencies and linkages with general education are included. Collaboration in the arts is a topic in Chapter 25.

ROLES OF SCHOOL ADMINISTRATORS, PARAEDUCATORS, AND PROFESSIONAL DEVELOPMENT PERSONNEL IN SCHOOL CONSULTATION AND COLLABORATION

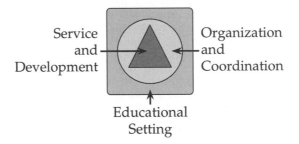

Service and Development — Educational Setting — Organization and Coordination

Much of our discussion about school consultation and collaboration to this point has been in reference to classroom teachers and special educators. Now we will focus on other significant partners, namely, school administrators, paraeducators, and professional development personnel.

Building administrators and special education directors are key people in establishing collaborative consultation and encouraging teamwork within their schools. They coordinate paraeducator selections and placements, and provide structure for professional development activities.

Teachers supervise and direct paraeducators (paras). Teachers and paras, in turn, are supervised and directed by building administrators. Yet, they are all partners, all working together to achieve common goals on behalf of the students in their educational settings.

Paraeducators and teachers have yet another type of relationship. They are partners in accomplishing the tasks assigned to the teacher; however, the teacher is responsible for supervising the para's work and for assessing outcomes of the para's performance. This could present problems, but it need not.

Professional development personnel can contribute significantly to the success of collaborative school consultation and working together in teams. Special education personnel are called on frequently to plan in-services and staff development that provide other school personnel with information about students' special needs.

Chapter 10 emphasizes services in the triangle for content. Supervision, organization, and coordination are important in the process circle. The context (square) provides the educational setting.

FOCUSING QUESTIONS

1. What can administrators do to facilitate effective collaboration and teamwork in their buildings?
2. Why is it important for the paraeducator role to be defined clearly?
3. How should teachers plan and communicate the para's responsibilities?
4. How are paraeducators selected and prepared for their roles?
5. In what ways do teachers supervise and direct para activities?
6. What are roles and responsibilities of the professional development staff in collaborative school consultation?
7. How can professional development personnel consult and collaborate effectively to prepare educators for serving special needs of students and their families?

KEY TERMS

adequate yearly progress
   (AYP)
confidentiality
in-service

needs assessment
needs sensing
paraeducator (para,
   paraprofessional)

professional development
staff development
supervising teacher

THE SCHOOL ADMINISTRATOR'S ROLE IN COLLABORATIVE, INCLUSIVE SCHOOLS

The building principal's role and concomitant responsibilities are just short of overwhelming. So many school issues compete for a principal's time and energy that consultants need to make special efforts to accommodate their principals' heavily committed schedules when asking for their participation in consultation and collaboration.

VIGNETTE 10.A

Margo is the principal of an elementary school where a collaborative school reform approach is being implemented. The approach is a bold attempt to turn around a low-achieving school that failed the NCLB-required adequate yearly progress (AYP). Teamwork is central to success of the program's four distinctive features:

- family and community partnerships in education;
- academic excellence with focus on reading, writing, math, and science instruction;
- citizenship efforts by which students are taught to develop responsible behaviors with emphasis on treating others with respect; and
- educator support that helps teachers make important decisions based on frequent reports throughout the year of each student's progress toward reading, writing, math, and science standards, which is in keeping with standardized testing requirements imposed by the NCLB legislation.

In Margo's building the teachers are extremely resistant toward making any changes. She has the challenge of leading them to a more positive and supportive attitude and to successful implementation of the approach. She makes it clear to the teachers that the approach *will* be implemented in the building and she is 100 percent behind it. She asks teachers who feel they cannot be supportive to consider transferring to another building in the district by the next school year. She invites teachers to discuss their concerns individually with her. She remains positive and supportive, yet firm in her goals for the school. She is careful to follow through to see that each implementation activity is completed and nothing slips through the cracks.

Margo confers with district administrators, including the director of special education, to provide additional personnel and material support to the teachers during the transition time. With the help of the school counselor and music teacher, she organizes schoolwide assemblies for Friday afternoons so teachers can have time for planning and teaming.

Margo also organizes a parent/community night for interacting with each other and showcasing the school's aims. She seeks written evidence of support from children, teachers, parents, and others. She continues to keep parents informed of changes taking place in the school and requests their input for significant decisions.

Ways Administrators Can Encourage Collaboration and Teamwork

Building administrators have key roles in allowing and encouraging collaboration and teamwork. They make allocations of time, space, and materials necessary for effective consultation and collaboration. They assign paraeducators and coordinate the teamwork that takes place among building personnel. They also arrange and promote staff development for educational reform and new programs.

Administrators can assist staff immeasurably by freeing up teacher time and arranging for substitutes so consultation and collaboration among school personnel can take place. They can work with consultants to clarify collaborative consultation roles, and to ensure that such roles have parity among the school staff.

Another major contribution is encouraging interaction and staff development for all school personnel. When in-service and staff development are arranged, promoted, and *attended* by building principals, the positive ripple effects can be profound.

In a review of educational research on the principal's role in creating inclusive schools for diverse learners, Riehl (2000) notes that school leadership has moved well beyond application of knowledge and skills as a science of administration would suggest, and beyond finesse with processes as an art of administrative performance, to school administration as a form of *practice.* School administration as a practice "creates a 'horizon' that envisions what schools create and where they might lead" (Riehl, 2000, p. 69).

A study by Foley and Lewis (1999) indicated that the secondary administrator role of manager and primary decision maker for operation and function of the school, with responsibility for centralized control of school activities and resources, is not congruent with the principles of collegiality, parity, and shared decision making that are underpinnings of collaborative-based structures. Foley and Lewis contend that a shift in authority is needed that allows the principal to be a team member and support others in leadership roles and collaboration.

In their handbook *A Principal's Guide,* Bateman and Bateman target the principal's role in special education and discuss what principals need to know in order to implement best practices in their schools. Topics covered include eligibility, assessments, and evaluations; inclusive schools; special education laws; policy issues concerning discipline, due process, accommodations, and adaptations; selection and evaluation of special education teachers; and more (*CEC Today,* 2001). It is vital for all school administrators, along with general and special education personnel, and related services and support personnel, to study and reflect on such issues. They also must be included as *participants* in professional development experiences so they are aware of special needs and the programs that can help serve those needs effectively.

Specific ways administrators can encourage collaboration include: providing resources for doing that; listening and gathering feedback from educators; serving as instructional resources themselves; being liaisons between school and community; providing released time for professional development; and participating themselves in professional development programs.

■ ■ ■ ■ ■ ■

APPLICATION 10.1
QUESTIONS FOR A BUILDING ADMINISTRATOR

Use these or similar questions to draw school administrators of inclusionary schools into dialogue about consultation, collaboration, and teamwork among all school personnel, and with families of students who have special needs.

1. Do I *have* to have a student with disabilities in my classroom? If so, who has the responsibility of developing curriculum and lessons for them?

2. If I don't agree with what the special education teachers or support staff have asked me to do and I've discussed the issues with them but still there is no change, what do I do next?

3. Why does the special ed teacher have a smaller caseload than I do?

4. Whose responsibility is it to supervise and evaluate the special education staff and support personnel staff?

5. How can I request services for a student that are not available now in our school?

6. Where will I find time to confer and collaborate with consulting teachers?

7. How can I go about setting up co-teaching with a colleague? Then, if it doesn't work out after a dedicated fair trial, what do we do?

8. What is my responsibility toward accountability for standardized test scores of all students in my room, including those with disabilities?

PARAEDUCATORS AS PARTNERS

Paraeducators are essential partners in providing special education services; therefore, teachers and consultants to whom these partners are assigned must give special consideration to their needs. Many of the concepts and skills presented in other parts of this book apply to working with paraeducators. In this section we emphasize special skills that relate specifically to supervising and communicating with paras.

VIGNETTE 10.B

Wanda, a nontraditional student in a university with an elementary school nearby, learned that the elementary school had implemented inclusionary classrooms. Part of the implementation plan for the school was getting assistance from volunteers to provide more help for classroom teachers. These assistants were to be called "volunteer paraprofessionals" and would do what paras typically do, but without salary.

As mother of two school-age children, Wanda had been considering teacher preparation as her field of study. She decided to volunteer for one afternoon of service each week at the school. This would give her a way to better understand the role of an educator as well as the inclusionary process in schools. It would help her decide if she wanted to apply now for a job as a paraeducator or enter a teacher preparation program at the university.

The building principal of the elementary school had made it clear to general classroom teachers that the volunteers were to be involved in instructional help, not mundane clerical tasks, just as the school's paras were. Teachers could request assistance on a form and turn it in to the principal each Friday. The principal would approve these requests and forward them to a special education teacher charged with responsibility for matching requests with volunteers.

So it was that Wanda was sent into a first-grade classroom to assist with a writing lesson. The teacher had presented a lesson earlier and Wanda's task was to help the students with disabilities write in their journals. It sounded simple enough. Very quickly several questions came to Wanda's mind. She made this checklist:

  ✓ Where are the writing supplies for the children to use?
  ✓ How can I help this child whose desk is facing away from the board? That makes it really difficult for the student to copy what the teacher wrote on the board.
  ✓ Will the teacher mind if I change the instructions a little so the student can be more successful?
  ✓ Who are the children with disabilities, anyway?
  ✓ What is the goal of the lesson?
  ✓ How will I know when the lesson goal is met?

"This is not as easy as it first seemed," Wanda concluded. It got easier as she became more familiar with the teachers and the students, but she soon learned that at times she tended toward overstepping her assigned role and going beyond what was expected. Teachers were forgiving and were not upset when she did this. They seemed to welcome her help and, after all, there were so very many student needs. She did have a significant list of responsibilities; however, it was not the ones she was expected to do that concerned her, but those that were outside her role boundaries that she wanted very much to do. She was finding out that a paraeducator has a subordinate (by-the-side) role when it comes to planning content and instructing students.

Wanda had always been a take-charge person, directing others in her home, church, and community life. She was beginning to think that, even though the teachers and students were glad to have another adult to help out, a para role probably would not be one for which she was well-suited. A better personal goal for her might be to earn teacher certification and focus on being a excellent teacher and an effective supervisor of the paraeducators assigned to assist her. But, for the moment, there was Randy's hand up, signaling his need for more help with the arithmetic assignment!

French and Pickett (1997) provide insight into the history of employing paraprofessionals. They cite the postwar shortage of teachers in the 1950s, federal legislation such as Title 1 and Head Start in the 1960s, P.L.94-142 in the 1970s, and IDEA in the 1980s, as catalysts for the increase of paras working alongside teachers. IDEA allows for paraprofessionals who are "appropriately trained and supervised" to serve students with disabilities.

Of the 500,000 paraeducators working in schools in 1995, some 250,000 to 280,000 were employed in special education programs (*CEC Today,* 1997). During the 1990s the number of paraeducators in U.S. schools grew at a faster rate than the numbers of students or teachers (*ASCD Update,* 2002). Part of this para explosion can be attributed to the movement toward inclusionary schools.

Reasons offered by French and Pickett (1997) for schools' increased reliance on paras include large caseloads of special education teachers, the need for more individualized attention to students at risk from economic disadvantage or other circumstances, and the cultural and linguistic fit with students by many paras who live right in the school's neighborhood. Paras are particularly important members of the teaching team in rural communities. They may be the most constant element in the school life of students with special needs if they stay there when teachers move on (Ashbaker & Morgan, 1997; Demchak & Morgan, 1998).

Concerns raised by French and Pickett (1997) about the preparation of paras brought out that at the time of their report in the mid-1990s, only one state—Kansas—was mandating training for its paraeducators. A few other states did have long-standing credentialing policies or funded training programs. Estimates of the number of special education paras now reach 300,000 and beyond; however, this has been one of the least studied and most significant aspects of special education in the last several years.

French and Pickett targeted training of teachers in para supervision as a concern. They called for more research on circumstances and issues affecting training, roles, supervision, community impact, and recruitment of paraeducators. Special education teachers often supervise at least one para and some may supervise as many as twenty (Council for Exceptional Children, 1997).

As one outcome of the No Child Left Behind Act, all paras hired after January 8, 2002 must meet one of three requirements:

- complete two years of study (48 semester hours) at an institution of higher education;
- obtain an associate's degree or higher;
- meet a rigorous standard of quality and be able to demonstrate, through a formal state or local assessment, knowledge of and ability to assist in instruction for reading, writing, and math (Christie, 2002).

Under the NCLB Act teachers will be held more accountable for supervising their paraeducators, and administrators will be expected to give paras more support, avoid mis-assignments of their responsibilities, and provide professional development to help them perform effectively. Neither paras nor teachers typically have had formal preparation for interacting with one another in productive ways. The relationship often is hampered by inadequate communication, lack of time for planning together, lack of clear job descriptions, and the opinion by too many others that paras are not that important to student learning (Demchak & Morgan, 1998).

Paraeducators themselves may feel lack of respect. Their salaries tend to be appallingly low. Some resent the absence of opportunity for advancement. Many articulate a need for more intensive clarification and preparation for the para role. Research by Giangreco, Edelman, and Broer (2001) identified six themes pertaining to how school personnel can respect, appreciate, and acknowledge paraprofessionals: nonmonetary signs and symbols of appreciation, adequate compensation, being entrusted with important responsibilities, having noninstructional responsibilities, being listened to, and having orientation experiences and support. Successful matches of role delineation, skill development, expectations, and support can help instill respect for and appreciation of the role.

Delineating the Role of Paraeducators

Paraeducators may be found in virtually any educational setting, ranging from a preschool class for children with special needs, to a first-grade classroom having students with disabilities, to a grocery store where adolescent students with developmental disabilities are learning a new job, to a resource room for gifted adolescents with needs for advanced and expanded curriculum. Paraeducator responsibilities vary widely, from teaching a lesson to grading homework and tests to participating in classroom activities to sometimes just "being there" for the students and teacher.

An extensive literature review by Giangreco and his colleagues (2001b) noted greatly expanding roles and duties for paraprofessionals over the past decade, especially those who serve students with disabilities in general education settings. They found that paras continue to work with students who have the most challenging behavioral and learning characteristics and to engage in a broad range of roles, many of which they have not been prepared to assume. The researchers listed eight major role categories of such duties:

- Providing instruction in academic subjects
- Teaching functional life skills
- Teaching vocational skills at community-based work sites
- Collection and management of data

- Supporting students with challenging behaviors
- Facilitating interactions with peers who don't have disabilities
- Providing personal care
- Engaging in clerical behavior

The relationship between the special education teacher and paraeducator differs somewhat from the other collaborative roles. Unlike the consulting teacher and the consultee teacher, classroom teachers and paraeducators do not have parity in the school program because they are not equally responsible for decisions about student needs and instructional interventions. The teacher is expected to supervise and direct the paraeducator. The paraeducator is employed to assist the teacher and, therefore, to follow the teacher's direction. Even so, the paraeducator is necessary as a partner to the teacher's success and to the success of the teacher's students. Indeed, the prefix *para-* means 'to come alongside,' or to help another.

Paraeducators are employed in schools to come alongside teachers and help them with the demands of their jobs. Some people use the term "instructional" paraprofessional to designate a person who helps with instruction of students. Nevertheless, paraeducators do not plan instruction nor are they responsible for evaluating student performance. But they can do a great deal to help students learn and gain confidence with their schoolwork.

Paraeducator Responsibilities

While every paraeducator position has its unique characteristics, there are four basic responsibilities to which virtually every paraeducator is assigned at one time or another:

- Student support and monitoring (reading to students and listening to them read, helping students with health care and personal needs, assisting with small group activities, supervising playground activities);
- Preparing instructional materials (materials for specific lessons, duplication of materials, bulletin boards, arrangements for field trips);
- communication support (participation in team meetings, preparation of student performance charts, feedback about student progress); and
- support of routine business (recording attendance, checking papers, filing materials) (Kaff & Dyck, 1999).

The inclusion movement has created a situation that causes some concern among special education teachers because paraeducators sometimes do their work in a general education classroom with individual students or small groups of students, whereas the special education teacher is not present to oversee day-to-day activities. Paraeducators may assume a range of job responsibilities in that setting, such as providing instruction in academic and social skills; making curricular modifications; managing student behavior; and developing working relationships with others. Many of them appear to assume primary responsibility for the included students, even though they are aware that it is more appropriate for the classroom teacher to carry out these responsibilities (Marks, Schrader, & Levine, 1999). Explanations for this behavior include:

- Paraeducators do not want students to be a "bother" to the teacher.
- Paraeducators feel an urgency to meet a student's immediate academic needs.

- Paras may believe their own performance will be based on positive relations with the teacher.
- Paras are often faced with the need to make "on the spot" modifications when teachers are not readily available.

Some paraeducators have become the primary vehicle for accommodation for students with severe or multiple disabilities in inclusive schools. In most instances the paraeducators stay in close proximity to the students with disabilities, attending to their students' physical needs such as toileting, for example, and to instructional needs such as reading aloud to students or recording their answers. Paraeducators may even adopt an advocacy role, taking it as their responsibility to work toward general acceptance of the included student, or to "represent" the student in ways that would support acceptance (Marks, et. al., 1999).

Supervision of Paraeducators

Supervision of paraeducators can be complex and challenging. Not many teacher education programs include the topic in their preparation programs. Salzberg and Morgan (1995) contend that few teachers were expecting to direct other adults and they have not been adequately prepared to supervise paraeducators. Even fewer have had practice in doing so.

One area of particular importance that Salzberg and Morgan (1995) target in regard to para and teacher relationships and success of the supervisory relationship is that of personality variables. (See Chapter 1 for a discussion of individual differences among adults in the work setting.) Individual differences also can be problematic when there are large discrepancies in age, culture, socioeconomic group, or ethnic background.

In spite of challenges in addressing the roles and responsibilities of paras, there are positive effects. As suggested earlier, many paras can be supportive links to the community. Their positions cost the schools relatively little. Laudably, most paras are pleased to work patiently and caringly with students who can be difficult at times and they often tend to view these students in different and positive ways. They frequently contribute information that helps teachers and consulting teachers provide appropriate learning experiences. Much more effort should be made to prepare professionals to collaborate with and supervise paraeducators, and to recruit exemplary paras and prepare them well.

Roles and responsibilities must be delineated clearly so that there will be mutual understanding among all concerned. The paraeducator and teacher relationship can be likened to a couple on the ballroom dance floor. The two gracefully perform together to the rhythm of the music, one partner leading and the other following. Both partners use the same basic dance steps, but the unique timing of special moves, as guided by the leading partner, keeps them from impeding others or digressing from their areas.

The para–supervisor relationship becomes less obvious when a para is employed to work with a team. In that case it can be likened to having an orchestra: the para plays an important role in a group performance directed by a conductor. Co-teachers, in contrast, can be thought of as engaging in a musical duet. Each follows the same score, but with different, preplanned parts. All must maintain the rhythm and harmony to create a pleasant experience.

The co-teaching team will need to determine who is to assume supervisory responsibilities for paraeducators. The best selection will likely be a person who

- holds ultimate responsibility for the outcomes,
- is in the best position to direct the para,

- can provide training for the assigned duties, and
- can observe and document para performance.

Supervision requires specific, sophisticated skills and behaviors. A supervisor must plan, schedule, coordinate, and evaluate another person's actions. It is not unusual for special education teachers to be assigned as many as five or six paras whom they direct and supervise. The supervisor is responsible for the para's actions and the para is accountable to the supervisor. No matter how much education or preparation a person has before taking a position as para (and, according to French and Pickett, 1997, many of them do bring very little formal preparation), a supervisor should provide on-the-job training. For example, co-teachers may develop a teaching plan that includes the para for part of the implementation. For the plan to be successful, the supervisor or co-teacher must ready the para for implementing the pertinent parts of the plan.

French (1997) lists seven functions associated with para supervision:

1. Planning;
2. Managing schedules (prioritizing tasks, preparing schedules);
3. Delegating responsibilities (assigning tasks, directing tasks, monitoring performance);
4. Orienting (introducing people, policies, procedures, job descriptions);
5. Providing on-the-job training (teaching, coaching new skills, giving feedback);
6. Evaluating (track performance, summative evaluation of job performance);
7. Managing work environment (maintaining communication, managing conflicts, solving problems).

The more individuals with whom the para works, the more complex the supervision processes. When paras are in a general classroom most of the school day, it is essential that the classroom teacher also is involved in the supervision. In some instances the classroom teacher may take major responsibility for the supervision. If communication processes among all parties are open, this arrangement can work well.

Selection and Preparation of Paraeducators

Most paraeducators have many useful skills that they bring into the job. Some are experienced as teachers themselves. When selecting a paraeducator, the administrator should look for a person with:

- a high school diploma, at least;
- evidence of good attendance at work;
- a sense of teaching ethics and the need for confidentiality;
- ability to follow the teacher's direction and written plans;
- ability to communicate effectively with students and adults;
- good relationships with students;
- willingness to learn new skills;
- flexibility; and
- a sense of humor.

With the rapidly increasing cultural and linguistic diversity of students in special education, attention should be given to the diversity of the paraeducators who support them.

Efforts should be made to create a staff of paraeducators who reflect the cultural and linguistic background of the students. This is especially crucial in communities where teachers may not be familiar with the culture and language of the students; paras have often fulfilled a role as a community partner in home–school relationships. They can serve as translators of the culture and language for both educators and families. Hispanic and Native American families especially rely on the interconnectedness of the extended family and informal community-based networks for emotional and social support (Geenen, Powers, & Lopez-Vasquez, 2001). Thus, paras from the community may be able to facilitate meaningful collaboration with CLD families. Paras who are not familiar with cultural and linguistic diversity should participate in the same relevant staff development and self-assessment as other educators.

Although IDEA 1997 *requires* states to provide appropriate training, preparation, and supervision for paraeducators, the type and amount of training that is provided varies from state to state. Using more than twenty-five years of experience as staff developers and data from a nationwide survey validating guidelines on standards and skills required by paraeducators and teachers, Lasater, Johnson, and Fitzgerald (2000) make several recommendations for school district staff development:

- Communicate that paraeducators are valued and important to the instructional process by conducting professional development in settings similar to those used in training other professionals, and offering professional credits and stipends.
- Direct any needs assessments for the para role to paras in particular, rather than including them in teacher-focused sessions that may not be of major interest or appropriate for them.
- Provide ongoing, responsive support to answer questions and discuss issues.
- Include numerous opportunities for sharing, interacting, and problem solving.
- Allow for venting while ensuring refocusing and action.
- Build a solid knowledge base that reflects students' needs and goals.
- Do not provide too much information but focus on the "best practices" they need to know.
- Offer concrete tools to take back to the classroom so they can implement them immediately.
- Offer practical alternatives for responding to implementation challenges. While both the teacher and the paraeducator partner should receive professional development together for most topics, there are instances where this would not be an effective use of time.
- Provide opportunities for partner teachers and paraeducators to experience professional development together. Include exploration of roles and responsibilities, team-building activities and communication skills.
- Celebrate their successes and recognize contributions made by the paraeducators.
- No matter how much advance preparation the paraeducator has received, teachers to whom a para is assigned must provide orientation and on-the-job training. The job of the supervising teacher is to provide training that will help the paraeducator function in the specific situation of the assignment.

The supervising teacher can create or obtain a guide that can be given to the paraeducator for self-study. One example of such a guide is *Essential Skills for Paras* (Kaff & Dyck, 1999). Topics addressed in this guide include: responsibilities of most paraeducators; labels used to categorize students with disabilities; terms and phrases frequently used in schools; a discussion of ethics for paras; basic principles of direct instruction methods; and guidelines for reporting student behavior.

Marks, Schrader, and Levine (1999) recommend that training be provided for both teachers and paraeducators on the goals of inclusive practices, including specific skill areas such as curricular and academic modifications and positive behavioral support strategies. If behavior management is a primary responsibility of the para, the teacher should provide a good behavior management resource. One example is *Behavior Management Guide for Paras* (Dyck, Zabel, & Zabel, 1998). For those whose paras who have responsibility for making text adaptations, *How to Adapt Text for Struggling Readers* (Dyck, 1999) is a useful resource. *The Positive Para: Helping Students Develop Positive Social Skills* (Thurston, 2000) is another helpful resource for paraeducators who work with students having social skill deficits. Other resources are listed in the For Further Reading section of this chapter.

Need for Confidentiality by the Paraeducator

It is of utmost importance that each paraeducator understands the necessity of confidentiality when working with students. The teacher needs to impress on the paraeducator the importance of keeping confidential and secure any information such as academic achievement, test scores, student behavior, attendance, family problems and other information of a personal nature.

Kaff and Dyck (1999) offer the following guidelines to help paraeducators decide whether to share information with other teachers.

1. Is the person requesting the information *directly involved* with the student's education?
2. Will the *student* benefit if the person receives the information?

If the answer to both of these questions is yes, the para can share information. However, if there is any doubt, the para should be instructed to just say "no."

Likewise, teachers must plan ahead to assure para confidentiality when substitute teachers are present. Fleury (2000) provides the following that can be helpful to the substitute teacher *and* the paraeducator when the regular teacher is absent.

- Discuss with paraeducators at the beginning of the year the guidelines for confidentiality and how to proceed when you are absent.
- Make sure paras know the limits on sharing more information than needed and the role they will have on days you require a substitute.
- Have a typed schedule of the day and duties you have for the day.
- Include notes on general information that will help the substitute.
- Point out the important role of the paras.
- Prepare a paper discussing the need for routine in your class and ways paraeducators can help the substitute with it.

Fleury (2000) makes these suggestions to help classroom teachers when a *paraeducator* is absent:

- Ask the para to call you at home to notify you personally that he or she will be absent.
- Go over the duties with the substitute assistant as soon as possible.

- Discuss issues of confidentiality at the beginning of the day.
- Provide the typed schedule of the day and methods you use, such as reinforcers and other classroom management routines. (Be class specific, not child specific, at this time.)
- If the absent para was assigned to a student with unpredictable behavior, consider reassigning that student temporarily to someone who does know the student.
- Encourage the substitute to ask questions about your teaching methods or behavior management tools. Be aware that sometimes you will not be able to fully answer the question because of the need to preserve confidentiality.

Framework for Working with Paraeducators

Para supervision requires skills beyond consulting, collaborating or teaching. The supervisor is responsible for the para's actions and the para is accountable to the supervisor. Whereas collaborating teachers mutually develop a teaching plan, the supervisor will tell the para what parts of the developed plan to implement. Most paraeducators are assigned to one supervising teacher who is responsible for planning what paraeducators should do from day to day, and for scheduling where and when the paras will do it, and communicating this information to others.

French (2000) suggests a number of practical ways a supervising teacher can select classroom tasks for delegating to a paraeducator. She describes delegation as getting things done through another who has been trained to handle them, by giving that person authority to do it but not giving up teacher responsibility. Selection of the task is determined by considering it in the light of time sensitivity and the consequences of *not* doing it. A task that needs to be done soon and that has major consequences should *not* be delegated. Such tasks include student behavior crises; meetings regarding the crises; student health crises, and monitoring students in nonclassroom settings. Tasks that are not time sensitive but have major consequences also should not be delegated. They include designing individual behavior plans; assessing students' progress; developing curriculum; and co-planning instruction.

French (2000) recommends six steps for delegation of para responsibilities:

1. Analyze the task, and if it can be delegated, identify the steps it contains.
2. Decide what to delegate, keeping in mind the skills and preferences of those involved.
3. Create a plan that tells how to do the task, purposes of the task, student needs to address, and criteria for completion.
4. If more than one para is available, choose the one best for that task.
5. Direct the task, being available to answer questions and provide clarification.
6. Monitor performance without hovering over the para, and then document and reinforce good work.

French also reminds teachers to be tolerant of the reality that the para may not do some things exactly the way they themselves would have done those things.

Special educators responsible for supervising paras need to define clearly and monitor carefully the paras' responsibilities. Zigmond (1997) observed in her study of inclusion classrooms that the least trained person (para) often is responsible for working with instructing the students who are hardest to teach. "Too often students with disabilities are placed in general education classrooms without clear expectations established among the team members regarding which professional staff will plan, implement, monitor, evaluate, and adjust instruction" (Giangreco, Edelman, Luiselli, & MacFarland, 1997, p. 15). These researchers suggest assigning paras as classroom assistants rather than as assistants for single students. They note that if co-teachers fail to plan instruction, the responsibility often falls on the para, which is clearly beyond reasonable expectation for them. Others recommend ongoing collaborative meetings for sharing expertise areas and for discussing and clarifying areas of responsibility, including strategies and a plan for "fading" the level of support provided by the paraeducator (Marks, Schrader, & Levine, M., 1999, p. 325).

Sometimes paras inappropriately take the students in their charge away from the general classroom group (Giangreco, et al, 1997). Paras must be instructed that students are to be physically, programatically and interactionally included in classroom activities planned by qualified teachers. To help instill this awareness, teachers need to make sure they consider the para's role when co-planning lessons, and whenever possible include the para in the planning process.

■ ■ ■ ■ ■ ▬▬▬▬▬▬▬▬▬▬▬▬▬▬▬▬▬▬▬▬▬▬▬▬

APPLICATION 10.2

CLARIFYING THE PARA ASSISTANT ROLE

Jane is one of three paras assigned to Martin, a teacher of students with behavior disorders. Jane is an experienced para and has clear notions of what she should do in the inclusive classroom where Martin has assigned her. Martin told Jane just to be in the classroom to intervene whenever a particular student, Bart, gets off task or refuses to do work. She is not to help him with his work, but only to take steps to keep him "under control." Jane doesn't think that is a good way to use her time. She wants to help this student and others who might be having difficulty with the assignment. She thinks she should help clarify confusing information and outline class lectures on the chalkboard as she did in the previous school where she was assigned. Is it appropriate for Martin to these somewhat limited expectations on Jane even when she isn't comfortable with it? Does Bart's classroom teacher have a voice in this? How could this conflict be addressed?

Managing Schedules.   We have discussed elsewhere the challenges of arranging consultant and co-teaching schedules. Those challenges are magnified when several paraeducators are part of the scheduling demands. Since schedules are likely to change from week to week, it is helpful for everyone to have a schedule each week that indicates who does what, and when, and where. The schedule should be available to all special service staff and the building secretary.

In the school described in Vignette 10.b, master schedules were drawn up for all support staff, including special teachers and paras. Another schedule was made for volunteer paras that focused on the teachers' reported needs. Every Friday morning teachers who wished volunteer para assistance would complete a request-for-support form indicating what type of support they needed the following week. This often was during an activity period when several students would need help. The requests were noted on a master schedule and paras were assigned accordingly. The system was particularly helpful to volunteer paras. They could check the schedule and go to assignments without further directions much of the time.

Finding Time. The challenge of finding time to plan and discuss student needs with a para mirrors those issues of time discussed elsewhere for collaborating teachers. Teachers and paras in self-contained special classes may have break periods at the same time, but that is not likely when the para is working in a different classroom, as is often the case in inclusive schools. In an ideal situation at least 20 minutes a day is set aside for para-supervisor planning.

The more individuals with whom a para works, the more complex the supervision process is. When paras are in the general classroom most of the school day, classroom teachers must also be in a supervisory role for them. If communication processes among all parties are open and ongoing, this arrangement can work well. Sometimes, however, much confusion can occur.

It is one thing to plan for oneself and quite another to organize and plan for another person such as a paraeducator. French (1997) provides several examples of forms teachers can use to plan for paras. Another type of plan would be a daily schedule that would list all time periods through the day, where the para is to be during each time period, (e.g., "room 25," or "the work room" and what activity or responsibility the para will have (e.g., co-teach the group with Martin or adapt the textbook for student Willy.) Plans of this nature can be printed on paper or put into a computer data base where the paraeducator and professional can easily add comments and provide feedback to one another.

Another challenging part of supervising paras will be to determine *when* the supervisory responsibilities will be performed. "Most teachers report that they spend time outside the student-contact day to plan the schedule, design or prescribe appropriate learning activities for the paraeducator to use with students, and provide the paraeducator with on-the-job training, coaching, and feedback. In return for the investment of their time outside of the students' school day, the presence of a paraeducator will double the amount of instructional time that teachers have available during school hours. Teachers who fail to spend outside time for planning, training, coaching, and feedback with paraeducators report that they are dissatisfied with the performance of the paraeducators with whom they work" (French, 1997, p.73).

Examples of other information to provide the paraeducator are:

- A copy of school handbook(s) providing school policies and regulations.
- Information about the students included in one's caseload
- Teachers' guides for instructional materials that will be used
- First Aid information
- Classroom rules and other expectations for classroom management
- Behavior management guidelines for specific students

Although supervising teachers are responsible for planning carefully and communicating responsibilities to paraeducators, it will not always happen. The following tips are useful to share with paraeducators who may be uncertain about their responsibilities (Kaff & Dyck, 1999, p.32):

- Use common sense.
- Don't ask for help too soon, but when in doubt, please do ask.

- Request details about your designated tasks.
- Practice good communication skills.
- Maintain a sense of humor.

■ ■ ■ ■ ■ ▬

APPLICATION 10.3
APPROPRIATE OR INAPPROPRIATE?

For the following situations, label the paraeducator's actions as (a) appropriate; (b) inappropriate; or (c) can't decide. Then discuss your viewpoints with your colleagues. There are no absolute answers to these situations. They can be interpreted differently within contrasting school philosophies.

1. A para works with a small group of students in the hallway every day. Students from another classroom walk past his group regularly on their way to music. The passing students sometimes make off-color jokes and comments about the para's small group of students. The para tells the offending students to stop talking in the hallway when he is working with students. If they do not stop, he says he will report them to the *principal* because they are breaking school conduct rules.
2. The special education teacher has set up a behavior management plan and the para is instructed to give the student a token every 10 minutes if working independently at that time. The para does not favor giving rewards for only meeting the minimum expectations. So she decides to dispense tokens if, and only if, the student demonstrates good behavior by *her* standards for the *entire 10 minutes*.

Evaluating the Paraeducator/Teacher Relationship.   Extensive use of paraeducators has changed the role of teachers. Supervising and directing the work of paraeducators is now added to the teacher's role. "Even though teachers are no longer solely responsible for providing instruction, they remain wholly accountable for the outcomes of the instructional process" (French, 1999, p. 70).

Teachers may find evaluating paras neither easy nor particularly pleasant, especially when performance is sub-standard. However, the task may be made less discomforting by following these suggestions:

1. *Be clear and concise in telling paras exactly what you expect.*   Preparing job descriptions will get you off to a good start. Say, "When you help co-teach in science, please refrain from responding to questions, and show the student instead how to find answers in the textbook or other resource materials," rather than, "Would you please help students in the science class during study time?"

2. *Tell paras what you like about the way they do their jobs.*   Everyone likes to have good performance acknowledged.

3. *Tell paras if there are things they are not doing well.*   Talking about what you don't like as well as what you do like is not only a teacher's responsibility, it also shows you care about the personal relationship. Many teachers do not feel comfortable talking about problems, so they dodge around troublesome issues far too long. But constructive feedback gives you and the para a chance to work out differences and misunderstandings. (Recall that Chapter 4 provided material to help with communication in sensitive areas.)

Feedback must relate to the task or action, not the person. Further suggestions provided by experts from the business world (GOAL/QPC & Joiner Associates, Inc., 1995, p.22) are:

- Review the actions and decisions that led up to the moment.
- Give feedback sooner rather than later.
- Choose an appropriate time and place. Be selective about when you share negative reactions in particular. Do it one-on-one when you will be around to follow up with the person. Hit-and-run feedback is not fair.
- Start by describing the context. "I'd like to talk with you about what happened in the meeting today."
- Describe your reactions and reasons. ("I was distracted by your side conversation and couldn't follow what others were saying.")
- Ask for the change you'd like to see. ("You often have good points to make and I'd like it if you would share them with the whole group rather than talking with just a few people.")
- Allow time for the other person to respond.

It is never easy to discuss problems. Other suggestions that may be helpful include:

- Review the guidelines above and plan or rehearse what you want to say before you meet with the para.
- Select a place to meet where you won't be overheard or interrupted (which usually is *not* the teacher's lounge or workroom!).
- Remember, you can only control what *you* say and what *you* do. You cannot control the other person.

Supervising teachers should listen to the para's input and suggestions that result from her or his observations and knowledge of the students. They need feedback from the para for two different purposes. The first is to learn what is happening with students assigned to the para's responsibility, and the second is to learn how the teacher is affecting the para and others with whom they work. Most paraeducators will feel uncomfortable providing the latter type of feedback unless the teacher makes it clear that the input is important and will be accepted without negative consequences. Accepting feedback does not mean that one automatically agrees with the other person. It only means you will make an effort to understand the other person's concerns. Here are suggestions for accepting feedback (GOAL/QPC and Joiner Associates, Inc., 1995, p. 27).

- Breathe deeply. This can help you relax.
- Listen carefully.
- Make sure you understand what the other person is saying. ("Can you describe what I do or say that seems aggressive to you?")
- Acknowledge valid points even if you don't agree with the other person's interpretation.
- Acknowledge the feedback but take time to sort out what you heard. (A simple "thank you" is all that is needed right away. Ask for time to think about what you heard. If possible, schedule a time to get back together with the person.)

Equally important is feedback to learn what is happening to and for the students assigned to the para's responsibility. Sometimes the paraeducator is the only adult who observes what a student does during a particular activity. The para's observations and the way these are communicated to the supervising teacher are important factors in the decisions that will be made about that student. The supervising teacher should direct the para to report outcomes related to specific goals and objectives on students' IEPs such as learning outcomes, specific behaviors and relationships with others. Ask the para to provide information to answer the following questions:

- What was the event?
- Who was there?
- When did it take place?
- Where did it take place?
- What was going on before the event?
- How did the event take place (what was said or done by all those mentioned in "Who" above)?
- What was the outcome (e.g., natural consequence), of your intervention?

Caution the paraeducator to avoid interpreting, judging, labeling, speculating about the student's motives, dwelling on covert behaviors, or making judgments about feelings. Ask for only the facts and get them written out if at all possible. Figure 10.1 shows examples of poorly written interpretations of behavior, followed by more objective behavioral descriptions suitable for an appropriate record of an event. Figure 10.2 provides a checklist that may be useful in guiding evaluation before or after instructional activities. Paraeducators should be encouraged to use a checklist such as that in Figure 10.3 as a way of demonstrating ethical behavior. Regular rechecks can allow them to monitor their continued performance in this vital area.

FIGURE 10.1 Behavioral Descriptions for Paraeducator Feedback

	Poor	Better
Motives	She was trying to get Marlene's attention.	She tapped Marlene's shoulder four times.
Feelings	She was embarrassed by the comment.	She looked down at the floor and her face turned red.
Covert behavior	He was daydreaming.	He stared at the bulletin board with a blank expression on his face.
Labels	His tone of voice was really obnoxious.	He answered, "No, why should I?"
Pseudodescription	She glared at Billy for a long time.	She stared at Billy for five seconds.
Dialogue	He said he didn't want to do his work.	He said, "This stuff is dumb. Nobody could do this."

FIGURE 10.2   Paraeducator Teaching Checklist

Ask yourself the following questions before and after teaching students. Identify those areas in need of improvement. Reward yourself for areas well done.

Getting Ready to Teach

Do I know the special instructional needs of all the students I will be teaching?
Is the teaching environment comfortable with no distractions?
Do I have all the necessary materials for this lesson?
Have I asked the teacher to clarify any parts of the lesson I do not understand?
Have I adapted material if needed?
Do I know the content I am preparing to teach?
Am I prepared to use at least three different activities related to the lesson goal?

While You Are Teaching

Do I take a few moments to establish rapport with students each time?
Have I verbally cued students to attend before starting the lesson (e.g., "Eyes up here")?
Are my instructions concise and clear?
Have I reviewed relevant past learning?
Is the lesson goal clear to me and my students?
Have I modeled a skill when appropriate?
Do I keep the student(s) engaged in the task at least 70% of the time?
Do I ask questions of selected students by name instead of calling on volunteers?
Do I provide praise for effort?
Do I give brief, immediate corrective feedback to the student who errs?
Does every student have an opportunity to respond many times during the lesson?
Do I provide questions and cues to help students use what they already know to discover new information?
Do students respond correctly 80–90% of the time?
Do I check for skill mastery before closing the lesson?
Do I change activities when it is clear a student is experiencing frustration?
Do I keep the lesson interesting by changing activities?
Am I using rewards for individual students correctly as instructed by my supervising teacher?

Teachers should provide students with information about para responsibilities and roles related to matters of discipline and classroom management. It is very important for supervising teachers of paras to keep in mind that paraeducators typically work very hard and are woefully underpaid, and yet their dedication to student welfare in most cases is considerable. The difficulty in attracting and retaining paras in special education may be indicative of these realities. And, as discussed earlier, teachers often have little preparation for and, therefore, considerable reluctance toward supervising paraeducators (French, 1998).

Paraeducators, according to Ernsperger (1998), can play key roles in helping students avoid going to or have a smoother return from more restrictive settings. However, to maximize the effectiveness of paraeductors specifically and special education in general, consultants and teacher teams should be keenly aware of the need for well-designed preparation programs, role clarification, appropriate supervision, and adequate compensation for their work.

Giangreco, et al. (2001b) suggest that education teams or schools strengthen paraprofessional support by examining their own status and priority needs and take constructive

FIGURE 10.3   Paraeducator Ethics Checklist

Ask yourself the following questions to identify areas in which you can improve yourself as a paraeducator.

Accepting Responsibilities

Do I recognize that the supervisor has the ultimate responsibility for the instruction and behavior management of children and follow the directions prescribed by him/her?

Do I engage only in noninstructional and instructional activities for which qualified or trained?

Am I careful to not communicate progress or concerns about students to parents unless directed to do so by the supervising teacher?

Do I refer concerns expressed by parents, students, or others to the supervising teacher?

Relationship with Students and Parents

Do I discuss a child's progress, limitations, and/or educational program only with the supervising teacher in the appropriate setting?

Do I discuss school problems and confidential matters only with appropriate personnel?

Do I refrain from engaging in discriminatory practices based on a student's disability, race, sex, cultural background, or religion?

Do I respect the dignity, privacy, and individuality of all students, parents, and staff members?

Do I present myself as a positive adult role model?

Relationship with the Teacher

Do I recognize the role of the teacher as supervisor and team leader?

Do I establish communication and a positive relationship with the teacher?

When problems cannot be resolved, do I utilize the school district's grievance procedures?

Do I discuss concerns about the teacher or teaching methods directly with the teacher?

Relationship with the School

Do I accept responsibility for improving my own skills?

Do I know school policies and procedures?

Do I represent the school district in a positive manner in the community?

Adapted from: Kaff, M. & Dyck, N. (1999). © 1999 permission granted by Curriculum Solutions, Inc

action to improve it. This assessment could begin, the researchers suggest, with an examination of the six issues they noted in their extensive review of the literature: Acknowledging paraprofessional work; orientation and training; hiring and assigning; interactions with students and staff; roles and responsibilities; and supervision and evaluation. Carrying out the assessment of progress with these six issues may be part of the special education administrator's role or it may be a responsibility of the school administrator.

ROLES, RESPONSIBILITIES, AND OPPORTUNITIES FOR PROFESSIONAL DEVELOPMENT

Educators are caught up in demands for school reform and restructuring efforts that emphasize consultation, collaboration and teamwork as goals. Professional development is a prime factor in the success of school consultation, collaboration, and co-teaching. When carefully planned, well delivered, and constructively evaluated, it catalyzes these interactive processes. School personnel now in the profession, and teacher education students preparing to become teachers, need professional development experiences to build scaffolding that will support their consultation, collaboration, and co-teaching efforts. Ideal professional development includes goals that address five purposes in personalizing the experience for each participant (see Figure 10.4). Unfortunately, attitudes toward professional development delivered by inservice and staff development presenters are not generally positive, often ranging from indifference to resentment to disdain. Criticisms cited by Davis (1985) and others in regard to inservice and staff development call attention to the *lack* of:

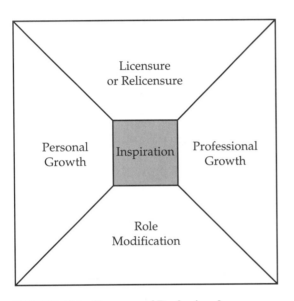

FIGURE 10.4   Purposes of Professional Development

- Clear purpose
- Relevance
- Sufficient scheduled time, on well-chosen days
- Meaningful objectives grounded in participant needs
- Integration into the total school program
- Structure and organization
- Emphasis on quality, not quantity
- Practicality and long-term applicability
- Flexibility and choices
- Interest and intrigue
- Attention to adult learner characteristics
- Support from administrators
- Most of all, follow-up activities with continuous evaluation of long-term benefits

VIGNETTE 10.C*

Several teachers at a middle school are conversing in the teachers' work room on Friday afternoon.

Social Studies Teacher: What a week! I feel like I've attended to everything this week but students and curriculum. Maybe things will slow down a bit next week.

Math Teacher: Guess you didn't look at your office memo yet, hmmm? There's a reminder about the staff development sessions next Tuesday and Thursday mornings before school. Something about working with consultants.

Social Studies Teacher: Consultants? You mean those people who drive over from the central office to borrow your clock and tell you what time it is? Or do you mean the imported experts breezing in from more than fifty miles away with their briefcases and stacks of transparencies?

Math Teacher: I believe this group involves our own special education staff. We're supposed to find out about school consultation service and collaborating with staff who will be consulting teachers.

Art Teacher: Oh, great. How does that involve me? I had my required course in special ed. What I *really* need is a bigger room and more supplies.

Social Studies Teacher: And if we're supposed to collaborate with these people, where will we find the time?

Physical Education Teacher: Uh-huh. It will be hard enough just carving out the time to go to the *meeting* about it.

Math Teacher: Now you know you'll just *love* sitting in that stuffy room trying to stay awake when you'd rather be in your classroom getting set for the day.

Social Studies Teacher: Well, let me put it this way. If they're not through by 8:20 sharp, I'm gone!

*adapted from Dettmer, 1990.

In order to provide the most constructive professional development experiences possible, planners and presenters need to address several points:

- What are characteristics of school personnel as adult learners?
- What are needs of school personnel in serving students with special needs?
- What kind of material is most helpful for them?
- How might the material be presented effectively and efficiently?
- How can follow-up and support be provided after the experiences? (This is *very* important.)

Characteristics of the Adult Learner

Participants in professional development experiences must be approached as the adult learners and professionals that they are. Participants demonstrate several basic characteristics as adult learners. They have (Knowles, 1978):

1. A desire and need to be self-directed in their learning
2. A wide experience base upon which to draw
3. A time perspective for learning that is oriented to the *here* and *now*
4. A problem-centered focus on learning

In his more recent research, Knowles indicates that the most definitive of these four characteristics for educators is the wide experience base they bring (Feuer & Geber, 1988). The participants will be self-directed, experienced, and interested primarily in material they can use at the present for real problems. They want ownership in the development process, and they resist aspects that are perceived as attacks on their competence. They can and should serve as resources for their colleagues during professional development activities. And although some fun and rewards are refreshing, adult learners respond best to intrinsic motivations rather than extrinsic motivations.

Professional developers can use knowledge of adult learner characteristics to work more productively with participants. The first step is to acknowledge that each person's perception of the environment reflects and is filtered through his or her own stage of development (Oja, 1980). Because of learning style preferences and variations in ways people process information, as discussed in Chapter 1, presenters must attend to different types of participants. These include (Garmston & Wellman, 1992):

- Those looking for facts, data, and references
- Those wishing to relate the topic to themselves through interactions with colleagues
- Those wanting to reason and explore
- Those who would like to adapt, modify, or create new ideas and procedures

With these adult learner characteristics and individual style variations in mind, professional developers will need to:

- Arrange for participant comfort
- Give participants options and choices
- Manage participants' time well
- Deliver practical, focused help
- Follow up on the effectiveness of the experience

Adult learners value activities in which they work toward realistic, job-related, useful goals. They need to see results for their efforts with follow-through and feedback experiences, and most of all, with success using the activities within their school context. Guskey (1985) stresses that staff development for busy school personnel must illustrate clearly ways in which new practices can improve student performance, and how these practices can be implemented without too much disruption or extra work. This is particularly important when focusing on consultation and collaboration, because this kind of professional activity often involves more time and effort initially. In Guskey's model of teacher change, staff development should be designed for the purpose of creating *change in classroom teaching practices.* This causes changes in student learning outcomes, which then results in changed teacher beliefs and attitudes. It is a promising concept for promoting collaboration as a way of helping students who have special needs.

Kelleher (2003) describes professional development as a form of adult learning that must be concerned primarily with student learning. A speaker or an activity might be interesting to participants, but the test of success is what teachers do with the new information they receive. He recommends allocating professional development budgets so as to encourage teachers to focus heavily on activities related to peer collaboration. A peer collaboration strand that features teachers collaborating in writing curriculum and assessments, examining student work, observing each other's classrooms, and mentoring new teachers, would have significant impact on student achievement.

Differentiating In-service from Staff Development

In-service and staff development are two necessary but distinctly different structures for professional growth. Inservice is ordinarily a single event or a series of short sessions on a topic of educational interest or school need. These one-shot sessions are most often provided by an expert who might be a state official, university professor, professional consultant, corporate leader, or educator from another district, on a topic of general appeal. In-service goals generally are directed toward awareness and information.

Staff development, on the other hand, is a process of long-term commitment to growth across a broad range of school goals. It should involve all school personnel and often includes local leadership in place of, or at least in addition to, service by outside consultants. Goals are directed toward involvement, commitment, and renewal. School personnel determine their own needs, develop steps to address those needs, and evaluate their professional growth.

Under ideal circumstances inservice would be only one useful component of a long-range, ongoing program to provide professional development that serves the needs of teachers, administrators, and support personnel in the school system. Staff development is a fundamental part of the general plan for improving education for all students. "Staff development will never have its intended impact as long as it is grafted onto schools in the form of discrete, unconnected projects" (Joyce, 1990, p. 21).

The consultant role is ideal for coordinating useful in-service and staff development (ISD) activities. Special education personnel often inherit these responsibilities either as a part of a plan or by default. There are disadvantages as well as advantages in being a "prophet in one's own land" for conducting professional development activities, but one of the biggest advantages is knowledge of the school context, along with what participants probably already know and still need to know.

Minninger and Goulter (1991) state that, besides knowing the information to be presented, a presenter needs to know the purpose of the presentation. Then, armed with purpose and information, the presenter must believe in oneself and believe in the material to be presented. They recommend that presenters look on presentations as opportunities and move through four stages of preparation to become confident:

- Prepare in head and heart. (Get ready.)
- Assess the audience. (On your mark.)
- Organize what you are going to do. (Get set.)
- Begin and end in an attention-getting way. (Go.)

They call this the Track-and-Field Model to be used for giving perfect presentations.

Determining Professional Development Needs

The consultant or consulting teacher who provides staff development will want to assess needs of other school personnel. What do they already know about a topic at this point? What do they want to learn? How can they be involved in planning, conducting, and evaluating experiences for their individual needs? This information should be solicited through needs assessment instruments. Before conducting needs assessment, however, the staff developer should engage in needs-sensing activities. In data gathering it is important to move beyond the surface data to get at what is *really* wanted and needed. What do participants *need* to want to know? School personnel may assess their needs as wanting classroom strategies for behavior management or for grouping high ability learners in productive but non-elitist ways. However, the staff developer may sense a need for addressing their concerns about inclusion and accountability for student performance. This radar-reading of what the participants-to-be "need to want to know" is a subtle but vital precursor to assessing needs. After all, if educators knew what they wanted or needed in every case, they probably would be doing it.

Needs Sensing.   Needs-sensing information allows planners to design formal needs assessment procedures that will reflect the true needs of all involved. For example, if a needs assessment questionnaire asks, "Which of the five topics do you want to know more about?" and the list includes discipline, motivation, computer literacy, alternative grouping structures, and inclusion, the ranked results will be somewhat predictable in a typical district. Alternative grouping structures probably would rank low, with discipline and motivation high.

Prior to the needs assessment activity, an interviewer or investigator might ask teachers if they would like to explore possibilities for structuring their classrooms to promote better discipline and stimulate self-regulated learning. If the answer is affirmative, staff development on modified grouping structures could be offered as an area of interest that promotes discipline as well as student motivation. As another example of needs sensing, teachers could be asked if they wish to explore ways in which children can work together, learn from each other, and share in the results of the learning. If the answer is yes, staff development on cooperative learning could be implemented. For a third example, it would be less helpful to assess needs with the question, "Do you want to know more about Advanced Placement possibilities at your high school?" than to sense where needs lie by asking first, "How might we extend learning of very able students beyond courses that cover grade level material they have already mastered?"

Needs sensing is a very important precursor to needs assessment. It can be carried out best through:

- Classroom observations
- Visits to successful programs, followed by a comparative analysis
- Dialogues and interviews with students, parents, support personnel, and others in the community
- Task force investigations
- Buzz group outcomes

■ ■ ■ ■ ■ ▬▬▬▬▬▬▬▬▬▬▬▬▬▬▬▬▬▬▬▬▬▬▬▬▬▬▬▬▬▬▬▬▬▬▬▬

APPLICATION 10.4
CONDUCTING NEEDS SENSING

Conduct a needs-sensing study by interviewing school personnel to obtain information on these concerns:

1. What do we need to know about to help students in our schools feel good about themselves?
√2. How important are test formats, designs, and reporting procedures in helping students learn to the best of their ability?
3. How can we determine which reinforcers work best at what ages and developmental levels and interests?
4. Are we using ancillary and support personnel to the greatest advantage for our students?
√5. Does our current material develop critical thinking, or do we need more effort in this area?
6. Do we have the resources for adapting materials to the needs of low-achieving students?
√ 7. In what ways can we build on students' strengths to remediate weaknesses?

Professional developers should develop instruments that allow target groups to feel able and willing to contribute information.

Needs Assessment.   After needs sensing has been conducted, needs assessment instruments procedures can be developed from the data. Most school personnel have had experience with completing needs assessments. Formats for needs assessments include:

- Checklists
- Questionnaires and surveys
- Open-ended surveys of areas of concern
- Interviews
- Brainstorm sessions

Needs assessment might ask personnel to check topics of need, or to describe their concerns which then can be developed into a staff development activity.

■ ■ ■ ■ ■

APPLICATION 10.5
CONDUCTING NEEDS ASSESSMENT

As a needs assessment procedure, ask teachers to check the topics that interest them most, rating them from 5 = greatest need, 4 = strong need, 3 = helpful, 2 = perhaps, and 1 = not needed:

___ How to create an an orderly, positive learning atmosphere ✓
___ How to develop critical thinking skills ✓
___ Alternative assessment procedure, including portfolios
___ Techniques of behavior management
___ Selecting and using resources beyond the basal texts
___ Working smarter, not harder, by using consulting teachers and resource personnel more effectively
___ How to modify classroom assignments and/or tests
___ Ways of dealing with the attention deficit and hyperactivity disorders

It is important to leave space on the instrument for open-ended responses, and to encourage them. After the needs assessments have been returned, summarize the information and use it to plan activities that will be meaningful for participants and relevant to the needs they specified.

Presenting Professional Development Activities

Garmston (1988) says that presenting in-service session or staff development is like giving presents. He suggests the "present" should be something participants (presentees) want or can utilize, personalized to individual taste as much as possible, attractively wrapped, and a bit suspenseful. The presenter should:

- Know audience needs and interests.
- Conduct the activity in an interesting, efficient, pleasant manner.

■ Package the ISD material attractively.

■ Provide an element of surprise and intrigue.

■ Deliver follow-up help, support, and additional information.

Formal and Informal In-service and Staff Development

Just as there are formal and informal approaches to consultation, as discussed in Chapter 2, there are formal and informal approaches to professional development. Formal activities can be conducted through scheduled sessions, conferences, programs, press releases, presentations, modules, courses, brochures, retreats, and other planned activities. Informal activities occur through conversations, observations, reports about one topic that include another aspect of education, memos, references to media productions, software programs and reading material. One very informal, convenient, and particularly effective in-service technique is to display information, explanations of procedures, invitations to collaborate, and morale-boosters on bulletin boards located in places that school personnel frequent.

The possibilities for both formal and informal ISD activities are limited only by the imagination of the personnel who provide them. Some special education consultants prepare bulletin boards of information about pertinent topics. Others provide staff members with newsletters, or columns within existing newsletters. Some request ten minutes in which to talk to the teachers at faculty meetings.

One enterprising group of teachers organized a series of sessions called "THT—Teachers Helping Teachers," in which they took turns delivering short sessions on topics in which they had expertise. Soon the idea caught on among other teachers. A teacher who had a school-related skill to share was given administrator support to prepare and present a half-day session to teachers in another school within the district. Other teachers followed suit at various times throughout the school year.

A popular practice with some gifted program consultants is to provide calendars of enrichment activities for classroom teachers. As these are used, they become vehicles for carrying out goals of the gifted program such as creative thinking, independent study, research, and small-group investigations. A productive inservice could be a brief session to explain the consultant role and what the consultant will be doing. Such endeavors often increase interest in consultation and collaboration dramatically. Consultants also might prepare Information Sheets of "Questions Frequently Asked About . . ." and suggest answers for the questions. A bagged treat or a package of peanuts could be stapled on as a friendly, caring gesture.

Learning is often a spontaneous event, occurring as a synergy of learner interest and need, teacher insight, and a supportive environment. This is the ideal "teachable moment." It is not stretching the comparison too much to suggest that there is an ideal "professional development moment." Perceptive consultants who seek ways of meeting students' special needs will find that inservice and staff development are appropriate tools. They need not expect all such experiences to be formal and planned. Both formal approaches and the informal, or "teachable moment for teachers" approaches, are needed.

When consultants work with one key teacher and their colleagues observe the results, that is informal staff development. As they ask what they can do to help teachers, then discuss their needs, and finally deliver on their promises to the best of their ability and the resources of their area, they are cultivating professional development among school personnel. (See Figure 10.5.)

FIGURE 10.5   Formal and Informal In-service and Staff Development

	Formal	Informal
Plan	Typically structured Example: Workshop	Usually casual Example: Newsletter column
Method	Designed with care Example: Speaker/discussion	Somewhat spontaneous Example: Hall chat
Evaluation	Data collection Example: Checklist	Reflection Example: Journal note

The Teachers' Workroom as a Forum for Professional Development

Very little has been written about the teachers' workroom, sometimes known as "the lounge" even though not much lounging goes on there. This lack of attention to the place is surprising, because most teachers drop in at some time or other. Of course, some go quite frequently, and others hardly ever do. Visits usually fall within one of three purposes—physical, social, or personal. There may be the physical benefit of refreshment, a quick "nap," or a rest room break. A few minutes of socialization with adults, squeezed between intensive hours with children and adolescents, is important to some. Professional benefits include attending to tasks such as grading papers or reading materials, or getting one's thoughts and plans together before the next barrage of youthful energy bursts into the classroom.

Oftentimes teachers just want an opportunity to interact with colleagues and share reflections about teaching practices and student needs. Occasionally this is problematic because the discourse can become quite negative and cynical. When this kind of talk affects one's morale negatively, then going there becomes iatrogenic and should probably be avoided. Nevertheless, the teachers' workroom has long been recognized as a useful hub of interaction, particularly by special education teachers. They have the opportunity to develop rapport with general education colleagues and learn more about their classrooms and students.

It is important that consulting teachers spend enough time in the teachers' workroom ("Don't the special ed people want to be a part of our faculty?"), but not too much ("Don't those special ed people have anything to do?"). Of course, care must be taken to keep professional conversation general in nature. Confidentiality and ethical treatment of information are necessary behaviors for all teachers, and special education teachers in particular. But in this room that is provided for relaxation, reflection, and refreshment, a collaborative spirit can be nurtured and carried out the door to classrooms and offices beyond.

Suggestions for improving the workroom/lounge in general, and making it more conducive to collegial interaction, in particular, include (Dettmer, 1989):

- Having a suggestion box in which staff could put ideas for time-savers, student-pleasers, or budget-easers.
- Having salad luncheon potluck once a month, perhaps on payday. (Set out different salads every half hour or so, if there are many people.) Simpson (1990) describes a

"Tuesday Luncheon" concept which has been in effect for nine years and supports teachers' efforts to reflect on their instruction.

- Holding a Friday afternoon snack time to encourage teachers to recap the week and think ahead to the next.
- Posting a "Brag Board" on which commendations could be displayed involving anyone and everyone connected with the school, from students to bus drivers to parents of students.
- Providing an "Orientation to Special Education" folder on an accessible table, changing its contents often.

APPLICATION 10.6
DESIGNING A TEACHERS' WORKROOM

In your thoughts or on sketch paper, create a "dream workroom" that would serve school personnel in their physical, social, and personal needs. What would it look like? What would it sound like? How might a consultant nurture the collaborative spirit there? What would it take to construct and furnish such a room? Could some of your suggestions be carried out right away, with little cost and disruption to the school?

More research is needed on the problems and possibilities of this important facet of school life. However, the consultant will find many opportunities there for developing rapport with consultees and initiating constructive interactions. This school place must be used wisely and judiciously.

Outline for Professional Development Activity

There is no single pattern for inservice and staff development format which will be appropriate for every school context. However, the following outline is one that can be adapted to a variety of schools and staff needs.

1. Engage in needs sensing
2. Conduct needs assessment
3. Select the topic to be featured
4. Determine the audience to be targeted
5. Choose a catchy, upbeat title for the activity
6. Determine presenters who will contribute
7. Decide on incentives, promotion, and publicity
8. Outline the presentation
9. List the equipment and room arrangement needed
10. Plan carefully the content to be covered
11. Prepare handouts and visual materials
12. Rehearse the presentation
13. Determine an evaluation procedure for the activity
14. Plan for the follow-up activity

Finding Time for Professional Development Activities

Time is the enemy when planning inservice and staff development activities. There is not enough of it at student-free times when teachers can concentrate and reflect. Before-school and after-school hours might seem workable because participants are coming to school anyway, or are required to stay after school for a specific length of time. But teachers find it hard to focus on their own learning at an early hour when their thoughts are centered on beginning the school day efficiently. By day's end, energy and emotions may be lagging and other responsibilities beckon. Saturday sessions are no more popular, and encroach upon the family and community life so necessary for sustaining teacher vitality and support.

The arrangement preferred by most teachers is released time. This means that their responsibilities with students will be assumed by others. Loucks-Horsley, Harding, Arbuckle, Murray, Dubea, and Williams (1987) recommend providing released time by using substitute teachers, a substitute cadre that conducts planned enrichment activities, roving substitute teachers, or arrangements where one teacher teaches two classes to free up the second teacher.

The substitute cadre eliminates the necessity for detailed lesson planning by the teacher, because the enrichment activities are planned and provided by the cadre. Roving substitutes allow released teachers to have short periods of time for observing, coaching, gathering research data, or assisting in another classroom. Loucks et al. (1987) counsel that the time issue is a "red herring," because the problem often lies in the constructive use of time, not its availability.

Presenter and Participant Responsibilities

Consultants who deliver inservice and staff development on their own professional turf may face some difficulty in being accepted as "prophets in their own land" (Smith-Westberry & Job, 1986). They will want to scrutinize their own capabilities and deficits first. Practice sessions can help presenters gain confidence and skill. Smith-Westberry and Job recommend videotaping the practice sessions, discomforting though that may be, and critiquing the taped sessions carefully to correct deficiencies.

Presenters have a responsibility to know their participants well. They should be experienced and confident with the content they are presenting. After assessing participant needs, they should develop the format and content carefully, rehearse for the presentation, plan the closing segment even more carefully, arrange for feedback and evaluation, and form ideas for follow-up to the presentation.

Participants, as presentees, have the responsibility to participate whole-heartedly in the activity, participate in the evaluation, and commit themselves to the follow-up activities. One of the most helpful contributions on their part is to defer any negative attitudes toward the event and anticipate that positive outcomes will come from it.

Follow-Up Activities to the Professional Development Experience

Follow-up is the breeze which fans any fires of change that were sparked by the activity (Dettmer, 1990). Educators sometimes avoid trying new concepts and techniques because they are uncomfortable with them or uncertain about the outcomes. It is easy to revert to business as usual once the activity is over. So follow-up is vital, just as it is with the consultation process. Follow-up should be a long-term practice of support for the innovation, and as such, might more appropriately be described as *follow-through* (Dettmer, 1990). The possibilities include peer coaching, discussion groups, visits to sites where the innovation is occurring, newsletters, and interviews. Data gathered during follow-up and follow-through can be used to plan future professional development projects. An example of one brief follow-up instrument is included in Figure 10.6. Of course, personal contact is best; therefore, the evaluator should consider conducting this follow-up as an interview.

One caution must be noted. When educators are introduced to new concepts and challenged to try new approaches, some discomfort is inevitable. Learning new skills involves greater effort than continuing to use old ones (Joyce & Showers, 1983). The adage that train-

FIGURE 10.6   Follow-Up Information for Professional Development

Please take a few minutes to respond to these questions about the recent staff development ___(date)___ on the topic of ___(topic)___. In doing so you will be helping staff developers and presenters plan effective staff development experiences for you and your colleagues.

1. Have you implemented any idea or strategy that was presented during the staff development? If so, please describe it briefly and rate the success level:

    _____

    _____

    _____

    _____ 1 = not effective   _____ 2 = somewhat effective   _____ 3 = very effective

2. Is there something more you would like to learn about this topic? If so, please describe your need.

    _____

    _____

    _____

3. If you did not use the staff development information, please tell why you did not.

    _____

    _____

    _____

4. This item is *very* important. Did the information or enthusiasm you received have positive ripple effects that you could identify and describe? If so, please do, and also rate the extent to which this happened.

    _____

    _____

    _____

    _____ 1 = a little   _____ 2 = somewhat   _____ 3 = to a great extent   _____ 4 = profoundly

ing may make one worse before it makes one better is an important point to consider. This accents the need for follow-through efforts and perseverance on the part of the consultant.

Evaluation of Professional Development

Evaluation of a professional development activity is imperative for at least two reasons. First, Guskey notes that because staff development is conducted to implement change, information must be gathered to assess the change (Todnem & Warner, 1994). Second, there is pressure more than ever now for accountability in education. Guskey warns that these needs will not be served by evaluation that is shallow and brief. Pertinent questions are (Gordon, 1992):

1. What are participants' reactions to the staff development?
2. What did participants learn?
3. Are participants using the new information in their roles and work?
4. What difference has the staff development made in the total system?

The tool used most often for evaluation is a questionnaire that participants complete immediately following the activity. The evaluation should include both objective responses and an invitation for open-ended responses. A Likert scale of five to seven values is preferable to a Yes/No format. The evaluation data should be used to design more meaningful activities as well as to improve presentation skills. See Figure 10.7 for an example of an evaluation tool, and consult Chapter 6 for additional information on evaluation.

FIGURE 10.7

In-service/Staff Development Evaluation

Date _____

Name (optional) _____ Teaching Area and Level (s) _____

Site of the In-service/Staff Development _____ Topic _____

Rate the following with a value from 1 through 5:

1 = None   2 = A little   3 = Somewhat   4 = Considerably   5 = Much

1. The event increased my understanding of the topic. _____
2. The goals and objectives of the event addressed needs I had identified. _____
3. The content was well developed and organized. _____
4. The material was presented effectively. _____
5. The environment was satisfactory. _____
6. I gained ideas to use in my own situation. _____
7. I will use at least one idea from this event. _____
8. Strengths of the event: _____
9. Ways the event could be improved: _____
10. I would like to know more about: _____

Presenters may want to complete a self-evaluation and evaluate the participants as well. By doing so, consultants ascertain participant preparedness and responsiveness toward the topic. This provides information that can help them and their host schools plan further consultation and collaboration directed to participant needs (See Figure 10.8).

Rewards of Professional Development

Professional development for consultation, collaboration, and special needs of students has the potential to create positive ripple effects that have no bounds. It can encourage:

- Increased respect for individual differences, creative approaches, and educational excellence
- Teacher proficiency in innovative curriculum and teacher strategies
- Staff and parent involvement, and satisfaction with the educational system
- Collegiality and collaboration among all school personnel as well as community and parents

In order to attain these positive outcomes, inservice and staff development must be planned, conducted, and evaluated thoroughly.

FIGURE 10.8   Presenter's Self-Assessment of Professional Development Activity

Rate the following items, using a scale of:

1 = inadequate, 2 = fair, 3 = satisfactory, 4 = good, 5 = excellent

_____   1. I was well-prepared.

_____   2. I was organized.

_____   3. My material was on target with their needs.

_____   4. I established rapport and got off to a good start.

_____   5. Participants seemed interested.

_____   6. Participants wanted to know even more about the topic(s).

_____   7. I had an accurate perspective of the audience.

_____   8. I got participants involved.

_____   9. I had the right kind and amount of handouts.

_____   10. My presentation materials were high quality.

_____   11. I did my very best in this activity.

_____   12. I have plans for follow-through with the participants.

_____   13. I learned from the experience, too.

_____   14. This is my overall rating of the staff development.

■ ■ ■ ■ ■ ▬▬

APPLICATION 10.7
PREPARING A STAFF DEVELOPMENT OUTLINE

Create an outline of a staff development activity that could be presented by special education consultants to cultivate a spirit of collaboration and teamwork among general classroom teachers, special education personnel, and related services and support personnel. Include a list of do's and don'ts that would be pertinent to this activity.

TIPS FOR CONSULTING, COLLABORATING, AND PROFESSIONAL GROWTH

1. Find ways to inform, support, and interact with principals of your schools, expecting that each will be a "prince-and-a-pal" or "princess-and-a-pal." We tend to get what we expect!
2. Discuss the school mission statement, building philosophy, and your own teaching philosophy and values with the paraeducators assigned to you before they begin working with you and the students.
3. Visit other schools where there are clear procedures for scheduling, directing, supervising, and evaluating the work of paraeducators. Implement such practices that are promising for your school setting.
4. Encourage paras to share their ideas on student behavior and learning, and incorporate those ideas into the instructional plan when appropriate.
5. Introduce family members to the paraeducators who will work with their child.
6. When a para asks for advice, first ask what the para has observed. This gets the para involved and encourages active participation in deciding on a plan and implementing that plan.
7. Advocate for well-designed, well-conducted, and well-evaluated staff development specifically prepared for paraeducators.
8. Enthusiastically take part in professional development activities, as a presenter or as a participant, vowing to take at least one idea away to use with students.
9. Keep remarks about teaching colleagues, staff, students, and families of students to a minimum and focused only on the instructional tasks at hand.
10. Practice the adage we all learned as children, "If you can't say something good (respectful, appreciative, supportive) about a colleague, then say nothing at all."
11. If an opportunity arises, suggest certain activities to teachers who might want them. Don't force. Sometimes, although not often, the distribution of material to teachers backfires because they resent the inference that they need it. So let them decide. Instead of stuffing teachers' mailboxes with things they may not want, lay out new books or activities on tables in the teachers' workroom with a sign that invites browsing.
12. Have an inservice on parent–teacher conferences for students with special needs. Ask teachers to submit "stumper" problems, then use them to determine how to react and deal with those situations. Have lots of ideas to distribute.
13. Do your very best to get administrators to *attend* and *participate* in the ISD activities.

14. About two months after the ISD, send a checklist of outcomes that were sought from the activity, and solicit feedback on progress toward those outcomes.

15. In the teachers' workroom, have treats and notecards with the directions, "Take a treat and take a sheet," meaning to take a sheet that has tips concerning student needs. A variation is "Take a treat and leave a sheet" in which the sheet is a needs assessment or evaluation you wish to collect (Dettmer & Landrum, 1997).

CHAPTER REVIEW

1. Administrators have a key role in paraeducator success by clarifying all personnel roles carefully, allocating time for teacher and para planning sessions together, and providing and encouraging staff development activities. When building administrators attend and participate in in-service and staff development sessions, that show of commitment is truly impressive to their staff!

2. When the paraeducator's role is clearly defined at the outset, the partnership between teacher and para is more likely to be smooth and productive. The paraeducator assists the special education teacher and follows that teacher's direction. The teacher directs and supervises the para. It is important that classroom teachers participate in supervising work of the paras as well.

3. Teachers must be permitted the time and the space needed to plan effectively with their paras. The IDEA legislation requires training for paraeducators; also, teachers need to provide specific, on-the-job orientation and training in their own school contexts.

4. Paraeducators should have a high school diploma, a sense of ethics and the need for confidentiality, ability to communicate with children and adults, ability to follow verbal directions and written plans of teachers, willingness to learn new skills, flexibility, sense of humor, and a good attendance record. Preparation will involve staff development sessions, teacher-provided instruction, and use of numerous materials available in the literature and professional resources.

5. Teachers supervise and direct para activities by planning with them, managing their schedules, delegating responsibilities, orienting them to their roles and work settings, providing training, managing their work environment, and evaluating their performance.

6. Consultants and consulting teachers have ideal roles for planning and implementing professional development activities. Through their involvement with ISD activities they can share content and help build processes that facilitate learning by students with special needs. They also will have the opportunity to develop consultation and collaboration networks in their local school context.

7. Professional development must be designed to address assessed needs of the participants. Before needs assessment is conducted, needs sensing should be undertaken. In-service and staff development for facilitating learning by students with special needs should be presented to a wide range of target groups—teachers, administrators, support personnel, policymakers, teacher educators, and others who are involved with learning programs and materials. ISD can be informal or formal. Formative and summative evaluation of professional development will provide accountability for resources expended and will help staff developers continue to plan and improve these services for school personnel needs.

TO DO AND THINK ABOUT

1. Given the careful planning and organization in principal Margo's school (described in Vignette 10.a), what would be most likely to happen next in that scenario? What will be some of the hurdles to progress within that educational setting and using that approach after one year, five years,

and beyond as a model for replication in other districts? What strategies and tactics might Margo and other school personnel employ to remove or surmount these hurdles?

2. Discuss the following activities and determine whether they should be done by the paraeducator, the teacher only, or by the person in either role.
Read to students.
Prepare homework assignments.
Observe and record student behaviors.
Administer and score standardized tests.
Check student papers.

3. Discuss the following situations and propose next steps for each.
■ The general classroom teacher asks the paraeducator to help a student complete his algebra assignment. It has been a long time since the paraeducator studied algebra and she feels uncertain about some of the steps involved.
■ During his break period in the staff lounge, a paraeducator overhears two teachers talking about one of the students with whom he works. The paraeducator is aware that some of the information the teachers are sharing is not correct.
■ The paraeducator is attending a meeting at her social club when someone says, "These people with mental problems should be locked up. They shouldn't be in school with my child."

4. React to these candid comments by a high school paraeducator during an interview with a graduate student in education. Then have a dialogue with your colleagues about any feelings and any concerns you have toward this revelation:

I help in a resource room where there are a number of different subjects being studied. Although I am not supposed to plan activities, I am more or less "in charge" of the kids taking world history, and I check in with the special ed teacher every so often to make sure what I am doing is okay. I handle quite a bit of paperwork, too, and make sure materials are copied on time. I adapt tests or worksheets for students needing differing materials, or administer tests orally if that is necessary.

We are not an inclusive school at this time. If we were, I would see my job evolving to one where I do no planning, but carry out the suggestions from the special ed teacher for specific students in the classroom. As I see it, the number of special ed students is growing so fast that certified special ed teachers will not be able to do direct consulting, but will have to rely instead on paras to carry out the goals of each student's IEP because paras are cheaper to hire.

5. Suppose that an in-service session on alternative grouping techniques is scheduled or an elementary school, with attendance by all building teachers required. The one-hour session is scheduled for Thursday after school, in the kindergarten room. A methods instructor from a nearby university will lecture to the group. Later this evening there is a high school play performance, and the next day is the end of term before the grading period. How does this in-service topic, time, location, and format violate principles of good adult learning experiences?

6. Design a bulletin board for the teachers' workroom that could be considered an informal inservice concerning a disability or an example of students at risk.

7. In a teacher's guide for a particular subject, locate instances where collaboration and use of a consultant are referred to, or better still, encouraged. Discuss these with classroom teachers relevant to the topic and grade level(s).

8. Talk about the following quotations as they might relate to in-service and staff development, and think of others to add to these:

"It is easier to produce ten volumes of philosophical writing than to put one principle into practice." (unknown)

"Our goal is not to think alike, but to think together." (anonymous)

"We're all in this boat together. If you don't care to help row, at least don't drill holes in the bottom of the boat." (some anonymous, wise person)

FOR FURTHER READING

Ashbaker, B., & Morgan, J. (1996). Paraeducators: Critical members of the rural education team. In D. Montgomery (Ed.), *The American Council on* *Rural Special Education Conference-Rural Goals 2000: Building programs that work* (pp. 130–136). Stillwater, OK: Oklahoma State University.

Dettmer, P., & Landrum, M. (1997). *Staff development: The key to effective gifted education programs.* Waco, TX: Prufrock.

Demchak, M. A., & Morgan, C. R. (1998). Effective collaboration between professionals and paraprofessionals. *Rural Special Education Quarterly, 17*(2), 10–15.

Doyle, M. B. (1997). *The paraprofessional's guide to the inclusive classroom: Working as a team.* Baltimore, MD: Brookes.

Dyck, N. (1999). *How to adapt text for struggling readers.* Lawrence, KS: Curriculum Solutions.

Dyck, N., & Pemberton, J. (1997). *A dozen tools for paras.* Lawrence, KS: Curriculum Solutions.

Dyck, N., & Thurston, L. P. (1998). *Getting the message across: A para's guide to communication.* Lawrence, KS: Curriculum Solutions.

Dyck, N., Zabel, M. K., & Zabel, R. H. (1998). *Behavior management guide for paras.* Lawrence, KS: Curriculum Solutions.

Foley, R. M., & Lewis, J. A. (1999). Self-perceived competence of secondary school principals to serve as school leaders in collaborative-based educational delivery systems. *Remedial and Special Education, 20*(4), 233–243.

French, N. K. (1997). Management of paraeducators. In A. L. Pickett & K. Gerlach (Eds.), *Supervising paraeducators in school settings.* Austin, TX: Pro-Ed.

French, N. K. (1999). Paraeducators and teachers: Shifting roles. *Teaching Exceptional Children, 2*(2), 69–73.

French, N. K. (2000). Taking time to save time: Delegating to paraeducators. *Teaching Exceptional Children, 32* (3) 79–83.

Garmston, R. J., & Wellman, B. M. (1992). *How to make presentations that teach and transform.* Alexandria, VA: Association for Supervision and Curriculum Development.

Giangreco, M. F., Edelman, S. W., & Broer, S. M. (2001). Respect, appreciation, and acknowledgment of paraprofessionals who support students with disabilities. *Exceptional Children, 67(4),* 485–498.

Idol, L. (1998). Collaboration in the schools: A master plan for staff development. *Journal of Educational and Psychological Consultation, 9*(2), 155–163. In this article Idol presents a master plan for helping school staff create a more collaborative school.

Journal for Staff Development. Manhattan, KS: Kansas State University. All issues.

Journal for Staff Development, 15(4). Results-oriented staff development. A topical, special issue on celebrating twenty-five years of service, 1969–1994. Oxford, OH: National Staff Development Council.

Joyce, B. (Ed.). (1990). *Changing school culture through staff development.* Alexandria, VA: Association for Supervision and Curriculum Development.

Joyce, B., & Showers, B. (1988). *Student achievement through staff development.* New York: Longman.

Kaff, M., & Dyck, N. (1999). *Essential skills for paras.* Lawrence, KS: Curriculum Solutions.

Kelleher, J. (2003). A model for assessment-driven professional development. *Phi Delta Kappan, 84*(10), 751–756. Kelleher offers a six-stage model of professional development that features four strands, including peer collaboration, individualized professional growth, research and leadership, and external experiences.

Kohm, B. (2002). Improving faculty conversations. *Educational Leadership, 59*(8), 31–33. Kohm offers strategies such as dot voting, round-robin, six points of view, and brainstorming for open discussions during which faculty colleagues discuss children's reading rather than "whether to use ketchup packets or bottles in the cafeteria" (p. 33).

Marks, S. U., Schrader, C., & Levine, M. (1999). Paraeducator experiences in inclusive settings: Helping, hovering, or holding their own? *Exceptional Children, 65(3),* 315–328.

Minninger, J., & Goulter, B. (1991). *The perfect presentation.* New York: Doubleday.

Mueller, P. H., & Murphy, F. V. (2001). Determining when a student requires paraeducator support. *Teaching Exceptional Children, 33*(6), 22–27. A process is outlined that helps IEP teams determine when to assign paraeducators to support students with disabilities.

Pickett, A. L. (1988). *The employment and training of paraprofessional personnel: A technical assistance manual for administrators and staff developers.* New York: City University of New York, National Resource Center for Paraprofessionals in Education and Related Services, Center for Advanced Studies in Education.

Riehl, C. J. (2000). The principal's role in creating inclusive schools for diverse students: A review of normative, empirical, and critical literature on the practice of educational administration. *Review of Educational Research, 70*(1), 55–81.

Riggs, C. G. (2001). Ask the paraprofessionals: What are your training needs? *Teaching Exceptional Children, 33*(3), 78–83.

Stanley, A. L., & Vasa, S. F. (1998). How paraeducators learn on the Web. *Teaching Exceptional Children, 30*(5), 54–59.

Thurston, L. P. (2000). *The positive para: Helping students develop positive social skills.* Lawrence, KS: Curriculum Solutions.

Wallace, T., Shin, J., Bartholomay, T., & Stahl, B. J. (2001). Knowledge and skills for teachers supervising the work of paraprofessionals. *Exceptional Children, 67*(4), 520–533.

CHAPTER ELEVEN

RELATED-SERVICES PERSONNEL, RESOURCES, AND TECHNOLOGY IN COLLABORATIVE SCHOOL ENVIRONMENTS

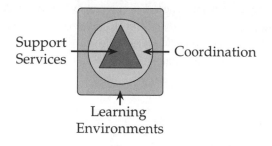

Resources for learning include people (experts, models, coaches, guides); places (sites, sources); and things (data, materials, artifacts, equipment, and technology systems and procedures). The possibilities are virtually unlimited—local colleges and universities; business, industry, and professions; special-interest groups in the community; city, county, and state agencies; homes with talented parents and grandparents; local service organizations; foreign student exchange; museums; libraries; vocational and technical schools; media; recreation; county extension offices; senior-citizen centers; even classrooms where students help other students. This wealth of resources is a rich pool from which to draw for students' special learning needs. As Helen Keller once said to remind us all, "Alone we can do so little, together we can do so much."

Consulting and collaborating teachers can be very effective catalysts for learning by finding multiple resources in and beyond school facilities and matching them with students' interests and needs. When consulting and collaborating, they have many opportunities to locate and coordinate the services of mentors, resource speakers, experts, adjudicators, and technology and media specialists.

Networking and interaction among general and special education teachers, paras, related-services and support personnel, administrators, and outside individuals and agencies will increase learning and production opportunities. In order to obtain even more resources for schools and students, school personnel should consider submitting proposals to funding agencies. Technology can be used in many and varied ways to help educators "work smarter, not harder" for student's learning needs.

Support services provide the content focus of this chapter (triangle). The process (circle) is coordination. Learning environments, within and beyond school sites, are the context (square).

FOCUSING QUESTIONS

1. What can related-services personnel and support personnel contribute to learning programs for students with special needs by collaborating on a team with general and special education teachers and who will coordinate these efforts?

2. What transition services are to be provided for students with special needs?

3. How can collaborative consultation solidify needed collaborative links among various agencies of home, school, and community to serve students' special needs?

4. How might school personnel seek out resources to enhance school environments and learning programs for special needs?

5. In what ways can technology assist school and home educators?

KEY TERMS

Educational Resources
    Information Center (ERIC)
*Federal Grants and Contracts
    Weekly*
Federal Register

grant funds
home-school-community
    collaboration
interagency collaboration
related-services personnel

Request for Proposal (RFP)
shell/template
support personnel
technology
transition services

RELATED-SERVICES AND SUPPORT PERSONNEL AS COLLABORATORS AND FACILITATORS

An ancient proverb counsels us that a child's life is like a piece of paper on which every passer-by leaves a mark. Bronfenbrenner (1973) stressed that all members of society have the responsibility to teach society's children. A typical community has three kinds of agencies for education—informal, nonformal, and formal (Seay, 1974). Families and neighborhoods are informal for education. Churches, media, and cultural centers are examples of nonformal agencies, and schools and universities are considered formal agencies.

VIGNETTE 11

The setting is the kitchen of a home where a middle-school student and mother are sitting at the kitchen table.

Mother: I see a note here from your teacher saying that you need to make up an important math test you missed yesterday.

Child: Uh-huh, I missed it because yesterday was Tuesday.

Mother: What does that have to do with the math test?

Child: Well, on Tuesdays I'm supposed to see Mrs. Evans, but she wasn't there. So I went to Mr. Bowman instead.

Mother: Who is Mrs. Evans?

Child: She's the reading teacher. I see her Tuesdays and Thursdays, from 1:30–2:30, but she was sick yesterday.

Mother: So you saw Mr. Bowman. Who is he?

Child: The special education teacher I see for more help with reading, but mostly with spelling and my workbooks. He got called to another school for a meeting, so he sent me to Jeanette.

Mother: Now wait a minute—who is Jeanette?

Child: Gee, mom, I thought you told the principal you and dad would keep up with my school program.

Mother: I'm *trying*!

Child: Anyway, Jeanette is the high school girl who tutors me in reading.

Mother: Oh?

Child: It's O.K. She's nice. She wants to be a teacher someday. Mrs. Bagley helped me work it out.

Mother: And *who* is Mrs. Bagley?

Child: The counselor. She says working with Jeanette is good for me, and for her, too.

Mother: And just what does Ms. Anderson think about all of this?

Child: Uh, who's she?

Mother: Your *classroom teacher*!

Child: Oh, yeah, I forgot all about her.

(This child's schedule underscores the complexity of the school day and accentuates the need for communication, cooperation, and coordination among an array of school personnel.)

—Adapted from Michelle Berg

Schools are required by the Individuals with Disabilities Education Act (IDEA, IDEA 1997), and Section 504 of the Rehabilitation Act of 1973, to provide an array of services for students with disabilities. These services range from health and medical services, to physical and occupational therapy, in-home services, transportation, speech pathology and audiology, psychological services, recreation and counseling services, and much more. (See Figure 11.1.) As mandated by P.L. 94-142, multidisciplinary teams determine student eligibility for special education, decide on the most appropriate placement, and monitor progress after placement. Collaboration is essential for identifying the needs or problems, and for exploring program adaptations that address them.

FIGURE 11.1 Related Services/Support Personnel

These roles can assist general and special education classroom teachers and school administrators in providing for students' academic, emotional, social, and physical needs:

Adaptive Physical Education	Parent Counseling Training
Art Therapy	Parent Volunteers
Assistive Technological Devices/Services	Physical Therapy (PT)
Audiology	Reading Specialist
Counseling	Recreational Services
Custodian	School Health Services
Dance Movement/Drama Therapy	School Psychologist
Food Services	Secretarial/Receptionist Services
Media/Library/Technology Specialists	Security Services
Medical Diagnosis	Senior Citizens/Grandparents
Mentors/Apprenticeship Supervisors	Social Work Services
Music Therapy	Special Education Administration/Supervision
Occupational Therapy (OT)	Speech/Language Services
Other Aides	Student Teachers
Paraeducator (para)	Transportation (Bus/Cab Services)

Services such as those displayed in Figure 11.1 are tapped to provide appropriate education programs for children having disabilities that range well beyond the traditional concept of basic education (Zirkel & Knapp, 1993). Such services must be real and substantial. They are defined and determined by how they relate to the student's IEP. Zirkel and Knapp cite numerous court cases, along with the background and outcomes for each case, that describe services school districts must provide. They make several recommendations for schools, including:

1. Do not reject parental requests for related services.
2. Separate related-services obligations under IDEA from those under Section 504.
3. Determine the school's obligation on a case-by-case basis according to the student's defined disability.
4. Distinguish between reasonable benefits and optimal education.
5. Follow due process considerations carefully to avoid grounds for an appeal.

TRANSITION SERVICES

Transition is an umbrella term for activities and opportunities that prepare students for significant changes in their lives. It can be described as the process of moving from one service delivery system to another (Fowler, Donegan, Lueke, Hadden, & Phillips, 2000). The changes and movements include transition in and out of preschool, transition from elementary to junior high or middle school and junior high to high school, and transition from high school to work or postsecondary education (*CEC Today,* April/May 1997, p. 1).

Transition most often is used to indicate change from school to adult living. This means going beyond job acquisition, to independent living, community participation, and financial management. Students with special needs must have early training to develop skills for making such changes and to move smoothly from one educational setting to another during their school years.

Transition in Early Childhood

Concern for preschoolers from poverty-level environments and other conditions of disadvantage gained momentum in the 1960s. Passage of Public Law 99-457 in 1986 expanded attention to preschoolers. Public schools now are required to provide special services for children age three and above who have disabilities. Public Law 99-457 has gone far beyond classroom concerns to include family, social workers, speech and language pathologists, medical personnel, and other professionals. The law authorizes funding for state grants and for experimental, demonstration, and outreach programs that are multidisciplinary in nature. An increase in services for preschool children with disabilities calls for cooperation among professionals, parents, and other caregivers. Collaboration, consultation, and teamwork are at the heart of these programs.

Early intervention programs for infants and toddlers with disabilities proliferated following the early childhood legislation. Parents and other caregivers outside the school now play a more integral part in the education and well-being of these children. Most disabilities of children in the early intervention programs are severe; therefore, services of specialists from several disciplines usually are necessary. Families play an integral part in the therapy through home-based programs. In these programs, therapists go into the homes to provide stimulation for the children, and guidance and instruction for the parents. Staff and parents are in collaboration with all available resources, including health and medical personnel, social services personnel, public school personnel, and community resources such as preschool and day-care centers.

Federal legislation (P.L. 102-119) requires that states develop interagency agreements to address roles and responsibilities for transition from early intervention services to preschool services and to provide guidance for local communities through specification of state level responsibilities (Fowler, Donegan, Lueke, Hadden, & Phillips, 2000). Preparation of such agreements is a daunting task, requiring skillful collaboration by team members. Issues to be dealt with include transmission of information from one agency to another, preparation of child and family for services, provision of services in least restrictive environments, service delivery for children who turn three late in the school year or during the summer, use of individualized family services plans (IFSPs), and consideration of the way eligibility for services is determined (Fowler, et al., 2000). The interagency agreement and its implementation should be monitored and evaluated on a regular basis.

Transition from the preschool settings to kindergarten school programs also calls for strong, continuous efforts in collaborative school consultation. While formal programs such as Head Start and Follow Through for young children have been successful in and of themselves, as stated earlier P.L. 99-457 reaches far beyond classroom interventions. Preschool teachers should identify essential skills needed in the local kindergarten in order to prepare children for that setting (Beckhoff & Bender, 1989; McCormick & Kawate, 1982; Salisbury

& Vincent, 1990). Their contributions to elementary school programs are invaluable for getting new kindergarten students off to a successful start.

Transition from School to Work

At the opposite end of the continuum from early childhood needs are the needs of students leaving school to enter the world of work and adult living. Heightened awareness of this important transition period for young people with disabilities grew in the 1980s, when program goals for serving students with disabilities focused on obtaining educational services that could help them lead meaningful and productive lives. One of the realities was that no one parent, teacher, or counselor can adequately provide all the necessary assistance. A team effort is needed by every party contributing services for the welfare of the students.

The 1990s educational and social reform movements directed considerable attention to youth who have special needs (Halpern, 1992). Requirements for transition services to this age-group population were modified by IDEA 1997. The IDEA amendments call for inclusion of a statement in the student's IEP by age fourteen that focuses on courses of study such as vocational education, and also a statement that the student has been informed of the legal rights that transfer to the student when reaching the age of majority. Transition services are to be a coordinated set of activities including instruction, related services, community experiences, employment and adult living objectives; therefore, extensive interagency collaboration is needed. Schools now are responsible for generating Individual Transition Plans (ITPs) to assess students' career interests and help them focus on career possibilities. Community support is given through vocational transition liaisons, job coaching, work-awareness classes, and school employment.

Without concerted team effort, students with disabilities will be hard-pressed to make a successful transition to adult life. More than 50 percent remain unemployed or underemployed. Students, parents, teachers, guidance counselors, and other support personnel need to contribute to development of the ITP. In order for the transition process to be successful, all parties and agencies must work together systematically to plan for it (Clark & Knowlton, 1988; Rusch & Menchett, 1988). Collaborative consultation has been helpful in providing this support (Sileo, Rude, & Luckner, 1988).

INTERAGENCY COLLABORATION

Clinical-school-community collaboration for delivery of services to children can be traced back to the end of the nineteenth century (McMahon, Ward, Pruett, Davidson, & Griffith, 2000), but the twenty-first century now demands better delivery of special services by agencies called on to assist with special needs. One model is the full-service school that guides organization of service delivery systems for children in high-risk environments (Dryfoos, 1994). However, some "flies in the ointment" of the collaboration needed for effective interagency services are legal and ethical questions about informed consent, confidentiality, and responsibility, as well as with defense of professional turf, and adherence to traditional modes of operating (McMahon, et al., 2000). Collaborative consultants must be attuned to factors that facilitate collaboration and then work toward skillful application of the best consultative and collaborative practices. Also, meaningful roles for classroom teachers, parents, *and* the students themselves in the collaborative activities must be defined.

ROLES FOR RELATED-SERVICES AND SUPPORT PERSONNEL

Two transition service providers in secondary schools are vocational education teachers and school counselors. Planning is to be coordinated among special education, vocational education, and out-of-school adult service agencies. Students and their families must be collaborating participants in the discussions. IDEA stipulates the need for setting transition goals and interagency linkages and for the integration of these into the IEP. In this way the linkages are made before the student exits the school environment. School administrators are responsible for facilitating the collaboration, outlining roles and responsibilities, and designating resources.

Related-services and support personnel for students also include those serving in areas coordinated with school programs such as transportation, speech pathology, audiology, psychological services, physical and occupational therapy, recreation, counseling, library and media service, medical and school health, social work, parent counseling and training, cultural agencies, and transition-to-work and internship supervisors. Special resource services from outside the school include a multitude of other roles, ranging from Scout leaders, to 4-H leaders, private music and art instructors, and synagogue or church-school teachers. There also are media representatives: speakers, mentors, tutors, judges of events and products, and community partners. Extender services can be provided by those in libraries, parks, colleges, industries, businesses, and professions. Special activities, managed through clubs, workshops, interests groups, travel, and the like, are an important part of special services for special needs. Doctors and dentists teach and advise within their professional roles, and some request information from school personnel for more insight prior to their medical interventions.

A frequently overlooked source of help that more and more schools are learning to value and use is senior citizens, including grandparents of students, to instruct, demonstrate, relate experiences, and model for children and youth. Schools and universities also house a variety of support personnel that can assist with student needs. In addition, they are catalysts for the increasingly popular practice of using community resources to accentuate learning (Dettmer, 1980). Another source for help with student learning is other students. Cooperative and collaborative learning activities, peer tutoring, and coaching give students opportunities to share their own new knowledge and provide service to others.

Consulting teachers find it helpful to have a resource notebook of potential resource personnel. A school-related group such as the Parent Teacher Organization or Association for Retarded Citizens, committee of teachers, or a students' group seeking a service project, could develop a Community Resources Information Page format for the school and compile individual pages into a Community Resources Notebook. Persons or agencies targeted for inclusion in the notebook could be contacted for their permission to be included and for information to enter on the page. Figure 11.2 shows an example of a resource template. The notebook should be reviewed and updated periodically to keep it current and useful.

Each school also has a number of ancillary personnel without whom school life would be uncomfortable and disorganized. These include people in support roles such as food-service staff, secretaries, transportation staff, paraeducators, custodians, and volunteer aides. Just as the roles of consultant, consultee, and client are interrelated and interchangeable according to the focus of the consultation, the roles and responsibilities of related, support, and ancillary service personnel interrelate and interchange according to the part each plays in the student's education. For example, transportation personnel are integral to the programs

FIGURE 11.2   Community Resources Information Page

Name of Individual or Agency _____

Phone Number _____   Fax _____   E-Mail _____

Address _____

Occupation or Emphasis _____

Area(s) of Expertise/Contribution _____

Preference for Grade Level or Staff Area _____

Preference for Group Size with Which to Work _____

Time of Day Preferred _____

Preference for Day(s) of Week and Month(s) of Year _____

Maximum Times Would Care to Assist in a Year _____

Special Arrangements Needed _____

Special Equipment Required _____

Any Further Clarifications _____

Record of Dates Contributed, with Description of Activities of the Contribution:

_____

_____

For More Information Contact (Resource Personnel) _____

(School Personnel) _____

of special education students beyond picking them up and delivering them home again. They are a key link between home and school, being the first to see the student in the morning and often the last of the school staff to see them in the afternoon. They transport students from school to school and program to program while adhering to tight schedules and sometimes unpredictable weather and traffic conditions. They can play an active role in a referral process for special education and can also help with intervention programs. They may be involved as partners in reward and reinforcement systems for students or in extending learning activities beyond the classroom.

Transportation staff further support students by respecting their differences and needs and by collaborating with other school staff for schedules, incentives, and other modifications. One driver of the special education bus displays school work in the bus. She also has a chart for the "Star" bus student of the week. She explains that because it is the special education bus, she wants to make their bus ride special. She makes an effort to collaborate with teachers, adhering carefully to special schedules so students are not late or left stranded at a building.

Sometimes transportation staff might be the consultant, and a teacher for a student with mental retardation could be the consultee who needs information about the student's social interaction or neighborhood environment. A librarian could be a consultant to help a gifted program teacher, as consultee, select and locate resources. The school psychologist could contribute valuable information about the purposes, interpretation, and uses of tests. The training of counselors in both individual guidance and group guidance techniques makes them helpful resources in staff development activities and problem-solving sessions. School nurses and social workers contribute valuable data in consultations and staffings. They are often able to target seemingly insignificant data toward important aspects of problem-identification. An understanding custodian has always been regarded as a teacher's best friend and helpmate in the school setting. This is especially relevant to the special education teacher's responsibilities. Consultants can encourage custodians to be involved in planning and monitoring special programs for students with special needs. All of these examples extend the concept of interchanging consultant, consultee, and client roles, as suggested in Chapter 1.

■ ■ ■ ■ ■

APPLICATION 11.1
IDENTIFYING ROLES TO HELP WITH STUDENT INTERESTS AND NEEDS

Think of other related- and support-services roles beyond those listed in Figure 11.1 that you might call on to assist with special needs and interests of students through consultation and collaboration with schools. Think "outside the box" to come up with people such as country extension agents, museum curators, and more. Describe practical ways in which they could be of special service with individual students or groups of students.

Array of Services for Inclusive, Collaborative Schools

Other chapters have focused on the teacher's restructured role in collaborative and inclusive schools, but roles of support services personnel also must be modified. When students need services such as physical therapy, occupational therapy, or speech therapy, a decision must be made about where to provide the service. In many inclusive schools the therapist removes the child from the group while providing the service directly in the classroom. This arrangement can cause considerable apprehension on the part of some teachers (Schlax, 1994). These fears can be reduced by having only one therapist at a time working with the child and by integrating therapies with the classroom routine.

In reality, the majority of students with special needs are assigned to general classrooms, even though they may attend resource rooms or work with consulting teachers for a portion of the school day. In order to serve their special learning and behavioral needs, support services and classroom extender services must be integrated into their educational programs. Pearce (1996) stresses the need to work with specialists in order to adapt curriculum to special needs. She recommends that special education teachers work with all students in the classroom to plan activities that classroom teachers may not be able to do on their own. Having another teacher alongside may take getting used to, but is well worth the effort when they can get twice as much done.

Sometimes therapists can work with all the students in the class to avoid singling out those with disabilities. When therapies such as physical therapy or occupational therapy require space, it might be possible to provide it in the classroom. Many classroom teachers welcome such a partnership, which can occur as a normal part of the classroom routine such as during "show-and-tell".

A group of teachers in a special project to include students with severe disabilities in their general education classrooms reported that the most helpful aspects of the specialist support they received included: Shared framework and goals; physical presence; validation of the teacher's contribution; and teamwork (Giangreco, Dennis, Cloninger, Edelman, & Schattman, 1993). When problems did appear, they tended to be caused by one or more of these:

- Separate goals by specialists
- Disruption to the class routine
- Overspecialization in special education practices

Both teacher and consultant needed to consider more fully the context of the regular classroom and to respect values and needs of that classroom, its students, and its teacher. In this study, which was to analyze the benefits of inclusion for students with severe disabilities, 17 of the 19 teachers reported that they were transformed by their experience. Not only were their attitudes toward the students changed, in some cases the teachers said their attitudes about themselves were changed as well (Giangreco et al., 1993).

Communication, cooperation, and coordination among general educators, special education teachers, support and related personnel, administrators, and ancillary staff will help ensure that collaboration has the best possible likelihood of success as an integral educational process. Several concrete steps can be taken. See Figure 11.3 on integrating efforts when collaborating with specific role groups.

Using Library and Media Resources

Libraries and media centers are repositories of tremendous amounts of information. Conceivably, no other public service center has changed more than the library in the past half-century. It now is a teaching and learning system, a network for interactive learning, a storehouse for artifacts to enhance learning, a workplace for development of interests and skills, and much more. The "Shhhhh!" of the librarian has been replaced with the hum and clicks of computers, the queries and responses of information-seekers and technical assistants, the sliding of printed materials into organizers, and the buzz of small groups sharing information or problem-solving. Many times corners and tables of libraries and media centers are set up for instructing students with special needs using modified curriculum materials and strategies.

FIGURE 11.3   Integrating Efforts through Collaboration

Collaborative consultants can integrate and collaborate with other educators in these ways:

With general education teachers:
1. Establish joint ownership of the student and the learning situation.
2. Respect the views of all.
3. Keep problems "in house."
4. Request regular interaction and feedback from them.

With other special education colleagues:
1. Openly deal with the discomfort of having others give critique and feedback.
2. Arrange and coordinate planned interactions.
3. Together develop support systems.

With support and related-services personnel:
1. Become more knowledgeable about their roles and responsibilities.
2. Make sure to integrate major ideas they produce.
3. Plan and implement student programs that reflect coordinated involvement and not fragmentation.

With building administrators:
1. Inform them in as brief and practical a manner as possible.
2. Don't carry tales from a school/district to others.
3. Don't be a spy, or judge, even if asked.
4. Request regular feedback as to your own effectiveness.

With attorneys/hearing officers:
1. State your credentials, certifications, training, and experiences relative to the case.
2. State the nature and extent of knowledge about the student.
3. Discuss assessments, curricula, and modifications used, and their reliability, validity, and appropriateness.
4. Explain all terms, using no acronyms or jargon.
5. Remain calm, honest, and cooperative.

With legislators:
1. Be brief, accurate, and substantiating with all material delivered.
2. Thank legislators for their past interest and help.
3. State situations realistically without unreasonable demands.
4. Consider the whole picture, as the legislator must, and not just one's own primary interest.

With the public:
1. Be perceptive about issues of culture, diversity, and conflicting interests.
2. Demonstrate reasonable expectations while upholding standards and delivering challenges.
3. Express your dedication to students and commitment to excellent schools.

In order to use this rich educational resource most efficiently, consultants and collaborators should be familiar with basic units, including:

Educational Resources Information Center (ERIC), a U.S. federal information system of 16 clearinghouses throughout the country, with the database available at www.eduref.org

Education Index, an index of titles and citations arranged by topic headings and author headings

Reader's Guide to Periodical Literature, titles and citations covering a wide variety of topics

CompuServe, Dialog, and similar on-line databases

Educational journals and reviews. See Vockell and Asher (1995) for a table of the fifteen most frequently cited journals by *Encyclopedia of Educational Research.*

Interlibrary loans, another useful source of information for the needs of consulting teachers working with wide ranges of student learning and behavioral needs

Consultants as Coordinators for an Array of Services

Labels and categories for school personnel are relatively unimportant within a collaborative climate. The service provided for a child's need determines the role. Thousand, Fox, Reid, Godek, Williams, and Fox (1986) emphasize that schools have many natural, untapped pools of skills and interest across a wide range of unassigned areas. When teachers can form teams and move among roles, positive ripple effects occur. Examples are increased adult-to-pupil ratio in a learning program and ability of the school to provide more personalized instruction (Nevin, Thousand, & Paolucci-Whitcomb, 1990).

In order to facilitate appropriate support services for students, consultants can do several things:

- Become knowledgeable about the roles and responsibilities of support personnel.
- Strive for IEPs and informal learning plans that include all facets of the student's learning and involve all roles that will help the student succeed.
- Within the bounds of necessary confidentiality and ethical school practices, ask support personnel for their viewpoints and opinions about helping students with special needs.
- Inform them about the consultation role, schedule, and responsibilities.
- Monitor the student's performance across all kinds of school, home, and community learning in a variety of situations.
- Provide time in the teachers' schedules for co-planning, co-teaching, and following up.
- Show ongoing support for inclusionary practices.
- Include support-services personnel in staff-development activities, encouraging their involvement and collaboration.
- Have specific in-services for them to provide awareness and encourage collaboration.

Lugg and Boyd (1993) caution against "contrived collegiality" that is administratively regulated and compulsory. They contend such an environment erodes trust and communication, even that which may already be in effect. Therefore, they recommend restructuring schools into schools-within-schools, where teachers and students are organized into teams that work and play together for sustained periods of time—perhaps over several years—so that strong interpersonal relationships can flourish.

Along these lines of schools-within-schools, Murphy (1995) proposes the whole-faculty study group concept as a way of implementing school-improvement initiatives. Teachers can be organized into small study groups of four to six individuals who meet weekly for about an hour to have collegial interchange that focuses on whole-school improvement and how to help students learn more.

Staff developers LaBonte, Leighty, Mills, and True (1995) set up study groups of teachers, creating collaborative time for them to improve programs and share new practices, and to link whole-school improvement with increased student achievement. One focus-team format consisted of having the principal and four or more teachers from each participating school attend a week-long institute and develop a plan for leading their schools in implementation of whole-faculty study groups. These educators believe that whole-faculty study groups are promising vehicles for school improvement that increases both student and teacher learning. They assert that professional development personnel must create interagency collaboration in order to bring about changes that increase student achievement.

Collaborative School Consultants as Coordinators for Interagency Collaboration

A vast array of social service agencies exists for serving students with special needs; however, their services often overlap and many are large, unwieldy bureaucracies with a maze of bewildering requirements (Guthrie & Guthrie, 1991; Hodgkinson, 1989). The situation calls for extensive collaboration among agencies for productive integration of services. Educators may be the most feasible link in cooperation and coordination among organizations and agencies that serve children with special needs. As budget constraints restrict the continuation or growth of many educational and social programs, special education consultants can play pivotal roles in the future for serving children with special needs. They are in good positions to become effective, cost-efficient links between education and other social agencies.

Home-School-Community Networks

Cross-agency collaboration among providers of education and providers of human services and other child- or family-based activities is a reform idea which has transformed services for students and families in many settings (Jensen & Kiley, 1998; Shaver, Golan, & Wagner, 1996). Because of overlapping needs, multiple needs, and inadequacies of many systems, such collaboration is a promising approach to meeting the complex needs of children and families. When agencies and community organizations connect to build on the strengths of each and respond to the needs and realities of students and their families, these efforts surpass the ability of any single institution to meet diverse and difficult needs.

For educational consultants, this means working directly with families, communities, and other agencies and promoting a shared responsibility among agencies. It means learning to relate more positively with other organizations and breaking out of institutional traditions, habits, and norms and embracing a new way of doing business (Shaver et al., 1996). This is not easy. There are many barriers to cross-agency collaboration; this is one reason it is not common practice in most communities. Capper (1996) suggests that barriers include power struggles among agencies; divided loyalties; shortages of time, funds, and personnel to collaborate; and threats to local control of pedagogy. However, students benefit when the perspective is holistic rather than isolating the student and student problems in the school. Collaboration can proactively address student and family needs beyond academics (Capper, 1996).

Consultants must consider how to work together with different services agencies, different professional cultures, and different norms and standards (Shaver et al., 1996). Many of the strategies, skills, and attitudes addressed in previous chapters can guide educators in developing good working relationships with noneducation colleagues and in resolving major obstacles to collaboration and service integration.

The twenty-first Century Community Learning Centers in schools across the nation are examples of collaborative efforts that combine the resources of schools, universities, families, volunteers, and community-based organizations to serve students beyond the school day. Communities in Schools unites community resources such as health care and mental health professionals with teachers, parents, principals, and volunteers on behalf of children (Barbour & Barbour, 2001). Many highly successful outcomes have been realized for students and families. Business-school partnerships have also shown promise for impacting schools, communities, and students. Several student entrepreneurship programs have boosted student achievement and the local economy (SEDL, 2000a). Critical features of these partnerships include: strong leadership and support from local power brokers; open communication; respect for differences in skills, ideas, cultures, and values of other partners; decision-making based on common ground; long range goals; careful planning; continuous assessment; and keeping the community informed (Barbour & Barbour, 2001).

The Southwest Educational Development Lab in Austin, TX, suggests these steps for collaborative interagency projects (SEDL, 2000b):

1. Convene a group
2. Assess student and community needs
3. Establish purposes and priorities
4. Learn to work together
5. Plan the project
6. Implement the plan
7. Assess the results
8. Sustain the achievement

Suggestions for increasing group members' capacity to work together include:

- Cross-train in each others' procedures and norms
- Build a sense of community
- Obtain and maintain high levels of support at all organizational levels
- Develop new joint procedures and eliminate conflicting ones
- Write policies that encourage integrated services and interagency collaboration
- Remember, the more democratic, the better
- Work to develop high levels of trust
- Define the decision-making process

School-community collaboration efforts require patience, diligence, and new perspectives about what is important in teaching and learning. Cross-agency collaboration creates multiple opportunities for learning and enhances the diversity of experiences for students with disabilities. It utilizes and exploits the informal curriculum of the community. The results will be longer-term, consistent, and community-developed educational supports for student success. The challenges may be great, but there are resources in educators' own "back yards" that will benefit students.

Home-School-Community Collaboration.   Schools, families, and communities can be considered overlapping spheres of influence on children's learning (Epstein, 1995). Much of what students learn comes from the experiences, associations, and interactions they have outside and beyond scheduled school activities. This secondary curriculum may be a dominant part of any student's life (Barbour & Barbour, 2001), especially when traditional or formal school curricula are not compatible with the special needs of many students. Community settings offer many alternative therapies or learning environments that promote socialization, language, and cognitive and physical development. Nonschool facilities in the community provide the added component of parental involvement, and linkages to the community and to other institutions in the community. This "curriculum of the community" (Barbour & Barbour, 2001) has great potential for enhancing the social networks of students and families, inculcating natural resources into the education of students, and providing services such as entertainment, recreation, and informal education. In addition, this informal curriculum provides involvement and collaboration of several organizations within a community (Barbour & Barbour, 2001).

Because family/school/community partnerships are often more difficult with parents of students with disabilities (Plunkett, 1997), educational consultants must consider the community an integral part of the preparation of all students for a successful adult life. Family-friendly educational programs should contain nonschool elements.

INTERAGENCY COORDINATION OF RELATED AND SUPPORT SERVICES

It will be a challenge for educators to form new paradigms that decompartmentalize services for students with special needs. Guthrie and Guthrie (1991) state that service providers must step outside the boundaries of their job descriptions on occasion to do what needs to be done for students. They suggest going to community centers, schools, and homes, devoting more time than usual to families and outside resources. These functions are compatible with the processes and content familiar to those in school-consultation roles. Guthrie and Guthrie warn against an "all-talk, no action" posture, excessive jargon, and failure to follow up. These points are readily recognizable to school consultants, who have developed skills in avoiding such pitfalls.

"If you think interpersonal and interagency consultation is challenging, wait until you try interagency collaboration!" says one experienced educational consultant. Turf issues, lack of clarity on fiscal responsibilities, and shared personnel, facilities, and equipment agreements are among the barriers to successful interagency collaboration. On the other hand, many educators have had experience with interagency collaboration while working with Interagency Coordinating Councils, as established under Part H of P.L. 99-457 (the Handicapped Infant and Toddler Program), and with Community Transition Councils, as established under P.L. 101-476. Others have valuable experience working with other human service agencies in developing programs such as "One-Stop Shopping" and "Wrap-around"

programs. These experiences in collaboration, difficult though they may have been, will
serve participants well as they assume new roles in interagency collaboration.

As a process, collaboration is a means to an end rather than an end in itself. The desired end is to engender more effective educational outcomes for students with special needs.
Schools are not alone in their responsibility for removing barriers that keep students from
succeeding in the adult world. Personnel in mental health, employment and training, child
development, recreation, health, and welfare services, as well as education, have a vital interest in promoting school success for all children. (See Figure 11.4.)

Many of the families of children with special needs face a multitude of problems and
require services beyond the realm of education. Too often these services are fragmented
without a coherent, binding strategy to meet basic family goals (Bruner, 1991). The Education and Human Services Consortium (Melaville & Blank, 1991) proposes that education,
health, and human service agencies join each other as co-equals in orchestrating the delivery of services to children and families. System-level collaboration is based on the reality

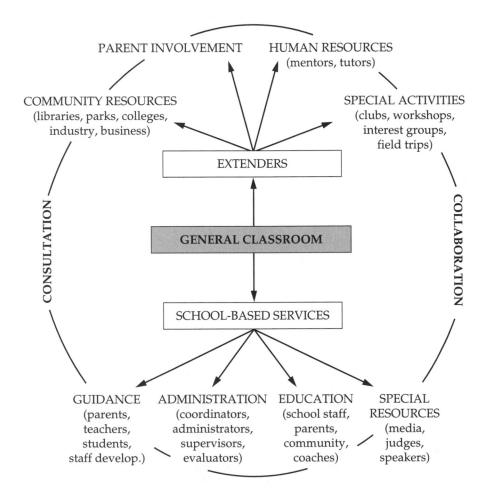

FIGURE 11.4   School-Based Extenders and Services

that no one agency can provide all necessary services for children with disabilities and their families. Collaborative strategies can:

- Help provide better services to families who are part of several human service systems.
- Keep children and families from falling through the cracks by ensuring that they receive needed services.
- Reduce environmental risks to children.

When personnel within systems collaborate, they avoid service duplication, reduce the total cost of services, ensure fewer gaps in services, minimize conflict, and clarify responsibility.

Interagency collaboration includes these elements (Bruner, 1991):

1. Jointly developing and agreeing to a set of common goals and directions.
2. Sharing responsibility for obtaining the goals.
3. Working together to achieve the goals, using the expertise of each collaborator.

APPLICATION 11.2

IMPORTANT ROLES FOR STUDENT DEVELOPMENT

Use the technique of brainstorming, or the Idea Checklist technique from Chapter 5 to think of ways the following roles can be accessed for fullest development of student potential. Add to the list of roles if other viable ones emerge.

Special Education Facilitators	Educational/Social/Psychological Researchers
General Classroom Teachers	Staff Developers/Curriculum Coordinators
Building Administrators	Diversity Specialists
School Psychologists	Media Specialists/Librarians
Educational Policy-makers	Textbook/Curriculum Materials Publishers
Advocates for Schools	and Authors
Educational Psychologists	Mentors/Talent Coaches
University Faculty for Teacher Education	Special Education Program Evaluators
Pediatricians	Families/Parents/Siblings/Extended Family
Entrepreneurs and Innovators	Senior Citizens/Statesmen and
in the Community	Stateswomen/Notables

Common elements of interagency collaboration that contribute to the effectiveness and efficiency of efforts are:

Collaborative attitude. Recognize the need for collaboration and take the time to develop positive relationships among the team. Joint ownership will reduce conflict and problems.

Written guidelines. Formulate a written statement of philosophy that stands as the measure of all policies and actions. Delineate roles, responsibilities, and agreements for shared resources.

Team leadership. Leadership roles should be assigned, but they can be shared. Coordination and technical assistance are important roles.

Staff development. Cross-agency training can foster positive relationships and promote the development of the skills and processes of collaboration.

Collective input and supportive environment (Weber, 1994). Clarity of purpose comes from sharing obstacles individuals and agencies face and solutions they envision. Sharing relevant experiences and insights reduces barriers from cultural differences and promotes understanding and empathy.

Identifying and implementing collaborative strategies and evaluating their impact can be challenging. The ultimate goal is ensuring the future success of students with special needs by eliminating or reducing difficulties that place them at risk—infant mortality, delinquency, youth unemployment, child abuse and neglect, drug involvement, suicide, mental illness, and poverty. Interagency collaboration is not a "quick fix." It is time-consuming and process-intensive. It takes commitment and flexibility to discover new roles and relationships. These new roles and responsibilities utilize collaborative skills that require wide knowledge and much practice.

■ ■ ■ ■ ■ ▬▬

APPLICATION 11.3
ASSESSING STRENGTHS OF THE TEAM

Organize into small groups of three to five persons. Discuss the strengths that this group as a team could provide toward a collaborative effort of planning interventions for a student with disability or giftedness in the inclusionary classroom. A second phase of this activity could involve using a case-study approach to demonstrate those strengths in preparing an IEP or a classroom adaptation for the student described in the case study.

Sources for Assistance

Every community, large or small, urban or rural, accessible or isolated, wealthy or poor, has agencies and potential resources that can contribute meaningfully to learning programs for the special needs of children and adolescents. The consulting teacher will find it helpful to develop a directory of referral agencies, with addresses and phone numbers, to have available for consultations and staffings. As one example, a consulting teacher in a mid-size town in the Midwest prepared a referral directory containing more than one hundred sources of assistance. Some were national sources which could be called with a hot-line or an 800 number, such as the Missing Children's Network. Others were state-level agencies, including the Resource Center for the Handicapped. Still others were county agencies, such as the County Family Planning Clinic. But within this average town, many sources were available "just down the street," including a crisis center and a community theater.

Another special education teacher in a large town with a land-grant university found more than 200 agencies, from Alcoholics Anonymous and ACLD (Association for Adults and Children with Learning Disabilities) to Living with Cancer Group and MADD (Mothers Against Drunk Driving), to World Friendship Organization and Young Mom's Group. Resourceful consultants will involve personnel regularly from a variety of agencies to collaborate in planning and implementing student programs that provide assistance for students' special needs.

APPLICATION 11.4
SEARCHING FOR RESOURCES

Have a personal scavenger hunt, or go with a small group of your classmates or colleagues, to discover new resources for student and adult learning. Find people, places, and things that can enhance special abilities and serve special needs. As you do this, if someone asks what you are doing, explain and then engage them in conversation about education. Invite them to be advocates and collaborators in enterprises that will help students succeed in school.

CONVENTIONS AND WORKSHOPS AS RESOURCES
FOR PROFESSIONAL GROWTH

A convention, conference, or workshop provides an ideal opportunity for personal and professional growth of educators. The atmosphere for well-conducted functions typically is charged with energy and enthusiasm. A smorgasbord of activity choices usually is available to whet the appetites of adult learners. Participants can learn from interacting with each other as they renew acquaintances and make new connections.

One way to gain ultimate benefit from the experience is to prepare a convention plan beforehand. It could be modeled on the IEP that most educators have helped to prepare for their students. This plan, which could be called an ICP, or Individual Convention (Conference) Plan could include goals and objectives for the event, any methods and materials needed, anticipated time line for parts of the event, and an evaluation. For example, two goals and accompanying objectives (Dettmer & Landrum, 1997) might be:

- I will acquire information to assist me with home–school collaboration.
    I will network with individuals from districts with successful family partnerships.
    I will visit the display and materials areas to seek out materials to help develop rapport with potential parent partners.

- I will enhance my multicultural sensitivity.
    I will explore at least one new place, interact with at least two participants from other cultural and geographic areas, and try some new foods and activities characteristic of the locale.
    I will compile a list of consultants and possible speakers with expertise in multicultural perspectives.

Materials needed could include a leave of absence from the school administrator, lesson plans for the substitute teacher, descriptions of professional materials colleagues would like to have brought back from the event, an empty disassembled box for bringing back or mailing back the resources, travel arrangements, and so forth. An evaluation could be a self-designed checklist, an interview by an interested colleague, or a report of the convention critiqued by the school administrator who granted released time to attend.

Many concomitant benefits are possible from a well-chosen and enthusiastically attended conference. Networks of collaboration can be established among educators with common interests and concerns. Leadership abilities are honed by submitting proposals and making presentations at the event. Partnerships can develop when colleagues or parents are invited to attend. One concept that is effective for some convention themes is a team model in which a classroom teacher, a special education teacher, and an administrator from the same building attend the event together.

Professional events are meant to be both invigorating and informative. Participants can gain the most from the experience by planning their time, getting to sessions early before they are closed, making sure to visit the exhibits area for new ideas and materials, going to any events that recognize outstanding educators or showcase student work, and setting one's sights on being rejuvenated by the entire experience. Preparing an ICP beforehand can help keep the convention-goer on track and focused.

GRANT PROPOSALS FOR EXTERNAL FUNDING

One of the most welcomed resources that school personnel can contribute is a funded grant proposal. Grant money is available from a wide variety of sources, including federal funds, state funds, private donations, foundations, local business, fund-raising activities, and corporations (Zimet, 1993). These sources provide funds with programs and projects in mind that fit their philosophies and goals. They set their own procedures, which must be followed explicitly by entrants if they wish to be in the running for receiving the grant.

Several benefits can be gained from submitting a collaborative grant proposal. The first is the collaboration experienced by the team, whether or not the grant proposal is funded. Few significant proposals are developed in these times that do not include a number of colleagues interacting to conceptualize and develop the plan and to carry out the project after it is funded. Some people have major roles and others serve in minor ways, but all can profit in tangible and intangible ways. Another benefit is the collection of resources and support needed to meet the goals of the grant. As resources are targeted, and letters of support are generated, more people become involved as supporters and advocates of school programs.

When a grant proposal is funded, then the benefits soar. Money and resources become available for carrying out projects that were only dreams or wishes before funding. This has an energizing, morale-boosting effect that can reverberate throughout a school system. The amounts of money do not need to be sizable for these positive outcomes to be realized. Some of the most invigorating projects have resulted from relatively small grant funds. The projects with the highest payoffs are those that generate ripple effects well beyond the grant funding.

School consultants and collaborators, particularly those who have significant professional development responsibilities, are in ideal positions to seek grant funds. Even larger districts that employ grant-writers can use the participation of these personnel productively. School districts should designate individuals to be trained in grant-seeking techniques, for there are some important procedures that are vital to success of the endeavor.

Successful proposals emanate from an identified need. A good match must be found between that need and the philosophy and goals of an appropriate funding source. The proposal must be prepared correctly and submitted on time. Proposals that are not funded should not be cast aside, but critiqued thoroughly for possible revision and resubmission.

Proposal development begins with an idea and has two phases: (1) planning; and (2) preparation. The most productive strategy usually is to spend about 80 percent of time and energy on planning the project, and the remaining 20 percent on writing the proposal. Those who switch these priorities often end up with weak projects that are hard to carry out even if funded.

Funding Sources

Two general sources of funding are available—public agencies and private foundations. Most companies give some money away as part of their tax structure, and the grant-developer's challenge is convincing companies to give part of it to them (Zimet, 1993). Experts in grant production advise that requirements for proposals are somewhat different between public and private sources, so they must be studied carefully.

Preparing the Proposal

Grant-writing is a combination of technical writing and creative writing (Zimet, 1993). Three mistakes must be avoided at all costs: Failing to read instructions diligently; failing to match grant goals with funding sources; and missing deadlines. Because proposal preparation is hard work, astute grant-writers follow basic steps to avoid major pitfalls. They:

1. *Identify a need.* What is the problem that stems from that need? Is it potentially fundable? For example, high-priority topics for successful grant proposals in the mid-1990s included: gangs, violence, drugs, world-class standards, teachers for providing education to meet those standards, math and science education, teen pregnancy, inclusion, integrated curriculum, diversity, and computer literacy for both young people and adults. Priorities for later decades will likely shift to other areas of interest and need.

2. *Explore the research base* for the identified need. Watch for trends and for connections that link trends and fields.

3. *Get together a team* of productive people. Note the points in Chapter 1 about having a variety of skills and learning styles on the team. Having multiple perspectives and a wide range of competencies will vastly improve the proposal. Teams are particularly helpful for collecting the demographic data that will be required for properly executed proposal preparation.

4. *Identify possible funding sources.* Funding sources are listed in the *Federal Register.* Find out if someone in your district has access to this document. If not, suggest that someone be in charge of that, because benefits might prove to be significant! Several sources are available at many libraries. With telecommunications software and a modem, some sources can be obtained online. The Internet includes sources such as the Department of Education at http://www.ed.gov *or* at http://www.fdncenter.org. Each site has links to other sites and additional, more specific information.

5. *Obtain the guidelines* for the selected funding source(s). A guidelines packet is called "Request for Proposal," or RFP. From this point on, each step of the process requires an admonition—*Read the guidelines*! At this stage read to be sure there is a good fit between your idea and the funding source. Look for the ability of that source to meet your budget request, for directions on how to apply, for criteria to be used in evaluating the proposal, and most of all, for the *application deadline.* A proposal, even a superior one, submitted late is no proposal at all. The second way to guarantee that the proposal will not be considered is failure to stay within the guidelines.

6. The next step is to *design the project.* As stressed earlier, this phase should take up the major time and energy directed toward the project. Again, read the guidelines thoroughly and often. Typical parts of a proposal are: Description of who will manage the project; personnel involved in implementing and maintaining the project; description of project activities; evaluation plan for assessing the project's effectiveness; dissemination of project results; budget and justification; continuation of the project beyond funding dates; letters of support; and of course, the ubiquitous forms that must be filled out accurately and completely. These parts are weighted by funding agencies in varying percentages to determine the proposal's ranking among all submitted proposals, and those weight values are listed in the guidelines. Subcategories under description of the project include expected outcomes that tie back to the problem, objectives that relate to each of the activities, plan of operation, time line, data-collection procedures, and activities.

7. *The budget must be adequate* for the project, but not "padded." All items should be tied to the activities of the project and the key personnel costs involved. If set too low, it would signal poor planning that could undermine the project. Budgets provide for indirect costs (overhead), any cost sharing or subcontracting for services, and primarily, direct costs of the proposed project—salaries and fringe benefits, equipment, supplies and materials, travel (which is getting quite restrictive with many funding agencies), consultant fees, computer expenses, printing and duplicating, postage and telecommunication, along with other direct costs specific to the focus of the project.

8. *Interagency collaborative support* is a very desirable component of most grant projects, and a requirement of some agencies for submitted proposals.

9. *Establish contact with the funding agency* and put to good use any suggestions their program officers have for proposal development.

10. The most singularly important step is to *meet the deadline.* If it is not met, the proposal is eliminated and the time, energy, and costs expended in producing it are wasted.

When proposals are received by the funding agency, they are scanned for ten or twelve key elements, with the first four or five receiving the most attention (Shanteau, 1997):

1. *Identity.* Are the persons submitting well known to the agency?
2. *Topic.* Is it an appropriate topic for the program?
3. *Funding level.* Is the requested amount within the guidelines?
4. *Duration.* Is it within acceptable time limits?
5. *Plan.* What is the approach?
6. *Procedure.* What procedures will be used?

7. *References.* Who is cited, and in what related fields?
8. *Identity of the developer.* What is the background?
9. *Budget.* Do the categories and amounts make sense?
10. *Consultants.* Who are they, and do they add to the team?
11. *Format.* Does the proposal meet requirements?
12. *Double check.* Is anything missing?

If a proposal is not funded, the developer(s) should ask to receive the reviews. Reading reviewer comments is a form of professional development and can help make the next attempt more productive. If the review marks were good, but not quite good enough for the proposal to be selected, the proposal might be revised or modified and resubmitted.

Proposals are funded because of:

The benefits they promise to a targeted population
The uniqueness of the proposal if it is educationally sound
A strong case for local need
Strong collaborative efforts
Local efforts to help with funding
The potential to benefit both local and state or regional efforts
Strong evaluative components
The potential for longevity and positive ripple effects
Justifiable and reasonable budget requests (Stephens, 1994)

Ingredients for pursuing external funding successfully are: An innovative idea, a team of qualified individuals, a close fit with the funding source, and a well-written, persuasive, potentially contributive proposal. Another ingredient is that precious commodity of time. Requests for a professional day, with phone unplugged and no distractions, often are permitted by an optimistic administrator who understands what external funds, even in small amounts, can do to energize teachers and school programs. Some teachers might want to pool resources, each doing part of the project, and enjoying positive outcomes as collaborators.

Collaborative school consultants can contribute to their school systems by learning about grant-writing and developing their skills in this area. A grant-writing workshop for the school district is an excellent professional-development activity. Not only are large-scale grants a boon to service for students, mini-grants to individual teachers or schools for innovative programs are invigorating for staff and students alike.

■ ■ ■ ■ ■

APPLICATION 11.5
TRYING OUT THE PROPOSAL PLAN

As the proposal is being developed, try explaining your plan in 3 minutes to some impartial, objective colleagues or, better yet, to individuals outside the profession whose perspectives you value. If they do not understand it and become enthused by it, your plan probably needs more work or a different focus.

TECHNOLOGY IN COLLABORATIVE SCHOOL ENVIRONMENTS

Technology is revolutionizing the processes of consultation, collaboration, and teamwork in school settings. Educators in technology-rich environments are able to engage in many of their collaborative efforts continuously throughout the day without leaving their classrooms or offices. Information can be exchanged instantly rather than waiting until a later time or day for face-to-face meetings. Technology, of course, does not eliminate the need for face-to-face interaction; rather, it frees the team members' time together to deal with major issues instead of day-to-day background information. It improves the efficiency of other routine tasks such as writing, material development or data collection so more time will be available for collaborative activities.

Many definitions of technology have been documented. Kipnis (1997) explains his perception of technology as the use of systematic procedures to produce intended effects, defining our world and both restricting and facilitating choices we can make. He states that this provides much latitude in some instances but almost none in others. Another definition that encompasses a wide range of applications comes from the International Technology Education Association's 1993 issue of *The Technology Teacher,* quoting Wright and Lauda:

> Technology is a body of knowledge and actions, used by people, to apply resources in designing, producing, and using products, structures, and systems to extend the human potential for controlling and modifying the natural and human-made (modified) environment.

Using technology as a team may be a major reason that full inclusion of students with disabilities in general classroom settings is a feasible option (Lipsky, 1994; Male, 1994). Educators who are concerned about students with special needs can be powerful influences in providing leadership for the use of technology in inclusive classrooms to accommodate the special instructional needs of all students.

Technology can improve achievement and self-esteem of many students with disabilities and can be a powerful motivator for students who have experienced failure and frustration in school. It can empower students with disabilities by enabling them to accomplish things never before thought possible:

> Telecommunications and multimedia technologies such as interactive video bring the world into the classroom. Electronic communication devices allow students to speak and add their voices to those of their classmates. Adapted computers provide access to instruction in myriad subject areas from learning to count to calculus (Lewis, 1993, p. 3).

Electronic Technology for Managing Responsibilities

Walls of classrooms can be expanded through technology. Consider the common stumbling block to collaboration—the need for time. Computers and telecommunications are major time-savers in many ways:

- Messages sent at the convenience of one party while others read and respond to them at their convenience.
- Databases and information on student progress stored in a file-server and accessed by any team member at a convenient time.

- Notes added by team members that keep everyone on the team apprised of information or items of concern.
- Computer adaptation of assignments by teachers or resource personnel for meet students' needs.
- Copies of special instructions or worksheets sent by a consultant in one building to a teacher in another by way of computer FAX.

Interactive teams that reach across organizational boundaries, sometimes even including customers and vendors, use technologies such as electronic mail, broadcast FAX, teleconferencing and video conferencing to communicate with one another consistently and quickly. Digital pagers and cellular phones make team members accessible regardless of their location and mobility. Information is gathered rapidly and exchanged through databases and electronic bulletin boards.

The possibilities are unlimited. Lewis (1993) states ". . . technology can increase teacher's professional productivity and reduce the amount of time that must be spent in non-instructional classroom duties" (p. 126).

Telecommunications and Electronic Networks

Computer networks and electronic mail might be the most useful applications of technology for school consultants. Wires or cables can link computers within the building, known as a local area network (LAN) or outside to other areas, known as a wide area network (WAN). Users share software and communicate with one another in an efficient manner. With electronic networks, a consultant could prepare an adapted lesson or test and send it to the classroom where needed. The adapted lesson or test would be "waiting" for the teacher or students in the classroom to access at the appropriate time without the presence of the consultant. Conversely, a student might prepare a product in the classroom and send it to the consultant for review and feedback. So a computer network allows monitoring of student work and makes feedback to the student more immediate.

Another advantage of the electronic network is facilitation of interaction among the users, in this case consultants, co-teachers or team members. In some systems users can work simultaneously with the same program. For instance, team members could use a word processor to collaborate in developing a lesson plan, with each team member accessing the work of others and making changes or adding notes. This reduces the number of time-consuming, face-to-face meetings for team members with a comparable or even better outcome.

Electronic mail can replace irritating, time-wasting "phone tag" with efficient communication. E-mail allows information prepared on one computer to be sent by network to another computer. When all members of a collaborative team are connected to the e-mail system and regularly access the system, a message can be sent to one or more persons faster than it takes to walk down the hall to speak to those individuals.

Although it is possible for individuals to arrange for e-mail, most educators have the e-mail service facilitated through internal networks set up by the school system. This ensures that all district e-mail participants are using the same or compatible systems. Some advanced e-mail systems are capable of providing real time conferencing. An IEP conference or team-planning meeting could use such a system, thus saving the time and expense of everyone traveling to a single location. Messages can be designed more carefully than those delivered by phone and left in the voice-mail box.

However, e-mail is not a substitute for face-to-face interaction and conversations. Some think it can make us inappropriately reactive rather than proactive. The all-important element of nonverbal communication is missing, which can lead to misunderstandings. E-mail also necessitates careful e-mail practices in selecting appropriate recipients and in refraining from entering anything there that we would not want disclosed. Neither should complex issues and immediate needs be handled in this way.

Kruger, Struzziero, Kaplan, Macklem, Watts, and Weksel (2001) found that e-mail messages between teachers and school psychologists enhanced teacher knowledge with regard to working with students, but the e-mail messages reduced their feelings of professional isolation even more than they enhanced knowledge. Teachers viewed the messages as more helpful than did the school psychologists, perhaps due to absence of nonverbal cues which made it hard for the school psychologists to determine effects of the e-mails.

Electronic Scheduling Programs

Many consultants find a scheduling program useful. These programs are electronic calendars in which appointments and other commitments are entered. One special advantage is the way the program can handle recurring appointments. For example, if a team planning meeting is scheduled for 2:00 Friday afternoons, the consultant can enter that information; the program will automatically write in meeting reminders on the appropriate dates. Another advantage is the ability to view and print out daily, weekly, or monthly calendars. These calendars can be shared through the network if desired. Sharing privileges can be customized to allow one or many individuals the right to view or schedule appointments for all or part of a colleague's calendar. Hand-held computers have made the work lives of many busy educators more efficient and less stressful.

Information Services

Consultants, teachers, and students can use computers with modems to engage in communication with large host computer information systems. These systems offer a variety of options to users, ranging from electronic bulletin boards to conferencing capabilities. Potential uses for consultants and teachers include library searches and information bulletins relating to special needs of students with disabilities. Special bulletin boards can be created to address unique audiences. It is even possible to create local bulletin boards that are used by teachers in a single building or school district. A creative consultant or teacher might consider developing such a bulletin board where ideas that have worked in other classrooms can be shared with fellow teachers and consultants.

Information bulletin boards can be interesting to special educators. Technology specialists and many librarians in a school district may provide currently available information services and bulletin boards.

Internet Resources

Consultants can find a wide array of useful information and resources through Internet searches. Many others will become available in the years ahead. Consultants and consultees will find it helpful to collaborate on generating lists of key words for conducting Internet searches, and to work as a team to locate promising Website addresses.

FAX Communication

FAX (facsimile) machines represent yet another form of technology that can enhance the consultation and collaboration processes. Many school buildings have at least one FAX machine. Consultants who serve more than one building can make efficient use of the machines by sending letters, reports and other written products for use in another building, city, or state, over telephone wires. As previously noted, computers on an electronic network can FAX a document directly from a computer, without requiring a printout.

Monitoring Student Records

Databases and other types of management software can help teachers keep track of important information. Databases are most useful for organizing large amounts of information. Being equivalent to electronic filing cabinets, they allow great flexibility in sorting and retrieving data. For example, a consultant might set up a database file on a caseload of students. That file would be made up of individual records, each containing a separate entry for categories selected, such as name, address, phone, age, grade, type of disability, parents' name(s), address, and phone number. Once the format is established, the consultant or an assistant can enter the information for each record. It then can be searched and sorted for different types of reports. This search-and-sort capability is what gives databases flexibility, an advantage over traditional paper-filing systems.

Grades and Attendance Records

Several software programs are available to manage records of students' grades. Most allow the teacher to enter students' scores, determine the weight of each assignment or quiz, and set standards for assigning grades. Final grades can be computed automatically. Many programs provide options for printing class rosters, grade reports by student or by assignment, and summary statistics and graphs. If special software is not available to a teacher or consultant, a standard spreadsheet can be used to accomplish many of these purposes.

Computerized Individual Educational Plans

Many special educators have shown interest in using computers to assist in the laborious process of writing Individual Educational Plans (IEPs). Software programs for producing IEPs have been developed and are available commercially. These programs are special types of databases tailored to the needs of special education professionals. The programs usually contain an IEP form and a collection of suggested annual goals and short-term objectives. Although the computerized availability of goals and objectives can alleviate much of the drudgery of writing IEPs, it is also the source of most of the criticism of computerized IEPs. Critics argue that the goals and objectives provided in the software are often isolated skills that are not relevant to an individual student or inconsistent with the local school curriculum.

However, effective software does not require use of the goals and objectives provided in the program. It allows the IEP team to develop others if they wish. Some systems even enable users to generate administrative reports and notices to teachers and parents.

Margolis and Free (2001) note that some computerized IEPs have been challenged successfully in court because they failed to individualize education to meet the student's special needs. They recommend that computerized IEP programs have three design features:

- Efficiency and consistency
- Adherence to the key legal requirement that each child's IEP be personalized for the student's needs
- Record keeping for the IEP content that will satisfy requirements for federal and state reports.

They recommend further that school personnel be trained adequately in preparing the computerized IEP.

Assessment and Evaluation

Assessment and evaluation issues in collaboration and consultation were discussed in Chapter 6. The data gathered in these processes can be stored in database or spreadsheet applications. They can be readily summarized in various formats, including meaningful graphs and charts. However, when educators store confidential information in computers, *careful steps must be taken to protect confidentiality of student information.* This issue is a major concern if data are to be shared with team members by way of computer networks. Computer technicians should be consulted to determine the safest and most efficient ways to make files secure.

Test-Scoring.   One of the most time-consuming parts of the assessment process is scoring standardized tests. Many test-developers provide software programs to assist in this task. "These programs are quick, accurate, and an excellent way for busy teachers to save time" (Lewis, 1993, p. 134). Monitoring Basic Skills Progress, by PRO-ED, Inc., is an example of a program that assists educators in generating, administering, and scoring probes that monitor student progress when using Curriculum-Based Measurement techniques. The results are graphed by computer over time so progress can be compared with the expected rate of improvement. The program also analyzes the results and makes recommendations about possible changes in instruction.

Consultants and collaborating teachers need to monitor student performance on computer tasks, especially when use of computers is specified on a student's IEP. Integrated learning systems (ILS) can be beneficial for this purpose. These systems provide instructional software for students and management tools for teachers. They are available in subject areas such as reading, writing, language arts, math and science. Teachers or consultants can easily monitor student progress and prescribe individualized activities based on the results of previous performance. These systems are growing in popularity with school districts as a tool for measuring outcomes. When available, and when relevant to student goals, these systems should be chosen by teachers and consultants for students in inclusive classrooms. Teachers and/or consultants then can refer to such data to make collaborative decisions about student progress and make changes as may be appropriate. If the software does not have built-in record-keeping capability, the student or paraprofessional can be taught to enter data in a database or spread sheet that can then be used to prepare summaries or graphs. A skilled consultant can provide valuable assistance to the classroom teacher in making these decisions and setting up the record-keeping tools.

Portfolios.   Use of portfolios is yet another way to monitor and evaluate student progress and document consultation activities. However, organizing and maintaining portfolio information can be very time-consuming. The convenience of filing information on a computer should not be overlooked. Products developed on the computer are easily filed. Other products and information can be scanned into the computer to be added to the portfolio. Many interesting possibilities exist for the innovative educator and students.

Several formats for recording consultation activities were discussed in Chapter 6. This type of information could be kept on the computer and would be more efficient than the paper-pencil format. Some of the information such as date, time, or name of student could be automatically entered, and the information searched and sorted in various ways, to provide valuable information for making decisions about students and collaboration processes. For example, if one wanted to know how many times a certain consultant or service provider worked with the student during the year, the data could be sorted to have all the entries for the service provider appearing together. Later, if one wanted to know who provided services on a particular date, the information could be sorted by the date field. Data can be sorted to produce valuable reports for making decisions about programs and services for students. Data also can be added to larger information bases for more extensive district-wide reports. Figure 11.5 illustrates a form that could be used in a classroom to record services provided

FIGURE 11.5   Service Provider Log

Student	Francisco, W.	Teacher	P. Webber

Date	Time	Service Provider	Comments
9-13-04	9:46 a.m.	N. Carney	Scripted paper for English
9-13-04	1:46 p.m.	L. Baker	Checked points earned, made
			suggestion to teacher
			about time-on-task
9-15-04	9:15 a.m.	K. Foster	PT—Worked on small motor
			during handwriting activity
9-15-04	1:44 p.m.	N. Carney	Helped with math instruction.
			Difficult. Try more manipulatives.
9-16-04	2:27 p.m.	N. Carney	Paraprofessional helped him
			with math. Spoke to
			teacher about next week's work.

for students with special needs. Figure 11.6 shows the information when recorded in a data base and sorted by a service provider.

Significant advances in technology-based assessment within special education have been made as a result of the Technology-Related Assistance for Individuals with Disabilities Act of 1988 (Greenwood, 1994). A special issue of *Exceptional Children* (October/November, 1994) that addresses this topic is but one example of its importance:

> Advances in software design enable expert-level assessment knowledge to be employed automatically in the context of data collection, data analysis, decision making, and prescription. Advances in the portability of computers (notebook and sub notebook computers) support classroom observational assessments by practitioners using quality instruments that routinely integrate data collection and numerical analyses with observer training and reliability assessment (Greenwood, 1994).

Adapting Materials and Tests

Another time-consuming activity for co-teachers and consultants is adapting written products for individuals with disabilities as was discussed in Chapter 8. A common example is to adapt

FIGURE 11.6   Service Provider Log Sorted by Service Provider

Student: *Francisco, W.*   **Teacher:** *P. Webber*

9/15/04   *9:15 AM*   **Service Provider:** *K. Foster*

Comments:

PT—Worked on small motor during handwriting activity

9/13/04   *1:46 PM*   **Service Provider:** *L. Baker*

Comments:

Checked points earned, made suggestion to teacher about time-on-task

---

9/16/04   *2:27 PM*   **Service Provider:** *N. Carney*

Comments:

Paraprofessional helped him with math. Spoke to teacher about next week's work.

9/15/03   *1:44 PM*   **Service Provider:** *N. Carney*

Comments:

Helped with math instruction. Difficult. Try more manipulatives.

9/13/04   *9:46 AM*   **Service Provider:** *N. Carney*

Comments:

Scripted paper for English

a worksheet used to supplement a math or science lesson. It is often felt there are too many work items for students with disabilities to complete in one setting. Moreover, the graphic material might be distracting from the relevant stimuli and needs to be removed. The old-fashioned way to deal with this situation is to make a copy of the worksheet, cut it apart with scissors, and paste it back together in a more usable format. However, if a scanner and computer with graphics software are available, the project can be completed more efficiently. The worksheet is scanned into the graphics program. The "cut and paste" function of the program is used to eliminate portions that are distracting or too difficult. Then the remaining portions are re-arranged as needed and the "new" worksheet printed out. This approach allows for making different adaptations for many different students in a relatively short amount of time.

Text also can be scanned into the computer if OCR software is installed. A consultant might scan a teacher-made test, for example, and then make adaptations as needed. The print can be enlarged or more space provided between items. Even better, if a classroom teacher prepares the test on the computer, the file can be shared with a consultant or co-teacher to make the adaptations.

There are a number of software programs that can be used to develop written tests. Test banks often accompany classroom texts. Teachers and consultants might find that the use of such programs is an efficient way to adapt a classroom test. For example, some soft-ware can produce several types of tests—matching, true-false, completion, and multiple choice. When questions have been typed into the program, they can be easily transferred from one of the formats to another. Other software can create paper-and-pencil tests as well as quizzes that students take at the computer.

Preparing Reports and Other Written Products

Word processors and desktop publishing programs are a *must* for busy consultants and other team members. Once text has been entered in a word processor, it can be changed easily, edited, added to, modified, or reformatted. This capability is particularly useful for routine writing such as consultation logs, letters to parents, memos to other team members, assess-ment reports, newsletters and classroom materials with adaptations made for specific stu-dents with disabilities.

Consultants and collaborating teachers might want to develop "shells" or "templates" for frequently used products. A shell or template is a word processing file that contains por-tions of a document that do not change. For example, most of the forms and checklists rec-ommended in this book could be scanned in or retyped to form shells. McLoughlin and Lewis (1990) suggest a shell for assessment reports. Permanent information would include the title, spaces for identifying information and headings such as Reason for Referral, Test Behavior, Results, and Recommendations. Brief descriptions of commonly administered tests could be included in the shell and simply omitted if not appropriate for a particular re-port. Male (1994) provides an example of a shell for homework assignments. When using a shell, the file is loaded into the word processor and relevant information is added before sav-ing the file under a new name.

Integrated software that combines word processing and database may be the most pow-erful tool for enhancing personal productivity of school personnel (Male, 1994). Software of this type allows the user to create a database such as the student information previously described. Any part or all of these data can be merged (or inserted) into word processing documents such as form letters or reports. Once the data for each student have been entered, a consultant can print out any lists needed. Academic or behavioral progress reports can be prepared for specific parents, or for all the parents in the caseload, with personalized information inserted automatically by the computer (Male, 1994).

PLANNING FOR USE OF TECHNOLOGY

Technology must save teachers time and labor. Furthermore, there are many teaching responsibilities that involve working with people, and technology cannot take the place of interactions with people. Teachers stand up and cheer when they have immediately and basically helpful teaching and management tools even when they are low-tech and not state-of-the-art. Such tools include, for example: Phones in every classroom; multiple FAX machines to eliminate wait for opportunities; automatic paper grading for more uniform assignments like spelling and arithmetic; video-and teleconferencing among teachers at other schools; databases of student records to look up previous schools, grades, and scores; and a database of educational specialists, organized by area of expertise, in the state or surrounding region to share ideas and viewpoints. (See Figure 11.7)

A software designer sympathetic to the harried schedules and multiple responsibilities of school personnel could find ways to help them automate their most tedious work and allow more time for people-work with students and co-teachers. Teachers do not need the "neatest" technology outfit in the store; they simply want something that helps them work smarter, not harder. Furthermore, they are distressed when computer labs replace art rooms. They shudder when computers arrive with no technical support and no budget for repairs and upgrades. Too many expensive machines stand idle in schools when they go "down" and help is not available to start them up.

Consultants should provide leadership for schools in three important ways to assure effective use of technology for professional uses and to accommodate the needs of students with disabilities in general classrooms:

- Participating in school-wide planning groups;
- Providing a role model in the use of technology; and
- Engaging in collaborative activities where technology is being used.

As one can see from the vast array of technology applications discussed in the preceding pages, there are many decisions to make about what, when, and how to invest in emerging technology. Right now, most schools do not have technology-rich environments to support consultation and collaboration. Thoughtful planning and invest-

FIGURE 11.7   Technology is for working smarter, not harder

By Jane More Loeb

ment decisions are needed to ensure that team members have the right technologies in their classrooms and offices for both management and instructional purposes.

Many decisions in education are based on reactions to problems or historical trends (Cain, 1985). This decision-making method does not work well for decisions about technology because of the rapid pace of change in the technology itself. Instead, a holistic and visionary method of planning is needed. Cain recommends a planning process for technology use in which individuals responsible for different program elements are brought together to pose questions and brainstorm for possible solutions.

TIPS FOR USING RELATED-SERVICES PERSONNEL, RESOURCES, AND TECHNOLOGY

1. Don't try to do it all by yourself.
2. Develop rapport with librarians. Give advance notice of upcoming topics and try not to make too many spur-of-the-moment requests.
3. Make friends with custodians and refrain from making excessive demands on their time and energy.
4. Keep public remarks about colleagues on a positive, professional level. If you must vent, try using a journal at home. Reviewing it now and then may show you the way to improve the situation.
5. Remember special things about the faculty in each school, and start a card file with comments that will be useful in personalizing the interactions. If you find a news article pertaining in a positive way to a colleague or a student, clip it out and send it along with a congratulatory note.
6. Advertise successes, both yours and those of classroom teachers. Sometimes teachers are amazed that a student or a situation has shown *any* progress at all.
7. Do not expect the same levels of involvement and commitment from everyone.
8. Before sending confidential information through electronic networks make sure steps have been taken to keep hackers and other would-be "technology thieves" from gaining access to the information.
9. Constantly monitor your habits of protecting confidential information. Make sure you do not leave information in files accessible to individuals who are not authorized to see them. When you use e-mail, be careful when selecting addresses for mail. It is very easy to accidentally include an unauthorized person. Most breaches of confidentiality result from carelessness of people, and not from lack of technology safeguards.
10. Consult a technology specialist on a regular basis to remain current in the ever-changing uses of technology.
11. Join or form a computer user's group to learn from one another about new uses for computers
12. Write a proposal that results in resources for sharing among schools.
13. Do not try to "go it alone," but look to colleagues for support and counsel.
14. Remember Ralph Waldo Emerson's words, "It is one of the most beautiful compensations of this life that no man can sincerely try to help another without helping himself."

CHAPTER REVIEW

1. Related-services personnel and support personnel represent a wide variety of fields, both in education and beyond. They can contribute to learning programs for students with special needs by collaborating as a team with general and special education teachers to address special needs (disabilities and/or high abilities), interests, talents, transition to school or to work, and achievement (low or high). Coordination of services and collaboration among school personnel and support personnel is an important responsibility for the collaborative school consultant.

2. Transition services help young children and adolescents make smooth adjustments at significant times in their education. The transition from preschool to kindergarten, from elementary to junior high or middle school, from junior high to high school, and ultimately from high school to work or postsecondary education can be eased for students with special needs through collaborative consultation.

3. Successful schools of the future will engage in interagency collaboration, with collaborators working together to achieve goals for serving all students' needs effectively. Bringing about needed school change requires greater emphasis on collaboration and teamwork. School consultation will be an important tool for coordinating health, social, and educational services to help all students, particularly those with special needs.

4. School personnel should seek out resources such as external funding to enhance school environments and learning programs for special needs. Such money, even if in small amounts, can be a strong motivational force in carrying out a learning project. Goals of the proposed project should match those of the funding source, and proposal writers must adhere to the guidelines and deadline stringently. Educators also can draw information and energy from participation in conferences and workshops.

5. Telecommunications and electronic networks are possibly the most valuable elements of technology that can revolutionize the way consultants and collaborating teachers engage in collaborative activities. Many time-consuming, routine tasks such as organizing schedules, keeping and sorting records, adapting materials, and developing IEPs can be done more efficiently with the use of technology. Consultants should provide leadership in schools to assure effective use of technology for professional uses and to accommodate the needs of students with disabilities in general classrooms by participating in schoolwide planning groups, being a role model in the use of technology, and engaging in collaborative activities when technology is being used. Planning should include applications for professional collaboration as well as instructional and student uses.

TO DO AND THINK ABOUT

1. Develop a plan for ways in which at least three related services and support personnel could work as a team to serve students with special needs.

2. Compile a reference list of referral agencies, support groups, and community resources in your area that could be helpful in meeting special needs of students. Preface the list with a brief description of the community where the school is located. Then compare your list with a colleague's list that represents a different type of geographic area.

3. Find out more about several related-services roles that you are not familiar with, for example, the

occupational therapist, the audiologist, the social worker, or the school psychologist. What are their responsibilities? What preparation did their roles require? What does a typical day entail for each of them? Interview them and ask their views about consultation and collaboration.

4. Invite consultants from businesses and other professions to participate in a class discussion or panel presentation to describe their roles and the skills that are required.

5. Survey your school building to determine the extent to which staff members are using telecom-

munications and electronic networks to engage in their collaborative activities. Then think about how you can get involved in this type of collaboration in your building. Or interview a person who uses electronic networks extensively and write a plan for yourself to learn more about their use for your work.

6. Use a computer to adapt an instructional material or a test.

7. Describe what you would want in a technology-infused inclusive environment if money were no object.

FOR FURTHER READING

Blackhurst, A. E. (1997). Perspectives on technology in special education. *Teaching Exceptional Children, 29*(5), 41–48.

Campbell, P., & Tierney, J. (1996). Sharing ideas about teaching effectively: Using technology to collaborate. *Teaching Exceptional Children, 29*(2), 4–8.

Carlson, M. (1995). *Winning grants step by step: Support centers of America's complete workbook for planning, developing, writing successful proposals.* San Francisco, CA: Jossey-Bass.

Collet-Klingenberg, L. L. (1998). The reality of best practices in transition: A case study. *Exceptional Children, 65*(1), 67–78.

Denham, A., & Lahm, E. A. (2001). Using technology to construct alternate portfolios of students with moderate and severe disabilities. *Teaching Exceptional Children, 33*(5), 10–17. In this article the authors provide a plan, with accompanying forms, for performance-based evaluation through alternate portfolios that use a multidisciplinary approach and holistic scoring. The portfolios also serve as instructional organizers for students' daily educational programs and as teaching tools for students to learn self-management, planning, and self-evaluation skills.

Educational Leadership. 55(3) (1997, November). Topical issue on Integrating Technology into Teaching.

Educational Leadership, (1995, October), *53*(2). Topical issue on How Technology Is Transforming Teaching.

Exceptional Children (October/November, 1994) Special Issue: Technology-Based Assessment within Special Education, *61*(2).

Geisert, P. G., & Futrell, M. K. (1995). *Teachers, computers, and curriculum: Microcomputers in the classroom*(2nd ed.). Boston: Allyn & Bacon.

Kurland, D. J., Sharp, R. M., & Sharp, V. F. (1997). *Introduction to the INTERNET for education.* Belmont, CA: Wadsworth.

Land, M., & Turner, S. (1997). *Tools for schools: Applications software for the classroom* (2nd ed.). Belmont, CA: Wadsworth.

Lewis, R. B. (1993). *Special education technology: Classroom applications.* Pacific Grove, CA: Brookes/Cole.

Lippitt, G., & Lippitt, R. (1978). *The consulting process in action.* San Diego: University Associates. Chapter 5 on ethical dilemmas and guidelines for consultants.

McMahon, T. J., Ward, N. L., Pruett, M. K., Davidson, L., & Griffith, E. E. H. (2000). Building full-service schools: Lessons learned in the development of interagency collaboratives. *Journal of Educational and Psychological Consultation, 11*(1), 65–92.

Phi Delta Kappan. (1992, December). A Special Section on "Technology in the Schools," *74*(4).

Short, R. J., & Talley, R. C. (1999). Services integration: An introduction. *Journal of Educational and Psychological Consultation, 10*(3), 193–200.

Teaching Exceptional Children, (1997, May/June), *29*(5). Topical issue on technology in special education.

Wienke, W. D. (1996). Book reviews: Current resources for grant writers. *Teacher Education and Special Education, 19*(3), 272–276. This article reviews books on grant proposal writing.

CHAPTER TWELVE

PUTTING IT ALL TOGETHER WITH COLLABORATIVE SCHOOL CONSULTATION AND TEAMWORK

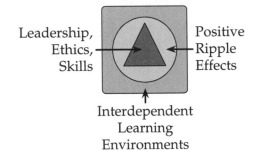

Leadership, Ethics, Skills → | Positive Ripple Effects

↑ Interdependent Learning Environments

Never in recorded history have so many facets of our world changed so rapidly and dramatically. No one can know for certain how these changes will affect schools and educators, but one thing is becoming more and more clear: Students who are at risk now because of special learning and behavior difficulties will be placed in greater jeopardy than ever by the accelerating demands on them to keep pace and measure up in competitive, high-pressure environments.

Teaching and learning are key elements in preparing students for such demands. Collaborative school consultation and teamwork among school, home, and community educators in partnerships will be a vital factor in enabling all students to be successful learners, happy individuals, and productive members of society.

In this last chapter of the book, the content (triangle) includes leadership, ethics, and skills. Positive ripple effects (the process circle) spread the benefits of consultation, collaboration, and teamwork for all students' special needs throughout interdependent learning environments (the square).

FOCUSING QUESTIONS

1. How is a visionary perspective for students with special needs relevant to the role of the collaborative consultant?

2. How do the skills of leading and following influence the effectiveness of collaborative school consultants in serving students' special needs?

3. How can a mentor relationship assist school personnel with collaboration, consultation, and teamwork?

4. How are collaborative consultation ethics evidenced?

5. What competencies are demonstrated by capable and effective collaborative school consultants?

6. What benefits and positive ripple effects can result from successful consultation, collaboration, and co-teaching in schools?

KEY TERMS

advocacy	ethics	multiplier effects
collaborative school consultation competencies	leadership/followership	positive ripple effects
	mentor/mentee	synergy

VIGNETTE 12.A

Another school day is over. The events of the past week are history. What happens beyond this moment is the future. As teachers finish their bus duties and other supervisory tasks and head for their rooms to pick up work they will take home for the weekend, their glances fall on a poster that hangs beside the door:

"THE FUTURE IS NOW!"

Below the poster in smaller type is the much-used maxim, "If we do what we have been doing, we will continue to get what we have been getting." Below that is a question, "Can we do better?" It is a good question to ponder over the weekend. . . .

A VISIONARY PERSPECTIVE FOR EDUCATION

A consensus is growing among educators and policymakers that in schools of the future there will be considerable role change, including increases in interaction through collaboration and consultation (Jenkins, Pious, & Jewell, 1990) and collegial relationships (West, 1990). New ways of thinking nurture a whole new way of viewing the world (Crowell, 1989, p. 60). The shift is away from the Newtonian ideas of simplicity, hierarchy, mechanics, assembly, and toward new views that are more integrative, holistic, collective, cooperative, and organizational. Such changes characterize scientific thinking, but they influence education as well (Crowell, 1989; Meyen & Skrtic, 1988).

Now is the time to have visionary scope. We should:

- look inward to analyze in microscopic detail;
- scan in all directions with periscopic breadth and depth;

- through kaleidoscopic colors and shapes, appreciate the beauty and usefulness of diversity; and
- look far beyond with telescopic range toward lofty goals and promising futures for our students. (See Figure 12.1.)

Schaps (1990) believes the public is seeing the necessity of changing the overall *system* for education, while acknowledging that such efforts will not work if they focus *only* on improved teaching processes, *or* content of the curriculum, *or* goals and policies of schools. Instead, process, content, and policy are strongly tied to one another so that change in any one necessitates change in all three. As stressed in earlier chapters, a growing number of special education leaders contend that students at risk of school failure in conventional settings are not disabled, deficient students. The problem lies primarily in a misfit between their abilities and the demands made on them in inflexible, depersonalized school situations. This is one reason for the success of collaborative consultation efforts in which educators work in partnerships to enhance student achievement.

Eisner counsels that an unknowable future is not a sound basis on which to plan curriculum and instruction, so we must prepare students to deal effectively in the *here* and *now* (Eisner, 2003/2004). He avers that our instruction must teach students to exercise judgment, to think critically, to acquire meaningful literacy, to serve, and to *collaborate* [emphasis added]. (See Chapter 9 for examples of activities that can serve these purposes.) Accountability is the responsibility of all. Test scores must be relegated to a back seat and the pursuit of educationally significant outcomes placed front and center. To address the challenges that lie ahead, Eisner emphasizes that we must prepare students for tomorrow by preparing them for today.

FIGURE 12.1   Education: A Visionary Scope

We have the knowledge, Marshak (2003) contends, to structure schools that educate all children and attend to their diverse needs. Furthermore, we know what schools' agenda must be:

> Digital age literacy (scientific, mathematical, technological, visual, informational, cultural, and global), inventive thinking (ability to manage complexity, creativity, risk-taking, higher-order thinking), effective communication (teaming, personal and social responsibility, communication skills), and high productivity (skills for prioritizing, planning, and managing for results, effective use of real-world tools) (p. 231).

Educators ought to abandon their never-ending searches for "something practical that works," Olson (2003) contends, because this is the time for the principles, impracticality, and passion. Hot topics that tend to fade away fast should be replaced by "the 'impracticality' of intellectual study, reflection, and collaboration built into every teacher's school day" (p. 308), so that teachers have time to read and discuss with colleagues in exchanges of experiences and ideas.

With school consultation and collaboration as an integral part of the educational program, there is hope for creating the flexibility and individualization students need by enhancing the repertoire of instructional and counseling practices that enable them to succeed. The best educators have always been those who expand, change, modify and tailor the requirements so that the important material is taught, but in a way and to the extent that serves each student's individual interests, needs, and talents.

Conoley (1989) emphasizes that teachers will need to assume some responsibility for achieving the outcomes they know are most important. However, they must also feel that the extra effort they give to planning, problem solving, and decision making in teams is not just an addendum to their load of responsibilities. They also need to regard this effort as having a positive effect on their daily professional lives.

The challenge of thinking in new ways about students, schools, and education is not a call to abandon our cherished values and history that have provided meaning and given us direction. Rather, it is a challenge to participate in creating a new vision of helping students to achieve their potential, not just crank out acceptable test scores. The time to begin is now. As the adage reminds us, "A journey of a thousand miles begins with a single step."

LEADERSHIP IN COLLABORATIVE SCHOOL CONSULTATION ENVIRONMENTS

Leadership is an enigmatic quality. For centuries sociologists, psychologists, and educators have tried to define leadership, with only marginal success. It is another one of those constructs where "we can't really describe it, but we know it when we see it." Perhaps the purposes of this book and its concluding chapter are well served by defining *leadership* as the capacity to influence people and/or to represent them, and to perform responsibilities on their behalf. Pure types of leadership probably do not exist; however, people function as leaders when their ideas and actions have effects on the thoughts and behaviors of others.

Certain clusters of behaviors seem to separate leaders from followers, and effective leaders from ineffective ones. These behaviors include a strong drive for responsibility and task completion, persistence in pursuing goals, self-confidence, willingness to accept consequences of their decisions and actions, and ability to influence others' thinking and doing. A saying attributed to that eminent leader Harry Truman is, "Great leaders have the ability to get others to do what they really don't want to do, and to like doing it." Effective leaders develop responsive followers. They make others feel more empowered. They thrive on the successes of followers. They take pleasure in seeing a collaborative team spirit coalesce and they constantly strive to help others improve and grow.

In the everyday work world, leaders use phrases and expressions that make others want to succeed. They avoid phrases such as "It'll never work in our district," "That's been tried before with no success," and "We are too new/old/big/small/inexperienced/set in our ways, etc., to do that in our school." Five expressions that dampen enthusiasm (Annunzio, 2001) are:

- "It's impossible—that idea could never work."
- "We've done that before."
- "If you had more experience, you'd understand why we can't do that."
- "It doesn't look like you put any thought behind that."
- "I'll tell you what you have to do."

As Annunzio sees it, rephrasing such "wet blanket" comments in somewhat the following manner will get better involvement and results:

- "Seems unworkable to me, so help me understand how it *could* work."
- "I'll explain what we tried before, and you can explain how your idea is different."
- "That sounds innovative, but there are some obstacles. How might we overcome those?"
- "Help me understand the reasoning behind your idea."
- "We need to accomplish the goal within these restraints. How might we do that?"

Not all leaders are openly active and dynamic. Some very successful leaders have reflective leadership styles, shaping others' values by teaching and modeling. Active leadership skills can be developed by: putting people in situations where they can lead; enhancing communication skills (including listening skills); honing creative problem solving and critical thinking skills; and practicing people skills of conflict resolution, management of meetings, and parliamentary procedure. Reflective leadership skills thrive on researching universal problems, learning how social policies are developed and implemented, and solving problems through interdisciplinary teamwork. In a collaborative environment, leadership often is diffused and passed around for individual contribution to what is needed for addressing the goals.

Envisioning collaborative environments is a relatively easy process; developing such environments and activating them require much more effort. The leadership role of the school administrator can be a catalyzing element in structuring the collaborative atmosphere. Administrators can steer researchers toward finding out why some students at risk *do* succeed, rather than dwelling on why students fail. Administrators as leaders can forge alliances with other social service agencies, with business, foundations, colleges and universities, and members of the community (Lugg & Boyd, 1993).

Leadership in schools is not a position, but a way of *doing* for everyone in the educational setting. Getting everyone involved in leadership builds leadership density in schools, which benefits all (McNulty, 2003).

As an educational and professional consultant with decades of experience in New York City public education, Monroe (1997) cautions that leaders can't wait around for consensus before they begin making innovations. She proposes that "school should not reflect what society is, but rather school should model what society should be" (Monroe, 1997, p. 208). Thus, the successful leader is an innovator and a change agent. Furthermore, effective leaders and followers are right for roles as mentors and mentees.

Collaborative Consultants in Mentorships

The mentorship concept originated and was recorded many centuries ago in Greek literature to explain the relationship of Telemachus, his son Odysseus, and a person named Mentor, chosen by Telemachus to be Odysseus' model and guide. Today the mentor relationship is best explained by describing the mentor.

A mentor is part "parent" and part peer—model, guide on the side, expert, diagnostician, appraiser, and advocate, all taking place in the full press of conducting daily business and accommodating the mentor's own work. The relationship between mentor and mentee (the mentored one), based on shared talent and passion for the field of common interest, is very special and quite personal. The mentor recognizes budding talent in the mentee, but does not campaign for commitments or push for greatness. However, the mentor has a sense of timing—when to bear down, or ease off, and take advantage of a teachable moment. The mentor coaches toward the bent of the mentee, facilitating advancement as rapidly as the mentee's competency allows, and modeling indirectly through experience rather than simply dispensing information to be ingested. A teacher tendency toward verbalism is cast aside to create instead a climate of experiential learning beside a master practitioner.

In studies of special education teacher attrition, Whitaker (2000) notes an alarming statistic that approximately 15 percent of new teachers will leave after their first year of teaching, and 10 percent to 15 percent more after the second year. This compares with an overall annual rate of 6 percent attrition for teachers nationally. Her studies show that effectiveness of mentoring correlates significantly with special education teachers' plans to remain in special education. Careful selection of a mentor as a special education teacher, and matching with one who teaches students with the same disabilities, are particularly relevant. Unstructured, informal, and frequent contacts are most important. (See Figure 12.2.)

Marsal (1997) proposes that through mentoring relationships, established between beginning teachers and experienced, effective peers can reduce the alarming rates of attrition from teaching during the first five years. She supports the CEC Guidelines for Developing a Mentorship for Beginning Special Education Teachers adopted at the 1997 CEC (Council for Exceptional Children) convention. She challenges each CEC member to find at least one person with possibilities and mentor that person in his or her local context. Knowledge and practice of consultation, collaboration, and co-teaching skills are superb conduits through which modeling and mentoring can occur.

Internships and career shadowing can be forms of mentorship, but only if the relationship involves deep understanding between those involved and their commitment in the field of interest. In the collaborative process both mentor and mentee will gain. Both roles must be voluntary. An unstructured and informal mentorship is often most effective. One caution pertaining to this special relationship is that there must be consideration of the duration of the relationship. This can prevent possible discomfort later, because mentorships

FIGURE 12.2   Mentorships Mean Sharing and Caring

By Jane More Loeb

do end. If this likelihood is addressed at the outset, most often as a set time limit of weeks or months, a way has been prepared for when and how it will be over. Then no one feels "stood up" or let down.

Advocacy for Students with Special Needs

At a well-attended conference on special needs in schools, a legislator active on a key educational committee for the legislature directed some strong remarks to participants who gathered to hear her speak. She asked pointedly from her place on the podium, "Can you name the representatives and senators who serve you in our state legislature? Do you know their positions on key issues?" She then charged each one to not spend one more day without knowing such important answers. It gave the educators much to ponder, and homework to do!

Getting to know policymakers and elected officials, communicating with them about the needs of students, and building bridges of communication are necessary steps of advocacy. When communicating, personal letters are more effective than form letters. *Many* letters, rather than one letter *signed* by many, gets more attention. The letters that are short, concise, friendly in tone, and free of stereotyped phrases and unreasonable requests, make a positive impact. Thanking legislators for their interest in the past and support they have given, along with descriptions of specific ways that support has helped communities, will be particularly powerful. Think of the letter as a vehicle of appreciation, information, and documentation, and as a message about action that would help, along with suggestions for how this might be done. Examples of student work and achievement provide convincing evidence when included with the letters (with parent and administrator permission, of course).

Student Self-Advocacy

Self-advocacy is knowing what one wants, what one is entitled to, and how to achieve one's goals (Kling, 2000). Students can be helped to become effective self-advocates by teaching them self-advocacy skills. The successful advocate knows her or his rights, needs, and best supports. It is important also to know the best time to approach others with requests that serve one's needs. Students who learn to do this can gain a sense of control and influence over their employment conditions and living situations. Kling offers a mnemonic acronym (ASSERT) to help students recall self-advocacy steps:

- *A*wareness of disability
- *S*tatement of disability
- *S*tatement of strengths and limitations
- *E*valuation of problems and solutions
- *R*ole-playing a situation
- *T*rying it in the real setting

A formal plan for teaching self-advocacy strategy is offered by Van Reusen, Bos, Schumaker, and Deshler (1994). The plan provides instructional methods for education planning conferences, transition planning conferences, verbal practice, group practice with feedback, and individual practice with feedback. Students are to have a great deal of involvement. As just one example of an instructional strategy included in the plan, the instructor will make no more than three statements without having students make a response, either orally or in written form.

ETHICS OF COLLABORATIVE CONSULTATION

Consultation, collaboration, and teamwork in the school setting require particular emphasis on ethical interaction for several reasons:

- Special needs of students are involved.
- Confidential data must be shared among several individuals.
- Consultants are out and about much more than classroom teachers, interfacing with many people in several buildings.
- Parent permission is not always required, but many of the issues to be dealt with approximate the sensitivity of issues that do necessitate parent consent.

- Consultants have complex roles with many demands upon them, but may have received little or no training in how to adapt to those roles.
- Consultation implies power and expertise until the collaborative spirit can be cultivated.
- Consultants may be asked on occasion to act inappropriately as a middle person, or to form alliances, or carry information, and they must respond ethically.
- Adults often have difficulty adapting to individual differences in teaching styles and preferences of colleagues, and many of them demonstrate resistance.
- There is some risk of having diminishing returns if collaborative efforts considerably reduce the amount of time available for direct service to the child (Friend & Cook, 1992).
- Just as with mentorships, it is important to recognize those rare times when it is in the best interest of all concerned, but of the student above all, to withdraw from a consulting situation. Disengagement is recognized in psychological consultation as the termination of a consultative relationship. This is reality, and having a transition plan for moving into other relationships and experiences can ease any feelings of loss and sadness, and dispel feelings of inadequacy or failure.

■ ■ ■ ■ ■

APPLICATION 12.1
"SELLING" A TEACHING CONCEPT

With a group of colleagues, or as a one-person agency, develop an advertisement for a concept from Chapter 7, 8, or 9, or another concept of interest. Promote that concept in an appealing, eye/ear-catching, ethical, and tastefully presented way that provides a compelling message for service to students with special needs. An ad might be created for the ideal co-teacher, or a particular classroom modification, or mentorship, or a paraeducator preparation program, or a multiplier effect of a collaborative school consultation program.

The persuasive aspects of consultation require a close, careful look at ethical practice (Ross, 1986). Ethical consultation is implemented by adhering to principles of confidentiality in acquisition and use of information about students, families, and individual school settings. It also includes a high regard for individual differences among colleagues and the constructive use of those differences to serve students' needs, concern and empathy for all, onedownsmanship (downplaying status differences and communicating as partners) in the consultative role, and mutual ownership of problems and rewards in the school environment.

Consultants and collaborators should review legal requirements relating to confidentiality, such as the Family Educational Rights and Privacy Act of 1974 (Buckley Amendment), and truth-in-testing laws within states that legislate them. Requirements such as these stipulate the need for confidentiality of student data and regulate parental access to information about their children.

Hansen, Himes, and Meier (1990) present several suggestions for school consultants to follow in order to exercise ethical behavior in their roles:

1. Promote professional attitudes and behaviors among staff about confidentiality and informed consent.

2. Take care with the quality of information they enter in written records.
3. Take care in discussing problems of children and their families.
4. Focus on strengths of clients and share information only with those who need it to serve the student's needs.

Educators will be more successful in their roles and more widely accepted by their professional colleagues if they base consultation, collaboration, and teamwork on a code of consultation ethics that includes the following recommendations:

- Avoid any activity that might embarrass colleagues.
- Do not violate confidences or carry tales.
- Limit the consultative activities to things for which one is trained.
- Take care not to distort or misrepresent information.
- Openly share helpful data, but only in ways that protect the rights of students and families.
- Make as few remarks about specific teaching practices as possible.
- Know when to stay in the consultation and when it would be best to get out and try another approach.
- Be open to new ideas and knowledge.
- Give colleagues the benefit of wanting to help.
- Leave therapy to therapists who are trained for it.
- Maintain good records that provide confidentiality.
- Keep consultative channels and doors open.
- Refrain from taking issues personally.
- Above all, advocate for the child, letting student needs guide one's actions and decisions.

Several well-known maxims apply to the implementation of planful, efficient, collegial, and ethical practices for consultation:

"Keep your words sweet, for you may have to eat them."
"Better to bend than to break."
"Only a fool would peel a grape with an ax."
"Eagles do not hunt flies."
"What breaks in a moment may take years to mend."

COMPETENCIES OF EFFECTIVE COLLABORATIVE SCHOOL CONSULTANTS

Consulting and collaborating require flexibility, adaptability, resilience, and the tolerance for getting delayed reinforcement or none at all. Effective school consultants are knowledgeable about special education and general education curriculum and methods. They are interested in current trends and topics, and innovative in generating new ideas. They recognize and value adult differences among colleagues. They understand how schools function, and have a panoramic view of the educational scene. They are practical and realistic at the same time that they are innovators. This requires that they be assertive, but diplomatic, and not pushy.

Successful school consultants relate well to teacher colleagues and staff members, administrators, students, and parents. They have good communication skills, a patient and understanding demeanor, and assertiveness when it is needed.

Effective collaborative school consultants have mature, objective viewpoints toward all aspects of education. While working to help students learn, they retain perspective on the entire school context and work within that larger framework to accomplish specific goals for individual students and their teachers.

The consultant links people with resources, refers people to other sources when necessary, and teaches when that is the most appropriate way to serve student needs. A consultant is self-confident, but if running low on resources and ideas, the consultant will not hesitate in finding a consultant for himself or herself!

Perhaps most of all, the consultant is a change agent. As one very experienced consulting teacher put it, "You have to be abrasive enough to create change, but pleasant enough to be asked back so you will do it some more," (Bradley, 1987). The ideal consultant encourages other educators, including parents, to help students with special needs succeed in school.

BENEFITS OF COLLABORATIVE SCHOOL CONSULTATION

School environments that promote collaborative consultation tend to involve all school personnel in the teaching and learning processes. Information is shared and knowledge levels about student characteristics and needs, and strategies for meeting those needs, are broadened. Importantly, many of the strategies are helpful with other students who have similar but less severe needs. A number of specific benefits of school consultation and collaboration can be anticipated.

First, there is much-needed support and assistance for students in the inclusive classroom. Consulting special education teachers help classroom teachers develop repertoires of materials and instructional strategies. Many find this more efficient than racing from one student to another in a resource room as all work on individual assignments. As one learning disabilities teacher succinctly put it, "In my resource room, by the time I get to the last student, I find that the first student is stuck and has made no progress. So I frantically run through the whole cycle again. Tennis shoes are a must for my job!" They also find ways of helping classroom teachers to be confident and successful with special needs students. At times they can assume an instructional role in the classroom, which frees the classroom teacher to study student progress, set up arrangements for special projects, or work intensively with a small group of students. When general classroom and special education teachers collaborate, each has ownership and involvement in serving special needs.

Collaborative efforts to serve students in heterogeneous settings help minimize stigmatizing effects of labels such as "handicapped," "exceptional," "disabled," or even, "gifted." It also can reduce referrals to remedial programs. In an early study to determine effects of consultation upon teacher referral patterns over a seven-year period, Ritter (1978) notes that the provision of consultation service resulted in decreasing referrals to programs for disabilities on the part of teachers over time. More recently, in a study of special education in an inclusionary middle school, Knowles (1997) found that collaboration and teamwork decreased special education referrals and grade retention of students. Fewer referrals for special education services means reduced expenditures for costly and time-consuming psychological assessments and special education interventions. Educators can focus more time and energy on teaching and facilitating, and less on testing and measuring. In addition, a ripple effect extends services to students by encouraging modifications and alternatives for their special needs.

When introduced to the concept of school consultation, some special education personnel are concerned that after a time they will work themselves out of a job. They fear their positions will be abolished if teachers become fully capable of serving the needs of mildly disabled, gifted, and underachieving students in the classroom. However, this possibility is extremely remote. Research since 1980 demonstrates that when consultation service is increased, there is more demand for the benefits generated by the service (Friend, 1988). A successful consultation process becomes a supportive tool that teachers increasingly value and use. As inclusive school systems become more prevalent, collaborative consultation will become even more critical for school program success. Consultation services contribute to the total school program as a bridge between the parallel systems of special education and general education (Greenburg, 1987) and are an effective way of alleviating confusion over goals and relationships of general and special education (Will, 1984).

Administrators can benefit from eased loads of pressure and planning when classroom teachers are efficient in working with a wide range of student needs. Principals find it stimulating to visit and observe in classrooms as team participants, collaborating on ways of helping every student succeed in the school and reinforcing teacher successes with all of their students. This is for many administrators a welcome change from the typical classroom visitations they make for purposes of teacher evaluation.

Another important and frequently overlooked benefit is the maintenance of continuity in learning programs as students progress through their school experiences. This, too, is a savings in time, energy, and resources of the educational staff and often the parents as well.

A collaborative consultation approach is a natural system for nurturing harmonious staff interactions. Teachers who have become isolated or autonomous in their teaching styles and instructional outlook often discover that working with other adults for common goals is quite stimulating. Sharing ideas can add to creativity, openendedness, and flexibility in developing educational programs for students with special needs. In addition, more emphasis and coordination can be given to cross-school and long-range planning, with an increased use of outside resources for student needs.

Collaborative consultants are catalysts for professional development. They can identify areas in which faculty need awareness and information sessions, and coordinate workshops to help all school personnel learn specific educational techniques (McKenzie, Egner, Knight, Perelman, Schneider, & Garvin, 1970). Just as removal of the catalyst stops a chemical process, so can the absence of consulting teachers curtail individualization of curriculum and differentiation of strategies for special needs (Bietau, 1994).

Parents or guardians of the exceptional student often become extremely frustrated with labeling, fragmented curriculum, and isolation from peers endured by their children. So they respond enthusiastically when they learn that several educators are functioning as a team for the student. Their attitudes toward school improve and they are more likely to become more involved in planning and carrying through with the interventions (Idol, 1988), more eager to share their ideas, and helpful in monitoring their child's learning. They are particularly supportive when consulting services allow students in special education programs to remain in their neighborhood schools.

School consultants and collaborators provide increased opportunities for communication, multiple sources of information, broadened perspectives on teaching strategies for special needs, expanded availability of resources, diminished isolation in the classroom, and more involvement with service agencies beyond the school. Benefits result when teacher skills are enhanced in preventing learning problems that might otherwise escalate into more serious needs (Idol, 1986; Heron & Kimball, 1988). Students with borderline special needs that are addressed successfully in classrooms represent single-case outcomes that can be replicated with an entire class or throughout a school.

Positive Ripple Effects of Collaborative School Consultation

Positive ripple effects, or multiplier effects as they have also been referred to from time to time in this book, provide compelling arguments for consultation, collaboration, and teaming. They create benefits beyond the immediate situation involving one student and that student's teachers. For example, by collaborating school personnel are modeling this powerful social tool for their students, who are quite likely to experience collaborative climates in their future workplaces.

As discussed earlier, consulting teachers who might be concerned that general education teachers will be given full responsibility for special learning needs and their own positions will be eliminated, should not fret. As teachers become more proficient in collaborating with consulting teachers, they tend to find those services more indispensable to their goals of serving all students' educational needs effectively. The use of specialized intervention techniques for many more students than the ones identified, categorized, and remediated in special education programs is a positive outcome to expect from collaborative school consultation. Multiple benefits can extend well beyond the immediate classroom because consulting teachers are in a unique position to facilitate interaction among many target groups. These effects that ripple out from mutual planning and problem solving across grade levels, subject areas, and schools are powerful instruments for initiating positive changes in the educational system.

Multiplier effects provide compelling arguments for consultation, collaboration, and teaming. They augment benefits beyond the immediate situation involving one student and that student's teachers. For example, when collaborating with colleagues, school personnel are modeling this powerful tool for their students who soon will be collaborating and teaming with others in their own workplaces.

Levels of Service

Direct services for consultees are one level of positive effects (see Figure 12.3). At this level the consultation and collaboration are most likely to have been initiated for one client's need. (Note that a client can be an entity such as a student group, school, family, or community, as well as a single student.) But consultation benefits often extend beyond level 1 of immediate need. At level 2, consultees use information and points of view generated during the collaboration to be more effective in similar but unrelated cases. Both consultant and consultee repertoires of knowledge and skills are enhanced so that they can function more effectively in the future. When consultation outcomes extend beyond single

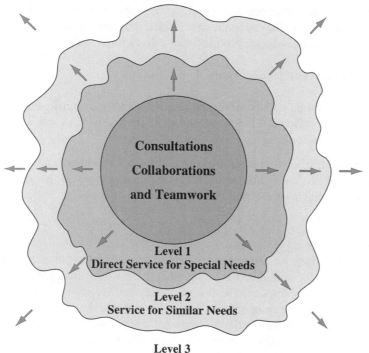

FIGURE 12.3   Positive Ripple Effects of Collaborative School Consultation

consultant/consultee situations of levels 1 and 2, the entire school system can be positively affected by level 3 outcomes. Organizational change and increased family involvement are potential results of level 3 outcomes.

Level 1 effects, for example, can result from the following types of school situations:

■ The consultant engages in problem-solving with a high-school teacher to determine ways of helping a severely learning-disabled student master minimum competencies required for graduation.

■ The audiologist helps the classroom teacher arrange the classroom environment to enable a hearing-impaired student to function comfortably in the regular classroom setting.

Level 2 effects include these examples:

■ The classroom teacher becomes more familiar with the concept of hyperactivity in children, subsequently regarding fewer children as attention-deficit disordered with hyperactivity, and adjusting the classroom curriculum to more appropriately address very active children's needs in that classroom setting.

■ The classroom teacher becomes comfortable with enrichment activities provided for gifted students through collaboration with the gifted program facilitator, and makes enriching activities available to a larger group of very able children in the classroom.

Level 3 effects enable these kinds of outcomes:

■ The efforts toward collaboration and teamwork result in a professional development plan called "Teachers Helping Teachers," during which teachers in a school system provide training for interested colleagues in their areas of expertise.

■ The school district's emphasis on consultation, collaboration, and teamwork pleases parents who find that their children are receiving more integrated, personalized instruction for their learning needs. Families become more active and interested in the school's programs.

Once again, it must be emphasized that when level 2 and 3 outcomes enable classroom teachers to handle some serious learning needs without consultant involvement, consultant positions should *not* be eliminated. It is important that the consulting role is not regarded as an add-on position to be dispensed with when money and personnel are in short supply, but rather as an indispensable component of each school's present and future context.

Use of specialized intervention techniques for many more students than those identified, categorized, and remediated in special education programs is an expected outcome of collaborative school consultation and co-teaching. All in all, the multiplier effect of these interactive processes is a powerful tool for progress in education.

SYNERGY OF CONTEXT, PROCESS, AND CONTENT

Effective school consultation results from the interaction of process skills and content methodology within the immediate school context. Contexts of a school setting are a "given" in the assessment of the educational scene. Schools without authentic content would be unnecessary. Schools without effective processes will flounder. Processes are the most malleable and promising of the parameters that delineate school consultation, but processes such as communication, problem solving, conflict resolution, time and resource management, and constructive use of adult differences tend to be either neglected or poorly carried out in too many school situations.

Can there be content-free processes for consultation? No, because process is composed of content (Tharp, 1975). This is one of the greatest strengths of consultation. Process incorporates content to provide services for students in each school context. Collaboration that occurs in conjunction with consultation requires harmonious, efficient teamwork. Thus, consultation with collaboration is not an oxymoron as some might suggest. It is *synergy*—"a behavior of whole systems unpredicted by the behavior of their parts taken separately" (Fuller, 1975, p. 3). When teamwork is effective, there is synergy. A synergistic combination of context, process, and content provides a recipe for success in the school setting. (See Figure 12.4.)

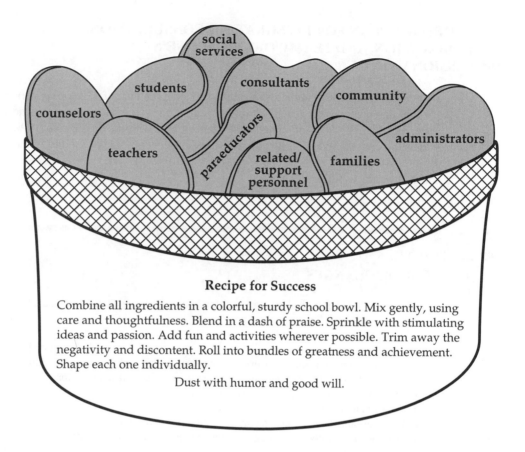

Recipe for Success

Combine all ingredients in a colorful, sturdy school bowl. Mix gently, using
care and thoughtfulness. Blend in a dash of praise. Sprinkle with stimulating
ideas and passion. Add fun and activities wherever possible. Trim away the
negativity and discontent. Roll into bundles of greatness and achievement.
Shape each one individually.

Dust with humor and good will.

FIGURE 12.4   Recipe for Success

APPLICATION 12.2

WHAT MIGHT BE DONE IN TEAMS?

With colleagues, compile a list of things that could be done effectively as teams in the school
context that would result in more expertise, higher enthusiasm, greater energy, and for that matter, more fun! Start with possibilities such as these, and add more innovative ones to the list.

- Sharing and trading of ideas, resources, information
- When things are not going so well, encouragement and support in the form of activities
  such as sharing compliments or playing a stimulating game
- Efficient task completion after responsibilities are assigned to match each person's area
  of expertise
- Identification of problems that need attention

DEVELOPING A PLAN FOR INTEGRATING CONSULTATION, COLLABORATION, AND TEAMWORK INTO ONE'S PROFESSIONAL ROLE

Individual differences abound when adults set about the task of developing personal plans for attaining professional goals. School reform, and the student success it is intended to generate, depend upon both individual and organization development (Sparks, 1992). In order to develop content and processes for consultation service contexts, and to initiate collaboration and teamwork in the school context, educators will want to construct their own personal plans for fulfilling these roles.

■ ■ ■ ■ ■

APPLICATION 12.3
MAKING SCHOOL CHANGES

Consider the following typical school needs, and ways that consultation and the collaborative ethic might assist in making school changes:

- Create opportunities to interface special education programs with the general program.
- Institute communication networks among school staff, parents, advocacy groups.
- Contribute to text selections, curriculum revisions, general school reform.
- Identify exemplary, successful teaching practices.
- Coordinate use of community resources for students' needs.
- Help parents identify ways to contribute to school programs.
- Help other educators and parents set realistic goals for students with learning and behavior problems.
- Contribute to planning and conducting professional development activities.
- Conduct formative and summative evaluation to improve school programs.

GETTING STARTED AS A COLLABORATIVE SCHOOL CONSULTANT AND TEAM MEMBER

Recall that four guiding questions were introduced in Chapter 1. It is time to reiterate those questions and formulate some responses. This will be a way to begin thinking of oneself as a consulting, collaborating school professional who often works in teams with others, for the purpose of helping students with special needs to learn, grow, and fulfill their promise. The questions are:

- Who am I in this role?
- How do I carry out responsibilities of the role?
- How do I know whether or not I am succeeding?
- How do I prepare for such a role?

Some, but of course not all, ways to address these questions are:

1. Read, study, think, interview others, and complete coursework if possible, to gain information and skills for the role.
2. Formulate one's own personal philosophy of school consultation, collaboration, and teamwork.
3. Meet with central administrators of one's school(s) to listen to their perceptions of the collaborative consultant role, if this possibility is open within the "chain of command" in that school context.
4. If an advisory council is available, engage the members in discussion about consultation and collaboration roles. The council should include general and special education teachers, support personnel, administrators, parents, and other community leaders.
5. Meet with each building administrator to whom assigned, engage in responsive listening and learn their viewpoints. Remember that this is a *very important* step.
6. After meeting with all principals, reorganize thoughts and ideas, and set about to gather more information if necessary.
7. Develop a tentative role description and goals based on central and building administrators' views as well as one's own perspective.
8. Return to central administration if appropriate in that district, trying out one's role description and goals with them, and revising if necessary.
9. Return to building administrators to share the revised package and obtain their approval and support. Again, this is *very* important.
10. After honing the document to a concise format, put it up for discussion, explaining it to teaching staff and non-teaching staff and refining it even further, based on their comments.
11. Ask for time during inservice or staff development meetings to discuss the program.
12. Begin to work first with receptive, enthusiastic teachers as consultees.
13. Begin right away to log consultations and related activities, and assess outcomes of collaborative consultation for improvement (formative evaluation), accountability, and decision-making (summative evaluation).
14. Solicit and welcome input from all, continually refining and reclarifying the role.
15. Get involved in each building to which assigned by accepting lunch, bus, playground duty. Offer to help during book fairs, school carnivals, ball games, as much as time and energy will allow.
16. Don't be seen around the building doing nothing, or *seeming* to be doing nothing. Spending time in the library to locate resources for a consultee or student may be misperceived by others.
17. Invite colleagues and family members of students to one's office or classroom. Have student work displayed, and occasionally serve refreshments.
18. Avoid hierarchical relationships by practicing the communicative art of "onedownsmanship."
19. Eat lunch with other staff members, and interact just enough, but not too much, in the staff workroom.
20. Ask teachers for their advice on educational issues, and encourage them to demonstrate some of their favorite techniques. However, do not share their personal techniques with others unless they grant permission to do so.

21. Dress for the school and the occasion. Variables such as high/low status, titles, and clothes can have a significant impact on consultation effectiveness (Kratochwill & Van Someren, 1985).

22. Ask colleagues the golden question: "What can I do for you and your students *that you don't have the time and materials to do?*"

23. Refrain from making any recommendations that conflict with administrative policy or teacher values.

24. Learn about content areas for the students who are to be served. Also, be knowledgeable about regulations and recommendations governing special education, education for students at risk of failure, and school improvement issues.

25. Develop a newsletter for school personnel and parents, taking care to preserve confidentiality of students and families.

26. Seek out and provide resources for teachers and parents.

27. Continue to read, study, attend conferences, and take courses in consultation and related professional development.

28. Observe students outside the classroom (playground, lunch, extracurricular events) to get a different perspective.

29. Make attractive bulletin boards that complement the goals of consultation and collaboration, stressing teamwork and partnerships.

30. With a colleague or two or three, brainstorm periodically for ways to improve services and enhance collaborative efforts among educators.

31. Reach out to more skeptical colleagues, asking for their views, and offering materials, information, and assistance as it fits into their plans.

32. Find basal texts and other materials that work best in collaborative efforts, and design curriculum materials and modifications to meet collaborator and student needs.

33. Engage in research efforts for new knowledge about consultation, collaboration, and team practices.

CHALLENGES FOR CONSULTATION, COLLABORATION, AND TEAMWORK IN THE FUTURE

As educational consultants struggle to establish themselves in school classrooms and buildings, they often find that they are sometimes trail-blazers and often pioneers in modeling consultation, collaboration, and teamwork. Establishing new collaborative roles is stressful and time-consuming (Newmann, 1991). No simple solution exists for the complex issues and concerns of the future. Now is the time to develop skills of consultation, collaboration and teamwork on behalf of students with special needs and the society in which they live, because collaboration is a process of the future. It is essential to school reform and restructuring, interagency cooperation, responses to changing student needs, and future global, economic, and technological productivity.

As consultants facilitate collaboration and teamwork within the school context to serve special needs each school day, they provide a basis and a framework for continued collaboration throughout the global village. This framework provides help and hope for our students of today who will be the citizens of tomorrow.

■ ■ ■ ■ ■

APPLICATION 12.4
AND NOW, THE PERSONAL PLAN

Develop your personal plan for using concepts of school consultation, collaboration, and co-teaching within the school context and the role responsibilities you anticipate for the future. Make a copy of the plan and mail it to yourself, or ask a course instructor, group leader, or valued colleague to mail it to you at a designated time in the future, to remind you of the commitment you made when you focused on these issues, set goals, and reflected on actions to achieve those goals.

TIPS FOR PUTTING IT ALL TOGETHER TO SERVE STUDENTS' SPECIAL NEEDS

1. Promote an exchange-of-roles day in which consultants teach classes and teachers observe, plan modifications, and consult with others.
2. Make a personal pledge to read at least an article a week from a professional journal.
3. Join a dynamic professional organization and become actively involved in it.
4. Learn a new technique and infect others with your enthusiasm for using it. Avoid just dropping off learning centers and activities with teachers. Instead, ask if you can help get them started.
5. Become acquainted with people in businesses and organizations who are field-testing products, materials, and processes.
6. Observe programs in other schools and share observations with key people in your own school context.
7. Remember that knowing how to consult does not guarantee one the opportunity to do it! *Create* the opportunity.

CHAPTER REVIEW

1. To acquire a visionary perspective on special education for student needs, educators are advised by authors and researchers in education to expect changing roles, to anticipate changes in the total educational system, to accept responsibility for accountability, and to build intellectual study, reflection, and collaboration into their professional days.

2. Leadership is a key element in successful implementation of the collaborative consultation process. Listening skills and followership behaviors enhance the likelihood of success. One important function of educational leaders is advocacy. Knowing key legislators, other policymakers, and community leaders, and communicating needs in clear, friendly, and assertive form will help ensure a receptive ear to the concerns. Students who are taught self-advocacy skills become more confident in demonstrating leadership, and independent in their work and living situations.

3. Mentorships among beginning special teachers and experienced, effective special education teachers can produce effective growth, development, changes in both mentor and mentee, and most promisingly, a reduced attrition rate among special education teachers in their early years in the profession.

4. Ethical and conscientious considerations must guide consultants in every consultative and collaborative effort. The primary aim of any school interaction is the welfare of the student. Confidentiality, respect for individual differences of students and adults, careful attention to student and family members' rights, appropriate advocacy, and close monitoring of one's own professionalism are foundations for solid ethical principles.

5. Collaborative school consultation requires skills and competencies of communication, empathy, diplomacy, organization, problem solving, change agentry, assessment, resourcefulness, and much more.

6. Benefits of collaborative school consultation include increased assistance for students; minimized labeling and stigmatizing; service to the spirit of inclusion; a more seamless curriculum; parent satisfaction with increased help for their children; enhanced skills through shared teaching; multiplier effects throughout the school context; increased interest among all teachers in helping all students succeed; and student satisfaction with having increased time with and attention from their teachers and resource personnel. Positive ripple effects create benefits well beyond the immediate learning and teaching situations that are the foci of consultation, collaboration, and team efforts.

TO DO AND THINK ABOUT

1. In a teacher's guide for a particular subject, locate instances when collaboration and use of a consultant are referred to, or, better still, encouraged. Discuss these with classroom teachers relevant to the topic and grade level(s).

2. Talk about the following quotations as they might relate to collaboration:
   - "It is easier to produce ten volumes of philosophical writing than to put one principle into practice." (unknown)
   - "Our goal is not to think alike, but to think together." (anonymous)
   - "We're all in this boat together. If you don't care to help row, at least don't drill holes in the bottom of the boat." (some wise, anonymous person)

3. If you were to pick up a newspaper and see a want-ad for a consulting teacher to assist students with learning and behavioral problems in any of the following school contexts, what would you expect that job description to include?
   - elementary school in a suburban area
   - large consolidated middle school in a rural area
   - high school in an inner-city area

4. A person's design for his or her workday puts a certain framework around the day and gives meaning to the rhythms of activity that help define the role. Using one of the settings in Activity 3 above, visualize an ideal day in a consulting teacher's life. Think of the context, the role, the schedule, the goals and activities for that day, and how the impact of that day's events might be appraised. You may want to review Chapters 1 and 2 as you do this.

5. Create a list of school improvement research questions for the future that might be explored within the context of strong school consultation programs and competent consulting personnel.

6. Now that you have studied the content, process, and context of collaborative schools that utilize consultation services and promote team efforts, what kind of schools would you build if you could start all over in a place where no schools exist?

7. Create a motivational bumper sticker that will proclaim the importance of school and home educators working together as partners for children and youth.

8. *And Now:* Where do we as school educators, family member educators, community citizens, and life-long learners, go from here? Lastly, if you are sharing this book in class time, or discussion with a group, how will the group's experience together end? Will you make a group collage to display and leave behind for the next ones who come along this path? Have you developed a new friendship while studying, attending class, carpooling with someone who *was* a stranger but is no more, and you want now to stay in touch? Will you

have a "group hug"? Or, on an agreed-on signal, will each leave to go on his or her own way, with

confidence renewed in the knowledge, skills, and resolve to help students with their special needs?

FOR FURTHER READING

Chernis, C. (1997). Teacher empowerment, consultation, and the creation of new programs in schools. *Journal of Educational and Psychological Consultation, 8*(2), 135–152. Points out that lack of teacher support is a major factor in failure of consultation as a school-based intervention. To increase teacher support, they should be involved in the change process, not just at the implementation stage, but at the time of adoption. Consultants must minimize any status difference by working with teachers as partners.

Darling-Hammond, L. (2003). Keeping good teachers: Why it matters, what leaders can do. *Educational Leadership, 60*(8), 6–13.

Denton, C. A., Hasbrouck, J. E., & Sekaquaptewa, S. (2003). The consulting teacher: A descriptive case study in responsive systems consultation. *Journal of Educational and Psychological Consultation, 14*(1), 41–73. Illustrates processes, relationships, and outcomes in implementation of the Responsive Systems Consultation (RSC) collaborative consultation model. Proposes that consulting teachers must be not only effective in communication, data collection, and problem-solving skills, but also in mentoring.

Foster, W. (1981). Leadership: A conceptual framework for recognizing and educating. *Gifted Child Quarterly, 25*(1), 17–25. This article from the early 1980s encourages reflection on recognition and use of "what works" for developing leadership skills, particularly for those in the field of gifted and talented education.

Friend, M., & Cook, L. (1992). The ethics of collaboration. *Journal of Educational and Psychological Consultation, 3*(2), 181–184.

Marsal, L. S. (1997). Mentoring & CEC guidelines for developing a mentorship program for beginning special education teachers. *Teaching Exceptional Children, 29*(6), 18–21.

Meyers, B., & Meyers, J. (2001). Observing leadership roles in shared decision making: A preliminary analysis of three teams. *Journal of Educational and Psychological Consultation, 12*(4), 277–312. Behaviors of leadership (defined as team member contributions to decisions), are described in regard to principals, team leaders, and other team members (teachers, parents, students). Suggestions are given for decision making, such as shared vision, streamlined data collection procedures by school consultants, and training that includes observations of team decision making.

Savelsbergh, M., & Staebler, B. (1995). Investigating leadership styles, personality preferences, and effective teacher consultation. *Journal of Educational and Psychological Consultation, 6*(3), 277–286. Individuals who are extraverted in communicating and acting to carry out solutions to problems, as determined by the Myers-Briggs Type Indicator, are deemed to be most effective.

Van Reusen, A. K., Bos, C. S., Schumaker, J. B., & Deshler, D. D. (1994). *The self-advocacy strategy: For education and transition planning.* Lawrence, KS: Edge Enterprises.

Whitaker, S. D. (2000). Mentoring beginning special education teachers and the relationship to attrition. *Exceptional Children, 66*(4), 546–566.

Also, professional periodicals, including, but certainly not limited to:

Educational Leadership
Phi Delta Kappan
Teacher Education and Special Education
Journal of Educational and Psychological Consultation

(Look for collaboration and team-teaching articles in subject-oriented journals and periodicals, such as *Science Education* or *Teacher.*)

REFERENCES

Adler, S. (1993). *Multicultural communication skills in the classroom.* Boston: Allyn & Bacon.

Adults and Attention Deficit Disorder (1997, September 2). *New York Times/Manhattan Mercury,* B-10.

Alberti, R. E., & Emmons, M. L. (1974). *Your perfect right: A guide to assertive behavior* (2nd ed.). San Luis Obispo, CA: Impact.

Allen, T. (2004). No school left unscathed. *Phi Delta Kappan, 85*(5), 396–397.

Allington, R. L., & Broikou, K. A. (1988). Development of shared knowledge: A new role for classroom and specialist teachers. *The Reading Teacher,* April 1988, 806–811.

Anderson, M., & Goldberg, P. (1991). *Cultural competence in screening and assessment: Implications for services to young children with special needs ages birth through five.* Minneapolis, MN: PACER Center.

Annunzio, S. (2001). *eLeadership.* New York: Free Press.

Arcia, E., Keys, L., Gallagher, J. J., & Herrick, H. (1992). *Potential underutilization of part H services: An empirical study of national demographic factors.* Chapel Hill, NC: Carolina Policy Studies Program.

Aronson, E. (1978). *The jigsaw classroom.* Beverly Hills, CA: Sage Publications.

ASCD. (2000). Finding time to collaborate. *Education Update, 42*(2), 1, 3, 8.

Association for Supervision and Curriculum Development. (1999). Partners in education: How schools and homeschoolers work together. *Education Update, 41*(4), 1, 4–5.

Association for Supervision and Curriculum Development. (2002). Teachers and paraeducators: Defining roles in an age of accountability. *Education Update, 44*(7), 1,6–8.

Ashbaker, B., & Morgan, J. (1996). Paraeducators: Critical members of the rural education team. In D. Montgomery (Ed.), *The American Council on Rural Special Education Conference-Rural Goals 2000: Building programs that work* (pp. 130–136). Stillwater, OK: Oklahoma State University.

August, D., & Hakuta, K. (1997). *Improving schooling for language-minority children.* Washington, DC: National Academy Press.

Babcock, N. L., & Pryzwansky, W. B. (1983). Models of consultation: Preferences of educational professionals at five stages of service. *Journal of School Psychology, 21,* 359–366.

Baca, L. M., & Cervantes, H. T. (1984). *The bilingual education interface.* Columbus, OH: Merrill.

Baca, L. M., & Cervantes, H. T. (1998). *The bilingual special education interface* (3rd ed.). Upper Saddle River, NJ: Merrill.

Baca, L. M., & de Valenzuela, J. S. (1998). Development of the bilingual special education interface. In L. Baca & H. T. Cervantes, *The bilingual special education interface* (pp. 336–357) (3rd ed.). Upper Saddle River, NJ: Merrill.

Bahamonde, C., & Friend, M. (1999). Teaching English language learners: A proposal for effective service delivery through collaboration and co-teaching. *Journal of Educational and Psychological Consultation, 10*(1), 1–24.

Bailey, G. D. (1981). Self-directed staff development. *Educational Considerations, 8*(1), 15–20.

Banks, J. A. (1988). *Multiethnic education and practice* (2nd ed.). Boston: Allyn & Bacon.

Banks, J. A., & Banks, C. A. (1989). *Multicultural education: Issues and Perspectives.* Boston: Allyn & Bacon.

Barbour, C., & Barbour, N. H. (2001). *Families, Schools, and Communities: Building Partnerships for Educating Children.* Upper Saddle River, NJ: Merrill Prentice Hall.

Bassett, D. S., Jackson, L., Ferrell, K. A., Luckner, J., Hagerty, P. J., Bunsen, T. D., & MacIsaac, D. (1996). Multiple perspectives on inclusive education: Reflections of a university faculty. *Teacher Education and Special Education, 19*(4), 355–386.

Bauch, J. P. (1989). The transParent school model: New technology for parent involvement. *Educational Leadership, 47*(2): 32–35.

Bauwens, J., & Hourcade, J. J. (1997). Cooperative teaching: Pictures of possibilities. *Intervention in school and clinic, 33*(2), 81–89.

Beakley, B. (1997). Inclusion: Theory, reality, survival. *The Delta Kappa Gamma Bulletin, 63*(3), 32–26.

Beckhoff, A. G., & Bender, W. N. (1989). Programming for mainstream kindergarten success in preschool: Teachers' perceptions of necessary prerequisite skills. *Journal of Early Intervention, 13*(3): 269–280.

Beebe, S. A., & Masterson, J. T. (1994). *Communicating in small groups: Principles and practices* (4th ed.). New York: Harper Collins.

Bender, W. N. (1988). The other side of placement decisions: Assessment of the mainstream learning environment. *Remedial and Special Education, 9*(5), 28–33.

Bennett, T., Deluca, D., & Bruns, D. (1997). Putting inclusion into practice: Perspectives of teachers and parents. *Exceptional Children, 64*(1), 115–131.

Bensky, J. M., Shaw, S. F., Gouse, A. S., Bates, H., Dixon, B. E., & Beane, W. E. (1980). Public Law 94-142 and stress: A problem for educators. *Exceptional Children, 47*(1), 24–29.

Berg, I. K. (1994). *Family-based services: A solution focused approach.* New York: W. W. Norton.

Bergan, J. R. (1977). *Behavioral consultation.* Columbus, OH: Merrill.

Bergan, J. R. (1995). Evolution of a problem-solving model of consultation. *Journal of Educational and Psychological Consultation, 6*(2), 111–123.

Bergan, J. R., & Tombari, M. L. (1976). Consultant skill and efficiency and the implementation and outcome of consultation. *Journal of School Psychology, 14*(1), 3–14.

Berger, E. H. (2000). *Parents as partners in education: Families and schools working together.* Upper Saddle River, NJ: Prentice-Hall.

Bevevino, M. (1988). The 87 percent factor. *Delta Kappa Gamma Bulletin, 54*(3), 9–16.

Bickel, W., & Bickel, D. (1986). Effective schools, classrooms and instruction: Implications for special education. *Exceptional Children, 20*(6), 489–519.

Bietau, L. (1994, December). Personal correspondence.

Blackhurst, A. E. (1997). Perspectives on technology in special education. *Teaching Exceptional Children, 29*(5), 41–48.

Blaylock, B. K. (1983). Teamwork in a simulated production environment. *Research in Psychological Type, 6,* 58–67.

Bloom, B. S., Engelhart, M. D., Furst, E. J., Hill, W. H., & Krathwohl, D. R. (1956). *Taxonomy of educational objectives; Handbook I: Cognitive domain.* New York: McKay.

Bocchino, R. (March, 1991). Using mind mapping as a note-taking tool. *The Developer, 1,* 4.

Bogdan, R. C., & Biklen, S. K. (1998). *Qualitative research in education: An introduction to theory and methods* (3rd ed.). Boston: Allyn & Bacon.

Bolton, R. (1986). *People skills: How to assert yourself, listen to others, and resolve conflicts.* New York: Simon and Schuster.

Boone, H. A. (1989). Preparing family specialists in early childhood special education. *Teacher Education and Special Education, 12*(3), 96–102.

Bos, C. S., Nahmias, M. L., & Urban, M. A. (1999). Targeting home-school collaboration for students with ADHD. *Teaching Exceptional Children, 31*(6), 4–11.

Bracey, G. W. (2002). The 12th Bracey Report on the condition of public education. *Phi Delta Kappan, 84*(2), 135–145.

Bradley, M. O. (1987). Personal communication.

Bramlett, R. K., & Murphy, J. J. (1998). School psychology perspectives on consultation: Key contributions to the field. *Journal of Educational and Psychological Consultation, 9*(1), 29–55.

Brandt, R. (1998). Listen first. *Educational Leadership, 55*(8), 25–30.

Bronfenbrenner, L. (1979). *The ecology of human development: Experiments by nature and design.* Cambridge, MA: Harvard University Press.

Bronfenbrenner, U. (October, 1973). Tear down the walls. *Scholastic Teacher, 78*–79.

Brown, A. L. (1994). The advancement of learning. *Educational Researcher, 23*(8), 4–12.

Brown, D., Pryzwansky, W. B., & Schulte, A. C. (1991). *Psychological consultation: Introduction to theory and practice.* Needham Heights, MA: Allyn & Bacon.

Brown, D., Wyne, M. D., Blackburn, J. E., & Powell, W. C. (1979). *Consultation: Strategy for improving education.* Boston: Allyn & Bacon.

Bruner, C. (1991). *Thinking collaboratively: Ten questions and answers to help policymakers improve children's services.* Washington, DC: Education and Human Service Consortium.

Bruns, D. A., & Fowler, S. A. (1999). Designing culturally sensitive transition plans for young children and their families. *Teaching Exceptional Children, 31*(5), 26–30.

Bursuck, W. D., & Lessen, E. (1987). A classroom-based model for assessing students with learning disabilities. *Learning Disabilities Focus, 3*(1), 17–29.

Buscaglia, L. (1986). *Loving each other: The challenges of human relationships.* Westminister, MD: Fawcett.

Buzan, T. (1983). *Use both sides of your brain.* New York: E. P. Dutton.

Cain, E. (1985). Developing an administrative plan for the implementation of micro-computers. *Selected Proceedings of Closing the Gap's 1985 National Conference,* 14–16.

Campbell, P., & Tierney, J. (1996). Sharing ideas about teaching effectively: Using technology to collaborate. *Teaching Exceptional Children, 29*(2), 4–8.

Canning, C. (1991). What teachers say about reflection. *Educational Leadership, 48*(6), 18–21.

Cantwell, D. P., Baker, L., & Rutter, M. (1979). Families of autistic and dysphasic children: Family life and interaction patterns. *Archives of General Psychiatry, 36,* 682–687.

Caplan, G. (1970). *The theory and practice of mental health consultation.* New York: Basic Books.

Caplan, G., & Caplan, R. (1993). *The theory and practice of mental health consultation* (2nd ed.). San Francisco: Jossey-Bass.

Caplan, G., Caplan, R. B., & Erchul, W. P. (1995). A contemporary view of mental health consultation: Comments on "Types of Mental Health Consultation."

Journal of Educational and Psychological Consultation, 6(1), 23–30.

Capper, C. A. (1996). We're not housed in an institution, we're housed in a community: Possibilities and consequences of neighborhood-based interagency collaboration. In J. G. Cibulka and W. J. Kritek (Eds), *Coordination among Schools, Families, and Communities: Prospects for Educational Reform* (pp. 299–322). Albany, NY: State University of New York Press.

Carlson, M. (1995). *Winning grants step by step: Support centers of America's complete workbook for planning, developing, writing successful proposals.* San Francisco, CA: Jossey-Bass.

Carlyn, M. (1977). An assessment of the Myers-Briggs Type Indicator. *Journal of Personality Assessment, 41*(5), 461–473.

Caro, D. J., & Robbins, P. (1991). Talkwalking—thinking on your feet. *Developer,* November 1991, 3–4.

Cawelti, G. (1997). Making the most of every minute. *ASCD Education Update, 39*(6), 1, 6, 8.

CEC Today, staff. (Fall, 1993). NEWS: CEC takes the lead for appropriate inclusive schools, *25*(2), 86.

CEC Today, staff. (April/May, 1997).

Center for Applied Special Technology (CAST). (1999–2004) Resources to help implement UDL and make curriculum adoptoins. Available on-line: www.cast.org

Chavkin, N. F. (1989). Debunking the myth about minority parents. *Educational Horizons, 67,* 119–123.

Cheney, D., Manning, B., & Upham, D. (1997). Project DESTINY: Engaging families of students with emotional and behavioral disabilities. *Teaching Exceptional Children, 30*(1) 24–29.

Chernis, C. (1997). Teacher empowerment, consultation, and the creation of new programs in schools. *Journal of Educational and Psychological Consultation, 8*(2), 135–152.

Christenson, S. L., & Cleary, M. (1990). Consultation and the parent-educator partnership: A perspective. *Journal of Educational and Psychological Consultation, 1,* 219–241.

Christie, K. (2002). States take on the training of paraprofessionals. *Phi Delta Kappan, 84*(3), 181–182.

Christie, K. (2004). AYP: The new purple pill for the slower learner. *Phi Delta Kappan, 85*(5), 341–342.

Cipani, E. (1985). The three phrases of behavioral consultation: Objectives, intervention, and quality assurance. *Teacher Education and Special Education, 8,* 144–152.

Clare, M. M. (2002). Diversity as a dependent variable: Considerations for research and practice in consultation. *Journal of Educational and Psychological Consultation, 13*(30), 251–263.

Clark, B. (2002). *Growing up gifted* (6th ed.). Upper Saddle River, NJ: Merrill.

Clark, G. M., & Knowlton, H. E. (1988). A Closer look at transition issues for the 1990's: A response to Rusch and Menchetti. *Exceptional Children, 54*(4): 365–367.

Clark, S. G. (2000). The IEP process as a tool for collaboration. *Teaching Exceptional Children, 33*(2), 56–66.

Cleveland, C. B. (1981). Coming to grips with memo mania. *Penton/I.P.C., Inc. Regency,* 33–87.

Cochran, M. (1987). The parent empowerment process: Building on family strengths. *Equality and Choice, 4,* 9–22.

Collet-Klingenberg, L. L. (1998). The reality of best practices in transition: A case study. *Exceptional Children, 65*(1), 67–78.

Collins, C. (1987). *Time management for teachers: Practical techniques and skills that give you more time to teach.* West Nyak, NY: Parker.

Conoley, J. C. (1985). Personal correspondence.

Conoley, J. C. (1987). National Symposium on School Consultation. Austin, TX: University of Texas.

Conoley, J. C. (1989). Professional communication and collaboration among educators. In M. C. Reynolds (Ed.), *Knowledge base for the beginning teacher,* (pp. 245–254). Oxford, England: Pergamon.

Conoley, J. C. (1994). You say potato, I say . . . : Part I. *Journal of Educational and Psychological Consultation, 5*(1), 45–49.

Conoley, J. C., & Conoley, C. W. (1982). *School consultation: A guide to practice and training.* New York: Pergamon Press.

Conoley, J. C., & Conoley, C. W. (1988). Useful theories in school-based consultation. *Remedial and Special Education, 9*(6), 14–20.

Corey, M. S., & Corey, G. (1992). *Groups: Process and practice* (4th ed.). Pacific Grove, CA: Brookes Cole.

Council for Exceptional Children. (1997). Working with paraeducators.*CEC Today, 4*(3), 1, 5.

Council for Exceptional Children. (1997). Working with paraeducators. *CEC Today, 4*(3), 1, 5.

Council for Exceptional Children. (2000). Home schooling—A viable alternative for students with special needs? *CEC Today, 7*(1), 1, 5, 10, 15.

Council for Exceptional Children. (2001). A principal's guide to special education. *CEC Today, 8*(2), 10.

Countryman, L. L., & Schroeder, M. (1996). When students lead parent–teacher conferences. *Educational Leadership, 53*(7), 64–68.

Covey, S. R. (1989). *The Seven Habits of Highly Effective People.* New York: Simon and Schuster.

Coyle, N. C. (2000). Conflict resolution: It's part of the job. *Delta Kappa Gamma Bulletin, 66*(4), 41–46.

Cramer, S., Erzkus, A., Mayweather, K., Pope, K., Roeder, J., & Tone, T. (1997). Connecting with siblings. *Teaching Exceptional Children, 30*(1), 46–49.

Cross, T. (1988). Services to minority populations: What does it mean to be a culturally competent professional? *Focal Point, 2,* 1–3.

Cross, T. (1996). Developing a knowledge base to support cultural competence. *Prevention Report, 1,* 2–5.

Crowell, S. (1989). A new way of thinking: The challenge of the future. *Educational Leadership, 47*(1), 60–63.

Curtis, M. J., Curtis, V. A., & Graden, J. L. (1988). Prevention and early intervention assistance programs. *School Psychology International, 9,* 257–264.

Daniels, H. (1996). The best practice project: Building parent partnerships in Chicago. *Educational Leadership, 53*(7), 38–43.

Darling-Hammond, L. (2003). Keeping good teachers: Why it matters, what leaders can do. *Educational Leadership, 60*(8), 6–13.

Davies, D. (1988). Low-income parents and the schools: A research report and plan for action. *Equity and Choice, 4,* 51–59.

Davis, G. A., & Rimm, S. B. (1989). *Education of the gifted and talented.* Englewood Cliffs, NJ: Prentice-Hall.

Davis, W. E. (1983a). Competencies and skills required to be an effective resource teacher. *Journal of Learning Disabilities, 16,* 596–598.

Davis, W. E. (1983b). *The special educator: Strategies for succeeding in today's world.* Austin: PRO-ED.

Davis, W. E. (1985). *The special educator: Meeting the challenge for professional growth.* Austin: PRO-ED.

de Valenzuela, J. S., Torres, R. L., & Chavez, R. L. (1998). Family involvement in bilingual special education: Challenging the norm. In L. M. Baca & H. T. Cervantes (Eds.), *The Bilingual Special Education Interface* (3rd ed.) (pp. 350–370). Upper Saddle River, NJ: Merrill.

DeBoer, A. L. (1986). *The art of consulting.* Chicago: Arcturus.

DeBoer, A. (1997). *Working together: The art of consulting and communicating.* Longmont, CO: Sopris West.

DeBoer, A., & Fister, S. (1998). *Working together: Tools for collaborative teaching.* Longmont, CO: Sopris West.

deBono, E. (1973). *Lateral thinking: Creativity step by step.* Boston: Little, Brown.

deBono, E. (1985). *Six thinking hats.* New York: Harper & Row.

deBono, E. (1986). *CORT thinking: Teacher's notes,* vols. 1–6 (2nd ed.). New York: Pergamon.

Delgado-Gaitan, C., & Ruiz, N. (1992). Parent mentorship: Socializing children to school culture. *Educational Foundations, 6*(2), 45–69.

Demchak, M. A., & Morgan, C. R. (1998). Effective collaboration between professionals and paraprofessionals. *Rural Special Education Quarterly, 17*(2), 10–15.

Denham, A., & Lahm, E. A. (2001). Using technology to construct alternate portfolios of students with moderate and severe disabilities. *Teaching Exceptional Children, 33*(5), 10–17.

Deno, S. L. (1987). Curriculum-based measurement. *Teaching Exceptional Children, 20*(1), 41–47.

Denton, C. A., Hasbrouck, J. E., & Sekaquaptewa, S. (2003). The consulting teacher: A descriptive case study in responsive systems consultation. *Journal of Educational and Psychological Consultation, 14*(1), 41–73.

Deshler, D. (1985). Metaphors and values in higher education. *Academe,* November–December, 1985, 22–29.

Deshler, D. D., & Schumaker, J. B. (1986). Learning strategies: An instructional alternative for low-achieving adolescents. *Exceptional Children, 52,* 583–590.

Dettmer, P. (1980). The extended classroom: A gold mine for gifted students. *Journal for the Education of the Gifted, 3*(3), 133–142.

Dettmer, P. (1981). The effects of teacher personality type on classroom values and perceptions of gifted students. *Research in Psychological Type, 3,* 48–54.

Dettmer. P. (1982). Preventing burnout in teachers of the gifted. *G/C/T, 21,* 37–40.

Dettmer, P. (1989). The consulting teacher in programs for gifted and talented students. *Arkansas Gifted Education Magazine, 3*(2), 4–7.

Dettmer, P. (1994). IEPs for gifted secondary students. *The Journal of Secondary Gifted Education, V*(4), 52–59.

Dettmer, P. (1997, September). *New blooms for established fields.* Presented at the annual conference of the Kansas Association for Gifted, Talented, and Creative, Hutchinson, KS.

Dettmer, P. (Ed.). (1990). *Staff development for gifted programs: Putting it together and making it work.* Washington, D.C.: National Association for Gifted Children.

Dettmer, P., & Landrum, M. (1997). *Staff development: The key to effective gifted education programs.* Waco, TX: Prufrock.

Dettmer, P., & Lane, J. (1989). An integrative model for educating very able students in rural school districts. *Educational Considerations, 17*(1), 36–39.

Dickens, V. J., & Jones, C. J. (1990). Regular/special education consultation: A teacher education training strategy for implementation. *Teacher Education and Special Education, 13*(3–4), 235–239.

Dishon, D., & O'Leary, P. W. (1989). Tips for teachers: Time saver options. *Cooperative Learning, 10*(2), 30.

Dorris, M. (1979). Why I'm not thankful for Thanksgiving. *Midwest Race Desegregation Assistance Center Horizons, 1*(5), 1.

Douglass, M. E., & Douglass, D. N. (1993). *Manage your time, manage your work, manage yourself.* New York: AMACOM.

Doyle, M. B. (1997). *The paraprofessional's guide to the inclusive classroom:* Working as a team. Baltimore, MD: Brookes.

Dryfoos, J. G. (1994). *Full-service schools: A revolution in health and social services for children, youth, and families.* San Francisco: Jossey-Bass.

Dunn, R., & Dunn, K. (1978). *Teaching students through their individual learning styles.* Reston, VA: Reston Publishing.

Dunst, C. J. (2000). Revisiting "Rethinking early intervention". *Topics in Early Childhood Special Education, 20*(2), 95–104.

Dyck, N. (1997). *Self advocacy form.* Lawrence, KS: Curriculum Solutions.

Dyck, N. (1999). *How to adapt text for struggling readers.* Lawrence, KS: Curriculum Solutions.

Dyck, N., & Dettmer, P. (1985–1987). *Special education consultation skills project.* Manhattan, KS: Kansas State University, College of Education unpublished manuscript.

Dyck, N., & Dettmer, P. (1989). Collaborative consultation: A promising tool for serving gifted learning-disabled students. *Journal of Reading, Writing, and Learning Disabilities, 5*(3), 253–264.

Dyck, N., & Pemberton, J. (1997). *A dozen tools for paras.* Lawrence, KS: Curriculum Solutions.

Dyck, N., & Thurston, L. P. (1998). *Getting the message across: A para's guide to communication.* Lawrence, KS: Curriculum Solutions.

Dyck, N., Pemberton, J., Woods, K., & Sundbye, N. (1996). *Creating inclusive schools: A new design for all students.* Lawrence, KS: Curriculum Solutions.

Dyck, N., Sundbye, N., & Pemberton, J. (1997). A recipe for efficient co-teaching. *Teaching Exceptional Children 30*(2), 42–45.

Dyck, N., Zabel, M. K., & Zabel, R. H. (1998). *Behavior management guide for paras.* Lawrence, KS: Curriculum Solutions.

Eberle, R. (1984). *Scamper on for creative imagination development.* Buffalo, NY: DOK.

Echevarria, J., & Graves, A. (1998). *Sheltered content instruction: Teaching English-language learners with diverse abilities.* Des Moines, IA: Allyn & Bacon.

Educational Leadership, 52(4). (December 1994/January 1995).

Educational Leadership, 53(2). (October, 1995). Topical issue, How Technology is Transforming Teaching.

Educational leadership, 55(3). (November, 1997). Topical issue on Integrating Technology into Teaching.

Educational Leadership, 55(8). Topical issue, Engaging Parents and the Community in Schools, May 1998.

Egan, G. (1982). *The skilled helper: A model for systematic helping and interpersonal relating* (2nd ed.). Monterey, CA: Brookes/Cole.

Eisner, E. W. (1988). The ecology of school improvement. *Educational Leadership, 45*(5), 24–29.

Eisner, E. W. (2003). *Questionable assumptions about schooling. Phi Delta Kappan, 84*(9), 348–357.

Eisner, E. W. (2003/2004). Preparing for today and tomorrow. *Educational Leadership, 61*(4), 6–10.

Elkind, D. (1994). *Ties that stress: The new family imbalance.* Cambridge: Harvard University Press.

Elmore, R. F. (2003). A plea for strong practice. *Educational Leadership, 61*(3), 6–10.

Epstein, J. L. (1995). School/family/community partnerships: Caring for the children we share. *Phi Delta Kappan, 76*(9), 701–712.

Erchul, W. P., & Martens, B. K. (1997). *School consultation: Conceptual and empirical bases of practice.* New York: Plenum.

ERIC Clearinghouse on Handicapped and Gifted Children (1987a). Critical presentation skills. *ERIC Digest #449.* Reston, VA: Council for Exceptional Children.

Ernsperger, L. (1998). Using a paraeducator to facilitate school reentry. *Reaching Today's Youth: The Community Circle Caring Journal, 2*(4), 9–12.

Evans, S. (1980). The consultant role of the resource teacher. *Exceptional Children, 46*(5), 402–404.

Exceptional Children (October/November, 1994) Special Issue: Technology-Based Assessment within Special Education. *61*(2).

Family Integration Resources. (1991). Second Family Leadership Conference. Washington, D.C.: U.S. Department of Education.

Federico, M. A., Herrold, Jr., W. G., & Venn, J. (1999). Helpful tips for successful inclusion: A checklist for educators. *Teaching Exceptional Children, 32*(1), 76–82.

Fennick, F. (2001). Coteaching: An inclusive curriculum for transition. *TEACHING Exceptional Children, 33(6),* 60–66.

Feuer, D., & Geber, B. (1988). Uh-Oh . . . Second thoughts about adult learning theory. *Training,* December 1988.

Field, S. L., & Hill, D. S. (1988). Contextual appraisal: A framework for meaningful evaluation of special education programs. *Remedial and Special Education, 9*(4), 22–30.

Finders, M., & Lewis, C. (1994). Why some parents don't come to school. *Educational Leadership, 51*(8), 50–54.

Fine, M. (1990). Facilitating home-school relationships: A family-oriented approach to collaborative consultation. *Journal of Educational and Psychological Consultation, 1*(2).

Fine, M. (1993). Apparent Involvement. *Equity and Choice, 9*(3), 4–8.

Finn, J. D. (1998). Parental engagement that makes a difference. *Educational Leadership, 55*(8), 20–24.

Fisher, D. (1993). *Communication in organizations* (2nd ed.) St Paul, MN: West Publishing Co.

Fisher, R., & Ury, W. (1991). *Getting past no: Negotiating agreement without giving in.* New York: Bantam Books.

Fleury, M. L. (2000). Confidentiality issues with substitutes and paraeducators. *Teaching Exceptional Children, 33*(1), 44–45.

Foley, R. M., & Lewis, J. A. (1999). Self-perceived competence of secondary school principals to serve as school leaders in collaborative-based educational delivery systems. *Remedial and Special Education, 20*(4), 233–243.

Foster, W. (1981). Leadership: A conceptual framework for recognizing and educating. *Gifted Child Quarterly, 25*(1), 17–25.

Fowler, S. A., Donegan, M., Lueke, B., Hadden, D. S., & Phillips, B. (2000). Evaluating community collaboration in writing interagency agreements on the age 3 transition. *Exceptional Children, 67*(1), 35–50.

Fox, L., Vaughn, B. J., Wyatte, M. L., & Dunlap, G. (2002). We can't expect other people to understand: Family perspectives on problem behavior. *Exceptional Children, 68*(4), 437–450.

French, N. K. (1997). Management of paraeducators. In A. L. Pickett & K. Gerlach, (Eds.), *Supervising Paraeducators in School Settings.* Austin, TX: PRO-ED.

French, N. K. (1998). Working together: Resource teachers and paraeducators. *Remedial and Special Education, 19,* 357–368.

French, N. K. (1999). Paraeducators and teachers: Shifting roles. *Teaching Exceptional Children, 2*(2) 69–73.

French, N. K. (2000). Taking time to save time: Delegating to paraeducators. *Teaching Exceptional Children, 32*(3) 79–83.

French, N. K., & Pickett, A. L. (1997). Paraprofessionals in special education: Issues for teacher educators. *Teacher Education and Special Education, 20*(1), 61–73.

Friend, M. (1984). Consultation skills for resource teachers. *Learning Disability Quarterly, 7,* 246–250.

Friend, M. (1988). Putting consultation into context: Historical and contemporary perspectives. *Remedial and special Education, 9*(6), 7–13.

Friend, M., & Bursuck, W. D. (1996). *Including students with special needs: A practical guide for classroom teachers.* Boston: Allyn and Bacon.

Friend, M., & Cook, L. (1990). Collaboration as a predictor for success in school reform. *Journal of Educational and Psychological Consultation, I*(1), 69–86.

Friend, M., & Cook, L. (1992). The ethics of collaboration. Journal of *Educational and Psychological Consultation, 3*(2), 181–184.

Fuchs, D., & Fuchs, L. S. (1994). Inclusive schools movement and the radicalization of special education reform. *Exceptional Children, 60*(4), 294–309.

Fuchs, D., Fuchs, L. S., Dulan, J., Roberts, H., & Fernston, P. (1992). Where is the research on consultation effectiveness? *Journal of Educational and Psychological Consultation; 3*(2), 151– 174.

Fuchs, L. L., Hamlett, C. L., & Fuchs, D. (1990). *Basic math, basic reading, basic spelling* [computer programs]. Austin, TX: PRO-ED.

Fuchs, L. S., Fuchs, D., & Hamlett, C. L. (1990). Curriculum-based measurement: A standardized, long-term goal approach to monitoring student progress. *Academic Therapy, 25*(5), 5, 615–632.

Fullan, M., & Miles, M. (June 1992). Getting reform right: What works and what doesn't. *Phi Delta Kappan,* 745–752.

Fuller, R. B. (1975). *Explorations in the geometry of thinking synergetics.* New York: Macmillan.

Futrell, M., Gomez, J., & Bedden, D. (2003). Teaching the children of a new America. *Phi Delta Kappan, 84*(5), 381–385.

Gallessich, J. (1973). Organizational factors influencing consultation in schools. *Journal of School Psychology, 11*(1), 57–65.

Gallessich, J. (1974). Training the school psychologist for consultation. *Journal of School Psychology, 12,* 138–149.

Gallessich, J. (1982). The profession and practice of consultation. San Francisco: Jossey-Bass.

Gardner, H. (1993). *Multiple intelligences: The theory in practice.* New York: Harper Collins.

Garmston, R. (1988, October). Giving gifts. *The Developer, 3,* 6.

Garmston, R. J. (1994). The persuasive art of presenting: What's a Meta Phor? *Journal of Staff Development, 15*(2), 60–61.

Garmston, R. J., & Wellman, B. M. (1992). *How to make presentations that teach and transform.* Alexandria, VA: Association for Supervision and Curriculum Development.

Gazda, G. M., Asbury, F. R., Balzer, F. J., Childers, W. C., Phelps, R. E., & Walters, R. P. (1999). *Human relations development: A manual for educators* (6th ed.). Boston: Allyn & Bacon.

Geenen, S., Powers, L. E., & Lopez-Vasquez, A. (2001). Multicultural aspects of parent involvement in transition planning. *Exceptional Children, 67*(2), 265–282.

Geisert, P. G., & Futrell, M. K. (1995). *Teachers, computers, and curriculum: Microcomputers in the classroom* (2nd ed.). Boston: Allyn & Bacon.

Gerber, M., & Kauffman, J. (1981). Peer tutoring in academic settings. In P. Strain (Ed.), *Utilization of classroom peers as behavior change agents,* (pp. 155–187). New York: Plenum Publishing.

Gerber, P. J., & Popp, P. A. (2000). Making collaborative teaching more effective for academically able students. *Learning Disability Quarterly, 23,* 229–236.

Gersten, R., & Baker, S. (2000). What we know about - effective instructional practices for English-language learners. *Exceptional Children, 66*(4), 454–470.

Gersten, R., Darch, C., Davis, G., & George, N. (1991). Apprenticeship and intensive training of consulting teachers: A naturalistic study. *Exceptional Children, 57*(3), 226–23.

Giangreco, M. F. (1993). Using creative problem-solving methods to include students with severe disabilities in general education activities. *Journal of Educational and Psychological Consultation, 4*(2), 113–135.

Giangreco, M. F., Dennis, R., Cloninger, C., Edelman, S., & Schattman, R. (1993). "I've counted Jon": Transformational experiences of teachers education students with disabilities. *Exceptional Children, 59*(4), 359–372.

Giangreco, M. F., Edelman, S. W., & Broer, S. M. (2001a). Respect, appreciation, and acknowledgment of paraprofessionals who support students with disabilities. *Exceptional Children, 67(4),* 485–498.

Giangreco, M. F., Edelman, S. W., Broer, S. M., & Doyle, M. B. (2001b). Paraprofessional support of students with disabilities: Literature from the past decade. *Exceptional Children, 68*(1), 45–63.

Giangreco, M. F., Edelman, S. W., Luiselli, T. E., & Mac-Farland, S. Z. C. (1997). Helping or hovering? Effects of instructional assistant proximity on students with disabilities. *Exceptional Children, 64*(1), 7–18.

Glasgow, N. A., & Hicks, C. D. (2003). *What SUCCESSFUL teachers do: 91 research-based classroom strategies for new and veteran teachers.* Thousand Oaks, CA: Corwin.

GOAL/QPC & Joiner Associates, Inc. (1995). *The team memory jogger: A pocket guide for team members.* Methune, MA: GOAL/QPC and Joiner Associates.

Goldberg, I. (1995). Implementing the consultant teacher model: Interfacing multiple linking relationships and roles with systematic conditions, *Journal of Educational and Psychological Consultation, 6*(2), 1975–190.

Gonzales, N., Moll, L. C., Floyd-Ternery, M., Rivera, A., Rendon, P., & Gonzales, R., & Amanti, C. (1993). *Teacher research on funds of knowledge: Learning from households.* Santa Cruz, CA: National Center for Research on Cultural Diversity and Second Language Learning.

Gordon, J. (1992). Measuring the goodness of training. *Training, 28*(8), 19–25.

Gordon, T. (1974). *T.E.T.: Teacher effectiveness training.* New York: Wyden.

Gordon, T. (1977). *Leader effectiveness training, L.E.T.: The no-lose way to release the productive potential in people.* Toronto: Bantam.

Gorman, J. C., & Balter, L. (1997). Culturally sensitive parent education: A critical review of quantitative research. *Review of Educational Research, 67*(3), 339–369.

Graubard, P. S., Rosenberg, H., & Miller, M. B. (1971). Student applications of behavior modification to teachers and environments or ecological approaches to deviancy. In E. A. Ramp & B. L. Hopkins (Eds.), *A new direction for education: Behavior analysis.* (pp. 80–101). Lawrence, KS: University of Kansas.

Greenburg, D. E. (1987). *A special educator's perspective on interfacing special and general education: A review for administrators.* Clearinghouse on Handicapped and Gifted Children. Reston, VA: The Council for Exceptional Children

Greenwood, C. R. (1994). Advances in technology-based assessment within special education. *Exceptional Children, 61*(2), 102–104.

Gregorc, A. F., & Ward, H. B. (1977). A new definition for individual: Implications for learning and teaching. *NASSP Bulletin, 61,* 20–26.

Gresham, F. M., & Kendell, G. K. (1987). School consultation research: Methodological critique and future research directions. *School Psychology Review, 16*(3), 306–316.

Gruskin, S., Silverman, K., & Bright, V. (1997). *Including your child.* Washington D.C.: Office of Educational Research and Improvement, U.S. Department of Education.

Guskey, T. R. (1985). Staff development and teacher change. *Educational Leadership, 42*(7), 57– 60.

Guthrie, G. P., & Guthrie, L. F. (1991). Streamlining interagency collaboration for youth at risk. *Educational Leadership, 49*(1), 17–22.

Gutkin, T. B., & Curtis, M. L. (1982). School-based consultation theory and techniques. In C. R. Reynolds & T. B. Gutkin (Eds.), *The handbook of school psychology* (pp. 796–828). New York: Wiley.

Haight, S. L. (1984). Special education teacher consultant: Idealism versus realism. *Exceptional Children, 50*(6), 507–515.

Halford, J. M. (1996). How parent liaisons connect families to schools. *Educational Leadership, 53*(7), 34–36.

Hall, C. S., & Lindzey, G. (1989). *Theories of personality* (3rd ed.). New York: John Wiley & Sons.

Hall, G. E., & Hord, S. M. (1987). *Change in schools: Facilitating the process.* Albany: State University of New York Press.

Hallahan, D. P., & Kauffman, J. M. (1991). *Exceptional children: Introduction to special education.* Englewood Cliffs, NJ: Prentice Hall.

Halpern, A. S. (1992). Transition: Old wine in new bottles. *Exceptional Children, 58*(3), 202–211.

Hammer, A. L. (1985). Typing or stereotyping: Unconscious bias in applications of psychological type theory. *Journal of Psychological Type, 10,* 14–18.

Hammond, H. (1999). Identifying best family-centered practices in early-intervention programs. *Teaching Exceptional Children, 31*(6), 42–46.

Hanna, G. S., & Dettmer, P. A. (2004). *Assessment for effective teaching: Using context-adaptive planning.* Boston: Allyn & Bacon.

Hansen, J. C., Himes, B. S., & Meier, S. (1990). *Consultation: Concepts and practices*. Englewood Cliffs, NJ: Prentice Hall.

Harris, A. J., & Sipay, E. R. (1990). *How to increase reading ability*. White Plains, NY: Longman.

Harris, K. C. (1998). How educational consultation can enhance instruction for culturally and linguistically exceptional (CLDE) students. In L. Baca & H. T. Cervantes (Eds.), *The bilingual special education interface* (3rd ed., pp. 336–357). Upper Saddle River, NJ: Merrill.

Harris, K. C., & Zetlin, A. G. (1993). Exploring the collaborative ethic in an urban school: A case study. *Journal of Educational and Psychological Consultation, 4*(4), 305–317.

Harry, B., Kalyanpur, M., & Day, M. (1999). *Building cultural reciprocity with families: Case studies in special education*. Baltimore, MD: Brookes.

Hay, C. A. (1984). One more time: What do I do all day? *Gifted Child Quarterly, 28*(1), 17–20.

Haynes, M. E. (1998). *Effective meeting skills: A practical guide for more productive meetings*. Los Altos, CA: Crisp.

Henkelman, J. (1991, February). Staff developers as consultants. *The Developer*. Oxford, OH: National Staff Development Council.

Henning-Stout, M. (1994). Consultation and connected knowing: What we know is determined by the questions we ask. *Journal of Educational and Psychological Consultation, 5*(1), 5–21.

Heron, T. E., & Harris, K. C. (1982). *The educational consultant: Helping professionals, parents, and mainstreamed students*. Boston: Allyn & Bacon.

Heron, T. E., & Harris, K. C. (1987). *The educational consultant: Helping professionals, parents, and mainstreamed students*. Austin, TX: PRO-ED.

Heron, T. E., & Kimball, W. H. (1988). Gaining perspective with the educational consultation research base: Ecological considerations and further recommendations. *Remedial and Special Education, 9*(6) 21–28, 47.

Hertzog, N. B. (2003). Impact of gifted programs from the students' perspectives. *Gifted Child Quarterly, 47*(2), 131–143.

Hildebrand, V., Phenice, L. A., Gray, M. M., & Hines, R. P. (2000). *Knowing and Serving Diverse Families*. Upper Saddle River, NJ: Merrill.

Hillerman, T. (1990). *Coyote waits*. New York: Harper & Row.

Hobbs, T., & Westling, D. L. (1998). Promoting successful inclusion through collaborative problem-solving. *Teaching Exceptional Children, 31*(1), 12–13.

Hodgkinson, H. (2000). Demographics—Ignore them at your peril. *Phi Delta Kappan, 84*(2), 300–303.

Hodgkinson, H. L. (1989). *The same client: The demographics of education and service delivery systems*. Washington, D.C.: Institute for Educational Leadership, Center for Demographic Policy.

Holloway, J. H. (2003). Managing culturally diverse classrooms. *Educational Leadership, 61*(1), 90–91.

Howard, T. C. (2001). Telling their side of the story: African-American students' perceptions of culturally relevant teaching. *Urban Review, 33*(2), 131–149.

Howley, A., Howley, C. B., & Pendarvis, E. D. (1986). *Teaching gifted children: Principles and strategies*. Boston: Little, Brown.

Hoy, W. K. (1990). Organizational climate and culture: A conceptual analysis of the school work place. *Journal of Educational and Psychological Consultation. 1*(2), 149–168.

Huefner, D. S. (1988). The consulting teacher model: Risks and opportunities. *Exceptional Children, 54*(5), 403–414.

Huff, B., & Telesford, M. C. (1994). Outreach efforts to involve families of color in the Federation of Families for Children's Mental Health. *Focal Point, 10,* 180–184.

Hughes, C. A., & Ruhl, K. L. (1987). The nature and extent of special educators' contacts with students' parents. *Teacher Education and Special Education, 10,* 180–184.

Hughes, C. E., & Murawski, W. A. (2001). Lessons from another field: Applying coteaching strategies to gifted education. *Gifted Child Quarterly, 45*(3), 195–204.

Hunter, M. (1985). Promising theories die young. *ASCD Update*, May 1985, 1, 3.

Idol, L. (1986). *Collaborative school consultation: Recommendations for state departments of education*. The Task Force on School Consultation, Teacher Education Division, Council for Exceptional Children.

Idol, L. (1988). A rationale and guidelines for establishing special education consultation programs. *Remedial and Special Education, 9*(6), 48–58.

Idol, L. (1998). Collaboration in the schools: A master plan for staff development. *Journal of Educational and Psychological Consultation, 9*(2), 155–163.

Idol, L., & West, J. F. (1987). Consultation in special education (Part II): Training and practices. *Journal of Learning Disabilities, 20,* 474–497.

Idol, L., Paolucci-Whitcomb, P., & Nevin, A. (1986). *Collaborative Consultation*. Austin, TX: PRO-ED.

Idol, L., Paolucci-Whitcomb, P., & Nevin, A. (1995). The collaborative consultation model. *Journal of Educational and Psychological Consultation, 6*(4), 329–346.

Idol, L., West, J. F., & Lloyd, S. R. (1988). Organizing and implementing specialized reading programs: A collaborative approach involving classroom, remedial, and special education teachers. *Remedial and Special Education, 9*(2) 54–61.

Idol-Maestas, L. (1981). A teacher training model: The resource/consulting teacher. *Behavioral Disorders, 6*(2), 108–121.

Idol-Maestas, L. (1983). *Special educator's consultation handbook.* Rockville, MD: Aspen.

Idol-Maestas, L., & Celentano, R. (1986). Teacher consultant services for advanced students. *Roeper Review, 9*(1), 34–36.

Idol-Maestas, L., & Ritter, S. (1985). A follow-up study of resource/consulting teachers: Factors that facilitate and inhibit teacher consultation. *Teacher Education and Special Education, 8,* 121– 131.

Idol-Maestes, L., Lloyd, S., & Lilly, M. S. (1981). Non-categorical approach to direct service and teachers education. *Exceptional Children, 48,* 213–20

Ingersoll, R. M. (2001). Teacher turnover and teacher shortages: An organizational analysis. *American Educational Research Journal, 38*(3), 499–534.

Ingoldsby, B. B., & Smith, S. (1995). *Families in multicultural perspective.* New York: The Guilford Press.

Jayanthi, M., & Friend, M. (1992). Interpersonal problem solving: A selective literature review to guide practice. *Journal of Educational and Psychological Consultation, 3*(1), 39–53.

Jenkins, J. R., & Jenkins, L. (1985). Peer tutoring in elementary and secondary programs. *Focus on Exceptional Children, 17*(6) 1–12.

Jenkins, J. R., Pious, C. G., & Jewell, M. (1990). Special education and the regular education initiative: Basic assumptions. *Exceptional Children, 56,* 479–491.

Jensen, R. A., & Kiley, T. J. (1998). Teams or torture?: Creating a climate for collaboration. ERIC Document ED 419-344.

Jersild, A. T. (1955). *When teachers face themselves.* New York: Teachers College Press, Columbia University.

Johnson, D. W., & Johnson, F. P. (1987) *Joining together: Group theory and group skills* (3rd ed.). Englewood Cliffs, NJ: Prentice-Hall.

Johnson, D. W., & Johnson, F. P. (2000). *Joining together: Group theory and group skills,* (7th ed.). Boston: Allyn & Bacon.

Johnson, D. W., & Johnson, R. T. (1987). *Learning together and alone: Cooperative, competitive, & individualistic learning* (2nd ed). Englewood Cliffs, NJ: Prentice Hall.

Johnson, L. J., & Pugach, M. C. (1996). Role of collaborative dialogue in teachers' conceptions of appropriate practice for students at risk. *Journal of Educational and Psychological Consultation, 7*(1), 9–24.

Johnson, L. J., Pugach, M. C., & Hammittee, D. J. (1988). Barriers to effective special education consultation. *Remedial and Special Education, 9*(6), 41–47.

Johnson, S. (1992). *"Yes" or "No": A guide to better decisions.* New York: HarperCollins.

Joint Committee on Teacher Planning for Students with Disabilities. (1995). *Planning for academic diversity in America's classrooms: Windows on reality, research, change, and practice.* Lawrence, KS: The University of Kansas Center for Research on Learning.

Journal for Staff Development, 15(4). Results-oriented staff development. A topical, special issue on celebrating 25 years of service, 1969–1994. Oxford OH: National Staff Development Council.

Journal for Staff Development. Manhattan, KS: Kansas State University. All issues.

Journal of Educational and Psychological Consultation, 4(4), (1993).

Joyce, B. (Ed.). (1990). *Changing school culture through staff development.* Alexandria, VA: The Association for Supervision and Curriculum Development.

Joyce, B. R., & Showers, B. (1983). *Power in staff development through research on training.* Alexandria, VA: The Association for Supervision and Curriculum Development.

Joyce, B., & Showers, B. (1988). *Student achievement through staff development.* Alexandria, VA: Association for Supervision and Curriculum Development.

Jung, C. G. (1923). *Psychological types.* New York: Harcourt Brace.

Jusjka, J. (1991). Observations. *Phi Delta Kappan, 72*(6), 468–470.

Kaff, M., & Dyck, N. (1999). *Essential Skills for Paras.* Lawrence, KS: Curriculum Solutions.

Kampwirth, T. J. (1999). *Collaborative consultation in the schools: Effective practices for students with learning and behavior problems.* Upper Saddle River, NJ: Prentice Hall.

Katz, N. H., & Lawyer, J. W. (1983). Communication and conflict management skills: Strategies for individual and systems changes. *Nonviolence and Change National Forum, 63:* 31.

Kauffman, J. M. (1994). Places of change: Special education's power and identity in an era of educational reform. *Journal of Learning Disabilities. 27*(10), 610–618.

Kay, P., & Fitzgerald, M. (1997). Parents + teachers + action research = real involvement. *Teaching Exceptional Children, 30*(1), 8–11.

Keirsey, D., & Bates, M. (1978). *Please understand me: Character and temperament types.* Del Mar, CA: Prometheus Nemesis.

Kelleher, J. (2003). A model for assessment-driven professional development. *Phi Delta Kappan, 84*(10), 751–756.

Keller, M. M., & Decoteau, G. T. (2000). *The military child: Mobility and education,* Fastback #463. Bloomington, Indiana: Phi Delta Kappa Educational Foundation.

Kerns, G. M. (1992). Helping professionals understand families. *Teacher Education and Special Education, 15*(1), 49–55.

Keyes, R. (1991). *Timelock: How life got so hectic and what you can do about it.* New York: Academic Press.

Kipnis, D. (1997). Ghosts, taxonomies, and social psychology. *American Psychologist, 52*(3), 205–211.

Kirschenbaum, R. J., Armstrong, D.C., & Landrum, M. S. (1999). Resource consultation model in gifted education to support talent development in today's inclusive schools. *Gifted Child Quarterly, 43*(1), 39–47.

Kling, B. (2000). ASSERT yourself: Helping students of all ages develop self-advocacy skills. *Teaching Exceptional Children, 30*(3), 66–71.

Kluth, P., & Straut, D. (2001). Standards for diverse learners. *Educational Leadership, 59*(1), 43–46.

Knight, M. T., Meyers, H. W., Paolucci-Whitcomb, P., Hasazi, S. E., & Nevin, A. (1981). A four- year evaluation of consulting teacher service. *Behavioral Disorders, 6,* 92–100.

Knowles, M. (1978). *The adult learner: A neglected species.* Houston, TX: Gulf Publishing.

Knowles, W. C. (1997). *An investigation of teachers' perceptions of special education placement and inclusion: A qualitative case study of two middle schools.* Unpublished doctoral dissertation, Kansas State University, Manhattan, KS.

Kohm, B. (2002). Improving faculty conversations. *Educational Leadership, 59*(8), 31–33.

Kolb, D. A. (1976). *Learning-style inventory: Technical manual.* Boston: McBer & Co.

Kozoll, C. E. (1982). *Time management for educators,* Fastback #175. Bloomington, IN: Phi Delta Kappa Educational Foundation.

Krathwohl, D. R., Bloom, B. S., & Masia, B. B. (1964). *Taxonomy of educational objectives; Handbook II: Affective domain.* New York: McKay.

Kratochwill, T. R., & Pittman, P. H. (2002). Expanding problem-solving consultation training: Prospects and frameworks. *Journal of Educational and Psychological Consultation, 13*(1 & 2), 69–95.

Kratochwill, T. R., & Van Someren, K. R. (1985). Barriers to treatment success in behavioral consultation: Current limitations and future directions. *Journal of School Psychology, 23,* 225– 239.

Kroth, R. L. (1985). *Communication with parents of exceptional children: Improving parent- teacher relationships.* Denver: Love.

Kruger, L. J., Struzziero, J., Kaplan, S. K., Macklem, G., Watts, R., & Weksel, T. (2001). The use of e-mail in consultation: An exploratory study of consultee outcomes. *Journal of Educational and Psychological Consultation, 12*(2), 133–149.

Kummerow, J. M., & McAllister, L. W. (1988). Team-building with the Myers-Briggs Type Indicator: Case studies. *Journal of Psychological Type, 15,* 25–32.

Kurland, D. J., Sharp, R. M., & Sharp, V. F. (1997). *Introduction to the INTERNET for education.* Belmont, CA: Wadsworth.

LaBonte, K., Leighty, C., Mills, S. J., & True, M. L. (1995). Whole-faculty study groups: Building the capacity for change through interagency collaboration. *Journal of Staff Development, 16*(3), 45–47.

Lakein, A. (1973). *How to get control of your time and your life.* New York: McKay.

Land, M., & Turner, S. (1997). *Tools for schools: Applications software for the classroom,* (2nd ed.). Belmont, CA: Wadsworth.

Landrum, M. S. (2001). An evaluation of the Catalyst program: Consultation and collaboration in gifted education. *Gifted Child Quarterly, 45*(2), 139–151.

Lanier, J. E. (1982). Teacher education: Needed research and practice for the preparation of teaching professionals. In D. C. Corrigin, D. J. Palmer, & P. A. Alexander, (Eds.), *The Future of Teacher Education* College Station, TX: Dean's Grant Project, College of Education, Texas A & M University.

Lasater, M. W., Johnson, M. M., & Fitzgerald, M. (2000). Completing the education mosaic: Paraeducator professional development options. *Teaching Exceptional Children. 33*(1) 46–51.

Lawren, B. (1989). Seating for success. *Psychology Today,* September 1989, (16) 18–19.

Lawrence, G. (1993). *People types and tiger stripes: A practical guide to learning styles,* (3rd ed.). Gainesville, FL: Center for Applications of Psychological Type, Inc.

Lawrence, G., & DeNovellis, R. (1974). *Correlation of teacher personality variables (Myers-Briggs) and classroom observation data.* Paper presented at American Educational Research Association conference.

Leitch, M. L., & Tangri, S. S. (1988). Barriers to home-school collaboration. *Educational Horizons, 66,* 70–75.

Levy-Shiff, R. (1986). Mother-father-child interactions in families with mentally retarded young child. *American Journal of Mental Deficiency, 91,* 141–142.

Lewis, A. C. (2002). The will to leave no child behind? *Phi Delta Kappa, 83*(5), 343–344.

Lewis, R. B. (1993). *Special education technology: Classroom applications.* Pacific Grove, CA: Brooks/Cole.

Lieberman, L. (1984). *Preventing special education . . . for those who don't need it.* Newtonville, MA: GloWorm.

Lightfoot, S. (1981). Toward conflict and resolution. Relationships between families and schools. *Theory into Practice, 20*(2), 97–104.

Lilly, M. S., & Givens-Ogle, L. B. (1981). Teacher consultation: Present, past, and future. *Behavioral Disorders, 6*(2), 73–77.

Linan-Thompson, S., & Jean, R. (1997). Completing the parent participation puzzle: Accepting diversity. *Teaching Exceptional Children, 30*(2), 46–50.

Lindle, J. C. (1989). What do parents want from principals and educators? *Educational Leadership, 47*(2), 12–14.

Lindsley, O. (1964). Direct measurement and prosthesis of retarded children. *Journal of Education, 147*, 62–81.

Lippitt, G. L. (March, 1983). Can conflict resolution be win-win? *The School Administrator,* pp. 20–22.

Lippitt, G., & Lippitt, R. (1978). *The consulting process in action.* San Diego: University Associates.

Lipsky, D. K. (1994). National survey gives insight into inclusive movement. *Inclusive Education Programs, LRP Publications, 1*, 3, 4–7.

Lloyd, J. W., Crowley, E. P., Kohler, F. W., & Strain, P. S. (1988). Redefining the applied research agenda: Cooperative learning, prereferral, teacher consultation, and peer-mediated interventions. *Journal of Learning Disabilities, 21*, 43–52.

Lopez, E. C., Dalal, S. M., & Yoshida, R. K. (1993). An examination of professional cultures: Implications for the collaborative consultation model. *Journal of Educational and Psychological Consultation, 4*(3), 197–213.

Loucks-Horsley, S., Harding, C. K., Arbuckle, M. A., Murray, L. B., Dubea, C., & Williams, M. K. (1987). *Continuing to learn: A guidebook for teacher development.* Andover, MA: The Regional Laboratory for Educational Improvement of the Northeast and Islands.

Lovett, H. (1996). *Learning to listen: Positive approaches and people with difficult behavior.* Baltimore, MD: Brookes.

Lovitt, T. C. (1995). *Tactics for teaching,* (2nd ed.). Englewood Cliffs, NJ: Merrill, Prentice Hall.

Lubetkin, B. (January, 1997). Master the art of apologizing. *The Manager's Intelligence Report.*

Lueder, D. C. (1989). Tennessee parents were invited to participate—and they did. *Educational Leadership, 47*(2), 15–17.

Lueder, D.C. (1998). *Creating partnerships with parents: An educators' guide.* Lancaster, PA: Technomic.

Lugg, C. A., & Boyd, W. L. (1993). Leadership for collaboration: Reducing risk and fostering resilience. *Phi Delta Kappan, 75*(3), 253–256, 258.

Lynch, E. W., & Hansen, M. J. (1992). *Developing cross-cultural competence: A guide for working with young children and their families.* Baltimore: Brookes.

Lynch, E. W., & Stein, R. C. (1990). Parent participation by ethnicity: Comparison of Hispanic, Black, and Anglo families. *Educating Exceptional Children* (5th ed.). Guilford, CT: Dushkin.

MacKenzie, A., & Waldo, K. C. (1981). *About time! A woman's guide to time management.* New York: McGraw Hill.

MacKenzie, R. A. (1975). *The time trap.* New York: McGraw Hill.

Madden, N. A., & Slavin, R. E. (1983). Cooperative learning and social acceptance of mainstreamed academically handicapped students. *Journal of Special Education, 17*, 171–182.

Maeroff, G. I. (1993). Building teams to rebuild schools. *Phi Delta Kappan, 74*(7), 512–519.

Maher, C. A. (1982). Time management training for providers of special services. *Exceptional Children, 48*, 523–528.

Maher, C. A. (1985). *Professional self-management: Techniques for services providers.* Baltimore: Brookes.

Male, M. (1994). *Technology for Inclusion: Meeting the special needs of all students* (2nd ed.). Boston: Allyn and Bacon.

Margolis, H. (1986) Resolving differences with angry people. *Urban Review, 18*(2), 125–136.

Margolis, H., & Brannigan, G. G. (1986). Building trust with parents. *Academic Therapy, 22*, 71–74.

Margolis, H., & Free, J. (2001). Computerized IEP programs: Guide for educational consultants. *Journal of Educational and Psychological Consultation, 12*(2), 171–178.

Margolis, H., & McGettigan, J. (1988). Managing resistance to instructional modifications in mainstream settings. *Remedial and Special Education, 9*, 15–21.

Marks, S. U., Schrader, C., & Levine, M. (1999). Paraeducator experiences in inclusive settings: Helping, hovering, or holding their own? *Exceptional Children, 65*, 315–328.

Marsal, L. S. (1997). Mentoring & CEC guidelines for developing a mentorship program for beginning special education teachers. *Teaching Exceptional Children, 29*(6), 18–21.

Marshak, D. (2003). No Child Left Behind: A foolish race into the past. Phi Delta Kappan, *85*(3), 229–231.

Martin, R. (1991). *Extraordinary children—ordinary lives.* Champaign, IL: Research Press.

Maslach, C. (1982). *Burnout: The cost of caring.* Englewood Cliffs, NJ: Prentice Hall.

Mason, J. L. (1994). Developing culturally competent organizations. *Focal Point, 8*, 1–8.

McCarthy, B. (1990). Using the 4MAT system to bring learning styles to schools. *Educational Leadership, 48*(2), 31–37.

McCormick, L., & Kawate, J. (1982). Kindergarten survival skills: New directions for preschool special education. *Education and Training of the Mentally Retarded, 17*(3), 247–252.

McDonald, J. P. (1989). When outsiders try to change schools from the inside. *Phi Delta Kappan, 71*(3), 206–212.

McGlothlin, J. E. (1981). The school consultation committee: An approach to implementing a teacher consultation model. *Behavioral Disorders, 6*(2), 101–107.

McGrew-Zoubi, R. R. (1998). I can take care of it myself. *The Delta Kappa Gamma Bulletin, 65*(1), 15–20.

McKenzie, H. S., Egner, A. N., Knight, M. F., Perelman, P. F., Schneider, B. M., & Garvin, J. S. (1970). Training consulting teachers to assist elementary teachers in the management and education of handicapped children. *Exceptional Children, 37*, pp. 137–143.

McLeskey, J., Henry, D., & Hodges, D. (1998). Inclusion: Where is it happening? *Teaching Exceptional Children, 31*(1), 4–10.

McLoughlin, J. A., & Kass, C. (1978). Resource teachers: Their role. Learning Disability Quarterly, 1(1), 56–62.

McLoughlin, J., & Kelly, D. (1982). Issues facing the resource teacher. *Learning Disabilities Quarterly, 5,* 58–64.

McLoughlin, J., & Lewis, J. A. (1990). *Assessing special students* (3rd ed.). Columbus, OH: Merrill.

McMahon, T. J., Ward, N. L., Pruett, M. K., Davidson, L., & Griffith, E. E. H. (2000). Building full-service schools: Lessons learned in the development of interagency collaboratives. *Journal of Educational and Psychological Consultation, 11*(1), 65–92.

McNulty, R. (2003). Making leadership everyone's responsibility. *Education Update, 45*(7), 2.

Medway, F. J. (1982). School consultation research: Past trends and future directions. *Professional Psychology, 13,* 422–430.

Medway, F. J., & Forman, S. G. (1980). Psychologists' and teachers' reactions to mental health and behavioral school consultation. *Journal of School Psychology, 18,* 338–348.

Melaville, A. I., & Blank, M. J. (1991). *What it takes: Structuring interagency partnerships to connect children and families with comprehensive services.* Washington, D.C.: Education and Human Resources Consortium.

Mercer, C. D., & Mercer, A. R. (1993). *Teaching students with learning problems* (4th ed.). Columbus, OH: Merrill.

Meyen, E. L., & Skrtic, T. (Eds.). (1988). *Exceptional children and youth: An introduction* (3rd ed.). Denver: Love.

Meyers, B., & Meyers, J. (2001). Observing leadership roles in shared decisionmaking: A preliminary analysis of three teams. *Journal of Educational and Psychological Consultation, 12*(4), 277–312.

Michaels, K. (1988). Caution: Second-wave reform taking place. *Educational Leadership, 45*(5), 3.

Miller, S., Miller, P., Nunnally, E. W., & Wackman, D. B. (1991). *Talking and listening together.* Littleton, CO: Interpersonal Communication Programs.

Miller, T. L., & Sabatino, D. (1978). An evaluation of the teacher consultant model as an approach to mainstreaming. *Exceptional Children, 45,* 86–91.

Mills, G. E., & Duff-Mallams, K. (2000). Special education mediation: A formula for success. *Teaching Exceptional Children, 32*(4), 72–78.

Minner, S., Minner, J., & Lepich, J. (1990). Maintaining pupil performance data: A guide. *Intervention in School and Clinic, 26*(1), 32–37.

Minninger, J., & Goulter, B. (1991). *The perfect presentation.* New York: Doubleday.

Moll, L. C., Amanti, C., Neff, D., & Gonzales, N. (1992). Funds of knowledge for teaching: Using a qualitative approach to connect homes and classrooms. *Theory and Practice, 31*(2), 132– 141.

Monroe, L. (1997). *Nothing's impossible: Leadership lessons from inside and outside the classroom.* New York: Times Books.

Morocco, C. C., & Aguilar, C. M. (2002). Coteaching for content understanding: A schoolwide model. *Journal of Educational and Psychological Consultation, 13*(4), 315–347.

Morris, A. (1999). *Teamwork.* New York: Lothrop, Lee, & Shepard.

Morsink, C. V., Soar, S., Soar, R., & Thomas, R. (1986). Research on teaching: Opening the door to special education classrooms. *Exceptional Children, 53*(1), 32–40.

Morsink, C. V., Thomas, C. C., & Correa, V. I. (1991). *Interactive teaming: Consultation and collaboration in special programs.* Columbus, OH: Merrill.

Mueller, P. H., & Murphy, F. V. (2001). Determining when a student requires paraeducator support. *TEACHING Exceptional Children, 33*(6), 22–27.

Munson, S. M. (1987). Regular education teacher modifications for mainstreamed mildly handicapped students. *Journal of Special Education, 20*(4):489–502.

Murphy, A. T. (1981). *Special children, special parents: Personal issues with handicapped children.* Englewood Cliffs, NJ: Prentice Hall.

Murphy, C. (1995). Whole-faculty study groups: Doing the seemingly undoable. *Journal of Staff Development, 16*(3), 37–44.

Murphy, E. (1987). *I am a good teacher.* Gainesville, FL: Center for Applications of Psychological Type.

Murphy, K. D. (1987). *Effective listening: Hearing what people say and making it work for you.* New York: Bantam Books.

Myers, I. B. (1962). *The Myers-Briggs Type Indicator manual.* Palo Alto, CA: Consulting Psychologists Press.

Myers, I. B. (1974). *Type and teamwork.* Gainesville, FL: Center for Applications of Psychological Type, Inc.

Myers, I. B. (1980a). *Gifts differing.* Palo Alto, CA: Consulting Psychologists Press, Inc.

Myers, I. B. (1980b). *Introduction to type.* Palo Alto, CA: Consulting Psychologists Press, Inc.

National Information Center for Children and Youth with Disabilities. The IDEA amendments of 1997. *NICHCY News Digest, 26,* 1–38.

Nazzaro, J. N. (1977). *Exceptional timetables: Historic events affecting the handicapped and gifted.* Reston, VA: The Council for Exceptional Children.

Neel, R. S. (1981). How to put the consultant to work in consulting teaching. *Behavioral Disorders, 6*(2), 78–81.

Neihart, M., Reis, S. M., Robinson, N. M., & Moon, S. M. (2002). *The social and emotional development of gifted children: What do we know?* Waco, TX: Prufrock.

Nelson, C. M., & Stevens, K. B. (1981). An accountable consultation model for mainstreaming behavioral disordered children. *Behavioral Disorders, 6,* 82–91.

Nevin, A., Thousand, J., Paolucci-Whitcomb, P., & Villa, R. (1990). Collaborative consultation: Empowering public school personnel to provide heterogeneous schooling for all—or, who rang that bell? *Journal of Educational and Psychological Consultation, 1*(1), 41–67.

Newman, J. E. (1992). *How to stay cool, calm, and collected when the pressure's on: A stress control plan for business people.* New York: American Management Association.

Newmann, F. M. (1991). Linking restructuring to authentic student achievement. *Phi Delta Kappan, 72,* 458–464.

Nichols, R. G., & Stevens, L. A. (1957). *Are you listening?* New York: McGraw-Hill.

Nuckolls, C. W. (1991). Culture and causal thinking: Diagnosis and prediction in a South Indian fishing village. *Ethos,* 19(1), 3–51.

Oja, S. N. (1980). Adult development is implicit in staff development. *Journal of Staff Development, 1*(1), 9–15.

Olson, D. L. (2003). Principles, impracticality, and passion. *Phi Delta Kappan, 85*(4), 307–309.

Osborn, A. F. (1963). *Applied imagination: Principles and procedures of creative problem-solving.* New York: Charles Scribner.

Osborne, S., & deOnis, A. (1997). Parent involvement in rural schools: Implications for educators. *Rural Educator, 19* (2), 20–25.

Parette, H. P., & Petch-Hogan, B. (2000). Approaching families: Facilitating culturally, linguistically diverse family involvement. *Teaching Exceptional Children, 33* (2), 4–12.

Park, J., Turnbull, A. P., & Turnbull, H. R. (2002). Impacts of poverty on quality of life in families of children with disabilities. *Exceptional Children, 68*(2), 151–170.

Pearce, M. (1996, September). Inclusion: Twelve secrets to making it work in your classroom. *Instructor,* 81–84.

PEATC (1991). *Partnership series.* Parent Educational Advocacy Training Center. Alexandria, VA.

Peterson, N. L., & Cooper, C. S. (1989). Parent education and involvement in early intervention programs for handicapped children: A different perspective on parent needs and parent-professional relationships. In M. J. Fine (Ed.), *The Second Handbook on Parent Education* (pp. 197–234). New York: Academic Press.

Pfeiffer, S. (1980). The school-based interprofessional team: Recurring problems and some possible solutions. *Journal of School Psychology, 18*(4):388–94.

Phelps, P. H. (1999). Creating a commitment to family involvement. *Rural Educator, 20,* 35–38.

Phillips, W. L., Allred, K., Brulle, A. R., & Shank, K. S. (1990). The regular education initiative: The will and skill of regular educators. *Teacher Education and Special Education, 13*(3–4), 182– 186.

Picket, A. L. (1988). *The employment and training of paraprofessional personnel: A technical assistance manual for administrators and staff developers.* New York: City University of New York, National Resource Center for Paraprofessionals in Education and Related Services, Center for Advanced Studies in Education.

Pines, A., & Aronson, E. (1988). *Career burnout: Causes and cures.* New York: Macmillan.

Plucker, J. A., & Yecke, C. P. (1999). The effect of relocation on gifted students. *Gifted Child Quarterly, 43*(2), 95–106.

Plunkett, V. R. L. (1997). Parents and schools: Partnerships that count. *Journal of Education for Students Placed At Risk, 2,* 325–327.

Pollio, H. (1987). Practical poetry: Metaphoric thinking in science, art, literature, and nearly everywhere else. *Teaching-Learning Issues,* Fall 1987, 3–17.

Polsgrove, L., & McNeil, M. (1989). The consultation process: Research and practice. *Remedial and Special Education, 10*(1), 6–13, 20.

Popham, W. J. (1988). *Educational evaluation* (2nd ed.). Englewood Cliffs, NJ: Prentice Hall.

Posavac, E. J., & Carey, R. G. (1989). *Program evaluation: Methods and case studies* (3rd ed.). Englewood Cliffs, NJ: Prentice Hall.

Price, M., and Goodman, L. (1980). Individualized education programs: A cost study. *Exceptional Children, 46*(6), 446–454.

Pryzwansky, W. B. (1974). A reconsideration of the consultation model for delivery of school- based psychological services. *American Journal of Orthopsychiatry, 44,* 579–583.

Pryzwansky, W. B. (1986). Indirect service delivery: Considerations for future research in consultation. *School Psychology Review, 15*(4), 479–488.

Pugach, M. C. (1988). The consulting teacher in the context of educational reform. *Educational Children, 55*(3), 273–275.

Pugach, M. C., & Johnson, L. J. (1990). Fostering the continued democratization of consultation through action research. *Teacher Education and Special Education, 13*(3–4), 240–245.

Pugach, M. C., & Johnson, L. J. (1995). *Collaborative practitioners, collaborative schools.* Denver, CO: Love.

Purcell, J. H., & Leppien, J. H. (1998). Building bridges between general practitioners and educators of the gifted: A study of collaboration. *Gifted Child Quarterly, 42*(3), 172–181.

Putnam, J. (1993). Make every minute count. *Instructor, 103*(1), 39–40.

Ramirez, S. Z., Lepage, K. M., Kratochwill, T. R., & Duffy, J. L. (1998). Multicultural issues in school-based consultation: Conceptual and research consierations. *Journal of School Psychology, 36,* 479–509.

Raschke, D., Dedrick, C., & DeVries, A. (1988). Coping with stress: The special educator's perspective. *Teaching Exceptional Children, 21*(1), 10–14.

Raymond, G. I., McIntosh, D. K., & Moore, Y. R. (1986). *Teacher consultation skills* (Report No. EC 182-912). Washington, D.C.: U.S. Department of Education. (ERIC Document Reproduction Service No. ED 170-915)

Raywid, M. A. (1993). Finding time for collaboration. *Educational Leadership, 51*(1), 30–34.

Reinhiller, N. (1996). Co-teaching: New variations on a not-so-new practice. *Teacher Education and Special Education, 19*(1), 34–48.

Reis, S. M. (2001). What can we do with talented readers? *Teaching for High Potential, 3*(1), 1–4.

Reis, S. M., & Westberg, K. L. (1994). The impact of staff development on teachers' ability to modify curriculum for gifted and talented students. *Gifted Child Quarterly, 38*(3), 127–135.

Reis, S. M., Burns, D. E., & Renzulli, J. S. (1992). *Facilitator's guide to help teachers compact curriculum.* Mansfield Center, CT: Creative Learning Press.

Renzulli, J. S. (1977). *The enrichment triad model: A guide for developing defensible programs for the gifted and talented.* Mansfield Center, CT: Creative Learning Press.

Renzulli, J. S., & Reis, S. M. (1985). *The schoolwide enrichment model: A comprehensive plan for educational excellence.* Mansfield Center, CT: Creative Learning Press.

Renzulli, J. S., & Reis, S. M. (1991). The reform movement and the quiet crisis in gifted education. *Gifted Child Quarterly, 35*(1), 26–35.

Reynolds, M. C., & Birch, J. W. (1988). *Adaptive mainstreaming: A primer for teachers and principals.* White Plains, NY: Longman.

Rich, D. (1987). *School and families: Issues and actions.* Washington, D.C.: National Education Association.

Riehl, C. J. (2000). The principal's role in creating inclusive schools for diverse students: A review of normative, empirical, and critical literature on the practice of educational administration. *Review of Educational Research, 70*(1), 55–81.

Riggs, C. G. (2001). Ask the paraprofessionals: What are your training needs? *Teaching Exceptional Children, 33*(3), 78–83.

Rinke, W. J. (1997). *Winning Management: 6 fail-safe strategies for building high-performance organizations.* Clarksville, MD: Achievement Publishers.

Ritter, D. R. (1978). Effects of a school consultation program upon referral patterns of teachers. *Psychology in the Schools, 15*(2), 239–243.

Robinson, A. (1990). Cooperation of exploitation? The argument against cooperative learning for talented students. *Journal for the Education of the Gifted, 14*(1):9–27.

Rogers, J. (1993). The inclusion revolution. *The Research Bulletin, Phi Delta Kappa, 11,* 1–6.

Rose, L. C. (2003). Public education's Trojan horse? *Phi Delta Kappan, 85*(1), 2.

Rose, L. C., & Gallup, A. M. (2003). The 35th annual Phi Delta Kappa/Gallup Poll of the public's attitudes toward the public schools. *Phi Delta Kappan, 85*(1), 41–52.

Rosenfield, S. (1995). Instructional consultation: A model for service delivery in the schools. *Journal of Educational and Psychological Consultation, 6*(4), 297–316.

Royster, A., & McLaughlin, T. (1996). Parent partnerships in special education: Purposes, models and barriers. *Journal of Special Education, 20*(2), 24–33.

Ross, R. G. (1986). *Communication consulting as persuasion: Issues and implications.* (Report No. CS506-027). Washington, D.C.: U.S. Department of Education. ERIC Document Reproduction Service No.ED 291–115.

Rule, S., Fodor-Davis, J., Morgan, R., Salzberg, C. L., & Chen, J. (1990). An inservice training model to encourage collaborative consultation. *Teacher Education and Special Education, 13*(3–4), 225–227.

Rusch, F. R., & Menchetti, B. M. (1988). Transition in the 1990s: A reply to Knowlton and Clark. *Exceptional Children, 54*(4), 363–364.

Safran, J. S. (1991). Communication in collaboration/consultation: Effective practices in schools. *Journal of Educational and Psychological Consultation, 1*(4), 371–386.

Safran, S. P. (1991). The communication process and school-based consultation: What does the research say? *Journal of Educational and Psychological Consultation, 1*(4), 343–370.

Salend, S. J. (1994). *Effective mainstreaming: Creating inclusive classrooms* (2nd ed.). New York: Macmillan.

Salend, S. J. (2001). *Creating inclusive classrooms: Effective and reflective practices* (4th ed.). Upper Saddle River, NJ: Merrill.

Salend, S. J., & Duhaney, L. M. G. (1999). The impact of inclusion on students with and without disabilities and their educators. *Remedial and Special Education, 20*(2), 114–126.

Salend, S. J., & Salend, S. (1984). Consulting with the regular teacher: Guidelines for special educators. *The Pointer, 25,* 25–28.

Salisbury, C. L., & Vincent, L. J. (1990). Criterion of the next environment and best practices: Mainstreaming and integration 10 years later. *Topics in Early Childhood Special Education, 10*(2), 78–89.

Salisbury, G., & Evans, I. M. (1988). Comparison of parental involvement in regular and special education. *Journal of the Association for Persons with Severe Handicaps, 13,* 268–272.

Salzberg, C. L., & Morgan, J. (1995). Preparing teachers to work with paraeducators. *Teacher Education and Special Education, 18*(1), 49–55.

Sandoval, J. (1996). Constructivism, consultee-centered consultation, and conceptual change. *Journal of Educational and Psychological Consultation, 7*(1). 89–97.

Sapolsky, R. (1994). *Why zebras don't get ulcers: A guide to stress, stress-related diseases, and coping.* New York: W. H. Freeman.

Savelsbergh, M., & Staebler, B. (1995). Investigating leadership styles, personality preferences, and effective teacher consultation. *Journal of Educational and Psychological Consultation, 6*(3), 277–286.

Schaps, E. (1990). Cooperative learning: The challenge in the 90s. *Cooperative Learning, 10*(4), 5–8.

Schatz, E. (1990). Ability grouping for gifted learners. *Educating Able Learners. 15*(3) 3,5,15. Denton, TX: Gifted Students Institute.

Schein, E. H. (1969). *Process consultation: Its role in organization development.* Reading, MA: Addison-Wesley.

Schein, E. H. (1978). The role of the consultant: Context expert or process facilitator? *Personnel and Guidance Journal,* February 1978.

Schenkat, R. (1988). The promise of restructuring for special education. *Education Week,* November 16, 1988.

Schindler, C., & Lapid, G. (1989). *The great turning: Personal peace, global victory.* Santa Fe: Bear and Company.

Schlax, K. (1994). Eight Tips for Effective Integration of Therapists. *Inclusive Education Programs 1*(2), 11.

Schuck, J. (1979). The parent-professional partnership: Myth or reality? *Education Unlimited, 1*(4): 26–28.

Schulte, A. C., Osborne, S. S., & Kauffman, J. M. (1993). Teacher responses to two types of consultative special education services. *Journal of Educational and Psychological Consultation, 4*(1), 1–27.

Schultz, E. W. (Fall, 1980). Teaching coping skills for stress and anxiety. *Teaching Exceptional Children,* Council for Exceptional Children, 12–15.

Schulz, J. B. (1987). *Parent and professional in special education.* Newton, MA: Allyn & Bacon.

Scollon, R. O. (1985). The machine stops: Silence in the metaphor of malfunction. In D. Tannen and M. Saville-Troike (Eds.), *Perspectives in silence.* Norwood, NJ: Ablex.

Scriven, M. (1967). The methodology of evaluation. In R. W. Tyler, R. M. Gagne., & M. Scriven (Eds.), *Perspectives of Curriculum Evaluation.* Chicago: Rand-McNally.

Scruggs, T. E., & Mastropieri, M. A. (1996). Teacher perceptions of mainstreaming/inclusion, 1958–1995: A research synthesis. *Exceptional Children, 63*(1), 59–74.

Seay, M. (1974). *Community education: A developing concept.* Midland, MI: Pendell.

SEDL (2000a). Rural student entrepreneurs: Linking commerce and community. *Benefits, 3.*

SEDL (2000b). Collaborative strategies for revitalizing rural schools and communities. *Benefits, 5.*

Seeley, D. S. (1985). *Education through partnership.* Washington, D.C.: American Enterprise Institute for Public Policy Research.

Shanteau, J. (1997, October). *ISBR Newletter, 7.* Kansas State University: Institute for Social and Behavioral Research.

Shaver, D., Golan, S., & Wagner, M. (1996) Connecting schools and communities through interagency collaboration for school-linked services. In J. G. Cibulka and W. J. Kritek (Eds), *Coordination among Schools, Families, and Communities: Prospects for Educational Reform* (pp. 349–378). Albany, NY: State University of New York Press.

Shaw, S. F., Bensky, J. M., & Dixon, B. (1981). *Stress and burnout: A primer for special education and special services personnel.* Reston, VA: Council for Exceptional Children.

Shea, T. M., & Bauer, A. M. (1985). *Parents and teachers of exceptional students.* Boston: Allyn & Bacon.

Short, R. J., & Talley, R. C. (1999). Services integration: An introduction. *Journal of Educational and Psychological Consultation, 10*(3), 193–200.

Sigband, N. B. (1987). The uses of meetings. *Nation's Business,* February 1987, 28R.

Sileo, T., Rude, H., & Luckner, J. (1988). Collaborative consultation: A Model for transition planning for handicapped youth. *Education and Training in Mental Retardation, 23*(4): 333–339.

Simpson, E. J. (1972). *The psychomotor domain, vol. 3.* Washington, DC: Gryphon House.

Simpson, G. W. (1990). Keeping it alive: Elements of school culture that sustain innovation. *Educational Leadership, 47*(8), 34–37.

Slavin, R. (1988). *The School Administrator, 45,* 9–13.

Slavin, R. E. (1986). *Using student team learning* (3rd ed.). Baltimore, MD: Center for Research on Elementary and Middle Schools, The Johns Hopkins University.

Slavin, R. E. (1990). Research on cooperative learning: Consensus and controversy. *Educational Leadership, December 47*(4), 52–54.

Slesser, R. A., Fine, M. J., & Tracy, D. B. (1990). Teacher reactions to two approaches to school-based psychological consultation. *Journal of Educational and Psychological Consultation, 1*(3), 243–258.

Smith, B. M. (2003). Who really needs educating? *Phi Delta Kappa, 85*(2), 99.

Smith, D. K. (1996). *Taking charge of change: 10 principles for managing people and performance.* Reading, MA: Addison-Wesley.

Smith, J. D. (1998). *Inclusion: Schools for all students.* Belmont, CA: Wadsworth.

Smith, S. C. (1987). The collaborative school takes shape. *Educational Leadership, 45*(3), 4–6.

Smith-Westberry, J., & Job, R. L. (1986). How to be a prophet in your own land: Providing gifted program inservice for the local district. *Gifted Child Quarterly, 30*(3), 135–137.

Sontag, J. C., & Schacht, R. (1994). An ethnic comparison of participation and information needs in early intervention. *Exceptional Children, 60,* 422–433.

Soodak, L. C., & Erwin, E. J. (1995). Parents, professionals, and inclusive education: A call for collaboration. *Journal of Educational and Psychological Consultation, 6*(3), 257–276).

Soo-Hoo, T. (1998). Applying frame of reference and reframing techniques to improve school consultation in multicultural settings. *Journal of Educational and Psychological Consultation, 9*(4), 325–345.

Sparks, D. (September, 1992). Some basic understandings. *The Developer* Oxford, OH: National Staff Development Council.

Speece, D. L., & Mandell, C. J. (1980). Resource room support services for regular teachers. *Learning Disability Quarterly, 3,* 49–53.

St. John, E. P., Griffith, A. I., & Allen-Hayes, L. (1997). *Families in Schools: A Chorus of Voices in Restructuring.* Portsmouth, M. H.: Heinemann.

Stainback, S., & Stainback, F. M. (1988). In M. C. Reynolds (Ed.), *Adaptive mainstreaming: A primer for teachers and principals.* White Plains, NY: Longman.

Stainback, W., & Stainback, S. (1984). A rationale for the merger of special and regular education. *Exceptional Children, 51*(2), 102–111.

Stanley, A. L., & Vasa, S. F. (1998). How paraeducators learn on the Web. *Teaching Exceptional Children, 30*(5), 54–59.

Stanovich, P. J. (1999). Conversations about inclusion. *Teaching Exceptional Children, 31*(6), 54–58.

Staples, L. (1990). Powerful ideas about empowerment. *Administration in Social Work, 14*(2), 29–42.

Starko, A. (1995). *Creativity in the classroom: Schools of curious delight.* Boston: White Plains, NY: Longman.

Stephens, P. (1994, October). *Developing a successful grant application.* Presented at United School Administrators conference in Emporia, KS.

Stephens, T. M. (1977). *Teaching skills to children with learning and behavioral disorders.* Columbus, OH: Merrill.

Stewart, J. C. (1978). *Counseling parents of exceptional children.* Columbus, OH: Merrill.

Stone, D., Patton, B., & Heen, S. (1999). *Difficult conversations: ow to discuss what matters most.* New York: Random House.

Sue, D. W., & Sue, D. (1990). *Counseling the culturally different: Theory and practice* (2nd ed.). New York: John Wiley.

Sugai, G. (Winter, 1986). Recording classroom events: Maintaining a critical incidents log. *Teaching Exceptional Children,* pp. 98–102.

Sundbye, N., & McCoy, L. (1997). *Helping the struggling reader: What to teach and how to teach it.* Lawrence, KS: Curriculum Solutions.

Sundel, S. S., & Sundel, M. (1980). *Be assertive: A practical guide for human service workers.* Beverly Hills: Sage.

Swap, S. M. (1987). *Enhancing parent involvement in schools.* New York: Teachers College Press.

Swicegood, P. (1994). Portfolio-based assessment practices. *Intervention in School and Clinic, 30*(1): 6–15.

Systma, R. (2001). Middle and high school student interests: Runway lights for outbound planes. *Teaching for High Potential, 3*(1), 3.

Talley, R. C., & Schrag, J. A. (1999). Legal and public foundations supporting service integration for students with disabilities. *Journal of Educational and Psychological Consultation, 10*(3), 229–249.

Tannen, D. (1991). *Gender and discourse.* New York: Oxford University Press.

Tannen, D. (1994). *You just don't understand: Women and men in conversation.* New York: William Morrow.

Teaching Exceptional Children (May/June, 1997), *29*(5). Topical Issue.

Tharp, R. (1975). The triadic model of consultation. In C. Parker (Ed.), *Psychological consultation in the schools: Helping teachers meet special needs.* Reston, VA: The Council for Exceptional Children.

Tharp, R. G., & Wetzel, R. J. (1969). *Behavior modification in the natural environment.* New York: Academic Press.

The Public Agenda. (1994). *First things first.* New York: Author.

The Technology Teacher, (1993). International Technology Education Association.

Thomas, C. C., Correa, V. I., & Morsink, C. V. (2001). *Interactive teaming: Enhancing programs for students with special needs* (3rd ed.). Upper Saddle River, NJ: Prentice Hall.

Thompson, L., Lobb, C., Elling, R., Herman, S., Jurkiewicz, T., & Hulleza, C. (1997). Pathways to family empowerment: Effects of family-centered delivery of early intervention services. *Exceptional Children, 64*(1), 99–113.

Thousand, J., Fox, T., Reid, R., Godek, J., Williams, W., & Fox, W. (1986). *The homecoming model: Educating students who present intensive educational challenges within regular education environments.* (Monograph No. 7-1). Burlington, VT: University of Vermont, Center for Developmental Disabilities.

Thurston, L. P (2000). *The positive para: Helping students develop positive social skills.* Lawrence, KS: Curriculum Solutions, Inc.

Thurston, L. P. (1987). *Survival skills for women: Facilitator manual.* Manhattan, KS: Survival Skills and Development.

Thurston, L. P., & Dover, W. (October, 1990). *Rural at-risk students.* Paper presented at the 12th annual Rural and Small Schools Conference, Manhattan, KS.

Thurston, L. P., & Kimsey, I. (1989). Rural special education teachers as consultants: Roles and responsibilities. *Educational Considerations, 17*(1): 40–43.

Thurston, L. P., & Navarrete, L. (1996). A tough row to hoe: Research on education and rural poor families. *In Proceedings of American Council on Rural Special Education (ACRES),* Baltimore, M.D.

Thurston, L. P., & Navarrete, L. A. (2003). Rural, poverty-level mothers: A comparative study of those with and without children who have special needs. *Rural Special Education Quarterly, 22*(2), 15–23.

Timar, T. (1989). The politics of school restructuring. *Phi Delta Kappan, 71*(4), 265–275.

Tindal, G., & Taylor-Pendergast, S. J. (1989). A taxonomy for objectively analyzing the consultation process. *Remedial and Special Education, 10*(2): 6–16.

Tobias, R. (1993). Underlying cultural issues that effect sound consultant/school collaboratives in developing multicultural programs. *Journal of Educational and Psychological Consultation, 4*(3), 237–251.

Todnem, G., & Warner, M. P. (1994, September). Demonstrating the benefits of staff development: An interview with Thomas R. Guskey. *Kansas Direct Connection,* September 1994. Hays, KS: Kansas Staff Development Council.

Tomlinson C. A. (1995). Deciding to differentiate instruction in middle school: One school's journey. *Gifted Child Quarterly, 39*(2), 77–87.

Tomlinson, C. A. (1996). Good teaching for one and all: Does gifted education have an instructional identity? *Journal for the Education of the Gifted, 20*(2), 155–174.

Tomlinson, C. (1999). *The differentiated classroom: Responding to the needs of all learners.* Alexandria, VA: Association for Supervision and Curriculum Development.

Tomlinson, C. A. (2000). *Reconcilable differences? Standards-based teaching and differentiation. Educational Leadership, 58*(1), 6–11.

Tomlinson, C. A., Coleman, M. R., Allan, S., Udall, A., & Landrum, M. (1996). Interface between gifted education and general education: Toward communication, cooperation and collaboration. *Gifted Child Quarterly, 40*(3), 165–170.

Tomlinson, G. (Ed.). (1984). *School administrator's complete letter book.* Englewood Cliffs, NJ: Prentice-Hall.

Torrance, E. P., & Safter, H. T. (1999). *Making the creative leap beyond . . . Buffalo, NY: Creative Education Foundation Press.*

Treat, M., & Dyck, N. (1997). *The TREAT program: Including students with high ability.* Lawrence, KS: Curriculum Solutions, Inc.

Treffinger, D. J. (1982). Gifted students, regular classrooms: Sixty ingredients for a better blend. *Elementary School Journal, 82*(3), 267–273.

Truesdell, L. A., & Lopez, E. C. (1995). Consultation models revisited: In conclusion. *Journal of Educational and Psychological Consultation, 6*(4), 385–395.

Tucker, J. A. (1985). Curriculum-based assessment: An introduction. *Exceptional Children, 52*(3): 199–204.

Turnbull, A. P., & Turnbull, H. R. (1998). *Families, professionals, and exceptionality.* (3rd ed.). Upper Saddle River, NJ: Merrill/Prentice Hall.

Turnbull, A. P., & Turnbull, H. R., III. (1997). *Families, professionals, and exceptionality: A special partnership* (3rd ed.). Upper Saddle River, NJ: Merrill.

Turnbull, H. R., III, Turnbull, A. P., & Wheat, M. J. (1992). Assumptions about parental participation: A legislative history. *Exceptional Education Quarterly, 3*(2), 1–8.

Turnbull, H. R., III., & Turnbull, A. P. (1985). *Parents speak out: Then and now* (2nd ed.). Columbus, OH: Merrill.

Turner, R. R. (April, 1987). Here's what teachers say. *Learning, 87,* 55–57.

Tyler, V. L. (1979). *Intercultural interacting.* Provo, UT: Brigham Young University, David Kennedy Center for International Studies.

Ury, W. (1991). *Getting past no: Negotiating with difficult people.* New York: Bantam Books.

Van Reusen, A. K., Bos, C. S., Schumaker, J. B., & Deshler, D. D. (1994). *The self-advocacy strategy: For education and transition planning.* Lawrence, KS: Edge Enterprises, Inc.

VanTassel-Baska, J. (1989). Appropriate curriculum for gifted learners. *Educational Leadership, 46*(6):13–15.

VanTassel-Baska, J. (1991). Gifted education in the balance: Building relationships with general education. *Gifted Child Quarterly, 35*(1), 20–25.

VanTassel-Baska, J. (1989). *Excellence in educating gifted and talented learners* (3rd ed.). Denver: Love.

Vasa, S. T. (1982). *The special education resource teacher as a consultant: Fact or fantasy?* Paper presented at the Sixth Annual Meeting of the Council for Exceptional Children, Houston. (ERIC Document Reproduction Service No. ED 218 918)

Vaughn, S., Schumm, J. S., & Arguelles, M. E. (1997). The ABCDEs of co-teaching. *Teaching Exceptional Children, 30*(2), 42–45.

Villa, R. A., & Thousand, J. S. (2003). Making inclusive education work. *Educational Leadership, 61*(2), 19–23.

Villa, R., Thousand, J., Meyers, H., & Nevin, A. (1996). Teacher and administrator perceptions of heterogeneous education. *Exceptional Children, 63*(1), 29–45.

Vockell, E. L.& Asher, W. J. (1995). *Educational research,* (2nd ed.). Englewood Cliffs, NJ: Prentice Hall.

Voltz, D. L., Elliott, Jr., R. N., & Cobb, H. B. (1994). Collaborative teacher roles: Special and general educators. *Journal of Learning Disabilities, 27*(8), 527–535.

Waldron, N. L., & McLesky, J. (1998). The effects of an inclusive school program on students with mild and severe learning disabilities. *Exceptional Children, 64*(3), 395–405.

Wallace, T., Shin, J., Bartholomay, T., & Stahl, B. J. (2001). Knowledge and skills for teachers supervising the work of paraprofessionals. *Exceptional Children, 67*(4), 520–533.

Wallings, D. R. (1990). *Meeting the needs of transient students,* Fastback #304. Bloomington, IN: Phi Delta Kappa Educational Foundation.

Wanat, C. L. (1997). Conceptualizing parental involvement from parents' perspectives: A case study. *Journal for a Just and Caring Education, 3*(4), 433–458.

Wang, M. C. (1987). Toward achieving educational excellence for all students: Program design and student outcomes. *Remedial and Special Education, 8,* 25–34.

Ward, S. B., & Landrum, M. S. (1994). Resource consultation: An alternative service delivery model for gifted education. *Roeper Review, 16,* 275–279.

Waters, D. B., & Lawrence, E. C. (1993). *Competence, courage, and change: An approach to family therapy.* New York: W. W. Norton.

Weber, L. (1994). Diversity and collaboration. *Center News.* Memphis: Center for Research on Women. University of Memphis, *13,* 2, 10.

Webster's new collegiate dictionary (8th ed.) (1996). Springfield, MA: Merriam-Webster.

Webster's third new international dictionary, unabridged: The great library of the English language. (1976). Springfield, MA: Merriam-Webster.

Welch, M. (1998). The IDEA of collaboration in special education: An introspective examination of paradigms and promise. *Journal of Educational and Psychological Consultation, 9*(2), 119– 142.

Welch, M. (2001). The O.F.T.E.N strategy for conflict management. *Journal of Educational and Psychological Consultation, 12*(3), 257–262.

Welch, M., & Sheridan, S. M. (1995). *Educational partnerships: Serving students at-risk.* Fort Worth, TX: Harcourt Brace.

Wesley, W. G., & Wesley, B. A. (1990). Conceptmapping: A brief introduction. *Teaching Professor, 4*(8), 3–4.

West, J. F. (1985). *Regular and special educators' preference for school-based consultation models: A statewide study* (Report No. 101). Austin, TX: The University of Texas, Research and Training Project on School Consultation.

West, J. F. (1990). Educational collaboration in the restructuring of schools. *Journal of Educational and Psychological Consultation, 1,* 23–41.

West, J. F., & Brown, P. A. (1987). State departments of education policies on consultation in special education: The state of the states. *Remedial and Special Education, 8*(3), 45–51.

West, J. F., & Idol, L. (1987). School consultation (Part i): An interdisciplinary perspective on theory, models, and research. *Journal of Learning Disabilities, 20*(7), 385–408.

Westby, C. E., & Ford, V. (1993). The role of team culture in assessment and intervention. *Journal of Educational and Psychological Consultation, 4*(4), 319–341.

Whitaker, S. D. (2000). Mentoring beginning special education teachers and the relationship to attrition. *Exceptional Children, 66*(4), 546–566.

Whitaker, S. D. (2000). What do first-year special education teachers need? Implications for induction programs. *Teaching Exceptional Children, 33(1),* 28–36.

White, G. W. (2000). Nonverbal communications: Key to improved teacher effectiveness. *Delta Kappa Gamma Bulletin, 66*(4), 12–16.

Wiederholt, J., Hammill, D., & Brown, V. (1983). *The resource teacher.* Austin, TX: PRO-ED.

Wienke, W. D. (1996). Book reviews: Current resources for grant writers. *Teacher Education and Special Education, 19*(3), 272–276.

Wikler, L., Wasow, M., & Hatfield, E. (1981). Chronic sorrow revisited: Parent vs. professional depiction of the adjustment of parents of mentally retarded children. *American Journal of Orthopsychiatry, 51,* 63–70.

Wildman, T. M., & Niles, J. A. (1987). Essentials of professional growth. *Educational Leadership, 44*(5), 4–10.

Will, M. (1984). Let us pause and reflect—but not too long. *Exceptional Children, 51,* 11–16.

Will, M. (1986). Educating children with learning problems: A shared responsibility. *Exceptional Children, 52*(5), 411–415.

Williams, J. M., & Martin, S. M. (2001). Implementing the Individuals with Disabilities Education Act of 1997: The consultant's role. *Journal of Educational and Psychological Consultation, 12*(1), 59–81.

Witt, J. C., & Elliott, S. N. (1985). Acceptability of classroom intervention strategies. In T. R. Kratochwill (Ed.), *Advances in School Psychology* (Vol.4, pp. 251–288). Hillsdale, NJ: Lawrence Erlbaum.

Wolf, D. P. (1989). Portfolio assessment: Sampling student work. *Educational Leadership 46*(7), 35–40.

Wolf, J. S., & Stephens, T. M. (1989). *Parent/teacher conferences: Finding common ground.* Educational Leadership, 47(2), 28–31.

Wood, M. (1998). Whose job is it anyway? Educational roles in inclusion. *Exceptional Children, 64*(2), 181–195.

Woolfolk, A. (2001). *Educational psychology* (8th ed.). Boston: Allyn & Bacon.

Working Forum on Inclusive Schools (1994). *Creating schools for all our students: What 12 schools have to say.* Reston, VA: Council for Exceptional Children.

Yocum, D. J., & Cossairt, A. (1996). Consultation courses offered in special education teacher training programs: A national survey. *Journal of Educational and Psychological Consultation, 7*(3), 251–258.

Ysseldyke, J. E. (1986). The use of assessment information to make decisions about students. In R. J. Morris and B. Blatt (Eds.), *Special education: Research and trends.* New York: Pergamon.

Ysseldyke, J. E., & Christenson, S. I. (1987). Evaluating students' instructional environments. *Remedial and Special Education, 8*(3), 17–24.

Ysseldyke, J., Thurlow, M., Wotruba, J., & Nania, P. (1990). Instructional arrangements: Perceptions from general education. *Teaching Exceptional Children, 22*(4), 4–8.

Zigmond, N., Levin, E., & Laurie, T. E. (1985). Managing the mainstream: An analysis of teacher attitudes and student performance in mainstream high school programs. *Journal of Learning Disabilities, 18*(9): 535–41.

Zimet, E. (1993). Grant-writing techniques for K–12 funding. *T.H.E.: Technological Horizons in Education,* November, 1993, 109–112.

Zirkel, P. A., & Knapp, S. (1993). Related services for students with disabilities: What educational consultants need to know. *Journal of Educational and Psychological Consultation, 4*(2), 137–15.

NAME INDEX